NEW TECHNOLOGIES AND HUMAN RIGHTS

New Technologies and Human Rights

Challenges to Regulation

Edited by

MARIO VIOLA DE AZEVEDO CUNHA
Rio de Janeiro State University, Brazil

NORBERTO NUNO GOMES DE ANDRADE
European Commission's Joint Research Centre, Spain

LUCAS LIXINSKI
University of New South Wales, Australia

LÚCIO TOMÉ FÉTEIRA
Dein Advogados, Portugal

Routledge
Taylor & Francis Group
LONDON AND NEW YORK

First published 2013 by Ashgate Publishing

2 Park Square, Milton Park, Abingdon, Oxfordshire OX14 4RN
52 Vanderbilt Avenue, New York, NY 10017

Routledge is an imprint of the Taylor & Francis Group, an informa business

First issued in paperback 2020

British Library Cataloguing in Publication Data
New technologies and human rights: challenges to regulation.
1. Technology and law. 2. Human rights. 3. International law and human rights–Southern Hemisphere. 4. International law and human rights–Northern Hemisphere. 5. Medical innovations–Law and legislation. 6. Technological innovations–Law and legislation. 7. Technological innovations–Social aspects.
I. Cunha, Mario Viola de Azevedo.
344'.095–dc23

Library of Congress Cataloging-in-Publication Data
New technologies and human rights: challenges to regulation/By Mario Viola de Azevedo Cunha, Norberto Nuno Gomes de Andrade, Lucas Lixinski, Lucio Tomo Feteira.
pages cm
Includes bibliographical references and index.
ISBN 978-1-4094-4216-5 (hardback : alk. paper) — ISBN 978-1-4094-4217-2 (ebook) — ISBN 978-1-4094-7370-1 (epub) 1. Human rights. 2. Technological innovations—Law and legislation. 3. Civil rights. I. Cunha, Mario Viola de Azevedo, editor of compilation.
K3240.N496 2013
342.08'5—dc23

2013000259

ISBN 13: 978-1-4094-4216-5 (hbk)
ISBN 13: 978-0-367-60140-9 (pbk)

Contents

List of Figures and Tables

Figures

Tables

About the Editors

Mario Viola de Azevedo Cunha is an Associate Professor of Private Law at the Centro de Estudos e Pesquisas no Ensino do Direito of the Rio de Janeiro State University (Brazil), and a State Attorney of the Municipality of Saquarema (Brazil). He holds a PhD in Law and a MRes from the European University Institute (Florence, Italy), an LLM in Private Law from Rio de Janeiro State University and has undertaken post-graduate studies in Consumer Law (Rio de Janeiro State University) and in Private Law (Fluminense Federal University, Brazil).

Norberto Nuno Gomes de Andrade is a Scientific Officer at the Information Society Unit of the Institute for Prospective Technological Studies (IPTS) of the European Commission's Joint Research Centre. He holds a PhD in Law and a Master of Research from the European University Institute (Florence, Italy). He also holds a Master of Arts in International Relations and European Studies from Central European University (Budapest, Hungary). He is a Member of the Editorial Board of the *International Journal of Human Rights and Constitutional Studies*. In 2009 he co-edited and published *Law and Technology: Looking into the Future – Selected Essays*.

Lucas Lixinski is a Lecturer at the University of New South Wales Law School (Sydney, Australia). Previously he was a Postgraduate Fellow at the Bernard and Audre Rapoport Center for Human Rights and Justice at the University of Texas School of Law (Austin, United States of America). He holds a PhD in Law from the European University Institute (Florence, Italy).

Lúcio Tomé Féteira is a part-time lecturer at the Faculté Libre de Droit (Paris) and works as a lawyer in Lisbon. He has undertaken post-graduate studies in Commercial and Corporate Law (Law Faculty of the University of Coimbra) and in Competition and Regulatory Law (Law Faculty of the University of Lisbon). He holds a PhD in Law from the European University Institute (Florence, Italy).

List of Contributors

Ana Eduarda Santos is an SJD Candidate, Duke Law School, L.L.M. Duke Law School (2008) and holds an L.L.M. from the Faculty of Law of the Portuguese Catholic University (2007).

Ana Nordberg is a trained lawyer. She is a Ph.D. candidate at the University of Copenhagen, Center for Information and Innovation Law.

Bruno Magrani is Professor of Law at the Centre of Law and Society (CTS) at *Fundação Getúlio Vargas* and coordinator of the Brazilian Observatory of Digital Policies. He holds an L.L.M. in Law and Technology from Harvard Law School.

Carlos Affonso Pereira de Souza holds an L.L.M and a Ph.D. in Private Law from Rio de Janeiro State University. He is currently a Professor of Private Law at the Centre of Law and Society (CTS) at *Fundação Getúlio Vargas*. He was a member of the ICANN board (2008–2009) and of the NCUC (non-commercial users constituency) executive committee (2009–2010).

Danilo Doneda is a Professor of Private Law at Getulio Vargas Foundation (Brazil) and holds an L.L.M. and a Ph.D. in Private Law from Rio de Janeiro State University. He was a visiting researcher at the *Garante per la protezione dei dati personali* in Italy. He is currently a General Coordinator at the National Consumer Secretariat of the Brazilian Ministry of Justice.

Giovanni Sartor is a Professor of Legal Informatics and Legal Theory at the Law Department of the European University Institute (Florence) and Professor of Computer and Law at the University of Bologna.

Joana Varon Ferraz holds an L.L.M. in Law and Development from Fundação Getúlio Vargas. She also holds postgraduate degrees in Law and Technology and Intellectual Property Law from Centro de Extensão Universitária. She is a researcher of the Centre of Law and Society (CTS) at Fundação Getúlio Vargas.

João Carlos Loureiro is member of the Centro de Direito Biomédico (Centre for Biomedical Law) and Associate Professor at the Faculty of Law of the University of Coimbra, where he teaches Constitutional Law and Social Security Law. He holds a PhD in Law from University of Coimbra, with a thesis entitled Constitution and biomedicine: contribution for a theory of bioconstitutional duties in the field of human genetics.

Judit Sándor is a professor at the Faculty of Political Science, Legal Studies and Gender Studies of the Central European University (CEU), Budapest. In 2004-2005 she served as the Chief of the Bioethics Section at the UNESCO. Since September 2005 she is a founding director of the Center for Ethics and Law in Biomedicine (CELAB) at the Central European University.

Luiz Edson Fachin is a Full Professor of Private Law at Universidade Federal do Paraná (Federal University of the State of Paraná) and Pontifícia Universidade Católica do Paraná (Pontifical

Catholic University of the State of Paraná) Schools of Law in Brazil; member of the Brazilian Academy of Constitutional Law; has a doctorate in 'Law of Social Relations' from the Pontifícia Universidade Católica de São Paulo (Pontifical Catholic University of the State of São Paulo); member of the International Society of Family Law; member of the Association Andrés Bello des juristes franco-latino-américains (Andrés Bello Association of Franco-Latin-American legal scholars); and visiting professor at the Universidad Pablo de Olavide, in Seville, Spain, in its Postgraduate Program in Law and New Technologies.

Maria da Glória F.P.D. Garcia is a Full Professor at the Faculty of Law at the Portuguese Catholic University.

Miguel Nogueira de Brito is a Professor at the Law Faculty of the University of Lisbon.

Paul De Hert is a recognized fundamental rights expert who devotes the majority of his work to human rights law, technology and criminal law. A human rights approach combined with a concern for theory is the common denominator of all his work. Paul De Hert has written extensively on the right to privacy and the right to fair trial. Currently his research also includes non-discrimination law, ethnic monitoring, diversity and religion and gross violations of human rights by states and firms. At the Brussels University (VUB), Paul De Hert teaches criminal law and constitutionalism. He is Director of the VUB-Research group on Fundamental Rights and Constitutionalism (FRC), Director of the Department of Interdisciplinary Studies of Law (Metajuridics) and core member of the Research group Law Science Technology and Society (LSTS) (see: www.vub.ac.be/LSTS). He holds a position as an associated-professor in the internationally renowned Institute of Law and Technology of Tilburg.

Pedro Ferreira holds an L.L.M. in Law and Technology (specialization in Data Protection, Privacy and Space Law). He is currently Head of Unit at the External Relations Department of the Portuguese Regulatory Authority for Communications, Lisbon – Portugal.

Walter Britto is a researcher at the Centre of Law and Society (CTS) at Fundação Getúlio Vargas.

Yaman Akdeniz is a Professor of Law at the Faculty of Law, Istanbul Bilgi University, Turkey. Akdeniz is also the founder of Cyber-Rights.Org (http://www.cyberrights.org) based in the UK, Cyber-Rights.Org.TR (http://www.cyber-rights.org.tr) based in Turkey, and the co-founder of BilgiEdinmeHakki.org (http://www.bilgiedinmehakki.org), a pressure group working in the field of freedom of information law in Turkey.

Preface

This book stems from a three-year project funded by several organizations, and spearheaded by the editors of the book, with the support of Professors Giovanni Sartor and Francesco Francioni from the European University Institute (Florence/Italy). Two major conferences sprang from this project, and they were devoted to analyzing the different ways in which human rights were being challenged by the deployment of emerging technologies. The first conference took place in Italy at the European University Institute (EUI), and the second was held in Brazil, at the Getúlio Vargas Foundation (FGV for its acronym in Portuguese). Both of these events managed to gather around the same table scholars from Europe and Latin America to discuss the impact of technology upon human rights that remain, academically speaking, relatively unexplored. Most prominent of these issues is the examination of the relationship between human rights and technologies across the North-South spectrum. This book includes papers presented at the two conferences and covers different aspects of the interaction between Human Rights and New Technologies. Many of the contributors are prominent scholars who have dedicated a substantial part of their academic careers to the field of Human Rights or to Law and Technology.

The Editors

Preface

Introduction

This volume discusses the multiple and multifaceted relationships between new technologies (both biotechnologies and information technologies) and human rights. In an age dominated by technology, almost every aspect of human life is deeply affected – and sometimes fundamentally reshaped – by modern technology. While scientific and technological developments have the enormous potential of providing better conditions of life for mankind, they can also easily give rise to world-scale problems; in other words, the use of technology can undoubtedly bring immense potential benefits for humanity, but can also have damaging and disastrous effects. Focusing on the latter scenario, the misuse of science and the perversion of technology has been a concern in many parts of the world for several decades. Nevertheless, and most unfortunately, it is still an issue demanding careful and urgent reflection.

As an instrument of power, control and manipulation, technology is changing the environment, exhausting natural resources, devastating landscapes, reshaping societies, restructuring the human body and pervading the human mind. In an unprecedented scale, present-day innovations in the domains of energy sciences, information and communication technologies, and genetic engineering are posing dangerous threats to the upholding and enhancement of human integrity, autonomy, freedom and dignity. Such scientific breakthroughs and advancements defy long-established moral values, re-evaluate ethical paradigms and, still, remain greatly immune to existing legal systems. Thus, the progression and, far more importantly, the direction of such technological developments must be subject to law, which must urgently evaluate and react to the multi-faceted threats and dangers posed by technology. Such task is a rather difficult one, as the rapid evolution of technology resonates against the classically slow pace of legal (particularly legislative) responsiveness.[1] Law has been constantly late in responding to the challenges and problems derived from the incessant march of technology, a problem that only tends to be aggravated by the exponential growth of technology. The fast and pervasive progress of technology has, thus, rendered some of the legal concepts, provisions and remedies outmoded. When confronted with the general inadequacy of legal systems, features and outputs of modern technology have often avoided legal control.

Within the long catalogue of threats posed by technology, the most troublesome and preoccupying ones are definitely those that jeopardize the universal and indivisible core of the most basic and primary rights of mankind – human rights. The danger of having uncontrolled technology circumventing or nullifying human rights is not merely prospective, but forcefully present. In this regard, the growth of science and technology has far-reaching human rights implications which are not being carefully accompanied by effective and updated legal remedies. Such lack of legal cover is extremely perilous, as human rights are being violated, more than ever, by technological advancements.

Despite the fact that international law has made important improvements in regulating many areas of technological danger (as, for example, in regard to nuclear technology, or privacy violations and data protection breaches inflicted by the new computerized ways of processing personal data), the impact of new technologies on human rights is still a rather unexplored area of research and analysis, continually evolving and demanding new legal answers and frameworks. As such, and

1 See for instance Lyria Bennett Moses, "Agents of Change: How the Law 'Copes' with Technological Change', (2011) 20(4) *Griffith Law Review* 763–794.

surprisingly enough, the far-reaching and multi-faceted effects of technology on human rights still remains a much neglected field of study. Therefore, the interpretation and enforcement of human rights in an increasingly technological environment remains a subject of large ambiguity and controversy. Moreover, there has not been a sufficiently profound discussion about how the international human rights regime should be protected and promoted with respect to the advancement of science and technology. Technology is being implemented with disregard for the relevance of its impact on internationally agreed human rights standards. There is therefore a pressing need to think about how these rights apply, and should evolve, in a progressively technological world, as well as a need to clarify their meaning and applicability under diverse conditions.

The articulation of modes of knowledge production brings with it complex politics, that are often unaccounted for, or even hidden behind a screen of scientific 'neutrality' or 'objectivity'. But the means through which risk is regulated, and technology is produced and distributed, indicate there is more at stake rather than a utopian quest for scientific bliss. Choices are constantly made in science and technology, and these choices carry with them politics. These choices and these politics create power relations which, taken globally, largely mirror the unbalanced relations between the Global North and the Global South. The contributions in this book articulate some of these tensions.

One might suggest a parallel between the proclaimed 'non-politics' of both science and technology, on the one hand, and human rights, on the other. On paper, both science and human rights advance and pursue the greater good, so goes the mainstream narrative, without regard to political contingencies. However, in making choices about what the common good is (the content of which, as we all know, gets fairly murky past the basic idea of 'we should strive for the common good'), politics inevitably comes into play, and to ignore that simple fact is to inevitably align with the dominant political project.

In this sense, the convergence between the regulation of technologies and human rights discourse runs deeper than what is commonly thought. While the central thrust of this volume is to look at how technologies impact the effectiveness and enjoyment of human rights, there is also an underlying set of issues that has to do with how both these sets of discourses converge. Namely, by proclaiming to be 'apolitical' or just transcending politics, there is a real danger in these narratives, and one that comes to light very clearly once its discussion is carried to the global perspective. More specifically, once we consider how technology moves globally, and how the Global South is usually placed in the subordinated position of grateful receiver of technologies (always part of a somewhat condescending and paternalistic narrative of progress), it becomes clear that the issue needs to be politicized, and that a double negation ('there is no politics in technology, and there is no politics in human rights') does not resolve the problem. To the contrary, it amplifies it.

The same can be said about the enjoyment of human rights in the Global South v. the Global North. The different aspirations of each hemisphere, as well as the power relations created between them, inform how human rights discourses travel. More specifically, if one thinks of human rights as a Global North fabrication imposed on the Global South,[2] it is to be expected that debates about how technologies and human rights interact will be riddled with a double bias (one from technological narratives, the other from human rights discourses) that is intended at creating, fostering and perpetuating inequality and subjection of the South to the North. The contributions of this book will attempt to uncover some of the ways in which these biases appear, largely by presenting narratives coming from the Global South (or that take the Global South perspective into account).

2 See, among others, M. Mutua, *Human Rights: A Political and Cultural Critique* (Philadelphia: University of Pennsylvania Press, 2008).

This is even more important if we take into account how the role the Global South countries play in the international scenario has changed in recent years, especially after the latest financial crises. As advocated by Trubek,[3] emerging economies, such as Brazil, are now playing a major role in trade law, investment law, and policies of the international financial institutions, which, according to him, will lead to significant changes in international economic law and policy. With new 'South' players participating actively in the international political debate, the narratives presented in this book will help to understand how these human rights are dealt with by the developing South countries.

Chapter summaries – bringing them back together

Giovanni Sartor's chapter analyses the relevance of human rights in the information society. Firstly, he introduces the opportunities and dangers posed by Information and communication technologies (ICTs) in the information society, referring to some famous literary work, which he calls 'nightmares' (he uses nine nightmares: Orwell's, Kafka's, Huxley's, Bradbury's, Capek's, Asimov's, Noziki's, Vonnegut's and Dick's). While discussing the role for politics, law and human rights in the ICT era, he argues that the development of new technologies opens new 'opportunities for individual and social action' which could not be anticipated, but this uncertainty about the possible future uses of technology 'does not eliminate our responsibility for governing the technology-driven social development, profiting of opportunities and preventing at least the most serious dangers'. Then, he concentrates on the 1948 Universal Declaration of Human Rights and the interaction ICTs have with the rights provided for in this document, presenting some European and US court cases, which dealt with some conflicts of human rights. He concludes his chapter by addressing some considerations 'on how ICT can contribute to constitute new human rights or dimensions of them'.

In her contribution, Maria da Glória F.P.D. Garcia departs from a philosophical and ethical analysis of the challenges posed by scientific and technological developments on what she calls 'crisis of power, a crisis of law'. According to her, this 'crisis' led society to think about sustainable development. In her opinion these challenges 'open the door to a new communitarian-based ethics, encompassing the future, which, thus, becomes our present responsibility'.

In her search for a solution, Garcia advocates that 'Nowadays the great challenge for political action is to foresee and plan, permanently adjusting the predictions and plans by adapting strategies for action'. For her, reviving old notions concerning man seems to be the answer to this 'crisis'. The rule of law must be reinvented, starting by a return to its origins; not only in terms of the voting citizen, but also the participating citizen, not only the subject of rights, but also the subject of duties.

Yaman Yakdeniz, in his chapter 'To block or not to block: European approaches to content regulation, and implications for freedom of expression', assesses significant developments at the pan-European level with regards to the development, and implementation of website and content blocking policies on the Internet. To highlight problems associated with access blocking, Yakdeniz used some adoption of blocking policies from certain member states of both the European Union and the Council of Europe.

In her contribution, Ana Eduarda Santos looks at the delicate balance between intellectual property and human rights, an equilibrium made even more precarious by the alignment of the former with trade policy. The author discusses two possible approaches to the topic – intellectual

3 David Trubek. Presentation delivered at the Global Governance and Development Workshop, organised at the European University Institute in 28 June 2012.

property rights *as* human rights v intellectual property rights *and* human rights – in light of the North/South contrast. While the North tends to regard intellectual property rights either as if they were property rights or merely from a utilitarian perspective, the South remains wary of the connection between trade policy and intellectual property rights. The author suggests that the same provisions that are the source of the South's mistrust and discomfort may also be turned to its advantage and provide a starting point for a more balanced approach between intellectual property rights and human rights.

Although it is widely recognized that development and access to technology work in tandem, the interaction between the two can be – and often is – disrupted by anticompetitive practices. In his chapter, Lúcio Féteira addresses some of the competition law issues raised by international transfer of technology analyzing what could be the possible role of competition law to ease the flow of technology and promote development. The multijurisdictional nature of anticompetitive effects associated with international transfer of technology expose the limitations of national competition laws to deal with these issues. Although the adoption of competition law regimes by developing countries is an important step, it is in itself insufficient in the absence of an international framework capable of protecting competition at a global scale. For this purpose, a multilateral commitment to the protection of competition as a global good may offer a valuable complement.

Departing from his previous work, labelled since the 1990s as 'bioconstitution', Loureiro provides in the chapter 'Prometheus, Golem & Co. – Bioconstitution and Bodiliness in a '(World) Risk Society'' a detailed overview of the possibilities and limits of a constitutional approach to the human bodiliness. In the context of the so-called GNR revolution – genetics, nanosciences and robotics – and, taking into account the constitutional evolution from a hierarchic and closed 'order of values' (*Wertordnung*) to an open land of fundamental values (*Grundwerte*), the scholar warns against the projects and the attempts to strip those values from dogmatic force or to establish an 'anarchy of values'. This is the case of the attempts to modify the human genome (genetic enhancement and other post-humanism ventures), or to pre-determine (cloning) the human being, jeopardizing the latter's genetic irreplicability and uniqueness; as well as the projects to abolish the differences between humans and animals, human/non-human (e.g. hybrids and chimeras), humans and machines (e.g. cyborgs), and the masculine/the feminine (e.g. utopian models of multiple sexualities or the sheer irrelevance of sexes as illustrated by the rediscovered androgyny). According to the author, many of these examples constitute genetic and neuroscientific-based reductionisms that refuse the foundations not only of constitutional law but of law as a whole, calling into question (if not dismounting the nature of) human autonomy, responsibility and freedom.

Given these technological developments, namely the ones observed in the field of biomedicine, along with the perspective of scientific reductionisms that undermine humankind, Loureiro poses the following and fundamental question: will we be able to maintain an ecologically open, personicentric and humanistic conception of constitution? In order to positively answer this question, and uphold such constitutional vision, the scholar proposes the conceptualization of a (partial) constitution based on the idea of bodiliness (the body as an essential modality of the human condition, rather than being a mere accident), i.e. a constitutional framework aimed at regulating interventions in the body. Bioconstitution is thus defined as the set of norms (principles and rules) formally and/or materially constitutional, whose subject is actions or omissions either from the state or from private entities, mainly centred on the protection of life, on identity and personal integrity, and on the health of today's or future human beings (understood as legally protected 'goods', having as their common feature the reference to bodiliness), especially as biomedical threats are at stake. In more detail, Loureiro presents and structures his constitutional theory of bodiliness along the following categories: subjects, goods, positions and principles. Regarding the latter, the scholar sketches the main guidelines for his bioconstitutional thesis by developing a list of core principles. With Dignity ranked as a foundational principle, Loureiro defines the following principles as bioconstitutional structuring ones: the Autonomy, the Integrity, the Familiarity, the Precautionary, the Cooperation and the Sustainability principles; along with the principles of Human Life Inviolability, of the Non-Commodification of the Human Body, and the one of Equal Access to Health Care.

In chapter 8, 'Protecting Persons v. Protecting Humans in Biobanks', Sándor describes the current basic uses and applications of genetic data in the ambit of research, discussing in particular the legal frameworks that have been developed in order to regulate biobanks. Regarding the latter, the author explains how they were established worldwide, distinguishes their different types and describes several national and regional biobanks/genome projects.

Taking into account the sporadic and fragmented nature of the different legal frameworks regulating the uses of genetic data, the author highlights the uncertainties they raise regarding the scope (the range of potential legal addressees) of protection, as well as the preferred procedural way to secure and enforce the rules of these regulatory frameworks, entering thus into the ownership debates on the human body. Sándor, in other words, discusses to whom and how biobank-related legislation ought to be applied, asking – respectively – if human tissues should be protected as persons, and if property rights on the DNA samples should be granted (or in what other way research participants rights could be framed).

In addition, Sándor also alludes to the controversial debate regarding the nature of genetic data, arguing that the two – classical and opposite – perspectives endorsed vis-à-vis its regulation (the enthusiastic and the passionate one, which emphasizes the novelty and specificity of this data; and the skeptical and critical perspective, which does not agree with the supposed novelty of this data and that argues against the reduction of individual attributes to genetic diagnosis) have prevented the creation of a friendly environment for good regulation. Regardless of the side taken on such theoretical debate, genes are increasingly being conceived as privileged sources of information, capable of revealing significant information about the individual. Hence, genes have thus become highly valuable assets, raising the issues of ownership and property.

Another obstacle presented by Sándor that has blocked the development of a sound regulatory framework in this area is the conceptual shift from the protection of *persons* to the protection of *humans* in legal discourse, that is, the unnoticed shift from the personality rights to a broad, *specie* specific protection of the human. In the ambit of the research conducted on human beings, and given the potential abuses or the possibilities of making psychological or physical harm, Sándor stresses the need for higher legal scrutiny in this field and, namely, to the need to define the boundaries of the human body. Taking into account that more and more human research is not conducted on human beings, on the human body, but on human bodily substance (human tissues, blood, samples and human DNA). In this respect, Sándor provides a word of caution, declaring that a more careful distinction should be established between the personal and human, between our socio-cultural and biological identities.

Miguel Nogueira de Brito's and Edson Fachin's contributions highlight the role of human dignity in debates about the role of law in stem cell research, and, more generally, in bioethics. While Fachin analyzes the topic from a cosmopolitan, Kantian standpoint, Brito chooses instead the critical path, relying on authors like Foucault and Habermas to provide his frame of analysis. Fachin focuses on the Brazilian debate about stem cell research, using the Brazilian Federal Supreme Court's judgment on a challenge to the constitutionality of a law on biomedical research as the background against which to discuss broader concepts such as personality rights, and the overall place of human dignity in the legal system. Brito, instead, starts from theoretical debates on the value of human life and biopolitics, using these concepts to discuss Portuguese and Brazilian takes on stem cell research and biomedical research more generally.

Despite their very different frames of analysis, though, both contributions reach strikingly similar conclusions, in defending a greater role of human dignity, and essentially conceding that the Kantian approach, however inspired by Judeo-Christian theology, is the one that offers the strongest protection to human dignity, an essential value that is undoubtedly at stake when it comes to bioethical research.

Pedro Ferreira, in his contribution 'Angels and Demons: Data protection and security in electronic communications', concentrates on the risks posed to individual privacy by the current 'networked world'. Departing from this perspective, he discusses the tensions between information/networks and community/identity, and the consequences it puts on human rights, affirming that 'this tension increases the closer we get to a world where to be on-line is not opposed to being off-line'. Then he moves to the different risks new technological devices pose to privacy, basing his analysis on four 'paradoxes': a) more communication, more disclosure; b) more participation, more exclusion; c) more security, less freedom; and, d) more communication, less control. Through these 'paradoxes' he criticizes the way governments and private companies are gathering enormous amounts of personal data for security purposes, letting aside any necessity or proportionality text. According to Ferreira, 'Data processing should only take place when the imperatives of security so require, in full implementation of the principle of proportionality (...)'. Finally, although not proposing a definitive solution for this dilemma, he suggests the enforcement of some data protection principles in order to ensure a minimum level of data protection.

Mario Viola de Azevedo Cunha and Danilo Doneda, in the chapter entitled 'Privacy, Security and new technologies: a Brazilian approach to privacy issues in the public security field', analyze the conflict between the right to privacy and security in the use of new technologies for the fight against crime. The scholars consider that one of the great challenges of the 21st century in the field of data protection is to establish an adequate balance between the need to ensure public security and the protection of individual privacy.

The authors draw the attention to the fact that, especially with the advent of the internet, a new facet of the right to privacy is being threatened, namely when personal information is collected and shared through the use of new technological tools for the purposes of fighting against or preventing crime. In effect, and following the terrorist attacks in the US and Europe, Viola de Azevedo Cunha and Doneda talk about a 'security threat' to privacy, according to which national security issues may unjustifiably trump the privacy protection of citizens. In this context, and focused on the Brazilian case, the scholars analyze the threats to privacy posed by new technological tools that play an important role in the fight against cybercrime, namely closed-circuit television (CCTV), body scanners and DNA databases.

The scholars thus move on to the critical description of the Brazilian Data Protection Framework and its most recent legislative and jurisprudential developments. In this respect, and despite the lack of a comprehensive data protection framework (Brazil has not yet a general data protection regulation, presenting only some general constitutional provisions and sectorial data protection rules), the authors note the fact that many Brazilian courts have recognized not only the protection of the traditional dimension of the right to privacy ('the right to be let alone') but also the protection of the informational aspect of privacy ('the ability of people to control information about themselves') and the right to self-determination ('the individuals should have the capacity to decide about circumstances that affect them').

Afterwards, Viola de Azevedo Cunha and Doneda make a brief survey of the main cases in which private and public bodies in Brazil have been resorting to new technologies in order to monitor people and process their personal data, raising thus legitimate concerns about privacy and data protection. This is the case of the monitoring of employee's emails in the workplace, wiretapping and other forms of government surveillance, as well as the Brazilian nationwide system for identifying vehicles (SINIAV) through the use of RFID technologies, video surveillance and DNA databases.

Norberto Andrade and Paul De Hert, in their article 'Proposing a Right to Identity within the international framework of Human Rights: Issues and Prospects', explain in detail the challenges posed to the legal regulation of personal identity and the importance of re-activating and re-conceptualizing a right to identity within the Human Rights' sphere. In order to do so, they start by examining how new (and prospective) technological developments are changing the old premises and paradigms of identity. They thus look into the impact that the so-called Ambient Intelligence (AmI) or Ubiquitous Computing environments (i.e., post-Internet scenarios) will exert upon personal identity and its legal framework. Afterwards, the scholars discuss a series of writings from authors that argue in favor of a re-conceptualization of the right to identity: Pino, Andrade, Oreg, Brownsword and others. They attach this doctrinarian movement to the ever expanding and more flexible manner through which law has been addressing and regulating identity, endowing individuals with more and more legal tools with which they can influence and change aspects of their identity. A comparative reading of these different writings allow the scholars to withdraw a number of interesting common positions and arguments regarding the right to identity, such as the identification of specific identity-related concerns, threats and dangers that: a) are not covered by the existing legal framework, namely by the right to privacy or other rights; b) that demand specific legal protection; and c) that require a new balancing of interests; and the argument in favor of an explicit and specific right to identity and the debate about the need and desirability of considering it (or upgrading it to) a human right. The rest of their chapter is devoted to this last question, debating a human rights-based approach to the emergent right to identity. Andrade and De Hert contextualize this question by: first, describing the existing legal framework on human rights law that regulates identity-related aspects, as well as the latest developments concerning the right to identity in the field of international human-rights framework; and second, by discussing a number of policy initiatives that call for new Information Society rights. The authors also provide us with several examples of recent human rights initiatives, which argue in favor of a right to Internet access, elderly, water and data protection, in order to then address the feasibility of a new right to personal identity. After examining the need and advantages (as well as possible disadvantages) of a human rights-based approach to the right to identity, Andrade and De Hert propose a comprehensive right to identity as fully-fledged human right, along the lines of Article 8 of 1989 UN Convention of Rights of the Child. This right should thus be applicable to all citizens, whether off-line or on-line.

In his contribution to this volume, Lucas Lixinski discusses the law and politics surrounding cyberwarfare, and the challenges this type of war pose to international human rights law. Much of the debate surrounding the need for regulating cyberwarfare points to the blurring of the public-private distinction, because of the special nature of cyberspace. The blurring of the public-private distinction is the reason he focuses his analysis on the privatization of cyberwarfare, arguing that both the newness of the technology and the use of private contractors create a double regulatory vacuum, which does little in the way of creating an opportunity for developing countries to counter empire.

Starting with a number of recent proposals that directly or indirectly restrict freedom of expression over the internet, Joana Varron Ferraz, Carlos Affonso Pereira de Souza, Bruno Magrani and Walter Britto undertake a comparative analysis of Argentina, Brazil, Chile, Colombia, Mexico and Venezuela. Their aim is to scrutinize the reasons behind these proposals, as well as to assess their impact on freedom of expression. For this purpose, the authors review the pertinent legislation, case law and public policy concerning Internet regulation, with a particular focus on filtering and cases involving content removal in Brazil. In this regard, the authors display well-grounded apprehension towards the skewed and abusive application of the current legal provisions, as it may lead to an unjustified restriction of freedom of expression in the Web. Their plea is one for a more careful and balanced approach to content filtering in South America.

Ana Nordberg writes on the cutting-edge topic of nanotechnologies, providing us with an overview of its implications in terms of human rights and patent law. The author starts by emphasizing how nanotechnology has become a much-coveted field of research both for the North and the Global South. In what concerns the latter, Ana reviews the advantages and potential dangers associated with the developing countries' investment in nanotechnologies, an option that may further deepen the development gap but that may also bring economic advantages. The author then focuses her attention on the implications of nanotechnologies on human rights and, in particular, on the interface between the right to health and patent law. In her view, a more balanced approach to patent law relying on a number of limitations, exclusions and exceptions would provide a more adequate legal answer to the challenges posed by the right to health.

All in all, this book is meant to inform, debate and problematize, in yet unexplored directions, the intricate relationship between new technologies and human rights. Be it by bringing into the discussion the latest technological advancements that were not included in earlier literature (because the technology was not present then in the same way it is today), be it by bringing new perspectives and horizons, we hope to make a collective contribution to discussions about the roles of technology and of human rights law, with a view of perhaps sparking novel projects that can rely on these discourses as a means of re-structuring the usual debate that comes from most thinking about technology across the North-South spectrum.

The Editors

PART I
General Legal and Philosophical Aspects of the Interaction between Human Rights and New Technologies

Chapter 1

Human Rights in the Information Society: Utopias, Dystopias and Human Values[1]

Giovanni Sartor

Introduction

Information and communication technologies (ICTs) are bringing about a pervasive economic, social, and anthropological transformation. They are changing productive processes: the production of physical commodities by means of other physical commodities is accompanied by, and integrated with, the production of information by means of information, i.e., new productive processes where information is both the rough stuff and the outcome (consider for instance, the creation of software, digital content, and web services such as searching, mining, filtering, aggregating, hosting and organising data, etc.). ICTs involve new ways of organizing economic activities: distances become largely irrelevant, flexible organization is enabled by the adaptable informational infrastructures, the enhanced capacity to produce and communicate favours new forms of cooperation. They support the integration between industry and culture, production and socialization, in the interlocked development of software and digital contents, through commercial firms, individual endeavours, or peer-based networks. ICTs drive the convergence between different technologies, pertaining to hardware, software, telecommunication, electronics, biotechnology, etc. Being based on knowledge, ICT provide the environment for producing new knowledge, in all other domains of culture, science and technology, including first of all ICTs themselves.

This emerging technological, economic and social framework (the so-called information society, or knowledge society),[2] offers new huge opportunities for individual and social development, as well as serious risks.

ICTs: Opportunities for Human Development

1. Economic development. First of all, ICTs provide many new opportunities for economic development. They support a vast increase in productivity, in industrial production as well as in related administrative and commercial processes. As machines for processing matter enabled a huge increase in productivity during the industrial revolution, so informational machines (the innumerable virtual machines realized by putting software on top of the hardware) now enable a similar increase in information-processing productivity – an increase that also affects the computer-driven production of material objects. Moreover, the fusion of computing and telecommunication allows innovation and development to be rapidly transmitted and distributed, transcending

1 I am very grateful to Jon Bing, for his many suggestions, which have enabled me to expand and refine this chapter.

2 See for all Castells, M. (2000). *The Rise of the Network Society*. Oxford: Oxford University Press.

geographical barriers. While centuries were necessary for industrial technologies to spread outside of Europe, ICTs have conquered all continents in a few decades.

2. Efficiency in the public sector. Second, ICTs can contribute to the efficiency of public organizations, reducing the administrative costs involved in delivering public services, and providing more information, transparency and accountability, so favouring equal access. Workflows can be redesigned and accelerated, mechanical activities can be automated, citizens' interactions with the administration can be facilitated, documents can be made publicly accessible, participation in administrative proceedings can be enhanced, and so can controls over the exercise of administrative and political functions. The preservation of a 'social state' under increasingly stringent economic constraints depends on the ability of using information technologies for reducing the cost of the delivery of public services.

3. Culture and education. ICTs can contribute to deliver information, education and knowledge to everybody. There is the possibility of packaging information and education as digital goods that can be distributed at zero marginal costs: once information goods are made available (and the cost for their creation has been sustained) providing them to additional on-line users is costless. This makes a significant difference as compared with traditional hardware-based media, where each new copy had production, transportation and commercialization costs. Moreover, new technologies dramatically reduce the costs involved in the production of intellectual goods (e.g., typesetting, recording, revising, modifying, processing data, etc.).

4. Creativity and progress. ICTs deliver unprecedented opportunities for individual creativity. Not only can individuals communicate more easily, but ICTs also provide new creative tools for producing information goods. Now it is possible to publish texts, make movies, record music, develop software at a much smaller cost, and with much greater effectiveness than ever before. An increasing section of humanity can contribute to the decentralized production of culture, creating contents that can be made accessible to everybody.

5. Social knowledge. ICTs enable the aggregation of individual efforts into social knowledge. In the so-called web 2.0,[3] content is mainly provided by the users, through platforms delivering and integrating their contributions. This happens in the simplest way through the non-organized 'crowd-sourcing' in the content repositories available on the web (YouTube, Twitter, etc.), which constitute collective works by aggregating separate individual contributions. It is not the first time that users appropriate a communication medium to transmit user-generated content. It happened with traditional phones, when public switchboards disappeared and communication costs dramatically decreased so that phones could be filled with commercial communications and the chatter of the subscriber.[4] In the Internet case, however, there is a major difference: user-generated content can be permanently stored and asynchronously accessed, becoming a shared source of information. More self-conscious kinds of participation in collaborative efforts are provided by open source projects for the production of software (Linux, Firefox, OpenOffice, Tex and Latex distributions, etc.), intellectual works (like Wikipedia), and peer-production of artistic or scientific contents.[5] Moreover, the combination of individual actions can generate new information content even without individual intentions, as it happens when individual choices are aggregated into outcomes relevant to others (blogs get clustered around relevant hubs, individual preferences are

3 O'Reilly, T. and J. Battelle (2009). *Web Squared: Web 2.0 Five Years On*. Beijing, Cambridge, Farnham, Köln, Sebastopol, Tokyo: O'Reilly Media.

4 Personal communication by John Bing.

5 Benkler, Y. (2006). *The Wealth of Networks: How Social Production Transforms Markets and Freedoms*. New Haven, Conn.: Yale University Press.

combined into reputation ratings, spam filtering systems aggregate user signals, links to web-pages are merged into relevance indexes, etc.).

6. Communication. Information technologies allow individuals to interact with their peers, regardless of physical distance. Here the focus is on the integration of computing and communication technologies, which diminishes the cost of telecommunications, makes them ubiquitously available (through digital phones, Internet connections, etc.), and consequently facilitates the interaction between individuals (from e-mail, to social network, to chats and voice over IP, etc.). This has expanded each one's chance to find and exchange opinions, and freely establish associative links having different degrees of intensity. In particular, it provides new opportunities for those belonging to minorities (in culture, ethnicity, attitudes, interests, etc.), enabling them to enter social networks where they can escape solitude and discrimination. In a way, ICTs realize the dream of Nozick,[6] i.e., the idea of a polity resulting from a network of multiple freely formed associations, built by the unconstrained choices of the concerned individuals.

7. Public dialogue and deliberation. ICTs (and in particular the Internet) have enabled the formation of a new public sphere, where individuals merge their opinions and build social knowledge in a variety of ways. Not only can individuals engage with one another, as they have always done in face-to-face interaction and debate. New ways of political communication have emerged, where one can post one's contribution to an unlimited number of hearers, or people can merge their cognitive efforts in a variety of ways. In a way the Internet realizes the dream of Habermas,[7] namely, the idea of polity whose choices result from open uncoerced dialogues, under conditions of equality and rationality. Equality can be enhanced by the fact that people can assume an on-line identity that abstracts from their particular condition, and thus be immune from the (racial, social, etc.) stereotypes associated to that condition. Competence can be enhanced by the fact that citizens can avail themselves of the evidence accessible through ICTs and of the insights obtainable by processing such data. The idea that media could be used not only for broadcasting, but also for communicating is not new. For instance, Brecht ([1932] 1990) argued that the radio should be used not only for transmitting but also receiving information, becoming 'the most wonderful public communication system', it should connect the listener rather than isolate him, transform him into a speaker, rather than a mere hearer. According to Brecht, the radio could include its users as main providers of information, it could become the place where democratic dialogue takes place, where citizens interact with political rulers and consumers with producers, where proposals are made, questions are asked, explanations and reasons are given. While these expectations have not been fulfilled by traditional media (such as the radio or the television), which have remained mainly or only within the broadcasting model, the Internet has shown the ability to fully integrate distribution and communication, effectively working as a two way many-to-many communication channel. It remains to be seen to what extent our social and political systems and our social networks will be able to profit from this opportunity for enhancing the quality of politics.[8]

8. Universalism and moral progress. ICTs may promote moral progress: by overcoming barriers to communication, offering people new forms of collaboration, by reducing costs involved in engaging in creative activities, it may favour attitudes inspired to universalism, (reasonable) altruism, and participation, beyond what may be expected from a merely self-interest individual.[9] In fact, when costs are removed, or limited to a minimum, then performing a creative activity

6 Nozick, R. (1974). *Anarchy, State and Utopia*. Oxford: Blackwell.

7 Habermas, J. ([1992] 1999). *Between Facts and Norms*. Cambridge, Mass.: MIT.

8 See Druckman et al. 2009, Chadwick 2009; on e-elections, see Trechsel 2007.

9 Benkler, Y. and H. Nissenbaum (2006). 'Commons-based peer production and virtue'. *Journal of Political Philosophy* 14: 394–419.

without expecting a direct monetary reward may become more attractive, even to those having only moderate moral (altruistic) motivation. Moreover, the idea of benefiting others through one's own work can become more appealing when the work to be done is rewarding in itself, there are little costs attached to it, and a universal audience can access it. Similarly, the idea of reciprocity can become more attractive (and free-riding on others less so) when reciprocation becomes easier, being included in a broader set of interactions. Altruism and reciprocation may indeed merge (as in the so-called indirect reciprocity), so that one may expect some reward from one's participation in a virtual community, but this reward is not conditioned to one's contribution, and comes from people different from those that have benefited from that contribution (as is the case for open source software, Wikipedia, etc.).

ICTs: Risks

The ICT opportunities outlined above need to be combined with the awareness of the risks related to use of information technologies. I shall summarize and emphasize these risks by linking them to some literary works, which give fantastic reality to dystopian perspectives. In fact science fiction writers have paid much more attention to dystopias than utopias, focusing on the dangers of a technological future.

1. The first risk is *Orwell's nightmare*, i.e., the use of technology for surveillance, from the story in the novel *Nineteen Eighty-Four*[10]. Orwell describes a society where every aspect of human life is controlled through telescreens and microphones located in houses and streets, so that people were forced not only to behave according to the expectations addressed to them but also to assume corresponding attitudes and beliefs. Today's ICTs have made surveillance much easier than before, since the costs of surveillance have dropped enormously, while its accuracy has increased. This is brought about by the increased possibility of using information technology for uploading information from life scenes, with or without human supervision, both in physical and virtual scenarios (consider for instance street cameras and the possibility of monitoring e-mail communication as well as any Internet-mediated activity). As *Dobrzeniecki*[11] observes, this nightmare may be viewed as a society-wide realization of Bentham's Panopticon (a prison where inmates would always be potentially visible to the invisible guardian in every moment of their life), which *Foucault*[12] sees as a paradigm of 'disciplinary' power (based on surveillance and control). In fact, information automatically uploaded from life scenes can be stored in digital form and processed automatically, enabling those in power to detect any unwanted behaviour. New forms of surveillance can be brought about by the combination of neuroscience and computing, such as the possibility of identifying states of mind on the basis of the electric activity of the brain.

2. The second risk is *Kafka's nightmare*, i.e., the use of technologies for cover control and judgment, from the novel *Trial*[13] where a man is prosecuted (and in the end executed) for a crime whose nature is never revealed to him.[14] As the trial goes on, the man progressively loses his autonomy and self

10 Orwell, G. ([1949] 2004). *Nineteen Eighty-Four*. London: Penguin.

11 Dobrzeniecki, K. (2008). 'A Janus-faced view of the electronic governance. between Foucault and Habermas'. In Schweighofer, E., ed., *Legal Informatics and e-Governance as Tools for the Knowledge Society*, pp. 25–41. Prensas Universitarias de Zaragoza, Zaragoza.

12 Foucault, M. (1975), *Discipline and Punish: The Birth of the Prison*, New York: Random House.

13 Kafka, F. (2007). *The Trial*. London: Penguin. (1st ed. 1925).

14 For the idea of a Kafka's nightmare, see Solove, D.J. (2008). '"I've got nothing to hide" and other misunderstandings of privacy'. *San Diego Law Review* 44: 745–72.

esteem, the very sense of his dignity. ICTs may contribute to this nightmare, since the information collected and stored can be used for assessing individual behaviour, according to any criteria, and make decisions on the concerned individuals (from minor one, such as those on giving a loan or an insurance policy, to those involving access to work or even to criminal prosecution or political repression). This issue has indeed been taken into account to some extent by the EU data protection directive (95/46/EC, art. 15), which grants every person the right 'not to be subject to a decision based solely on automated processing'. We may possibly say that what is at issue is not just the possibility of a negative judgment, but also a double attack on one's position as a legal and moral agent. On the one hand, one is deprived from the possibility of articulating one's perspective, of expressing one's point of view of one's own case, as a partner in a legal or moral dialogue. Thus one is denied the status of a moral subject, namely, the capacity of bringing one's arguments upon one's case, as an input the decision-maker should take into account. On the other hand one may also be denied the status of a moral object, being viewed as a mere thing, rather than as an 'end in itself': a comprehensive consideration of one's interests, the personality of individuals (as they can be captured by the empathic understanding of another person) plays no role in the decision. It is true, disregard for one's comprehensive personality is a necessary feature of all rule-based decisional processes. However, the recognition of one's dignity requires that, at least in extreme cases (when the application of the rule would involve a completely unjustified or unbalanced sacrifice of the individual), the possibility of an individual exception should be considered.

3. The third risk is *Huxley's nightmare*, i.e., technologies for discrimination and exclusion, from the novel *Brave New World*,[15] which delineates a world where humans are divided into castes, produced by applying certain technologies to human foetuses (genetics was not yet known, so Huxley considered differentiation being produced by giving foetuses different substances and putting them in different temperatures, etc.). Each caste would be specifically destined and confined to a particular occupation and kind of life. This dystopia raises two issues concerning ICTs. The first issue concerns the possibility that the emerging combination of ICTs and biotechnologies may be used in the future not for therapeutic purposes, nor even for enhancing human possibilities but rather for limiting and constraining the very biological bases of human freedom and equal dignity (an aspect addressed, for instance, in the movie *Gattaca*, issued in 1997). A second issue concerns the fact that moral equality of humans is also based on their factual quasi-equality, namely, on the fact that our physical and cognitive capacities are quite similar (even though the arrangement of an advanced society can make even small differences highly significant, and give a high marked values to differential talents). Where such differences have expanded through the differentiated access to enhancement technologies, one may wonder whether humans could continue to see themselves as equal members of the same community. The third aspect, which has a more concrete bearing for the issues addressed here, concerns the possibility that the information stored in computer systems (e.g., genetic or health information) is used for distinguishing and discriminating individuals, by classifying them into stereotypes without regard for their individual features, or taking into invidious consideration certain features of them, subjecting them to unjust treatment with regard to employment and other social goods.

4. The fourth risk is *Bradbury's nightmare*, i.e., technologies causing ignorance and indifference, from the novel *Fahrenheit 451*,[16] which inspired the homonymous movie by François Truffaut. The novel describes a world where books are forbidden, and people are only fed the information that the political power wants to provide them, in order to produce pleasurable emotions while

15 Huxley, A. ([1932] 1994). *Brave New World*. Flamingo. (1st ed. 1932).

16 Bradbury, R. ([1953] 1996). *Fahrenheit 451*. London: HarperCollins. (First Ed. 1954).

preventing any critical thinking. Interestingly, there is some degree of interactivity, but biased and manipulative: soap operas float on wall-sized screens and the viewer is mailed lines in order to slot his or her own words into the plot. One may argue that something similar may be already happening in the television domain, at least to some extent and in some places. Advanced ICTs could enable malevolent political-economic powers to achieve such an outcome to a higher extent: advanced technologies for the identification of content could allow unwanted materials to be tracked and eliminated, and at the same time, people could be provided with whatever information was considered to be useful for distraction or indoctrination.

5. The fifth risk is *Capek's nightmare*, from the play *R.U.R. (Rossum's Universal Robots)*,[17] the first text where the word 'robot' was used (from the Czech *robota*, meaning work, or *robtnik*, meaning servant). The play describes how artificial 'men' are constructed, first with the intention of helping humans, but then with the purpose of substituting them.[18] The widespread use of the robots makes human work redundant, and with work the engagements and commitments that give meaning to human life are also lost. In the end the robotic slaves will rebel and wipe out humanity. While an anticipation of this idea can be found the myth of the Golem (expounded in the homonymous novel by Gustav Meyrink[19] (and movie by Paul Wagener) or in the Frankenstein story,[20] the idea of the rebellion of the slaves can also be traced back to the famous pages of Hegel's *Phenomenology of Mind*,[21] where the Master, after delegating all work to the Slave, loses the ability to interact with nature and with his fellows, the capacity to act as the intermediary between his desires and their satisfaction. By becoming dependent on ICTs, we may similarly lose our ability to think and act on our own, become completely passive, a mere 'desire machine', relying on machines for all productive and communicative initiatives. This idea can also be found in Asimov's Robot-Saga,[22] where peoples who have decided to rely on robots progressively become so dependent on them that they will lose the ability to act on their own, as well as their initiative and interest in life. Human passivity may be promoted by the fact that automated technologies are really superior to humans in an increasing number of tasks. We may therefore fall into what Guenther Anders called 'Promethean shame', namely, be ashamed for being inferior to our artefacts. We may view ourselves as antiquated beings, outperformed by our technologies, as inappropriate inhabitants of the society of our objects, as an antique piece of furniture in a new room. We may even feel embarrassed for resulting from an inferior and imperfect method of production, for having been born instead of made.[23]

6. I reserve *Asimov's nightmare* for the sixth risk, i.e., technologies causing separation and loss of communication between humans, from the novels *The Naked Sun*[24] and *Foundation and Earth*,[25] where a planet (Solaria) is described whose culture rejects every physical contact. Its inhabitants (humans transformed through genetic engineering) only engage in face-to-face contact with their robots, with whom they have developed a symbiotic interdependence. Their supreme moral ideal

17 Capek, K. ([1920] 2004). *R.U.R. (Rossum's Universal Robots)*. London: Penguin.

18 On robots and the law, see Bing, J. (2008). 'The riddle of the robots'. *Journal of International Commercial Law and Technology*, pp. 197–206.

19 Mayrink, G. ([1914] 2000). *The Golem*. Dedalus, Sawtry.

20 Shelley, M. (1818). *Frankenstein; or, The Modern Prometheus*. Lackington, Hughes, Harding, Mavor and Jones, pp. 315–56.

21 Hegel, G.W.F. ([1807] 1931). *The Phenomenology of Mind*. London: Allen and Unwin.

22 See in particular Asimov, I. (1985). *Robots and Empire*. London: Collins.

23 Anders, G. (1961). *The Antiquiertheit des Menschen*. Muenchen: Beck.

24 Asimov, I. (1957). *The Naked Sun*. Doubleday, New York, N.Y.

25 Asimov, I. (1986). *Foundation and Earth*. London: Collins.

of individual autonomy requires refusing all contacts with other humans, and in the few instances where contact is necessary to use telecommunication tools.[26] This social arrangement corresponds to some present trends: Internet surfing and the solitary access to digital contents, games and other interactive programs, can become a substitute to face-to-face human interaction (as in the case of the reclusive young Japanese called hikikomori, who remain in their computer-connected rooms, rejecting any social contact). The separation dystopia may also take a group rather than individual-based perspective. In a flexible information infrastructure, individuals (at least those empowered to do that) may establish with whom to interact, what kind of information to access and in what social networks to participate. The possibility of engaging in social interaction transcending geographic limits may lead us to rejecting physical proximity as a source of social bonds. Thus, individuals may lose contact with their broader social environment, with the political and social problems in which their fellows are involved, and choose to avoid unanticipated encounters and unfamiliar topics or points of views. Sunstein[27] has argued that democracy may be at risk under such conditions, and that an active (though not authoritarian) public intervention may be justified to promote a broader exposure to information and social interaction.

7. The seventh risk is *Nozick's nightmare*, i.e., technologies for illusion and artificial pleasure, from the story of the *Experience Machine*, contained in Nozick,[28] where 'super-duper neuropsychologists' have figured out a way to stimulate a person's brain to induce pleasurable experiences, which that person cannot distinguish from real ones (as in the early science fiction tale *The Chamber of Life*).[29] Thus virtual experience could become a substitute for real experience, providing easier and deeper satisfaction than real life, it could become an electronic drug susceptible of taking possession of human minds. Humans indeed may become indifferent to their natural and social environment (the landscape, the art, the architecture around them), to their relations with other people (e.g., friendships and even sexual relationships), substituting them with virtual experiences. The idea of a technology-induced exchange illusion for reality can be found in various science fiction works, such as Philip Dick's novel 'We Can Remember It for You Wholesale',[30] from which the movie *Total Recall* (1990), directed by Paul Verhoeven, was inspired. It was also addressed in movies such as *eXistenZ* (1999), directed by David Cronemberg and the *Matrix* movies (1999–2003), by Larry and Andy Wachowski.

8. The eighth risk is *Vonnegut's nightmare*, i.e., technologies causing class division and exclusion, from the novel *Player's piano*,[31] which depicts a society where technology, by substituting most human labour, divides society into two separate classes. An upper, well educated class includes those having the knowledge and skills to operate the new technological environment, governing the machines and addressing the problems of a complex technological society, while the rest of the people (those whose work could be substituted by a computer or a robot) would be made redundant, deprived of meaningful life and forced into the army or in the most menial jobs. In fact, there are many new work opportunities opened by ICT, but unless everybody is enabled to profit from them, through education and social organization (unless the digital divide, broadly

26 A similar future has been recently described in Houellebecq, M. (2006). *The Possibility of an Island*. London: Phoenix.

27 Sunstein, C.R. (2001). *Republic.com*. Princeton, N.J.: Princeton University Press.

28 Nozick, R. (1974). *Anarchy, State and Utopia*. Oxford: Blackwell.

29 See Wertenbaker, G.P. (1929, October). 'The chamber of life'. *Amazing Stories*. Manchester: Experimenter Publishing Co., Inc

30 Dick, P.K. ([1966] 2002b). 'We can remember it for you wholesale'. In *Minority Report*, pp. 267–90. London: Gollancz. (1st ed. 1966).

31 Vonnegut, K. (1952). *Player's Piano*. New York, N.Y.: Charles Scribner's Sons.

understood, is addressed) Vonnegut's dystopia remains a likely outcome. The idea that technologies may contribute to class division can also be found in the movie *Metropolis* by Fritz Lang (1927), and took a different, less likely, but more sinister, turn in Wells's *Time Machine* (Wells 1895), when humanity has split into two distinct species, one of which is used as food by the other, which has maintained the ability to work and use machines. A twist, with regard to class division, consists of the use of humanoids as disposable slaves, even though they have human-like cognitive and affective capabilities. Such slavery, involving the exploitation-consumption of the servants as well as the degradation of their masters, is described in Philip Dick's novel *Do Androids Dream Of Electric Sheep*,[32] which inspired the *Blade Runner* movie (1982), by Ridley Scott, and to some extent also the movie *AI*, by Steven Spielberg.

9. The ninth risk is *Dick's nightmare*, i.e., ICT technologies for war and human destruction. From the many dystopias emerging from the work of Philip Dick the most extreme one is probably provided by his short story *Second Variety* (to which movie *Screamers*, issued in 1995, is inspired),[33] where intelligent killer weapons developed for global warfare acquire the ability to construct and perfect themselves, become more and more similar to humans, and end by wiping out humanity. The recent developments in intelligent weapons may be just the beginning of a new arms race, based on ICTs: warfare (but not its impacts on innocent human lives) will be increasingly delegated to technological devices, of growing destructive power and precision, with outcomes engendering not only the lives of particular individuals and communities, but potentially the very future of humanity. This dystopian perspective is also developed by Stanislaw Lem's novel *The Upside-down Evolution*,[34] which describes a future where war is delegated to synthetic insects (synsects), namely 'ceramic microcrustacea, titanium annelids, and flying pseudo-hymenoptera with nerve centers made of arsenic compounds and with stingers of heavy, fissionable elements'. Such microsoldiers are endowed with swarm intelligence and can build themselves: they are designed, combat-tested, and sent to be mass-produced by 'construction battalions' of non-living microdesigners. The artificial insects establish pervasive surveillance (thanks to them anything can be a covert agent: a nail in the wall, a laundry detergent, etc.) and they dominate the world, and even merge with nature, to produce apparently natural disasters. The idea that intelligent machines may rebel against humanity and wage war against them has been developed in many further novels, such as the recent *Robocalypse*[35] and movies, such as *Terminator* (1984), by James Cameron, or *I, Robot* (2004), by Alex Proyasm.

What role for politics, law and human rights?

The opportunities and the risks described above raise a fundamental issue: what range of action do we have, as individuals and as societies, when facing the information technologies? Can we anticipate the impacts of information technologies? And can we direct such impacts, by channelling technological progress of its societal application?

32 See Dick, P.K. (1968). *Do Androids Dream Of Electric Sheep*. New York, N.Y.: Doubleday.

33 See Dick, P.K. ([1953] 2002a). 'Second variety'. In *Minority Report*, pp. 61–101. London: Gollancz.

34 In Lem, S. (1986). *One Human Minute*. Harcourt.

35 Wilson, D. H. (2011). *Robocalypse*. New York, N.Y.: Doubleday.

When facing informational technologies we should avoid the risks of inventing another philosophy of history, falling back on what Karl Popper called the 'poverty of historicism',[36] i.e., the pretension of detecting a necessary and inescapable trend in the technology-driven social development.

In fact we cannot imagine the outcomes emerging from the aggregation of infinite individual choices nor the creative responses of individual minds to the complexity of their social and technological environment. In fact, many uses of information technologies, opening new unpredictable opportunities for individual and social action, were not anticipated by the very people building those technologies. For instance, the inventors of the computer did not imagine that each of us would have multiple computers at our disposal (in one's personal computer, in the mobile phone, in the car, in the kitchen, etc.), as the constructors of the Internet did not think about its many applications (e-mail, chats, web-browsing, electronic commerce, Wikipedia, cloud computing, social networks, etc.).

Uncertainty concerning technological and social development does not eliminate our responsibility for governing the technology-driven social development, profiting of opportunities and preventing at least the most serious dangers. It also does not exclude the attempt to anticipate change, prospecting future scenarios and advancing possible solutions, even though we should be cautious since our forecasts (and moral-political judgments based on them) may be mistaken, and even the obvious assessments may be contradicted by reality. What if only a few decades ago, somebody would have said that the future informational infrastructure of humanity would not be controlled by any political body and would be run by a weird mixture of associations, working groups, and companies? Who could have imagined the spread of the mobile phone in African countries, the development of Internet centres in Brazilian favelas, the activity of bloggers during the Iranian protest, the Iraqi war, the recent popular movements in Tunisia and Egypt?

Addressing the issues of the information society requires the integration of different legal measures (concerning issues such as data protection, security, electronic commerce, electronic documents, etc.), as well as appropriate public policies (addressing economical, political, social, educational issues), combined with self-regulation by the involved social actors and groups of them. However, the need to respect and promote the so-called generativity of the Internet, namely, the fact that in its open environment new ideas, technologies, ways of interacting emerge through accumulation of free individual initiatives,[37] makes Internet Governance a process of trial and error, of piecemeal tinkering. But then having broad and open guidelines, such as human rights, may provide the right kind of guidance. Human rights are indeed important since they provide us with a framework for articulating some basic normative structures for the governance of the information society, in the awareness of the human values at stake. It is true, authoritative formulations, doctrinal developments and social understanding of human rights cannot provide us with a complete regulatory framework: economical and technological consideration must be taken into account, while legal traditions and political choices play a decisive role in many regards (even with regard to the very understanding of human rights and their balance). However, the human-rights discourse still play an important role: it identifies some basic fundamental needs and entitlements, it links our understanding of such needs and entitlements to successes and failures of human history, it enables us to provide a context for our analysis of the new issues emerging in the information society, linking such analysis to a rich background including legal cases as well as social, political and legal debates.

---

36 Popper, K.R. (1959). *The Logic of Scientific Discovery*. London: Hutchinson. (1st ed. in German 1934).

37 Zittrain, J. (1994). 'The generative Internet'. *Harvard Law Review* 119: 1974–2006.

Specific human rights involved

Even a superficial reading of the main human rights sources reveals that number of human rights are involved in the opportunities and risks of the information society. Here I shall only focus on the 1948 Universal Declaration of Human Rights, and I shall limit myself to some general considerations.[38]

In article 1 of the Declaration ('All human beings are born free and equal in dignity and rights') we find two broadest (though most vague and controversial) rights, the right to freedom and the right to dignity. Freedom – broadly understood as the opportunity for self-determination – and dignity – broadly understood as the opportunity to enjoy the consideration and respect that each human deserves – identify the fundamental, though largely undetermined, references for assessing the opportunities and risks considered above. These two rights provide background justifications for more specific rights, having a high and specific relevance in the information society, the right to freedom of expression and the right to privacy. Freedom and dignity provide the deepest rationales for such specific rights, even though these rationales are often controversial, multifaceted, and pulling in opposite directions (e.g. by exercising the freedom to collect information and express facts and views about other people, one may violate their privacy, whose protection, in its turn, may be a condition for the freedom of action of the concerned people). Concern for freedom would require us to take care of all the opportunities we have listed in section 2 while preventing the 'nightmares' mentioned in section 3. Providing such opportunities would also contribute to human dignity, as our presence in the virtual sphere gets an increasing importance for our life. Dignity is at risk when we become mere objects of social and computational processes exploiting the Internet, such as subjecting people to persistent and pervasive surveillance (Orwell's nightmare, n. 1) or to automated assessments (Kafka's nightmare, n. 2).

The combination of freedom and dignity may provide a reference (though a very partial and undetermined one) for approaching issues that go beyond specific individual rights and which can only be addressed through collective action, such as the need to provide virtual resources that enable multiple activities and engagements as well as the integration between the virtual and physical reality, so favouring human flourishing and commitment, rather than isolation and escape in virtual illusion. In fact, dignity is also at risk, in a different way, by the prospect that humans are substituted by machines and lose the opportunity (and maybe also the desire) of engaging an active life (Capek's nightmare, n. 5) and interacting with their peers (Asimov's nightmare, n. 6).

The ideas of liberty and dignity are coupled with the further right mentioned in art. 2, the right to non discrimination ('Everyone is entitled to all the rights and freedoms ... without distinction of any kind ...'). This is relevant with regard to the exclusion from access to the Internet, when some groups or kinds of persons are differentially affected. It also impinges on limitation of access to informational resources, when this can increase the underprivileged status of communities and peoples. Non-discrimination is also at issue with regards to the increased possibilities of treating people differently on the bases of classifications of them, performed on the basis of stored data (such as data concerning health conditions, and in particular genetic data), an in Huxleys' nightmare (n.3). Non-discrimination can also sometimes justify (though this is highly controversial and differently appreciated in different legal and political cultures) some limitations to other rights (as enabled by ICTs), such as freedom of expression when used to incite to hatred and discrimination

38 For a detailed account of the connection between human rights and new technologies, see for instance Joergensen, R.F. (ed.) (2006). *Human Rights in the Global Information Society*. Cambridge, Mass.: MIT; and Klang, M. and A. Murray (eds.) (2005). *Human Rights in the Digital Age*. London: Routledge.

against particular groups or communities. Equality with regard to the enjoyment of social rights is also at issue with regard to the possibility that technologies create huge differences in resources and social status, depriving most people of the possibility of decent work and of corresponding social opportunities (Vonnegut's nightmare, n.8).

Art. 3 of the Declaration grants the right to the 'Security of person' ('Everyone has the right to life, liberty and security of person'), which may be understood as covering first of all the body of a person, his or her physical integrity (which will be at issue first of all in the use of technological weapons, as in Dick's nightmare, n. 9). However we may understand this right as covering not only his 'embodied' mind (what one has stored inside one's head), but also one's 'extended mind', that is the computer memory where one has stored one's thoughts and memories and the tools one uses for developing one's cognitive efforts, alone or with others. This is an idea that has been developed by epistemologists, philosophers and experts in cognitive science, which have observed how human cognition (and memory) does not take place only inside one's head, but requires interacting with external tools.[39] It is true, there is nothing new in this idea (consider for instance how detainees in prisons or concentration camps could be hit by the prohibition to read, or to take notes), but in the information age we tend to work in symbiosis with automatic tools, so that interference with them is going to deprive us of a part of our mind, not only in a figured sense. In fact I shudder if I imagine that my computer and my backups were destroyed. I would lose all my work, the thoughts and projects I have stored, the links to people I know, etc. Besides the idea of security the idea of property could also be relevant in this connection, and the protection of property provided by art. 17 ('Everyone has the right to own property alone as well as in association with others').

Art. 12 of the Declaration sets out a cluster of rights particularly significant with regard to information technologies: the rights to privacy, to correspondence, honour and reputation ('No one shall be subjected to arbitrary interference with his privacy, family, home or correspondence, nor to attacks upon his honour and reputation'). Here one aspect of the right to privacy broadly understood is at issue, i.e., informational privacy, understood as one's right to have control over information concerning oneself (the right that this information is processed only when needed for legitimate purpose, that one can assess it and control its accuracy, and so on), the right underlying data protection legislation. Orwell's nightmare (n. 1) shows indeed how the complete deprivation of privacy may impair all individual freedoms. It has also been argued that this right can be assimilated to the *habeas corpus*, i.e., the right to our bodily integrity and freedom, since we have not only a physical dimension, but also an informational dimension. This is our 'information shadow', i.e., the aura of data that accompanies each one of us and is constitutive of our social personality (determining how others see us). In the information society our information shadows have become larger, thicker and more connected, as an increasing amount of personal information can be automatically captured, stored, linked and processed in multiple ways. Information privacy is related through a complex web with other human rights, sometimes being in conflict with them (e.g. with the right to access and impart information) and sometimes, on the contrary, providing the background for their exercise (again, the right not to be discriminated, to hold opinion, etc.). The right to communication (to the respect of correspondence) needs obviously to also apply to electronic correspondence, which has now almost completely substituted the traditional exchange of paper messages. The right to reputation is also highly relevant, considering that today one's reputation can be interfered with by publishing information on-line and this information is going to be accessible for ever, even if false or inaccurate, or no longer corresponding to the identity of the person.

39 See Clark, A. and D.J. Chalmers (1998). 'The extended mind'. *Analysis* 58: 10–23.

Art. 19 of the Declaration addresses the relation between humans and information content, by granting freedom of opinion, expression and access to information ('Everyone has the right to freedom of opinion and expression; this right includes freedom to hold opinions without interference and to seek, receive and impart information and ideas through any media and regardless of frontiers'). The Internet has indeed expanded unprecedentedly our ability to express and transmit opinions, by enabling everyone to reach a universal audience through web pages, blogs, discussion groups, and other ways of delivering one's communications and intellectual creations. Recently the so-called web 2.0 has emerged, a new socio-technical framework where everyone can, and often does, contribute to the creation of on-line content, expressing one's opinion and making it accessible to a universal audience. This expanded liberty has often been countered by oppressive regimes, which have restricted this liberty for the purpose of political control. As in Bradbury's nightmare (n. 4), information technology, while enhancing access to information, also offers new possibilities for restricting access to content and also for changing and falsifying information (even for rewriting the past, as Orwell imagined in his novel *1984*, though he did not envisage how much cheaper and quicker this could be thanks to information technologies fully controlled by political power). Therefore all limitations to freedom of information must be subject to very strict scrutiny, even though this liberty may be subject to the limitations provided for by art. 29 of the Declaration, i.e., 'the just requirements of morality, public order and the general welfare in a democratic society', or rather with the different ways in which these limitations are understood in different societies and by different people (for instance, limitations concerning pornography, glorification of violence and terrorist propaganda, incitation to racial, religious or ethnic hatred have been invoked against particular content posted on-line).

The exercise of the right to 'receive and impart information' (art. 19) is hugely facilitated by the Internet, which allows costless universal distribution of information, as well as by computer technologies for producing digital content. Similarly, the right to participate in culture and science (art. 27: 'Everyone has the right freely to participate in the cultural life of the community, to enjoy the arts and to share in scientific advancement and its benefits'), is supported by ICTs, which facilitate access to existing intellectual and artistic works, as well as the creation of new content to an unprecedented level.

By enabling the reproduction and the modification of existing content, ICTs interfere with the rights of authors and inventors (art. 27: 'Everyone has the right to the protection of the moral and material interests resulting from any scientific, literary or artistic production of which he is the author)'. In particular there is a tension between participation in culture and copyright, namely, the exclusive entitlement currently attributed to authors over the duplication and distribution of their works (though copyright is not mentioned in the Universal Declaration, and many have observed that its current regulation fails to adequately protect the rights of authors). How can we enable the widest access to digital content (software, texts, music, movies, audio-visual materials) and the widest opportunities for creation (also by reusing and modifying contents produced by others) while recognising the rights of the authors (and the role of cultural industry)? While many interesting initiatives, such as open source software and creative common licences, provide for innovative ways to promote access and enhance participatory aspects the regulation of copyright and patents remains a highly controversial area. It should be noted in this regard, that besides the tension between copyright and access to culture, there is a conflict that is intrinsic to copyright itself. This is related to the authors' exclusive right over the modified versions of their works, which may impede others from exercising their creativity in elaborating and developing pre-existing work.[40] Similar

40 Lessig, L. (2008). *Remix: Making Art and Commerce Thrive in the Hybrid Economy*. Penguin Press.

considerations also apply to the right to education (art. 26): by facilitating the production and worldwide distribution of educational resources (textbooks, e-learning materials, on-line courses), ICTs can contribute to the provision of knowledge and education to everybody. Implementing the right to education in the information society requires making this opportunity real, while taking into account the interests of the authors of educational resources, courses and tools (even providing them with new incentives). A beautiful example of how much can be achieved by combining ICTs and human creativity and generosity is provided by Wikipedia, the largest encyclopaedia now available, containing a huge range of high quality content. Wikipedia results from the cooperative efforts of millions of authors and is freely available through the Internet, to anyone in the world. Though the Wikipedia model may be extensible to a limited extent (since the need to provide an adequate remuneration to authors and educators must also be taken into account) it shows how ICTs in the educational-cultural domain can provide outcomes beyond all expectations.

The Internet is also having an impact on political participation (art. 21: 'Everyone has the right to take part in the government of his country, directly or through freely chosen representatives'), providing new forms of political communication between citizens, with their representatives and with the administration, new opportunities for civic engagement and participation. Even though results in e-democracy are so far limited and often disappointing, there are solid hopes for an increased informed participation of citizens to political and social debates and to legislative and regulatory procedures. In fact the Internet, coupled with various technologies for producing and delivering contents and for social networking, enables everyone to communicate his or her view and interact with others. The political arena has been enriched by discussion forums, blogs and interactive debates and comments. Where political debate and communication are constrained by repressive Government, the Internet and various ICTs (from setting up web sites and blogs, to using encryption for having secret communications and hacking techniques for overcoming informational barriers and monitor governmental activities) have enabled citizens to exercise, at least partially, their right to know about Governmental behaviour, to comment, diffuse criticisms and build political action. This has been particularly apparent in the recent uprisings in Tunisia and Egypt, which have succeeded in forcing out long-lasting dictatorships. In both cases, the Internet has played a crucial role in enabling protesters to distribute information and opinions, communicate, and get organised. However, it has often been observed that new technologies also allow pervasive political controls, meant to curb oppositions and restrict communications (websites can be closed, Internet traffic can be filtered, on-line behaviour can be monitored, etc.). In the EU worries have been raised in particular with regard to the Data Retention directive (2006/24/EC), which requires telecommunications companies to store data about all of their customers' communications, in order to facilitate criminal investigations. The collection of this data involves quite an invasive form of surveillance, since phone records provide a map of the social contacts of each citizen.

The Internet and ICTs produce various impacts on other rights and dimensions of them, such as the right to work (Art. 23): ICTs create new jobs, but make many traditional work activities redundant, undermining the lives of those practicing them; they enhance human creativity and productivity, but also enable new forms of monitoring and control endangering workers' freedom (as in Vonnegut's nightmare, n. 8). Similarly, ICTs facilitate cultural, technological and economic development, by enabling a costless world-wide distribution of knowledge and a borderless articulation of productive activities, but also create new dependencies from the owners of the relevant technologies and infrastructures, even though these dependencies, however, are alleviated for the broad availability of open source software and digital resources, and by the decreasing cost of development tools (the disastrous effect of political control over culture were an aspect of Bradbury's nightmare, n. 3). Also with regard to the protection of minorities, ICTs may provide a significant contribution: by facilitating the production and distribution of knowledge, as well as the articulation of social networks, they enable ethnic, cultural or social minorities to articulate their language and self-understanding, This is indeed happening in the Internet domain where, rather than the feared cultural homogenization, we are seeing an increasing diversity of linguistic and cultural expressions. On the contrary, the phenomenon of the so-called long tail – the fact that the Internet, reaching a global public, enables the distribution of niche products, to which a very small proportion of the population are interested – applies not only to commercial distributors but also to no-profit initiatives. For instance, Wikipedia, originally only in English, is now available in an increasing number of languages (more than 200), and contributions in different languages often reflect different cultural perspectives. Another example of the emergence of cultural differences is represented by international generic top level domains and domain names, now available not only in multiple languages, but also in multiple writing systems (Cyrillic, Arabic, Chinese, etc.).

ICTs and the concept of a human right

In the above section the connection between human rights and ICTs has been addressed in general 'political' terms, without considering the strictly legal dimension of such rights, namely, the extent to which they provide justiciable constraints over public and private action. I believe that indeed a merely legalistic understanding of such rights would fail to grasp their relevance as moral and political guidelines for a humanistic information society, for realising the opportunities indicated in Section 2 while avoiding the risks mentioned in Section 3. On this point I will follow Sen[41] who argues that human rights are primarily an ethical demand, concerning human freedoms or opportunities which satisfy some 'threshold conditions', with regard to their importance for the concerned individuals and their social influenceability. According to this author human rights may generate different kinds of obligations. Firstly such obligations may be only moral or also legal. Secondly they may have different degrees of stringency: in Kantian terms they may be imperfect duties, i.e., duties to consider the right in deliberation, or perfect duties, i.e., duty to perform certain actions or omissions (this distinction corresponds to Alexy's[42] distinction between rules and principles or to the distinction between action-duties and goal-duties in Sartor[43]). By adopting Sen's idea of human rights, we can understand how ICTs not only provide new ways of satisfying or interfering with human rights, but they also contribute to the very existence of certain human rights or at least to the identification of their content. ICTs themselves can transform a mere human opportunity into a moral human right in two complementary ways: (1) by endowing a certain human opportunity with importance and (2) by making it socially influenceable.

Let us consider, for instance, the right to have access to the Internet under fair conditions. It seems to me that this right indeed satisfies the condition for it to be at least a moral human right. Firstly, this right concerns a liberty or opportunity greatly important for each individual, i.e., participating in the network that unifies humanity and provides unique opportunities for information, communication and participation. Obviously, the importance of this opportunity does not pre-exist the Internet, but it is constituted by the Internet itself: according to the so-called network effect, the value of a network for its participants increases (in an accelerated way) as the

41 Sen, A. (2004). 'Elements of a theory of human rights'. *Philosophy and Publi Affais,* 32, 4. 315-356.

42 Alexy, R. ([1985] 2002). *A Theory of Constitutional Rights*. Oxford: Oxford University Press.

43 Sartor, G. (2010). 'Doing justice to rights and values: teleological reasoning and proportionality'. *Artificial Intelligence and Law* 18: 175–215.

number of participants increases. The Internet has already reached billions of people, embracing a huge amount of cultural/educational content and providing opportunities to communicate and publish to everybody; thus being able to access the Internet has become greatly important for each human being and being excluded from it appears to be an unacceptable diminution/discrimination. Secondly, the recent technological evolution has made the realization of this right socially influenceable, with a moderate effort, in all parts of the world: now that the web has spread over the whole earth and the costs for cables, machinery and software have gone down, we really have the means for giving everybody the opportunity of enjoying Internet access. The moral obligation for the implementation of this right would fall upon the State whose citizens need access, but also other states, organizations, and individuals would have an obligation to contribute and support the implementation of this right.

Let us now consider whether this right may be considered just a moral right or whether it is a legal right, and a legal right *de lege lata*, that should already influence institutional decision-making, rather than only a right *de lege ferenda*, i.e., something we would like to make legal through future legal instruments. I think that in this regard one has to distinguish the negative dimension of this right, namely its protection through an obligation not to impede Internet access, and its positive dimension, namely its protection through the obligation to provide the means for access (to those who are unable to obtain them on the market). With regard to the negative dimension one could argue for the existence of a perfect and enforceable obligation: forcefully excluding somebody from the Internet would amount to depriving him or her the most effective way to participate in culture and express opinion (and exercise other fundamental liberties, such as the liberty of association, political liberty, etc.). The issue has recently emerged not only when the use of the Internet for political criticism has been met with repression (as in China, and in some countries in Northern Africa and in the Middle East), but also when exclusion from the Internet is imposed as a sanction against repeated copyright violation (as in French and British legislations).

With regard to the positive dimension of the right, ensuring the means for universal Internet access may be viewed as an imperfect obligation upon States, namely, as a goal that needs to be duly taken into account in political (legislative and regulatory) decision-making, alongside other goals, within the opportunity space determined by the available resources. Failure to take it into consideration, giving it the importance it deserves, may still involve a human-rights violation (though the discretion of the legislature in articulating and prioritising human rights should be duly taken into account).

These two dimensions of such a human right can, I think, be considered existent even when positive law has not yet been explicit about it. Here is a recent statement by Frank la Rue, Special Rapporteur on the promotion and protection of the right to freedom of opinion and expression (16 May 2011),[44] who upholds a negative right to access the internet and connects it to freedom of expression, affirming that: 'cutting off users from internet access, regardless of the justification provided, including on the grounds of violating intellectual property rights law' is to be disproportionate and thus a violation of article 19, paragraph 3, of the International Covenant on Civil and Political Rights.

The fact that a right to access the Internet may be considered as already existing, on the basis of the current instruments does not exclude the utility of explicitly including such a right into international charters or national constitutions, so as to transform it into an explicitly recognized

44 UN Human Rights Council, Report of the Special Rapporteur on the promotion and protection of the right to freedom of opinion and expression, Frank La Rue, 6 May 2011, A/HRC/17/27, http://www2.ohchr.org/english/bodies/hrcouncil/docs/17session/A.HRC.17.27_en.pdf.

fundamental right. This is the aim of the initiatives concerning the creation of an Internet Bill of Rights (in particular in connection with the Internet Governance Forum and the ensuing Dynamic Coalitions). Among the national initiatives I would like to recall the one sponsored by Stefano Rodotà, to include in the Italian constitution an additional article, supplementing the existing paragraph on freedom of expression: 'Everybody has equal right to access the Internet, in condition of equality, and under technologically adequate modalities, which overcome every social or economical obstacle.'

Similar considerations on how ICTs contribute to constitute new human rights or new dimensions of them can be developed for other human rights but these will be left to future investigation.

Chapter 2

Knowledge and New Technologies: From Ethics to Politics and Law

Maria da Glória F.P.D. Garcia

Introduction

The scientific and technological challenges posed today have given rise to a knowledge crisis, a crisis of power, a crisis of law. At the same time, those challenges have raised many questions that must be answered not by politicians, philosophers or experts, but by citizens, by all of us. And this opens the door to a new community-based ethics, encompassing the future, which thus becomes our present responsibility.

Reviving old concepts of Man seems to be the answer to overcoming the crisis. The rule of law must be reinvented, starting with a return to its origins. This means summoning not only the voting citizen but also, and especially, the participating citizen, not only the subject of rights but also, and especially, the subject of duties.

We are living in times of rupture between a 'before' and an 'after', times where the search for truth, the fight for power and the quest for the meaning of law are becoming strained and renewing themselves in the wake of a rediscovered power of governance.

The southern countries are now experiencing different problems and those that we are dealing with in this chapter may appear very distant from them, as typical problems of the industrialized countries. But the question that has to be asked is this: can the southern countries anticipate the future and learn from the errors of others? Can the southern countries solve problems without having to go through them? In other words, can they prevent the problems so as not to waste time solving them, and gain a better life more easily?

The quest for education is therefore of great importance. The new ethics needs better informed citizens, who are curious about the future and inquisitive, and who exercise their rights and duties so that they can shape their destiny and be part of community solutions.

This new ethics, open to the future, and the rediscovery of the power of governance to deal with this new ethics, on the one hand, and the development of multiple public policies at various levels, led by that power of governance, on the other hand, will give people hope and confidence in the continuous preservation of the rule of law in our globalized world.

In short, we may say that due to the scientific and technological challenges we are currently facing, within the political society, there are not only fears and problems but also hopes and ways of solving problems by means of law.

Scientific and technological challenges and the risk society

Science, considered in very wide and diversified terms, and the technological developments driven by it and infinitely linked with it, have taken over our daily life.

Every day we are surprised by the progress of microbiology and all its consequences for improving our health and welfare. Over the past decades, microbiology has opened paths for the understanding of genetic codes and molecular mechanisms involved in DNA and protein synthesis, fostering the growth and development of genetics and genome engineering and enabling further progress in biotechnology. Everybody acknowledges the giant steps taken by research in the field of telecommunications, alternative energies, clean technologies and surgical medicine. And not a day goes by without our being confronted with neologisms coined in order to facilitate the communication of newly-discovered, decomposed and reassembled scientific ideas, movements, facts and phenomena.

This new reality is accompanied by an odd feeling that the concepts and assertions that we thought to be firm and unshakeable are going through a process of disintegration and are becoming worn out, and even gradually losing touch with the life that inspired them.

Questioning what we have learnt and experienced and what kind of impact that knowledge and experience has in the construction of our future has become unavoidable. No more unavoidable is the need to reflect on the fast scientific and technological development that is taking place, though we are left with little room to think it over and adapt ourselves to it. It is also true that such reflection is accompanied by the age-old certainty that nobody can predict the future or, therefore, teach us how to deal with it. The head-spinning pace of development, and the little time we are therefore left with for serious planning, consequently makes it very hard, if not totally impossible, to shape our human future collectively. This is even truer when we realize that even the normal risk of living has increased exponentially in our technical society.

In particular, since Ulrich Beck published his emblematic *Risikogesellschaft* in 1986, months after the Chernobyl accident, it has become evident that the increased welfare of society has multiplied the risk of living in a society. And the 9/11 attack on the Twin Towers in 2001 has shown how easily terror can penetrate technical society and spread within it, diversifying the means used for striking at a great number of human lives. Climatic changes, largely associated with the way of life we have created, have intensified our fears about the future, now at the global level. Increased risk and the resulting ignorance about the effects of life in society intermingle with the extended well-being of a society, where science and technology do not cease to amaze us.

This is the context of time where we find ourselves today.

And the first step towards reflecting seriously on politics and law is to allow the feeling of discomfort that stems from not knowing the value of our knowledge and from our uncertainty about the consequences of our actions, to settle within us. We must shake off the obstinacy which has, for decades, characterized the culture of western democracies and imbued our way of being in this world, the obstinacy of wanting to live with certainties.

This reflection is also a stimulus for a journey in search of greater self-awareness among citizens, awareness of the space where answers to the community should be given. This community questions and calls upon each of us daily, within the very singleness on which we are founded and where we exist. It is a space of responsibility where each person, while gaining self-awareness, seeks a global understanding of his way of being in the world, together with all the others, and tries to contribute to the transformation and excellence of the community.

Political thought and knowledge in the *polis*

The notion that when we are in community we benefit from knowledge and abilities that we do not possess but that others do, dates back to ancient times.

In classical Antiquity, Plato constructed the republic on the basis of that notion, using it to fashion justice in the city. Sophiocracy or the government of wise men was built on the need to assign tasks in accordance with the 'natural' abilities of each member of society. The fact that each person only performed the task for which he was predestined made it possible to attain justice and strengthened the whole of society. Aristotle, for his part, although starting from different premises, also maintains the underlying notion of action in the *polis*, the perfect city *par excellence*. As a matter of fact, his understanding is that it is within the *polis* that each citizen becomes, in freedom, distinct from others, as 'being with others' who complements and completes them, and thus aims at happiness. Happiness is constructed individually, by appealing to a 'virtue' which can only emerge and manifest itself in the city; hence it is seen as the virtue of citizenship. The knowledge of others enables a dialogue with one's own knowledge, fosters reciprocal enrichment and allows us to overcome the permanent social imbalances upon which justice is continuously being woven.

At a later time, during the High Middle Ages, St. Thomas Aquinas retrieved the notion and Christianized it, that is, he let it share in God's transcendence: each member of the community has diverse talents and skills, which have been granted by God. They must be used for one's own good, but at the same time for the common good.

During the Enlightenment, secularization of society and a boundless belief in Man and his potential were accompanied by the spread of rationalism. United by reason, men sedimented the idea that knowledge and individual experience combine forces in the community, in order to overcome iniquitous and despotic political regimes.

More recently, the idea that we benefit from knowledge that we do not have but that others possess, has conquered the welfare society, as Friedrich Hayek[1] has tirelessly pointed out. The way in which we fit into the world rests on that notion. We are resigned to what we do not know or have not experienced, but reach confidently for the benefits of knowledge and experience acquired by others, certain of thus contributing, in the uniqueness of each individual's knowledge and experience, towards the trust that others bring into their own interaction with us.

The banalization of ignorance and the elites

It is no surprise, within this context, that the welfare and technical society, in which we still live, continues to unfold before our eyes at a maddening pace, with its increasingly complex and specialized sciences and techniques and its discoveries and inventions. The products and goods that these generate are delivered *en masse* by means of a powerful marketing and media machinery. Yet, it is also no surprise that, at the same time, it gradually desensitizes the community in relation to the knowledge that sustains them. Ignorance becomes trivial and no longer worries those who live in this society.

Since individuals are unable to gain access to the full range of available knowledge they tend to accept without question every scientific wonder or technological innovation, one after another. As a result, not only does a steadily widening gap develop between the restricted groups of experts and the immense group of those who benefit from their end products, but the way is also paved for the deification of the former. The community bows before them, and busies itself performing the new tasks that have been conceived in order to respond to the social needs which have been created in the meantime and engendered by the growing number of new discoveries. The complexity of

1 *Law, Legislation and Liberty: a new statement of the liberal principles of justice and political economy* (Routledge and Kegan Paul, London 1982). See, in particular, 'Rules and Order'.

mathematical equations, physics assessments or chemistry experiments is growing exponentially. Understanding all this would demand so much knowledge that it has now become a habit, as well as a potential source of well-being, to applaud, integrate within our culture and consider as components of our civilization, fields such as transgenic foods, chlorofluorocarbons, nuclear energy or third-generation phones, without feeling any particular distress or need to ask any questions. Trust in sciences, in the technologies they allow us to develop and in their end products has gradually become the cement that structures community life.

The uncertainty principle and the resulting scientific scepticism

When Werner Heisenberg raised doubts in the field of quantum mechanics, in 1927, as to the exactitude of mathematical sciences, when he formulated the uncertainty principle, scepticism began to germinate in society. This grew with the notion of the dimension of 'chance' present in mankind, as described by Nobel-prize winner Jacques Monod in 1965.[2]

Nowadays, scientists and technicians tend to display increasing uncertainty as to the consequences of extracting from nature the materials needed to manufacture the goods they design. They reject former assertions about the usefulness of those goods and detect formerly unforeseen negative consequences both for those who benefit directly from the goods and for those who only experience the effects of the destruction. Scientists and technicians are confronted with the problem of waste, its accumulation and how to treat it. Moreover, it is also scientists and technicians who alert us to the slow degradation of the quality of life on earth and to the imbalances and injustice afflicting those who suffer the evils of civilization without benefiting from its advantages. It is these scientists and technicians who point out the ambiguities and weaknesses of the global knowledge of phenomena, in their variety and synergies, particularly when multiplied around the planet, our common home. It is they who spread the notion that the common home is becoming a place which is less and less pleasant to live in as a result of the activities we have been engaging in.

It is no longer possible to consider scientific progress and technological challenges in a different light to that of the present, where there is more personal and social well-being than ever and, at the same time, uncertainty as to the effects of this. The space of ignorance that goes with the aforementioned progress and challenges has now become apparent, a space of ignorance where the possibility of having a future is being gambled with. The substances that the technological society has placed in the atmosphere, water and soil may be agents of illness, if not of death,[3] and they tend to multiply, while we continue to be unaware of the reciprocal relations that may flow from them in connection with the

2 Nobel Prize Winner in medicine, this French biochemist wrote a book that would become famous, *L'hasard et la nécessité: essai sur la philosophie naturelle de la biologie moderne* (Seuil, Paris 1970). In it he argues that 'l'ancienne alliance est rompue: l'homme sait enfin qu'il est seul dans l'immensité indifférente de l'Univers d'où il a émergé purement par hasard. Non plus que son destin, son devoir n'est écrit nulle part. A lui de choisir entre le royaume des cieux et les ténébres' ('The old alliance has been broken; man is at last aware that he is alone in an immense universe that is quite indifferent to him, where he appeared by chance. No destiny awaits him, no obligations are imposed on him. He alone must choose between the Kingdom and eternal night').

3 By means of gaseous chromotography, a chemical analysis technique, perfected by an electron capture detector, it was possible to verify that all creatures on earth carry pesticide residues in their bodies. The alert given in the 1960s by the biologist Rachel Carson in *Silent Spring* regarding the presence of toxic chemical products in living beings led to research that culminated in James Lovelock's essay, *Gaia, a new look at life on Earth* (1979), translated into Portuguese and published by edições 70, under the title *Gaia. Um novo olhar sobre a vida na Terra*.

sustainability of life. The perception that traditional sources of energy have run out and that waste, in particular toxic waste, is not easily treated and that there is no consensus about its treatment, together with the various inadequacies in dealing with soil contamination, have all shown it is no longer possible to continue to blindly place our trust in those who *know* or *believe they know*.

In short, while the expansion of scientific and technical knowledge, by prolonging life and the quality of that life, has enabled the welfare we enjoy nowadays, in our advanced societies, it has also given rise to injustice and produced serious political problems, particularly between industrialized and developing countries. In a certain sense, it seems to have opened a 'Pandora's box', throwing wide open the gates to the unknown and to consequences that are now 'on the loose' in the world we know.

In addition, the expansion of scientific and technical knowledge has exposed another reality: what each individual does not know is not necessarily compensated for by the knowledge of others. There is a lack of knowledge about the effects of human action, that is, there are areas of ignorance that no one can offset. This is why we must come to the conclusion that knowledge is not the reality which globally unifies men. In my view, that reality is ignorance.

Furthermore, ignorance is no longer exclusively restricted to issues which are seen as lateral or peripheral. Despite the huge amount of knowledge we possess these days, there is a perception that the space of ignorance, or of *chance* (Monod), coincides with the space where the definitive issues in the community are decided i.e. life and its future. It is no longer conceivable to accept ignorance with indifference, carelessly, as something banal, as something that others may compensate for in our place.

Scientific elites have ceased to transmit certainties or simple formulas for increasing personal and social welfare. Neither do they broadcast the safety of a better world. On the contrary, they spread doubt, demonstrate vulnerability and draw attention to the unreliability of their knowledge.

Pause for questioning. Ignorance as a challenge

What kind of consequences should be drawn from this development?

I would answer that Man's relationship with other men, and with himself, should profoundly change. Shakespeare's immortal prince of Denmark would say that time 'is unhinged' and the poet Hölderlin that time has ceased to 'rhyme'. One thing appears certain: this is a time of rupture or, quoting Gilles Deleuze, it is a time of '*césure*' between a 'before', understood as a succession of events in sequence or repeated, and an 'after', the image of which confronts mankind today apparently as a task that is 'too large for me'[4] and which has now, in the gathering dusk, a dimension that may be hindering *Minerva's owl*[5] to take off on its flight.

Ignorance of the effects of human action is a discovery of the second half of the 20th century that has turned, in the 21st century, into a challenge. Symbolically, it is similar to Hamlet's sea voyage and, like that voyage, it leads to a profound reflection conducted by each individual within himself. On the other hand, we are heading towards a reflection to be conducted within the community, 'looking at ourselves' as the writer David Grossman argued for, on November 4, 2006, in Tel

4 Gilles Deleuze, *Diferença e Repetição* (ed. Relógio d'Água, 2000) pp. 168–9.

5 António Castanheira Neves, focusing his analysis on law and on the crisis it is going through, alerts us to the risk we run, if nothing is done, of being the ones who shall have to '... write law's epitaph'. See 'O funcionalismo jurídico – Caracterização fundamental e consideração crítica no contexto actual do sentido da juridicidade' in *Revista de Legislação e Jurisprudência* (2007): 136–3942, p. 151.

Aviv, on the occasion of a tribute to Yitzhak Rabin.[6] At issue is the present of the metamorphosis, a connecting bridge towards the rupture or '*césure*' between the 'before' and the 'after', between equal parts that complete each other in the time of Man, since concern about the future is the key to human existence.

The outcome of this pondering may, nevertheless, be a mere shrug of the shoulders, that is, it may lead to the conclusion that the scientific community is wrong and that we can carry on as usual. However, given that what is in question is life, we are inclined to think, with Peter Singer, that 'to believe in that possibility is a risky strategy'[7] and we shall probably not be alive to learn how it will end.

Concern about the future demands that we be twice as alert, that we learn to deal with probabilities, that we be careful with our actions, and that we transform experience into a way of acting. There are no certainties for any of us.

However, since no one is sure, what was until now a scientific and technical issue has become a challenge posed to every individual, as a person, in a community. All this can be set against the backdrop of humanity that everyone carries along, conditions and is responsible for. In other words, the space of scientific and technical questioning is transformed into a space of ethical and philosophical questioning.[8]

The transformation of the scientific and technical issue into an ethical issue

The transformation of the scientific and technical issue, i.e. the question of the consequences of human action, into an ethical challenge, i.e. living in a political and legal community, resembles the shiver that a gust of wind sends through one's body.

Around our body there is a layer of hot and wet air that slowly climbs from our feet up to our head and encloses us in an atmosphere created by our own metabolism. When blowing through us, the wind causes that layer of hot air to disappear and the body is exposed to a number of different temperatures and degrees of humidity. Thus, a shivering effect is produced.[9] That is why, when one shivers, there is an adage that says: 'death has passed through me but found me still strong'. The body has been able to overcome the imbalance caused by the elimination of the protecting hot air layer and has recovered its stability.

For the parallel drawn between an individual shiver and the challenge posed by ethical questioning of the community to be appropriate, it is necessary to examine how one's balance in the community can be recovered after such a shake.

Three decades ago it seemed possible to recover it merely by using good sense and with the help of scientific progress. Even today, some optimists believe that everything can be fixed by virtue of technological innovation, focusing their attention on economic growth, the only reality – so they say – that human communities really need.

---

6 See the text of David Grossman's conference in *The New York Review of Books* (11 January 2007).

7 Peter Singer, *Um só mundo. A ética da globalização*, translated by Maria de Fátima St. Aubyn (Gradiva 2004): 44.

8 It should be borne in mind, as pointed out in the report of the High-level Panel on Financing for Development, appointed by the Secretary-General of the UN, United Nations General Assembly, 55th session, agenda item 101, June 26, 2001, that: 'In the global village, someone else's poverty very soon becomes one's own problem: lack of markets for one's products, illegal immigration, pollution, contagious disease, insecurity, fanaticism, terrorism.'

9 R.C. Lewontin, *Biologia como ideologia*, 124.

However, if we examine the matter in greater depth, we are led to the conclusion that this is not exactly the case.

In fact, this kind of 'shiver' calls for a perception about living in community which is different to the traditional one. There are two reasons for this: firstly, due to the eradication of distance between people and the resulting globalization of the community, including the economic community; and, secondly, because decisions are no longer taken based on personal interests but rather according to the interests of future generations, given that the consequences that any decision may have on the distant future are taken into consideration, which means that the timeframe to be considered when making the decision is still a human timeframe, but it goes beyond the life of the actual person taking that decision.

Personal ethics become community ethics. Indifferent to risk and to the possibility of a future, Kantian ethics are gradually being replaced by a type of ethics which encompasses precisely that risk and, along with it, the possibility of a future. The element of chance, as a result of a personal action, affects both the one who acts and others, including not only those who are close by, in terms of distance, but also those who are distant, in terms of time. The possibility that others may continue to exist and that others will exist in the future conditions every action. These actions are conditioned by introducing a special concern as to the probable effects at the moment immediately preceding the decision to act.

From ethical questioning to political and legal questioning

If that is the case, then the acceptance of community ethics – which encompasses the future transformed into present responsibility within the daily freely built continuity of being – implies the reconstruction of the political and legal community. It implies a reorganization of power according to the intentionality of a historical and human notion of what 'should be', which is external to it; an intentionality accepted as a right which, since it 'should be', can legitimate power as a power of freedom.

Yet, the metaphor of the shivering organism allows us to progress a little further in the knowledge of existing boundaries in the political and legal community and the resulting need for human intervention.

Indeed, it clearly shows that living beings define their own environment. They build it rather than adapt to it and, at the same time, they gradually destroy the conditions of their existence. We might say that the environment is permanently being rebuilt during the lifetime of the various beings, not only human, but also each and every living being.

Thus, when plants grow roots, they alter the physical nature of the soil, expanding it, and transforming its chemical nature by means of the organic molecules they release. At the same time, they allow fungi to penetrate their rooting system, humidity to rise and their leaves to alter the quantity of light around them. This means that no organism may live without bringing changes to the environment, without defining its own environment.

On the other hand, living beings not only modify the environment, they also manage to stabilize average conditions over time. This is what happens when the oak, by bearing acorns, allows squirrels to keep them for the winter and when the potato plant, by producing potatoes, similarly allows men to hoard them in order to eat them throughout the year, whenever they need to and not only when they harvest them.

Man, however, has a capacity that is not shared by any other living being: that of making predictions and designing life projects according to those predictions. He has an added power, the power of shaping the future, using his will, beyond merely stabilizing average environmental conditions over time. This is not in the sense that he may hinder the world from transforming itself, which, as we have observed, would be an impossible task, but in the sense that he may achieve behavioural changes he views as beneficial to the aims he has set, owing to the theoretical knowledge and skills acquired by experience.

As a result, it appears to be within our reach to establish environmentally sustainable social and economic development as a political aim to be pursued, within a framework of ethical responsibility, and to legally safeguard that aim.

Prospective analysis as a condition for political action

The aforementioned capacity, an eminently human one, involves, nevertheless, two problems.

In the first place, it is a capacity which man, over the years, has not particularly exercised. Considering it unnecessary, he has not developed it. That is why it has become atrophied in the brain, unlike other, better-trained capacities, namely the ability to use memory and to associate data and experiences from the past. Consequently, it is nowadays difficult to make predictions or conduct prospective analyses.

Secondly, since this capacity is not yet very well developed, it is unable to deal with the immense and global task before it. The dimension and synergies resulting from the environmental movements interfere, therefore, with the training of that capacity.

In short, it is not only the novelty of the task that makes it difficult. Its very scale generates problems with regard to the understanding of the phenomena and renders conclusions difficult; hence the need to invest in this capacity to predict and plan and to use it. Nowadays the great challenge for political action is to foresee and plan, permanently adjusting the predictions and plans by adapting strategies for action.

There is, however, another no less complex problem which results from the first: after developing strategies for action, it is essential to exercise the power of will by deciding to alter behaviours and to act accordingly. Predictions and action plans are worth little or nothing at all if they are not able to change reality. On the other hand, if the prediction is uncertain, the programme or plan that frames the action will echo that uncertainty. The programme or plan, despite being formalized, is not exhaustive. It remains open, with the imprecision resulting from the weakness of the prediction and the incompleteness stemming from ignorance about the very 'becoming' it is addressing. In this way, planning gains strength as a process of both elaboration and implementation of the plan or programme.

In that process, in which elaboration and implementation are closely intertwined, the strategies for action are permanently renewing themselves and they do that in a time that can only be the present. It is never the past and much less the future. This is because the time of the action that transforms what is, the time of power, is the time of will. The time of power coincides with that of action, and the latter becomes mingled with the present. It is in the present, that 'eternal now' in the meaningful words of Fernando Pessoa, that action is decided and pursued by the will and the power inherent to it.

Consequently, the difficulty lies in knowing how to exercise the power of will against a background of uncertainty, imprecision and incompleteness. This difficulty must be culturally accepted since it results from a traditionally lived experience comprising certainties, precise definitions, and political and normative systems that tend to be complete.

The need for a new political and legal paradigm

For this reason, we are forced to ask ourselves, in the radical way its decisive character demands: Do we wish to go on living as we have done until now, 'trusting', as we are reminded by James Lovelock, 'that the air is here for breathing, constant in its composition, as constant as sunrise and sunset',[10] now that we have become aware that we are the actors in a life-destroying process? And, should the answer to this be negative, then we must immediately add another question: How must we organize ourselves in the political and legal community so as to enable the 'continuum' of life presently threatened? How are we supposed to reinvent our life in community on the basis of uncertainties and imprecision? How can we build up a certain degree of confidence within the community and guarantee its freedom?

It seems that the need for a new paradigm for life in community is beginning to be felt both at the level of the state and of the world. And the starting point for changing the status quo, within the biological limitations of each individual or of the available biological information, is only to be found inside ourselves and in our understanding of mankind living together, in the distance that separates us from that other one who is close to us, that other one who is farther away and that other one whom we will certainly never meet.

Replacing the state's political power in the sphere of global ethics

We have built the state and the state's sovereignty. We have granted legitimacy to state action in law. However, the absolute sovereignty of states, enshrined in the Treaty of Westphalia, signed in 1648 in Osnabrück, is now hard pressed to answer the questions we have been raising. The old stereotypes of the nation-state, confined within territorial boundaries and whose power imposes itself as sovereign, internally and externally, have been slowly undermined, as has, consequently, the traditional relationship between states.

Given that this is clearly inevitable, relocating the state's political power within a framework of global ethics is urgently needed. In this global ethics, action is local, since the boundaries between science, economics and politics are fading, leading to more mature, participative and aware citizens.

Community life tends to be more complex, open, and uncertain. However, this does not mean that everything will become frightening or critical and the citizen will feel distanced from the decision-making process. In other words, the complexity and uncertainty of evolution that each of us incorporates in our own knowledge through life experiences do not and cannot justify bestowing on the scientists or more or less highly-placed elites the decision-making power with regard to changing behaviours and cultures. Indeed, as we have seen before, the elites, beyond the boundaries of what they know, have only their position to offer, and that does not hold much value within the described framework. Ignorance and uncertainties also weigh on the elites, albeit in different fields. If they were to accede to political power, even on a democratic mandate, and start directing other people's actions, this would be tantamount to signing a blank cheque. Power would be exercised in personal terms, in a totalitarian drift, and not even those in power would be able to foresee where it would lead or how it would end.

---

10 *Gaia. Um novo olhar...*, 16.

The generalization of ignorance brings on the generalization of the desire to know and the generalized sharing of risk

When you do not have the knowledge, the solution is to look for information and explanations. When in possession of the available information and knowledge and aware of the impossibility of acquiring, at that moment, further knowledge, alternatives are examined and probabilities weighed up. Subsequently, will is exercised and this puts us at risk with respect to what we do not know. For, what is inaccessible to knowledge may only be revealed to the will. As Hannah Arendt[11] reminds us, 'Not knowing is at the root of having to will'[12], and hence it is also at the root of running risks. This is the reason why, if, at the ultimate limit of what each of us knows, ignorance reigns, then everyone must "will". Everyone must run risks. Sharing ignorance leads to sharing the will, the power of wanting, and to sharing risks.

Consequently, in order to achieve the much-discussed renewal of democracy the best way would probably be through the enhancement of participative, informed and knowledgeable citizenship, which is to say, through the sharing of social responsibility.

Ethical reinvention of politics and law. The original responsibility for knowledge and political and legal responsibility

Generalized ignorance about the 'what' and the 'how' of the behavioural or cultural change that one seeks to achieve, in view of the environmental sustainability of development or on other grounds, such as security, nowadays threatened by terrorist phenomena, calls for the integration in action of a heuristic need to question that action and to learn continuously and creatively from its results. From another perspective, it compels us to expand the span of attention to our surroundings and to deal with uncertainty, taking as our starting point the one certainty that inspires us, as people: ethical responsibility for the continuity of life, the life that was transmitted to us and that we carry.

Focusing on the moment preceding action, so as to avoid acting after the irremediable has occurred, requires a careful preventive attitude. Action, for its part, reflects constant self-limitation. It results from the exercise of a contained but responsible freedom to build or recreate, in the knowledge that the past begins when the future vanishes: 'The past, the "having-been-ness"', contends Heidegger, 'has its origin in a certain sense in the future.'[13]

In short, in the present state of unpredictability with regard to human destiny, to trust, without another thought, people or set programmes of behavioural change aimed at maintaining sustainable development – whatever may be meant by that – is tantamount to entering a process of dictatorial powers; in the face of the many ambiguities of knowledge, to share the responsibility for ignorance keeps us from lapsing into meaningless projects of merely personal power.

Along with Castanheira Neves, we would like, therefore, to point out that '… today's man, and all of us with him, will have to ask ourselves what meaning we intend to confer on our praxis'.[14]

The community-based historical existence projected by that praxis is indissolubly linked to the 'I' and to the 'other' through comparison, that *tertium genus* that generates responsibility and

11 Hannah Arendt comments, on this topic, the Jaspers' thought. See... *A vida do espírito. Vol. II, Querer* (Instituto Piaget ed. Pensamento e filosofia 2000) 28.

12 Jaspers, in Hannah Arendt's analysis, *op. cit.* 28.

13 *Die Gewesenheit entspringt in gewisser Weise der Zukunft.* Quoted by Hannah Arendt, *op. cit.*, 49.

14 António Castanheira Neves, *O actual problema metodológico. Da interpretação jurídica – I* (Coimbra Editora, 2003) 203 ff.

a *continuum* of alterity. Indeed it is that existence that nowadays enables the consolidation of pluralism and the sustainability of the *polis* rather than the traditional state, through the voting citizen, or the law that ensures justice, through the subject of rights. The comparative element that brings up the question and, thereby, obtains an answer, demands that the answer be based on political reflections. This is a power-based response centred on social justice that should emerge out of continued ruptures in a community turned global – *political responsibility*. On the other hand, the comparative element, the *tertium genus*, changes the question into a claim for an answer; it demands a formal answer. From this it follows that the answer is a legal answer, focused on justice, expressed in the act of dispensing justice – a *legal responsibility*. And lastly, the comparative element, the *tertium genus*, when it transforms the query into an obligation to answer, invites us to permanently learn, to build autonomously the knowledge that enables us to give an answer – a *philosophical responsibility for knowledge*. In short, everything points to the fact that the traditional rule of law is being left behind, as a result of direct appeals not only to the voting citizen, but also to the citizen who shares in the decision-making, not only to the subject of rights but also to the subject of duties.

The revival of old ideas about Man, dictated by the moment of rupture or '*césure*' we are currently experiencing, is a consequence of this *moment of crisis of political power*, now decentred and divided into multiple infra-state powers that submerge it and supra-state ones that dilute it. It is also a consequence of this *moment of crisis of the law* and of its guiding or pedagogical function. It is also a consequence of this *moment of crisis of knowledge* and orphaning of the sciences, due to the feeling of loss of certainties.

Therefore, it is urgent to let go, in a critical manner, of the cultural and civilizational devices that surround and mould us every day, just as it is imperative to open the way to an ethical reinvention of politics and law, in the constitutive dimension dictated by the original responsibility, which shapes and conditions our being in the world, in a creative reciprocity.

Participative democracy: public policies and law

Consequently, it is necessary to go in search of Man's humanity, not in the way Diogenes went, incapable of seeing in the other – any other – even with a lighted lamp in full daylight, what he intuitively sensed was the notion of Man, but in the sense of a challenge to understand the ethical call to think the other – any other – in his absolute self, his radical concreteness of being a person, as the reflection of a 'self', which, despite repeating himself, is never the same and, therefore, never able to be made relative.

It is on the basis of that absoluteness of reason and emotion, conservation and creativity that it is possible to establish a guiding thread for a new political community. This new community shall be reinvented as a democracy by virtue of a participative citizenship of quality, living in uncertainty. This shall include a law that is acknowledged as an argumentative mediator, with the law being laid down along the way rather than being laid down once and for all.

The commitment to a different concept of law joins here the commitment to a notion of the state's power. This power goes beyond representative democracy. Indeed, as we have seen, when we do not know, and there is a human question, it is impossible to delegate because the answer asks for the original powers. Therefore it is necessary to guarantee a citizenship that has an ethical dimension expressed in the act of observing and judging, seeking information and participating. And the search for the other in the distance, separating him from each of us and allowing the recognition and the safeguarding of the difference, opens the way to overcoming the problem of validity, viewed, since rationalism, as an intrinsic problem of the law – *the law as validity.*[15] At the same time, the exteriority of the other and his radical distance from himself, within a self-reflecting law, enables the construction of duties without the corresponding rights[16] or, from another perspective, the construction of rights in a different subject, up to now unrecognizable: the 'generation subject'.[17]

Whatever the approach to the analysis of the problem and the conclusions that are reached, there is a common link between them all: the future and future generations empower law. Through them, law opens itself to take on uncertainty, imprecision and complexity, but also responsibility for achieving deeper and more extensive justice.

The enhancement of the principle of sustainable development or of intra and intergenerational justice by means of corollaries that integrate our daily actions in a valuative manner contains the promise of more humane actions, heedful of unjustified imbalances and of not reasonably founded differences, and which shall manifest themselves in a 'continuum' of awareness and precaution. The sense of justice is built up over a succession of ruptures and incites each individual to self-restraint in his argumentation – far from the certainty and rigour of the '*dura lex, sed lex*', but near what is best in each of us – out of a sense of responsibility for the other and following the thematization of that difference.

Lifelong learning, the state and the law

Investing in knowledge and continuing learning, in search of the available control mechanisms against uncertainty and insecurity, and looking for new approaches to truth is no longer the call of only a few. It has become the duty of all. In a certain sense, it means heightening the humanity that each of us carries inside himself and the philosophical responsibility into which we project our knowledge, in the same sense that can be found, although more elaborately, in Karl Popper's statement that we are all philosophers, 'albeit some more than others'.[18] Our wish is that the responsibility for knowing – invoked by the now so frequently mentioned lifelong learning process – may spread and take root alongside legal responsibility and political responsibility.

Lifelong learning enables the establishment of a citizenry which is attentive to detail but open to universal thinking, informed but not entirely certain, tolerant but based on values, and participative but aware of man's irreducible freedom in the distance that separates him from the other.

By absorbing and expressing justice constructed in that manner, democratic legislative power does not separate the law from the open evaluative system under which justice is administered, in a shaky equilibrium, always on the verge of losing its balance and causing new imbalances. Unfinished by nature, the law opens itself to those arguments which the community has generally viewed as fair throughout history.

The judge, for his part, since he is the one who administers the law, takes on a key role in the community. This is not because he is technically more knowledgeable, reasonable or prudent, but because he is the person who is in a privileged position when it comes to understanding the

15 António Castanheira Neves, *O actual problema metodológico. Da interpretação jurídica – I* (Coimbra Editora, 2003) 203 ff.

16 José Manuel Aroso Linhares, 'O dito do direito e o dizer da justiça. Diálogo com Levinas e Derrida', in *Studia Jurídica, 89, Entre discursos e culturas jurídicas* (Coimbra Editora, 2006): 213.

17 José Joaquim Gomes Canotilho, 'O direito ao ambiente como direito subjectivo', in *A tutela jurídica do meio ambiente: presente e futuro* (Coimbra Editora, 2005): 47.

18 *Sociedade Aberta. Universo Aberto* (ed. Dom Quixote, 1991): 9.

meaning of the law and the principles of the legal system to which it belongs, and capturing what the community, through him, means, hopes and feels. Perhaps the reason therefore is not so much that he administers the law by resolving disputes or controversies, but rather that he promotes and consolidates the culture of an open society.

Making judgements, social psychology and the danger of the *rule of thumb*

However, here too, things are not as simple as they seem. As the decisions of judges, particularly those of the higher courts, tend to reflect the way the community that they belong to thinks and feels, they also mirror back to that community their own way of thinking and feeling, with the inherent consequences. This is why we should keep in mind Cass R. Sunstein and his conclusions concerning the amplification of ideology and minimization of reality in the courts' decisions. These conclusions help us gain insight into legal behaviours and a better understanding of cultural movements in the community.[19]

After examining the voting patterns of judges in panels and the resulting decisions, Cass R. Sunstein comes to the conclusion that the ideological leanings of a judge grow stronger when he makes decisions on a panel with other judges who embrace the same ideals. The group decision-making reflects that fact. However, his leanings become weaker when the same judge makes group decisions on a panel with other judges whose ideals are different to his own but identical among themselves. In the latter case, the judge votes in a similar way to the other judges and the verdict reflects the minimization of his ideological beliefs.[20]

Social psychology explains this phenomenon. As a general rule, each of us feels safer in his knowledge and convictions when others share them. Conversely, when we are in a minority, we doubt our knowledge and are inclined, in that case, to conform to the others. The reason appears to be that when we are in a minority, we usually attribute this to a lack of information and believe that the others have what we lack. When we are not sure what the best solution is, we follow the others according to a rule that social psychologists call the *rule of thumb*.[21]

This leaning toward conformism or consensus stems, on the one hand, from a lack of information or knowledge or, at least, little conviction regarding what we know, and, on the other hand, from a particular conception of power, the original power, applied at the periphery of inter-subjectivity by the expression of will. The 'I' assumes his 'being with the others', expressing his own will in an interaction with the others' expressions of will. I decide with the others because I believe that their decision is a 'plus' that adds a certain authority to my will which I feel is missing from it.

19 *Why societies need dissent?* (Harvard University Press, London), 2003.

20 *Op cit.*, 5.

21 Amos Tversky and Daniel Kahneman, *Judgment under uncertainty. Heuristics and biases*, in Daniel Kahneman, Paul Slovic and Amos Tversky, *Judgment under uncertainty: Heuristics and biases* (Cambridge University Press, 1999): 3–20.

The discourse of power and the legitimation of its exercise

The preceding arguments lead us to reflect on this topic, firstly because the introduction of changes in reality belongs to the realm of the expression of will and, consequently, of the exercise of power; and, secondly, because that expression has a tendency towards expansion.[22]

The exercise of power leads to changes since it is the expression, in the present, of a will that generates futures. Whatever the conceptions regarding its origin and limits, power gains meaning from that capacity to intervene by altering the reality which it addresses.

In fact, it is that capacity to shape behaviours aimed at safeguarding justice and the 'continuum' of quality life that marks us as persons, in our being in the world with others. We should add that this is a particularly demanding capacity, given the imbalances between the various generations living in different parts of the globe and the awareness of the potential disequilibrium between present-day and future generations. The reinvention of the discourse of power in the public space and of legitimation of its limited exercise by virtue of a refreshed law, in the sphere of justice, implies the availability of enlarged and extended information and knowledge capable of sustaining a well-founded dialogue that rejects easy consensus and, in particular, empty conformism.

While, until recently, it was acceptable to view the structures of community life with no great concern, trusting in the institutions of power and conceptual categories, that is no longer the case today, due to the reflection it requires. The complexity of the phenomena is so profound and what is at stake with regard to the consequences of action is so huge that if every one of us remained unconcerned and resigned himself to the will expressed by others without querying it and, furthermore, amplified that will, we would certainly not be overcoming deficiencies in information and knowledge, but rather demonstrating our belief in the claim made by the Geneva-born philosopher Jean-Jacques Rousseau that the majority, because it is a majority, is correct; hence we would be provoking a chain of errors. Seen from a different perspective, we would be handing the future over to pure chance since, as we have seen, what is definitive is decided in community, by the changes we make to reality.

With regard to this, Hans Christian Andersen's brilliant description in *The King's New Clothes* is particularly appropriate: if everybody conforms to what everyone else says and no one makes an effort to get acquainted with, to seek information or, at least, to become aware of what he sees, hears, breathes and feels, and act accordingly, perhaps it will no longer be possible to awake from the lethargic sleep when the voice of the child exclaiming 'the king is naked' is heard.[23] Meanwhile, time may have gone mad.

Conformism and liberty

To fight against conformism and an unconcerned attitude in action does not mean to deify dissent and pluralism of opinion. It means to pay attention to the dangers of consensus, especially when it is formal or tends to be empty and, above all, it suggests the need to reflect seriously on action

---

22 The example quoted, of the manner in which the judges of higher courts arrive at a group decision, has enabled us to better understand the distortions and deviations that accompany the formation of consensus due to the lack of conviction about one's knowledge. And it compels the judges to invest in technical knowledge in order to reduce their zones of ignorance and allow a better control of the risk of deciding. The effects of judicial decisions on the manner in which the notion of what is fair is shaped in the community require it to be so.

23 This example is quoted by Cass R. Sunstein. See *op cit.*, 6.

and its implications. Each of us must reflect on his own, with the knowledge that he possesses and takes responsibility for enlarging.

At a time when sciences proclaim their doubts and express ambiguity, rejecting one day what they have categorically stated the day before, at a time when technological innovations have been caught in a vortex, if not in a process of schizophrenia, inviting changes in methodologies they have previously recommended, it has become urgent to pose questions – questions that bring us together and situate us according to our values – and to intervene accordingly in the political community through the power that is exerted in it, the power to construct what is fair; the power to constrain, command, modify; a power that becomes also – as opposed to the power of liberty – a power to act impelled by the daily pursued truth.[24]

The search for truth, the fight for power in the political community and the quest for a meaning for law

Hans Georg Gadamer, basing himself on Vico, has already stated that more than the imaginary will of the law, and more than the quest for the truth of facts, what really matters is the unfolding of action, the ongoing process, the recovery of its *meaning*, the learning through its causes, and what allows us to find the evident or *verisimilar* (*vero + simile*, i.e. with the appearance of truth). If, on the one hand, this directs us to the knowledge of the past – 'evidence belongs to tradition', says Gadamer – on the other, it challenges us to deal with the uncertainty of the future resulting from the effects of present-day action.[25]

It is just as necessary to find out why the synchronized explosion occurred on March 11, 2004, in Madrid, or the *tsunami* off the Asian coast on December 26, 2004, or the reason for the enduring drought affecting the Maghreb, or the Columbia accident or the bomb attack on the Hyderabad (India) mosque, on May 18, 2007, as it is to understand the consequences of the loss of biodiversity, rising sea levels or the intensive planting of eucalyptus. It is our aptitude to acquire knowledge and the manner in which we cope with the uncertainty of our knowledge that incites us, also through reasoning, to learn and to carry out the heuristic process, in order to arrive at a decision.

In this eminently political field, the social contract does not end with elections. It renews itself daily, calling for the original participation of all. Winning spaces of knowledge from ignorance does not follow so much, as we have seen, from the acquisition of new and more advanced scientific knowledge by restricted groups of experts, but from the aggregation of scattered and localized knowledge. The latter, after being made available and discussed, is converted into an enlarged form of knowing, to be used for decision-making. Political action programmes become strategic, open and adaptive, thereby making all people co-responsible for action. Public policies are generated in this framework.

---

24 We do not deny how difficult this manner of acting is, at the global scale, particularly when one is faced with cultures for which the death of the other is considered more important than one's own life. However, neither should it be forgotten that what matters nowadays is to draw attention to the problems that derive from understanding man's humanity, to enter into dialogue with the other, rather than to counter extreme positions by taking other positions which are equally extreme. For, since no one owns the truth, we cannot, therefore, act as if we did. In fact, as Karl Popper argues, quoting Claude Bernard, 'those who place excessive faith in their ideas are not apt to make discoveries'. See *O mito do contexto. Em defesa da ciência e da racionalidade* (Biblioteca de Filosofia Contemporânea 1999): 26.

25 *Wahrheit und Methode: Grundzüge einer philosophischen Hermeneutik*, 5th ed. II (Mohr,Tübingen 1986).

Yet the quest for truth that nourishes knowledge and the fight for power that nourishes politics are not the same as the search for meaning that nourishes the law.

And perhaps something else should be added. Knowledge for knowledge's sake holds little value. The value of knowledge lies in the potential basis it provides for making informed decisions, encouraging us to take positions where, in the context of the game of probabilities and of risk-sharing, the best argument, in the sense of Jürgen Habermas[26] is determinant, albeit not always easy to obtain. The influence of certain information and the managing of social pressure may contribute to multiplying errors and to cascading effects, as well as to the polarization of groups[27] and they may sway us away from making the best decisions.[28]

One thing now seems certain: it is not by chance that argumentation is not popular under dictatorships or regimes of absolute power, where evident truth and syllogistic, straight and linear inferences have a more successful career, as Chaim Perelman aptly pointed out.[29]

Argumentation is linked to the problematicity of law. It may be the means to overcome the traditional paradigm, considering the realities we are faced with in the future, which force us to turn our attention to prevention rather than reaction, to the individual and concrete rather than to the general and abstract, to what is different rather than to what is equal, to the possible consequences rather than to the causes.

The approach to the case, to the real situation, makes the law problematic and dampens the enthusiasm of those who see in the law the point of arrival dreamt of by nineteenth century philosophers, 'the safe harbour against our uncertainties and worries, the shield of our freedom'.[30]

Criticizing the notion that the norm must have only one correct answer, Robert Alexy teaches that not only would this imply that human knowledge is capable of vanquishing a 'Dworkian Hercules', but, in order to do this, it would also need to fulfil five unattainable conditions: unlimited time, unlimited information, unlimited linguistic clarity, unlimited capacity of adaptation to change and the equally unlimited absence of pre-comprehension.[31].

Thus, law recovers problematic sense. And, as it carefully examines a case, it is offered the opportunity to refresh its arguments in the quest for justice, supported namely by tendentially universal legal principles, on the basis of which it instils confidence in the community.

Public policies, law and legal technique as safeguards

It follows that our time is one of reflection and rupture between a 'before', which repeats itself, and an 'after', which is getting closer, in the form of a new paradigm for the 'being with the other' of man: the other he knows, the other he does not know but knows is somewhere in this world and the other who, by definition, he does not know and shall never be in a position to know.

---

26 See, in particular, *Between facts and norms: contributions to a discourse theory of law and democracy* (Polity Press, Cambridge, 1996).

27 Ovídio A. Baptista da Silva, *op. cit.*, 105.

28 *Derecho y razon prática* (2nd ed, Mexico 2002): 20–23.

29 Neither should one forget the story recounted by Karl Popper in the introduction to his work 'The myth of the framework ...' already cited, where he states that that story may have sown the seeds of his most important work, *Open Society*. Around the year 1933, the year when Hitler ascended to power, a young member of the National Socialist Party is quoted as having said the following to Karl Popper: 'So, you want to discuss? I don't discuss, I shoot.'

30 Ovídio A. Baptista da Silva, *op. cit.*, 105.

31 *Derecho y razon prática* (2nd ed. Mexico 2002): 20–23.

The change of paradigm of political and legal life does not stem from the sole awareness of the other who, in the distance, shares with us the globalized world. It also stems from the awareness of the other who, far away in the future, questions us about his life potentially carried by us. It follows from this that the challenge that faces today's risk society is the introduction into politics and the law of the global space and future time, with all the associated uncertainties resulting from generalized ignorance about the synergy of the phenomena produced by our actions and about their evolution.

Responsibility for knowledge has highlighted the existence of vast areas of political responsibility that do not allow for intermediaries because they represent an original responsibility, which cannot be delegated. This being the case, as we have seen, it is then among public policies, laid down within the community framework and coordinated by the state power – be it original or delegated – that the new paradigm seeks room to settle down and grow. For that purpose it attempts a different, subtler formula for the exercise of power, encouraging everybody to intervene in the community, providing means for research and scientific and technological development, carefully monitoring the social movements without hindering them or preventing their multiplication; in a word, a reinvented formula for the exercise of the political and state power, which is now being called governance or good governance.

Recently, in Portugal, the flourishing of public policies, within the realm of the state and in the most diverse fields, concentrating the efforts of various sectors of the community in order to make the best choices in the face of a wide range of alternatives, has opened new ways and announced a different form of exercising political power. However, since the state's legitimacy, when pursuing public policy and in its relationship with other political powers, rests on the law – we speak, of course, of the state governed by the rule of law that is culturally embedded in Western civilization – it is conceivable that it may be compelled to learn anew how to act. Consequently, in the context in which public policies are carried out, ignoring the effects of their actions, one should be doubly careful about ensuring that the government's action is founded on the law and is hence legitimate.

The law that legitimizes the government's action does not – and cannot – rest fundamentally on legislation and on the certainty and security the latter has been capable of providing over the years.[32] That is not to say, however, that legislation should be discarded. To address the uncertainty of one's knowledge, in the most diverse fields, the uncertainty with regard to evolution and to social movements, as well as the ignorance of the complexities that characterize real-life situations and determine what are good choices, requires a different conception of law, one that emphasizes precaution and its guiding and pedagogical mission, and that is founded on principles and the rights of the people.

The principles are broad and flexible and, because they are broad and flexible, their development and approach to problematic issues require not only that a particular technique be applied to their resolution (a legal technique) but also prudential action on the part of jurists, who shall act in a rational manner, argumentatively, 'in situation', according to commonly accepted standards of action.

The state's power to define, implement and evaluate public policies is no longer, as was formerly the case, the government's power, a power that acts centrally, in a chain of subordination and is implemented according to a vertical logic, as required by Hans Kelsen's legal pyramid. On the contrary, the state's power to define, implement and evaluate public policies is the power to give coherence to the social actions and sweeping social movements, which is known today as the power of governance.

---

32 On the 'uprising of facts against the code' as 'uprising of the law against the code', António Castanheira Neves, *Introdução ao Estudo do Direito* (extracts), (Coimbra 1971–1972): 138 ff.

In a state governed by the rule of law, the power of governance must be regarded as the power to realize the law, this being secured by the general principles of law and the freedoms and safeguards of the rights of the people. To gain a full understanding of the latter, one must attempt successive approaches to the problematic reality of the facts, argumentatively, thus enriching the legal framework leading to the fair decision required by the case at issue.

The rigour of the employed technique, the density of the range of arguments deployed and the caution with which the correct solution is sought, within the framework of the acknowledged principles and rights of the people, instil confidence in the law's addressees and, despite the complexity and uncertainty of our world in the beginning of the 21st century, vouch for the correctness of the solution. In times of complexity and uncertainty, the autonomy of law lies in the hands of the jurist inasmuch as he is the technician to whom the task of caring for the law has been entrusted. In the apparent imprecision of the legal principles and fluid configuration of the acknowledged rights, it is up to the law expert to interpret them adequately and pass them on to the law's addressees with clarity and precision. In large measure, the trust the law so strongly needs and claims as a source of peace and of a future for man and the community to which he belongs depends on achieving that aim.

PART II
Freedom of Expression in the Online Environment

Chapter 3

To Block or Not to Block: European Approaches to Content Regulation, and Implications for Freedom of Expression

Yaman Akdeniz

Introduction

New media historically face suspicion and are liable to excessive regulation as they spark fear of potential detrimental effects on society. This has proved true of the publication and transmission of sexually explicit content[1] through the printing press,[2] the telegraph, telephone, post, cinema,[3] theatre,[4] radio, television, satellite and video.[5] During the 1990s, as attention turned to the Internet, the widespread availability of sexually explicit content stirred up a moral panic[6] shared by law enforcement agencies and large sections of the media.[7] Consequently, during the 2000s, attention turned to the development of peer-to-peer networks and illegal distribution of digital copyrighted content. During the early 2010s, this was followed by the development and widespread use of web 2.0 based technologies and services such as YouTube, Facebook and Twitter and the impact of these user-driven services on political movement and speech. The dissemination of so called state secrets on influential websites such as Wikileaks caused major state level embarrassment across the globe.

The regulation of Internet content whether illegal, harmful, offensive, morally objectionable, desirable or undesirable, consequently became a key focus of governments, supranational bodies and international organizations across the globe.

Today, many European states are reacting to the availability and dissemination of certain types of content through the Internet, and there is major concern about the availability of sexually explicit

1 See generally Travis, A., *Bound and Gagged: A Secret History of Obscenity in Britain*, Profile Books, 2000.

2 See generally Sutherland, J., *Offensive Literature: Decensorship in Britain 1960–1982*, Barnes & Noble Books, 1982.

3 See generally Smith, S.J., *Children, Cinema & Censorship*, I.B. Tauris, 2005.

4 See generally Aldgate, A., and Robertson, J.C., *Censorship in Theatre and Cinema*, Edinburgh University Press, 2005.

5 See for example Egan, K., *Trash or Treasure?: Censorship and the Changing Meanings of the Video Nasties*, Manchester University Press, 2007.

6 Cohen, S., *Folk Devils and Moral Panics: Creation of Mods and Rockers*, Routledge: 30th Anniversary edition, 2002; Jenkins, P., *Intimate Enemies: Moral Panics in Contemporary Great Britain*, Aldine De Gruyter, 1992.

7 The House of Commons Home Affairs Committee described computer pornography as a new horror in 1994: House of Commons, *Home Affairs Committee: First Report on Computer Pornography* (London: HMSO), 1994 p. V, para. 1.

content including child pornography,[8] racist content,[9] hate speech, and terrorist propaganda on the Internet.[10] This chapter will provide an overview of policies and recommendations adopted at the pan-European level covering both the European Union and Council of Europe levels with regards to illegal and harmful Internet content.

The governance of illegal as well as harmful (which falls short of illegality) Internet content may differ from one country to another and variations exist within the pan-European region.[11] Harm criteria remain distinct within different jurisdictions, albeit within the same European region, with individual states deciding what is legal and illegal based upon different cultural, moral, religious, historical and legal differences and variations. The Council of Europe member states have a certain margin of appreciation in assessing whether a 'pressing social need' exists to introduce speech-based restrictions to their national laws based on Article 10 of the European Convention on Human Rights principles as laid down by the jurisprudence of the European Court of Human Rights.[12]

Furthermore, harmonization efforts to combat illegal Internet content, even for universally condemned content such as child pornography, have been protracted and are ongoing.[13] Efforts to harmonize laws to combat racist content on the Internet have proved to be even more problematic.[14] The availability of glorification of violence and terrorist propaganda[15] on the Internet, and content which may encourage terrorist activities[16] such as bomb-making instructions also triggered policy action at the international level, and new laws and policies are being developed to combat the availability of such content on the Internet. At the same time, the music industry is pressuring governments and international organizations to address the problem of Internet piracy and the

8 For a detailed assessment of legal issues surrounding child pornography see Akdeniz, Y., *Internet Child Pornography and the Law: National and International Responses*, Ashgate, 2008.

9 For a detailed assessment of legal issues surrounding racist content and hate speech on the Internet see Akdeniz, Y., *Racism on the Internet*, Council of Europe Publishing (forthcoming in 2009); Akdeniz, Y., 'Introduction,' in *Legal Instruments for Combating Racism on the Internet*, Council of Europe Publishing, Human Rights and Democracy Series, 2009, pp. 7–37.

10 See generally Weimann, G., *Terror on the Internet: The New Arena, the New Challenges* (Washington: US Institute of Peace, 2006).

11 Harm is a criterion which depends upon cultural differences and this is accepted within the jurisprudence of the European Court of Human Rights. See for example *Handyside v UK*, App. no. no. 5493/72, Ser A vol. 24, (1976) 1 EHRR 737. Nevertheless, the availability of harmful Internet content is a politically sensitive area and a cause for concern for European regulators.

12 *Handyside v. UK* (1976), App. No. 5493/72, Ser A vol. 24; *Castells v. Spain* (1992), App. No. 11798/85, Ser. A vol. 236. Note also *Lingens v. Austria*, judgment of 8 July 1986, Series A, No. 103.

13 Rights of the Child: Report submitted by Mr. Juan Miguel Petit, Special Rapporteur on the sale of children, child prostitution and child pornography, E/CN.4/2005/78, 23 December, 2004. Note also the Addendum to this report: E/CN.4/2005/78/Add.3, 8 March, 2005. Note further Akdeniz, Y., *Internet Child Pornography and the Law: National and International Responses*, 2008, Ashgate.

14 Akdeniz, Y., *Racism on the Internet*, Council of Europe Publishing, 2010; and Akdeniz, Y., 'Governing Racist Content on the Internet: National and International Responses,' (2007) *University of New Brunswick Law Journal* (Canada), Vol. 56, Spring: 103–161.

15 Note articles 5–7 of the Council of Europe Convention on the Prevention of Terrorism (CETS No. 196), which came into force in June 2007.

16 Publications such as Mujahideen *Explosive Handbook and the Encyclopaedia of the Afghan Jihad* are examples of some of the publications disseminated and distributed through the Internet. Note 'Terror law vague, accused to argue', *The Globe and Mail* (Canada), 30 August 2006 and 'Abu Hamza trial: Islamic cleric had terror handbook, court told', *The Guardian*, London, 12 January 2006.

distribution of pirated content through the Internet. User access blocking policies are developed in several countries including in France and United Kingdom.

However, the major question that is being faced by international organizations and state level regulators is how to control the free flow of content deemed illegal or harmful over the Internet. As mentioned above, the question becomes even more complex by the fact that different political, moral, cultural, historical and constitutional values exist between different states. For example, while countries such as Germany, France, and Austria criminalize the denial of the Jewish Holocaust, not all the member states of the European Union or Council of Europe criminalize such conduct or content. In 2008, Fredrick Töben, a well known Holocaust denier from Australia was arrested at the Heathrow Airport in London because of a pending European arrest warrant issued by the German authorities. The warrant was issued because of Töben's writings on his website denying the existence of the Jewish Holocaust.[17] Töben was subsequently released after the German government gave up its legal battle to extradite him from Britain.[18] Such an example shows that certain acts may be regarded as morally wrong or considered to be offensive by many, or illegal in some countries, but nevertheless are not criminalized by law within certain jurisdictions. Evidently differences exist between states even within the pan-European region.

Once within the strict boundaries and control of individual states, whether through paper-based publications (such as pamphlets, local papers and even books), or audio-visual transmissions limited to a particular area (such as local radio), or public demonstrations and talks, currently with its digital transmission and availability through the Internet such content respects neither national rules nor boundaries. Nowadays, the increasing popularity of user driven interactive Web 2.0 applications and services such as YouTube, Facebook and Twitter seem to eliminate virtual Internet borders even further. This, undoubtedly complicates efforts to find an appropriate balance between the right to freedom of opinion and expression and to receive and impart information and the prohibition on certain types of content deemed to be illegal by state authorities or international organizations.

Typically the stance taken by governments is that what is illegal and punishable in an offline form must also be treated equally online. There are, however, several features of the Internet which fundamentally affect approaches to its governance, and while rules and boundaries still exist, enforcement of the existing rules to digital content becomes evidently problematic on the Internet.

Based on the limited effectiveness of state laws, and lack of harmonization at international level (despite some efforts at regional level[19]) a number of states (including in the pan-European region) started to introduce policies to block access to Internet content and websites deemed illegal which are situated outside their legal jurisdiction. In short, the new trend in Internet regulation seems to be blocking access to content if state authorities are not in a position to reach the perpetrators or criminals for prosecution, or if their request for removal or take down of such content is rejected or ignored by hosting or content providers outside their jurisdiction.

However, blocking policies are not always subject to due process principles, decisions are not necessarily taken by the courts of law, and often administrative bodies or Internet hotlines run by the private sector decide which content or website should be subject to blocking. Often blocking policies lack transparency, and the administrative bodies lack accountability. Therefore,

---

17 *The Daily Telegraph*, 'Alleged Holocaust denier allowed bail,' 29 October, 2008; BBC News, 'Holocaust key to extradition case,' 03 October, 2008, at <http://news.bbc.co.uk/1/hi/uk/7648980.stm>.

18 *The Times*, 'Holocaust denier Fredrick Toben wins German extradition fight,' 20 November, 2008.

19 Note the Council of Europe Convention on Cybercrime (ETS No. 185), and the *Additional Protocol Concerning the Criminalisation of Acts of a Racist and Xenophobic Nature Committed Through Computer Systems* (ETS No. 189).

increasingly, the compatibility of blocking action is questioned with regards to the fundamental right of freedom of expression.

This chapter will assess pan-European level of development and implementation of blocking policies. Adaptation of blocking policies from certain member states of both the EU and CoE will be used to highlight the above mentioned problems associated with blocking policies.

European Union perspectives on content regulation

Content related problems have been divided into two categories by the European Commission ever since 1996. These two categories involve illegal and harmful content. The European Commission in its October 1996 communication on *Illegal and Harmful Content on the Internet* stated that:

> These different categories of content pose radically different issues of principle, and call for very different legal and technological responses. It would be dangerous to amalgamate separate issues such as children accessing pornographic content for adults, and adults accessing pornography about children.[20]

The European Commission developed an *Action Plan for a safer use of the Internet* in 1998,[21] and suggested that 'harmful content needs to be treated differently from illegal content'. Tackling these two distinctive categories separately was a welcome move by the European Commission even though what is illegal, or for that matter harmful was predominantly a Member States' decision. That is why these categories have never been clearly defined by the Commission in its Action Plan.

Usually, the difference between illegal and harmful content is that the former is criminalized by national laws, while the latter is considered offensive, objectionable, unwanted, or disgusting by some people but is generally not criminalized by national laws. While child pornography could be regarded as a clear example of illegal content, Internet content that may be labelled 'harmful' especially with regards to children's access includes sexually explicit material, graphically violent material, and content advocating illegal activity, such as drug use, bomb making, or underage drinking and gambling. Certain strong or extreme political views or religious views are also regarded as harmful by many state regulators. Furthermore, certain states differ in terms of labelling or categorizing certain types of content. Content advocating hate or racist views, and content involving terrorist propaganda are for example treated differently by different states.

Therefore, harm is a criterion which depends upon cultural differences and this is accepted within the jurisprudence of the European Court of Human Rights.[22] It should however be noted that in the *Handyside*[23] case the European Court of Human Rights confirmed that freedom of expression extends not only to ideas and information generally regarded as inoffensive but even to those that might offend, shock, or disturb. As established in *Castells v. Spain*, 'such are the demands of that pluralism, tolerance or broadmindedness without which there is no democratic society'.[24] In *Editorial Board of Pravoye Delo and Shtekel v. Ukraine*, the European Court stated that:

---

20 *European Commission Communication on Illegal and Harmful Content on the Internet* (1996), p. 10.

21 Action Plan on promoting safer use of the Internet by combating illegal and harmful content on global networks, December 1998.

22 See *Handyside v UK*, App. no. 5493/72, Ser A vol. 24, (1976) 1 EHRR 737.

23 Ibid.

24 *Castells v. Spain*, App. no.11798/85, Ser. A vol. 236, (1992) 14 EHRR 445.

> … the Internet is an information and communication tool particularly distinct from the printed media, in particular as regards the capacity to store and transmit information. The electronic network serving billions of users worldwide is not and potentially cannot be subject to the same regulations and control. The risk of harm posed by content and communications on the Internet to the exercise and enjoyment of human rights and freedoms … is certainly higher than that posed by the press.[25]

Nevertheless, the availability of harmful Internet content is a politically sensitive area and a cause for concern for European regulators.

European Union Perspectives on Blocking Access to Illegal Content

With regards to illegal Internet activity, the European Union developed a separate policy on combating child pornography through a Council Framework decision,[26] and addressed the conduct related criminal activity through the Council Framework Decision on Attacks against Information Systems.[27] The EU addressed the liability of Internet Service Providers with regards to carrying or providing access to illegal content through its E-Commerce Directive.[28]

Furthermore, on 28 November, 2008, the Framework Decision on combating racism and xenophobia was adopted through the Council of the European Union. The Framework Decision is designed to ensure that racism and xenophobia are punishable in all member states by effective, proportionate and dissuasive criminal penalties. The Framework Decision deals with such crimes as incitement to hatred and violence, and publicly condoning, denying or grossly trivializing crimes of genocide, crimes against humanity and war crimes.[29] The crimes covered within the Framework Decision will also apply to the Internet and the Member States of the European Union had time until 28.11.2010 to transpose[30] the Framework Decision into national law.

Furthermore, the European Union's May 2006 revised Action Plan on Terrorism[31] included the development of policies and measures to detect misuse of the Internet by extremist websites, and to enhance co-operation of States against terrorist use of the Internet. This initiative involved the development of a new strategy for combating radicalization as it is believed that increasingly more terrorist propaganda and information which could be useful for terrorist use will be produced and distributed over the Internet.[32]

---

25 See *Editorial Board of Pravoye Delo and Shtekel v. Ukraine*, Application no. 33014/05, Jusdgment of 05.05.2011, para 63.

26 Council Framework Decision 2004/68/JHA of 22 December 2003 on combating the sexual exploitation of children and child pornography (see OJ L 013 20.01.2004, p. 0044-0048), at <http://register.consilium.europa.eu/pdf/en/03/st10/st10748en03.pdf>.

27 Council Framework Decision 2005/222/JHA of 24 February 2005 on attacks against information systems, at <http://eur-lex.europa.eu/LexUriServ/site/en/oj/2005/l_069/l_06920050316en00670071.pdf>.

28 This issue will be discussed later in the book.

29 Ibid., section 1(d).

30 There is no detailed information yet on whether all the EU Member States transposed the Directive, and how this Directive was implemented into national laws.

31 Council of the European Union, Revised Action Plan on Terrorism, 10043/06, Brussels, 31 May, 2006.

32 Note the Communication from the European Commission to the European Parliament and the Council concerning Terrorist recruitment: addressing the factors contributing to violent radicalisation, Brussels, 21.9.2005, COM(2005) 313 final.

Within this context the EU considered 'adopting legal measures obliging Internet service providers to remove or disable access to the dissemination of terrorist propaganda they host'[33] but this policy option has been ruled out during the Impact Assessment work done by the European Commission with regards to the proposal for a Council Framework Decision amending Framework Decision 2002/475/JHA on combating terrorism.[34] The Commission also ruled out 'encouraging blocking through the industry's self-regulation or through agreements with industry, without the previous adoption of legal measures outlawing the dissemination of terrorist propaganda and terrorist expertise'.[35]

The European Commission cited 'the issue of the speedy re-apparition of websites that have been closed down' as the main reason for not recommending a blocking policy. The Commission argued that blocking policies are ineffective as in most cases blocked websites reappear under another name outside the jurisdiction of the European Union in order to avoid the eventuality of being closed down or blocked once more.[36] The Commission also acknowledged that existing methods of filtering can be circumvented,[37] and they are designed specifically for websites and are not capable of blocking the distribution of objectionable content through other Internet services such as P2P networks.

The European Commission in its assessment concluded that the removal or disablement of access to terrorist propaganda or terrorist expertise by Internet service providers hosting such information, without the possibility to open an investigation and prosecute the one responsible behind such content, appears inefficient. The Commission reached the conclusion that the dissemination of such content would only be hindered rather than eliminated.[38] The Commission expressed that:

> the adoption of blocking measures necessarily implies a restriction of human rights, in particular the freedom of expression and therefore, it can only be imposed by law, subject to the principle of proportionality, with respect to the legitimate aims pursued and to their necessity in a democratic society, excluding any form of arbitrariness or discriminatory or racist treatment.[39]

The European Commission also expressed concern with regards to the cost of implementing blocking and filtering systems by ISPs and concluded that the implementation of such a system would have direct economic impact not only on ISPs but also on consumers.[40] Furthermore, partially declassified documents in relation to the secretive EU Check the Web Project which monitors the use of the Internet for terrorist purposes through Europol suggest that 'Member States will not be obliged to monitor, interrupt or shut down specific Internet sites' in the fight against terrorist use of

33 European Commission Staff Working Document, Accompanying document to the proposal for a Council Framework Decision amending Framework Decision 2002/475/JHA on combating terrorism: Impact Assessment, 14960/07 ADD1, Brussels, 13 November, 2007, para 4.2, pp. 29–30.

34 Ibid.

35 Ibid.

36 See ibid. See further Communication from the Commission to the European Parliament, the Council and the Committee of the Regions 'Towards a general policy on the fight against cyber crime' of 22 May, 2007 – COM(2007) 267.

37 Ibid., p. 41.

38 See further *European Commission Staff Working Document*, section 5.2, pp. 41–2.

39 Ibid., p 29.

40 Ibid, pp. 42–5.

the Internet.[41] Therefore, blocking access to websites and Internet content is not a common policy adopted within the European Union region and there are no EU policies actively encouraging blocking access to websites.[42]

Blocking considered by the EU with regard to combating child pornography

However, despite there exists no such general policy at the EU level, more recently with regards to amending its policy framework with regards to combating the sexual abuse, sexual exploitation of children and child pornography, the European Commission proposed to have EU wide mechanisms to block access from the Union's territory to Internet websites identified as containing or disseminating child pornography especially where the original materials are not located within the EU Member States' jurisdiction.[43] The Draft Council Framework Decision, through Article 18, stated that Member States would take the necessary measures to enable the competent judicial or police authorities to order or similarly obtain the blocking of access by Internet users to Internet websites containing or disseminating child pornography, subject to adequate safeguards.

While this blocking measure was proposed, a European Commission Staff Working Document referred to the risks of blocking access to content without a legal basis and recommended that to respect fundamental rights such as that of freedom of expression (Article 10 ECHR, Article 11 of the EU Charter), an interference with such an important right needs to be prescribed by law and be necessary in a democratic society.[44] The European Commission Staff Working Document argued that the 'proportionality of the measure would be ensured, as the blocking would only apply to specific websites identified by public authorities as containing such material'.[45] On the one hand, the requirement for 'a legal basis' for blocking is a desired and welcome move from a European Convention on Human Rights point of view. On the other hand, this highlights the fact that currently many hotlines within the European Union region function and order blocking access to content and websites without a legal basis, triggering legitimate accusations of vigilantism. These fundamental concerns needed to be addressed by the European Union before adopting a blocking policy even though this would only apply to content involving child pornography.

41 Council of the European Union, document no. 13930/06 RESTREINT UE, 13930/06, EXT 2, ENFOPOL 169, Brussels, 10 November, 2008, Conclusions of the Kick-off conference 'Check the Web' – Berlin, 26–27 September 2006: This is a partially de-classified document following a request to access the document made by Yaman Akdeniz.

42 The Commission, however, proposed to criminalize the public provocation to commit terrorist offences, recruitment for terrorism and training for terrorism by amending the Framework Decision on combating terrorism. It is expected that the amendments will take place during 2008. See Proposal for a Council Framework Decision amending Framework Decision 2002/475/JHA on combating terrorism, 2007/0236 (CNS), COM(2007) 650 final, Brussels, 6 November, 2007, at <http://ec.europa.eu/commission_barroso/frattini/archive/COM(2007)650%20EN.pdf>.

43 See Proposal for a Council Framework Decision on combating the sexual abuse, sexual exploitation of children and child pornography, repealing Framework Decision 2004/68/JHA, paragraph 12 and draft Article 18 entitled Blocking access to websites containing child pornography.

44 Commission Staff Working Document, Accompanying document to the proposal for a Council Framework Decision on combating the sexual abuse, sexual exploitation of children and child pornography, repealing Framework Decision 2004/68/JHA, Impact assessment, 8150/09 ADD 1, Brussels, 30 March, 2009, p. 30.

45 Ibid.

Having said that the above mentioned European Commission Staff Working Document further stated that 'there is also a risk, depending on the technology used, that the systems in place may occasionally block legitimate content too'[46] which raised further concerns for proportionality.

In February 2011, the European Parliament's Committee on Civil Liberties, Justice and Home Affairs Committee (LIBE) adopted a text[47] in response to the European Commission's proposal on Internet blocking.[48] According to the amendments made by LIBE 'child pornography or child abuse material on the web must be removed at the source in all EU countries'.[49] The Committee, therefore, did not recommend 'mandatory blocking' of websites containing child pornography but rather took the position that such content should be taken down entirely. However, where removal is impossible, e.g. because websites are hosted outside the EU jurisdiction or where the state that hosts the servers in question is unwilling to co-operate or because its procedure for removing the material from servers is particularly long, Member States 'may take the necessary measures in accordance with national legislation to prevent access to such content in their territory'.[50] This would mean that EU Member States may, if necessary, decide to introduce measures involving blocking. National measures preventing access 'must be set by transparent procedures and provide adequate safeguards, in particular to ensure that the restriction is limited to what is necessary and proportionate, and that users are informed of the reason for the restriction'.[51] Content providers and users must also be informed of the possibility to appeal, and to whom to appeal under a judicial redress procedure. It is important to mention that, according to the Committee, the EU must also co-operate with third countries to secure the prompt removal of such material from servers hosted in those countries.

The European Parliament voted on 27 October 2011, and adopted a compromise amendment to the initial proposal. The adopted amendment corresponds to what was agreed between the three European institutions (Council, the European Parliament and the Commission).[52] The amended version of the blocking measure is provided below:

46 Ibid.

47 Committee vote on report of Roberta Angelilli (EPP, IT): 40 in favour, none against, 5 abstentions. See draft report of the European Parliament's Committee on Civil Liberties, Justice and Home Affairs (Rapporteur: Roberta Angelilli) on the proposal for a Council Framework Decision on combating the sexual abuse, sexual exploitation of children and child pornography, repealing Framework Decision 2004/68/JHA, (COM(2010)0094 – C7-0088/2010 – 2010/0064(COD)), 2010/0064(COD), 16.12.2010.

48 Article 21 and Recital 13. Committee on Civil Liberties, Justice and Home Affairs, *Press Release: Delete child pornography web pages across the EU, says Civil Liberties Committee*, 14.02.2011, at <http://www.europarl.europa.eu/en/pressroom/content/20110131IPR12841/html/Delete-child-pornography-web-pages-across-the-EU-says-Civil-Liberties-Committee>. New forms of abuse and exploitation, such as 'grooming' (befriending children through the web with the intention of sexually abusing them), or making children pose sexually in front of web cameras, will also be criminalised.

49 Civil Liberties, Justice and Home Affairs Committee, Press Release, 'Delete child pornography web pages across the EU, says Civil Liberties Committee,' 14.02.2011, at <http://www.europarl.europa.eu/en/pressroom/content/20110131IPR12841/html/Delete-child-pornography-web-pages-across-the-EU-says-Civil-Liberties-Committee>.

50 Committee on Civil Liberties, Justice and Home Affairs, Press Release: Delete child pornography web pages across the EU, says Civil Liberties Committee, 14.02.2011.

51 Ibid.

52 European Parliament legislative resolution of 27 October 2011 on the proposal for a directive of the European Parliament and of the Council on combating the sexual abuse, sexual exploitation of children and child pornography, repealing Framework Decision 2004/68/JHA (COM(2010)0094 – C7-0088/2010 – 2010/0064(COD)).

> Article 25: Measures against websites containing or disseminating child pornography: (1) Member States shall take the necessary measures to ensure the prompt removal of webpages containing or disseminating child pornography hosted in their territory and to endeavour to obtain the removal of such pages hosted outside of their territory. (2) Member States may take measures to block access to webpages containing or disseminating child pornography towards the internet users within their territory. These measures must be set by transparent procedures and provide adequate safeguards, in particular to ensure that the restriction is limited to what is necessary and proportionate, and that users are informed of the reason for the restriction. Those safeguards shall also include the possibility of judicial redress.[53]

The new Directive 2011/92/EU of the European Parliament and of the Council of 13 December 2011 on combating the sexual abuse and sexual exploitation of children and child pornography, and replacing Council Framework Decision 2004/68/JHA was published in the *Official Journal of the European Union* on 17 December 2011.[54] Member States shall bring into force the laws, regulations and administrative provisions necessary to comply with this Directive by 18 December 2013. The European Commission shall, by 18 December 2015, submit a report to the European Parliament and the Council assessing the extent to which the Member States have taken the necessary measures in order to comply with this Directive, accompanied, if necessary, by a legislative proposal.

EU Member States Blocking Practices

While a general blocking policy does not exist at the European Union level, a general monitoring obligation cannot be imposed upon ISPs through Article 15 of the EU E-Commerce Directive.[55] In *L'Oréal* the European Court of Justice stated that:

> it follows from Article 15(1) of Directive 2000/31, in conjunction with Article 2(3) of Directive 2004/48, that the measures required of the online service provider concerned cannot consist in an active monitoring of all the data of each of its customers in order to prevent any future infringement of intellectual property rights via that provider's website.[56]

Despite having no EU-wide general blocking policy, nor an obligation to monitor at the ISP level, EU Member States started to develop their own blocking policies and practices. In Germany, a general blocking policy with regard to child pornography was considered by the parliament. However, in April 2011, after almost a year of discussions, the German government decided

53 Directive of the European Parliament and of the Council on combating the sexual abuse and sexual exploitation of children and child pornography, and replacing Council Framework Decision 2004/68/JHA, PE-COS 51/11, Brussels, 4 November 2011.

54 OJ L 335, 17.12.2011, p. 1.

55 'A general monitoring obligation would be incompatible with Article 3 of Directive 2004/48, which states that the measures referred to by the directive must be fair and proportionate and must not be excessively costly.' See further Judgment of the Court (Grand Chamber) of 12 July 2011, Case C-324/09: *L'Oréal SA and Others v eBay International AG and Others*. Reference for a preliminary ruling: High Court of Justice (England and Wales), Chancery Division – United Kingdom.

56 See paragraph 139 of the Judgment of the Court (Grand Chamber) of 12 July 2011, Case C-324/09: *L'Oréal SA and Others v eBay International AG and Others*. Reference for a preliminary ruling: High Court of Justice (England and Wales), Chancery Division – United Kingdom.

that removal rather than access blocking will be the policy to tackle the problem of online child pornography.[57] During discussions there were concerns that merely blocking material could open the door to wider censorship on the Internet.[58] However, it should also be noted that during 2002, North Rhine Westphalia, Germany's most populous state, issued a blocking-order to prevent German-based ISPs from providing access to Web sites based outside Germany (mainly in the US) if those sites host racist and neo-Nazi content.[59] The blocking-order affected approximately 76 ISPs within that region.[60] Although there have been legal cases and appeals surrounding the blocking-orders, a number of administrative courts have ruled that German authorities can continue to ask ISPs to block such websites. Between 2002–2004 the Düsseldorf District Administration issued 90 ordinances against Internet providers in North Rhine – Westphalia forcing them to block access to certain websites with right-wing extremist content. More recent statistics are not available but the German authorities continue to issue blocking orders, however as highlighted above, the effectiveness of such orders is questioned by the European Commission assessment of blocking as a policy.

Furthermore, the German authorities through the Jugendschutz.net hotline monitor the extent of the criminal Internet activity with regards to propaganda crimes.[61] In 2004, Jugendschutz. Net's activities resulted in the blocking or removal of 131 extreme right-wing websites.[62] During 2007 Jugendschutz.net contacted service and content providers 252 times and was successful in the closure of websites and take down of content in 232 occasions.[63] In 2008, Jugendschutz.net encountered 1,707 right-wing extremist websites online and more than 1,500 illegal videos and profiles with extreme right-wing content. The organization claimed success in the removal of content in 80 percent of all illegal cases.[64]

Germany is not the only EU Member State where blocking has been used as a measure. In the United Kingdom, British Telecom ('BT') in partnership with the Internet Watch Foundation ('IWF'), developed the CleanFeed Project[65] in late 2003. This follows the decision of the IWF to assist its subscribing ISP members in filtering potentially illegal content from their client services

57 See Deutsche Welle, Deleting trumps blocking in fight against online child porn, 06.04.2011, at <http://www.dw-world.de/popups/popup_lupe/0,,14968970,00.html>. According to Deutsche Welle, a law from the previous coalition of Christian Democrats (CDU) and Social Democrats stated that Germany would fight the spread of child pornography on the Internet by blocking sites with pornographic content involving children. The current CDU-Free Democrats (FDP) coalition believes deleting the sites is a better way to solve the problem and had previously announced it would test out the policy over the course of one year.

58 See ibid.

59 *National Journal's Technology Daily*, 'Ban On Neo-Nazi Web Content In German State; Upheld', 22 December, 2004.

60 See US Bureau of Democracy, *Human Rights, and Labor, Report on Global Anti-Semitism*, January 2005, at <http://www.state.gov/g/drl/rls/40258.htm>. Note also Combating racism, racial discrimination, xenophobia and related intolerance and comprehensive implementation of and follow-up to the Durban Declaration and Programme of Action Note by the UN Secretary-General, A/59/330, 4 October, 2004.

61 Section 86, German Criminal Code.

62 Jugendschutz.Net, 'Right-wing Extremism on the Internet' – successful strategies against Online-Hate, 2004 Annual Report, at <http://www.inach.net/content/jgs-annual-report2004.pdf>.

63 Jugendschutz.net Annual Report 2007, Right-wing extremism on the Internet, 15 June, 2008.

64 Jugendschutz.Net report, Cyber Hate 2008: Right-Wing Extremism Online – Targeting teenagers with stylish websites: Trends and Counter-Strategies, 2009, at <http://www.jugendschutz.net/pdf/report_cyberhate_2008.pdf>.

65 IWF/BT Project CleanFeed, at <http://www.iwf.org.uk/media/news.archive-2004.39.htm>.

through the use of the Child Abuse Images URL service.[66] The CleanFeed Project is aimed towards blocking access to any images or websites that contain child pornography within the IWF database. Customers of BT (and other UK ISPs that use the system) are prevented from accessing the blocked content and websites. In 2006, BT claimed that its CleanFeed system was blocking 35,000 attempts to access websites known to carry child pornography every day.[67] According to the Register, 'the announcement caused a flurry of media attention raising fears that thousands of people in the UK are trying to access illegal child abuse websites'.[68] Subsequently, the British government attempted to ensure that all British ISPs offering broadband internet connectivity to the UK public use the CleanFeed system to restrict access to the sites identified by the IWF by the end of 2007.[69] At present, the use of such a blocking system by British ISPs is voluntary and there is no legal requirement to implement such a system, but it is estimated that the 'biggest UK ISPs who between them provide over 90 percent of domestic broadband connections are either currently blocking or had plans to implement blocking systems to by the end of 2006'.[70] The government has hinted that it will review 'the options for stopping UK residents accessing websites on the IWF list'[71] if ISPs elect not to use blocking systems.

In December 2008, the Internet Watch Foundation blocked access to Wikipedia from the UK because of a single image (had been available on the Internet for years) involving the cover of an album called Virgin Killer by German heavy metal band Scorpions.[72] Even though the IWF revoked its decision after five days subsequent to an appeal by the Wikipedia Foundation[73] the incidence highlighted problems associated with this kind of privatized unaccountable regulation. It is often forgotten that the IWF does not have legal authority to require ISPs to block access to such content, and ISPs did not have to comply with a decision to block access to Wikipedia. It is therefore surprising that no British ISP challenged the decision.

---

66 See generally Child Abuse Images URL database at <http://www.iwf.org.uk/public/page.148.htm>. See further the IWF discussion paper, *Commercialising the CAI URL Database*, June 2004, at <http://www.iwf.org.uk/corporate/page.94.176.htm>, and Addendum to the discussion paper at <http://www.iwf.org.uk/corporate/page.94.177.htm>. Note further *Recommendations from the Board and FC Working Group on Commercialising the CAI Database*, February 2005, at <http://www.iwf.org.uk/corporate/page.128.277.htm>, as well as the revised recommendations of May 2005, at <http://www.iwf.org.uk/corporate/page.141.304.htm>.

67 'Porn blocks', *The Evening Chronicle*, 07 February, 2006.

68 Richardson, T., 'ISPA seeks analysis of BT's 'Cleanfeed' stats,' The Register, 21 July, 2004, at <http://www.theregister.co.uk/2004/07/21/ispa_bt_cleanfeed/>. See further Richardson, T., 'BT blocks 230k attempts to access child porn,' The Register, 20 July, 2004, at <http://www.theregister.co.uk/2004/07/20/bt_internet_block/>.

69 Child Abuse (Internet), House of Commons Hansard Debates for 30 April, 2007. Note further Child Pornography, House of Commons Hansard Written Answers for 07 November, 2006; Internet Service Providers, House of Commons Hansard Written Answers for 25 October, 2006.

70 Child Abuse (Internet), House of Commons Hansard Written Answers for 15 May, 2006.

71 Ibid.

72 *The Observer*, 'Wikipedia censorship highlights a lingering sting in the tail,' 14 December, 2008, at <http://www.guardian.co.uk/technology/2008/dec/14/wikipedia-censorship-scorpions-virgin-killer>.

73 Wikimedia Foundation, 'Censorship in the United Kingdom disenfranchises tens of thousands of Wikipedia editors,' 07 December, 2008, at <http://wikimediafoundation.org/wiki/Press_releases/Censorship_of_WP_in_the_UK_Dec_2008>. See further Wikinews, 'Wikimedia, IWF respond to block of Wikipedia over child pornography allegations,' 08 December, 2008, at <http://en.wikinews.org/wiki/Wikimedia,_IWF_respond_to_block_of_Wikipedia_over_child_pornography_allegations>.

Similarly, during January 2009, it was reported that access to the Internet Archive (Wayback Machine)[74] which includes around 85 billion pages had been blocked from the UK subsequent to a blocking decision issued by the IWF.[75] The incidence was described as a technical hitch but once again raised questions with regard to the IWF and lack of due process principles or legal basis with regards to the issuing of blocking decisions at the UK level.

In terms of copyright infringements, in April 2010, the Chancery Division of the High Court in *Twentieth Century Fox Film Corp and others v Newzbin Ltd*[76] held that the claimants would be granted the injunction sought since the defendant's website service had infringed the claimants' copyrights. The service had authorized acts of infringement, had entered into a common design to infringe with those members and had communicated the claimants' copyright works to the public. Subsequently, on 28 July 2011 the High Court of Justice decided that[77] British Telecom ('BT') should block access to the website known as Newzbin2, its domains and sub-domains and including payments.newzbin.com and any other IP address or URL whose sole or predominant purpose is to enable or facilitate access to the Newzbin2 website. The Court decided by reference to section 97A of the Copyright, Designs and Patents Act 1988.[78] The technical details for the blocking measure were adopted in a subsequent judgment on 26 October 2011:[79]

> (i) IP address re-routing in respect of each and every IP address from which the said website operates and which is notified in writing to the Respondent by the Applicants or their agents; and
> (ii) DPI-based[80] URL blocking utilizing at least summary analysis in respect of each and every

74 See http://www.archive.org/

75 The Register, 'IWF confirms Wayback Machine porn blacklisting,' 14 January, 2009, at <http://www.theregister.co.uk/2009/01/14/iwf_details_archive_blacklisting/>.

76 See *Twentieth Century Fox Film Corp and others v Newzbin Ltd* [2010] All ER (D) 43 (Apr); [2010] EWHC 608 (Ch).

77 *Twentieth Century Fox Film Corp and others v Newzbin Ltd* [2011] EWHC 1981 (Ch).

78 Section 97A of the Copyright, Designs and Patents Act 1988 provides that the High Court (in Scotland, the Court of Session) shall have power to grant an injunction against a service provider, where that service provider has actual knowledge of another person using their service to infringe copyright. However, the 'mere (or even knowing) assistance or facilitation of the primary infringement is not enough' to hold service providers liable. See *L'Oréal v eBay* [2009] EWHC 1094, [2009] RPC 21; *Sabaf SpA v MFI Furniture Centres Ltd* [2002] EWCA Civ 976, [2003] RPC 264; *Credit Lyonnais Bank Nederland NV v Export Credits Guarantee Dept* [1998] 1 Lloyd's Rep 19. The joint tortfeasor 'must have so involved himself in the tort as to make it his own. This will be the case if he has induced, incited or persuaded the primary infringer to engage in the infringing act or if there is a common design or concerted action or agreement on a common action to secure the doing of the infringing act'. See *Twentieth Century Fox Film Corp and others v Newzbin Ltd* [2010] EWHC 608 (Ch).

79 *Twentieth Century Fox Film Corp and others v Newzbin Ltd* [2011] EWHC 2714 (Ch).

80 DPI stands for deep packet inspection. According to the High Court, 'this mechanism involves configuring the ISP's network management system to monitor traffic by means of Deep Packet Inspection (DPI) and reset or block a customer's connection to specific Uniform Resource Locators (URLs) as defined in the network management system's Access Control Lists. A URL is an IP address, which usually consists of the access protocol (e.g. http), the domain name and the resource (i.e. the page). This mechanism can also be used to implement IP address blocking as an alternative to the router method described above. DPI-based URL blocking is necessary in cases where a website to be blocked shares an IP address with other websites which are not to be blocked. Further, this mechanism is necessary to block access to only a portion of a website. For example, blocking only the URL 'www.example.com/home.html' would block access to the specific page named 'home.html' on the website 'www.example.com' while leaving the remainder of the site accessible'. See *Twentieth Century Fox Film Corp and others v Newzbin Ltd* [2011] EWHC 1981 (Ch).

URL available at the said website and its domains and sub-domains and which is notified in writing to the Respondent by the Applicants or their agents.[81]

In February 2012, the High Court in *Dramatico Entertainment Ltd & Ors v British Sky Broadcasting Ltd & Ors*[82] ruled that the operators of the infamous *The Pirate Bay* (TPB) website induce, incite or persuade its users to commit infringements of copyright, and that they and the users act pursuant to a common design to infringe. The Court also ruled that 'in this regard that the operators profit from their activities'.[83] Therefore, in May 2012, in *Dramatico Entertainment Ltd & Ors v British Sky Broadcasting Ltd & Ors*,[84] the High Court ordered the blocking of the Pirate Bay website from within the UK through the servers of six ISPs including British Sky Broadcasting Limited, British Telecommunications PLC, Everything Everywhere Limited, Talktalk Telecom Group PLC, Telefónica UK Limited and Virgin Media Limited. The Court also ruled that IP address blocking in addition to DNS blocking was appropriate in this case as the Pirate Bay website IP address is not a shared IP address.

In France, since March 2011, it is possible to require ISPs to block websites containing child pornographic content under the LOPPSI Project (Law on Guidelines and Programming for the Performance of Internal Security).[85] A blacklist of websites, not made public, is established by the administration. ISPs in turn are required to block access to these sites.

In Finland, since January 2007, the Act on Measures to Restrict the Distribution of Child Pornography[86] restricts access to child pornography on the Internet through confidential blacklists prepared by the police. Some ISPs, since early 2008, decided to use the police-maintained blacklist to block access to websites containing child pornography. In June 2011, it was reported that the Helsinki Administrative Court had ruled that domestic websites may not be placed on the blocking blacklist maintained by the police.[87] The administrative court action started in February 2008 when lapsiporno.info ('childporn.info') website was included to the police maintained blacklist and has remained on the list ever since. Lapsiporno.info discovered a large part of the blacklist and circulated the findings on its website.[88] The lapsiporno.info revealed that the top five Google search results for 'gay porn' were all blacklisted even though there was nothing related to children on those sites. The World Wide Web Consortium's website[89] and the memorial page of a deceased Thai princess was among the blacklisted websites. The police, however, accused the website owner

81 The blocking order applies to BT and its customers whether the Cleanfeed system is applied optionally or otherwise. If BT uses the Cleanfeed system, then BT is not required to adopt DPI-based URL blocking utilising detailed analysis.

82 [2012] EWHC 268 (Ch) (20 February 2012).

83 Ibid, para 83.

84 [2012] EWHC 1152 (Ch) (02 May 2012).

85 Loi no. 2011-267 du 14 Mars 2011 d'orientation et de programmation pour la performance de la sécurité intérieure [Internal Security Law]. LOPPSI was announced in the *French Official Gazette* on 15 March 2011. The Law is known as 'Loppsi 2', in reference to a law with a similar name and objective that was passed in 2002. The constitutionality of the 2011 Law was reviewed prior to its promulgation by the Constitutional Council, which struck down 13 of its articles, none of them essential (Conseil Constitutionnel, Décision no. 2011-625 DC du 10 Mars 2011.)

86 Laki lapsipornografian levittämisen estotoimista, lagen om åtgärder som hindrar spridning av barnpornografi; no. 1068/2006.

87 See EDRi-gram, Finland: Blocking of domestic websites ruled illegal, 01 June, 2011, at <http://www.edri.org/edrigram/number9.11/blocking-case-finland-court>.

88 See The Finnish Internet Censorship List at <http://lapsiporno.info/suodatuslista/english.html>.

89 www.w3.org

of distributing child pornography and eventually put the website on the blacklist. The website owner therefore lodged an appeal with an administrative court because his website was blacklisted without a valid legal basis.

In Italy, the competent judicial authority can order seizure, either to prevent an offence or to collect evidence, of a website with illegal content or which is used to commit an offence.[90] Since 2006, online gambling has been permitted only via state-licensed websites, and ISPs are required to block access to international or unlicensed gambling sites identified on a blacklist compiled by the Autonomous Administration of State Monopolies (AAMS).[91] As of May 2012, access to 4,025 gambling sites are blocked from Italy. The authority transparently makes the updated blocked gambling websites list available through its website.[92] A similar blacklist for known child pornography websites is maintained by the National Center for the Fight against Child Pornography on the Internet within the Postal and Communications Police Service[93] since February 2006.

In Norway, access to websites depicting child sex abuse has been blocked at ISP level since 2004 with the establishment of the Child Sexual Abuse Anti Distribution filter (CSAADF). The law enforcement agency NCIS Norway evaluates and verifies illegal sites and provides a list of domains to the ISPs based on a written agreement between NCIS Norway and the ISPs. The agreement has been developed by the Internet Service Providers Association of Norway.[94] The number of websites subject to blocking varies on average between 800–1200 websites at any given time. With regards to Internet piracy, a Norwegian District Court ruled that there were no grounds for ordering the Norwegian ISP Telenor to block access to the popular Pirate Bay website in November 2009. The Court of Appeal rejected an appeal filed by the music and film industry in February 2010. The appeal court held that Telenor did not unlawfully contribute to the infringement of copyright by providing access to the Pirate Bay website.[95]

---

90 Sections 253 and 321 of the *Italian* Code of Criminal Procedure.

91 See further Freedom House, Freedom on the Net 2011: *A Global Assessment of Internet and Digital Media*, April 2011, at <http://www.freedomhouse.org/uploads/fotn/2011/FOTN2011.pdf>.

92 See <http://www.aams.gov.it/site.php?id=2484>.

93 See <http://www.poliziadistato.it/articolo/view/10232/>. Chapter II of Act 38/2006 provides for the setting up within the Postal and Communications Police Service of the National Centre for the Fight against Child Pornography on the Internet – a body of the Ministry of the Interior – having the task to guide, monitor and fights minors' sexual exploitation on the Internet.

94 NCIS Norway receives statistics on a daily basis from the largest ISPs in Norway. The report is based on anonymous log files where NCIS Norway is able to see the referral site, search words leading to the illegal sites, time of day, browser and operation system. NCIS Norway does not receive the IP information, a point exclusively mentioned in the contract with the ISPs.

95 Borgarting Court of Appeal, LB-2010-6542 (10-006542ASK-BORG/04), 9 February 2010. See Winsvold, L., Telenor not Obliged to Block Access to The Pirate Bay, IRIS 2010-4:1/34. See also Winsvold, L., *Unsuccessful Attempt to Block the Pirate Bay*, IRIS 2010-1:1/33.

It should also be noted that leaked secret 'child pornography' access blocking blacklists published on Wikileaks from Finland,[96] Denmark[97] and Italy[98] (as well as from China,[99] Thailand,[100] Australia[101]) have demonstrated that majority (apart from Denmark) censor non-child pornographic content, including political content. Therefore, often, secrecy and unaccountability of such private hotlines lead into blocking and censorship of content which is not deemed to be illegal. In the absence of openness, and transparency of the work of the hotlines as well as the secrecy surrounding the blocking criteria and the list of blocked websites, concerns will continue to exist about the work of such organizations.

Blocking and Filtering Related Litigation at the European Court of Justice Level

Furthermore, policies and practices adopted in a number of European countries resulted with legal challenges through the courts.

In Belgium, the courts may, under national legislation, issue an order for any infringement of an intellectual property right to be brought to an end. In particular, the legislation provides that, where a third party uses the services of an intermediary to perpetrate an infringement of that type, the courts are authorized to issue such an order against that intermediary. The Société belge des auteurs compositeurs et éditeurs (Sabam) applied for interim relief against Scarlet Extended SA, an Internet Service Provider.[102] Sabam sought first of all a declaration that the copyright in musical works contained in its repertoire had been infringed because of the unauthorized sharing, through the use of Scarlet's services, of music files – in particular, by means of peer-to-peer software. Sabam also sought an order requiring Scarlet to bring such infringements to an end, on pain of a penalty payment, by blocking or making impossible the sending or the receiving by its customers in any way of files containing a musical work, using peer-to-peer software, without the permission of the copyright holders. By a judgment of 26 November 2004, such copyright infringements were found to have taken place. After a report had been obtained from a technical expert, Scarlet was ordered, by another judgment, delivered on 29 June 2007, to bring those copyright infringements to an end by making it impossible for its customers to send or to receive in any way, by means of P2P software in particular, files containing a musical work in Sabam's repertoire, and to do so within a period of six months, on pain of a penalty payment of €2,500 per day should Scarlet fail to comply

96 Wikileaks, '797 domains on Finnish Internet censorship list, including censorship critic, 2008,' 05 January, 2009, at <http://www.wikileaks.com/wiki/797_domains_on_Finnish_Internet_censorship_list%2C_including_censorship_critic%2C_2008>.

97 Wikileaks, 'Denmark: 3863 sites on censorship list,' February, 2008, at <http://wikileaks.org/wiki/Denmark:_3863_sites_on_censorship_list%2C_Feb_2008>.

98 Wikileaks, 'Italian secret internet censorship list, 287 site subset, 21 June, 2009, at <http://wikileaks.org/wiki/Italian_secret_internet_censorship_list%2C_287_site_subset%2C_21_Jun_2009>.

99 Wikileaks, 'China: censorship keywords, policies and blacklists for leading search engine Baidu, 2006-2009,' 02 May, 2009, at <http://www.wikileaks.com/wiki/China:_censorship_keywords%2C_policies_and_blacklists_for_leading_search_engine_Baidu%2C_2006-2009>.

100 Wikileaks, 'Thailand official MICT censorship list,' 20 December, 2008, at <http://wikileaks.org/wiki/Thailand_official_MICT_censorship_list%2C_20_Dec_2008>.

101 Wikileaks, 'Leaked Australian blacklist reveals banned sites,' 19 March, 2009, at <http://wikileaks.org/wiki/Leaked_Australian_blacklist_reveals_banned_sites>.

102 Court of Justice of the European Union, Press Release: Advocate General's Opinion in Case C-70/10 *Scarlet Extended v Société belge des auteurs compositeurs et* éditeurs (Sabam), No 37/11, Luxembourg, 14 April 2011.

with the judgment. Scarlet has appealed against that judgment to the Court of Appeal in Brussels, which must decide whether to uphold the measure adopted against Scarlet. In that context, the Court of Appeal sought a ruling from the Court of Justice on whether the European Union law and, in particular, the fundamental rights guaranteed by the Charter of Fundamental Rights, permit a national court to order an ISP to install a system for filtering and blocking electronic communications.[103]

In its ruling of 24 November 2011,[104] the European Court of Justice stated that the EU law precludes the imposition of an injunction by a national court which requires an Internet Service Provider to install a filtering system which applies indiscriminately to all its customers exclusively at the expense of the ISP with a view to preventing the illegal downloading of files containing a musical, cinematographic or audio-visual work in respect of which the applicant claims to hold intellectual-property rights. According to the Court, the injunction imposed on the ISP concerned requiring it to install the contested filtering system would oblige it to actively monitor all the data relating to each of its customers in order to prevent any future infringement of intellectual-property rights. It follows that that injunction would require the ISP to carry out general monitoring, something which is prohibited by Article 15(1) of Directive 2000/31.[105]

Another case that reached the European Court of Justice from Belgium involves Sabam, the Belgian management company which represents authors, composers and publishers of musical works as in the above mentioned case and Netlog NV runs an online social networking platform based in Belgium. Users of this service can also share audio-visual files through their own profile pages. Sabam claimed that unauthorized distribution of music files took place without their consent nor a licence fee paid by Netlog NV. In June 2009 Sabam requested from the President of the Court of First Instance of Brussels (Belgium) that Netlog be ordered immediately to cease unlawfully making available musical or audio-visual works from Sabam's repertoire and to pay a penalty of €1000 for each day of delay in complying with that order. In that regard, Netlog submitted that granting Sabam's injunction would be tantamount to imposing on Netlog a general obligation to monitor, which is prohibited by the E-Commerce Directive. In those circumstances, the Court of First Instance of Brussels made a reference for a preliminary ruling to the Court of Justice.

103 Reference for a preliminary ruling from the Cour d'appel de Bruxelles (Belgium) lodged on 5 February 2010 — *Scarlet Extended SA v Société Belge des auteurs, compositeurs et* éditeurs (SABAM), Case C-70/10, 2010/C 113/30: A reference for a preliminary ruling allows the courts and tribunals of the Member States, in disputes which have been brought before them, to refer questions to the Court of Justice about the interpretation of European Union law or the validity of a European Union act. The Court of Justice does not decide the dispute itself. It is for the national court or tribunal to dispose of the case in accordance with the Court's decision, which is similarly binding on other national courts or tribunals before which a similar issue is raised.

104 Judgment of the Court (Third Chamber) of 24 November 2011, Case C-70/10: *Scarlet Extended SA v Société belge des auteurs, compositeurs et* éditeurs *SCRL* (SABAM). Reference for a preliminary ruling: Cour d'appel de Bruxelles – Belgium. Note also Advocate General's Opinion in Case C-70/10 *Scarlet Extended v Société belge des auteurs compositeurs et éditeurs* (Sabam), No 37/11, Luxembourg, 14 April 2011. According to Advocate General Cruz Villalón, a measure ordering an ISP to install a system for filtering and blocking electronic communications in order to protect intellectual property rights in principle infringes fundamental human rights. Villalón opined that in order to be permissible, such a measure must comply with the conditions laid down in the Charter of Fundamental Rights to govern restrictions on the exercise of rights. It must therefore be adopted, inter alia, on a legal basis that meets the requirements concerning 'the quality of the law' at issue.

105 Ibid, para 40. Note further Judgment of the Court (Grand Chamber) of 12 July 2011, Case C-324/09: *L'Oréal SA and Others v eBay International AG and Others. Reference for a preliminary ruling: High Court of Justice* (England and Wales), Chancery Division – United Kingdom.

The Belgian Court asked the European Court of Justice whether European Union law precludes a national court from issuing an injunction against a hosting service provider, such as an owner of an online social network, which requires it to install a system for filtering information stored on its servers by its service users, which applies indiscriminately to all of those users, as a preventative measure, exclusively at its expense and for an unlimited period.

The European Court of Justice ruled in February 2012 in the case of *Sabam v. Netlog NV*[106] that the owner of an online social network cannot be obliged to install a general filtering system, covering all its users, in order to prevent the unlawful use of musical and audio-visual work. According to the Court, such a preventive monitoring would require active observation of the files stored by users with the owner of the social network. Accordingly, the filtering system would require the owner to carry out general monitoring of the information stored on its servers, something which is prohibited by the E-Commerce Directive. The European Court of Justice, therefore, did not approve of an injunction would result in a serious infringement of Netlog's freedom to conduct its business since it would require Netlog to install a complicated, costly, permanent computer system at its own expense. The Court was also concerned that the injunction could potentially undermine freedom of information, since that system might not distinguish adequately between unlawful content and lawful content, with the result that its introduction could lead to the blocking of lawful communications.

Notice Based Liability System

Going back to the official European Union policy, rather than advocating or requiring a general blocking policy for illegal content, the European Union favours a notice based liability system for EU based hosting companies and access providers. Therefore, the EU adopted a notice based liability system in 2000 through the European Union Directive on certain legal aspects of information society services, in particular electronic commerce, in the Internal Market ('Directive on electronic commerce').[107] The Directive suggested that 'it is in the interest of all parties involved in the provision of information society services to adopt and implement procedures',[108] to remove and disable access to illegal information. As far as hosting issues by ISPs or information society service providers are concerned, Article 14(1) of the E-Commerce Directive requires Member States to:

> 'ensure that the service provider is not liable for the information stored at the request of a recipient of the service, on condition that:

106 Judgment of the Court (Third Chamber) of 16 February 2012, Case C-360/10: *Belgische Vereniging van Auteurs, Componisten en Uitgevers (SABAM) v Netlog NV*. Reference for a preliminary ruling under Article 267 TFEU from the rechtbank van eerste aanleg te Brussel (Belgium), made by decision of 28 June 2010, received at the Court on 19 July 2010, in the proceedings.

107 Directive 2000/31/EC of the European Parliament and of the Council of 8 June 2000 on certain legal aspects of information society services, in particular electronic commerce, in the Internal Market, Official Journal of the European Communities, v. 43, OJ L 178 17 July, 2000 p.1. Note also Common Position (EC) No 22/2000 of 28 February 2000 adopted by the Council, acting in accordance with the procedure referred to in Article 251 of the Treaty establishing the European Community, with a view to adopting a Directive on electronic commerce, Official Journal C 128, 08/05/2000 p. 0032–0050.

108 Ibid.

> (a) the provider does not have actual knowledge of illegal activity or information and, as regards claims for damages, is not aware of facts or circumstances from which the illegal activity or information is apparent; or
> (b) the provider, upon obtaining such knowledge or awareness, acts expeditiously to remove or to disable access to the information.'

This means that there is no absolute protection provided within the Directive for ISPs and the ISPs are required to act expeditiously 'upon obtaining actual knowledge' of illegal activity or content 'to remove or to disable access to the information concerned'.[109] Such removal or disabling of access 'has to be undertaken in the observance of the principle of freedom of expression and of procedures established for this purpose at national level'[110] according to the Directive. Termination or prevention of an infringement is also possible by a court or administrative authority order. Article 14(3) also states that the provisions of Article 14 do not 'affect the possibility for Member States of establishing procedures governing the removal or disabling of access to information'. It was decided that the notice and take down procedures would not be regulated in the Directive itself.[111] Rather, the Directive, through Recital 40 and Article 16, encourages self-regulatory solutions and procedures to be developed by the Internet industry to implement and bring into action notice and takedown procedures.[112]

In addition to the notice based limited liability exceptions, the Directive prevents Member States from imposing a monitoring obligation on service providers only with respect to obligations of a general nature but 'this does not concern monitoring obligations in a specific case, and in particular, does not affect orders by national authorities in accordance with national legislation'.[113] Under article 15, the Directive specifically requires Member States not to 'impose a general obligation on providers, when providing the services covered by Articles 12, 13 and 14, to monitor the information which they transmit or store, nor impose a general obligation actively to seek facts or circumstances indicating illegal activity'. However, Member States 'may establish obligations for information society service providers promptly to inform the competent public authorities of alleged illegal activities undertaken or information provided by recipients of their service or obligations to communicate to the competent authorities, at their request'.[114]

Overall, the E-Commerce Directive provides limited and notice based liability with take down procedures for illegal content and requires Member States and the Commission to encourage the development of codes of conduct.[115] However, various studies so far showed that ISPs based in Europe tend to remove and take down content without challenging the notices they receive. A Dutch study claimed that 'it only takes a Hotmail account to bring a website down, and freedom of

109 Ibid, para. 46.

110 Ibid.

111 See Report from the Commission to the European Parliament, the Council and the European Economic and Social Committee – 'First report on the application of Directive 2000/31/EC on electronic commerce'), COM(2003) 702 final, Brussels, 21 November, 2003, at <http://europa.eu.int/eur-lex/en/com/rpt/2003/com2003_0702en01.pdf>, section 4.7.

112 Out of those Member States which have transposed the Directive, only Finland has included a legal provision setting out a notice and take down procedure concerning copyright infringements only: This information has been taken from the above mentioned Commission Report: COM(2003) 702 final.

113 Ibid, para. 47.

114 Article 14(2).

115 Ibid, para. 49.

speech stands no chance in front of the cowboy-style private ISP justice'.[116] As mentioned briefly above, there was no challenge from any ISPs based in the UK with regards to the Wikipedia blocking decision imposed by the Internet Watch Foundation during December 2008. The ISPs complied with the order even though the blocking decision has no legal basis under UK law. For clarity, UK based ISPs could be exposed to legal liability for knowingly carrying child pornography on their servers.[117] However, the picture the IWF complained about was hosted on the Wikipedia servers rather than on the servers of the UK based ISPs, but 'access blocking' is currently not a legal remedy provided by law even with regards to content involving child pornography in the UK.

Within this context it is important to note that an application from Estonia has been made to the European Court of Human Rights. In Estonia, the provisions on liability limitation in case of mere conduit and caching services have been harmonized with the EU E-Commerce Directive 2000/31/EC. Estonia has transposed the EU principles into the Information Society Services Act (*Infoühiskonna teenuse seadus*).[118] Similar to other EU states that implemented the EU E-Commerce Directive, the Estonian law includes limited liability for mere transmission of information and provision of access to public data communications network,[119] limited liability for temporary storage of information in cache memory,[120] and limited liability upon provision of information storage service.[121] Furthermore, the providers are not obliged to monitor their

116 Nas, S., *(Bits of Freedom), The Multatuli Project: ISP Notice & take down*, 2004, at <http://www.bof.nl/docs/researchpaperSANE.pdf>. Note also Ahlert, C., Marsden, C. and Yung, C., *How 'Liberty' Disappeared from Cyberspace: The Mystery Shopper Tests Internet Content Self-Regulation*, at <http://pcmlp.socleg.ox.ac.uk/text/liberty.pdf>.

117 See generally Akdeniz, Y., *Internet Child Pornography and the Law: National and International Responses*, (Ashgate, 2008), pp. 17–92 and 227–45.

118 14 April 2004 (Riigi Teataja 2004, 29, 191).

119 Section 8(1): Where a service is provided that consists of the mere transmission in a public data communication network of information provided by a recipient of the service, or the provision of access to a public data communication network, the service provider is not liable for the information transmitted, on condition that the provider: 1) does not initiate the transmission; 2) does not select the receiver of the transmission; 3) does not select or modify the information contained in the transmission. (2) The acts of transmission and of provision of access in the meaning of paragraph 1 of this section include the automatic, intermediate and transient storage of the information transmitted, in so far as this takes place for the sole purpose of carrying out the transmission in the public data communication network, and provided that the information is not stored for any period longer than is reasonably necessary for the transmission.

120 Section 9(1): Where a service is provided that consists of the transmission in a public data communication network of information provided by a recipient of the service, the service provider is not liable for the automatic, intermediate and temporary storage of that information, if the method of transmission concerned requires caching for technical reasons and the caching is performed for the sole purpose of making more efficient the information's onward transmission to other recipients of the service at their request, on condition that: 1) the provider does not modify the information; 2) the provider complies with conditions on access to the information; 3) the provider complies with rules regarding the updating of the information, specified in a manner widely recognised and used in the industry; 4) the provider does not interfere with the lawful use of technology, widely recognized and used by the industry, to obtain data on the use of the information; 5) the provider acts expeditiously to remove or to disable access to the information it has stored upon obtaining actual knowledge of the fact that the information at the initial source of the transmission has been removed from the network, or access to it has been disabled, or that a court, the police or a state supervisory authority has ordered such removal.

121 Section 10(1): Where a service is provided that consists of the storage of information provided by a recipient of the service, the service provider is not liable for the information stored at the request of a recipient of the service, on condition that: 1) the provider does not have actual knowledge of the contents of

servers.[122] An application with the European Court of Human Rights against Estonia was lodged in December 2009 by Delfi AS, an Internet news portal that publishes up to 330 news articles a day. The case involves the posting of third party comments on the Delfi portal with regards to the published articles on the website. Delfi received a complaint and subsequently removed the allegedly defamatory comments according to the notice-and-take-down obligation. However, Delfi refused to pay damages claimed. In June 2009, the Supreme Court of Estonia ruled that both Delfi and the authors of the comments were to be considered publishers of the comments. In this context, the Court also referred to the economic interest of an Internet portal administrator, defining the publisher as an entrepreneur, similar to a publisher of printed media. The European Court of Human Rights will consider[123] whether there has been a violation of the applicant company's right to freedom of expression, in particular its right to impart information and ideas as guaranteed by Article 10 of the European Convention on Human Rights. The case is significantly important as it will lay down liability principles with regards to third-party comments published on news portals and social media platforms. The Court will also have the opportunity to scrutinize the 'notice-based liability' measures of the E-Commerce Directive.

Council of Europe perspectives on content regulation

Moving on to the Council of Europe (CoE) policy initiatives, the Council of Europe's Cybercrime Convention 2001[124] is the first international treaty to address criminal law and procedural aspects of various types of offensive behaviour directed against computer systems, networks or data in addition to content related crimes such as child pornography. In general, the Convention aims to harmonize national legislation with regards to criminal activity conducted by computers or through the Internet, facilitate investigations related to such crimes, and allow efficient levels of co-operation between the authorities of different Member States of the CoE and other third party states who would be party to the Convention following a ratification process at the national level.

Following the first five ratifications, the Cybercrime Convention came into force on July 1, 2004. The signing and ratification process for the Cybercrime Convention resulted with 46

---

the information and, as regards claims for damages, is not aware of facts or circumstances from which the illegal activity or information is apparent; 2) the provider, upon obtaining knowledge or awareness of the facts specified in subparagraph 1 of this paragraph, acts expeditiously to remove or to disable access to the information. (2) Paragraph 1 of this section shall not apply when the recipient of the service is acting under the authority or the control of the provider.

122 Section 11(1): A service provider specified in sections 8 to 10 of this Act is not obliged to monitor information upon the mere transmission thereof or provision of access thereto, temporary storage thereof in cache memory or storage thereof at the request of the recipient of the service, nor is the service provider obliged to actively seek information or circumstances indicating illegal activity. (2) The provisions of paragraph 1 of this section do not restrict the right of an official exercising supervision to request the disclosure of such information by a service provider. (3) Service providers are required to promptly inform the competent supervisory authorities of alleged illegal activities undertaken or information provided by recipients of their services specified in sections 8 to 10 of this Act, and to communicate to the competent authorities information enabling the identification of recipients of their service with whom they have storage agreements.

123 The statement of facts was published by the Strasbourg court on 11 February 2011.

124 The text of the CyberCrime Convention can be found at <http://conventions.coe.int/treaty/en/projects/cybercrime.htm>.

Member States[125] signing and 33 countries[126] ratifying the Convention as of May 2012 out of the potential 47 CoE Member States as well as the external supporters.[127] Only Andorra, Monaco, Russia and San Marino are yet to sign the Convention from the CoE Member States. Austria, Azerbaijan, Belgium, Czech Republic, Georgia, Greece, Ireland, Liechtenstein, Luxembourg, Malta, Montenegro, Poland, Portugal, Spain, Sweden, Switzerland and the United Kingdom are yet to ratify the Convention despite signature.

Subsequently, the CoE also developed the first Additional Protocol to the Cybercrime Convention on the criminalization of acts of a racist or xenophobic nature committed through computer systems (ETS No. 189).[128] This Additional Protocol entails an extension of the Cybercrime Convention's scope, including its substantive, procedural and international cooperation provisions, so as to cover offences of racist or xenophobic propaganda. Thirty-five Member States[129] have signed the Additional Protocol since it was opened to signature in January 2003, but only 20 Member States[130] have ratified the Additional Protocol as of may 2012. Following the initial five ratifications the Additional Protocol came into force on 1 March, 2006.

Furthermore, the Council of Europe Convention on the Prevention of Terrorism (CETS 196) which came into force in June 2007 provides for a harmonized legal basis to fight the use of the Internet as a means for public provocation to commit terrorist offences,[131] recruitment for terrorism,[132] and training for terrorism[133] including through the Internet. Therefore, if signed and ratified by the Member States, the distribution and publication of certain types of content deemed to be related to terrorist activity could be criminalized. While 43 Member States signed the Convention, 29 of them ratified it as of May 2012.

The content specific crimes within the Cybercrime Convention and the Additional Protocol, namely, the offences related to child pornography (Article 9), and the dissemination of racist and xenophobic material through computer systems (AP, Article 3) do not include any blocking provisions. Similarly the provisions of the Convention on the Prevention of Terrorism do not provide for blocking, and instead concentrate on the criminal activity of dissemination and publication.

Access and hosting providers are also protected under the provisions of these three CoE Conventions, and it 'is not sufficient, for example, for a service provider to be held criminally liable' under these provisions, and 'that such a service provider served as a conduit for, or hosted a

125 Plus the external supporters United States, Canada, South Africa, and Japan and Montenegro.

126 Albania, Armenia, Azerbaijan, Bosnia and Herzegovina, Bulgaria, Croatia, Cyprus, Denmark, Estonia, Finland, France, Germany, Hungary, Iceland, Italy, Latvia, Lithuania, Moldova, Montenegro, Netherlands, Norway, Portugal, Romania, Serbia, Slovakia, Slovenia, Spain, Switzerland, Ukraine, United Kingdom, United States of America, and the former Yugoslav Republic of Macedonia.

127 See generally Akdeniz, Y., 'An Advocacy Handbook for the Non Governmental Organizations: The Council of Europe's Cyber-Crime Convention 2001 and the additional protocol on the criminalisation of acts of a racist or xenophobic nature committed through computer systems', *Cyber-Rights & Cyber-Liberties*, 2003 (revised May 2008), at <http://www.cyber-rights.org/cybercrime/coe_handbook_crcl.pdf>.

128 See generally Akdeniz, Y., *Racism on the Internet, Council of Europe Publishing*, 2010.

129 Including the external supporters Canada, and South Africa.

130 Albania, Armenia, Bosnia and Herzegovina, Croatia, Cyprus, Denmark, Finland, France, Germany, Latvia, Lithuania, Montenegro, Netherlands, Norway, Portugal, Romania, Serbia, Slovenia, Ukraine and the former Yugoslav Republic of Macedonia.

131 Article 5 of the Council of Europe Convention on the prevention of terrorism (CETS 196).

132 Ibid., article 6.

133 Ibid., article 7.

website or newsroom containing such material, without the required intent under domestic law'[134] in any particular case under the CoE provisions. Moreover, as provided by the EU E-Commerce Directive, a service provider is not required to monitor conduct to avoid criminal liability under the CoE provisions.

CoE Recommendations on Blocking and Filtering Systems

With regards to the deployment and use of blocking and filtering systems CoE Cybercrime Convention Committee (T-CY) recognized the legal difficulties which could arise when attempting to block certain sites with illegal content.[135] More importantly, a CoE Committee of Ministers Recommendation of 2007[136] called upon the Member States to promote freedom of communication and creation on the Internet regardless of frontiers, in particular by not subjecting individuals to any licensing or other requirements having a similar effect, nor any general blocking or filtering measures by public authorities, or restrictions that go further than those applied to other means of content delivery.[137]

More recently, in March 2008, the Committee of Ministers in a new Recommendation[138] recalled the Declaration of the Committee of Ministers on freedom of communication on the Internet of 28 May, 2003,[139] which stressed that public authorities should not, through general blocking or filtering measures, deny access to the public information and other communication on the Internet regardless of frontiers.[140] The Committee of Ministers in its March 2008 Recommendation stated that 'there is a tendency to block access to the population to content on certain foreign or domestic web sites for political reasons. This and similar practices of prior State control should be strongly condemned'. Equally, the 2003 Declaration emphasized that exceptions must be allowed for the protection of minors, and states can consider the installation of filters for the protection of minors, in particular in places accessible to them, such as schools or libraries.

Furthermore, CoE Recommendation of March 2008 stated that any intervention by Member States that forbids access to specific Internet content may constitute a restriction on freedom of expression and access to information in the online environment and that such a restriction would have to fulfil the conditions in Article 10(2) of the European Convention on Human Rights and the relevant case law of the European Court of Human Rights. The Recommendation noted that the

---

134 Council of Europe, 'Committee of Ministers, Explanatory Report of the Additional Protocol to the Convention on CyberCrime, concerning the criminalisation of acts of a racist and xenophobic nature committed through computer systems' (2002) at para. 25, at <http://conventions.coe.int/Treaty/en/Reports/Html/189.htm>.

135 CoE Cybercrime Convention Committee (T-CY), 2nd Multilateral Consultation of the Parties, Strasbourg, 13 and 14 June, 2007, Strasbourg, 15 June, 2007, T-CY (2007) 03, para. 29.

136 CM/Rec (2007)16 of November, 2007.

137 Recommendation CM/Rec (2007)16 of the Committee of Ministers to member states on measures to promote the public service value of the Internet: Adopted by the Committee of Ministers on 7 November, 2007 at the 1010th meeting of the Ministers' Deputies.

138 Recommendation CM/Rec (2008)6 of the Committee of Ministers to member states on measures to promote the respect for freedom of expression and information with regard to Internet filters: Adopted by the Committee of Ministers on 26 March, 2008 at the 1022nd meeting of the Ministers' Deputies.

139 Freedom of communication on the Internet, Declaration adopted by the Council of Europe Committee of Ministers on 28 May, 2003 at the 840th meeting of the Ministers' Deputies.

140 Ibid, Principle 3.

voluntary and responsible use of Internet filters (products, systems and measures to block or filter Internet content) can promote confidence and security on the Internet for users, in particular for children and young people, while also noting that the use of such filters can seriously impact on the right to freedom of expression and information as protected by Article 10 of the ECHR.

The Guidelines provided within the March 2008 Recommendation[141] stated that the Internet users should have the possibility to challenge the blocking decisions or filtering of content and be able to seek clarifications and remedies.[142] The Guidelines called upon the Member States to refrain from filtering Internet content in electronic communications networks operated by public actors for reasons other than those laid down in Article 10(2) of the ECHR as interpreted by the European Court of Human Rights.

The Guidelines, further, called upon the Member States to guarantee that nationwide general blocking or filtering measures are only introduced by the states if the conditions of Article 10(2) of the ECHR are fulfilled. According to the Guidelines such action by the state should only be taken if the filtering concerns specific and clearly identifiable content, a competent national authority has taken a decision on its illegality and the decision can be reviewed by an independent and impartial tribunal or regulatory body in accordance with the requirements of Article 6 of the ECHR. The Guidelines also called upon the Member States to ensure that all filters are assessed both before and during their implementation to ensure that the effects of the filtering are proportionate to the purpose of the restriction and thus necessary in a democratic society, in order to avoid unreasonable blocking of content.

According to the CoE Guidelines the universal and general blocking of offensive or harmful content for users who are not part of a specific vulnerable group (such as children) which a filter has been activated to protect should be avoided. This recommendation therefore distinguishes between the adults' use of the Internet and vulnerable groups use of the Internet. Therefore, the need to limit children's access to certain specific types of Internet content deemed as harmful should not also result in blocking adults' access to the same content available on the Internet.

With regards to protection of children from harmful content the Committee of Ministers recommended in July 2009[143] that Member States, in co-operation with private sector actors and civil society, develop and promote coherent strategies to protect children against content and behaviour carrying a risk of harm. The Committee of Ministers also recommended that safe and secure spaces similar to walled gardens should be developed for children on the Internet. While doing so the Committee of Ministers noted that 'every action to restrict access to content is potentially in conflict with the right to freedom of expression and information as enshrined in Article 10 of the European Convention on Human Rights'.[144] Therefore, while the need to protect children from harmful content was highlighted, and walled gardens and the development of a pan-European trustmark and labelling systems[145] was encouraged, the Committee did not recommend

141 Recommendation CM/Rec(2008)6 of the Committee of Ministers to member states on measures to promote the respect for freedom of expression and information with regard to Internet filters: Adopted by the Committee of Ministers on 26 March, 2008 at the 1022nd meeting of the Ministers' Deputies.

142 Ibid., Guideline I.

143 Recommendation CM/Rec(2009)5 of the Committee of Ministers to member states on measures to protect children against harmful content and behaviour and to promote their active participation in the new information and communications environment, adopted by the Committee of Ministers on 8 July 2009 at the 1063rd meeting of the Ministers' Deputies.

144 See Guidelines 7, Recommendation CM/Rec(2009)5 of the Committee of Ministers.

145 To be prepared in full compliance with the right to freedom of expression and information in accordance with Article 10 of the European Convention on Human Rights. See Guidelines 12, Recommendation

state level blocking or filtering mechanisms for the protection of children. Similarly, the Committee stated that 'online content which is not labelled should not however be considered dangerous or less valuable for children, parents and educators'.[146]

More recently, the CoE Committee of Experts on New Media (MC-NM) developed guidelines for search engines[147] and social networking providers.[148] Both guidelines were approved by the Committee of Ministers of the Council of Europe in April 2012[149] and recommend that Member States should guarantee that blocking and filtering, in particular nationwide general blocking or filtering measures, are only introduced if the conditions of Article 10, paragraph 2, of the European Convention on Human Rights are fulfilled. Within this context Member States should avoid general blocking of offensive or harmful content for users who are not part of the groups for which a filter has been activated to protect. The Committee of Experts believes that search engines and social network providers should be encouraged to offer adequate voluntary individual filter mechanisms which would suffice to protect vulnerable groups such as children.

Conclusion

Having assessed the nature of blocking policies at the pan-European region certain conclusions and recommendations are reached. These are explained below.

Blocking is an inadequate method to combat illegal content

Although the criminalization of certain types of content is encouraged through the policies of both organizations, neither the EU nor the CoE encourage blocking access to websites as a feasible solution to encounter criminal use of the Internet. In fact, serious concerns have been raised with regards to adopting state level blocking and filtering policies and this crude measure as a potential solution has been found to be inadequate, and explicitly dismissed by the European Union.

However, as noted above, a recent Council Framework Decision on combating the sexual abuse, sexual exploitation of children and child pornography[150] established that EU Member States may, if necessary, decide to introduce measures involving blocking from the Union's territory to Internet pages identified as containing or disseminating child pornography especially where the original materials are not located within the EU. National measures preventing access 'must be set by transparent procedures and provide adequate safeguards, in particular to ensure that the restriction

---

CM/Rec(2009)5 of the Committee of Ministers.

146 See Guidelines 13, Recommendation CM/Rec(2009)5 of the Committee of Ministers.

147 See CoE Committee of Experts on New Media (MC-NM), draft Guidelines for Search Engine Providers, MC-NM(2010)009_en, Strasbourg, 5 October 2010.

148 See CoE Committee of Experts on New Media (MC-NM), Proposal for draft Guidelines for Social Networking Providers, MC-NM(2010)008_en, Strasbourg, 5 October 2010.

149 See Recommendation CM/Rec(2012)3 of the Committee of Ministers to member states on the protection of human rights with regard to search engines; Recommendation CM/Rec(2012)4 of the Committee of Ministers to member States on the protection of human rights with regard to social networking services, 4 April 2012.

150 The new Directive 2011/92/EU of the European Parliament and of the Council of 13 December 2011 on combating the sexual abuse and sexual exploitation of children and child pornography, and replacing Council Framework Decision 2004/68/JHA was published on the *Official Journal of the European Union* on 17 December 2011, OJ L 335, 17.12.2011, p. 1.

is limited to what is necessary and proportionate, and that users are informed of the reason for the restriction'. [151] However, a mandatory blocking policy was not introduced at the EU level.

Furthermore, the Council of Europe through the Cybercrime Convention and its Additional Protocol, as well as through the Convention on the Prevention of Terrorism did not adopt any policy which encourage or recommend blocking as a feasible way of combating illegal content disseminated through the Internet. Through certain declarations and recommendations the CoE Committee of Ministers concluded that public authorities should not deploy general blocking or filtering measures to combat illegal content.

In any case the futility of the blocking systems should also be highlighted as circumvention technologies are developed hand to hand with blocking and filtering technologies, and Internet users are capable of circumventing blocking mechanisms and accessing supposedly blocked pages as long as those pages continue to be available over the Internet and not taken-down by those who host them. It should be noted that there are several freely available tools and services that the Internet users can use to circumvent access blocking methods. Several alternative DNS servers (such as OpenDNS) are available to circumvent DNS blocking and tampering mechanisms while several anonymous proxy servers such as Anonymizer.com, Ktunnel.com, Vtunnel.com, and Electronic Frontier Foundation's TOR network,[152] and several other systems are available and used to bypass IP address blocking mechanisms.

Privatized Blocking and the role of Hotlines

In terms of blocking and take-down decisions taken by administrative bodies and private Internet hotlines set up in Europe, such public or private organizations may not always be in a position to judge the suitability or illegality of Internet content. In fact, such hotlines are often criticized as serious concerns remain about the policing role they inevitably play. Many commentators maintain that decisions involving illegality should be decided by the courts of law only rather than hotline operators. It has been argued that 'these hotlines violate due process concepts that are also enshrined in international, regional, and national guarantees around the world'. [153]

While it may be tempting to identify and attempt to block content posted to particular websites, or other Internet forums that seems devoted to illegality, such measures could set dangerous precedents if hotlines or administrative bodies assume the role of the courts. Over time, such an approach could result in a form of privatized censorship with no limit on its application. Although hotlines and certain administrative bodies could play an important role in combating illegal Internet content, there remain significant questions about their operation as was highlighted in this article. As the Martabit report to the UN stated 'while encouraging these initiatives, States should ensure that the due process of law is respected and effective remedies remain available in relation to measures enforced'.[154] Therefore, the operation of private hotlines formed through self-regulatory means should be consistent with the principles underlying the European Convention on Human Rights. States may have a positive obligation to guarantee that hotlines respect due

151 Committee on Civil Liberties, Justice and Home Affairs, Press Release: Delete child pornography web pages across the EU, says Civil Liberties Committee, 14.02.2011.

152 See <http://tor.eff.org/>.

153 American Civil Liberties Union, Press Release, 'ACLU Joins International Protest Against Global Internet Censorship Plans,' 9 September ,1999.

154 See Report of the Intergovernmental Working Group on the effective implementation of the Durban Declaration and Programme of Action on its fourth session, UN ESCOR, 62d Sess., UN Doc. E/CN.4/2006/18 (2006), at <http://daccessdds.un.org/doc/UNDOC/GEN/ G06/119/23/PDF/G0611923.pdf >, para. 47.

process principles, and their functions and practice do not contravene the principles underlying the European Convention.[155] States must furthermore provide adequate and effective safeguards against abuse. These should include procedures for effective judicial scrutiny of the decisions taken by the hotlines.[156]

Web 2.0 based applications and services

Although not specifically addressed by any European policy, blocking access to any Web 2.0 based applications and services such as YouTube, Facebook, Twitter, WordPress, Google Groups, DailyMotion, Blogger, Myspace, and Last.fm may have extreme side effects.[157] It should be noted that blocking of such services not only result in the blocking of access to the allegedly illegal content (usually a single file or page) but also results in the blocking of millions of legitimate pages, files and content under the single domain that these systems operate. Therefore, blocking access to web 2.0 based systems and services should be avoided at all costs as the damage caused by blocking access to such sites would be higher than the public good that would be achieved by blocking and censoring access to thousand (if not millions) of legitimate content.

Furthermore, blocking access to socially useful websites such as YouTube, Twitter and others could also have very strong implications on political expression. Such platforms provide a venue which is popular all around the world for alternative and dissenting views. According to the Strasbourg Court, while political and social news 'might be the most important information protected by Article 10, the freedom to receive information does not extend only to reports of events of public concern, but covers in principle also cultural expressions as well as pure entertainment'.[158]

Development of 'Three-strikes' Measures is Worrisome

It should also be noted that the development of so-called 'three-strikes' legal measures to combat Internet piracy in a number of participating States is worrisome given the growing importance of the Internet in daily life. 'Three-strikes' measures provide a 'graduated response' resulting in restricting or cutting off the users' access to the Internet in cases where a user has attempted to download allegedly illegal copyright protected (pirated) material. The third strike usually leads to the user's access to the Internet being completely cut off. This disproportionate response is incompatible with fundamental human rights such as freedom to seek, receive and impart information, which are vital to democracy, and in fact are strengthened by Internet access. An interference with such a fundamental human right must be motivated by a pressing social need, whose existence must be demonstrated by the participating States and such interference must be proportionate to the legitimate aim pursued.[159]

---

155 See *Özgür Gündem v. Turkey*, no. 23144/93, §§ 42–46, ECHR 2000-III, and *Fuentes Bobo v. Spain*, no. 39293/98, § 38, 29 February 2000.

156 See *Lupsa v. Romania*, no. 10337/04, § 34, 8 June 2006.

157 Note examples of such blocking activity taking place in Turkey: Akdeniz, Y., Report of the OSCE Representative on Freedom of the Media on Turkey and Internet Censorship, January 2010, at <http://www.osce.org/documents/rfm/2010/01/42294_en.pdf>.

158 Khurshid Mustafa and Tarzibachi v. Sweden, App. no. 23883/06, judgment of 16 December, 2008.

159 See *Olsson v. Sweden (No. 1)*, judgment of 24 March 1988, Series A no. 130, § 67, and *Bladet Tromsø and Stensaas v. Norway* [GC], no. 21980/93, ECHR 1999-III.

Filtering is an inadequate method to combat harmful content

With regards to the availability of harmful content (which falls short of illegality) both the EU and CoE encourage self-regulatory measures for the protection of vulnerable groups such as children rather than offering legislative solutions. Within this context both organizations strongly emphasize the adoption of policies which do not result in adult citizens being prevented from accessing legal content which may be deemed inappropriate for children to access. Therefore, while Member States should encourage the use of filtering software on home computers, and in schools, the deployment of state level filtering systems should be avoided at all costs. Furthermore, users should be made aware of the potential limitations of filtering software. It should also be noted that none of the currently available filtering methods or tools offer a suitable solution for blocking access to allegedly illegal content or content which may be regarded as undesirable or unsuitable for children.

Originally promoted as technological alternatives that would prevent the enactment of national laws regulating Internet speech, filtering systems have been shown to pose their own significant threats to free expression. When closely scrutinized, these systems should be viewed more realistically as fundamental architectural changes that may, in fact, facilitate the suppression of speech far more effectively than national laws alone ever could.[160] Therefore, the deployment and use of filtering tools is unacceptable at state level. Filters are limited, defective, ineffective, and easy to circumvent.[161] Filters do not offer full protection to concerned citizens. As a result of various defects massive over-blocking is usually witnessed in filtering software. Apart from over-blocking, under-blocking is also witnessed with certain filtering software which raise further questions marks about the reliability of such tools as stand-alone solutions.

Therefore, no filtering system should be deployed at the country access level (whether index based,[162] analysis based filtering,[163] or both) or used by individual ISPs. Within this context, although not within the European region, the controversial Australian plans to introduce a mandatory filtering system for all users to block access to allegedly illegal Internet content must be criticized. Opponents of the proposed system argue that the government has not demonstrated a need for such an online censorship system. If the system is implemented, there will be concern for its potential domino effect and consideration for the implementation of similar filtering systems elsewhere. It is submitted that filters should only be used by individuals on their home computers if their use is deemed necessary.

Filtering is Limited in Functionality

Furthermore, filtering software (including ISP level filtering products) offer limited functionality as they are predominantly designed to filter out websites while by design exclude other Internet-related communication systems such as chat environments, file transfer protocol servers (FTP), peer-to-peer networks (P2P), Usenet discussion groups, and VOIP systems. Users, for example, increasingly obtain content through P2P systems such as BitTorrent. Furthermore, users increasingly exchange files through the Internet chat protocol (MSN, etc.) as well as through popular VOIP systems such as Skype and Gizmo. Therefore, the assumption that filtering systems would make

160 Global Internet Liberty Campaign, 1999.

161 Schulz, W., 'Regulating the Code? Using ISPs to block banned web-sites in Germany', 14th Computers, Freedom & Privacy Conference, 22 April, 2004, at <http://www.cfp2004.org/program/materials/c7-schulz.ppt>.

162 Blacklists prepared by government bodies or by commercial organizations.

163 Developed to meet a set of criteria intended to determine the acceptability of content.

the Internet a 'safer environment' especially for children is false as World Wide Web content represents only a fraction of the whole of the Internet.

It should also be noted that ISP level filter products can also cause performance degradation, and have a detrimental impact upon Internet access and speed.[164]

Content based restrictions and the European Convention on Human Rights

With regards to content based restrictions, the state response should be proportionate,[165] correspond to a 'pressing social need',[166] be necessary in a democratic society,[167] and be compatible with Article 10 of the European Convention on Human Rights and the jurisprudence of the European Court of Human Rights.

Having said that, States enjoy a 'certain but limited' margin of appreciation[168] in assessing the need for an interference. However, this limited margin goes hand in hand with European supervision through the European Court of Human Rights whose extent will vary according to each case. The Strasbourg Court is therefore empowered to give the final ruling on whether a 'restriction' is reconcilable with freedom of expression as protected by Article 10.[169] However, the Court's supervision will be strict because of the importance given to freedom of expression. While the measure taken need not be shown to be 'indispensable', the necessity for restricting the right must be convincingly established at state level.[170]

Furthermore, blocking access to content on websites indefinitely could result to 'prior restraint'. Although the Strasbourg Court does not prohibit the imposition of prior restraints on publications, the dangers inherent in prior restraints are such that they call for the most careful scrutiny on the part of the European Court.[171] This is particularly valid for the press as news is a perishable commodity and to delay its publication, even for a short period, may well deprive it of all its value and interest.[172] Same principles also apply to new media and Internet publications. In this connection, it is argued that prior restraints and bans imposed on the future publication of entire newspapers, or for that matter websites are incompatible with the Convention rights. The Strasbourg Court requires the consideration of less draconian measures such as the confiscation of particular issues of publications including newspapers, or restrictions on the publication of specific

---

164 See Australian Communications and Media Authority (ACMA) report, Closed Environment Testing of ISP-Level Internet Content Filtering, June 2008, at <http://www.acma.gov.au/webwr/_assets/main/lib310554/isp-level_internet_content_filtering_trial-report.pdf>.

165 See Bladet Tromsø and Stensaas judgment of 20 May 1999, Reports 1999.

166 See Sürek v. Turkey (No. 1) (application no. 26682/95), judgment of 8 July 1999, Reports 1999; Sürek (No. 3) judgment of 8 July 1999.

167 See *Sunday Times v. UK* (No. 2), Series A no. 217, 26.11.1991, para. 50; *Okçuoğlu v. Turkey*, No. 24246/94, 8.7.1999, para. 43.

168 Handyside judgment of 7 December 1976, Series A No. 24, §49; *Castells v. Spain* judgment of 23 April 1992, Series A No. 236.

169 *Lingens v. Austria*, 8 July 1986, Series A no. 103, p. 26, § 41.

170 Autronic AG judgment of 22 May 1990, Series A No. 178, § 61.

171 Case of Ürper *and Others v. Turkey* (Applications nos. 14526/07, 14747/07, 15022/07, 15737/07, 36137/07, 47245/07, 50371/07, 50372/07 and 54637/07), Chamber Judgment of 20.10.2009, paras 39–45.

172 Observer *and* Guardian *v. the United Kingdom*, 26 November 1991, § 59, Series A no. 216).

articles.[173] It stems from the Strasbourg principles that by suspending access to websites indefinitely the Member States could largely overstep the narrow margin of appreciation afforded to them.[174] In December 2012, in its first access blocking related decision, in *Ahmet Yildirim v. Turkey*,[175] the European Court of Human Rights found a violation of Article 10 of the European Convention on Human Rights. The application to the European Court involved a Turkish court decision to block access to Google Sites, which hosted an Internet site whose owner was facing criminal proceedings for insulting the memory of Atatürk. As a result of the court decision, access to all other sites hosted by Google Sites was also blocked including the applicant's websites hosted on Google Sites. The responsible public authority made it technically impossible to access any content on Google Sites in order to implement the measure ordered by the local court. The measure in question therefore amounted to interference by the public authorities with the applicant's right to freedom of expression. Such interference would breach Article 10 unless it was prescribed by law, pursued one or more legitimate aims and was necessary in a democratic society to achieve such aims. The European Court reiterated that a restriction on access to a source of information was only compatible with the Convention if a strict legal framework was in place regulating the scope of a ban and affording the guarantee of judicial review to prevent possible abuses. The Court further observed that there was no indication that the Criminal Court had made any attempt to weigh up the various interests at stake, in particular by assessing whether it had been necessary to block all access to Google Sites. In the Court's view, this shortcoming was a consequence of the domestic law, which did not lay down any obligation for the courts to examine whether the wholesale blocking of Google Sites was justified. The courts should have had regard to the fact that such a measure would render large amounts of information inaccessible, thus directly affecting the rights of Internet users and having a significant collateral effect.

It is hereby argued that, following the decision of the European Court of Human Rights in *Ahmet Yildirim v. Turkey*, there could be a breach of Article 10 if blocking measures or filtering tools are used at state level to silence politically motivated speech on the Internet, or the criteria for blocking or filtering is secret, or the decisions of the administrative bodies and hotlines are not publicly made available for legal challenge.

Despite having reached the above conclusions, many will continue to argue that in the absence of universal laws and agreements blocking and filtering is the 'best that can be done' to combat the dissemination of illegal Internet content. On the other hand, many support the view that the small amount of illegal content available through websites does not warrant a huge investment for blocking. In fact, more often such content including child pornography is distributed by other means, including through private forums, ftp servers and peer to peer networks. In a similar vein, it is claimed that blocking systems have their limitations[176] as circumvention is technically possible. The UK's Internet Service Providers Association stated that it supported the government's action

173 Case of Ürper *and Others v. Turkey* (Applications nos. 14526/07, 14747/07, 15022/07, 15737/07, 36137/07, 47245/07, 50371/07, 50372/07 and 54637/07), Chamber Judgment of 20.10.2009, paras 39–45.

174 *Cumpănă and Mazăre v. Romania*, no. 33348/96, § 119, 10 June 2003; *Obukhova v. Russia*, no. 34736/03, § 28, 8 January 2009, and Case of Ürper *and Others v. Turkey* (Applications nos. 14526/07, 14747/07, 15022/07, 15737/07, 36137/07, 47245/07, 50371/07, 50372/07 and 54637/07), Chamber Judgment of 20.10.2009, paras 39–45.

175 Application No.3111/10, decision of 18.12.2012.

176 See generally Ryan, J., *Countering Militant Islamist Radicalisation on the Internet: A User Driven Strategy to Recover the Web*, Dublin: Institute of European Affairs, 2007.

against child-abuse sites but cautioned it would 'only curtail casual browsing and will not hinder organized distribution of such images'.[177]

Ultimately it is argued that censorship and blocking should not be pursued. Having said that, in reality states will continue to develop blocking mechanisms and policies. It should however be recalled that openness, transparency, and accountability are important elements of a healthy democratic system. As the development of blocking policies have serious implications for censorship, the need for openness and transparency are even greater. The states may not, in the name of the struggle against illegal Internet content adopt whatever actions or measures they deem appropriate[178] especially if such measures lead into censorship and arbitrary blocking of websites as the secret 'child pornography' access blocking blacklists published on Wikileaks from Finland,[179] Denmark[180] and Italy[181] (as well as from China,[182] Thailand[183] and Australia[184]) have demonstrated. The narrow margin of appreciation afforded to the Member States by the European Court of Human Rights should not be broadly interpreted. Therefore, without a doubt, such blocking systems, if developed and deployed by the states, as well as the reasons behind blocking decisions, and the criteria for blocking should respect the rule of law and fundamental human rights.

177 *The Guardian*, 'Surfing with a safety net: The government is leaning on ISPs to install web filters for home broadband, at huge cost', 29 June, 2006.

178 Note for example the case of *Klass v. Federal Republic of Germany* within this context: judgment of 18 November 1977, European Court of Human Rights, Series A No 28.

179 Wikileaks, '797 domains on Finnish Internet censorship list, including censorship critic, 2008', 05 January, 2009, at <http://www.wikileaks.com/wiki/797_domains_on_Finnish_Internet_censorship_list%2C_including_censorship_critic%2C_2008>.

180 Wikileaks, 'Denmark: 3863 sites on censorship list,' February, 2008, at <http://wikileaks.org/wiki/Denmark:_3863_sites_on_censorship_list%2C_Feb_2008>.

181 Wikileaks, 'Italian secret internet censorship list, 287 site subset, 21 June, 2009, at <http://wikileaks.org/wiki/Italian_secret_internet_censorship_list%2C_287_site_subset%2C_21_Jun_2009>.

182 Wikileaks, 'China: censorship keywords, policies and blacklists for leading search engine Baidu, 2006-2009,' 02 May, 2009, at <http://www.wikileaks.com/wiki/China:_censorship_keywords%2C_policies_and_blacklists_for_leading_search_engine_Baidu%2C_2006-2009>.

183 Wikileaks, 'Thailand official MICT censorship list,' 20 December, 2008, at <http://wikileaks.org/wiki/Thailand_official_MICT_censorship_list%2C_20_Dec_2008>.

184 Wikileaks, 'Leaked Australian blacklist reveals banned sites,' 19 March, 2009, at <http://wikileaks.org/wiki/Leaked_Australian_blacklist_reveals_banned_sites>.

PART III
Intellectual Property, Competition Rules and New Technologies

Chapter 4

Intellectual Property and Human Rights: Northern and Southern Perspectives

Ana E. Santos

Introduction

As developments in skill and technology brought down the marginal cost of copying, creators and related industries began worrying that non-rivalrousness and non-excludability[1] would soon lead to the following scenario: if anybody (and especially *everybody*) could easily appropriate the goods that they produced, then no one would have the incentive to spend time and money producing them.[2] Intellectual property was designed as a balancing mechanism that would solve this particular kind of market failure: through the grant of a monopoly (the copyright that will last the life of the author plus a few more decades,[3] the patent that will give lead time to the inventor) it keeps alive the economic incentive that will lead to the production of public goods, therefore ensuring that the general public will have access to books and medicines that otherwise it may not have had. The catch is that when that period of exclusivity ends these goods will fall into the public domain, where anyone can use or re-use them for free.[4]

A different, less utilitarian approach tells us that intellectual property is rooted in natural law and has its oldest coordinates in the labour theory of property.[5] Wendy Gordon summarises Locke's arguments in the following way:

> Labor is mine and when I appropriate objects from the common I join my labor to them. If you take the objects I have gathered you have also taken my labor, since I have attached my labor to the objects in question. This harms me, and you should not harm me. You therefore have a duty to leave these objects alone. Therefore I have property in the objects. Similarly, if I use the public domain to create a new intangible work of authorship or invention, you should not harm me by copying it and interfering with my plans for it. I therefore have property in the intangible as well.[6]

1 See Joseph Stiglitz, 'Knowledge as a Global Public Good' in Inge Kaul, Isabelle Grunberg and Marc A. Stern (eds) *Global Public Goods: International Cooperation in the 21st Century* (United Nations Development Programme, OUP 1999): 308–325.

2 A problem that is often referred to as 'the tragedy of the commons', a variation of the dilemma first described by Garrett Hardin. See Garrett Hardin, 'The Tragedy of the Commons' (1968) 162 *Science* 1243, 1248.

3 Usually it lasts for the life of the author plus 50 or 70 years (both Europe and the United States have adopted the latter standard). Mexico has stretched it to life plus 100 years.

4 For a theory on the multiple configurations of the public domain see e.g., P Samuelson, 'Enriching Discourse on Public Domains' (2006) 55 *Duke Law Journal*, 102.

5 See J. Locke, *Second Treatise of Government*, in *Two Treatises of Government*, first published 1689.

6 W. Gordon, 'A Property Right in Self-Expression: Equality and Individualism in the Natural Law of Intellectual Property' (1993) 102 *Yale L.J.* 1533, 1544–1555.

Locke's notion of property, although subject to many reinterpretations, has remained influential in framing intellectual property as a set of rights that orbit around the sphere of human rights,[7] as yet another manifestation of Justinian's *jus suum cuique tribuendi*. In copyright theory, for instance, it is acknowledged that each author leaves his or her personal imprint in a given work and it is in deference to this seed of one's personality that copyright law seeks to protect original expression. However, the fact that intellectual property deals with non-rivalrous and non-excludable goods poses some insurmountable problems to its assimilation into a strictly Lockean philosophy.[8] Human rights approaches to intellectual property that assume that the latter should be regarded as a human right because it is akin to property are fatally flawed because they rely on a defective analogy, confusing the tangible goods in which the intellectual work is embodied with the intangible goods themselves.

Regardless of which one of these approaches one may choose – and the truth is that legal systems are not aseptic ecosystems, with contamination working both ways[9] – there is a balancing feature that is implicit in each one of them. An analysis of a possible dialectics between human rights and intellectual property must therefore pay attention to the current status of this balance and on the external disruptive effects that an ill-calibrated ratio between protected and unprotected elements will cause.

Despite its half-blood affiliation with natural law, it took a long time before intellectual property was first scrutinised through the lens of human rights. This does not mean that there have not always been tensions between these two fields (think how copyright can apply pressure on freedom of expression,[10] or how the proprietary enclosure of science may affect traditional knowledge or the right to health[11]), but only recently did the first claims arise for a 'comprehensive and coherent "human rights framework" for intellectual property law and policy'.[12] One of the reasons which has lead to the emergence of this new approach has been the worrisome impact that the 'progressive alignment of trade and intellectual property policy'[13] has had in the past few years. The TRIPS

7 For further developments and critical analysis of this theory see, in general, J. Schroeder, 'Unnatural Rights: Hegel and Intellectual Property' (2005) 60 *University of Miami Law Review* 453; M. Vivant, '"Authors" Rights, Human Rights' (1997) 174 *Revue Internationale du Droit D'Auteur* 60. For copyright in particular and the contrast between civil law and common law systems, see J. Ginsburg, 'A Tale of Two Copyrights: Literary Property in Revolutionary France and America' [1990] *Tulane Law Review* 64.

8 Cf. n. 1. A good and recent example of how a purely proprietary framework for intellectual property leads to conceptual confusion is the campaign led by the movie industry across Europe and the United States, asking 'You wouldn't steal a movie/a car/a purse, would you?'. The conclusion that followed in the ads showed in cinemas before the feature presentation was that *because* you wouldn't steal any of those physical goods, you wouldn't download illegal music or movies either. The incongruence is that if one steals a cd from a music store, there is one less cd in the store, whereas if one downloads a song, that very same song is still available for others to hear and download.

9 See n. 7.

10 See P.B. Hugenholtz, 'Copyright and Freedom of Expression in Europe' in R.C. Dreyfuss, H. First and D.L. Zimmerman (eds), *Innovation Policy in an Information Age* (OUP 2000).

11 See e.g., S. Musungu, 'The Right to Health, Intellectual Property and Competition Principles' in Cottier, Paulwelyn and Bonanomi (eds), *Human Rights and International Trade* (OUP 2005).

12 See L. Helfer, 'Toward a Human Rights Framework for Intellectual Property' (2007) *U.C. Davis Law Review* 971, 977.

13 D. Gervais, 'Intellectual Property and Human Rights: Learning to Live Together' in Paul L.C. Torremans (ed.), *Intellectual Property and Human Rights* (Kluwer 2008) 6.

Agreement (Agreement on Trade-Related Aspects of Intellectual Property Rights[14]) has, in this regard, a self-explanatory name. As Daniel Gervais explains, 'Intellectual property rights holders ask for the linkage with trade essentially to benefit from the protection of trade sanctions and cross-sectoral trade-offs in trade agreements'.[15] For those who believe that intellectual property and human rights are indissolubly tied, embracing the trade paradigm has at least two disruptive consequences, as the same author further explains: 'unlike human rights, trade law is essentially pragmatic and results-based,'[16] and 'trade remedies are generally predicated on a showing of actual adverse impact on trade. The protection of intellectual property by trade rules does not seem to mesh with its ideological deference either as a "property" or a human right'.[17]

At the same time that trade was becoming a magnetic force, intellectual property rights became stronger than ever before: for instance, the term of protection afforded by copyright law was extended in the United States,[18] Europe created *sui generis* rights over databases, the scope of patentability kept stretching and stretching over time.[19] All these phenomena raise serious concerns that the balance inherent to intellectual property may have been destroyed and that anti-commons effects[20] may be hindering future creation and innovation. And, in this regard, for the sake of some human rights – or some components of these rights – it is crucial to rethink intellectual property in light of a much-needed balance.

What do we Talk about when we Talk about Intellectual Property and Human Rights

One can think about the connection between intellectual property and human rights in two different ways: intellectual property rights *as* human rights; or intellectual property *and* human rights as separate but overlapping areas. The first notion has direct roots in natural law and personalistic conceptions of intellectual property and it places the creator at the centre of the system: in copyright theory, civil law countries are called *droit d'auteur* countries, an expression that literally translates as 'the rights *of the* author'. Therefore, it is not surprising that the first time that European courts examined the relationship between intellectual property and human rights, their main concern was to make intellectual property rights fit the concept of 'property' as it appeared in the European Convention on Human Rights.[21] In recent years, academics, non-governmental organizations and the civil society have started to voice concerns about the negative effects of over-protective legislation in the copyright and patent fields, but the debate has so far remained detached from a human rights framework. The emphasis is therefore on a *static* perspective – copyrights, patents and trademarks as rights, and possibly as human rights – rather than on the *dynamic* interplay

14 Annex 1C of the Marrakesh Agreement Establishing the World Trade Organization, signed in Marrakesh, Morocco on 15 April 1994. Hereinafter referred to as TRIPS. Text available at <http://www.wto.org/english/tratop_e/trips_e/t_agm0_e.htm> accessed 12 June 2012.

15 Gervais, 'Intellectual Property and Human Rights' 6.

16 Ibid, 7.

17 Ibid.

18 Commonly known as the Sonny Bono Copyright Term Extension Act.

19 See e.g., M Heller and R Eisenberg, 'Can Patents Deter Innovation? The Anticommons in Biomedical Research' (1998) 280 *Science* 698.

20 The existence of a plethora of intellectual property rights and its consequent web of transaction costs, which would slow down subsequent innovation. See Heller and Eisenberg n.19.

21 See n. 30.

between intellectual property and the areas affected by the grant of these exclusive rights (which, in many cases, are areas of incidence of classic human rights doctrine).

Common law countries, known as copyright countries, have built their intellectual property frameworks around the concepts of market failure and incentives to creation and innovation. The main difference between a *droit d'auteur* system and a copyright system is that the latter tends to recognise weaker moral rights, if any at all.[22] Because less emphasis is given to the centrality of the author or the inventor, the discussion is not centred on the possibility of copyright or patents qualifying as human rights per se. Much of the critical thinking about the appropriate degree of patent and copyright protection fuelled by the recent trend towards overprotection in both these fields[23] revolves around the detrimental effects that intellectual property rights have had on the access to data or medicines – to name but two examples – but it does so from an internal viewpoint: that of intellectual property (in the United States, usually based upon an analysis of the Copyright and Patent clause).[24] The current state of the debate amounts to what Graeme Austin and Laurence Helfer have aptly described as a 'historical isolation of the Human Rights and Intellectual Property regimes'.[25]

In recent years, movements like 'Free Culture'[26] or 'Access to Knowledge'[27] have promoted a narrowing of the gap between copyrights and human rights. Also, with the growth of the generic industry, both in the developed and in the developing worlds, together with the renewed concern with orphan diseases and drugs,[28] the linkage between patents and human rights has become even more apparent and one can only hope that it will continue to expand in the near future.

The North: Intellectual Property as a Human Right? – The Debate Surrounding the European Convention on Human Rights

The Convention for the Protection of Human Rights and Fundamental Freedoms, also known as European Convention on Human Rights (ECHR), was signed in 1950 and established the European Court of Human Rights. Protocol 1 of the ECHR protects (physical) property, stating that everybody is 'entitled to the peaceful enjoyment of his possessions'.[29] Until very recently,

22 See article 6bis of the Berne Convention for the Protection of Literary and Artistic Works, 1 B.D.I.E.L. 715: 'Independent of the author's economic rights, and even after the transfer of the said rights, the author shall have the right to claim authorship of the work and to object to any distortion, mutilation or other modification of, or other derogatory action in relation to the said work, which would be prejudicial to the author's honor or reputation.'

23 See, for instance, J. Boyle, 'A Manifesto on WIPO and the Future of Intellectual Property' (2004) *Duke L. & Tech. Rev.* 9.

24 Art I, s 8, cl 8 of the United States Constitution, which empowers the Congress to pass laws 'To promote the Progress of Science and useful Arts, by securing for limited Times to Authors and Inventors the exclusive Right to their respective Writings and Discoveries'.

25 See L. Helfer and G. Austin, *Human Rights and Intellectual Property: Maping the Global Interface* (CUP 2011) 31.

26 See L. Lessig, *Free Culture: The Nature and Future of Creativity* (Penguin 2005).

27 See <http://a2knetwork.org/> accessed 12 June 2012.

28 See Kevin Outterson, 'Patent Buy-Outs for Global Disease Innovations for Low- and Middle-Income Countries' (2006) 32 *American Journal of Law and Medicine* 159.

29 ECHR Protocol 1 art 1: 'Every natural or legal person is entitled to the peaceful enjoyment of his possessions. No one shall be deprived of his possessions except in the public interest and subject to the conditions provided for by law and by the general principles of international law.

the Court did not hear any cases on intellectual property, a scenario that changed with *Dima v. Romania*[30] and *Anheuser-Busch v. Portugal*.[31]

In *Dima v. Romania*, an admissibility decision, the Court addressed the case of a Romanian graphic artist who worked in the Defence Ministry's plastic arts studio and created a new State emblem for a competition supported by the Romanian Parliament. In 1992, his design was approved by the Parliament. Dima developed it and it was later published in the *Official Gazette*, which identified him as being 'the graphic designer'. In 1996, Dima brought suit against two private companies that had reproduced and distributed his design and a State-owned company that minted Romanian coins, claiming that he was entitled to a statutory percentage of the profits. The Romanian Supreme Court dismissed his claims, considering that, although Dima had created the State emblem, it was the Parliament who had commissioned it and therefore the Parliament should be deemed the 'author' of the design.

Dima claimed before the European Court of Human Rights that Romanian national law protected 'works of graphic art' and that it established that the 'author' of a work was 'the person who [had] created [it]'. He also claimed that copyright arose when the work took 'concrete form'.

The Court held that Dima was not entitled to any 'legitimate expectation' to 'acquire a possession' as author of the emblem because the existence of a valid copyright was, in the first place, an unresolved issue. In such cases, the European Court defers to domestic courts, and the Romanian Supreme Court had ruled against Dima.

As Laurence Helfer points out,[32] it is relevant that the Court has not tried to 'second-guess the Romanian court's interpretation of domestic copyright law in a case whose facts were sympathetic to the creator'. Moreover, it is also worthwhile noticing that the European Court, while deferring judgment to domestic courts, did say that article 1 of Protocol 1 protected copyrighted works, a step forward in arguing that some components of intellectual property rights – at least where copyright is concerned – might have a human rights dimension.

In *Anheuser-Busch v. Portugal* the European Court of Human Rights dealt with trademarks. In 1981, Anheuser-Busch Inc. sought to register *Budweiser* as a trademark with the Portuguese National Institute for Industrial Property. The application was not immediately granted because *Budweiser Bier* had already been registered as a designation of origin by Budejovicky Budvar, a Czechoslovak beer producer. In 1995, Anheuser-Busch obtained a court order cancelling the registration of Budejovicky Budvar's designation of origin and Anheuser-Busch was therefore allowed to register *Budweiser* as a trademark. Budejovicky Budvar, however, invoked a 1986 bilateral agreement between Portugal and Czechoslovakia protecting designations of origin and argued that Portugal had the obligation to register its beer as geographical indication. Budejovicky Budvar lost at the lower level[33] but won in appeal, which lead to the cancellation of Anheuser-Busch's trademark. At this stage, Anheuser-Busch filled a complaint with the European Court of Human Rights, stating that Portugal had violated article 1.

The preceding provisions shall not, however, in any way impair the right of a State to enforce such laws as it deems necessary to control the use of property in accordance with the general interest or to secure the payment of taxes or other contributions or penalties.'

30 App. No. 58472/00 (ECtHR, 16 November 2006).

31 App. No. 73049/01 (ECtHR, 11 October 2005).

32 See L. Helfer, 'Intellectual Property and the European Court of Human Rights' in Paul L.C. Torremans (ed) *Intellectual Property and Human Rights* (Kluwer 2008) 41.

33 The lower court reasoned that only the Czech version of the beer name could be considered a designation of origin and Budweiser was its German form.

The Court had to decide whether article 1 protected not only registered marks but also trademark applications. The Chamber ruled that article 1 did not apply, because Budejovicky Budvar had already contested Anheuser-Busch's trademark when the latter filled its 1981 application and because of the bilateral agreement, which had been in effect for over two years when Anheuser-Busch challenged the geographical indication. In 2007, the Grand Chamber revised the Chamber's decision and held that Portugal had not violated article 1 and it also declared that it applies to both registered marks and trademark applications.

The Meaning of the Decisions of the European Court of Human Rights

The jurisprudence in Europe is now clear: intellectual property rights claims can find shelter under the European Convention on Human Rights. It remains to be seen how far a doctrine of intellectual property rights *as* human rights may stretch, but it is nonetheless worth pointing out that the reasoning followed by the Court is premised upon an erroneous construction of what intellectual property actually is. Protocol 1 of the ECHR refers to 'peaceful enjoyment' of one's 'possessions'. This language is alien to the intellectual property field, and with good reason: the analogy between property *stricto sensu* and intangible property may be helpful to understand certain problems,[34] but it is certainly not accurate.[35] Intellectual property rights were not created to promote 'peaceful enjoyment' of works or inventions; they were created to promote their existence, meaning that they confer to their holders precisely the ability to exclude others from enjoying the protected intangible good at all, if they so wish to do.

This is not to say that the Court overstepped into an area which it was not supposed to enter. Instead, it was more a clever and slightly twisted construction meant to encompass a field that the drafters of the ECHR were not particularly concerned about, rather than a truly meaningful statement that intellectual property rights should be treated as human rights *per se*.

Interaction Between Intellectual Property and Human Rights: the International Framework

There are a few provisions in other international agreements that are also often alluded to in the debate between the relationship between intellectual property and human rights. One of the most quoted provisions in this debate is article 27 of the Universal Declaration of Human Rights (UDHR):

> (1) Everyone has the right freely to participate in the cultural life of the community, to enjoy the arts and to share in scientific advancement and its benefits.
> (2) Everyone has the right to the protection of the moral and material interests resulting from any scientific, literary or artistic production of which he is the author.

Although the UDHR is said to have no binding effect (given that it is a Recommendation of the United Nations General Assembly), several authors[36] point out that in fact it possesses the force

34 See n. 2.

35 See n. 1.

36 See C Geiger, The Constitutional Dimension of Intellectual Property in Paul L.C. Torremans (ed.) *Intellectual Property and Human Rights* (Kluwer 2008) 113.

of international customary law. This provision would be relevant both in copyrights ('cultural life', 'literary or artistic production') and patents ('scientific advancement'), but too broad an interpretation of number 2, or an overuse thereof, could reduce the understanding of the dynamics between human rights and intellectual property to a vision in which the property aspects of the debate would ultimately prevail.

Article 15 of the International Covenant on Economic, Social and Cultural Rights (ICESCR) is also often mentioned is this debate. 15.1 is very similar to article 27 UDHR in recognising the right of 'everyone' to:

> (a) take part in cultural life; (b) enjoy the benefits of scientific progress and its applications; (c) benefit from the protection of the moral and material interests resulting from any scientific, literary or artistic production of which he is the author.

Also, article 15.2 of the ICESCR states that 'the steps to be taken by the States Parties to the present Covenant to achieve the full realization of this right shall include those necessary for the conservation, the development and the diffusion of science and culture'. Article 15.3, on the other hand, proclaims that 'the States Parties to the present Covenant undertake to respect the freedom indispensable for scientific research and creative activity'. Finally, article 15.4 states that 'the States Parties to the present Covenant recognize the benefits to be derived from the encouragement and development of international contacts and co-operation in the scientific and cultural fields'.

Audrey Chapman has pointed out that in order [t]o be consistent with the full provisions of article 15 [of the ICESCR], the type and level of protection afforded under any intellectual property regime must facilitate and promote cultural participation and scientific progress and do so in a manner that will broadly benefit members of society both on an individual and collective level."[37] However, it is highly doubtful that many of today's intellectual property policies are consistent with this proviso.

Some of the recommendations made in 2000 by a United Nations Sub-Commission on a Resolution with regarding 'Intellectual Property and Human Rights'[38] are worth highlighting as well. The recommendations advise governments to protect 'the social functions of intellectual property'[39] consentaneously with international human-rights obligations and principles. Chapman suggests that 'one way to do so would be to have a mechanism for a human rights review/appeal of decisions by patent and copyright procedures'.[40] The Resolution also calls for the WTO in general and the TRIPS Council (Agreement on Trade-Related Aspects of Intellectual Property) in particular to take 'fully into account existing state obligations under international human rights instruments' during its review of the TRIPS agreement. Chapman argues that 'for this to happen in a meaningful way, however, it would first be necessary to gain recognition for the principle that human rights are fundamental and prior to free trade itself'.[41] Lastly, the Resolution encourages the Committee

37 See Chapman, A. 2001. *Approaching Intellectual Property as a Human Right*, in Copyright Bulletin, volume XXXV, no. 3, 14 <http://unesdoc.unesco.org/images/0012/001255/125505e.pdf> accessed 12 June 2012.

38 See Office of the High Commissioner for Human Rights, Sub-Commission on Human Rights Resolution 2000/7, hereinafter Resolution, <http://www.unhchr.ch/Huridocda/Huridoca.nsf/0/c462b62cf8a07b13c12569700046704e?Opendocument>, accessed 12 June 2012.

39 See Resolution n. 40 para 6.

40 See Chapman n. 39, 30.

41 Ibid.

on Economic, Social and Cultural Rights 'to clarify the relationship between intellectual property rights and human rights, including through the drafting of a general comment on this subject'.[42]

Finally, article 7 of TRIPS, entitled 'Objectives', establishes that:

> The protection and enforcement of intellectual property rights should contribute to the promotion of technological innovation and to the transfer and dissemination of technology, to the mutual advantage of producers and users of technological knowledge and in a manner conducive to social and economic welfare, and to a *balance* of rights and obligations.[43]

Authors suggesting that the proper connection between intellectual property and human rights lies in a balancing effect of the latter over the former often quote article 7 to substantiate their claim.[44] According to them, article 7 TRIPS would:

> encourage (…) WTO Member States to build their IP systems in equilibrium between the two key interests at stake: Providing an incentive for the creation of new innovations through rewards (…) [and] secure the transfer and diffusion of innovations to the public. (…) The proportional balance of these two interests should be determined in accordance with the overall aim of promoting progress in science, arts and technology (…).[45]

It is also worth pointing out that in the following article, which lists the principles of the TRIPS Agreement, there is an explicit allusion to abuse of intellectual property rights by right holders:

> Appropriate measures, provided that they are consistent with the provisions of this Agreement, may be needed to *prevent the abuse of intellectual property rights* by right holders or the resort to practices which unreasonably restrain trade or adversely affect the international transfer of technology.[46]

Although still largely underused by judicial bodies[47] and regulators alike, articles 7 and 8 have recently attracted the attention of the literature that advocates a more balanced interpretation and implementations of the TRIPS Agreement. Among others, Peter Yu has identified 'five ways in which the[se] provisions can be put into effective use':[48]

> (1) as a *guiding light* for the interpretation and implementation of the Agreement; (2) as a *shield* against aggressive expansion of intellectual property rights and demands for TRIPS-plus protections; (3) as a *sword* to challenge the lack of balance in the international intellectual property

42 See Resolution n. 40 para 11.

43 Art 7 TRIPS (emphasis added).

44 See, for instance, H.G. Ruse-Khan, 'Proportionality and Balancing within the Objectives', in Paul L.C. Torremans (ed.), *Intellectual Property and Human Rights* (Kluwer 2008).

45 Ibid., 174.

46 Art 8.2 TRIPS (emphasis added).

47 One exception is the case Canada-Patent Protection of Pharmaceutical Products, WT/DS114/R where the Panel, while examining art 30 TRIPS, which deals with exceptions to the rights conferred by the Agreement, declared that 'the goals and the limitations' stated in articles 7 and 8 should 'obviously be borne in mind'. See the Panel Report para 7.26, WT/DS114/R , March 17, 2000

48 P. Yu, 'The Objectives and Principles of the TRIPs Agreement' (2009) 46 *Houston Law Review* 797–1046, 1019.

system; (4) as a *bridge* to connect the TRIPS regime with intellectual property and other related international regimes; and (5) as a *seed* for the development of new international intellectual property norms.[49]

The South: Tensions between Intellectual Property Rights and Human Rights

It is in the context of themes that are usually associated with the Global South that intellectual property is more often thought of as being at odds with such human rights as the right to health, to food, to education or freedom of expression. In intellectual property scholarship, the attempt to provide a systematic articulation of these tensions is a fairly recent phenomenon.[50] Tellingly, it is also in international agreements dealing with problems that usually affect either exclusively or predominantly countries from the Global South that we encounter most references to articles like Articles 7 and 8 TRIPS.

A clear example of this is the Doha Declaration, adopted by the 2001 WTO Ministerial Conference, and dealing with matters of public health. During the negotiation process, articles 7 and 8 of TRIPS were 'singled out'.[51] The Ministerial Declaration explicitly states that the TRIPS Council 'shall be guided by the objectives and principles set out in Articles 7 and 8 of the TRIPS Agreement and shall take fully into account the *development dimension*'.[52] Furthermore, the Doha Declaration establishes that the TRIPS Agreement 'can and should be interpreted and implemented in a manner supportive of WTO Members' right to protect public health and, in particular, to promote access to medicines for all'.[53]

As explained by Carlos Correa:

> [t]here are different possible interpretations for [paragraph 4]. On the one hand, it may be viewed as a statement of fact rather than a rebalancing of the Agreement. On the other, it may be regarded as an indication that in cases where there is conflict, IPRs (intellectual property rights) should not be an obstacle to the realization of public health.[54]

It would be encouraging to see more and more developing countries placing articles 7 and 8 at the centre of their development policies, instead of allowing that provisions that can potentially *balance* an agreement that aligns intellectual property with trade interests turn into mere empty statements. Of course one may argue that provisions like paragraph 4 should not be read as statements of fact: rather than mirroring the existing Agreement, they should somehow change it, either by limiting or expanding a fraction of its scope. Should this be the case, it seems more probable that the explicit allusion to public health values and to access to medicines would not be construed as a merely duplicative addendum to TRIPS, but rather as a way of recalibrating it.

---

49 Ibid., 1019–1020 (emphasis added).

50 See, for all, Helfer and Austin n. 27.

51 See D. Gervais, *The TRIPS Agreement: Drafting History and Analysis* (2nd edn, Sweet and Maxwell 2003) 120.

52 World Trade Organization, Ministerial Declaration of 14 November 2001, WT/MIN(01)/DEC/1, 41 I.L.M. 746 (2002) para 16 (emphasis added).

53 World Trade Organization, Declaration on the TRIPS Agreement and Public Health, WT/MIN(01)/DEC/2, 41 I.L.M. 755 (2002), at paragraph 4.

54 C.M. Correa, *Trade Related Aspects of Intellectual Property Rights* (OUP 2007) 105.

Returning to Peter Yu's colourful distinction[55] of the possible purposes served by articles 7 and 8 of TRIPS, the idea of a *shield* seems particularly appealing for developing and least developed countries. As a rule, these countries are also the party with less bargaining power in trade negotiations with the developed world. Many of them have agreed to free trade agreements (FTAs) in which the more developed countries, such as the United States and the European Union, push for the implementation of heightened intellectual property regimes in the developing world.[56] These regimes, known as TRIPS-plus on account of the fact that they establish levels of protection for intellectual property that go beyond the TRIPS Agreement minimums (e.g. by granting terms of patent protection superior to the minimum 20 years set by TRIPS), are particularly harmful to developing economies. In the patent field, TRIPS-plus clauses contained in most FTAs range from a limitation to the grounds allowing compulsory licensing, to restrictions in the use of trial data in the process of approval of generic drugs. The results of this kind of provisions can be catastrophic. Take the case of restrictions on the use of trial data: they cripple the generic industry at birth because, even when a drug is off-patent, it might well not enter the market until very late (or, in some cases, never) on account of the need to replicate costly and time-consuming tests for which data is already available but cannot be used for market approval purposes.

It is therefore in the developing countries' best interest to start holding on to whatever balancing provisions they can find, with Articles 7 and 8 TRIPS coming first to mind. Ideally, the countries that form the Global South should build their innovation and developmental policies with the idea of a *shield* in mind. It is questionable to what extent can they expand this *shield* or even, at a later stage, evolve from a *shield* into a *sword*-like bargaining position. However, it is crucial that, in voicing their problems and discontents in areas covered by intellectual property regulations, they also start pointing out possible solutions within the law – and this is where balancing mechanisms might serve to reconcile intellectual property with human rights theory.

Conclusion: Intellectual Property and Human Rights – a Dialectic Relationship?

Some scholars have suggested that 'Human rights and intellectual property were natural law cousins owing to their shared filiation in equity'.[57] Others have expressed doubts about the possibility of a long lasting 'marriage'[58] between these two spheres. As a matter of fact, international and regional agreements do provide us with a place for rooting intellectual property claims based on humans rights violations – and, as seen above, some courts might actually be willing to explore this connection – but it is nonetheless a fragile liaison. It should suffice to remember that the European Court of Human Rights' interpretation of article 1 is based on the concept of 'peaceful enjoyment of possessions', which resonates with proprietary notions ill-suited to the universe and *raison d'être* of intellectual property. Also, as Helfer points out,[59] decisions like *Dima v. Romania* and *Anheuser-Busch v. Portugal* only serve to bind the parties involved in a particular case. Cases

55 See n. 50.

56 See, for instance, R.L. Okediji, 'Back to Bilateralism? Pendulum Swings in International Intellectual Property Protection' (2003–2004) 1 *University of Ottawa Law & Technology Journal* 125.

57 See Gervais, 'Intellectual Property and Human Rights' 12.

58 To use Peter Yu's expression. See Peter Yu, 'Reconceptualizing Intellectual Property Interests in a Human-Rights Framework' (2007) 40 *U.C. Davis L. Rev.* 1039, 1128.

59 L. Helfer, 'Intellectual Property and the European Court of Human Rights' in Paul L.C. Torremans (ed.), *Intellectual Property and Human Rights* (Kluwer 2008) 48.

like these were very fact-specific[60] and therefore the jump forward that the Court chose to give in applying article 1 to intellectual property may in practice have a more limited scope.

Likewise, the UDHR's call for everyone to be able to freely 'participate in cultural life'[61] and 'share in scientific advancement'[62] should be understood with a grain of salt. The fact that it may be international customary law is certainly relevant in many other areas (areas that have always been at the core of human rights protection), but one should notice that the same article 27, at number 2, also mentions 'the right to the protection of the *moral* and material interests resulting from any scientific, literary or artistic production of which he is the author'.[63] It so happens that moral rights were expressly excluded by article 9.1 TRIPS,[64] the reason being not to deter those countries that embraced a more utilitarian approach to intellectual property – i.e. copyright countries – from joining the Agreement.

It should also be mentioned that although a balancing approach to intellectual property in general is certainly welcome, there are also some disadvantages in this new trend. Indeed, some literature suggests that bringing intellectual property rights too close to the human rights sphere would not result in a smoothening of intellectual property-generated imbalances, but rather in the sharpening of these asymmetries. As Peter Yu pointed out:

> [a]n emphasis of the human rights attributes in intellectual property rights is also likely to further strengthen intellectual property rights, especially in civil law countries where judges are more likely to uphold rights that are considered human rights. As a result, the development of a human rights framework for intellectual property would result in the undesirable "human rights" ratchet of intellectual property protection.[65]

Other potential problems could include the 'undesirable capture of the human rights forum by intellectual property right holders'[66] and 'the framework's potential bias against non-Western cultures and traditional communities'.[67]

Nonetheless, it is perhaps too late to ignore that a significant part of the international community has embraced this quest for a so-called 'human rights framework' to intellectual property. At the very least, this quest should lead us to look carefully into areas where intellectual property over-protectionism may in practice endanger human rights: an unbalanced patent regime may directly affect the right to health, access to medicines or the right to food; an unbalanced copyright regime

60 Ibid., 49.

61 Art 27.1 UDHR.

62 Ibid.

63 Art 27.2 UDHR (emphasis added).

64 Art 9.1 TRIPS states that 'Members shall comply with Articles 1 through 21 of the Berne Convention (1971) and the Appendix thereto. *However, Members shall not have rights or obligations under this Agreement in respect of the rights conferred under Article 6bis of that Convention* or of the rights derived therefrom.' Art 6 bis.1 of the Berne Convention states that 'Independently of the author's economic rights, and even after the transfer of the said rights, the *author shall have the right to claim authorship of the work and to object to any distortion, mutilation or other modification of, or other derogatory action in relation to, the said work, which would be prejudicial to his honor or reputation*' (emphasis added).

65 See Peter Yu, 'Reconceptualizing Intellectual Property Interests in a Human-Rights Framework', 1125. The author considers, nonetheless, that this risk is mitigated by the approach that existing international instruments have been careful enough 'to have recognized only certain attributes of existing intellectual property rights as human rights' (ibid.).

66 Ibid., 1047.

67 Ibid. See n 49.

may impact freedom of speech, the right to education, to cultural participation and to benefit from scientific advancements. How can human rights theory help? By illuminating the debate about the appropriate levels of intellectual property protection, particularly when the field affected by the exclusive right is one of the mentioned above. The first step in any discussion over the possible interface between intellectual property and human rights should be an assessment of the current impact that intellectual property law and policy have on the core areas that they are supposed to balance and nurture, some of which are inherently at the core of human rights protection.

The language in article 7 TRIPS is a very good example of how human rights concerns can add a new layer to intellectual property legislation. It calls for the '*promotion* of technological innovation', the '*transfer and dissemination* of technology', while alluding to the need of a '*mutual advantage* of producers and users of technological knowledge' and highlighting that intellectual property rights should be set at a level that is '*conducive to social and economic welfare*' and to 'a *balance* of rights and obligations'.[68]

The recent debate surrounding intellectual property and human rights is therefore far more estimable if seen as the raising of a powerful red flag rather than the search for a unified theoretical human rights frame for intellectual property. The relationship between intellectual property and human rights is akin to one of two distinct spheres or planets with different resources and different trajectories; one cannot be assimilated into the other, but they are able to exert some effects on each other and it is this distant but continuous gravitational force that keeps each one of them on the right track. That is why it is important to keep monitoring intellectual property's routes, so as to prevent it from deviating from its original goals. Ultimately, the reason that should lead us to keep looking for more contact points between intellectual and human rights is exactly the same that led to the emergence of the first intellectual property rules: the search for balance, for an equilibrium of inputs and outputs that will benefit copyrights and patents' internal systems and prevent them from colliding with other spheres.

68 Art 7 TRIPS (emphasis added).

Chapter 5
(Right to) Development and International Transfer of Technology: A Competition Law Perspective

Lúcio Tomé Féteira[1]

Introduction

One of the issues that developing countries often bring to the foreground in international forums is the critical association between development and access to technology. The substance of the claim is that development and access to technology should work in tandem, with the latter being considered 'a prerequisite, even an imperative, for desirable economic and social development'.[2] Although the details behind the interplay between development and access to technology are a complex and contentious issue,[3] this chapter will address the combination between development and technology from three complementary perspectives: the right to development (henceforth 'R2D'), international transfer of technology (henceforth 'ITT') and competition law.

The reference to the R2D is arguably the one that requires fewer justifications, as it purports to reflect the human rights approach that underlies the remaining chapters of this book. In this context, it can be said that access to technology is one of the components of a wider and expanding notion of development incorporated into the R2D. The limitation inherent to this approach is that, as it will be argued in a brief incursion into the topic, the enduring debate concerning the contents and legal nature of the R2D does not provide solid ground for widening and fostering access to technology.

The reference to ITT can easily be explained on account of its role as a vehicle to promote access to technology. More specifically, this chapter will be focussing on ITT via licensing agreements. These concepts and their economic relevance will be explained in some detail and provide the background for the third and last perspective: competition law.

Including competition law as part of a chapter dedicated to development and access to technology may invite perplexity, if not downright scepticism from the readers. However, if one thinks that ITT

---

1 This chapter is an extended and revised version of a paper originally presented at the Conference on Human Rights and New Technologies, which took place on 23–24 November 2009 at the Law School of the Fundação Getúlio Vargas in Rio de Janeiro. The general cut-off point of the research is the 20 June 2012. A special word of gratitude is due to Holger Hestermeyer for his comments and suggestions on an earlier version of this paper, the quality of which should only reinforce the usual disclaimer.

2 Michael Blakeney, *Legal Aspects of the Transfer of Technology to Developing Countries* (ESC Publishing Limited 1989) 57. See also Keith E. Maskus, *Intellectual Property Rights in the Global Economy* (Institute for International Economics 2000), 143 ff.

3 It is not so much the positive impact of technology upon development that is debated, but rather a number of related questions, namely the choice of the appropriate technology and the adequate mode of transfer; generally on this point, see the introduction to Edward K.Y. Chen (ed.), *Technology Transfer to Developing Countries* (United Nations Library on Transnational Corporations Series, vol 18, Routledge 1994) 14–20; and, specially, G.K. Helleiner, 'The Role of Multinational Corporations in the Less Developed Countries' Trade in Technology' ibid., 62–71.

agreements and, in particular, licensing agreements, may be the source of anticompetitive effects that can be particularly damaging to countries that are highly dependent upon imported technology, then competition law might not appear as implausible as it did at first glance. Such is, in fact, the situation in most developing countries, as became painfully clear during the ill-fated negotiations of the 'Draft International Code of Conduct on the Transfer of Technology' (henceforth 'TOT Draft Code'),[4] when developing countries complained about the detrimental effect of unfair and restrictive conditions included in – or deriving from – ITT.[5] The role that competition law can play both in stimulating the inward flow of technology to developing countries and in fighting against the effects of anticompetitive practices associated with ITT provides the background of this chapter while purporting to be, by the same token, an illustration of how to combine three apparently unrelated topics: development, ITT and competition law.

In addition to what has been said, the reference to competition law should be contextualized as part of the growing debate amidst competition law scholars concerning the design and implementation of competition rules adjusted to the context of developing countries.[6] Discussing the anticompetitive implications of ITT provides a welcome opportunity to take part in this on-going debate and deal with the question of whether it is appropriate[7] to include developmental concerns in competition law and, this being the case, how and to which extent this can be achieved. While dealing with these issues, the more practical aspects relating to the enforcement of competition law should not be forsaken – a point that is not always taken into due account by the literature – as they amount to a considerable portion of the difficulties that developing countries face when dealing with anticompetitive conduct that has an extra-territorial effect in multiple jurisdictions.

This chapter will be structured as follows: the ensuing section will introduce the basic features of the R2D (§ 2) merely with the aim of providing an overview of its notion, nature and present significance. The following section (§ 3) will be dedicated to briefly discussing the notion, as well as the economic and legal aspects of ITT. The latter can take place through different arrangements, licensing agreements being one of the available options. Though generally considered as being pro-competitive, licensing agreements may have a restrictive impact on competition (they can involve price-fixing, restrictions of output, etc.) and thus call for the intervention of competition law. The competition law issues that may generally arise from technology transfer will be addressed in § 4.

4 The TOT Draft Code was an attempt to regulate ITT at the international level under the auspices of UNCTAD. The draft document never made it to the final stages and the chapter on restrictive practices – whose very title was the subject of lively debate between the negotiating parties – was greatly responsible for the failure of the negotiations. The matter will be developed below in § 5.

5 Such grievances were part of a broader claim for an equitable international economic order, which came to be known as the New International Economic Order ('NIEO'), of which access to technology was an important part. The defining elements of the NIEO are contained in the 'Declaration on the Establishment of a New Economic Order', adopted by the General Assembly of the United Nations in December 1974. It rested on three main elements: (i) the elimination of dependence of developing countries on the undertaking's of developed countries; (ii) the promotion of accelerated development of the economies of developing countries on the basis of the principle of self-reliance; and (iii) the need for an institutional reform of the global management of world resources in the interests of mankind as a whole. See Blakeney n. 1, 59–67; and also, contextualising ITT within the NIEO, Peter-Tobias Stoll, *Technologietransfer: Internationalisierungs- und Nationalisierungstendenzen* (Springer 1994) 12 ff.

6 In this sense but adding the IPR dimension, see e.g., R. Ian McEwin, 'Editor's Introduction' in R. Ian McEwin (ed.), *Intellectual Property, Competition Law and Economics in Asia* (Hart 2011) 6.

7 The question does not address the possibility but rather the appropriateness of including developmental concerns in CL because competition policy can and has indeed been used to implement a number of very different policies. See, in general, Massimo Motta *Competition Policy: Theory and Practice* (CUP 2004) 17–30.

This section will take as reference points, on the one hand, the approach under US antitrust and EU competition law (§ 4 a)) and, on the other hand, article 40 of the TRIPS Agreement (§ 4 b)). In both cases the purpose is to expose the inherent limitations of both national jurisdictions and international instruments regarding anticompetitive effects of ITT, namely in developing countries (§ 4 c)). Against this background, § 5 will explore the possible role of competition law in addressing these issues, while accommodating some of the developmental concerns voiced by developing countries. The chapter will end with some closing remarks and conclusions in § 6.

Before bringing this introduction to an end, two final words of caution should be added. Firstly, there are a number of issues that have to be excluded at the outset from the scope of this chapter so as to keep it reasonably within space limits. The excluded subjects include human rights issues pertaining to the connection between the R2D and ITT;[8] economic issues relating to developing economies, most of them addressed by the literature on development economics and technology economics;[9] and the developmental impact of intellectual property rights ('IPR'), a subject closely associated with ITT and a topic on its own right.[10] Secondly, a word of caution concerning the use of the expression 'developing countries'. Despite being aware that the notion – and indeed the term itself – falls short of gathering international consensus,[11] practical reasons owing to its wide use explain why it will be kept throughout this chapter, whilst trying to avoid the pitfalls associated with the expression (namely the fact that it refers to a heterogeneous group of countries but masks the complexity of the underlying realities,[12] as well as the fact that the expression may acquire different meanings according to the context in which it is deployed).[13] These general considerations extend to

8 On the interplay between human rights and IPR, including a brief reference to the R2D, see Flávia Piovesan, 'Direitos humanos e propriedade intelectual: protecção internacional e constitucional' in Patrícia Luciane de Carvalho (ed.), *Propriedade Intelectual: Estudos em homenagem à Professora Maristela Basso*, vol 2 (2nd edition, Juruá Editora 2008) 13 ff. See also Jakob Cornides 'Human Rights and Intellectual Property: Conflict or Convergence?' (2004) 7 *Journal of World Intellectual Property* 135.

9 See, e.g., Jang-Sup Shin, *The Economics of Latecomers: Catching-up, technology transfer and institutions in Germany, Japan and South Korea* (Routledge 1996). Taking as reference point two industries – the iron and steel industry and the semiconductor industry – across Germany, Japan and South Korea, the author analyses the internal conditions that have permitted the catching-up of the industrialization process in these three countries.

10 Since ITT agreements frequently involve the temporary transmission of IPR. On this topic see, e.g., Keith E. Maskus, 'Incorporating a Globalized Intellectual Property Rights Regime into an Economic Development Strategy' in Keith E. Maskus (ed.), *Intellectual Property, Growth and Trade* (Frontiers of Economics and Globalization, vol 2, Elsevier 2008) 497. In any case, it should be stressed that ITT is not confined to the transmission of IPR but rather 'combines elements of intellectual property law, competition law, international trade law and the law of international legal organisations' (Blakeney n. 1, xi).

11 One of the most commonly used criterion – though not the most consensual – is the one deployed by the World Bank which relies on income per capita (see the data and statistics section in <http://www.worldbank.org> accessed 20 June 2012. See also IMF 'World Economic Outlook – 2009' <http://www.imf.org/external/data.htm> accessed 20 June 2012). More comprehensive and perhaps more consensual is the Human Development Index proposed by the United Nations Development Programme, which combines (i) GDP per capita, (ii) life expectancy and (iii) educational standards (see <http://hdr.undp.org/en/statistics/hdi/> accessed 20 June 2012).

12 Although very different amidst themselves, Brazil, China, India, South Africa, Albania and Azerbaijan are all examples of developing countries.

13 Not the least because the expression is sometimes deployed for strategic purposes in different international contexts through the use of the designation 'on a *ad hoc* basis and primarily through self-selection' (Mitsuo Matsushita, Thomas J. Schoenbaum and Petros C. Mavroidis, *The World Trade Organization: Law Practice, and Policy* (2nd edition, OUP 2006) 764).

the field of competition law, as one quickly realizes when comparing the mixed results delivered by competition law in Latin American countries with the profound limitations of competition regimes in Sub-Saharan Africa.[14] Since it would be impossible to attend to the specificities of each developing country, this chapter will strive to circumvent the difficulties by addressing some of the issues that may be of relevance to a large number of developing countries.

(Right to) Development: Overview of its Background, Notion and Present Significance

The first express reference to the R2D as a human right can be found in the 1986 Declaration on the Right to Development (hereinafter 'Declaration on the R2D'),[15] whose article 1 paragraph 1 states:

> 1. The right to development is an inalienable human right by virtue of which every human person and all peoples are entitled to participate in, contribute to, and enjoy economic, social, cultural and political development, in which all human rights and fundamental freedoms can be fully realized.

The Declaration on the R2D was meant as a bridge that would cover the gap between civil and political rights, on the one hand, and economic, social and cultural rights on the other, thus reflecting an integrated and indivisible conception of human rights, arguably in consonance with their original understanding in the Universal Declaration of Human Rights.[16] Although the latter addresses both civil and political rights (articles 1–21) and economic, social and cultural rights (articles 22–28) under the common roof of human rights, it was the Declaration on the R2D that rendered explicit the underlying unity.[17]

The Declaration on the R2D was further complemented in 1993, during the Second UN World Conference on Human Rights that took place in Vienna. The Conference dealt extensively with the R2D, leading to the adoption of the Vienna Declaration and Programme of Action,[18] which

14 However, South Africa is an important exception to the general failure of competition law in Sub-Saharan Africa. On these points, see David J. Gerber, *Global Competition: Law, Markets and Globalization* (OUP 2010) 236–258.

15 UN Resolution 41/128 (adopted 4 December 1986) < http://www.un.org/documents/ga/res/41/a41r128.htm> accessed 20 June 2012. On the political, ethical and legal origins of the R2D, see Isabella D. Bunn, *The Right to Development and International Economic Law: Legal and Moral Dimensions* (*Studies in International Trade Law* 13, Hart 2012) 13 ff.

16 Art 6 para 2 of the Declaration on the R2D states that '[a]ll human rights and fundamental freedoms are indivisible and interdependent; equal attention and urgent consideration should be given to the implementation, promotion and protection of civil, political, economic, social and cultural rights'. On this point, see Arjun Sengupta, 'The Right to Development as a Human Right' working paper no 7 (Harvard School of Public Health, François-Xavier Bagnoud Centre for Health and Human Rights, 2000) 1-2 <http://www.harvardfxbcenter.org/resources/working-papers/FXBC_WP7--Sengupta.pdf> accessed 20 June 2012. Arguing that Art 28 of the UDHR is the 'ultimate premise' of the R2D, see Ibrahim Salama, 'The Right to Development: Renewal and Potential' in Stephen P. Marks (ed.), *Implementing the Right to Development. The Role of International Law* (Friedrich Ebert Stiftung/Harvard School of Public Health – Program on Human Rights and Development, 2008) 118 <http://library.fes.de/pdf-files/bueros/genf/05659.pdf> accessed 20 June 2012.

17 Referring in this context to the 'integrative function' of the R2D, see Anna E. Gouwenberg, 'The Legal Implementation of the Right to Development' (2009) Grotius Centre for International Legal Studies Leiden University, 30 quoted in Bunn n. 14.

18 Partially similar references can be found in the 1986 Declaration in the second and tenth paragraphs of the preamble read in combination with Art 6 paras 2 and 3 of the Declaration on the R2D. According to

emphasized R2D as a universal and inalienable right and the facilitating role of development for the enjoyment of all human rights. None of the Declarations[19] that followed the Vienna Conference conferred legally binding effect to the R2D. As it became increasingly clear, the implementation of the R2D hinged upon the coordinated action of the developing countries and the international community (donor countries and international financial institutions) through what would be later designated as a 'development compact'.[20] The implementation of the 'development compact' would require a number of steps to be taken by the international community, with ITT being one of those steps.

In spite of the implicit, and occasionally explicit, references to the R2D at the international level,[21] the legal[22] obstacles to the recognition of the R2D remain practically unchanged since its inception and can be summarized in two major points: on the one hand, the lack of a legally binding instrument addressing the R2D; and on the other hand, the (vague) content of the R2D and its implications for the right holders and the duty bearers. Concerning the first objection, it is generally recognized that neither the Declaration on the R2D, nor any of the ensuing international instruments dealing with the R2D, have legally binding force, so the discussion that follows is whether the R2D, in its present formulation, has developed 'sufficient normative power'[23] that would compel its transformation into an internationally binding right. The second objection relates to the content of the R2D. Although it is possible to identify the core elements of the R2D,[24] it becomes much harder to derive from them specific rights and obligations.[25] While reference to development as 'a comprehensive economic, social, cultural and political process' in the Preamble of the Declaration on the R2D makes clear that

---

Sengupta n. 15, with the Vienna Declaration and Program of Action, 'the right to development emerged as a human right which integrated economic, social, and cultural rights with civil and political rights in the manner that was envisaged at the beginning of the post-World War II human rights movement' (ibid 2).

19 These include the Millennium Declaration (2000), the Monterrey Consensus (2002), the Paris Declaration on Aid Effectiveness (2005), the Accra Agenda for Action (2008) and the World Summit Outcome Document (2005). Conversely, the Cotonou Agreement (2000) is an example of a legally binding agreement concerning cooperation for development between the ACP countries, the EC and its Member States. Although not conducive to the R2D, the Cotonou Agreement integrates obligations very much related to the elements that integrate the latter. For an overview of the evolution of the R2D, see Gouwenberg (2009) 10–17 quoted in Bunn n. 14.

20 The 'development compact' would bring together the developing countries' endeavours to fulfil their national human rights obligations with the international community's effort to provide resources and share the related costs. In this context, ITT would be part of a possible set of actions to be undertaken by the international community – along with free trade and access to markets, debt adjustment, etc. – to implement the 'development compact' taking into account the particular needs of each developing country. <http://www.ohchr.org/EN/ABOUTUS/Pages/ViennaWC.aspx> accessed 20 June 2012. For an overview of the legal development of the R2D, see generally Bunn n 14, 31–57.

21 See Bunn n. 15, 44–57.

22 For additional references to other obstacles (political, practical and epistemological), see Stephen Marks, 'Obstacles to the Right to Development' (Harvard School of Public Health François-Xavier Bagnoud Centre for Health and Human Rights, 2003) <http://www.harvardfxbcenter.org/resources/working-papers/FXBC_WP17--Marks.pdf> accessed 20 June 2012.

23 The expression is taken from Upendra Baxi, 'Normative Content of a Treaty as Opposed to the Declaration on the Right to Development: Marginal Observations' in Marks *Implementing the Right to Development* 47. Discussing the legal status of the R2D, see Bunn n. 15, 127–150. Proposing alternative ways to strengthen the R2D and suggesting that guidelines for the implementation of the R2D might be best option, see Gouwenberg (2009) 34 ff quoted in Bunn n. 14.

24 See Gouwenberg (2009) 30–33 quoted in Bunn n. 14.

25 On these issues, see Bunn n. 14, 107–126.

development is neither confined to economic growth nor to developing countries,[26] it remains of very little avail in what concerns its implementation.

Rather than approaching development and access to technology from the much discussed and excessively vague R2D, it seems thus preferable to step on firmer ground. If the beneficial effects of technology are undisputed, the negative developmental impact arising from restrictions to the dissemination of knowledge seem equally straightforward. Anticompetitive conduct may be one of such restrictions, as it will become increasingly clear in the following sections.

Technology Transfer: Notion, Economic and Legal Aspects

The transmission of knowledge can occur through a number of ways, one of them being technology transfer. For the purposes of this chapter, technology transfer is to be understood as the transmission of a particular form of knowledge – technology – from a transferor (A) to a recipient (B). The transfer acquires an international dimension through the participation of a multinational corporation[27] based in a developed country acting as the transferor, and an institution or undertaking in a developing country that act as the recipient of technology. It usually implies 'an integrated sequence of commercial transactions'[28] that takes the shape of a consensual legal arrangement involving the temporary use of technology against the periodic payment of an agreed fee (royalties). In this context, the term technology encompasses all knowledge useful in production, frequently though not necessarily protected under IPR.[29] It follows that ITT frequently, though not necessarily involves the temporary transmission of IPR.

So far we have only emphasized the private transaction side of ITT. However, there is an equally important dimension to ITT: the transfer of technology as a communication and learning process.[30] The latter perspective is complementary to the transaction side of ITT, and it brings to the forefront two interrelated problems: firstly, the transmission of knowledge cannot be completed

26 In the Declaration on the R2D, a specific reference to developing countries is only to be found in the eleventh paragraph of the preamble and in arts 4 para 2 and 7. But the R2D is by no means restricted to developing countries, as results from art 1 itself and is confirmed throughout the Declaration on the R2D.

27 The fundamental role of transnational corporations in the transmission of knowledge via ITT provided the background to a comprehensive study on the topic conducted under the auspices of the United Nations Conference on Trade and Development (UNCTAD). See Chen n. 2.

28 See Blakeney n. 1, 3. The author exemplifies the integrated sequence of transactions that integrate technology transfer by describing the steps that are typically required to get a plant into industrial production, which include: 'the grant or assignment of industrial property rights; the communication of technical know-how in a documentary form; the communication of technical or other know-how in the supply of services; assistance in the commissioning of an industrial plant; the sale or lease of machinery or the provision of services in relation to the sale or lease of machinery; providing services to assist in the recruitment and training of staff and the institution of managerial and accounting procedures; providing services in relation to the marketing and distribution of the product of the plant.' (ibid).

29 The description of ITT advanced in the main text combines the elements proposed by Chen n. 2, 1–2, Stoll n. 4, 9–10 and Blakeney n. 1, 33.

30 See Stoll n 4, 8–9. As the author rightly points out (ibid 10), referring to the private transaction dimension of TT, '[d]iese Betrachtungsweise geht also einerseits weiter als die Vorstellung eines Lernprozesses, indem sie auch die rechtlichen Verwertungs- und Nutzbefugnisse an einer Technologie einbezieht. Sie ist aber andererseits weniger präzise, weil sie von wirtschaftlichen Zusammenhängen und Transaktionsformen ausgeht, bei denen es in erster Linie um die kommerzielle Nutzung von Technologien geht. Ob und in welchem Umfang technologisches Wissen vermittelt wird, ergibt sich allein aus der Betrachtung der verschiedenen

without the recipient actually being able to receive and process the information transferred; secondly, since technology involves immaterial knowledge beyond its material applications, one of the major difficulties that ITT poses is the assessment whether the process of transmission has been completed.[31] Both problems are related because developing countries, for the most part greatly dependent on ITT for technological progress,[32] frequently face considerable difficulties in selecting the appropriate technology, absorbing it and optimizing its exploitation.[33] These difficulties may be created or exacerbated by anticompetitive effects associated with ITT agreements, since certain practices that restrict competition may also reinforce the choice of inadequate technology (e.g. when the sale of one product or service is made conditional on the purchase of an unrelated good or service; this practice is usually known as 'tying'), hamper its absorption (e.g. restrictions on research imposed upon the recipient) and/or prevent its optimal exploitation (e.g. restrictions of output imposed upon the recipient).

The transmission of technology through ITT can take place through several methods. The basic option is usually put in terms of international trade, foreign direct investment ('FDI') and licensing,[34] although in practice these options are frequently combined and supplemented by a number of additional features taken from other legal instruments. As it has been advanced in the introductory section of the chapter, we will focus our attention on licensing – which comprises both 'pure' and mixed licensing agreements[35] – since it remains a widely used legal instrument for the acquisition and exploitation of technology[36] and it may be the source of a number of competitive concerns.[37] In

---

Transaktionsformen nicht.' See also, from an economic perspective, Shin n. 8, 27–31, who underlines the neo-Schumpeterian contribution underlying the approach to ITT as an 'ongoing process'.

31 See Chen n. 2, 2. The author further adds that 'the transfer of technology is not complete until the recipient can operate and maintain, i.e. absorb the process entirely independently of outside assistance and, above all, can improve, extend and develop the technology originally transferred. In that sense, technology transfer is not just the acquiring of a knowledge in production, but also the building up of a nation's technological capability' (ibid).

32 As explained by Shin n. 8, 26, the forerunners in technological progress rely mostly on innovation, while the latecomers are dependent on TT to have access to technological progress.

33 Compare with Blakeney n. 1, 3.

34 See Walter G. Park, 'Intellectual Property Rights and International Innovation' in Maskus *Intellectual Property, Growth and Trade* n. 9, 314 ff. In more detail, see Chen n. 2, 10, who quotes P. Buckley, 'New forms of international industrial co-operation' in P.J. Buckley and M. Casson, *The Economic Theory of the Multinational Enterprise* (Macmillan 1985). Buckley identifies ten types of technology transfer: '(1) wholly-owned foreign subsidiaries; (2) joint ventures; (3) foreign minority holdings; (4) "fading-out" agreements; (5) licensing; (6) franchising; (7) management contracts; (8) "turnkey ventures"; (9) contractual joint ventures; and (10) international subcontracting.' From an economic perspective, what sets these different methods of ITT apart is 'whether the mode of technology transfer is internal or external, i.e., whether the transfer is intra-firm (from the TNC [transnational corporation] to its affiliates or through the market (arm's-length)' (Chen n. 2, 10).

35 Licensing can be combined with a number of other agreements, most notably franchising, or be itself part of a wider turnkey agreement.

36 Blakeney n. 1, 34. Although it has been observed a general 'decline in the importance of contractual or non-equity modes of technology transfer' when compared to FDI. Explaining the declining importance of licensing agreements for ITT, see Carlos M. Correa, 'Emerging Trends: New Patterns of Technology Transfer' in Surendra J. Patel, P. Roffe and A. Yusuf (eds), *International Technology Transfer* (*Kluwer Law International* 2001) 268–270.

37 See, inter alia, S.K. Verma, 'The TRIPS Agreement and Development' in Patel, Roffe and Yusuf n. 35, 344–345. Dealing with these points in the context of the TOT Draft Code, see Wolfgang Fikentscher, *The Draft International Code of Conduct on the Transfer of Technology* (Verlag Chemie 1980) 64 ff.

any case, given the absence of a fixed boundary between licensing and FDI,[38] or between external (through the market) and internal (intra-firm) modes of ITT for that matter, licensing agreements may involve unaffiliated undertakings or institutions in developing countries as the recipients.

From an economic perspective, licensing is considered to be an external mode of ITT because it takes place through the market, as opposed to intra-firm (internal) modes of ITT.[39] According to a study conducted by the United Nations Centre for Transnational Corporation ('UNCTC')[40] the choice between different modes of ITT is influenced by the combination of three variables: (i) the strategies pursued by transnational corporations, (ii) the host country's environment, and (iii) the characteristics of a particular industry.[41] The study distinguished between 'internalized' and 'externalized' modes of foreign involvement,[42] concluding that externalized modes of ITT such as licensing of unaffiliated enterprises 'tend to be used in cases where transnational corporations desire to continue to earn rents on standardized technology or where the absorptive capacity of domestic enterprises is strong'.[43] The same study concludes that, although the form of ITT varies considerably from industry to industry and from country to country, licensing to both affiliated and unaffiliated undertakings appear particularly relevant in the sectors of food and beverage processing (branded food and beverage), textiles and clothing (man-made fibres and branded clothing), pharmaceuticals, electric power equipment and automobiles, just to name a few.[44]

More recent studies[45] dealing with the relationship between the process of industrialization and the methods (and contents) of ITT indicate that licensing is first used for the transfer of 'mature' technologies during the initial stages of industrialization in cases relating to large-scale industries and

38 Since both can be combined in the same commercial arrangement (e.g. intra-enterprise transfers). See Blakeney n. 1, 46–7.

39 See Chen n. 2, 10. For a complementary approach, considering licensing as a formal and direct mode of TT, see Correa in Patel, Roffe and Yusuf (eds) n. 35, 259.

40 The UNCTC is nowadays part of UNCTAD. The study, conducted by the UNTC in 1987 and entitled 'Determinants of the Form of Technology Transfer', is included in Chen n. 2, 171 ff. The study should be complemented with other surveys conducted by the UNTC and, more recently, by the UNCTAD, and dealing with technology transfer involving specific sectors and countries, such as the aircraft manufacturing in Brazil, pharmaceuticals in India and the automobile industry in South Africa.

41 Arriving to similar conclusions, see Farok J. Contractor, 'Technology Acquisition Policies in Emerging Countries' in Farok J. Contractor (ed.), *Economic Transformation in Emerging Countries: The Role of Investment, Trade and Finance* (Elsevier 1998) 321 ff.

42 The distinction between internalized and externalized modes of ITT is between 'those that involve continuing direct ownership, control and use of the technological assets within the context of the firm's foreign production operations, and those that do not. Broadly speaking, this distinction corresponds to the one between foreign direct investment in wholly owned or majority-owned affiliates and other forms of technology transfer such as joint venturing and licensing of unaffiliated enterprises' (Chen n. 2, 172).

43 Ibid., 173. The UNTC study further denoted that there was an 'increased willingness of transnational corporations to use externalized forms of technology transfer', with a particular rise of 'joint ventures in which host country enterprises own a part of the capital' (ibid., 174).

44 The same study added that: 'There are other instances where the use of externalized modes may be more advantageous than internalized modes. These arise in cases where foreign direct investment is relatively unprofitable, carries an unacceptable degree of risk to the parent firm, or is simply not allowed by the host country. When markets are small and relatively unimportant for overall corporate strategies, externalized modes of technology transfer may tend to minimize co-ordination costs, while still allowing the firm to earn rents on their technological assets' (ibid., 174). The study focuses on how are the different modes of ITT distributed throughout economic sectors, with a particular emphasis in selected manufacturing industries (ibid., 174, 176–192). More cautious in his conclusions, see Farok in Farok n. 40, 345.

45 See Correa in Patel, Roffe and Yusuf n. 35, 263–265.

tends to become more relevant as the industrialization process advances. When compared to other modes of ITT, it would seem that:

> [L]icenses will always provide an economical way of transfer – from the transferor view point – of standardized, relatively simple and mature, technologies to recipients having absorptive capacities. Licensing will also be the first option for small and medium enterprises lacking the financial resources to enter into equity venture of FDI. Licensing is also likely to be used in transactions between large industrial groups with comparable technological levels.[46]

Licensing agreements are usually part of larger arrangements, which involve not only the transfer of IP rights or know-how, but may also include the provision of 'finance, raw materials, skilled labour, engineering and management services and marketing assistance'.[47] The inclusion of different inputs combined with the economic conditions and legal structure in the host country[48] will favour the choice of a particular commercial arrangement (turn-key contract, joint venture arrangement, industrial co-operation agreement, intra-enterprise transfers, product purchase or marketing arrangements).[49]

Although it can generally be stated that developing countries, both at the government and at the industry level, find themselves in a weaker bargaining position vis-à-vis multinational enterprises – and thus more exposed to restrictive or disproportionate conditions – this assertion bequeaths qualification. In fact, certain developing countries have managed to develop endogenous capabilities under relative isolation from external competition and have thus succeeded in increasing their bargaining power.[50] The latter are, however, the exception that confirms the rule, as in most cases the combination of dependency on foreign technology with a wide set of endemic institutional weaknesses[51] pose severe constrains to the bargaining position of developing countries.

Certain clauses and practices that are frequently included in or associated with ITT agreements – including but not limited to licensing agreements –, have been consistently contested by developing countries as being detrimental to their development on account of the significant limitations they

---

46 Ibid., 279–280. On the impact of product life-cycle and other factors on the choice between different modes of ITT, see ibid., 272–276. It is worth complementing these conclusions with those drawn by Park in Maskus *Intellectual Property, Growth and Trade* n. 9, 321–323.

47 Blakeney n. 1, 43.

48 Ibid., 43. The author refers to 'the nature of any economic planning, ownership requirements, rules on the repatriation of capital and income and the nature of the legal rules within which the transfer will occur'. See also Farok in Farok n. 40, 321 ff.

49 Blakeney n. 1, 43–7.

50 See Correa in Patel, Roffe and Yusuf n. 35, 276–9, who concludes that such an increase of bargaining power is nevertheless insufficient to offset other adverse factors to ITT, such as increased technology prices. Also voicing some scepticism as to the ability to achieve innovation through local endogenous development, see Jorge Mario Martínez-Piva, 'Protection of Intellectual Property Rights, Innovation and Development' in Jorge Mario Martínez-Piva (ed.), *Knowledge Generation and Protection: Intellectual Property, Innovation and Economic Development* (Springer 2009) 27 ff.

51 Blakeney n. 1, 31 refers to '(a) inadequate facilities for the evaluation of technology needs, for assessing the feasibility of proposed projects and for identifying the available sources of comparable technology; (b) capital shortages, which often restricts the selection of sources of technology to those which are willing to provide credit facilities; (c) limited availability of skilled labour and management personnel; (d) lack of access to non-technology inputs, such as raw materials, components, transport facilities; (e) lack of access to export markets, including lack of marketing skills'. These weaknesses will inevitably have its negative impact on the transferor, hindering a stable investment environment and creating additional costs. More generally on the institutional context, see Shin n. 8, 38 ff.

impose to access to technology.[52] However, given the multi-jurisdictional effect of ITT, transnational anticompetitive effects cannot be fully captured by any set of national legislation.[53] The developmental and the anticompetitive impact of ITT was clearly acknowledged in Chapter 4 of the TOT Draft Code,[54] which included a number of provisions dealing with several restrictive business practices adopted in ITT. Examples of such restrictive practices include grant-back provisions, prohibitions of challenge to the validity, exclusive dealing, restrictions on research, price fixing, exclusivity agreements, tying arrangements, export restrictions, restrictions of output, etc.

In the next section we will review some of these anticompetitive concerns both from the perspective of the two most important antitrust jurisdictions – the US and the EU – and within the context of article 40 TRIPS.

Technology Transfer and Anticompetitive Effects

The facilitating role of technology dissemination for the promotion of development justifies placing anticompetitive practices that impair or restrict the former at the centre of our concerns. From an economic perspective, restrictive practices or conditions entail indirect costs and have welfare-reducing effects for developing countries, be it directly as the recipient of technology or at the place where the recipient is located.[55] They restrict the export capacity of the recipient, raise its import costs and restrain the expansion of its technological capacity.[56] Furthermore, such practices have an overall impact on the country's balance of payments and generally impair economic development.[57] They may, for instance, take the shape of an abuse (unilateral conduct) of IPR, build upon overly protective (both in duration and scope) IP legislation that restricts competition,[58] or relate to restrictive clauses included in ITT agreements. Competition law has a prominent role to play in fighting against restrictive practices. Either as the result of internal initiative or as the consequence of external

---

52 See Blakeney n. 1, 35 and 67. For an overview of the anticompetitive practices that may be associated with ITT, see Philip Y. Bacher, *Entwicklungsperspektiven des Kartellrechts im Rahmen des TRIPS-Abkommens* (Stämpfli 2009) 109–131.

53 See generally, explaining the reasons behind the TOT Draft Code and including a reference to competition issues, UNCTAD Secretariat, 'The Rationale for Regulatory Action' included in Patel, Roffe and Yusuf n. 35, 3–15; and also Bacher n. 51, 406–407.

54 Chapter 4 of the TOT Draft Code was structured around a general clause followed by a list of unlawful practices, but the matter was highly contentious and ultimately led to the breakdown of negotiations. See Fikentscher *The Draft International Code of Conduct on the Transfer of Technology* n. 36, 64–121.

55 Generally on the importance of ITT for developing countries and the role of competition law in fostering innovation through transfer of technology, see Mor Bakhoum, 'Reflections on the concepts of "economic freedom", "free competition" and "efficiency" from the perspective of developing countries' in Daniel Zimmer (ed.), *The Goals of Competition Law* (The Fifth ASCOLA Workshop on Comparative Competition Law, Edward Elgar 2012), 412 and 436–9. Referring to indirect costs borne by the recipients of technology in the context of the difficulty of assessing the total resource costs required for the successful completion of the ITT, see Chen n. 2, 12.

56 Chen n. 2, 13.

57 Ibid., 13. This point also goes back to the problem of selecting the appropriate technology, absorbing it and exploiting it in optimal terms. On the latter point see G.K. Helleiner, 'The Role of Multinational Corporations in the Less Developed Countries' Trade in Technology' in Chen n. 2, 62–71.

58 Although there is no inherent conflict between competition law and IP. On this topic see, e.g., J. Gregory Sidak and David Teece, 'Favouring Dynamic Competition over Static Competition in Antitrust Law' in McEwin n. 5, 53 ff.

pressure, the widespread adoption of competition law regimes[59] should not be dissociated from the idea that competition policy forms an integral part of development policy that requires a 'complex sets of market institutions to support economic growth and policy management capability'.[60]

The response to multi-jurisdictional effects of anticompetitive practices has been twofold: convergence and multilateral agreements.[61] The first endeavours to bring national competition laws closer through non-binding instruments such as policy papers, recommendations, 'best practices', reports, etc. The most important forum for convergence has been the International Competition Network ('ICN') – composed of national and multinational competition authorities – whose convergence efforts are directed at bringing national competition laws closer to the template of US antitrust and EU competition law.[62] For this reason, we shall briefly review the approach of US antitrust and EU competition law to technology transfer, with a particular emphasis on its jurisdictional limitations (sub-section a)) and, at a later stage (§ 5), assess whether they provide an adequate template for competition law in developing countries.

A second strategy to deal with multi-jurisdictional anticompetitive effects consists in multilateral agreements, namely against the background of trade liberalization. Attempts to introduce competition issues in the WTO agenda came to a standstill in the 2003 Cancún ministerial conference, only to be dropped altogether in July 2004.[63] Nevertheless, the TRIPS Agreement deals with a number of competition issues that are relevant in the context of ITT and will therefore be included in this chapter (sub-section b)).

Technology Transfer under US Antitrust and EU Competition Law: an overview

Agreements for the transfer of technology, including licensing arrangements, are generally considered to have pro-competitive effects. Under EU competition law, they are covered by the Technology Transfer Block Exemption Regulation (hereinafter 'TTBER')[64] which, together with the Technology

59 See, e.g., McEwin in McEwin n. 5, 10, as well as the ensuing country chapters (ibid., 95 ff). And also Franz Kronthaler, *Implementation of Competition Law in Developing and Transition Countries* (Nomos 2007) 26–31.

60 Taimoon Stewart, Julian Clarke and Susan Joekes, 'Competition Policy in Action: Experiences from Developing Countries' (Ottawa, International Development Research Centre 2007) 3 and 13–20 <http://web.idrc.ca/in_focus_environment/ev-111677-201-1-DO_TOPIC.html> accessed 20 June 2012. Dealing with the positive impact of competition policy on the standards of living via the increase of local competition intensity, see Michael Krakowski, 'Competition Policy Works: the Effect of Competition Policy on the Intensity of Competition: An International Cross-Country Perspective' (HWWA Discussion Paper 332, 2005) <http://www.econstor.eu/handle/10419/19300> accessed 20 June 2012.

61 See Gerber n. 13, 9–10. As Gerber rightly emphasises, even if successful convergence would still not solve the problems posed by conflicting national competition laws and 'unilateral jurisdictionalism' (ibid., 290).

62 Ibid., 273–292; and also Bakhoum 'Reflections on the concepts of "economic freedom", "free competition" and "efficiency" from the perspective of developing countries', 419. The OECD and the UNCTAD also take part in the convergence effort, but their role has been overshadowed by the creation of the ICN in 2001 (ibid., 111–116). However, the alignment of ICN with US antitrust and EU competition law has attracted growing mistrust from developing countries; on this point, see Angela Wigger, 'The Convergence Crusade: The Politics of Global Competition Law and Practices' (paper prepared for the 46th Annual ISA Convention, 2005) <http://convention2.allacademic.com/one/isa/isa05/index.php?click_key=5> accessed 20 June 2012.

63 See Gerber n. 13, 101–111.

64 Commission Regulation (EC) No 772/2004 of 27 April 2004 on the application of Article 81(3) of the Treaty to categories of technology transfer agreements [2004] OJ L123/11. The TTBER will expire on 27 April 2014 and the Commission, with the input from stakeholders, is currently conducting a review of the

Transfer Guidelines[65] issued by the Commission, unequivocally state that: 'Most licence agreements do not restrict competition and create pro-competitive efficiencies. Indeed, licensing as such is pro-competitive as it leads to dissemination of technology and promotes innovation.'[66]

In the same vein, the 'Antitrust Guidelines for the Licensing of Intellectual Property'[67] jointly issued by the US the Department of Justice and the Federal Trade Commission include explicit references to the pro-competitive benefits of licensing as facilitating the 'integration of the licensed property with complementary factors of production'[68] and 'benefiting consumers through the reduction of costs and the introduction of new products'.[69]

Notwithstanding the common shared goal of promoting dynamic competition[70] and the acknowledgement of numerous benefits provided by licensing agreements – including but not restricted to improvement of economic efficiency, reduction or avoidance of duplication of investments in R&D, encouragement of incremental innovation, diffusion of knowledge and creation of product market competition[71] – both jurisdictions also recognize that licensing agreements have the potential to restrict competition.[72] In the most serious cases, they may involve price fixing, reduction of output and allocation of markets (or customers), all of them banned as 'hardcore restrictions' under the TTBER,[73] and subject to per se prohibitions under the Sherman Act.[74] In other cases, certain contractual provisions – that include grant-back obligations, obligations to assign or the obligation not to challenge the validity of an IPR[75] – though not outright detrimental to competition, may nevertheless have a negative impact on the latter.

Reg. See <http://ec.europa.eu/competition/consultations/2012_technology_transfer/index_en.html> accessed 20 June 2012.

65 Commission Notice – 'Guidelines on the application of article 81 of the EC Treaty to technology transfer agreements' [OJ/2004 C101/2] <http://eur-lex.europa.eu/LexUriServ/LexUriServ.do?uri=OJ:C:2004:101:0002:0042:EN:PDF> accessed 20 June 2012.

66 Technology Transfer Guidelines n. 64, para 9; in the same vein, see also rec 5 TTBER n. 63.

67 Issued by the US Department of Justice and the Federal Trade Commission on 6 April 1995 <http://www.justice.gov/atr/public/guidelines/0558.htm> accessed 20 June 2012. For a general comparison between the Antitrust Guidelines and the TTBER, see Alicia del Tiempo Matanzo, *Kartellrechtliche Beurteilung horizontaler Technologietransfer Vereinbarungen nach Europäischem Recht* (Stämpfli 2008) 12 ff.

68 See Antitrust Guidelines n. 66, 4–6.

69 Ibid.

70 See, respectively, TTBER n. 63, para 7 ('[i]ntellectual property rights promote dynamic competition by encouraging undertakings to invest in developing new or improved products and processes. So does competition, by putting pressure on undertakings to innovate') and Antitrust Guidelines n. 66, 2 ('[t]he intellectual property laws and the antitrust laws share the common purpose of promoting innovation and enhancing consumer welfare').

71 TTBER n. 63, 4–6; and also Technology Transfer Guidelines n. 64, para 17.

72 See Blakeney n. 1, 67 ff; and also Bacher n. 51, 109–131.

73 See art 4 TTBER n 63. The provision distinguishes whether the undertakings that entered into the agreement are competitors or not, showing greater leniency in the latter case.

74 See Antitrust Guidelines n. 66, 16: 'Among the restraints that have been held per se unlawful are naked price-fixing, output restraints, and market division amidst horizontal competitors, as well as certain group boycotts and resale price maintenance.' It should be noted, however, that since the *Leegin* case (*Leegin Creative Leather Products, Inc. v PSKS, Inc.* 127 S. Ct. 2705 (2007)) minimum resale price maintenance is no longer subjected to a per se prohibition, but instead evaluated under the rule of reason.

75 Under the TTBER (n. 63) they are considered 'excluded restrictions' under art 5 thereof. Under the Antitrust Guidelines (n. 66), they fall under the rule of reason. Specifically on grant-backs, see Antitrust Guidelines n. 66, 30 para 5.6.

Both jurisdictions take market power – including the market share in the relevant market and whether the undertakings involved are competitors[76] – as the pivotal element for an economic balance between the pro- and the anti-competitive effects of transfer of technology agreements. Market shares below 20 percent of the affected relevant market are generally considered unproblematic from a competition law standpoint.

However, even in those cases where technology transfer does have anticompetitive effects, the application of national competition rules is invariably limited by their territorial scope of application. This means that neither EU competition law nor US antitrust will be applicable to anticompetitive conduct that fails to produce an effect within their respective scope of application. The territorial scope of application of competition law is usually defined by the principle of territoriality, but both the EU and the US allow for an extension of jurisdiction under certain circumstances in what can be described as 'unilateral jurisdictionalism'.[77] In the US courts rely on the so-called 'effects doctrine'[78] to support the extraterritorial application of antitrust rules to those cases that produce a direct and substantial effect within the US. In the EU, the Court of Justice has allowed for the extraterritorial application of European competition law in cases that involve an anticompetitive practice implemented within the EU ('implementation doctrine').[79] Minor differences apart,[80] both the effects and the implementation doctrines allow for the extraterritorial application of national competition rules in similar cases,[81] since implementation generally implies effect and the latter relates in both jurisdictions to the impact on inter-state trade.[82] A practical implication of this selective application of extraterritoriality with direct relevance for our topic is, for example, the exclusion of export cartels from the scope of application of competition law.[83] In the event that the anti-competitive effects associated with ITT were the result of an export cartel, this would mean that such effects would take place outside the territorial scope of application of competition law and, therefore, beyond its grasp.

---

76 See Technology Transfer Guidelines n. 64, paras 19–33; and Antitrust Guidelines n. 66, paras 22–23.

77 Gerber n. 13, 5.

78 Established by the leading case *United States v Aluminum Co of America* [*Alcoa*] 148 F2d 416 (2d Cir 1945) and later developed in *Timberlane Lumber Co v Bank of America* 549 F.2d 597 (9th Circ. 1976), *Metro Industries Inc v Sammi Corp* 82 F.3d 839, 845 (9th Cir. 1996) and *Hartford Fire Insurance Co v California*, 509 U.S. 764 (1993), which coupled an element of comity to the effects-criterion. See also Gerber n. 13, 63–74.

79 See joined cases C-89 & 104 & 114 & 116 & 117 & 125-129/85 *Åhlström v Commission* [1988] ECR I-5193 (commonly referred to as the 'Woodpulp I' decision) and case T-102/96 *Gencor v Commission* [1999] ECR II-753.

80 Though reluctant to endorse the effects doctrine due to its potential implications in terms of public international law, in practical terms the case law of the Court of Justice comes very close to the latter. See generally Peter Roth and Vivien Rose (eds), *Bellamy & Child: European Community Law of Competition* (6th edition, OUP 2008) 61 ff.

81 An exception could be a boycott cartel that, while implemented within a given jurisdiction, would produce effects elsewhere.

82 See, respectively, arts 101 TFEU (ex 81 EC) and 102 TFEU (ex 82 EC) and Sections 1 and 2 of the Sherman Act.

83 More generally, on the pursuit of trade policy through the 'strategic' expansion and retraction of the enforcement of national competition rules, see Beatriz Conde Gallego, *Handelsbezogene Aspekte des Lizenzkartellrechts* (Stämpfli 2003) 182 ff.

Technology Transfer and the TRIPS Agreement

Another strategy to deal with multi-jurisdictional anticompetitive effects is multilateral agreements. Although this sub-section proposes to review the provisions of TRIPS that deal with the anticompetitive effects of ITT,[84] it should be said that TRIPS was not the first attempt to address the matter at the international level,[85] though it was the first to become a legally binding instrument. Previous attempts[86] testify to the limitations of multilateral agreements for dealing with transnational competition issues. They include the previously mentioned TOT Draft Code, as well as the Draft International Antitrust Code (known under the acronym 'DIAC'), a bold but equally ill-fated attempt to establish international antitrust rules that took place in the first half of the 1990s, under the auspices of the WTO.[87] In this context, and despite its scarce practical significance, we should also mention the Restrictive Business Practices Code ('RBP Code') approved by the UN General Assembly in 1980.[88] In the case of the RBP Code, the necessary minimum consensus that was necessary for its approval was obtained at the expense of its contents, which amounts to little more than a set of non-binding recommendations dealing only partially with the least contentious aspects of antitrust.[89]

Despite the fact that the WTO regime contains several provisions that touch upon competition matters,[90] article 40 TRIPS is the only provision that expressly deals with the interplay between ITT

---

84 For a general introduction to the TRIPS Agreement, see Matsushita, Schoenbaum and Mavroidis n. 12, 695 ff. Specifically on the driving force behind the TRIPS Agreement and the 'link between trade and IP through IP rights transfer agreements', the authors refer to the US concern that 'burdensome registration and approval requirements [of IP rights transfer agreements] in some countries inhibited investment and IP licensing and, therefore, trade' (ibid., 697) For an integrated approach to TRIPS, ITT and competition rules, see Tu Thanh Nguyen, *Competition Law, Technology Transfer and the TRIPS Agreement: Implications for Developing Countries* (Edward Elgar 2011) 32 ff.

85 On the antecedents and legislative history of art 40 TRIPS see, generally, the commentary of O. Brand and F. Lehmann to this provision in Peter-Tobias Stoll, Jan Busche and Katrin Arend (eds), *WTO - Trade-Related Aspects of Intellectual Property Rights* (Max Planck Commentaries on World Trade Law Series, vol 7, Max Planck Institute for Comparative Public Law and International Law, Martinus Nijhoff Publishers 2009) 660–662, paras 7–10.

86 For an overview of the various attempts to adopt an international code dealing with restrictive practices, see Wolfgang Fikentscher, 'United Nations Codes of Conduct: New Paths in International Law' in Wolfgang Fikentscher, *Recht und wirtschaftliche Freiheit: Transnationales Marktrecht*, 2nd vol (Mohr Siebeck 1993) 197 ff.

87 On the topic see Wolfgang Fikentscher and Ulrich Immenga (eds), *Draft International Antitrust Code* (Nomos 1995). The political sensitiveness of the matter – competition rules – was certainly an important but not the sole explanation for the failure of the DIAC. The dissent went even deeper and touched upon the very necessity – or desirability – of having a comprehensive body of legislation dealing with competition rules.

88 U.N. Conference on Restrictive Business Practices, The Set of Multilaterally Agreed Equitable Principles and Rules for the Control of Restrictive Business Practices, U.N. Doc. TD/RBP/CONF/0 (1980), repr in (1980) 19 Int'l Legal Materials 815.

89 On the RBP Code see Wolfgang Fikentscher and Wolfgang Straub, 'Der RBP-Kodex der Vereinten Nationen: Weltkartellrechtlinien (I-II)' in Fikentscher *Recht und wirtschaftliche Freiheit* n. 85, 239 ff and 260 ff. For a comparison between the RBP Code and the TOT Draft Code, see Debra L. Miller and Joel Davidow, 'Antitrust at the United Nations: a Tale of Two Codes' in Patel, Roffe and Yusuf (eds) n. 35, 77–100.

90 It should be said that the WTO regime lacks a comprehensive competition regime, having instead several provisions that deal with different aspects of CL. Outside TRIPS, such provisions include: Art 8.1 of the Agreement on Technical Barriers to Trade (TBT), Arts VIII:1–5 and IX:1–2 of the General Agreement on Trade in Services (GATS), Art 9 of the Agreement on Trade-Related Aspects of Investment Measures

and competition law, and it does so against the background of ensuring free trade.[91] However, article 40 TRIPS addresses only some of the issues of ITT[92] and, furthermore, it does so within the rather limited perspective of protecting free trade and ensuring a minimum threshold of the protection for IPR. While developed countries had since long strived for the introduction in developing countries of a minimum threshold of protection of IPR, article 40 TRIPS was seen as a concession to the latter aimed at appeasing concerns that the strengthening of IPR regime would open the way to anticompetitive practices adopted by multinationals from developed countries.[93] In this respect article 40 TRIPS states as follows:[94]

> 1. Members agree that some licensing practices or conditions pertaining to intellectual property rights which restrain competition may have adverse effects on trade and may impede the transfer and dissemination of technology.
> 2. Nothing in this Agreement shall prevent Members from specifying in their legislation licensing practices or conditions that may in particular cases constitute *an abuse of intellectual property rights having an adverse effect on competition in the relevant market*. As provided above, a Member may adopt, *consistently with the other provisions of this Agreement*, appropriate measures to prevent or control such practices, which may include *for example* exclusive grantback conditions, conditions preventing challenges to validity and coercive package licensing, in the light of the relevant laws and regulations of that Member. [emphasis added]

As it becomes immediately noticeable upon reading the provision, it deals only with anticompetitive implications of 'licensing practices and conditions' of IPR.[95] It covers restrictive clauses included in licensing agreements, as well as the granting and execution of the license, but excludes from its scope other anticompetitive practices associated with ITT, namely those that do not involve IPR.[96] Article

(TRIMS) and Arts 11:1 and 11:3 of the Safeguards Agreement. See generally Matsushita, Schoenbaum and Mavroidis n. 12, 858–64.

91 See Hanns Ullrich, 'Technology Protection According to TRIPs: Principles and Problems' in Friedrich-Karl Beier and Gerhard Schricker (eds), *From GATT to TRIPs: The Agreement on Trade-Related Aspects of Intellectual Property* (IIC Studies, Max-Planck Institute for Foreign and International Patent Law, Copyright and Competition, VHC 1996) 360 ff.

92 For an account of restrictive licensing practices with an impact on international trade, see Gallego n. 82, 77–101.

93 See, e.g., Pedro Roffe and Cristoph Spennemann, 'Control of Anti-competitive Practices in Contractual Licenses under the TRIPS Agreement' in Carlos M. Correa and Abdulqawi Yusuf (eds), *Intellectual Property and International Trade: The TRIPS Agreement* (2nd edition, Wolters Kluwer 2008) 298, 311–313.

94 Paras 3 and 4 of the provision are of lesser interest to the topic of this chapter since they deal with the consultation procedures following a violation by one of the Members of its duty to control anti-competitive practices in contractual licenses. For an in-depth analysis of art 40 TRIPS see especially the commentary by Brand and Lehmann in Stoll, Busche and Arend n. 84, 656–76. Specifically on art 40 paras 3 and 4 see Roffe and Spennemann in Correa and Yusuf n. 92, 318–319.

95 Criticising this option, see Hanns Ullrich, 'Expansionist Intellectual Property Protection and Reductionist Competition Rules: A TRIPS Perspective' (2004), EUI Working Paper LAW No 2004/03, 8 <http://cadmus.eui.eu/bitstream/handle/1814/1883/law04-3.pdf?sequence=1> accessed 20 June 2012.

However, though referring mostly to patents and trademarks, art 40 para 2 TRIPS does not exclude other IPR.

96 Also in this sense, see Roffe and Spennemann in Correa and Yusuf n. 92, 316–317.

40 TRIPS is to be seen as developing the general principle enunciated in article 8 paragraph 2 TRIPS, which states:[97]

> 2. Appropriate measures, provided that they are consistent with the provisions of this Agreement, may be needed to prevent the abuse of intellectual property rights by right holders or the resort to practices which unreasonably restrain trade or adversely affect the international transfer of technology.[98]

What article 40 paragraph 1 conveys is the WTO Members' shared understanding that certain licensing practices and conditions with anti-competitive effect may equally have an adverse effect on trade and on the dissemination of technology. In this context, article 40 paragraph 2 authorizes the same Members to introduce competition rules that address the anticompetitive aspects of licensing practices and conditions. However, the adoption of national provisions in the context of article 40 TRIPS is subject to several constraints: firstly, it presupposes that the licensing practice or condition restrains competition (the 'competition test')[99] and has a negative impact on trade or on the transfer and dissemination of technology;[100] secondly, national provisions must be generally consistent with other provisions of TRIPS, which would arguably mean that national provisions should not erode upon the substantive minimum standards of IP protection established in TRIPS.[101]

Though article 40 TRIPS is silent on the type of national provisions that Members are allowed to adopt, its paragraph 2 expresses nevertheless a preference[102] towards a rule of reason approach ('may in particular cases') to anticompetitive conduct. At the same time, it illustrates some of the cases of anticompetitive conduct that the Members may decide to address ('exclusive grantback conditions, conditions preventing challenges to validity and coercive package licensing'). However, the provision is of no avail concerning the notions of abuse or relevant market (where the abuse takes place). Furthermore, even if restricted to contractual 'licensing practices and conditions', article 40

97 It has been suggested that art 40 TRIPS should be read as *lex specialis* vis-à-vis art 8 para 2 TRIPS. See UNCTAD/ICTSD, *Resource Book on Trips and Development* (CUP 2005) 554: 'Whilst some authors hold the view that Article 8.2 contains a policy statement, which is implemented by Article 40, a more consistent interpretation seems to be that Article 40 represents a *lex specialis* provision' [italic in the original]. See also Brand and Lehmann in Stoll, Busche and Arend n. 84, 663, para 12.

98 Art 8 is entitled 'Principles' and its number 1 states: '1. Members may, in formulating or amending their laws and regulations, adopt measures necessary to protect public health and nutrition, and to promote the public interest in sectors of vital importance to their socio-economic and technological development, provided that such measures are consistent with the provisions of this Agreement.'

99 The debate over the adoption of a 'competition test' as opposed to a 'development test' goes back to the discussion around the TOT Draft Code and concerns the choice between competition or development as the standard to assess the abusive nature of the conduct. On these points, see Stoll n. 3, 121–3; and also Hanns Ullrich, 'Competition, Intellectual Property Rights and Transfer of Technology' in Patel, Roffe and Yusuf n. 35, 366–7.

100 Convincingly arguing that the criteria are meant to be applied alternatively rather than cumulatively, see Brand and Lehmann in Stoll, Busche and Arend n. 84, 666–7, para 22. The authors advance two justifications for their claim: i) the fact that the scope of art 40 para 1 goes beyond ITT and generally covers licensing of IP rights; and ii) that the same provision – as art 8 para 2 – applies only to ITT.

101 See Roffe and Spennemann in Correa and Yusuf n. 92, 317–18.

102 See Ullrich 'Expansionist Intellectual Property Protection and Reductionist Competition Rules' n. 94, 6.

TRIPS does not provide any clarification as to the contractual nature of ITT agreements covered by the provision, nor does it clarify whether it can be applied to mixed agreements.[103]

An additional difficulty is assessing the nature of the obligation that arises from article 40 paragraph 1 TRIPS. The more detailed nature of this provision, when contrasted with the general principle enunciated in article 8 paragraph 2 TRIPS, seems to suggest that article 40 paragraph 1 imposes a minimum obligation to act,[104] which could be translated into 'a duty to protect national IPR systems against practices that undermine their proper operation on domestic markets'.[105] However, should this be the case, the provision could hardly be seen as 'a minimum step toward minimum harmonization of IPR-related competition rules for global markets'.[106] In addition, and to make the situation even more complex, Members are also obliged 'to respect whatever measures other Members legitimately take pursuant to Art. 40.2'.[107]

If the general tone adopted in TRIPS is already one that hardly incentivizes licensing,[108] article 40 TRIPS is of very limited avail concerning the possibility to foster the dissemination of technology through the adoption of national legislation against anticompetitive practices associated with ITT.[109] The most salient shortcomings of the provision lie in its excessively vague and unclear wording, combined with the fact that it cannot be directly applied.[110] All things considered, it seems hardly surprising that article 40 TRIPS has had scarce – if any – practical relevance.[111] The context in which ITT is addressed – free trade and the guarantee of a minimum threshold of protection for IP rights –

103 The contractual nature refers to the license as the outcome of mutual consent between licensor and licensee, but in cases such as compulsory licenses the point is ultimately one of dogmatic approach taken by each legal system. As to the licensing nature of the agreement (as opposed to assignment), difficulties can arise in cases involving mix agreements (e.g. franchising), since licensing is but an element of the contract. On both points, see generally Brand and Lehmann in Stoll, Busche and Arend n. 84, 663–65, paras 13–17. Specifically on the second point, advancing criteria to assess if a mix agreement falls within the scope of art 40 TRIPS, see UNCTAD/ICTSD n. 96, 556.

104 In this sense and striving to extract such minimum obligation from the commitment of Members under art 1 para 1 TRIPS to give effect to the provisions of TRIPS, as well as from the objectives set in art 7 TRIPS, see Brand and Lehmann in Stoll, Busche and Arend n. 92, 665–66, para 19; and also Ullrich 'Expansionist Intellectual Property Protection and Reductionist Competition Rules' n. 94, 7–10. See also UNCTAD/ICTSD n. 96, 555: 'Reading Article 40.1 in conjunction with Article 7 may well be understood as imposing a obligation on Members to address certain forms of anticompetitive practices in licensing agreements'.

105 Ullrich 'Expansionist Intellectual Property Protection and Reductionist Competition Rules' n. 94, 8.

106 Ibid., 8.

107 Brand and Lehmann in Stoll, Busche and Arend n. 84, 666, para 20.

108 See Verma in Patel, Roffe and Yusuf n. 35, 344. And also, more generally, Carlos M. Correa, 'Can the TRIPS Agreement foster technology transfer to developing countries?' in Keith E. Maskus and Jerome H. Reichman (eds), 'International Public Goods and Transfer of Technology Under a Globalized Intellectual Property Regime' (CUP 2005) 227–56.

109 Voicing an extremely critical view both on the contents and on the form chosen to address the problem, see especially Ullrich in Patel, Roffe and Yusuf n. 35; and again Ullrich 'Expansionist Intellectual Property Protection and Reductionist Competition Rules' n. 94.

110 See Brand and Lehmann in Stoll, Busche and Arend n. 84, 662, para 11, taking issue against those who claim that the provision has mere declaratory value (ibid 665, para 19). In the latter sense, see Andreas Heinemann, 'Antitrust Law of Intellectual Property in the TRIPs Agreement of the World Trade Organization' in Beier and Schricker n. 90, 245.

111 Qualifying the practical relevance of art 40 paras 1 and 2 as 'negligible' since it 'does not force Members, at least the industrialized countries, to amend their substantive competition law', see Brand and Lehmann in Stoll, Busche and Arend n. 84, 675, para 45.

has deviated TRIPS from the most topical issue in ITT:[112] access to knowledge. Instead, the provision adopts a selective approach to anticompetitive practices, dealing only with licensing and, within the latter, only with a fraction of the problems at stake. Furthermore, the question of inferior bargaining power of developing countries is left completely unattended since article 40 paragraph 2 TRIPS leaves the adoption and enforcement of competition rules entirely to the sphere of the WTO Members.[113]

Competition Law in Developing Countries: Legal Framework and Enforcement

The 1990s witnessed an exponential growth in the number of competition law regimes, many of them introduced in developing countries for the first time, a surge that can be explained as the combined result of internal impetus – namely liberalization – and external pressure.[114] However, the enactment of competition rules has frequently not been translated into an effective application of those rules,[115] thus bearing witness to the well-known gap that separates 'law in books' from 'law in action'. The explanations behind this gap concerning enacted and applied competition rules have been frequently addressed by the literature. They encompass a number of factors such as deficiencies at the level of substantive law, frailties on the institutional level (institutional design),[116] absence of a competition culture,[117] lack of expertise, absence of autonomy and/or financial means to ensure a non-biased application of competition rules,[118] political instability, strong presence of informal economy, as well as more general problems afflicting the overall functioning of the judicial system.[119]

In what concerns transnational anticompetitive effects, namely those associated with ITT, developing countries face at least two types of difficulties. The first concerns the design of an appropriate legal framework to deal with such issues. This is the question of what type of competition law would be better suited to the social, economic and legal context of these countries, as well as to meet their specific needs. The second major difficulty concerns the enforcement of such rules against

112 Denoting the 'backwards looking character' that art 40 TRIPS displays, see Brand and Lehmann in Stoll, Busche and Arend n. 84, 675, para 45. In the same sense, qualifying as 'obsolete' the 'principles of competition embodied in the TRIPS Agreement', see Ullrich 'Expansionist Intellectual Property Protection and Reductionist Competition Rules' n. 94, 23. On the inherent limitations of the competition rules included in the WTO Agreements, see also Carlos M. Correa, 'Competition Law and Development Policies' in Roger Zäch (ed.), *Towards WTO Competition Rules: Key Issues and Comments on the WTO Report (1998) on Trade and Competition* (proceedings of the seminar at the Zurich University, 8–10 July 1999, Stämpfli/Kluwer Law International 1999) 380–85.

113 On this point, see Ullrich, in Patel, Roffe and Yusuf n. 35, 367.

114 See Gerber n 13, 85–89.

115 On this point see Kronthaler n. 58, 26–31.

116 See, in particular, Stewart, Clark and Joekes n. 59, 26–32. See also Michal S. Gal, *Competition Policy for Small Market Economies* (Harvard University Press 2003) 255–57.

117 See Kronthaler n. 58, 75 ff.

118 See Michael J. Trebilcock and Edward M. Iacobucci, 'Designing Competition Law Institutions' (2002) 25 *World Competition* 363–68.

119 Generally, on the importance for development of the existence of an effective legal system, see Robert Cooter, 'Direito e desenvolvimento: inovação, informação e a pobreza das nações' in Luciano Benetti Timm e Pedro Paranaguá (org), *Propriedade intelectual, antitruste e desenvolvimento: O caso da transferência de tecnologia e do software* (Editora FGV 2009) 9 ff. Providing an overview of these and other factors that have conditioned of competition policy in Latin America, see Julián Peña, 'The Limits of Competition Law in Latin America' in Ioannis Lianos and D. Daniel Sokol (eds), *The Global Limits of Competition Law* (Stanford Law Books 2012) 236–51.

anticompetitive practices that are implemented by a foreign (and usually stronger) business partner and which have a multi-jurisdictional reach. A solution to the latter problem remains beyond the reach of national competition laws being bound as they are by a strict – in the absence of any realistic chance of resorting to 'unilateral jurisdictionalism' – principle of territoriality. At the same time, these problems are not adequately dealt with at the international level by any of the existing instruments of international law. This section will address both issues in turn.

Designing Adequate Competition Rules for Developing Countries

Behind competition law stands a particular type of competition policy responsible for the selection of the goal or set of goals that legal provisions should pursue. This selection is influenced by the embedment of competition culture in society and, ultimately, by the overall cultural setting.[120] Taking these general thoughts into consideration and moving from competition policy to competition law, it has been rightly argued a 'one size fits all' solution may not, and frequently will not, deliver the best results for the design of the appropriate legal framework[121] in the context of small market economies,[122] developing countries or transition countries.[123] The point can be illustrated by the limited results achieved through legal transplants of competition law from developed to developing countries or by the modest success attained by models of competition law designed at the international level.[124] Furthermore, 'one size fits all' solutions follow the approach adopted by US antitrust and EU competition law, a feature that frequently gives rise to suspicion – if not outright hostility – from developing countries. However, most of the complaints[125] voiced by developing countries against competition policy and competition law are in fact directed against US or EU-modelled

---

120 Dealing with this point from the perspective of behavioural economics, see Thomas K. Cheng, 'How Culture May Change Assumptions in Antitrust Policy' in Lianos and Sokol *The Global Limits of Competition Law* n. 118, 205–220. For a more broad and enriching perspective, see Wolfgang Fikentscher, *Culture, Law and Economics: Three Berkeley Lectures* (Münchener Schriften zum Europäischen und Internationalen Kartellrecht vol 6, Staempfli 2004).

121 Both the UNCTAD and the World Bank/OECD provide examples of model laws on competition. Critically assessing the latter see Wolfgang Fikentscher, 'Model Laws on Technology Transfer to developing Countries: A Survey' in Fikentscher *Recht und wirtschaftliche Freiheit* n. 85, 293, 297 ff.

122 See Gal n. 115, 13 ff. As Bakhoum rightly points out ('Reflections on the concepts of "economic freedom", "free competition" and "efficiency" from the perspective of developing countries' n. 54, 428), while developing countries often have small market economies, the existence of the latter extends beyond developing countries (e.g. Israel).

123 See, for example, Kronthaler n. 58, 88, including additional references to other authors; Maher M. Dabbah, 'Competition Policy and Law in Developing Countries: A Critical Assessment of the Challenges to Establishing an Effective Competition Law Regime' in (2010) 33 *World Competition* 457; and Mor Bakhoum, 'A Dual Language in Modern Competition Law? *Efficiency Approach* versus *Development Approach* and Implications for Developing Countries' (2011) 34 *World Competition* 495.

124 Kronthaler n. 58, 89–90.

125 For a discussion of these complaints, see Kronthaler n. 58, 32–57. Kronthaler divides them into four main categories: 'claims with respect to developing strategies, claims with respect to potential substitutes, claims with respect to competing priorities, and claims around the issue of competition law building' (p. 32). On the same topic, see also Frédéric Jenny, 'Globalization, Competition and Trade Policy: Issues and Challenges' in Zäch n. 111, 15–25. A good illustration of this point is the extremely critical assessment of the results achieved by competition laws adopted by developing countries and modelled after US antitrust by A.E. Rodriguez and Ashok Menon, *The Limits of Competition Policy: The Shortcomings of Antitrust in Developing and Reforming Economies* (International Competition Law Series vol 43, Wolters Kluwer 2010).

competition law rather than arguments against competition law per se.[126] Essentially, the underlying issue is that the 'particularities of developing and transition countries have to be taken into account when designing and implementing competition law'.[127] These 'particularities' comprise a number of issues that are, to a greater or lesser extent, specific of or at least more intensely experienced by developing countries and which constitute major impediments to the effective implementation of competition law. These specific features have been introduced at the beginning of § 5 and they can be divided into internal and external obstacles.[128] The first category covers issues such as lack of capacity, Government interference, weak institutional structure, political instability, absence of competition culture, protectionism and strong vested interests. The second category covers issues from political and economic pressure from foreign Governments and multinationals to bilateral trade and investment agreements that neutralize the effectiveness of national competition law.[129]

Although an internal obstacle in itself, there is one specific feature of developing countries that deserves a separate reference on account of its intimate correlation with competition law: market structure. The latter may serve to explain why certain types of anticompetitive conduct should be of greater concern to developing countries and, for that reason, should deserve particular attention from competition law. Mainstream competition policy has been tailored for large economies, such as the US and the EU, thus fitting uneasily with the specific features of developing countries with small market economies.[130] The latter are the outcome of 'the large size of minimum efficient scales of production relative to demand' and generally include:[131] (1) high industrial concentration levels; (2) high entry barriers; and (3) below minimum efficient scale (MES) production levels.[132]

---

126 Also in this sense, see Josef Drexl, 'International Competition Policy after Cancún: Placing a Singapore Issue on the WTO Development Agenda (2004) 27 World Competition 419, 435–37. Drexl contextualises the opposition of developing countries to the introduction of competition law issues in the WTO agenda in connection with excessive reliance on US antitrust and EU competition law as the blueprint. See also Gerber n. 13, 106–107.

127 Kronthaler n. 69, 57.

128 Dealing with these issues see Kronthaler n. 69, 75 ff.; Peña in Lianos and Sokol n. 118; Dabbah n. 122, 463–73; and Nguyen n. 83, 244–55.

129 The most obvious examples are bilateral/regional trade, investment or economic partnership agreements containing TRIPS-plus standards. On this point see Nguyen n. 103, 251–53. See also Andrés Moncayo von Hase, 'The Flexibility of TRIPS and Its Possible Erosion in Bilateral, Multilateral and Regional Negotiations' in Martínez-Piva n. 49, 59; and, for a case-study of a Free Trade Agreement with TRIPS-plus standards, Pedro Roffe, 'Intellectual Property and the New Generation of Free Trade Agreements: The Agreement Between Chile and the United States of America' in Martínez-Piva n. 49, 85.

130 Defined as 'independent sovereign economy that can support only a small number of competitors in most of its industries' (Gal n. 115, 1). The definition captures the highly concentrated nature of most of the industries in these markets – a feature that should be decisive in the design of an appropriate competition policy – as a result of three mains factors: population size, population dispersion and openness to trade (ibid at 1). In any case, the definition is sufficiently broad to encompass examples such as Malta, Israel, Australia, New Zealand and South Africa. For a similar argument viewed from the perspective of the theory of institutional design, see Kronthaler n. 58, 89–90.

131 Gal n. 115, 57. On these points, see also Kronthaler n. 58, 91; and Peña in Lianos and Sokol n. 118, 237 ff.

132 With these features in mind, Gal n. 115, 47–55 argues that competition policy in small market economies should have a clear focus on economic efficiency as its primary goal, approach cooperative conduct taking into account its potential to increase productive and dynamic efficiency and display a preference towards conduct regulation (to the detriment of structural remedies). Irrespective of espousing the author's views on the solution – and the author is admittedly not dealing specifically with developing countries, but

It follows that the enactment of competition law cannot be preceded by an assessment of a number of factors including the level of economic development, the size of the economy, the degree of reliance on market forces, the role of FDI, openness to trade, the level of corruption and the role of trade agreements and international organizations.[133] However, even if there is a relative consensus that competition law from developed countries cannot be simply transplanted to developing countries, there are considerable divergences as to the extent to which the former should be adapted to the reality of developing countries.[134] A more conservative approach would mean keeping competition law in developing countries as close as possible to the US and EU counterparts,[135] assuming that the economic benefits of competition would by themselves entail a positive impact on development.

Others, by contrast, sustain that competition law in developing countries should explicitly pursue a specific development agenda,[136] either directly through the inclusion of non-competition goals or indirectly through the re-interpretation of 'traditional' competition goals such as efficiency or welfare. In practice, this would mean including a number of goals that are not traditionally pursued by competition law, such as redistribution and participation of disadvantaged segments of the population, all in an attempt to bridge part of the developmental gap through competition law.[137] The South African Competition Act[138] is often referred as an example of a competition statute that has successfully integrated these types of concerns into competition law, though its practical achievements can be disputed. According to its section 2, the purpose of the Act is to promote and maintain competition in order to, amidst other goals, 'promote employment' (sub-section c)), ensure that small and medium-sized enterprises 'have an equitable opportunity to participate in the economy' (sub-section e)) and

---

only with small market economies – the diagnosis of the specific problems that small market economies face is extendable to developing countries with the same market features.

133 See especially Kronthaler n. 58, 58–74 and 75–87. Without the purpose of exhausting the subject, the author also includes the role of social policies, the existence and extent of state aid and subsidies, and the degree of political intervention in foreign trade as factors that influence the decision to enact competition rules (ibid., 63–64); and time as a factor influencing the implementation of the aforesaid rules (ibid., 80).

134 Compare, for example, Stewart, Clarke and Joekes n. 59, 7–11; Gal n 115, 46–57; and Ajit Singh, 'Competition and Competition Policy in Emerging Markets: International and Developmental Issues' (ESRC Centre for Business Research, University of Cambridge, working paper No 246, December 2002) 24 ff <http://www.cbr.cam.ac.uk/pdf/WP246.pdf> accessed 20 June 2012.

135 See ICN, 'Special Project for the 8th Annual Conference: Competition in Small Economies', prepared by the Swiss Competition Commission and the Israel Antitrust Authority, 5–10 <http://www.internationalcompetitionnetwork.org/uploads/library/doc385.pdf> accessed 20 June 2012. The ICN meeting had small market economies as one of the topics and although it did not address specifically the issue of developing countries, the differences of opinion between developed and developing countries were obvious.

136 Bakhoum 'A Dual Language in Modern Competition Law?' n. 122 refers, respectively, to an 'efficiency approach' and a 'development approach' as two different competition law languages. See also Bakhoum 'Reflections on the concepts of "economic freedom", "free competition" and "efficiency" from the perspective of developing countries' n. 54, 413 ff.; and Correa in Zäch n. 111, 386–87 ('The best option for [developing] countries would be to keep the possibility of establishing their own competition regimes, according to their own situation and policy objectives').

137 In this sense, with further references to the relevant literature, see Bakhoum 'A Dual Language in Modern Competition Law?' n. 122, 512–16; and Bakhoum 'Reflections on the concepts of "economic freedom", "free competition" and "efficiency" from the perspective of developing countries' n. 54, 413 ff.

138 <http://www.compcom.co.za/assets/Files/pocket-book-2005-R.pdf> accessed 20 June 2012. The Act was last amended in 2009 by the Competition Amendment Act <http://www.compcom.co.za/assets/Files/Competition-Amendment-Act.pdf> accessed 20 June 2012.

promote the dispersion of ownership 'in particular to increase the ownership stakes of historically disadvantaged persons' (sub-section f)).[139]

While an approach to competition law that mimics the one adopted in developed countries ('efficiency approach')[140] may be unadjusted to the problems that developing countries face, one should be careful about introducing non-competition goals into competition policy. It is highly doubtful that competition law is the most suitable instrument to pursue affirmative action or address equity issues, with the additional disadvantage that an all-encompassing 'development approach' to competition law – as it ends up being – risks blurring the limits of competition policy and ultimately chill the positive effects of competition.[141] For one thing, broadly sketched goals are more easily prone to discretionary behaviour of political actors, rent-seeking by vested interests groups and erroneous decisions adopted by administrative authorities (the so-called type I errors or false positives). In the context of developing countries, where competition culture is recent and hardly a political priority, informal economy bears a considerable weight and the necessary expertise to deal with competition issues is often lacking, opening competition law to the pursuit of vague and excessively wide goals may produce the opposite effect and invite a skewed application of the law. The very process that competition law is supposed to protect will be subject to twists and turns that, while capable of delivering short-term advantages, may in the medium or long term produce detrimental effects, namely ossify market structures and deter new entrants.[142]

Instead, it would seem preferable to reflect the specificity of competition law in developing countries at the level of the anticompetitive concerns they address and the remedies adopted.[143] The research undertaken on the features of small market economies has brought to the foreground a number of issues that could be usefully taken into account when it comes to prioritizing competitive concerns in developing countries. It is arguably at this level that developmental concerns can be best addressed, namely by first dealing with those anticompetitive practices that bear the greatest negative

139 According to sec 1 sub-sec 4: '(4) For the purposes of this Act, a person is a historically disadvantaged person if that person – *(a)* is one of a category of individuals who were disadvantaged by unfair discrimination on the basis of race before the Constitution of 25 the Republic of South Africa, 1993 (Act No. 200 of 1993), came into operation; *(b)* is an association, a majority of whose members are individuals contemplated in paragraph *(a)*; *(c)* is a juristic person, other than an association, in which the 30 individuals contemplated in paragraph *(a)* own and control a majority of its issued share capital or members' interest and are able to control a majority of its votes; or *(d)* is a juristic person or association in which the individuals contemplated in paragraph *(a)* own and control a majority of its 35 issued share capital or members' interest and are able to control a majority of its votes.'

140 As suggested by Gal n. 124, 47–51 with respect to small market economies.

141 As in the case of the South African Competition Act and Indonesian competition law; in this sense, see Bakhoum 'A Dual Language in Modern Competition Law?' n. 122, 517. As generally referred by Motta n. 6, 30, the question is not whether other non-competition objectives and public policies are important, but rather that competition policy is an inadequate instrument to pursue them. Expressing some reservations concerning the pursuit of public interest objectives through competition law, see Trudi Hartzenberg 'Competition policy and enterprise development: the role of public interest objectives in South Africa's competition policy' in Paul Cook, Raul Fabella and Cassey Lee (eds), *Competitive Advantages and Competition Policy in Developing Countries* (Edward Elgar 2007) 136 ff.

142 For a contrasting opinion on the topic, see Kim Kampel, 'The role of the South African competition law in supporting SMEs' in Cook, Fabella and Lee n. 140, 237–59.

143 The practice of the South African Competition Commission provides, in this regard, an interesting example as how to reflect developmental concerns in the remedies adopted; see Tembinkosi Bonakele and Liberty Mncube, 'Designing Appropriate Remedies for Competition Law Enforcement: The *Pioneer Foods* Settlement Agreement' in (2012) 8 *Journal of Competition Law and Economics* 425.

impact on developing countries because, amidst other reasons, they prevent access to technology. In what concerns ITT, this would mean paying particular attention to four types of anticompetitive conduct: (i) refusal to licence; (ii) excessive pricing; (iii) tying; and (iv) restrictions of use on downstream purchasers.[144] Whether developing countries should adopt a laissez faire approach, a quasi per se prohibition approach, a rule of reason approach or a combination of the three[145] would very much depend on the specific context of the developing country and cannot be addressed in this context. Identifying priorities in competition law enforcement may also prove a more reasonable and manageable policy choice as opposed to the adoption of overly ambitious goals in competition policy.[146] The latter may prove excessively burdensome in terms of resources, available expertise and economic impact (for example, in combination with deregulation policies, they may lead to high unemployment rates). Focussing on the most serious competition issues rather than attempting to grasp a wide range of competition-related problems may prove particularly appropriate, especially when competition policy is being implemented in combination with other economic policies of liberalization and structural adjustment.[147]

The mainstay of the argument is that, although it is unquestionable that the socio-economic, political and cultural context of developing countries is significantly different from that of industrialized countries – which are also those where the principles of competition law have first been developed[148] – different enforcement priorities, progressive implementation[149] and simpler rules ('lighter' competition rules) seem preferable to a discretionary inclusion of non-competition goals. It is believed that this approach would better suit the concerns of developing countries without the danger of an inadequate deployment of competition law.[150] For example: while competition law in developed countries tends to focus on exclusionary abuses, exploitative abuses by dominant firms may be an issue of particular relevance to developing countries,[151] namely in the context of ITT. The

144 In this sense, see Nguyen n. 83, 296–99. These have indeed been the issues addressed by a number of competition authorities in developing countries such as Korea, South Africa, Taiwan, Thailand and Vietnam; for an account of these case studies, see ibid 174 ff. See also UNCTAD, 'Competition Policy and the Exercise of Intellectual Property Rights' (2008) TD/B/COM.2/CLP/68 1, 9-11 <http://unctad.org/en/docs/c2clpd68_en.pdf> accessed 20 June 2012.

145 In this sense, with examples of developing countries that have implemented these different models, see Nguyen n. 83, 169–174.

146 On this point, see Dabbah n. 122, 474.

147 Ibid. It may be the case, however, that developing countries are being encouraged or simply pressured by developed countries or key international economic institutions to adopt competition policies and/or to effectively enforce them (see Gerber n. 13, 87–89), in which case there is very little they can do about it.

148 Emphasising the problem of market dominance, barriers to entry and lack of competitiveness of national undertakings from developing countries vis-à-vis foreign multinationals, see Max Planck Institute for Intellectual Property, Competition and Tax Law, 'ICN Unilateral Conduct Working Group: Responses to the Questionnaire' (31 October 2006) 26–27 <http://www.internationalcompetitionnetwork.org/uploads/questionnaires/uc%20objectives/drexl.pdf> accessed 20 June 2012.

149 The underlying argument is that a gradual and selective implementation of competition law may be preferable taking into account the institutional setting, poor experience, weakness of competition culture, and lack of resources in developing countries. On this point, see Kronthaler n. 58, 92–93 and also, although referring specifically to the implementation of TRIPS provisions on anticompetitive practices, Roffe and Spennemann in Correa and Yusuf n. 92, 324.

150 On this point, see Kronthaler n. 58, 96.

151 Drexl n. 125, 3: 'for social reasons, exploitation is a much greater concern in developing and emerging markets, where large parts of the population may be more easily and directly affected by supra-competitive pricing.'

market structure of developing countries, in which barriers to entry are a sizeable issue, may serve to explain why exploitation is of particular competitive concern: the consumer's lower average ability to pay in developing countries, combined with the existence of barriers to entry, deters the entry of new competitors and will tend to perpetuate the exploitative abuse.[152] At the same time, rules on exploitative abuses are easier to apply than, say, merger control, while allowing the necessary time for capacity building and the introduction of more complex rules. Also, they can work with lower market power thresholds as sometimes happens with rules on unilateral conduct in certain jurisdictions,[153] thus making rules on unilateral conduct easier to apply. Conversely, if the market power threshold is set at the level of dominance,[154] this may deprive enacting rules on unilateral conduct of its usefulness because, as the EU experience goes to show, assessing dominance may prove a more challenging task.[155]

Another point concerns the distinction between collusive and non-collusive practices, a distinction that may pose some challenges in the case of restrictive practices associated with ITT. On the one hand, it may happen that the restrictive practice may not be included in the agreement from the outset, but rather be the outcome of the way it's implemented in the context of, let's say, a mixed agreement.[156] On the other hand, it may also be the case that as a result of the recipient's weak bargaining position, it becomes difficult to assess whether we are dealing with a collusive or a non-collusive conduct.[157] This would suggest the need to address the anticompetitive effects of ITT using provisions both on collusive conduct and on unilateral conduct. In the latter case, the relevant market power threshold may be set below dominance because, as suggested, the market structure of developing countries is particularly prone to high concentration ratios that while easier to achieve, are harder to erode.[158]

---

152 The point is explained in Drexl n. 125, 5–7, who departs from the question of whether or not 'pure exploitation (without any exclusion) is within the ambit of protecting competition'.

153 Take the case of abuse of economic dependence/superior bargaining power; on this topic, see ICN, 'Report on Abuse of Superior Bargaining Position' (ICN 7th Annual conference, 2008) <http://www.internationalcompetitionnetwork.org/uploads/library/doc386.pdf> accessed 20 June 2012.

154 Dominance generally presupposes a market share not lower than 40 percent in the relevant market; see Commission (EC), 'Guidance on the Commission's Enforcement Priorities in Applying Article 82 EC Treaty to Abusive Exclusionary Conduct by Dominant Undertakings' (Communication) [2009] OJ C45/02, 7, para 14. For US antitrust, see Phillip Areeda, Louis Kaplow and Aaron Edlin, *Antitrust Analysis: Problems, Text and Cases* (6th edition, Aspen 2004) 483 ff.

155 In this context, see Matanzo n. 66, 198.

156 The example is not accidental as this is precisely one of the questions that art 40 TRIPS raises, namely whether the provision is applicable to mixed agreements, which include licensing provisions. On this point, see Brand and Lehmann in Stoll, Busche and Arend 84, 664).

157 A similar question arises in the context of EU competition law; see generally Hannes Schwinn, *Einseitige Maßnahmen in Abgrenzung zum europäischen Kartellverbot* (Nomos 2009).

158 As Gal n. 115, 93 comments, referring to the particularly damaging effect of artificial restrictions of competition by dominant firms: 'Dominant position is much easier to achieve and, once achieved, much more difficult to erode in many markets in small economies, given that competition is already limited by the natural conditions of the market: high concentration barriers protected by high natural barriers to entry. Unnatural barriers may even strengthen a dominant position even further, to the point where it is almost impossible to challenge it. Moreover, downstream and upstream markets in small economies are often also concentrated, so it might be easier for the monopolist operating at one level of the chain of supply to abuse its monopoly power in such markets.' However, Gal does not seem to espouse the view that competition law should work with a market power criterion below dominance (ibid 95).

Enforcement of Competition Law in Developing Countries

The previous sub-section focussed on the design of competition rules in developing countries, particularly aimed at tackling the detrimental effects associated with ITT while attempting to incorporate certain specificities of these countries. Along with the difficulties of enacting an appropriate legal framework we have an even greater – and arguably more relevant – problem concerning its enforcement.[159] This enforcement-deficit has an internal and an external dimension. The internal dimension relates to issues that have been already mentioned, such as absence of a competition culture, lack of expertise and resources, institutional capture, etc. The external dimension concerns the absence of effective instruments at the international level that can ensure the enforcement of competition rules. It is upon this external dimension that ultimately hinges the effective deterrence of multi-jurisdictional anticompetitive effects. In the absence of international instruments that ensure, for example, cooperation between competition authorities for the collection of evidence, the effectiveness of the enforcement conducted by national authorities in developing countries is seriously jeopardized.[160] Although different developing countries tell different stories in what comes to the degree of success obtained in the enforcement of competition law,[161] the extraterritorial and multijurisdictional nature of ITT makes it difficult to expect any consistent rate of success without the prior establishment of an international cooperation of some sort.

The projects for building up global competition rules have failed so far to deliver any palpable result and neither the OECD nor the UNCTAD seem to offer promising solutions for promoting the development of competition law at a global scale: the OECD is widely regarded as representing the interests of developed countries, while UNCTAD seems excessively connoted with developmental concerns and thus not very appealing to developed countries.[162] The possibility of convergence through the efforts of the ICN remains suspicious to some developing countries that frequently perceive it as surreptitious harmonization according to the blueprint of US antitrust and EU competition law.[163]

As for multilateralism through the WTO,[164] the perspectives seem equally dim. Although it is true that the WTO 'is currently the only international institution that has IPR-related competition rules under the TRIPS Agreement as hard law',[165] it has still to recover from the failure of the Cancún Ministerial Conference of September 2003,[166] during which no agreement on antitrust issues was achieved between the WTO members. This failure was confirmed in July 2004, when the Working

159 In the same vein, see Kronthaler n. 58, 88.

160 On this point, see Stewart, Clarke and Joekes n. 59, 43–46.

161 For a comparative study on the effectiveness of competition policy in South Africa, Poland and Ukraine, see Kronthaler n. 58, 93 ff

162 See Gerber n. 13, 112–114; and Nguyen n. 83, 273.

163 See Wigger n. 61; and Bakhoum 'Reflections on the concepts of "economic freedom", "free competition" and "efficiency" from the perspective of developing countries' n. 54, 419. The same could be said about the OECD, who has the additional disadvantage of being almost entirely composed by developed countries; on this point, see Nguyen n. 83, 271–72.

164 Exploring this solution, see Philip Marsden, *A Competition Policy for the WTO* (Cameron May 2003). Arguing against a WTO antitrust discipline, see Bernard Hoekman and Petros C. Mavroidis, 'Economic Development, Competition Policy and the WTO' (World Bank Policy Research Working Paper 2917, 2002) <http://www-wds.worldbank.org/external/default/WDSContentServer/IW3P/IB/2002/11/22/000094946_021 11404425138/Rendered/PDF/multi0page.pdf> accessed 20 June 2012.

165 Nguyen n. 83, 267.

166 Generally on this topic, see the account provided in Drexl n. 125; and also Gerber n. 13, 103–107.

Group on the Interaction between Trade and Competition Policy (WGTCP) was disbanded[167] and antitrust issues dropped from the WTO agenda.[168]

The observation that the WTO seems to remain the most appropriate forum to enact international antitrust rules,[169] including those dealing with anticompetitive conduct related to ITT, may very well be accurate but is presently of very little avail to reintroduce competition issues in the WTO agenda. Although multilateral agreements remain a more promising path than convergence, the challenges of global competition law would require a change of perspective. Amidst the ever-growing literature on the topic, the remainder of this section will deal with two contributions to the field that, while endorsing the suggested change of perspective, can be seen as complementary in the way they tackle the issue. Their potential complementarity arises from the fact that the first is more concerned with substantive issues – how to reconceptualize international competition law [170]– whilst the second is primarily concerned with procedural issues – how to address competition law as a global issue.[171]

The mainstay of the first perspective is to detach the approach to international competition from trade issues based on the perception that the (constitutional) value and importance of competition should not be subordinated to the liberalization of worldwide trade. The underlying change of perspective would be one from a trade-related approach to international competition to considering the latter as an essential element of 'quasi-constitutional character'[172] within the WTO system. This change of perspective is, to a considerable extent, the logical consequence of combining the recognition by the UN Development Programme (UNDP) of the international trading system as one of the global public goods,[173] with the acknowledged complementarity between the objectives of trade law and those of competition law.[174] As a public good, international competition would share the traits of non-rivalry and non-excludability commonly referred to in the economic literature, but having at the same time a global projection, meaning that it benefits more than one country, one people or one generation.[175] It is not difficult to recognize the potential of this approach, particularly

167 Nevertheless, during its mandate the WGTCP identified a number of trade-related restrictions of competition, distinguishing between (i) practices affecting market access for imports, (ii) practices affecting international markets, where different countries are affected largely in the same way (e.g. horizontal price-fixing), and (iii) practices having a differential impact on the national market of countries (e.g. export cartels). On these points, see Drexl n. 125, 425–431; and also Ullrich in Patel, Roffe and Yusuf n. 35, 372–73.

168 The last development was the Decision adopted on 1 August 2004 ("the July Package"), in which the WTO General Council expressed the following view: '*Relationship between Trade and Investment, Interaction between Trade and Competition Policy and Transparency in Government Procurement:* the Council agrees that these issues, mentioned in the Doha Ministerial Declaration in paragraphs 20–22, 23–25 and 26 respectively, will not form part of the Work Programme set out in that Declaration and therefore no work towards negotiations on any of these issues will take place within the WTO during the Doha Round.' [emphasis in original] <http://www.wto.org/english/tratop_e/dda_e/draft_text_gc_dg_31july04_e.htm> accessed 20 June 2012.

169 Exploring the possibility of developing international antitrust rules from the TRIPS Agreement, see especially Bacher n. 51, 449 ff. See also, with a focus on international licensing agreements, Gallego n. 82, 165 ff.

170 The argument is developed by Drexl n. 125, 437 ff.

171 The argument is developed by Gerber n. 13, 293 ff.

172 Drexl n. 125, 456.

173 See Office of Development Studies (UNDP), 'Profiling the Provision Status of Global Public Goods. An ODS Staff Paper' (December 2002) 13 ff <http://web.undp.org/globalpublicgoods/globalization/pdfs/background-paper-profiles.pdf> accessed 20 June 2012.

174 As developed by the WGTCP; see Drexl n. 125, 424–25.

175 Ibid 438–41.

if one takes into consideration that the most problematic features of transnational anticompetitive practices are its multijurisdictional effects. At the same time, it seems hopeless to insist on a solution that relies solely upon national competition when markets, as well as anticompetitive effects, are increasingly transnational by nature. But the recognition of international competition as a global public good would only be the beginning, as its effective implementation within the WTO system would require concessions both from developed countries (for example, tackling export cartels and other anticompetitive practices that escape the territorial scope of application of competition law) as well as from developing countries (for instance, compliance with the general WTO principle of non-discrimination when enforcing competition law domestically).[176]

The second approach endorses much of the premises of the first – it neither builds upon a specific competition law regime nor views competition law issues as an appendage to international trade[177] – and advances a strategy to supplement the limitations of convergence and provide new impetus to multilateralism. This strategy would be a 'commitment pathway' whose basic concept is that:

> [P]articipants sketch a path towards agreed goals and establish obligations to support movement towards these goals. Elements of the pathway are expected to take on sharper form as states interact in moving along it. The strategy would establish shared commitments to create and maintain an effective regime for global competition. Commitments would be "shared" in the sense that the projects' success would depend on the commitments of all participants to the project's goals.[178]

What is being suggested is a procedural strategy that would work as a gradualist and non-linear approach to widely defined common goals. Rather than setting precise goals that would be bound to stir opposition from one side or the other, the 'commitment pathway' suggests that only a number of widely shared goals can attract and maintain commitment.[179] These are defined as neutrally as possible and comprise (i) deterrence of anticompetitive conduct, (ii) protection of the process of competition and (iii) providing durable benefits for consumers.[180] Such a strategy should remain flexible and adaptable so as to deliver high benefits at a low cost and thus harness internal and international support to maintain and further the commitment.[181] While vague on the substantive issues, this second approach may supplement and provide a pathway for the implementation of the first.

Conclusion

Although the connection between development and access to technology is undeniable, approaching the subject from the perspective of the highly disputed R2D may not be the most rewarding strategy. Instead, this chapter has taken a different path building upon the widely accepted association between

176 More in detail as to how such a system could work, see Drexl n. 125, 447 ff.

177 See Gerber n. 13, 293–94. In fact, Gerber argues that the 'pathway strategy can be pursued on its own, but it may also be possible to create a separate competition law regime within the WTO' (ibid., 325).

178 Ibid., 295.

179 Ibid., 300 ff. There is indeed a fair degree of convergence regarding the basic goals of competition law, which include protection of consumer welfare, efficiency and freedom of competition; on this point, see Bakhoum 'Reflections on the concepts of "economic freedom", "free competition" and "efficiency" from the perspective of developing countries' n. 54, 414–17.

180 Gerber n. 13, 308. And Bakhoum 'Reflections on the concepts of "economic freedom", "free competition" and "efficiency" from the perspective of developing countries' n. 54, 414–17.

181 Gerber n. 13, 301–304.

development and technology. Within the later, it focussed on ITT and, in particular, on licensing agreements as one of the most relevant forms of ITT. Anticompetitive conduct associated with ITT often minimizes or thwarts the developmental benefits of transmission of technology. This issue is of particular concern to developing countries since they are frequently net importers of technology and thus highly dependent on transfers of technology originating from developed countries. However, we presently lack an adequate legal framework to address anticompetitive conduct with multijurisdictional effects, as is the case with ITT: at the national level, national competition laws are bound by the principle of territoriality; at the international level, attempts to address this issue have remained inconsequential and only article 40 TRIPS provides a partial and utterly unsatisfactory solution.

While it is increasingly acknowledged that a 'one-size-fits-all' solution would be an inadequate response to the challenges of designing and implementing competition law in developing countries, identifying the internal and external obstacles that prevent an effective application of competition law in developing countries is only the first albeit important step. The specificities of developing countries should be taken into account when prioritizing those anticompetitive practices that are particularly detrimental to developing countries and when defining the appropriate remedies. Conversely, opening competition to a number of vaguely defined non-competition goals may not only fail to deliver the desired results but also increase the probability of opportunistic behaviour, rent-seeking and political arbitrariness.

Remedying the weaknesses of competition law in developing countries is only part of the answer to the problem, and arguably not the most relevant part. Equally indispensable but much more difficult is setting up international mechanisms for the enforcement of competition law against multijurisdictional restraints of competition. Only a global competition law could adequately keep up with globalized restrictions of competition, but attaining the former seems further away given the inherent limitations of international convergence and the presently dim perspectives for a WTO competition regime. A possible way out would require a change of perspective and, following suggestions advanced in the literature, these should take place at two levels: at a substantial level, by considering international competition as a global public good rather than an appendage to trade liberalization; and at the procedural level, by settling for a more modest but probably more effective 'commitment pathway' instead of the classical framework of multilateral agreements.

PART IV
Biobanks, Bioethics and Human Rights

Chapter 6

Prometheus, Golem & Co.: Bioconstitution and Bodiliness in a '(World) Risk Society'[1]

João Carlos Loureiro

Within the mythological plot which shapes Western culture, at a unique intersection of Jewish-Christian and Greco-Latin matrixes, Prometheus stands as a symbol of rebellion against the gods.[2] He is often seen also as an archetype of a (self)creator. In Modernity the Promethean or Titanic principle has come to assert itself, refusing divinity and exalting human nature[3] and contrasting itself with the Dionysian principle, also reflected in a vision of the body.

As for Golem, a Jewish concept, the different versions of this humanlike figure evoke the production of artificial life.[4] The search for the capacity to create bodies is now simply the result of a vast technical and scientific project which aims at going beyond the limits of knowledge by creating life in a laboratory. In a time of genetics and genomes, of DNA sequencing, one must recall that in the process of creating one of the most famous Golems, the Prague Golem, the Rabbi curiously uses Heaven-revealed letters.[5] A number of traditional Jewish debates about Golem find some sort of parallel in the controversy about life arising from the somatic nuclear cell transfer (cloning).[6]

According to some reports, Golem emerged as a possible answer to the question of Jewish survival, by means of 'a Jew without death'.[7] As we know, there have been interventions meant to overcome body limits – and its telomere-written temporality – in a sort of a new pursuit of Methuselah's project, the Old Testament hero who lived almost 1000 years. In terms of its ethical and legal translation, the door is thus open to discuss the duty to die, so as to allow the *novum* of birth, so well reflected upon by Hannah Arendt.[8]

---

1 English translation from Portuguese by Isabel Gil and Isaías Hipólito.

2 About the variations on Prometheus' myth see Gregório Luri Medrano, *Prometeos: biografias de un mito* (Madrid 2001); Wolfgang Storch/ Burghard Damerau (Hrsg.), *Mythos Prometheus: Texte von Hesiod bis René Char* (Leipzig 1995).

3 See Hans Urs von Balthasar's reflections, namely *Apokalypse der deutschen Seele: Studien zu einer Lehre von letzen Haltungen* (Freiburg 1998), although we use these formulations in a more vast sense.

4 By itself, this Jewish word refers not only to the body's external form, but also to the structure (*zelem*): Moshe Idel, *Golem: Jewish magical and mystical traditions on the artificial anthropoid* (Albany 1990) 6.

5 Chayim Bloch, *Golem: legends of the ghetto of Prague* (1997) 65.

6 J. David Bleich, *Bioethical dilemmas: a Jewish Perspective – II* (Southfield 2006) 21.

7 Laurie Zoloth, 'Born again: faith and yearning in the clone controversy', in Paul Lauritzen (ed.), *Cloning and the future of human embryo research* (Oxford/ New York 2001) 137.

8 *The human condition* (Chicago 1958) [transl.: *A condição humana* (S. Paulo 1981) 17]. For a philosophy of birth see Ludger Lütkehaus, *Natalität: Philosophie der Geburt*, Kusterdingen, 2006. See also Hans Saner, 'El significado político de la natalidade en la obra de Hannah Arendt', in Marco Estrada Saavedra (ed.), *Pensando y actuando en el mundo: ensayos críticos sobre la obra de Hannah Arendt* (México 2003) 19–37, 28–29.

The idea of a Golem – which according to many accounts ended up turning against his creator, as in Mary Shelley's *Frankenstein*, a book published with the interesting subtitle 'the modern Prometheus' – allows us to revisit also the 'heuristics of fear' proposed in Hans Jonas' *Das Prinzip Verantwortung.*[9] As a matter of fact, some of the ethical or legal discussion on technology evokes a sort of 'no control land', epitomized by the sorcerer's apprentice, as well as models of analysis of risk. Granted that technology inheres the human condition, there is in modern technique a *novum* that might be summarized in Dieter Birnbacher's[10] three key-words:

a. *Technicality* – which questions value-centred models of rationality and models of a 'rationality of the dignity',[11] thereby jeopardizing the 'image of the human being' which underlies Western law and ethics (the Heideggerean analysis of the *Gestell* as well as the instrumental reason triumph might be recalled in this connection);
b. *Globalism*, i.e. the worldwide reach of acts and their consequences, which forces us to wrestle with issues such as the shortcomings of self-centred, closed states and normativities, or the meaning of state laws at a time in which the borders appear so flexible, with the exception of North Korea and the like;
c. *Destruction potential* – in addition to the nuclear, chemical and biological weapons, a new threat comes from the biotechnological field, where the possibility to alter the human (biological) nature is being pursued. As we turn to the legal implications of such issues, we have to wrestle with debates over the human genome as part of the common heritage of Humanity, debates over the limits to medical interventions in the human body, and over the tension between the individual genome and the collective one.

In this chapter I will tentatively propose some thoughts on the possibilities and limits of a constitutional approach to the human bodiliness, with a focus on what I have labelled, since the 1990s[12] as 'bioconstitution'.[13] I will proceed in two steps.

a. To start out I shall focus on national constitutions' performance in the context of both fragmentary societies and a world in which borders are being relativized (if pushed to the limit, this latter situation leads to the irrelevance of space, i.e., 'atopia'[14]). The normative and constitutional sphere is being envisaged by and large as a network system,[15] combining

9 Subtitle: *Versuch ein Ethik für die technologische Zivilisation* (Frankfurt am Main 1979) [transl.: *Imperative of responsibility: in search of an ethics for the technological age* (Chicago/ London 1985)].

10 'Technik', in E. Martens/H. Schnädelbach (Hg.), *Philosophie: ein Grundkurs*, 2 (Hamburg 1998) specially 608-613.

11 Pierpaolo Donati, *Oltre il multiculturalismo: la ragione relazionale per un mondo comune* (Roma/ Bari 2008), XVII.

12 João Carlos Loureiro, 'O direito à identidade genética do ser humano', in *Portugal-Brasil Ano 2000* (Coimbra 1999), 263–389, 294.

13 The term 'biconstitutionalism' is used in a book recently edited by Sheila Jasanoff [*Reframing rights: bioconstitutionalism in the genetic age* (Cambridge, Mass./ London 2011). We cannot go into detail here, but her views, despite some issues and interests in common with ours, prove substantial different from my own bioconstitutional project.

14 Helmut Willke, *Atopie: Studien zur atopischen Gesellschaft* (Frankfurt am Main 2001).

15 François Ost/ Michael Van de Kerchove, *De la pyramide au réseau: pour une théorie dialectique du droit*, (Bruxelles 2002); for doctrine see José Joaquim Gomes Canotilho, *'Brancosos' e interconstitucionalidade: itinerários dos discursos sobre a historicidade constitucional* (2nd edn, Coimbra 2008; João Carlos Loureiro, '«É bom morar no azul»: a constituição mundial revisitada', (2006) 82 *Boletim da Faculdade de Direito*,

both state regulations with the social ones and the *hard* with the *soft law*;

b. afterwards, I shall consider some of the challenges to a constitutional theory of bodiliness. I will focus on the following interventions to the human body, as they seek to: (1) alter, even eliminate, as an elixir of eternal life, any boundaries between life and death; (2) heterodeterminate the other as a double (cloning), or to select certain features, by means of genetics, and within a hybridization and technologization process of the body. Such analysis highlights a bioconstitutional approach to the following items: subjects, goods, positions and principles.

Since the body is a recurrent metaphor in political and normative thought, there is the need to determine what sort of normative *corpus* is at stake here, especially as far as the constitutional field is concerned.

Technique, Bodiliness and the Constitution: Some Challenges

In the last decades, biomedical interventions have been approached within the framework of fundamental and human rights. Constitutional scholarship has always played a central role and constitutional justice is still regarded by many with hope. A cursory look at the doctrine allows us to realize the trend toward constitutionalization:

a. at the internal level, the conceptualization of new fundamental rights and duties, or at least fundamental rights' dimensions,[16] are seen as signs of constitutionalization;
b. in the (trans)temporal axis, the future generations (and the extremely long-term and distant future generations) are credited with a new relevance in the constitutional field, as asserted by the project labelled constitution of distance (*Fernverfassung*),[17] inspired by analogy with the 'ethics of distance' (*Fernethik*),[18] asserts. In a first moment, part of the modern French-inspired constitutionalism – somewhat different from the evolutionary constitution, which the Anglo-Saxon case brilliantly illustrates – reflected about a constitution that would govern us to the end of centuries,[19] while simultaneously there was an ongoing debate about

181–212; also in the constitutional area see Andrea Hamann/ Hélène Ruiz Fabri, 'Transnational networks and constitutionalism' (2008) 6 *International Journal of Constitutional Law* 481–508.

16 José Carlos Vieira de Andrade, *Os direitos fundamentais na Constituição portuguesa de 1976* (5th edn, Coimbra 2012), 163–64.

17 João Carlos Loureiro *O direito à identidade genética*, cit., 275–76; idem, 'Fernverfassung, Konstitutionalismus und Weltverfassung: Achtzig Jahre nach der Weimarer Verfassung, fünfzig Jahre nach der Bonner Verfassung und am Anfang der Berliner Republik', (2001) 77 *Boletim da Faculdade de Direito* 549–73.

18 *Das Prinzip Verantwortung*, cit.; see also Peter Kemp, *Das Unersetzliche: eine Technologie-Ethik* (Berlin 1992); for an evaluation, Jörg Schubert, *'Das Prinzip Verantwortung' als verfassungsstaatliches Rechtsprinzip: Rechtsphilosophische und verfassungsrechtliche Betrachtungen zur Verantwortungsethik von Hans Jonas* (Baden-Baden 1998); Gilbert Hottois (éd.), *Aux fondements d'une éthique contemporaine: Hans Jonas et H.T. Engelhardt en perspective* (Paris 1993).

19 Borges Carneiro mentioned by José Joaquim Gomes Canotilho, *Direito constitucional e teoria da constituição* (7th edn, Coimbra 2003) 108.

the legitimacy to bind future generations.[20]

Currently, though, the problem is quite different: to what extent are we bound by future, naturally non-existent generations? Time has, indeed, acquired a new density of its own: the beginning of the atomic age has brought about, along with huge amounts of long-lasting (for thousands of years) waste, tremendous risks as well. Along the line of Hans Jonas' *Fernethik*, an 'ethics of distance' has asserted itself. It is one which compels constitutional doctrine to develop a constitution of distance (*Fernverfassung*), one which seriously takes into account not only the extremely long-lasting effects derived from a set of interventions, but also the transterritoriality of risks.

Parameter and Circumstance: (In)ability of Constitutional Enforcement?

A preliminary issue is the ability of enforcing the constitution. As a matter of fact, different strategies in this field can be found in late Modernity, namely reduction, destruction or conversion of the constitutional norm.[21] The first case can be illustrated by the transposition of Engelhardt's[22] position to the (bio-)constitutional field. In a society of *moral strangers*,[23] marked by a concern with procedure and with an emphasis on the principle of permission, a great number of issues would undergo a process of privatization and commitment to the communities that the individuals belong to.[24] As for the destruction of the constitutional measure, some expressions found in *Critical Legal Studies* portray a deconstructionist matrix that elects indetermination and inconsistence as fundamental tenets of law. With regard to the conversion of the constitutional measure, rooted in the Economic Analysis of Law, the image of the *homo oeconomicus* is assumed to be a beneficial one.

However, despite the growing fragmentation and complementarity, and without jeopardizing constitutional openness, I believe that it is possible, at a constitutional level, to find fundamental values that may provide a framework for the resolution of clashes over bodiliness.

The Forsaken Image? On the Constitutional Icon, or the Diatribes of Neoscientisms

Linked to the above discussion, though somehow independent from it, is the issue of the human image. As a matter of fact, underlying Western legal discourse there is a freedom and responsibility

20 See Article 28 of the French Constitution of 1793: '(…) Une génération ne peut assujettir à ses lois les générations futures' ('A generation must not subject future generations to its rules').

21 About such perspectives see, with other references, João Carlos Loureiro, *Constituição e biomedicina*, vol. I, part I.

22 *The foundations of bioethics* (2nd edn, New York/Oxford, 1996).

23 For further details on the opposite view, i.e. about opponents who consider that we are 'moral friends' see Francesco D'Agostino, idem, *Il diritto come problema teologico ed altri saggi di filosofia e teologia del diritto* (3th edn, Torino 1997) 84–89; also, in the Anglo-Saxon context, Erich Lowevy, *Moral strangers, moral acquaintance, and moral friends: connectedness and its conditions* (Albany, N.Y. 1997), who, although using the expression, considers that we are 'moral acquaintances', starting from common needs and experiences (p. 3); for this model see also Kevin W. Wildes, *Moral acquaintances: methodology in bioethics* (Notre Dame 2000). In a recently published work Stephen Hanson, *Moral acquaintances and moral decisions: resolving moral conflicts in medical ethics* (New York 2009) 149, underlines that '(…) the moral friends would be able to agree on the justifications of their decisions, while the moral acquaintances could not'.

24 For lack of space, a thorough examination of this position will be set aside.

paradigm. It was gradually woven into History, and while recognizing the constraints of the human condition, such paradigm does not interpret them under a deterministic light.

In the Jewish (and Christian) narrative of Genesis, the image of the human being was understood as *imago Dei*.[25] The Enlightenment significantly contributed to the shaping of an image of autonomy, albeit in a universalizing key, *maxime* Kantian (this sort of autonomy should not be confused with the Anglo-Saxon idea of empirical autonomy that eventually marked medical law so decisively).

In Western constitutionalism, particularly after Second World War barbarity, the image of a free, responsible and solidary human being asserted itself, while human dignity assumed the role of a foundational principle.[26] This is why, as far as human rights are concerned – i.e., within the perspective of philosophy of law and international law[27] – both the economic, social and cultural rights, and freedom rights and political participation rights came to the forefront, exorcising the idea of a state reduced to a mere 'watchdog of property'.[28] Along with the ambiguous 'generations of rights' formula, and owing to the ecological awareness and technological development, a new set, or at least new dimensions, of rights[29] eventually emerged.

However, this image of the human being is now subjected both to purifying fire and to destructive blaze. A corrosive scepticism, one which is beyond good and evil (in Nietzsche's words), has dominated our values. Thanks to a challenging interculturality and to the acceptance of the 'new diversity' of a world where, in each city, there is a tendency to clone such multiplicity,[30] this image of the human being was purged from the inadequate waste it carried with it. In many cases, though, instead of reaching an 'overlapping consensus',[31] this process opened the gates to a fragmented neo-tribalization stemming from a radicalization of multiculturalism.[32] The resources of a taken for granted value-centered consensus are now considered baseless, a vestige from some mythology of modern reason, unable to overcome the challenges of late modernity, or post-modernity, as some would have it.

The hierarchic and closed 'order of values' (*Wertordnung*) as a constitutional reading tool, gave way to the recognition of the constitution as an open land of fundamental values (*Grundwerte*), within which one may strike different balances. However, attempts to strip those values from dogmatic force and to develop projects grounded upon an 'anarchy of values',[33] have come to light.

25 For the different modes of filling up this formula, with the correspondent bibliographic references, see João Carlos Loureiro, 'Pessoa, dignidade e cristianismo', in Jorge de Figueiredo Dias/ José Joaquim Gomes Canotilho/ José de Faria Costa (Org.), *ARS IVDICANDI: Estudos em homenagem ao Prof. Doutor António Castanheira Neves*, vol. I: *Filosofia, teoria e metodologia* (Coimbra 2008) 669–723.

26 On the relation between the image of human being and the constitution see Peter Häberle, *Das Menschenbild im Verfassungsstaat* (Berlin 1988).

27 José Carlos Vieira de Andrade, *Os direitos fundamentais*, cit., 15–49.

28 Francisco Lucas Pires, *O problema da constituição* (Coimbra 1970).

29 About the ambiguity of the notion of new rights, with other references, see João Carlos Loureiro, 'O nosso pai é o dador n.º xxx:»: a questão do anonimato dos dadores de gâmetas na procriação medicamente assistida heterológa', (2010/13) 7 *Lex Medicinae – Revista Portuguesa de Direito da Saúde*, 5–42. Bearing in mind Murphy's analysis trilogy (repetition, revolution and resonance), and drawing on a paper by Hélène Boussard, arguing that several questions seen as examples of new rights lead again to 'old rights' applied in new contexts, see Thérèse Murphy, 'Repetition, revolution and resonance: an introduction to new technologies and human rights', in Thérèse Murphy (ed.), *New technologies and human rights* (New York 2009) 1–18, 9.

30 Ulrich Beck, 'Vorwort', in *Perspektiven der Weltgesellschaft* (Frankfurt a. M. 1998) 7.

31 John Rawls, *Political liberalism* (New York 1993).

32 For the various senses of the expression and a counterproposal grounded on a relational theory see Pierpaolo Donati, *Oltre il multiculturalismo*, cit.

33 Paul Valadier, *L'anarchie des valeurs: le relativisme est-il fatal?* (Paris 1997).

On science's side, naturalism(s) has increasingly gained visibility and virulence. Reductionisms from genetic and neuroscientific matrices[34] act as though they were the keys to understanding the human being, reaching the point of assigning themselves the role of dismounting the nature of freedom and responsibility. In practice, attempts to pre-determinate (cloning) and modify the human genome (genetic enhancement) would jeopardise human autonomy, through a process of illegitimate heterodetermination. The human being would become moulding stuff, artifact or product, opening the doors to genetical dominance of humans over humans, as in dystopias like *Brave New World.* Generally speaking, the technological revolution does not leave the human being's image[35] unscathed.

The abolition of the human being, such as in the Hobbesian *homo homini lupus* image, has been settled all around in different forms, and now with a new sociobiological twist.[36] In dogmatic terms, such a natural state, built upon a selfish individual, is expressed by an 'autonomist' reading of fundamental rights; such radicalization would transform the individual, not the person, into a *prius*. In the biomedical field there have been illustrative instances of denial of alterity.

The so-called GNR revolution – genetics, nanosciences and robotics[37] – is out there. Biosciences, especially genetics and currently neurosciences, are moving toward new reductionisms that refuse the foundations not only of constitutional law but of law as a whole, by calling into question human responsibility and freedom. The utopian models of multiple sexualities propose to alter the foundations supporting the human being, as they forsake the traditional distinctiveness of sexes (the masculine/the feminine).

Such interventions, often viewed as the abolition of the human being, seem to give way to the abolition of differences:[38] differences between humans and animals (e.g. hybrids and chimeras), humans and machines (cyborg, opposition between body and spirit in terms of *hardware* and *software*), Man and Woman (the irrelevance of sexes as illustrated by the rediscovered androgyny) and Creator and creature. All this somewhat mirrors a (post-) secular worldview[39] (e.g. the anthropotechniques[40]).

Will we be able to maintain an ecologically open, personicentric and humanistic conception of constitution?

This chapter proposes a core thesis: the criticism of anthropocentrism does not necessarily need to degenerate into any sort of post-humanism.[41] Thus, where xenotransplants are concerned, there

---

34 Literature about the neurosciences and its impact is vast. Regarding the discussions around a neuroethics and a neurolaw, see Stephan Schleim/ Tade Matthias Spranger/ Henrik Walter (Hg.), *Von der Neuroethik zum Neurorecht?*, Göttingen, 2009).

35 See essays published in Luca Consoli/ Rolf Hoekstra (red.), *Technologie en mensbeeld* (Nijmegen 2008).

36 Thomas Mohrs, *Vom Weltstaat: Hobbes's Sozialphilosophie, Soziobiologie, Realpolitik* (Berlin 1995).

37 Andrea Vaccaro, 'Filosofie dell' immortalità' (2008) 49 *Rassegna di Teologia* 459–71; idem, *L'ultimo esorcismo: filosofie dell'imortalità terrena* (Bologna 2009).

38 C.S. Lewis, *The abolition of man, or, Reflections on education with special reference to the teaching of English in the upper forms of schools* (London, 1978).

39 Jürgen Habermas, *Glauben und Wissen* (Frankfurt am Main 2001) [transl.: 'Faith and knowledge', in *The future of human nature* (Oxford, 2002)].

40 Peter Sloterdijk, *Regeln für den Menschenpark: ein Antwortschreiben zum Brief über den Humanismus* (Frankfurt a. M., 1999).

41 For different approaches towards post-humanism, from its militant defence to its categorical rejection, see Brent Waters' synthesis, *This mortal flesh: incarnation and bioethics* (Grand Rapids 2009), esp. 96–102.

is no conflict between, for example, the purported fundamental rights of the pig[42] and of the human being. Using swines or other animals, like simians, is essentially a question of risk, of viruses, in the first place, while also a question of impact on the representations of the human being and body.

Human Rights and Biomedicine: Discursive Illusion?

Since this project is placed within the framework of human rights, just as the new technologies (namely those within the biomedical field) have done, one cannot but wonder about the capacity of a category such as human rights. The fundamental rights perspective is basically conceived in state terms, without disregard for other usages (e.g. the Charter of Fundamental Rights of the European Union). Human rights evoke both a legal philosophical perspective – the one having to do with rational foundations – and, most importantly, a legal international perspective.[43]

Some might consider this approach as doomed, since human rights would not withstand the two following accusations:

a. ethnocentrism (i.e., deficit of interculturality). Human rights emerge as a Western construct, ultimately a weapon of imperialism to subdue and illegitimately interfere in the politics of other states;
b. religiousness (i.e., deficit of universalization). Human rights appear as a Christian construct rendered obsolete due to the advent of secularization, or perhaps more accurately, secularism and state neutrality.

Furthermore, one may question if this category may be effectively enforced, as – due to their level of abstraction – human rights would hardly serve any purpose from a legal viewpoint.

Since I cannot proceed to develop the latter, I argue:

1. against anthropological relativism: for every human being there is a core of values of good and evil; against epistemological relativism, it is possible to reach a reasonable degree of consensus no matter cultural specificities; as for cultural relativism, the context-driven enforcement of values will not hinder the universality of a set of core legal positions (on a foundational level);[44]
2. that interconstitutionality-based interaction may pave the way to a macro-regional (e.g. European constitutional law), world constitutional law, through intercultural dialogue. This process would allow human rights to be included within the constitutional core and to be enhanced *via* a dynamics interfundamentality of rights.[45]

---

42 For one of the figure's criticism in philosophical discussion, showing the main tendencies fundamenting the theory of animals' rights, see David S. Oderberg, *Applied ethics: a non-consequentialist approach* (Oxford 2000) [transl.: *Ética aplicada: uma abordagem não consequencialista* (Parede 2009) 125–178].

43 See, for all, José Carlos Vieira de Andrade, *Os direitos fundamentais*, cit., 15–49.

44 On this point we pay a special tribute to Michael Perry, *The idea of human rights: four inquiries* (New York 1998) 81–82.

45 Concept used by Gomes Canotilho: see José Joaquim Gomes Canotilho, with the collaboration of Suzana Tavares da Silva, *Competência intercultural e interjusfundamentalidade: Master na Faculdade de Direito de Coimbra no âmbito da cadeira de direitos fundamentais* (Coimbra 2008).

In summary, I posit a material 'parameter', the degree of density of which might be arguable, but that, at the end (and even if it does not legitimize the constitution's imperialist and colonizing models of other branches of law), would render the constitution the central *locus* of discourse. As to mankind's image, I assert that plurality is not necessarily a hindrance to an 'overlapping consensus'[46] on fundamental issues and that the perspective of scientific reductionisms undermines humankind. Finally, against those who claim ethnocentricity or religiosity as evidence for the inexistence of human rights, I defend their existence within the framework of multilevel constitutional networks.

Bioconstitution: for a Theory of Bodiliness, especially in Biomedical Law

Body's Memory, Frailty and Vulnerability

Frailty and Vulnerability

A discussion on legal issues involving the notion and limits of bodiliness necessarily has to be rooted in reality's analysis, within a framework that intertwines text and context. What we have before us is none other than the '*a priori* of the lived body' (*Leibapriori*[47]), characterized by frailty, magnificently symbolized by the Genesis narrative of Adam's creation out of clay. Frailty is, thus, a structural feature of the human being's nature; the human being experiences pain, suffering and finitude, alongside with threats to bodiliness. Herbert Hart[48] states that, where frailty (structural frailty, as advanced in this approach) is concerned, it would be quite different if human beings had a different physical shell-like structure that would render them immune to attacks. In his words: 'If men were to lose their vulnerability to each other there would vanish one obvious reason for the most characteristic provision of law and morals: *Thou shall not kill.*'[49]

Frailty is not only structural but also circumstantial and epochal. Our questioning arises in a '(world) risk society'[50] in which biomedicine, like Janus, suppresses certain risks while creating others. The medical-industrial paraphernalia generates situations where patients are left, in a limbo between life and death, in a persistent vegetative state, leaving us wondering whether this metaphor is of a personal or vegetal nature.[51] The advances in human genetics create new categories of patients, those with 'a healthy life but an ill genome'.[52] Furthermore, genetic intervention may jeopardize the human being's inviolability, the genetic irreplicability and uniqueness (cloning) and humanhood itself (hybrids).[53] If, on the one hand, the new information technologies applied to

46 Formula used by John Rawls, *Political liberalism*, cit.

47 Expression by Karl-Otto Apel, who prefers the linguistic *a priori*. Its roots are found in a text where Kant criticizes Leibnizians for forgetting the body (*Ak* XX, 7, 282–83): *vide* Domingo Blanco Fernandéz, 'El *a priori* corporal: insuficiencia de la ética discursiva', in Domingo Blanco Fernández/ José A. Pérez Tapias/ Luis Sáez Rueda (ed.), *Discurso y realidad: en debate con K.-O. Apel* (Madrid 1994) 46–74.

48 Herbert Hart, *The concept of law* (2nd edn Oxford 1994) 194–95.

49 On the commandment *Thou shall not kill*, see Adriana Cavarero/Angelo Scola, *Non uccidere* (Bologna 2011).

50 Ulrich Beck, *World Risk society*, Cambridge, 1999; idem, *Weltrisikogesellschaft: auf der Suche nach der verlorenen Sicherheit*, Frankfurt am Main, 2007.

51 For more elaboration on the subject see João Carlos Loureiro, 'Metáfora do vegetal ou metáfora do pessoal? Considerações jurídicas em torno do estado vegetativo crónico', (1993/ 8) *Cadernos de Bioética*, 27–65.

52 Luís Archer, 'Genoma e intimidade' (1994/7) *Cadernos de Bioética*, 63–69, 67.

53 For a detailed explanation see our *O direito à identidade genética*, cit.

health care deepen our knowledge and capability of intervention, on the other hand they bear the fear of the informational *Big Brother*.

The frailty inherent to specific steps and conditions is what we call vulnerability. This is the frailty we experience deep in the flesh, i.e. in bodiliness; this frailty calls upon law and rights to protect the fundamental goods. While making us more aware of others and of care, ethically and legally speaking in particular where human and fundamental rights are concerned, this frailty and incompleteness also claims for the assertion of fundamental duties.

Body

Pedro Laín Entralgo[54] defined the human body as 'the material makeup which enables the human being to live, to fall sick, to get cured and to die.

Let us point out some fundamental issues on bodiliness:

a. The bodiliness experience is essentially based on *being* a body, not on *having* a body: 'I am my body', said Gabriel Marcel; and this is decisive in the juridical realm (e.g. the issue of the so-called 'rights over the body');
b. the human body as objective reality (*Körper*) should be distinguished from the human body as flesh (*Leib*). During the 20th century, new perspectives on the former emerged: there were major breakthroughs in genetics, namely the DNA knowledge increase and the human genome mapping.[55] The latter derives from the intimate experience of one's own body.
c. The animated body is a sexed body, i.e. there is no such thing as a generic asexual human being. The experience of humankind is, to this extent, disjunctive and not divisive, sex thus being a binding element. Human existence, characterized as polar[56] in terms of masculine/ feminine,[57] is a material presupposition of law.
d. Bodiliness is temporality and historicity. The experience of temporality is an experience of finitude, of awareness of death, the ultimate frailty. The human being deals with this biological finitude as an '*animal quaerens*'[58] by raising the issue of the meaning of life, and with the frailty of his/her condition, by craving for longevity, at which law also aims.
e. Bodiliness is a mediation process necessary to the human being's relation with others and the world, an essential alterity dimension.

The animated bodiliness is legally protected[59] in its various dimensions, which gained some degree of autonomy. As a general rule, the following goods are at stake: life, personal integrity – not merely physical, which is a plain external view of the body – personal identity, sex and health.

---

54 *Antropologia medica* (Barcelona 1984) [transl.: *Antropologia medica* (Milano 1988) 71].

55 Though James F. Keenan ['Genetic research and the elusive body', in Lisa Sowle Cahill/ Margarte A. Farley (ed.), *Embodiment, morality and medicine* (Dordrecht/Boston/London 1995) 59–73] underlines that, in this area, we are witnessing a 'suppression of the body', as geneticists seldom work in a 'recognizable body' (p. 61).

56 As a matter of fact, as Romano Guardini remarks [*Ethik: Vorlesungen an der Universität München* (Mainz 1993): transl.: *Ética: lecciones en la Universidade de Múnich* (Madrid 1999) 503], we are faced with relations of polarity, not contradiction.

57 On the importance of this distinction, see Julián Marías, *Antropologia metafísica* (Madrid 1973) 148–49 [transl.: *Metaphysical anthropology: the empirical structure of human life* (University Park 1971)].

58 Pedro Laín Entralgo, *Idea del hombre* (Barcelona 1996) 49–50.

59 Concerning the legal framework of the living body, we should avoid integrating it in the universe of things: for Portugal, see Rabindranath Capelo de Sousa, *O direito geral de personalidade* (Coimbra 1995)

What the Bioconstitution Is (not): Approaches

Back in the 1990s, the word *bioconstitution* referred to the legal constitutional framework connected to bioethical issues. However, it soon became clear that it was necessary, heuristically, to develop a consistent concept on which to build a partial constitution, with a field of its own, independent from bioethics. This formula, shaped either as a 'bioethical constitution'[60] or as an autonomous version,[61] eventually made its way in Portuguese-speaking countries, especially in Brazil (although in this process there were misunderstandings and even oblivion as to its origins).

Bioconstitution is the set of norms (principles and rules) formally and/or materially constitutional, which has as its object actions or omissions either from the state or from private entities, mainly centred on the protection of life, on identity and personal integrity, and on the health of today's or future human beings, especially as biomedical threats are at stake.[62]

This constitution stands on a set of fundamental goods and has great potential for comparison at the constitutional law level. The core of this partial constitution is bodiliness.

Limits of Bodiliness

Taking into account the limits of the human body, I shall begin by tracing some guidelines for a bioconstitutional perspective.

The word *limits* is, in any dictionary, polysemic.[63] Limit evokes differentiation and also limitations, incapacities or insufficiencies. This word conveys yet another sense, that of 'should not be trespassed',[64] which allows for the difference between the possible and the permissible/acceptable (the latter will further be developed in connection with the normative limits to body interventions).

Concerning difference, the pressure by the several post-humanisms challenges the human body's specificity and the human/non-human code, illustrated, for instance, by hybridation and interspecific chimeras phenomena.[65]

As to the limits of the human body, there are several important distinctions to be made:

a. absolute common limits, pertaining to the human condition: human beings have no wings,

211–228; for a synthesis of German doctrine, with reference to reifying, personalist and mixed theories, see Nadine Bock, *Rechtliche Voraussetzungen der Organentnahme von Lebenden und Verstorbenen* (Frankfurt a. M. 1999) 86–89; for the current French doctrine, rejecting reification, see Irma Arnoux, *Les droits de l'être humain sur son corps*, (Bourdeaux 1994) specially 35 ss.; see also Stéphane Prieur, *La disposition par l'individu de son corps* (Bordeaux 1999) 48–58.

60 Paolo Martelli, 'Bioetica, pluralismo morale e futuro della cittadinanza', in Stefano Rodotà, *Questioni di bioetica* (Roma, 1993) 11. In this sense, João Carlos Loureiro, 'Portugal II – Bioethical legislation', in EU Project Biomed II, *Working papers: Biolaw in Europe (Meeting, June 1–4, 1996, Copenhagen)* (Copenhagen 1997) 71–90, 72.

61 João Carlos Loureiro, *O direito à identidade genética*, cit., 294.

62 Notion explained in *O direito à identidade genética*, cit., 294. In detail, idem, *Constituição e biomedicina*, vol. I, cit., part III.

63 E.g. *Dicionário Houaiss da língua portuguesa* (Lisboa 2003) IV 2279.

64 E.g. *Dicionário Houaiss da língua portuguesa*, cit., 2279.

65 Alessandro BLASIMME, 'La creazione di ibridi e chimere tra scienza e bioetica' (2008/1) 16 *Bioetica* 21–45.

although they can follow Icarus by technological means;

b. relative common limits, characteristic of certain steps in human life; these limits may affect all human beings or a certain category (women, for example, cannot achieve postmenopausal pregnancy without technological aid);
c. specific limits, that some human beings experience while others do not (i.e. more or less severe disability).

In the first case, these so-called limits refer to impossibilities inherent to the human condition and nature; in the second and third cases, limits are abilities that the human species or one of the sexes possess but eventually lose or never acquire.

However, technology may surpass some of these limits, firstly and foremost by medically restoring normal abilities. For those who view deficiencies as nothing but differences, it would be legitimate for a deaf-mute couple to use pre-implantation diagnosis for deficiency-carrying embryo selection.[66]

Body limits are essentially those inherent to the human condition: finitude and frailty. The former unveil a *mortal body*, while the latter are attributes of a *frail* or vulnerable body in the etymological sense, i.e. a *body that may be wounded*, and also a body liable to illness and ageing.

Body Interventions

The anthropological experience of illness underlies medicine as care for the 'other', while death is behind attempts to overcome, or at least postponing it, and ageing has driven the pursuit for youth. However, these attempts were traditionally viewed as some sort of magical or even devilish pact ('selling the soul') forsaking the Jewish-Christian alliance.[67] Nowadays, 'invulnerability'[68] is pursued by more material means.

Medicine is, thus, an *ars* that confronts body limits. Medicine surpassed its helplessness with the emergence of the 'medical-technical power'[69] that has provided a broad range of treatments for disease. Now that society idolatrizes the body, medicine offers solutions to rejuvenate and mould a perfect body; death would be overcome or at least postponed by an amazing life expectancy increase (eternalized body), while genetic enhancement is well under way.

There is an asserted technical-scientific paradigm underlying all these attempts to overcome death. In fact, these attempts are one of Humankind's oldest aspirations, which – according to Condorcet,[70] in the context of the Enlightenment metanarrative of progress – medicine was obliged to fulfil. The notion of an *eternalized body* has Methuselahian contours and sees cryopreservation as a means to turn a corpse back to a living body, an inversion of the human being's natural trajectory. Eternity technologies increasingly resort to genetic intervention, although cloning is just

66 See Jonathan Glover, *Choosing children: genes, disability, and design* (Oxford/ New York 2008).

67 About this category see Scott Hahn, *Kinship by covenant: a canonical approach to the fulfilment of God's saving promises* (New Haven and London 2009).

68 Stuart Spicker, 'Invulnerability and medicine's «promise» of immortality: changing images of the human body during the growth of medical knowledge', in Henk A.M.J. Ten Have/ Gerrit K. Kimsma/ Stuart Spicker (ed.), *The growth of medical knowledge* (Dordrecht/Boston/London 1990) 163–175.

69 As explained by Jan Hendrik van den Berg, *Medische macht en medische ethiek*, 1969 *apud* Stuart Spicker, *Invulnerability*, cit., 163–64.

70 *Esquisse d'un tableau historique des progrès de l'esprit humain*, Paris, 1794 [*apud* Hans Küng, *Ewiges Leben?*, (6th edn München/ Zürich 1996) 21; transl.: *Eternal life?* (London 1984)].

an illusion[71] since human identity is unreplicable.[72] As a general rule, these projects aim to achieve a kind of quasi-immortality, whereby quasi means long life expectancy but not immortality, and immortality does not mean invulnerability,[73] since external factors like accidents and infectious diseases[74] are the new Achilles' heel.

As for medically assisted reproduction, for certain people sterility is now a limit that medical intervention may overcome. The availability of techniques targeted at new customers led to the demand for medically assisted reproduction rights, even for homosexual couples and single mothers. Moreover, postmenopausal pregnancies are now the banner for those who are past their fertile age.[75]

The defence of an enhanced body encompasses not only risk factors but also legal issues, as it paves the way for genetic type differentiation. State-of-the-art diagnosis techniques originate talk of a 'transparent body'. Traditionally speaking, medicine is all about correct diagnosis and information, wherein symptoms are a key element to medical practice. Now at stake is the creation of a *diagnosing body*, one which would have nanotechnologies integrate sensors in the biological system as a means for monitoring and promptly giving answers to various parameters.[76]

Nonetheless, (bio)medicine generates new limits to the human condition, due to error and risk in general, but also due to the possibility of survival with no chances of recovery or even in a persistent or chronic vegetative state. Such scenarios deepen human anguish and legitimize the limitation of intervention, provided that specific principles are met.

Bodiliness and Bioconstitutional Subjects

As far as subjects are concerned, the humanistic personicentrism of the bioconstitution is being increasingly criticized. If, on the one hand, many stumble upon its excessive inclusiveness, insofar as human beings are therein viewed as identical with persons, on the other hand we find those who accuse it of being anthropocentrically exclusivist, since it recognizes no legal personality whatsoever neither to animals nor to nature. With regard to the first question it is worth noting that any denial of subjectiveness to embryos or foetuses does not necessarily mean their 'annihilation' when it comes to their protection. Nonetheless, we ought to stress that any sort of 'fabricated life', any *in vitro* achievement, demand a previous densification of the concept of life, duly articulated with reality.

The bioconstitutional subjects issue has gained increasing relevance in both the intrahuman and the extrahuman realm. Though collective persons are beyond our concerns here, we must stress their instrumental and by no means irrelevant character, which ultimately allows for the self-accomplishment of the human person.

I am in disagreement with Teubner's[77] systemic view, as he bends toward recognizing partial legal personality to animals and other entities, and does so within the framework of a 'fragmentation

71 Béatrice de Montera, 'La génétique et l'illusion d'immortalité', in C. Hervé/ J.J. Rosenberg (ed.), *Vers la fin de l'homme?* (Bruxelles, 2006) 102.

72 Béatrice de Montera, *La génétique et l'illusion d'immortalité*, cit., 118–119.

73 John Harris, *Enhancing evolution*, cit., 60.

74 John Harris, *Enhancing evolution*, cit., 60.

75 For this question see, *inter alia*, Francesco D'Agostino, 'Menopausa', in idem, *Parole di bioetica* (Torino 2004) 121–28.

76 James R. Baker, 'Nanotechnology for biology and medicine', in William Sims Bainbridge/ Mihail C. Roco (ed.), *Managing nano-bio-cogno-innovations: converging biotechnologies in society* (Dordrecht 2006) 119–132, 122.

77 *Elektronische Agenten und grosse Menschenaffen: zur Ausweitung des Akteursstatus in Recht und Politik* (Zürich/ Basel/Genf 2007) 6.

of legal subjectivity'. Drawing upon Bruno Latour, Teubner further proposes the idea of 'actant' as a hybrid – a blend of object and human subject, in which the latter acts as 'person', in the very etymological sense of 'mask'.[78]

Human Life

The Referent Question

As we seek to define the constitutional subjects, we must stress at once that the very meaning of 'human life' stands as the first and foremost source of ambiguity. Strictly speaking, human life may refer to very different self-integrating levels, such as: cell, organism, population and species.[79] Although primarily concerned with the life of organisms, we are aware of the fact that legal consideration has also been devoted to the life of the species. In this case Humanity would be understood as a specific holder of rights; the human genome, taken as a common heritage of Humanity, is illustrative in this connection.[80]

Fabricated Human Life: What Framework?

The possibility of *in vitro* reproduction gave rise to a new set of issues. Our concern here is to assess whether the biological product of cloning processes by means of somatic nuclear transfer is a human embryo, or another entity unworthy of the same respect. This is also the case with altered nucleus transfer (ANT), whether by means of the 'switching off' of gene Cdx2 to prevent its normal development, or by 'oocyte-assisted reprogramming' (ANT-OAR[81]) so as to obtain pluripotent cells skipping the totipotent phase.[82]

Still concerned with the humanhood of lab-generated life or '*in vitro* humanity',[83] let us take the recent example of a type of cloning in which an animal oocyte is used, though the transferred nucleus is a human one. Cybrids[84] are used for stem cell harvesting and also for sheer experimentation. The word chimbrids[85] has thus been proposed to encompass hybrids, chimeras and other 'similar genetic mixtures'.[86]

---

78 Gunther Teubner, *Elektronische Agenten und grosse Menschenaffen*, cit., 15.

79 Angelo Serra/ Roberto Colombo, 'Identità e statuto dell'embrione umano: il contributo della biologia', in *Identità e statuto dell'embrione umano* (Città del Vaticano 1998) 106–158.

80 See, with other references, João Carlos Loureiro, *O direito à identidade genética do ser humano*, cit., especially 334–50.

81 OAR stands for oocyte-assisted reprogramming.

82 José Granados, 'ANT-OAR: it is underlying philosophy of biology sound?' 32 (2005) 32 *Communio* 724–43, 724–25.

83 Jesus Ballesteros (ed.), *La humanidad* in vitro (Granada 2002).

84 As to the *cybrids*, where the *c* relates to the cytoplasm and *ybrids* comes from hybrid, one should note that we are not faced with real hybrids. From the genetic point of view, we are confronted with an embryo that has more than 99 percent of human DNA – with an exception at the mitochondrial level. For its evaluation see, in an ethical perspective, Thomas Heinemann, 'Ethische Beurteilungskriterien für die Forschung an Stammzellen', in Thomas Heinemann/ Jens Kersten, *Stammzellforschung: naturwissenschaftliche, rechtliche und ethische Aspekte* (Freiburg/ München 2007), 236–38.

85 'The chimbrids project' (2008) 16 *Jahrbuch für Rechts und Ethik/ Annual Review of Law and Ethics* 499–519; now Jochen Taupitz/ Marion Weschka (ed.), *Chimbrids – chimeras and hybrids in comparative, European and International research: scientific, ethical, philosophical and legal aspects* (Berlin/ Heidelberg 2009).

86 As underlined in the project, the traditional distinction between hybrids and chimeras became itself problematic (*The chimbrids project*, cit., 501).

Post-Humanism(s)

Voices from the post-humanism trend have proposed a number of candidates for legal personality. First and foremost among such candidates are animals, but Nature and even robots are also included in such list. Actually, the following post-humanistic views are quite diverse:[87] a) the zoological or animalist; b) the biocentric, i.e. the one under the sign of Gaia; c) the (biologically) hybrid; d) the cyborgian vision; e) and the informational.

Regarding the issue of robots, and as we all know, the cybernetic reductionism sought to view the body as mere hardware and the mind as software. Drawing upon some of the puritan views on the body as an unclean reality,[88] such cybernetic reductionism might be summarized in the following set of equations: 1) human being = brain; 2) brain = machine; 3) human being = machine.[89] While an analysis of these propositions cannot be undertaken here, we can at least point out that any reduction of human beings to their brain is tantamount to mutilation, for one should bear in mind that we are 'sentient intelligence.'[90] The body, rather than being a mere accident, is an essential modality of the human condition. Hence, any attempt to transcend the limits of the body ought to be confronted with the notion of human body as a limit where as a set of interventions is concerned.

Another quite different question is whether non-human persons could be holders of rights. We do know that, in the theological discussions that eventually led to the definition of the concept of person in order to solve the question of God's triunity, 'person' also designated God and the angels. Borrowing the example of Data, in the *Star Trek* series, we might debate whether a robot holds rights.[91] Along with the criterion of intelligence, we also assume love as a distinctive mark. Thus, we cannot rule out that, granted they could ever be, robots like David – the one featuring in *Artificial Intelligence* by Spielberg[92] – should eventually be considered as persons holding rights.

87 We use herein this formula in a wide context, considering that only for a minority the 'overstepping of the species' boundaries' are at stake [Dieter Birnbacher, *Natürlichkeit* (Berlin/ New York 2006) 174]. See also João Carlos Loureiro, 'Bios, tempo(s) e mundo(s): algumas reflexões sobre valores, interesses e riscos no campo biomédico', in José de Faria Costa/ Inês Fernandes Godinho (org.), *As novas questões em torno da vida e da morte em direito penal: uma perspectiva integrada* (Coimbra 2010) 195–230.

88 Derrick de Kerchove [*apud* Jesús Ballesteros, 'Biotecnología, biolítica y posthumanismo', in Jesús Ballesteros/ Encarnación Fernández (Coord.), *Biotecnologia y posthumanismo* (Navarra 2007) 21–46, 37] recalls the puritan perspective of the body as 'imperfect, dirty, sinful and absolutely non-indispensable'.

89 We evoke Juan L. Ruiz De La Peña, *Las nuevas antropologías: un reto a la teología* (2nd edn Santander, 1983).

90 Xavier Zubiri, *Inteligencia sentiente* (Madrid 1980), *Inteligencia y* logos (Madrid 1982), *Inteligencia y razón* (Madrid 1983) [transl.: *Sentient intelligence* (Washington, DC 1999)].

91 Robert Alexy, *Data und die Menschenrechte: positronisches Gehirn und doppeltriadischer Personenbegriff*, Beitrag im Rahmen der 'Ringvorlesung des Instituts für Neuere Deutsche Literatur und Medien zur Erforschung von Populärkultur am Beispiel von STAR TREK', de 8.2.2000, Kiel University, available at http://www.uni-kiel.de/alexy/startrek/index.htm; there is a Spanish translation, with an introductory study by Alfonso García Figueroa: *Star Trek y los derechos humanos* (Valencia 2007).

92 We cannot explore herein other films suitable for discussing the concept of personality: see Stephen Coleman/Richard Hanley, *Homo sapiens, robots, and persons* in *I, Robot* and *Bicentennial Man*', in Sandra Shapshay (ed.), *Bioethics at the movies* (Baltimore 2009), 44–55.

Bioconstitutional Goods and Interventions: Possibilities

Prior to discussing goods, let me start by clarifying their meaning, for unlike in criminal law, this concept seems to be taken for granted in the constitutional field.[93] I take goods as physical (objective) or (subjective) ideal entities that are positively estimated;[94] they can be either personal or communitarian, final or instrumental, single or systemic, disposable and undisposable; they eventually allow for the 'dynamism of living together'[95] and also, in some direct or indirect way, for the flourishing[96] of the human being. When considered from the constitutional (formal and/ or material) viewpoint, i.e., as something received and developed in the law system, they may be called juridical goods.

As to the *determination* of bioconstitutional goods, let us point out first of all the reference to bodiliness as their common feature. The discussion of a new set of goods, genetic identity included, is well under way. As a matter of fact, the possibilities of genetic intervention have given rise to an autonomous good which explicitly asserts itself in some constitutional texts (the Portuguese[97] and also the Greek[98]). It also enjoys some degree of acceptance in other legal systems, though within the framework of more general constitutional norms.[99]

Within a typological approach, one may find objective as well as subjective goods. The former have as referents, according to Josef Isensee, 'physical or ideal substances, which are protected as such; they ought not to be subjected to the self-determination of the holder of fundamental rights, insofar as they are inherent to him (like life), or in any case bear some sort of relationship with him (...)'.[100] Regarding subjective goods, they point toward the self-determination of the holder in certain domains or spheres.[101] The bulk of this debate has been on whether goods traditionally considered as plainly objective (like life or physical integrity) are to be subjectivized.

Of special relevance in the bioconstitutional field is the distinction between disposable and undisposable goods. The former are those which the holder may alienate with or without payment, or even destroy. Undisposable goods are the ones withdrawn from its holder's will. Disposability concerns the good as a whole, rather than any part of it. Accordingly, the living body ought to be understood as a totally undisposable good, even though some partial disposal of it is admissible, provided body unity is not jeopardized.

93 For more developments see *Constituição e biomedicina*, cit., vol. I, part I, the study where this notion was proposed.

94 Revisiting the notion of good proposed by Günther Jakob, *Strafrecht, Allgemeiner Teil: die Grundlage und die Zurechnungslehre: Lehrbuch* (2th edn Berlin/New York 1993) 39.

95 Xavier Zubiri, *Estructura dinámica de la realidad* (Madrid, 1989) [transl.: *Dynamic structure of reality*, Urbana 2003) 162.

96 For this notion see John Finnis, *Natural law and natural rights* (Oxford 1982).

97 Art. 26/nr. 3.

98 Art. 5/nr. 5.

99 For Brazil, see João Carlos Loureiro, *O direito à identidade genética do ser humano*, cit., 351–59; Selma Petterle, *O direito fundamental à identidade genética na Constituição brasileira* (Porto Alegre 2007); idem, 'Notas sobre a fundamentação e a titularidade do direito fundamental à identidade genética na Constituição brasileira', in Ingo Wolfgang Sarlet/ George Salomão Leite (org.), *Direitos fundamentais e biotecnologia* (São Paulo, 2008) 237–61.

100 'Der Grundrecht als Abwehrrecht und staatliche Schutzpflicht', in Josef Isensee/ Paul Kirchhof (Hrsg.), *Handbuch des Staatsrechts der Bundesrepublik Deutschland*, Bd. V, *Allgemeine Grundrechtslehren* (Heidelberg 1992) 143–240, 166.

101 Josef Isensee, *Der Grundrecht als Abwehrrecht*, cit., which we will follow very closely on this aspect.

Bioconstitutional Positions

The protection of bioconstitutional goods presupposes the recognition of a set of constitutional positions (e.g. rights and duties). As for rights, we may observe that the classical list of rights is expanding itself, *via* hermeneutics and other means, so as to include other positions. Even core rights, like the very right *to* life, are (re)discussed within the framework of autonomy, in an attempt to find out whether they also ought to include a right *over* life.

Moreover, since rights may also enter in conflict among themselves, a set of limits to the so-called fundamental positions has also asserted itself. Alongside the concrete constitutional framework, it is by no means indifferent how both (*a priori* or *a posteriori*) legal limits and any previous determination of the scope of protection of a given right, are to be understood in juridical dogmatics. Although a right to refuse medical treatment is nowadays recognized, the existence of cases of coercive treatment should not be ignored.[102]

The door is thus being opened not just to the traditional rights but more specifically to a broad theory of the fundamental duties[103] that encompasses both the personal duties – *stricto sensu* duties – and the different duties of the state (protective duties, positive state action duties, and also duties to ensure).

In the bioconstitutional field one finds expressed the need to cooperate in health protection. The Portuguese constitution, for instance, lays down a duty to defend and promote it.[104] With regard to the human genetics field, one may take a look at the ongoing discussion on the determination of the newest duties. Thus, along with the tension between duties of non-interference in the human genome and the case of a certain view on freedom of procreation, one also finds a case for both conception avoidance duties and even for embryo discarding. To such end, the foremost argument would be so-called 'right not to be born handicapped' coupled with a broad reflection on the value of non-existence.[105] In one word, we have entered the realm of so-called *wrongful life*.

Within a rather futuristic scenario, the case is also made whether parents would not be required to use, when available, instruments for therapy and also for genetic enhancing, lest they be liable for a *wrongful genetic makeup*.

Regarding projects for (quasi-)immortality, the point now at stake is the duty to die,[106] as the condition of possibility for the *novum* that every birth entails. The debate, however, is over the scarcity of resource and over the fact that the growing life expectancy entails an expenditure boom in terminal disease cases. Besides, the duty to die,[107] here understood as one's renouncing to the use of available technologies, would also assert itself under the cover of solidarity at family and/ or the national level.

---

102 Jean-Marie Auby, 'Le corps humain et le droit: les droits de l'homme sur son corps', in *Direito da saúde e bioética* (Lisboa 1991) 169–181, 180–181.

103 For details, see João Carlos Loureiro, *Constituição e biomedicina*, vol. I, cit., part II.

104 Art. 64/nr. 1. For an elaboration, see João Carlos Loureiro, *Constituição e biomedicina*, vol. II, cit., part V.

105 For other indications, see João Carlos Loureiro, 'Genética, moinhos e gigantes: Quixote revisitado: deveres fundamentais, «sociedade de risco» e biomedicina', in Agustín Jorge Barreiro (ed.), *Derecho y genética: un reto a la sociedad del siglo XXI* (Madrid 2006) 29–48, 43–45.

106 John Harris [*Enhancing evolution: the ethical case for making better people* (Princeton, N.J. Woodstock 2007) 69], a defender of these techniques, points out the need of a 'generational cleansing' to be decided collectively.

107 John Hardwig, *Is there a duty to die?* (New York/London 2000); James M. Humber / Robert F. Almeder, *Is there a duty to die*? (Totowa/ New Jersey, 2000).

Bioconstitutional Principles

While recognizing the autonomy of bioconstitutional principles vis-à-vis the bioethical ones – themselves as controversial – it is our contention that, given the existent points of convergence between both types of principles, a number of the former should be underscored in connection with the latter. The foundational principle is, thus, the dignity of the human person.

Dignity as a Foundational Principle
Since a thorough treatment will not be possible here, I start by presenting one notion and a few theses. Thus, human dignity – here taken as synonymous with the dignity of the human person, a view which is far from being consensual[108] – means the intrinsic value which is accorded to every human being from the outset, grounded in his/her ethical autonomy and grounding the general obligation of owing respect to every single person, an obligation enforcing certain correlative rights and duties.

I propose the following theses:

1. regarding the *systemic* level, an *open* and *dynamic*[109] theory of the human dignity, one that reaches beyond the strict limits of 'comprehensive doctrine' (borrowing the all too well-known expression by Rawls[110]);
3. as to the *scope of protection*, a theory of differentiation between the human person's dignity and the whole range of fundamental rights. In other words, the different rights harbour some 'content of human dignity' and this dignity operates, as a rule, through each of the fundamental positions. In the Portuguese constitution's case, the vast list of rights therein recognized only in a subsidiary and exceptional mode allows us to speak of autonomous violation of dignity;
4. the recognition, in *juridical-structural terms*, of the objective and subjective dimension of the principle; the former allows for *postmortem* projection of human dignity and the corresponding corpse protection;
5. concerning the *perspectives*, dignity viewed in terms of one's relation toward others as its beneficiaries (*alterity*), there is an obligation of respect, and the state plays a fundamental role as to the protection and promotion of dignity. In terms of *selfhood* (rights-holding viewpoint) – that is, given our narrative identity as a process – not only are we entitled to bodiliness safeguarding and to positive state aid duties, but we also have a dimension which is grounded in our personal self-determination. The latter dimension makes the person belong *ab initio* to the realm of coexistentiality, with limits directly and indirectly stemming from other individuals, but stemming also from the systemic and communitarian realms. Such coexistentiality is key to personal flourishing. The fewer the possibilities for a person's autonomy and the greater his/her vulnerability is, the greater the demand to protect and provide, both on the state's part and on the part of those – for example parents – who in

108 The theses of differentiation recommend: (1) either the inclusion, in human dignity, of the so-called dignity of Mankind; (2) or consider that not all human beings are persons, following a line that for instance Jürgen Habermas (*Die Zukunft der menschlichen Natur*: *auf dem Weg zur liberalen Eugenik?*, Frankfurt am Main, 2002, 71–80; transl.: *The future of the human nature*, cit.), translates as the differentiation between human dignity and the dignity of human life.

109 For instance Carlos Romeo Casabona in Comité de Expertos sobre Bioética y Clonación, *Informe sobre la clonación*: *en las fronteras de la vida* (Madrid 1999), 175.

110 *Political liberalism*, cit.

legal terms may have any special duties of care.[111]

Bioconstitutional Structuring Principles

The Principle of Human Life's Inviolability As a basic good, although not an absolute one, life exhibits an all-or-nothing structure. Nonetheless, a case for 'euthanasia with indications'[112] is being made based upon the argument of body limits coupled with an idea of self-determination. Moreover, malformations taken as unacceptable limits of the body have opened the door to the selection of *in vitro* embryos and also to the upholding in many legal systems of an embryopathic indication, autonomized or operating *via* therapeutic indication.

By and large, an underestimation of seriously disabled bodies coupled with the principle of equality claim has dramatically undermined the principle of human life's inviolability. Obviously, such undermining is stretching out even beyond birth, in so-called early or neonatal euthanasia.[113]

The Autonomy Principle The autonomy principle is key, within the framework of the bioconstitution, as it encompasses different dimensions or sub-principles. Of particular importance for our purposes is the health care professionals' situation, which all too often has to deal both with the informed consent-related issues and with conscientious objection. Along with the end of the axiological consensus over principles such as the inviolability of human life – in euthanasia – and abortion-related situations – for instance, the multiplication of possibilities stemming from medically assisted procreation, and from widespread access to so-called emergency contraception (e.g.), has dramatically widened the grounds for health care professionals to resort to conscientious objection, as well as for the fuelling of a burning controversy over its limits. Where abortion is concerned, conscientious objection is, by and large,[114] acknowledged; controversy, however, is ignited, for instance, by the refusal, on conscientious objection grounds, of *in vitro* fertilization to a lesbian where it is legally possible. In a time of hyperdiversity, we may also face situations where, for instance, a Muslim female physician invokes conscientious objection and religious freedom as grounds for her refusal to provide medical treatment to male patients in the emergency room. Another issue hearkening back to the autonomy principle is a right not to know, bearing on self-

---

111 On this question, in a more detailed manner and with the correspondent bibliographic references, see João Carlos Loureiro, 'Os genes do nosso (des)contentamento (Dignidade humana e genética: notas de um roteiro)', in Rui Nunes/ Helena Melo/ Cristina Melo, *Genoma e dignidade humana* (Coimbra 2002), 205–249.

112 Hans Küng, 'Menschenwürdig sterben', in Walter Jens/ Hans Küng, *Menschenwürdig sterben: ein Plädoyer für Selbstverantwortung* (München/ Zürich 1995) 13–85 [transl.: *Dying with dignity: a plea for personal responsibility* (New York 1995)].

113 Miriam Saati, *Früheuthanasie* (Frankfurt am Main 2001); Reinhard Merkel, *Früheuthanasie: rechtsethische und strafrechtliche Grundlagen ärztlicher Entscheidungen über Leben und Tod in der Neonatalmedizin* (Baden-Baden 2002); on the Portuguese doctrine, see Manuel da Costa Andrade, *Consentimento e acordo*, cit.; Fernando Araújo, *A procriação assistida e o problema da santidade da vida* (Coimbra 1999) 125–128; Helena Moniz, 'Eutanásia precoce: dúvidas e interrogações', in Jorge de Figueiredo Dias/ Nuno Brandão [Comentário conimbricense ao Código penal, I (2nd edn, Coimbra 2012) 294].

114 See, however, the hypothesis of the so-called strict therapeutic indication, with the intervention of the conscientious objectors doctors 'constituting the only mean of eliminating the risk of death or serious or irreversible lesion for the body or the physical or psychic health of a pregnant woman' (art. 142/1/a) of the Portuguese Criminal Code). For doctrine, on all these aspects, see Jorge de Figueiredo Dias [*Comentário conimbricense ao Código penal*, I (Coimbra 1999) 199–200].

determination and the right to the disposal of one's body (e.g. organ selling, 'renting' uterus).

The Integrity Principle Starting with the psychosomatic unity of the human being, our focus is the defence of personal integrity, rather than the integrity of the human species. The etymological stem of integrity (*integritas*) is *tag*, which conveys the notion of 'untouchability' along with the idea of remaining 'whole' and 'not corrupted.[115] So, when it comes to the normative field that same concept may be usefully brought into the identity issue, be it the biological (genetic and bodily) – an identity as sameness – or the narrative, personal identity (identity as selfhood).[116] From a legal perspective, not every affecting of one's integrity entails the affecting of identity.

The contention is made that, with exception made to *post-mortem* usages (and the latter should only apply within some very restricted limits), a right to whole-body disposal is non-existent. Even in what concerns parts of the body there are limits. As Mariachiara Tallacchini argues,[117] it is important to avoid a legally relevant double reductionism, to wit: the 'downward reductionism', one that reduces the body to just the mere sum of its parts; the 'upward reductionism', that sacralizes every single element of it, by taking as human everything that has human origin (e.g., the case she advances in this respect is the method for producing insulin by inserting a human gene in the *Escherichia coli* bacteria).

The Principle of the Non-Commodification of the Human Body The case for the non-commodification of the human body assumes that an issue such as the determination of limits to one's disposal of the whole, or part, of the human body is already settled. Michael Walzer's complex model of the spheres of justice[118] would help us to see how, within a framework of 'blocked exchanges',[119] some specific zones lie outside the market sphere. The donation or gift paradigm is useful here,[120] and as Courtney Campbell has stated,[121] it encompasses four key notes: 'altruistic intent', 'therapeutic expectation', 're-incorporation' and 'receiver's responsibility'. With regard to scientific research purposes, he prefers to speak of a 'resource paradigm'[122] which is based on the *body surplus*, and aimed at generating information, that is, a symbolic 'reincorporation', the focus

---

115 Jean Bouffartigue/ Anne-Marie Delrieu, *Trésors des racines latines* (Paris 1981) 194.

116 Following Paul Ricoeur, *Soi-même comme un autre* (Paris 1990) [transl.: *Oneself as another* (Chicago, 1992)].

117 'Il corpo e le sue parti: l'allocazione giuridica dei materiali biologici umani' (1998/3) 48 *Medicina e Morale* 499–544, 514.

118 *Spheres of justice: a defence of pluralism and equality* (Oxford/Cambridge 1983). Michael Walzer does not treat the health's sphere autonomously. However, for the establishment of an autonomous domain within the theoretical framework proposed by Walzer, see Margo Trappenburg's work, *Soorten van gelijk: medisch-ethische discussies in Nederland* (Zwolle 1993) 269–336; in English language and in short, see idem, 'Defining the medical sphere', 6 (1997) *Cambridge Quarterly of Health Care Ethics* 416–34.

119 Michael Walzer, *Spheres of justice*, cit., 100, which refers to Okun.

120 This principle leads Gilda Ferrando ('Il principio di gratuità, biotecnologie e 'atti di disposizione del corpo' (2002) *Europa e diritto privato* 761–84, 767) to consider that, instead of speaking of 'acts of disposition of the body', it would be more appropriate to refer to 'acts of destination'.

121 *Vide* 'Research on human tissue: religious perspectives', in National Bioethics Advisory Commission, *Research involving human biological materials: ethical issues and policy guidance*, vol. II, Commissioned papers (Rockville, Maryland 2000), C-5 e C-6.

122 *Research on human tissue*, cit., C-7 to 9.

of which is insertion of the results into the 'body of scientific knowledge'.[123]

The *rationale* for this includes the ideas of human dignity and autonomy itself, and also a consequentialist approach. The Kantian contraposition between dignity and price ought to be recalled in connection with the idea of human dignity;[124] as to autonomy, suffice it to say that autonomy's guarantee would require, in view of protecting the weakest ones, the existence of a domain of 'blocked exchanges'; the consequentialist approach, in its turn, calls to mind the so-called *slippery slope* argument, also labelled as the 'dam break' effect (*Dammbrucheffekt*). The end result would therefore be a sort of 'domino theory'[125]: the commodification of certain goods (e.g., blood) could not take place without causing negative effects in the very goods being donated.[126]

As to the *legislative* plan, article 21 of the Convention on Human Rights and Biomedicine from the Council of Europe should be referred: 'The human body and its parts shall not, as such, give rise to financial gain'.

Nonetheless, markets of human organs and tissues are out there,[127] like a true 'body bazaar',[128] the basic rule of which is a distinction between the rich and the poor. Actually, the case for the commercialization of the body is on the rise, as manifested in the following examples: uterus 'renting', a form of paid surrogacy motherhood, already accepted by a number of legal systems; cell use targeting the formation of a cell lineage to be traded by some pharmaceutical company – most illustrative on this, is the John Moore case, known as the 'man with the golden cells'.[129]

The 'body as matter' view[130] is thus giving way to 'a logic of the 'economic-managing' sort'[131] – just think of the discussion on genome patenting, or the creation and diversification of a set of products from a human source (bioengineered products).

The Principle of Equal Access to Health Care The principle of equal access to health care is the expression of a principle of sociality. Given today's context, so marked by an escalation of costs, by so disparate answers, and by a significant population ageing, one cannot overlook the discussion over health care rationing, within a universe of scarcity. One of the foremost fears is the using of age – medically-prescribed cases are obviously not meant here – as a criterion for access, or restricting, the services provided. Even the latest developments in the genetic- and nano-technology field[132]

123 *Research on human tissue*, cit., C-8.

124 *Grundlegung zur Metaphysik der Sitten*, 1786 [transl.: *Grounding for the metaphysics of morals* (3rd edn, Indianapolis 1993].

125 Margaret Jane Radin, *Contested commodities: the trouble with trade in sex, children, body parts and other things*, (Cambridge (Mass.)/London 1996), cit., 95–101.

126 Predictably enough, empiric data availability is scarce. However, a study made in 1990 in Kuwait, based on an analysis of 72 transplantation cases performed abroad, revealed, in addition to other negative consequences, that there was among relatives a lesser predisposition for donations from the moment on that alternatives were found for obtaining an organ [see Erwin Bernat, 'Verso la commercializzazione di organi umani?', in Cosimo Marco Mazzoni, *Una norma giuridica per la bioetica* (Bologna 1998), 193–206, 205–206].

127 For all references see Giovanni Berlinguer/ Volnei Garrafa, *La merce finale: saggio sulla compravendita di parti del corpo umano* (Milano 1997) (transl.: *A mercadoria final: ensaio sobre a compra e venda de partes do corpo humano* (Lisboa 1997).

128 Lori Andrews/ Dorothy Nelkin, *Body bazaar: the market of human tissue in the biotechnology age* (transl.: *Il mercato del corpo: il commercio dei tessuti umani nell'era biotecnologica* (Milano 2002).

129 Bernard Edelman, 'L'homme aux celulles d'or', *Recueil Dalloz* (1989).

130 Bruno Cadoré, *L'expérience bioéthique de la responsabilité* (Bruxelles 1994) 76–78, who considers other 'body states' in medicine, like the '«exploited» body', the 'technical body' and the 'fragile body'.

131 Bruno Cadoré, *L'expérience bioéthique de la responsabilité*, cit., 77.

132 James R. Baker, *Nanotechnology for biology and medicine*, cit., 130.

are likely to give room not only for discriminations, but also for juridical issues implicating the constitution itself. Scholarship refers the following examples as illustrative: within the labor market field, the 'optimized' candidates for whom a 'genetic enhancement certificate' would be required;[133] in a scenario of xenotransplantation, the differentiated access to organs (e.g., porcine or humans[134]); and, in case immortality should be a possibility, the coexistence of mortals and immortals.

The so-called gender differentiation view rightly observes that, under the cloak of equality, some specific needs (women's specific needs,[135] for instance) are being overlooked.

The issue of (un)equal health care access, both in absolute (refusal of access) and relative terms (the need to pay for access), is being more and more debated with regard to patients with high-risk lifestyles (smokers, for instance). Actually, the solidarity dimension, as a basic feature of the 'European constitutional state type',[136] would find itself confronted with the merit principle as far medical care access is concerned.[137]

The Familiarity Principle Especially stressed by some Italian authors,[138] the familiarity principle has been advanced in the area of genetic information and mainly in connection with medically assisted procreation matters. Typical of the latter are traditional requirements such as biparenthood – so-called 'independent production' is ruled out – and heterosexuality, while the access of homosexual couples is ruled out altogether. Since both biparenthood and heterosexuality requirements are nowadays under the fire of criticism, it is no wonder that several legal systems have adopted solutions allowing for the aforementioned techniques to be available, not only to single mothers and homosexual partners, by and large lesbians, but also to male partners, provided surrogate motherhood is accepted by the legal system. This familiarity principle is also advanced so as to prohibit the use of gametes that might violate the interdict of incest and also question the symbolic value of family relations.

The Precautionary Principle In a '(world) risk society', and since the principle of prevention has proven itself to be insufficient in so many fields as it takes the idea of danger as its starting point, the precautionary principle ought to be taken seriously[139] to evaluate interventions in the body. Initially developed in the environmental sphere, the principle under consideration has been applied to broaden the realm of the relevant risks, so as to take into account situations in which a causal nexus has not (yet?) been found. This principle requires an evaluation of the proceedings used (for example ICSI techniques for medically assisted procreation) and, for now, it legitimates the

133 Allen Buchanan/ Dan W. Brock/ Norman Daniels/ Daniel Wikler, *From chance to choice: genetics and justice* (Cambridge 2001) 3–4.

134 François Pothier, 'Y-a-t-il une limite à la modification biotechnologique de l'être humain?', in Jean-Pierre Béland (Dir.), *L'homme biotech: humain ou posthumain*? (Québec 2006) 35–44, 39.

135 Marjet J. Gunning, 'Discriminatie in de gezondheidszorg: eigen bijdrage in strijd med het vrouwenverdrag' (1996) 71 *Nederlands Juristenblad* 1362–1367.

136 Peter Häberle, 'Die europäische Verfassungsstaatlichkeit', 78 (1995), *Kritische Vierteljahresschrift für Gesetzgebung und Rechtswissenschaft* 298–312.

137 Margo Trappenburg, 'Lifestyle solidarity in the healthcare system', 8 (2000) *Health Care Analysis* 65–75.

138 E.g. Francesco D'Agostino, *Bioetica nella prospettiva della filosofia del diritto* (Torino 1998).

139 For other references and developments see João Carlos Loureiro, 'Da sociedade técnica de massas à sociedade de risco: prevenção, precaução e tecnociência. Algumas questões juspublicísticas', in *Estudos em homenagem ao Prof. Doutor Rogério Soares* (Coimbra 2001) 797–891.

prohibition of germinal gene therapy and somatic cell nuclear transfer (SCNT) to produce children.

The Cooperation Principle In the health care sphere, the cooperation principle can be seen at the interdisciplinary level (one should bear in mind the multiplicity of actors involved in today's health care systems) and at the institutional level (articulation of the different providers) in the network creation of scientific knowledge, in the ethical and scientific procedures evaluation, and when duties are concerned: either general duties, i.e. community members' ones (think of the aforementioned duty to defend and promote health), or specific duties, i.e. the patients' duties.[140] A noteworthy example is, in what health policies are concerned, the growing number of hearings of patients associations.

The Sustainability Principle To the above list we may add a 'sustainability principle',[141] especially relevant for risk societies and for societies where new dimensions of scarcity are being reached. Ecological or environmental sustainability,[142] as a condition of possibility for human life; financial sustainability, within a framework where access to health care faces a rationing of the services provided; social sustainability, given the challenges arising from either dramatic demographic changes (on account of which the foundations of so-called 'generational contract' are endangered), or from the scenarios that somehow suggest a *mimesis* of Methuselah, one that might dramatically increase life expectancy.

An exemplary way of expressing the first dimension, i.e. environmental sustainability, would be by means of a new categorical imperative, in the wake of Hans Jonas: 'act so that the effects of your action are compatible with the permanence of genuine human life'; or, negatively put: 'act so that the effects of your action are not destructive of the future possibility of such life'.[143]

The second one, i.e. financial sustainability, which often touches upon the equal access to health care principle, is leading some scholars to suggest age as a way of differentiation (among other criteria) and to reflect upon the scope of medicine.

The third dimension – social sustainability – has led some scholars to make the case of a duty to die, so as to ensure the Earth's habitability (on this, they are crossing paths with environmental sustainability) as well as the *novum* which natality entails, a topic so masterfully dealt with by Hannah Arendt.

Epilogue

In closing this chapter, I can say that a bioconstitutional *corpus* has been developed, one which aims at frameworking interventions in the body, and at the same time faces new challenges. Bodiliness, actually, signals the condition of a human being that laughs and mourns, tastes pleasure and drinks the cup of sorrow and suffering and that yearns for health whilst often experiencing illness too.

---

140 For instance, the obligation of the beneficiaries, provided for in art. 13/2 of the Portuguese Medically Assisted Procreation Law (Law nr. 32/2006, of July the 26th, concerning the results' evaluation, notably 'to provide all information related with health and the development of children born using these techniques'.

141 Markus Vogt, *Prinzip Nachhaltigkeit: ein Entwurf aus theologisch-ethischer Perspektive* (München 2009).

142 About the complexity of sustainability see for all Wolfgang Kahl (Hrsg.), *Nachhaltigkeit als Verbundbegriff*, (Tübingen 2008).

143 *Das Prinzip Verantwortung*, cit., 11.

Chapter 7

Protecting Persons v. Protecting Humans in Biobanks

Judit Sándor

Introduction

In this chapter I would like to explore the ambiguous and fragmented legal framework that has developed in the field of genetic data since the Human Genome Project. In my view, ambiguity stems partly from some of the current legal developments in biomedical research on the human tissue and on biobanks: these legal norms originally set out to protect *persons* (in the legal sense), but also were intended to protect *humans* (in the biological sense) as they exist in tissues, cells and DNA, because they have 'human origin'. This dual aim of the new legal norms often remained hidden or, at least, was left without significant reflection. Furthermore, it contributed to the prolonged ambiguities and uncertainties related to the privacy and ownership debates on the human body. Therefore, I intend to unfold the reasons and scope of this dual aim by identifying some of the obstacles that hinder the thorough assessment of the main fields in which we now routinely use genetic data. Despite the widespread application of genetic data in research,[1] legal frameworks of biobanks remain uncertain as to whom to protect and how to protect. Thus, should we protect *human tissues* as *persons*? Should we grant property rights on the DNA samples? Are there any alternative to respect the rights of research participants?

Public discourse on genetics is greatly influenced by the emblematic nature and powerful symbolism of the human DNA. One may assume that it is this symbolic character of the *human* DNA that played a crucial role in the conceptual shift from the protection of *persons* to the protection of *humans* in the legal discourses on genetic data. In response to advances in genetics during the past two decades after the completion of the Human Genome Project, law has provided two sharply distinguishable solutions to the emerging legal challenges. The first one developed a 'rhetoric of skepticism' and argued that there is nothing new and nothing special about genetic research and genetic data, therefore already existing legal reasoning can be applicable to these fields. The other position passionately claimed the novel character of genetic research and emphasized the unique specificities of genetic data.

Molecular biologists and social scientists have enthusiastically attached various labels on genes from 'Holy Grail'[2] to 'Rosetta Stone of Life'.[3] But one can see that critics of genetic studies have also applied strong and colorful vocabulary, such as 'gene fetishism'[4] used by Haraway, while

1 http://www.businessweek.com/2000/00_15/b3676117.htm last accessed: 28.03.2012.

2 Allison Morse (1998) *Searching for the Holy Grail: The Human Genome Project and Its Implications* in: Journal of Law and Health, Vol. 13. No. 2

3 Kaushik Sunder Rajan, *Biocapital: The Constitution of Postgenomic Life* (Durham: Duke University Press, 2006), 138.

4 Donna Haraway, *Modest_Witness@Second_Millenium. FemaleMan@_Meets_Oncomouse* (London and New York: Routledge, 1997), 215, (London and New York: Routledge, 1989), 142–148.

some others mention 'geneticization'[5] which refers to an ideology that reduces individual attributes to genetic diagnosis. Since the beginning of the debates on the regulation of genetic research and use of genetic data exaggerating tones on both sides prevented to create a friendly environment for good regulation.

The other obstacles to the coherent normative framework can be identified in the multiple uses of genetics, from paternity tests, to criminal investigations, from assessing susceptibility to certain diseases to genetic discoveries that may result in developing intellectual property; from collecting genetic data for uncertain future research to the direct therapeutic benefit for the patients. All these distinct domains require different legal assessment and often different normative solutions, as well. Regardless of the critical reflections, genes are conceived more and more as sources of information for biomedical or forensic research; they are applied as tools for diagnosis or therapy; and they are also used as data in actuarial calculi and many other fields. What is relevant that genes can be interpreted as sensitive personal data that are capable to reveal significant information about the individual. In any case, genes are seen as precious entities, valuables and, as such, raise the issues of ownership and property.

Interventions with the aim to cure children's suffering, (for example, from cancer) are accepted more easily by the general public, even if they call for the use of genetic engineering, than scientific researches that do not promise immediate therapeutic benefits. The situation is different when genetic information is not intended to be used for therapeutic or research purposes, but in connection with insurance, the creation of patents or the establishment of business-oriented biobanks. In these fields of activities, the general public tends to be even more suspicious, and the law also tends to stipulate stricter conditions for the use of genetic knowledge.

Another source of ambiguity is the false perception that laws have to be renewed whenever a new technology appears on the horizon. In the face of new challenges, the law should not set up new legal institutions automatically, but rather endeavour to insert the new knowledge among the existing legal principles with a view to maintaining the proper consistency. If the legal system were turned upside down for every technical novelty or innovation, the basic construction of the rule of law would collapse due to the loss of predictability. For this reason, the extent of legal innovation tends to be much smaller than the strong drive of science for innovation. If a technical or scientific novelty emerges, legal thinking will turn to incorporation and interpretation, rather than to the establishment of a new legal institution.[6]

This approach also explains why the most significant European document on biomedicine is based on the already existing norms of human rights. Adopted in 1997 in Oviedo, after several years of consultations, the convention is the key pan-European source of law in relation to the issues of biomedicine.[7] It follows from this convention, as well as from the European Convention on Human Rights that the principle right that can be applied in the field of biobanks and genetic research is the right to privacy (or right to private and family life). So we should examine this right more closely.

---

5 Rayna Rapp (1999), *Testing women, testing the fetus: the social impact of amniocentesis in America* (London.: Routledge).

6 Judit Sándor, 'Human Rights and Bioethics: Competitors or Allies? The Role of International Law in Shaping the Contours of a New Discipline'. *Medicine and Law*, vol. 27, no. 1 (March 2008): 15–28.

7 Convention on Human Rights and Biomedicine of 4 April 1997 is known as the Oviedo Convention. It has now been ratified by 21 member states and entered into force in 1999. This is the first binding instrument that explicitly links human rights and bioethics.

Right to privacy in the biobank

In order to assess the relevance of privacy in biobanks we have to go back to the history of the right to privacy, especially to its function to protect individuals against technical intrusions into their private spheres. The legendary article written by Samuel D. Warren and Louis D. Brandeis on the right to privacy was published in 1890 in the *Harvard Law Review*.[8] It is one of the most frequently cited and most accepted justifications for the right to privacy. The passionate tone of the article, which had been motivated by the private injuries suffered by the authors' families, is still forceful and today it is not only part of the American legal literature but its reasoning is often cited in international legal scholarship as well.

In their groundbreaking article, the authors made the famous argument that the right to privacy should strengthen simultaneously with technological development. Without technological means of forwarding, a simple gossip, though unpleasant, can cause only limited injuries, but publishing the same information in a newspaper raises completely new challenges to the protection of privacy and personality. As property rights are also widening to encompass not only titles to physical objects but also to intellectual achievements, the protection of the persons' intellectual and emotional expressions are required to be extended in the same way. Brandeis' and Warren's argument has proven to be so flexible that it is applicable to every new situation that a technological advancement creates from telephone tapping through surveillance by street cameras to DNA sample collection. Contemporary legal instruments all refer to the notion of privacy as a major principle that justifies protection and restricted use of the biological samples in biobanks.

Right to private life and data protection in Europe

Article 10 (2) of the Oviedo Convention states clearly that '[e]veryone is entitled to know any information collected about his or her health. However, the wishes of individuals not to be so informed shall be observed.'[9]

In connection with genetic research, there has emerged a growing demand for the establishment of genetic databanks operated in national or other institutional frameworks. These genetic databanks call for special regulations even if they are only involved in data storage and data management, or operate as tissue banks. Genetic tests provide specific challenges to the protection of private life.[10]

Though the rights to privacy were already appeared in the American jurisprudence at the end of the 19th century, the legal concept of data protection has appeared much later. The first law on data protection was introduced in continental Europe only in the 1970s. Early laws on the protection of data primarily focused on the technical aspects of the management of information and the safety of data management.[11] The first law on the protection of data was adopted in the State of Hessen in Germany in 1970, and it was only the beginning of a long list of laws and institutions created for a better protection of data on individuals. In Sweden, the Act on Data Protection established the

8 Samuel D. Warren and Louis D. Brandeis, 'The Right to Privacy'. *Harvard Law Review*, vol. 4, no. 5 (December 15, 1890): 193–220.

9 Oviedo Convention, *op.cit.*

10 Rebecca F. Furlong, 'Ethical, Legal and Social Issues: Out in the Open'. Editorial. *Genome Medicine* vol. 4, no. 2 (2012): 18 (Published online on February 27, 2012 at genomemedicine.com/content/4/2/18).

11 Viktor Mayer-Schönberger, General Development of Data Protection in Europe. In Philip E. Agre and Marc Rotenberg (eds), *Technology and Privacy: The New Landscape* (Cambridge, MA: MIT Press, 1997), 219–247.

Data Protection Council in 1973; and in Germany the 1990 amendment of the 1977 Data Protection Act created the office of the Data Protection Commissioner. This first generation of data protection norms was created on the basis of the concerns about the centralized collection of data. Since the beginning of the 1970s the legal norms formerly drafted in rather technical terms were replaced by the connection of the rights to privacy and the data protection norms. This phenomenon could be detected in the Austrian, Spanish and Portuguese regulations,[12] and led to the connection of data protection to constitutional rights.

What is so special about genetic data?

For a long time it was believed that anonym data could guarantee the highest level of protection for genetic data. However, many problems were identified in respect of systematic anonymization of genetic samples and data. First of all, anonym data cannot be matched with other health data and as such it is less relevant for scientific research. But taking into account the participants' interests it is also contestable as with anonymization a further feedback based on the request of the owner of the sample would be usually impossible.

One difficulty that laws on the biotechnologies always face is how to balance between legal and scientific definitions of certain terms. While science may develop comfortably without laying down strict legal definitions of the terms 'biobank' or 'genetic data', lawmaking requires these definitions to be exact and understood unequivocally, even across the related legal instruments. This, however, brings about the problem of inflexibility: as biotechnological inventions develop, such as in the fields of cloning or stem cell research, new advances might not fit the old definitions.

Genetic information has brought about specific legal problems in data processing, as well as in data protection.[13] The scope of genetic data itself is difficult to define. Certain family-related medical data should be viewed to belong to this category alongside susceptibility factors or *monogenic* disorders (caused by the defect or deficiency of a single gene). The accuracy of and potential for using these data are highly variable. Information on any hereditary disease has a serious impact on the lives and decisions of family members who may not have wanted to subject themselves to test examinations.

Genetic data have their implications on lifestyles, routines, selection of spouses, decisions to have children, career preferences and even the learning ambitions of people. Whoever decides to become acquainted with these parameters has the opportunity to become informed within the limits that the healthcare system can offer. In legal terms, the question is rather how to ensure the right to control genetic data. [14]

The main argument behind genetic exceptionalism is that personal genetic data should be processed under special legal guarantees, as genetic data can be considered not only as a simple health care data,[15] but it can also be used for identification purposes. In comparison with

12 See Section 35 of the Constitution of Portugal, the 1978 Act on data protection in Austria, and the 1978 Constitution of Spain.

13 William F. Mulholland and Amy S. Jaeger, 'Genetic Privacy and Discrimination: A Survey of State Legislation'. *Jurimetrics*, vol. 39, no. 3 (Spring 1999): 317–326.

14 Wolfram Henn, 'Genetic Screening with the DNA Chip: A New Pandora's Box?', *Journal of Medical Ethics*, vol. 25, no.2 (April 1999): 200–203.

15 In the sense as it is treated under Article 8 of the of the European Parliament and Council Directive 95/46/EC of 24 October 1995 on the Protection of individuals with regard to the processing of personal data and on the free movement of such data.

conventional medical data, another major difference is that genetic data do not only refer to the medical status of the examined person, but may reveal the medical characteristics of the affected family members or even children about to be born. Therefore, it can be claimed that medical data are generated without the persons concerned knowing about the existence of the data.

A key condition of the legislative act on data protection is that any data processing should be bound to a specific purpose. Thus, personal data may only be processed for stated purposes, towards the proper exercise of rights and fulfillment of obligations. Data processing should comply with the given purpose in all its phases. Furthermore, only such personal data can be managed that are essential to accomplish the given objective of data management, suitable for the purpose stated, but only to the extent and for the duration actually required for the accomplishment of the underlying objective. So in strict interpretation medical data – not to mention genetic information – generated for medical purposes, and – for instance – forming parts of a given documentation, cannot be disclosed in their original form to insurance companies, but may be revealed only to the extent they are absolutely necessary for the insurance activities.

Many distinguished social scientists, even bioethicists,[16] however, did not subscribe to these special claims associated with regulation on genetics. In order to challenge the legitimacy of the particular regulation they pointed out that many characteristics of the data – predictive, particular, sensitive – can be also seen in other types of health care data. In the European jurisprudence, especially in the decisions of the European Court of Human Rights protections of health care data together with the data on private and family life have been acknowledged in several important court decisions.[17]

Legal scholars are also hesitant to jump to enact special legal provisions to genetic data.[18] Usually health care professionals, especially those who work in the field of biobanks favour *tabula rasa* and are eager to seek specific a law that governs their situation so that they do not have to worry about often vague legal interpretations of general legal norms on data protection.

The importance of the genetic data motivated several legislations worldwide. For instance, regarding the Hungarian Parliamentary *Act No XXI of 2008 on the protection of human genetic data and the regulation of human genetic studies, research and biobanks*, one may state that it has become shorter and simpler than in the original policy paper in a desperate effort to avoid sensitive issues. Thus, the law addresses the use of genetic information only in the very narrow biomedical sector: in the fields of genetic testing, screening, and research. The law restricts the use of genetic data only in this biomedical context so even in the lack of regulation of the broader use of genetic data based on the Act genetic data processed for diagnostic or research purposes cannot be disseminated for the purposes of insurance. Despite the intended laconic law the mere word 'genetics' was a calling for a vehement debate by various political actors. Fears of genetic discrimination, exploitation or trafficking data to foreign countries were the major concerns in the political debate. Maybe it is not an exaggeration to say that this law served as a learning

16 For example, Søren Holm challenged genetic exceptionalism already in 1997, see Søren Holm, 'There is Nothing Special about Genetic Information'. In Alison K. Thomson, Ruth Chadwick (eds) *Genetic Information* (Dordrecht and New York: Kluwer Academic Publishers, 1997).

17 *Z. v. Finland*, no. 9/1996/627/811, § 95; ECtHR 27 August 1997, *M.S. v. Sweden*, no.74/1996/693/885, § 41; ECtHR 17 July 2008, *I. v. Finland*, no. 20511/03, § 38; ECtHR 25 November 2008, *Biriuk v. Lithuania*, no. 23373/03, § 39; ECtHR 25 November 2008, *Armonienė v. Lithuania*, no. 36919/02, § 40; ECtHR 28 April 2009, *K.H. and others v. Slovakia*, no. 32881/04, § 55; ECtHR 2 June 2009, *Szuluk v. The United Kingdom*, no. 36936/05, § 47; ECtHR 2 November 2010

18 Atina Krajewska, 'Conceptual Quandaries about Genetic Data: A Comparative Perspective', *European Journal of Health Law* 16 (2009): 7–26.

exercise for the wider public on contemporary ethical issues in genetics. In addition to regulating and interpreting privacy protection in the field of genetics, the other consideration of why rights are re-interpreted in this domain is the prohibition of discrimination.

It follows from the spirit of data protection norms that even rules on biomedical research have to be developed in order to respond to different kinds of uses of genetic data. For instance, consent for collection and for specific use of genetic data is a precondition for the research. But then legal policy should differentiate whether the research material still carries personal information or not. When human tissue samples are anonymized in the sense that it is no longer possible to trace back the identity of the person from whom these tissues have been harvested then legal concerns are minimized to governing the tissue management.

Prohibition of genetic discrimination

The threat of genetic discrimination is existent in several fields of life, yet the interpretation of this concept is not as evident as that of racial discrimination.[19] Any person belonging to the genetic minority with respect to a specific characteristic may belong to the genetic majority in terms of another property. Nevertheless, being a part of some genetic minority may even bring about some advantages, or in the case of rare diseases researchers often hunt for these conditions for studies and that might also offer some therapeutic advantages to the previously discriminated group.[20]

The European Union has been surprisingly quick in including genetic discrimination in the list of forms of discrimination that are conventionally subject to prohibition in the Charter of Fundamental Rights.[21]

On the other hand, discrimination on the basis of genetic properties is partly different from the cases and instances of discrimination that have emerged so far; although they are also unalterable characteristics, in most cases they remain invisible. If, however, others know about them, they may cause uncertain and unforeseeable disadvantages to the person concerned, and serve as a basis for uncertain abuses. For example, if the employer becomes aware that some employees are genetically more susceptible to certain illnesses or diseases, it can be easily presumed that, entirely due to the higher risks, these employees would find themselves in a less favorable situation in spite of the fact that these characteristics do not constitute any monogenic irregularity, but just an increased level of susceptibility.

Possibility of stigmatization and discrimination poses a great danger especially in serious late onset diseases where efficient therapy or prevention is not yet known.[22]

---

19 See also Paul R. Billings, Mel A. Kohn, Margaret de Cuevas, Jonathan Beckwith, Joseph S. Alper and Marvin R. Natowicz, 'Discrimination as a Consequence of Genetic Testing'. *American Journal of Human Genetics*, vol. 50, no. 3 (March 1992): 476–482.

20 Jonathan Beckwith and Joseph S. Alper, 'Reconsidering Genetic Discrimination Legislation'. *Journal of Law, Medicine and Ethics*, vol. 26, no. 3 (September 1998): 205–210.

21 Charter of Fundamental Rights of the European Union 2000/C 364/01, Article 21 on Non-discrimination states that 'Any discrimination based on any ground such as sex, race, color, ethnic or social origin, genetic features, language, religion or belief, political or any other opinion, membership of a national minority, property, birth, disability, age or sexual orientation shall be prohibited'.

22 Janet K. Williams, Cheryl Erwin, Andrew R. Juhl, Michelle Mengeling, Yvonne Bombard, Michael R. Hayden, Kimberly Quaid, Ira Shoulson, Sandra Taylor and Jane S. Paulsen, 'In Their Own Words: Reports of Stigma and Genetic Discrimination by People at Risk for Huntington Disease in the International

Access to insurance

In 2012 Council of Europe launched a public consultation on the predictivity, genetic testing and insurance. The aim of the consultation was a preparation of a further legal instrument that would cover the application of genetic data beyond health purposes (in the field of insurance and work). Mapping the needs and principles of insurance industry, as such is a very ambitious project as in Europe various types of private insurance models and social welfare schemes do not necessarily exclude each other. Private insurance is based on the joint sharing of risks within a certain (standardized) pool of clients. Therefore, insurance companies have compelling interests in assessing the future risks carried by the persons to be insured as accurately as possible.[23]

In most parts of Europe, distribution of basic medical services are based on general insurance scheme and on the principle of solidarity. For this reason, the assessment of genetic risks still has little significance here, as it would not result in larger insurance fees or exclusion from the insurance. The situation is completely different in the case of insurance policies for life, accident or inability to work. In this field, the general legal principle is *uberrimae fides*,[24] which should be based on the largest possible degree of trust between the contracting partners. Consequently, the person to be insured must not conceal any information that is deemed to be significant in the assessment of the associated risks.[25]

If anyone has such a genetic 'finding' that, in life insurance, would affect the risks to be assumed by the insurer, this information – in theory – may not be hidden from the insurance company.[26] There may be cases when the genetic test should mean preferential insurance fees for the insured person in comparison with the fee calculated in the conventional manner. For instance, if – within the scope of questions of the insurance company pertaining to medical status illnesses and diseases having already occurred in the family – the person to be insured makes up a less positive picture; but the genetic test can prove that the same person does not carry the genes being responsible for the occurrence of the specific disease, the fee to be imposed in view of the higher estimated risks may be avoided.

Under Article 12 of the Oviedo Convention, predictive genetic tests[27] may be performed on the basis of appropriate genetic counselling, and solely for health purposes or scientific research. Consequently, the insurance company cannot obligate the person to be insured to take part in any genetic examination. Yet, this requirement does not fully solve the problem, because the few people who have already had unfavorable genetic 'findings' may be disadvantaged in insurance affairs. If the above-referenced article and data protection norms are related to each other, the fact that the registration of any data should be bound to a specific purpose implies that available data may be used for other purposes only with the special consent of the person concerned.

RESPOND-HD Study'. *American Journal of Medical Genetics*, Part B: Neuropsychiatric Genetics, vol. 153, no. 6 (September 2010):1150–1159.

23 House of Commons, Science and insurance companies have added to my better understanding the perspectives of insurers. I would express my particular gratitude to Ildikó Takács, who assisted me in conducting the interviews. Technology Committee, *Genetics and Insurance* (London: HMSO, 2001).

24 Utmost good faith.

25 Tony McGleenan, Urban Wiesing, and François Ewald, *Genetics and Insurance* (Oxford: Bios Scientific Publishers, 1999).

26 Neil A. Doherty and Lisa L. Posey, 'On the Value of a Checkup: Adverse Selection, Moral Hazard and the Value of Information'. *Journal of Risk and Insurance*, vol. 65, no. 2 (June 1998), 189–211.

27 Currently Council of Europe launched a public consultation on the use of genetic data in insurance.

Another problem is that insurance companies tend to request the submission of medical information over a fairly broad scope. Although the large majority of these medical data focus on conventional medical information, in the future a broadening set of information will have a genetic character. In other words, the more we know about the genetic backgrounds of individual diseases, the more the genetic component of these data strengthens. The regulation may also differ as to concerns the scope of the use of genetic tests. Here, access to the test results of medical records, genetic tests for diagnostic purposes, predictive genetic tests that reveal genetic susceptibility should be assessed distinctively.[28]

It is worth observing that life insurance companies have long been interested in diseases and illnesses within the family. The ages reached by parents, brothers, sisters, as well as the causes of their death. In fact, these details can be regarded as a kind of genetic data, as they do not rely on the medical data of the person concerned, but consider the anamnesis in the family. Although they tend to be different between the various insurance companies, medical sheets often inquire about the occurrence of specifically heritable diseases within the family. It is evident that the insurance company asks for these details because the assessment of the future medical status is at the core of the approach of insurers. Some of the insurance companies evaluate these data as the influence of the family environment, while others consider them to be indirect evidence for higher medical risks. For example, if cancer or diabetes has occurred in the family on several occasions, this fact may have its implications on the life insurance.

Use of genetic information in the health care of the family members

A serious and still unsolved ethical and legal problem is posed by the issue of to what extent consenting relatives may be informed on the results generated by the research. If they are informed of any family disposition to suicide, depression or other psychiatric diseases, this information would seriously affect them and the wider family as well. Thus, the information may contribute to conflicts and tragedies within the family.

Without the proper identification of genetic factors and environmental influences, this information may be seen as a destiny. This line of thinking potentially leads to the conclusion that relatives should not be provided with the research results. However, the question is not as simple as that. There may be cases when relatives have legally confirmable motivations for the receipt of the associated information. Under the Hungarian legal regulations, relatives may not be banned from becoming informed of medical data that concern them.

In recent decades, legal rules of informed consent have tended to follow the individual based model to a growing extent: it means that information is only provided to the patient provided that s/he is capable to act, while family members may only be informed if the patient expressly consents. It seems, however, that genetic information will potentially re-establish the role of information provision to the family.[29] In the case of certain diseases, there are just a few people who undergo routine medical screening. Yet, when such a disease appears in a family, it is regarded as a reason for family members to take screening examinations and prevention more seriously, especially

28 For understanding the differences between these categories across Scandinavian countries see: Marcus Radetzki, Marian Radetzi, and Niklas Juth, *Genes and Insurance: Ethical, Legal, and Economic Issues* (Cambridge: Cambridge University Press, 2003), 36.

29 Bobbi McGivern, Jessica Everett, Geoffrey G. Yager, Robert C. Baumiller, Amanda Hafertepen and Howard M. Saal, 'Family Communication about Positive BRCA1 and BRCA2 Genetic Test Results'. *Genetics in Medicine*, vol. 6, no. 6 (November–December 2004): 503–509.

when the disease is known to be hereditary.[30] With the enlarging scope of genetic knowledge, more and more diseases are likely to involve the obligation of physicians to warn the family members.[31]

Already in several early judicial cases on genetic data the intergenerational character of genetic data has been recognized. In the *Munro v. Regents of University of California* case, for instance, the Court of Appeal of the State of California claimed the defendant physician to be responsible for failing to conduct the Tay-Sachs test. In the *Safer v. Pack* case,[32] the court ascertained the liability of the physician for the failure to provide information when he did not warn the relatives of a patient who had been treated for a known hereditary disease of the associated risks. In the *Pate v. Threlkel*[33] case, the Court of Appeal of the State of Florida also confirmed the obligation of the physician to warn the children of the patient.

In the case of genetics, the individual consent model is also often challenged.[34] It follows from the recognition of the interest of several third parties in genetic data that justification of the individual consent model is problematic or, at least, requires some adjustments.

Forensic use of genetic data

DNA is a very useful piece of evidence in criminal justice system. Still, from the moment of collection, storage and retention all of these episodes have distinct legal aspects; how to ensure the security and authenticity of the data and how to protect the innocent or unconvicted party's privacy, as well as how to prevent the discriminatory use of this data.

In the case of *S. and Marper*[35] the European Court for Human Rights made a decision for the first time on the retention of the genetic data in the criminal justice system. The Court found that there had been a violation of Article 8 of the European Convention for the Protection of Human Rights and Fundamental Freedoms, stating:

> […] the Court finds that the blanket and indiscriminate nature of the powers of retention of the fingerprints, cellular samples and DNA profiles of persons suspected but not convicted of offences, as applied in the case of the present applicants, fails to strike a fair balance between the competing public and private interests and that the respondent State has overstepped any acceptable margin of appreciation in this regard. Accordingly, the retention at issue constitutes a disproportionate interference with the applicants' right to respect for private life and cannot be regarded as necessary in a democratic society.

Although in the forensic use of the genetic data the primary concern is not property law, still in the *People v. Rodriguez*, the New York Supreme Court's Criminal Term in King's County

30 Caryn Lerman, Beth N. Peshkin, Chanita Hughes, Claudine Isaacs, 'Family Disclosure in Genetic Testing for Cancer Susceptibility: Determinants and Consequences'. *Journal of Health Care Law and Policy*, vol. 1, no. 2 (1998): 353–72.

31 Sharon J. Durfy, Trisha E. Buchanan and Wylie Burke, 'Testing for Inherited Susceptibility to Breast Cancer: A Survey of Informed Consent Forms for BRCA1 and BRCA2 Mutation Testing'. *American Journal of Medical Genetics*, vol. 75, no. 1 (January 6, 1998): 82–87.

32 Superior Court of New Jersey, Appellate Division, 1996 291 N.J. Super A.2d 1188.

33 *Pate v. Threlkel* 661 So 2d 278) Fla. (1995).

34 Maartje Schermer, *The Different Faces of Autonomy: Patient Autonomy in Ethical Theory and Hospital Practice* (Dordrecht: Kluwer Academic Publishers, 2012).

35 *S. and Marper v. United Kingdom* (Applications no. 30562/04 and 30566/04).

directly recognized a DNA contributor's property right in preventing the genetic information's dissemination in its decision to limit the use of defendant's DNA in solving uncharged crimes.[36]

Forensic use of biobanks constitute one of the most contested fields as searching for evidence in a biobank is a clear alteration from the original purpose of collection, while – in case of violent crimes – police is often under pressure to look for all possibilities.[37]

Use of genetic information in family law

Elements in personhood and kinship can be seen in those DNA debates, when paternity and maternity is challenged, or biological parenthood is to be established. If genetic evidence is used in legal disputes within the family, the establishment of parenthood may become more certain, and there may be broader potential for posthumous identification of family relations.

These purposes in themselves are understandable, but if the process leads to the overstatement of genetic family relations, it may carry the risk of the underestimation of non-biological family ties.

It seems that the skeptical phrase of *pater semper incertus est*[38] has been fading into the past, and the underlying reasons include not only the spread of genetic identification tests, but the fact that the person of the mother has become subject to legal disputes as well. In the *Johnson v. Calvert* case[39] in the USA, both mothers grounded their relations with the newborn child on 'natural' parentage. Both Anna Johnson, as the delivering mother, and Crispina Calvert, as the genetic mother (she had provided the ovum), requested the recognition of their motherhood. In comparison with other similar cases, this latter case is interesting and typical because both mothers intended to evidence exclusive motherhood with the use of medical expert opinions. According to the expert opinion presented by Anna Johnson, natural parentage should be based on the physical contact and bond during pregnancy, development of the fetus in the womb and the delivery of the child. For Crispina Calvert, genetic identity lay in the core of professional argumentation. It is striking that the announcement of the human genome project immediately triggered legal claims on the basis of the DNA evidence worldwide. Even applicants over 60 years old renewed paternity claims with the aim to seek for their biological father by using the new DNA tests. DNA as a tool to establish or to challenge family ties within a reasonable time also appeared in several cases in front of the European Court of Human Rights, such as *Mikulić v. Croatia*,[40] *Szarapo v. Poland*,[41] *Paulík v. Slovakia*,[42] or *Jäggi v. Switzerland*.[43] When post-mortem DNA identification was raised in the case *Estate of Kresten Filtenborg Mortensen v. Denmark*[44] the Court found that the private life of a deceased person from whom a DNA sample was to be taken could not be adversely affected by a request made after his death. Courts were, in general, receptive to these new DNA-based claims and recognized the uncovering of the biological truth about someone's identity as an important aspect of the legally protected private life. In the establishment of the biological kinship

36 *People v. Rodriguez* 196 Misc. 2d 217, 224–25 (N.Y. Sup. Ct. 2003).

37 Claudio Tamburrini, 'What's Wrong with Forensic Uses of Biobanks?' In Christian Lenk, Judit Sandor, Bert Gordijn (eds.) *Biobanks and Tissue Research* (Dordrecht: Springer, 2011), 127–140.

38 The father is always uncertain.

39 5 Cal.4th 84, 851 P.2d 776.

40 *Application no. 53176/99*, § 54, ECHR 2002-I.

41 *Application no. 40835/98*, Judgment of May 23, 2002.

42 *Application no. 10699/05*. Judgment of October 10, 2006, Final *10/01/2007*.

43 *Application no. 58757/00*. Judgment of July 13, 2006, Final *13/10/2006*.

44 *Application no. 1338/03*, ECHR 2006-V.

personality rights can be clearly identified. When human biological tissues, including human DNA are collected, stored and used for research it is more difficult to establish the connection between the sample and the person.

International legal norms

In the field of biomedicine several special organizations within the *United Nations* adopted relevant legal declarations. UNESCO adopted three major declarations, two of them had specific content in the field of genetics: The Universal Declaration on the Human Genome and Human Rights,[45] and the International Declaration on the Human Genetic Data.[46] Article 4 of the International Declaration on Genetic Data grants a special status to the human genetic data because they can be predictive of genetic dispositions concerning individuals; furthermore they may have a significant impact on the family, including offspring, extending over generations, and in some instances on the whole group to which the person concerned belongs. Genetic data may contain information of which significance is not necessarily known at the time of the collection of the biological samples; and they may have cultural significance for persons or groups.[47]

In the framework of the *Council of Europe* the following documents are of primary importance: the Convention for the Protection of Human Rights and Dignity of the Human Being with regard to the Application of Biology and Medicine: Convention on Human Rights and Biomedicine, signed in Oviedo in 1997, and its protocols, such as the Additional Protocol concerning Biomedical Research of 2005, the Additional Protocol Concerning Transplantation of Organs and Tissues of Human Origin of 2002, or the Additional Protocol with regard to the Application of Biology and Medicine, on the Prohibition of Cloning Human Beings of 1998. One of the most relevant Protocol in the field of genetics, the Additional Protocol to the Convention on Human Rights and Biomedicine concerning Genetic Testing for Health Purposes[48] (CETS No.: 203), was adopted in 2008.

Among the primary sources of *European Union law*, the Charter of Fundamental Rights of the European Union of 2000 is to be mentioned. The Charter can be regarded as the Bill of Rights of the European Union, but opposed to most national constitutions listing fundamental rights, it is a novel document and, therefore, it is rather progressive. Article 1 on human dignity, and more specifically Article 3 on the right to the integrity of the person are of great relevance. As to the sources of secondary legislation, the following documents are relevant: Regulation (EC) No 45/2001 of the European Parliament and of the Council of 18 December 2000 on the protection of individuals with regard to the processing of personal data by the Community institutions and bodies and on the free movement of such data, the Directive 98/44/EC of the European Parliament and of the Council of 6 July 1998 on the legal protection of biotechnological inventions, and finally Directive 95/46/EC of the European Parliament and the European Commission on the protection of individuals with regard to the processing of personal data and on the free movement of such data.[49]

---

45 The Universal Declaration on the Human Genome and Human Rights was adopted unanimously and by acclamation at UNESCO's 29th General Conference on 11 November 1997. The following year, the United Nations General Assembly endorsed the Declaration.

46 To address these concerns, the International Declaration on Human Genetic Data was adopted unanimously and by acclamation at UNESCO's 32nd General Conference on 16 October 2003.

47 Article 4 of the International Declaration on Genetic Data.

48 (CETS No.: 203).

49 Final Report of the GeneBanC Project (2009) in: European Ethical-Legal Papers No.17. Leuven 15.

The *European Group on Ethics in Science and New Technologies (EGE)* is also highly authoritative in questions related to biobanking. Amidst its opinions, one should mention the following: Opinion n°19 on the ethical aspects of umbilical cord blood banking, Opinion n°15 on ethical aspects of human stem cell research and use, and Opinion n°11 on the ethical aspects of human tissue banking are of great relevance.

The Parliamentary Assembly of the Council of Europe adopted Additional Protocol on genetic testing for health purposes[50] to the Oviedo Convention covering the field related to the genetic testing, with the exception of genetic research.

Although data protection is applicable in the field of protection of genetic data, still the most specific legal instrument in Europe was adopted in 2006: the Recommendation Rec(2006) 4 of the Committee of Ministers to Member States on research on biological materials of human origins. The extension of the human rights language to the field of human tissues is clear in the stated objective of the Recommendation. Dignity and identity of all human beings without discrimination, as well as respect for private life belong to the classical human rights, personality rights.

Article 11 of the Recommendation distinctly harmonizes the rules on the research on human beings with the rules on human tissues:

> An intervention should only be carried out to obtain biological materials for storage for research purposes if it complies with the Additional Protocol concerning biomedical research …[51]

The Additional Protocol to the Convention on Human Rights and Biomedicine concerning Genetic Testing for Health Purposes[52] applies to tests which are carried out for health purposes, involving analysis of biological samples of human origin and aiming specifically to identify the genetic characteristics of a person which are inherited or acquired during early prenatal development. The Protocol does not apply to genetic tests carried out on the human embryo or foetus; to genetic tests carried out for research purposes.

Biobank typology worldwide

It is a peculiar fact in the history of medical sciences that the word 'bank' has already appeared in a medical context before: its usage in reference to blood banks dates back to the 1930s. The expression was coined by Bernard Fantus, an American physician of Hungarian descent who ran a blood bank[53] already before the outbreak of World War Two. Blood banks played a major role in the treatment of soldiers wounded in the war. Naturally, the technology of preserving blood has changed a great deal since then, resulting in blood products that last much longer.

Although the expression 'biobank' continues to elicit critical comments, invariably seizing on the commercial connotation of the word 'bank', the expression 'blood bank' failed to raise similar

50 Additional Protocol to the Convention on Human Rights and Biomedicine concerning Genetic Testing for Health Purposes (Strasbourg, 27.XI.2008).

51 CETS No. 195, 2005.

52 Adopted in Strasbourg, 27.XI.2008

53 Bernard Fantus, 'The Therapy of the Cook County Hospital', *Journal of the American Medical Association*, vol. 109, no. 2 (July 10, 1937): 128–131. Reprinted in vol. 251, no. 5 (February 3, 1984): 647–649.

moral concerns at the time: no one seemed to object to the application of a commercial term to human matter.[54]

The term 'biobank' appears in numerous policy and legal texts. The scope and meaning show a very diverse picture. For instance, OECD provides the following definition of the term:

> Biobanks or Biological Resources centers are an essential part of the infrastructure underpinning life sciences and biotechnology. They consist of service providers and repositories of the living cells, genomes of organism, and information relating to heredity and the functions of biological systems. Biobanks or BRCs contain collections of culturable organisms (e.g. micro-organisms, plant, animal and human cells), replicable parts of these (e.g. genomes, plasmids, viruses, cDNAs), viable but not yet culturable organisms, cells and tissues, as well as databases containing molecular, physiological and structural information.[55]

The term 'population biobank' is based on the definition of the Council of Europe. It is a collection of biological materials that has the following characteristics:

> (i) the collection has a population basis; (ii) it is established, or has been converted, to supply biological materials or data derived therefrom for multiple future research projects; (iii) it contains biological materials and associated personal data, which may include or be linked to genealogical, medical and lifestyle data and which may be regularly updated; and (iv) it receives and supplies materials in an organized manner.[56]

Robert F. Weir and Robert S. Olick define biomedical (clinical) research databases, in the classical databases, as the following: a database that is developed by and restricted to authorized clinical investigations (e.g. oncology, pathology, etc.) in several academic medical centers. These databases contain genetics and other biomedical information connecting individual patients, derived from their clinically collected tissues, with the electronic data sometimes being transmitted to a central database. The above mentioned scholars differentiate commercial databases, which are human tissue databases that are restricted to scientists willing to pay to have access to DNA sequences and the other protected information contained in the database.

In 2012 European Commission aimed to map biobanks from a new focus; instead of looking at the legal challenges across Europe, examined the biobank as a challenge to governance[57]. A report submitted by Herbert Gottweis and Jane Kaye highlighted nine major recommendations relevant to the governance of biobanks. Among them many new aspects, such as the sustainable governance mechanisms for creating a relationship of reciprocity between biobanks were also mentioned.

The activities of a biobank may be directed at studying the genetic background of a specific disease, as well as at conducting comprehensive surveys among the population of a given country, province or region. One of the most important differences between the biobanks and the earlier

---

54 Judit Sándor, Petra Bárd, Claudio Tamburrini, and Thorbjörn Tännsjö, 'The Case of Biobank with the Law: Between a Legal and Scientific Fiction', *Journal of Medical Ethics*, Online First, September 24, 2011.

55 OECD (2009) OECD Guidelines on Human Biobanks and Genetic Research Databases http://www.oecd.org/dataoecd/41/47/44054609.pdf

56 https://wcd.coe.int/ViewDoc.jsp?id=977859

57 Biobanks for Europe: A Challenge for Governance(2012) *Report of the Expert Group on Dealing with Ethical and Regulatory Challenges of International Biobank Research* (chair: Herbert Gottweis, Rapporteur: Jane Kaye, Members: Fabrizia Bignami, Emmanuelle Rial-Sebbag, Roberto Lattanzi, Milan Macek) doi:10.2777/68942

sample collections is that while the latter basically use samples resulting from operations and autopsies, biobanks engage in the systematic acquisition of information and tissue samples on the basis of a previously formulated concept. Beside their infrastructure and freezing capacity, biobanks also need to have a certain institutional and administrative background. While the sample collections are generally established in a single hospital unit, usually a pathology department, and usually remain closed to the outside world, biobanks tend to be both independent and open, willing to provide samples and information in accordance with certain protocols. Despite conceptual and legal heterogeneity, several countries have already regulated biobanks, tissue banks or the protection of genetic data in a special law. Among them are Estonia,[5859] Belgium,[60] Hungary[6162], Latvia,[63] Sweden,[64] Portugal[65] and Spain.[66] Many European countries still apply a kind of mosaic regulation, so instead of a distinct law several types of health laws (transplantation, data protection, etc.) are applicable in the field of biobanks. Fragmented, mosaic like regulation can be seen in France, Italy, Cyprus and Greece for instance. In several countries, however, national ethics committees have adopted opinions or guidelines on biobanks.[67] Different kinds of biobanks may need different types of regulation. For instance, in countries where there are many local biobanks and virtual network of biobanks exist (such as in Germany or Hungary), the focus of the law can be shifted to the general legal treatment of genetic data and not just biobanks. When there is one major National Biobank Project such as in the United Kingdom, Estonia or Latvia, the whole network and institution as such needs a standard regulation, as well as linking and access.

The Icelandic Biobank Project

The first project known by that name was the biobank of Iceland.[68] Since the majority of Iceland's population has lived here in total isolation from the rest of the world for more than a thousand years,

58 Judit Sándor and Petra Bárd (2009) *The Legal Regulation of Biobanks. National Report: Estonia.* CELAB Paper Series No. 5. Budapest: CEU CELAB. available: http://web.ceu.hu/celab/Genebank/GeneBanC_est.pdf

59 Human Genes Research Act http://www.legaltext.ee/text/en/X50010.htm

60 Law of 19 December 2008 regulation the procurement and the use of human bodily material for medical application in humans or for scientific research.

61 Judit Sándor and Petra Bárd (2009) *The Legal Regulation of Biobanks. National Report: Hungary.* CELAB Paper Series No. 1. Budapest: CEU CELAB. available: http://web.ceu.hu/celab/GeneBanc_hu.pdf

62 Judit Sándor and Petra Bárd (2009) *The Legal Regulation of Biobanks. National Report: Latvia.* CELAB Paper Series No. 4. Budapest: CEU CELAB available: http://web.ceu.hu/celab/Genebank/GeneBanC_Lett.pdf

63 Human Genome Research Law, adopted by the Saeima on 13 June, 2002 (amended in 2003 and 2005) in original language: Latvijas populăcijas genofonda pětíjumi un to izmantošana cilvěka patolo+ijas diagnostikă un profilaksë; available at: http://phoebe.vm.gov.lv/misc_db/web.nsf/bf25ab0f47ba5dd785256499006b15a4/17cb8c1218bf81cdc2257313001f391a/$FILE/genoms.pdf

64 The Swedish Act on Biobanks (SF 2002: 297).

65 Portuguese Law Nr. 12/2005 on Personal Genetic Information and Health Information.

66 Biomedical Research Act (2007) http://www.isciii.es/ISCIII/es/contenidos/fd-investigacion/SpanishLawonBiomedicalResearchEnglish.pdf

67 For instance in France the French National Ethics Committee (CCNE) in Opinion No 77 on the Ethical Issues raised by collections of biological material and related data 'biobank', biolibraries (2005).

68 Act on Biobanks No. 110 (2000): http://ministryofhealth.is/laws-and-regulations/nr/31 see also: Regulations on the Keeping and Utilization of Biological Samples in Biobanks No. 134 (2001).

researchers anticipated great results from collecting the samples of this rare population. Another important factor was the fact that the conditions for gathering a complete and accurate medical family history were excellent, considering that genealogical data going back ten centuries were available, together with information compiled by a traditional tissue bank that had been in business since 1940. The initiative to establish a Health Sector Database on the Icelandic population was largely associated with Kari Stefansson, who returned to Iceland from Harvard Medical School.[69] He founded the Reykjavik-based company DeCODE Genetics, becoming the chief project manager of the Iceland biobank.[70] However, there have been ethical and legal concerns in connection with this scientific and business project from the start.[71] One of the most serious moral concerns raised the point that, in view of the country's very small population, the involvement of the country's total population of 270,000 – while technically simpler than procuring the participation of a larger and more heterogeneous society – would make it possible in some instances to identify members of the community even on the basis of limited health information. The other problem arose from the method of processing the participants' consent, as individuals who rejected participation in the research had to state it in a separate form. However, according to the Supreme Court of Iceland the opt-out model in itself was not in conflict with the Constitution of Iceland.

From the first moment, the Iceland biobank project was based on the cooperation of the private and the public sector.[72] However, in exchange for the patent licenses, the company Hoffmann-La Roche agreed to provide samples from the new medicines developed using the project's patents. The Icelandic database does not make the publication of individual research data or feedback possible. The hospitals' existing data can be used in the project without the consent of the parties concerned.

UK Biobank

Today one of the largest DNA collections is the UK Biobank.[73] It is not just a collection of the DNA samples. It is a resource that links many different sources of information on individuals for research. Furthermore participants have to complete a long questionnaire about their lifestyle. Participants visit the local UK Biobank assessment center; the visit lasts about 90 minutes. First, information is given to the participant then health and lifestyle data will be collected, some standard medical tests will be conducted and blood and urine samples will be taken. Subsequently, with the permission of the participant the UK Biobank will follow medical and other health-related records of the participant. In 2006 the UK Biobank started recruiting people aged 40–69. Researchers set up assessment centres in shopping malls, where volunteers gave blood and urine samples and spent 2–3 hours answering medical questions and undergoing measures of height, weight and body fat and tests of hearing, grip strength and lung function. The study also included tracking the participants through follow-up questionnaires and through the United Kingdom's National Health Service.

The UK Biobank Project aims to enable studies to be carried out on the relationships between genes, lifestyle and health through the collection of DNA samples and information from half

69 Gísli Pálsson, 'The Rise and Fall of a Biobank'. In Herbert Gottweis and Alan Petersen (eds.) *Biobanks: Governance in Comparative Perspective* (Abingdon and New York: Routledge, 2008), 41–55, at 43.

70 Weir and Olick, *op. cit.*, 260–261.

71 Hilary Rose, *The Commodification of Bioinformation: The Icelandic Health Sector Database* (London: The Wellcome Trust, 2001) WC10-2220/tbcK/03-2001/JM.

72 In November 2009 the Icelandic biobank project ran into an economic difficulties.

73 Alan Doyle, Frances Rawle, Peter Greenaway, 'The UK Biobank'. In Judit Sándor (ed.) *Society and Genetic Information* (Budapest and New York: Central European University Press, 2003), 247–267.

a million people across the UK. The UK Biobank model tends to avoid regulation and instead follows the ethical oversight model.[74]

If the given genetic databank is established in relation to researches that serve the examination of the genetic backgrounds of psychiatric diseases or human behaviour, even more complex legal problems arise. In a 1994 Recommendation of the Committee of Ministers of the European Council, the following aspects were highlighted.[75] The establishment of any tissue bank should provide for the proper separation of the following functions: organization, procedures, conservation, internal quality control, storage, distribution and use. These functions may be undertaken only by organizations that operate in non-profit legal forms and hold the official permits of the national healthcare authorities.

The British Nuffield Council on Bioethics has compiled a 127-page study under the title of *Mental Disorders and Genetics* that focuses on the genetic implications of certain psychiatric diseases.[76] One of the final conclusions of the Work Group has been that, in the near future, genetic tests are not likely to prove to be specifically useful in the diagnosis of mental disorders. The aim of these researches has rather been the description of more efficient medication. Genetic information pertaining to individuals should be handled as medical secrets, but according to the Work Group in certain cases the disclosure of this information to the family members may be justified.

In view of the increased risk of stigmatization, specific research on mental disorders should examine whether the identification of genetic factors would not result in further discrimination. The genetic studies of mental disorders invariably consider that these diseases can be interpreted in several different theoretical approaches, and the genetic explanation is only one of them. Genetic research into mental disorders carries an especially high risk of genetic reductionism.

The Estonian Genome Project

The Estonian Genome Project[77] was also one of the earliest genome projects, as it was launched already in 2002. The Project was based on the so called Human Genes Research Act. The rights of the gene donors were broadly elaborated in the Act and several legal innovations were also made.

The Estonian Genome Project started its operations in 2003. While the costs of its establishment were initially met from both public and private resources, in its subsequent funding it became increasingly reliant on the public sector. It operates on the basis of the Law on Human Genetic Research. The participants give a general consent and their genetic information can be used in various research projects. In the planning phase of the Estonian genome program, the general practitioners received training in data protection, as they were going to be the chief data providers at the later stages. In addition to taking blood samples from the volunteers, it was also their job to inform the biobank about any medical problems the volunteers may have developed.

---

74 UK Biobank (2007) Ethics and Governance Framework http://www.ukbiobank.ac.uk accessed March 25, 2012.

75 Recommendation R (94) 1 of the Committee of Ministers to Member States on Human Tissue Banks.

76 The head of the Work Group was Fiona Caldicott, psychiatrist.

77 Krista Kruuv and Ants Nomper, 'The Estonian Genome Project'. In Judit Sándor (ed.) *Society and Genetic Information* (Budapest and New York: Central European University Press, 2003), 213–225.

The Latvian Genome Project

The Latvian Genome Project was, since the beginning, a public project,[78] while the Human Genome Research Act was very similar to the Estonian law. Its main aim was to provide research tool to certain genetic diseases.

Here one can observe that countries of Central Europe seemed to have even stronger motivation not to lag behind the mainstream of science and to remove all possible obstacles from scientific development. As medical profession was dominant during the socialist area, medical doctors and researchers developed some immunity from social scrutiny and their apolitical image raised their social appreciation in the totalitarian regimes. However, because of this social isolation and public admiration, paternalism remained the main guiding principle until the post-transitional patients' rights bills.

Was it too early or too late to regulate biobanks, it is hard to tell. It was too early in the sense that the public had only little knowledge about biobanks and the popular interpretation of what genetics is about is quite ambiguous. For instance, since the beginning of the debate experts had to explain that this law is not about human cloning, the law does not cover forensic use, does not deal with paternity testing, genetically modified organism and many other contemporary biotechnologies.

The Hungarian approach to the broad protection of genetic data in health care and in research

After many years of debate a very short and simplified version of the original concept was adopted in April 2008, as Parliamentary Act No. XXI of 2008 on the Protection of human genetic data and on the regulation of human genetic studies, research and biobanks[79] (hereinafter, Human Genetics Act). This law engages with the strong protection of genetic data and, as such, follows the tradition of the data protection norms in Hungary. The Act entered into force on July 1, 2008.

The official *Explanatory Note* to the 2008 Parliamentary Act tried to strike a balance between two major interests: the freedom of science, on the one hand, and the need to secure the rights of the individuals, on the other. The *Explanatory Note* emphasizes that as early as the 1990s, the profession and, later on, society demanded legal regulation for the field of genetics. The 'right not to know' is respected by the law by saying that the person concerned may withdraw from knowing their genetic data through a declaration. The declaration can be withdrawn at any time without restriction. The person concerned shall be informed about this right.[80]

Biobanks based on comparative genomics

Other biobanks follow a different logic; instead of collecting samples from a homogenous population they build their research on heterogeneity. For instance, the idea of the Indonesian

---

78 Valdis Pirags and Elmars Grens, 'The Latvian Genome Project'. In Judit Sándor (ed.) *Society and Genetic Information* (Budapest and New York: Central European University Press, 2003), 225–233.

79 In the original Hungarian language: 2008. évi XXI. törvény a humángenetikai adatok védelméről, a humángenetikai vizsgálatok és kutatások, valamint a biobankok működésének szabályairól, official text available at http://net.jogtar.hu/jr/gen/hjegy_doc.cgi?docid=A0800021.TV

80 Human Genetics Act, Article 6 (7).

Biobank that dates back to 2002[81] is in sharp contrast with the Estonian and Icelandic biobanks, (which were based on relatively homogeneous populations). The Indonesian biobank benefited from the ethnic diversity of this multi-colored archipelago that proved irresistible to researchers. However, the sudden interest of the Dutch and international researchers caught the inhabitants of Indonesia unprepared; neither the ethical nor the legal principles of genetic research had crystallized sufficiently so as to pave the way for the collection of samples. Moreover, since there had not been any local discourse about the social interpretation of genetics, the conditions for the emergence of some form of a biosocial identity were not ready. The engagement of a pre-genetic society in genetic research can, therefore, be regarded as a form of genetic colonization.

Regional genome projects

Regional specificities can be seen, for instance, in the establishment of the Southern African Human Genome Programme (hereafter: SAHGP). The Program which was officially launched in 2011, aims to collect sufficient data to examine specific genetic risk factors, such as connection between certain infectious diseases and lifestyle. In some indigenous groups, collections of certain bodily materials may be seen as a source of witchcraft[82] and collection of blood may be seen as controversial in Kenya and in Gambia.[83] The European Union had to face the challenges of many biobanks operating in Europe under different definitions and legal framework. BBMRI is not a regional biobank in the physical sense; it provides rather a tool for harmonization and communication between the already established biobanks within Europe.

Organ and tissue banks for research

It is not unusual that a biobank is established for the collection of a particular type of organ or tissue. The research into psychiatric and neurological conditions is often based on data provided by the so-called 'brain banks'. Such research is being conducted in several countries. The tissues come from cadavers. The *Netherlands Brain Bank* was founded in 1985.[84] The brain tissue samples were initially used in research directed at the Alzheimer disease. Later on, study on the collected brain tissues was extended to also include Parkinson's and Huntington's disease, as well as other neurological and psychiatric conditions.

Biobanks are frequently established to store tissues related to a certain type of cancer, along with the results of the tissues' genetic analysis and the patients' medical data. There are numerous examples in Austria and Germany while clinical biobanks specializing in a particular type of cancer exist all over the world.

---

81 Margaret Sleeboom Faulkner, 'Human Genetic Samples in Indonesia: The Interplay between Biosocieties and Non-Biosocieties'. In Margaret Sleeboom Faulkner (ed.) *Human Genetic Biobanks in Asia: Politics of Trust and Scientific Advancement* (Abingdon and New York: Routledge, 2009), 117–141.

82 Jantina de Vries, Melodie Slabbert, Michael S. Pepper, 'Ethical, Legal and Social Issues in the Context of the Planning Stages of the Southern African Human Genome Programme'. *Medicine and Law* 31 (2012): 119–152.

83 James Fairhead, Melissa Leach, Mary Small, 'Where Techno-Science meets poverty: Medical Research and the Economy of Blood in The Gambia, West Africa'. *Social Science & Medicine*, vol. 63, no. 4 2006: 1109–1120; Molyneux et al.

84 Netherlands Brain Bank Progress Report 2007–2008, Amsterdam.

Biobanks for the study of special group of people

The collection of biological samples can also be conducted on the basis of special populations, indigenous groups or members of a certain ethnic minority, as well as in relations to a peculiar biological characteristic. One example of this type of biobanks is *GenomEUtwins*.[85] Financed by the European Union, this project has been designed to collect genetic samples from twins in Denmark, Finland, Italy, The Netherlands, Great Britain, Austria and Sweden. Focusing on five major health factors – obesity, height, longevity, stroke and cardiovascular diseases – the project examines the genetic as well as non-genetic background of these conditions on the basis of twin research.

Intellectual property and human biological material

Article 7 of the 2006 Recommendation[86] states that '(b)iological materials should not, as such, give rise to financial gain'. This article reflects the principle of non-payment usually cited in the context of organ transplantation, which is a different legal field than the research on human tissues. Biobank research has never excluded the possibility to be engaged in a lucrative biotechnological business. On the contrary since the beginning of the biobank projects the hope that this type of research would not only produce scientific but also economic results were openly expressed.[87]

Legal guarantees of research performed on human beings have been a significant part of medical ethics, bioethics and, moreover, universal human rights since World War II. The legal requirement that no one shall be subject to research without their express consent arises from the basic right to human dignity. The interests of the individual prevail over scientific interests,[88] i.e. no one may be treated as an instrument, even in the most important biomedical research. Needless to say, that the rules adopted 50 years ago were primarily aimed at avoiding physical suffering and humiliation, as well as the use of human beings as trial subjects. It was declared in the *United Nations International Covenant on Civil and Political Rights*, adopted in 1996, that 'No one shall be subjected to torture or to cruel, inhuman or degrading treatment or punishment'. In particular, no one shall be subjected without his free consent to medical or scientific experimentation.[89]

During the last 50 years both medical research and the rules related thereto significantly expanded; today not only humans but also guinea pigs used in experimentation are granted more protection than was found at the dawn of biomedical research. Presumably one of the most significant changes is that nowadays a major part of the researches is implemented months or even years after the patient received medical treatment. In the era of biobanks,[90] it is also increasingly frequent that someone in perfect health voluntarily provides a blood sample, for example, to a biological sample collection.

---

85 An international twin research database was launched in 2002 in Stockholm but in 2004 centers join to this research decided to retain their data http://www.genomeutwin.org, downloaded on January 12, 2010.

86 Council of Europe Recommendation Rec(2006)4 of the Committee of Ministers to member states on research on biological materials of human origin.

87 Henry Etzkowitz, *The Triple Helix* (London and New York: Routledge, 2008).

88 Article 2 of the Oviedo Convention: 'The interests and welfare of the human being shall prevail over the sole interest of society or science.'

89 Article 7 entered into force on March 23, 1976.

90 Since the establishment of the first biological sample collections for epidemiologic purposes, after the Human Genome Programme, there were thousands of biological sample collections and DNA banks established worldwide in the hope of serious research and trade possibilities.

Whose property?

Organs and tissues removed from deceased persons were, for a long time, classified as hazardous waste, but these biological materials have gradually become valuable for scientific research – even long after the determination of the cause of death. Research human biological samples collected in biobanks have become more common than research on living human beings and the wider public has also started to pay attention to the latest scientific developments.

Today a DNA sample of a rare or serious disease together with its health anamnesis can serve as a basis for research and also promises of considerable financial benefit.[91] Nevertheless, the situation is that the person providing the sample may not directly receive a share of such financial benefits. Moreover, she/he usually has no therapeutic benefit from that at all. When European law started to apply the prohibition of financial gain on samples, they initially wanted to avoid a trade in organs as well as the sale and purchase of human organs and tissues.

The first internationally relevant legal debate on the benefit sharing in relation to the use of human tissues followed after the (American) Moore case.[92] John Moore had leukemia and, following his father's advice, he underwent treatment at the clinic of a prestigious university, the Los Angeles University Hospital, between 1976 and 1983. His disease was successfully treated by Dr. David Golde, head of the medical team there but besides this, the doctor made important studies of the patient's tissue samples. The patient's spleen had to be removed in the course of the series of treatments but many times blood, sperm, bone-marrow and other biological samples were also taken from the patient for the purpose of examination. Since Moore was satisfied with the treatment, he travelled from Seattle to Los Angeles for treatment for many years.

John Moore began to become suspicious in 1983, seven years after the commencement of the treatments, when he had to fill a statement of consent, stating that he voluntarily consented to transfer all his rights over his cell lines and other biological samples to the university. He marked the sentence 'I do not consent to it' with a circle. When the clinic thereafter phoned him and asked him to change his opinion, seeing the great excitement about his tissues, Moore turned to a lawyer. His lawyer found a patent concerning a cell line called 'Mo'[93] which produced a large profit for the research team. Then Moore announced a claim for irregular ownership, and sought a share in the profits received from the invention, stating that it was based upon his biological samples. The court refused to accept this pecuniary claim but established that the doctor's conduct, i.e. non-disclosure of research and business interests to the patient, should be considered as infringement of the relationship of trust between doctor and patient.

Due to the fact that the court applied the rules on objects and property in this case, it seems that it finally recognized the possibility of owning human cells or tissues even if the lack of disclosed information rather refers to bad faith. Although there are moral concerns regarding biotechnological inventions of human origin to date, some say this debate was decided a long time ago, in 1980, in the *Chakrabarty* case.[94] Although in that case the subject of the lawsuit was only an invention on GM micro-organisms, it seemed that such a decision made it possible to grant legal protection to inventions regarding living organisms. Due to the fact that an invention regarding living organisms was established, now doors are open to the registration of patents on human cells or DNA samples. The Chakrabarty case was of great importance because the Supreme Court forced the Patent Office

91 Graeme Laurie, et al., 'Managing Access to Biobanks: How Can We Reconcile Individual Privacy and Public Interests in Genetic Research?' *Medical Law International* 10 (September 2010): 315–37

92 *Moore v. Regents of the University* of California, 793 P.2d 479 (Cal.,1990): 490.

93 Later on it was called RCL Cell Line.

94 *Diamond v. Chakrabarty* 447 U.S. 303 (1980).

to license the patentability of new intellectual products created from living organisms with human cooperation, which was contrary to its former position.

To come back to the use of human biological samples for trade purposes, what if the invention based on human tissues is not created secretly but with the express consent or moreover with the intellectual or financial support of the subject participating in the project and providing the sample? Should the donor be considered as a voluntary provider of the sample in this case, too?

In 1981 Hideaki Hagiwara participated in developing a biotechnological invention to a greater extent than merely providing samples for it, in that she acted as an 'originator'. Hideaki Hagiwara offered the researchers of the University of California the use of the lymphocytes of her mother, who was suffering from cervical cancer, for the purpose of producing a so-called immortal cell line. The research work was followed by a great success for they managed to create very important antibodies in the treatment of cancer. Due to the settlement out of court, the Hagiwara family obtained an Asian patent right for its invention.[95]

The organizations of the parents of children suffering from Canavan disease[96] participated in its research even more intensively; they not only organized the gathering of samples but also supported researchers with significant financial resources so they could create genetic tests as soon as possible. Groups of relevant patients and non-profit organizations offered their help in the research activities concerning Canavan disease.[97] They not only provided their own tissue samples for the research but also contributed to it financially. As a result of the research a patent was issued, which could be obtained for payment by the contributing patients themselves; and therefore the patients group initiated a lawsuit in October 2000. The Court of Florida acting in the case confirmed the former court decision adopted in the Moore case, and refused to recognize the plaintiffs' claim to title.[98] In the Catalona case,[99] the main issue was who can possess the sample collection: the researcher who has created it or the university who employed the researcher and whether patient may have a vote on this issue.[100]

One of the ethically challenging elements of the biobanks lies in the fact that the contribution to it is often a dreadful disease.[101]

Perhaps the greatest recognition of a non-professional participant occurred in 2004. Sharon Terry, mother of two children, was the first 'non-professional' who was registered as a 'co-inventor' for a biotechnological invention.[102] The mother's seven-year-old child suffered from what is known as *pseudoxanthoma elasticum* (PXE) disease, which was not recognized even by the doctor, at first sight. However the mother felt her child had a special and serious disease, whereas the pediatrician

95 Robert F. Weir and Robert S. Olick, *The Stored Tissue Issue* (Oxford: Oxford University Press, 2004), 163.

96 The Canavan disease (OMIM 271900) is an autosomal recessive form of hereditary leukodystrophy, it is a fungal degeneration of the white substance of the central nervous system which is generally assumed to develop due to the genetic error in the aspartoacylase enzyme (mutation of the gene). This is a genetic disease with a very bad prognosis i.e. only a few patients live to the age of two.

97 This case is referred to by Weir and Olick, *op. cit.*, 164.

98 *Greenberg v Miami Children's Hospital Research Institute* 264 F Supp 2d 1064 (SD Fla 2003).

99 The Washington University v. William J. Catalona, et al., Case No. 4:03 CV 01065 SNL.

100 Donna Dickenson, *Property in the Body* (Cambridge: Cambridge University Press, 2007).

101 'By 2022, an estimated 10,000 of the cohort will have breast cancer, 9,000 will have Alzheimer's disease and some 28,000 will have died from heart disease. Scientists can look back at data collected at the beginning and work out what distinguishes those who develop disease from those who stay healthy.' UK. Biobank Project.

102 http://www.pxe.org/sharon-terry (last visited: 25 March, 2012).

believed her child had a simple skin condition. Later on, a rare genetic disease was revealed, due only to the mother's persistence. Sharon Terry had behaved not only as a worried mother but she had also visited libraries and collected medical books and donations for research. During her research work conducted in libraries, she discovered that the disease under discussion was of unknown cause and so she and her husband obtained significant support for the purpose of research.

For the time being the question is still open on how human tissue should be considered if it serves the purpose of creating valuable biological inventions in biobanks or via international cooperation, i.e. should it be considered as a contribution in kind or a common heritage?

Currently there seem to be three solutions in this field, the first one is the way of creating an open market, which is so far inconsistent with the approach of European law[103] and really has dangerous consequences. This would be the case when research subjects, organ donors, DNA and other donors provided samples for money or other direct financial benefits.[104] The other solution is when the benefit or reimbursement is more symbolic and does not mean any direct financial benefit. It can be expressed as the provision of free genetic tests, medical treatment or medicine at a reduced price for the persons participating in the creation of the relevant biotechnological or pharmaceutical product. They can also be health benefits providing for early diagnosis or prevention.

The third solution is a new kind of ownership construction e.g. extension of the concept of common heritage. There are several arguments in support of public ownership too, e.g. in the event of an epidemic all virus samples belong to the public. If the virus sample is not provided immediately and for free but only after protracted negotiations, it might entail consequences that are difficult to foresee. With the sale and purchase of biological samples comes an increasing danger of bioterrorism if the biological samples are provided to unscrupulous persons.

Furthermore, if research falls under the direct influence of trade, this effect might even increase in other fields, e.g. solidarity and altruism might disappear in fields based thereon, such as in the case of transplantation, or that stem cell banks would operate only as so-called autologous banks i.e. banks established exclusively for the participants' own purposes.

Human DNA may be considered as some kind of *common heritage* of mankind. The concept of mankind's common heritage, as well as the specific ownership category thereof, had been inspired by environmental protection. Arvid Pardo, Ambassador of Malta, mentioned this first officially at the United Nations General Assembly, serving as a model to date for everyone keeping the protection of future generations in mind[105]. However Arvid Pardo's famous sentences at that time referred to the treasures of the ocean.

This concept related to the human genome came up in 1997 when the Universal Declaration of UNESCO on the Human Genome and Human Rights was drafted in Paris. The idea can be traced back in Article 1 of this Declaration 'the human genome underlies the fundamental unity of all members of the human family, as well as the recognition of their inherent dignity and diversity. In a symbolic sense, it is the heritage of humanity'. It is not accidental that ownership disputes became more and more conspicuous after the increase in genetic research. Namely, upon the enlargement of genetic examinations, a smaller unit of observation, i.e. the gene, became the centre of interest. Due to the fragmentation in biology, embryos, tissues, spermatozoa, genes and proteins became

103 Article 21of the Oviedo Convention: 'The human body and its parts shall not, as such, give rise to financial gain.'

104 These disputes have also reached the field of intellectual property law. In 2010, a US district court invalidated Myriad Genetics' BRCA gene patent claims, finding that human intervention and isolation did not produce markedly different characteristics than those possessed by genes in the human body.

105 Jasper A. Bovenberg (2006) *Property Rights in Blood, Genes and Data Naturally Yours*? Leiden. Martinus Nijhoff Publisher p. 57.

the subjects of scientific observation. The genes that can be studied independently from the body, but which include hereditary properties revealing a lot of information, have not only scientific and therapeutic but also serious social and cultural meanings. If we considered a property as a genetic one, then several scientific meanings, as well as social and cultural meanings completely independent from science, have been attached to it to date. If it comes to legislation we find that the legislator has to cope with both the real possibilities of science and the risks to human rights arising from it, and with the prejudices and fears not necessarily resulting from the scientifically verifiable achievements of genetics.

Whatever the solution will be, we should see that the increasing use of DNA samples and biological tissue samples for research and biotechnological purposes confronted not only the researchers with a new situation, but radically rearranged the legal issues, and last but not least the research subjects' (today rather participants) attitude to the research. According to David Price, *biological interpersonal relations*[106] are increasing so intensively today as never before. Citizens get in contact with each other not only through services and the labour market but we are connected to each other with more and more biological strings. Since it seems that the common genome and the researches arising from that are hopefully to everyone's advantage, the organs offered for transplantation, biobanks, stem cells and umbilical cord blood are all important primary materials and elements of diagnosis and therapy. In my opinion, as a result of the above-mentioned, people that recognize those possibilities somehow become part of the research/creative process and, moreover, not only as until today, i.e. as research subjects (on whom the research is conducted), but also as active partners.

What will happen if the passive research subjects wish to become co-creators in research? If they provide not only biological sample but also knowledge, experience and money, and in return they request cheap, accessible tests, health provision, treatment or recognition of their intellectual contribution and experience? In addition, science is no longer perceived as the unquestionable common good, it is seen more as a result of the combination of both private and public investment and common knowledge production. It follows from the extension of the personal rights to the sphere of human tissues that participants' interests should be considered more relevant also in the field of benefit sharing.

Conclusions

It follows from the complexity of genetic data that, when we deal with its legal implications, a preliminary legal question has to be addressed, namely whether we are facing a human rights problem or we are in the field that requires a simple technical regulation on safety and logistics of research on the human DNA.[107]

106 David Price, *Legal and Ethical Aspects of Organ Transplantation* (Cambridge: Cambridge University Press, 2000).

107 Directive 2004/23/EC of the European Parliament and of the Council of 31 March 2004 on setting standards of quality and safety for the donation, procurement, testing, processing, preservation, storage and distribution of human tissues and cells, Strasbourg, March 31st 2004. Commission Directive 2006/17/EC of February 8th 2006 implementing Directive 2004/23/EC of the European Parliament and of the Council as regards certain technical requirements for the donation, procurement and testing of human tissues and cells. Commission Directive 2006/86/EC implementing Directive 2004/23/EC of the European Parliament and of the Council as regards traceability requirements, notification of serious adverse reactions and events and

The second relevant discourse is the (so far mainly) unnoticed shift from the personality rights to a broad, *specie specific* protection of 'human'. Defining the boundaries of the human body is especially relevant when we look at research conducted on human beings, as the potential abuses or the possibilities of making psychological or physical harm justifies legal scrutiny in this field.[108] Most of the research carried out today is not conducted on *human beings* but on *human tissues*, blood samples, human DNA. Humans as research subjects are not even in the labs when research 'on them' is carried out. In other words, more and more human research is done *not on the human body but on human bodily substance.* As a consequence, pain and suffering and humiliation are usually not relevant concerns here as scientific observations are made not *on* human body but *about* the human body.

In the field of the application of genetic knowledge, legal issues are mostly concentrated around the problem of how new genetic information affects our basic human relations, family ties, decisions over the reproduction, insurance, employment and intellectual property. To be more precise, how genetic information should be qualified, what kinds of rights can be established on this knowledge, who should hold this knowledge and who is to control this intrinsically individual, wide-ranging information that can easily be obtained by others? Is it the genetic sample itself that should be protected, or rather the data that can be revealed during any examination of the sample? Or is it both of them in an identical manner, the sample as a set of data or separately as human tissue, or that the DNA information should be regarded as a special type of personal data?

The fine-tuning and detailed scrutiny of our biological and genetic view on humans, as well as the mapping of the entire human genome, originate from a generally understandable scientific drive, and at first sight it produces mostly neutral information. Serious ethical and legal dilemmas arise especially when this knowledge is applied in a broader social context.

Now, more than ten years after the landmark research on the Human Genome – perhaps in a less passionate manner than in the beginning of the 21st century— we can better see the various issues within the legal landscape of genetic research and particularly of biobanks. Now we should make more careful distinction between *personal* and *human*, between our social-cultural and biological identities. Rights over the human tissues do not make us (persons) equal with our (human) samples. On the other hand, biobank research should value more the individuals who participate in research by granting them a more emancipated status.

certain technical requirements for the coding, processing, preservation, storage and distribution of human tissues and cells, October 26th 2006.

108 Judit Sándor, 'Body Immortal'. In Jennifer Gunning, Søren Holm (eds), *Ethics, Law, and Society* (Aldershot: Ashgate, 2007), 123–135.

PART V
Reproductive Technologies and Human Dignity

Chapter 8
Human Reproduction and Human Dignity as a Constitutional Concept

Miguel Nogueira de Brito

A philosophical dependent concept?

Even if the concept of human dignity is contained in the Constitution, in truth at the very beginning and as the foundation of almost every Constitution following the Second World War,[1] its content is not comprehensible without the help of philosophical traditions. The most immediately perceptible of those traditions are inherent in what we can call the deontologist and the consequentialist approaches to human dignity. It is even possible to say that 'all conflicts of interpretation at last gravitate around the content construction of a dignity violation and its categorical or open to consideration character'.[2] No doubt, the 'categorical' refers to the deontologist, and the 'open to consideration' to the consequentialist approach.

In this article, I argue, having in mind the uses of human dignity in the field of genetics, that beyond the opposition between a deontologist and a consequentialist conception of human dignity lays a more profound connection: both conceptions are instruments of the 'governmental reason' of the liberal state, a well known concept developed by Michel Foucault. Furthermore, I argue, also following Foucault, that the consequentialist approach tends to expand over the deontologist one, especially if one considers the legal articulation of both approaches. I illustrate these aspects by means of recent decisions of the Portuguese Constitutional Court as well as of the Brazilian Supreme Federal Court on the issue of scientific research on human embryos. In the following pages, I begin by explaining how biopolitics arises in the same historical moment in which human dignity assumes a central role in legal and moral discourses. After that I expose two radically different conceptions of human dignity and their alignment with the consequentialist and deontologist approaches. Subsequently I argue that liberal political theory, in either its libertarian or more egalitarian varieties, tends to adopt the consequentialist approach on human dignity. I then turn to the legal articulation of the two previously exposed conceptions of human dignity, before analyzing two recent judicial decisions on the issue of artificial procreation.

1 See, for example, article 1 of the Portuguese Constitution of 1976, which says that 'Portugal is a Sovereign Republic based upon human dignity and the popular will and committed to building a free, just and solidary society'. In the same vein, article 1-III of the Brazilian Constitution of 1988 establishes human dignity as one of the foundations of the Republic.

2 Cf. Herdegen, Matthias 2008. 'Deutungen der Menschenwürde im Staatsrecht', in *Menschenwürde: Begrundung, Konturen, Geschichte*, edited by Gerd Brudermüller and Kurt Seelmann. Würzburg: Königshausen & Neumann, 57.

Biopolitics

The strains on the concept of human dignity have their immediate source in the advances of biotechnology and of genetics in particular.[3] More remotely but also more structurally one can explain the strains on the concept of human dignity as a result of the emergence of biopolitics as a new form of governmentality from the eighteenth century on, as pointed out by Michel Foucault.

The new challenges made by genetics to the concept of human dignity are to be understood in the context of new forms of biopolitics, the political managing of human life itself.[4] But in fact the encounter between politics and the law, on the one hand, and genetics, on the other hand, is not one in which politics and law undertake a mere passive role in the face of scientific developments; on the contrary, this encounter is also a consequence of the internal development of political power. Biopolitics simply means that the human body goes through being an object of political power, that phenomena peculiar to life itself finally enter the reach of political calculation.[5]

Since at least the end of the eighteenth century onwards it has been shown that political power is acted upon the population at large, understood not merely as a large human group but as an assembly of living beings ruled by biological processes and laws. A population has a birth-rate and a death-rate, an age pyramid, a health condition and so on. The political discovery of population is, according to Foucault, the great technological axis around which all political procedures of the Occident were transformed. As Foucault says:

> life enters the domain of power: capital mutation, one of the most important ones, without doubt, in the history of human societies; and it can clearly be seen that sex has become from that moment on, that is, from the eighteenth century on, a capital part since sex is most correctly put on the intersection between the individual disciplining of the body and the regulations of the population.[6]

It is easy to understand how this conception of governmentality provides the ideal frame for eugenics, a word of Greek origin that means 'well born' and was regained in 1833 by Sir Francis Dalton, a cousin of Charles Darwin, who applied statistical methods to the study of heredity. The dictionaries tell us that eugenics corresponds to the applied biological science whose purpose is the improvement of human genetic qualities, but also the study and practice of selective breeding applied to humans with the aim of improving the human species, including the medical intervention on human reproduction.[7] This rather consensual definition conceals a fundamental distinction between an old and a new eugenics.

---

3 As stressed by Wolfgang Graf Vitzthum, the endangerment of human dignity by means of genetics acquires a new dimension – *homo faber*'s destructive capacity of disposition over the identity and evolution of the human species (see Vitzthum, 1985. Die Menschenwürde als Verfassungsbegriff. *Juristen Zeitung*, 1985, 201).

4 See Ladeur, Karl-Heinz and Augsberg, Ino 2008. *Die Funktion der Menschenwürde im Verfassungsstaat. Humangenetik – Neurowissenschaft – Medien*. Tübingen: Mohr Siebeck, Tübingen, 41; Ogien, Ruwen, 2009. *La Vie, la Mort, l'État: Le Débat Bioéthique*. Paris: Grasset, Paris, 22 note 2.

5 See Allen, Barry, 1998. Foucault and Modern Political Philosophy, in *The Later Foucault: Politics and Philosophy*, edited by Jeremy Moss. London: SAGE Publications, 187.

6 See Foucault, Michel 1994. Les Mailles du Pouvor, in *Dits et Écrits*, IV – 1980–1988, edited by Daniel Defert and François Ewald. Paris: Éditions Gallimard, 193–194; Neyrat, Frédéric, 2008. *Biopolitique des Catastrophes*. Éditions MF, 41 ff.

7 See *Dicionário da Língua Portuguesa Contemporânea da Academia das Ciências de Lisboa*. 2001. Lisboa: Verbo.

Old eugenics was the one in which the government would actively restrain the reproduction of people with 'bad genes', through the forced sterilization of disabled persons or persons belonging to degenerate social groups, such as convicts and vagrants. In the first years of the twentieth century 'old eugenics' has lead to the forced sterilization of thousands of people in Nazi Germany, but also in the United States and in social-democrat Sweden.

In face of the old stands the new genetics: the distinction between the two turns around the line that separates a eugenics envisaged as state coercive interfering in the lives of individuals in the name of public health and well-being, as a public policy, and a clinic genetics, considered as a service provided to individuals. New eugenics claims itself to be a liberal eugenics, which provides uncoercive genetic improvements and does not go against the autonomy of the children it helps to give birth to.[8]

It is important to underline at this stage the fitting not only of the old but also of the new eugenics to biopolitics as a specific conception of governmentality. In fact when Foucault refers to biopolitics he is careful to note that biopolitics governmentality is a special case of liberal governmentality. The liberal state is not quite opposed to absolutist reason of state, but rather modifies it without questioning its foundations.[9] Hence, according to Foucault liberalism does not amount to the setting aside of reason of state but only to the acknowledgment of the 'reason of less government as the very organizing principle of the reason of state'.[10] Liberal eugenics means the recognition of the reason of less government in the realm of genetic improvement of the population. Less government means precisely the rejection of a coercive intervention of the public powers towards the goal of genetic improvement, but not the relinquishment of an efficient pursuit of the same goal.

An example of this is the policy developed by the government of Singapore which included the offering of $4.000 as down payment on a low cost apartment to low income and low educated women provided they were willing to be sterilized. At the same time, the same policy included several measures to encourage college graduates to marry and have children, from a state-run computer dating service, to courtship classes in the undergraduate curriculum and free 'love boat' cruises for single college graduates.[11] These rather bad taste measures show that the rejection of state imposition does not stop social pressure, through the establishment of social habits.

The modern concept of dignity shows up at exactly the same time as biopolitics emerges as an art of government. Peter Berger points out the central importance the concept of dignity acquires with modernity. Whilst the concept of honor is associated with a hierarchical order of society, the concept of dignity presupposes the discovery of the individual man and it is precisely this solitary self that modern consciousness has perceived as the bearer of human dignity and of inalienable human rights. According to Berger, the modern discovery of dignity took place precisely amid the wreckage of debunked conceptions of honor. What is modern, however, is not the discovery that there is humanity behind the roles and norms imposed by society, but the assumption that

8 On this distinction, see Buchanan, Allen Brock, Dan W. Daniels, Norman and Wikler, Daniel, 2001. *From Chance to Choice: Genetics and Justice*. Cambridge: Cambridge University Press, 27 ff. and 53, which also allude to the difference between a Public Service Model and a Personal Service Model; Sandel, Michael J., 2007. *The Case Against Perfection: Ethics in the Age of Genetic Engineering*. Cambridge, Massachusetts: The Belknap Press of Harvard University Press, 63 ff.; Habermas, Jürgen 2003. *The Future of Human Nature*, Cambridge: Polity Press, 60 ff.

9 See Foucault, Michel 2004. *Naissance de la Biopolitique: Cours au Collège de France, 1978–1979*, Paris: Seuil/Gallimard, 23–24.

10 See Foucault, Michel Foucault 2004, 30.

11 See Sandel, Michael J., 2007, 69–70.

intrinsic humanity makes irrelevant all social differentiations among men. This is particularly clear, according to Peter Berger, in all classic formulations of human rights, from the Preamble to the Declaration of Independence to the Universal Declaration of Human Rights of the United Nations from 1948. Human rights are individual rights, independent of any social status.[12] At the same time the bearer of human rights is the individual which is also, considered as a member of a population, the subject of biopolitics.

So biopolitics and human dignity are connatural concepts. This is acutely described by Hannah Arendt when she says that 'man had hardly appeared as a completely emancipated, completely isolated being who carried his dignity within himself without reference to some larger encompassing order, when he disappeared again into a member of a people'.[13] Arendt primarily views the fact that the question of human rights was inextricably blended from the beginning with the question of national emancipation. Only human beings who had their own government had human rights, even if these had been solemnly defined as inalienable and independent of all governments. But with the appurtenance to a people came inextricably blended the appurtenance to a population. And as history has tragically demonstrated, even when the individual is not considered as member of a people who respects the rights of man their appurtenance to a population to be coped with by the political power is never denied. In the same vein, Habermas asks why human dignity appears so late in constitutional and international law, at least when compared with human rights. To Habermas the answer is simple: the inclusion of human dignity in the Universal Declaration of Human Rights and in almost all Constitutions subsequent to the Second World War was a response to mass murder and genocide,[14] in sum, to the most radical forms of biopolitics.[15]

There is however a missing element in the above sketched picture: science and technology are also essential parts of the overall scheme in which biopolitics and human dignity take part. In fact, one can even say that science and technology are manifestations of human dignity, at least in its specific modern interpretation. According to this interpretation the three fundamental components of human dignity are rationality, perfectibility and autonomy. Reason is the most characteristic feature of the human race, sure no longer in the sense of knowledge about the goal and purpose of human existence, as in the Ancient Times and the Middle Ages, but in the sense, devoid of any teleology, of control over nature. This also means that the human being has no fixed place in God's plan of creation but its essence is permanent self-alteration and self-perfection. With this comes autonomy, in the sense developed by Kant: the human being is capable of shaping not only its environment but also of creating its own norms and values.[16] In this context science and technology are without doubt a strong expression of reason, perfectibility and autonomy. But the relation of

---

12 See Berger, Peter 1985. *On the Obsolescence of the Concept of Honor in Revisions*, edited by Stanley Hauervas and Alasdair MacIntyre. Notre Dame, Indiana: University of Notre Dame Press, 176; Taylor, Charles 1992. 'The Politics of Recognition', in *Multiculturalism and 'The Politics of Recognition*, edited by Amy Gutmann. Princeton, New Jersey: Princeton University Press, 27, 37 and 49–51; Habermas, Jürgen, 2003, p. 37. Alexander Welsh attempts to salvage the concept of honor in our times (see Welsh, Alexander, 2008. *What is Honor? A Question of Moral Imperatives*. New Haven: Yale University Press, 199 ff.)

13 See Arendt, Hannah 2004. *The Origins of Totalitarianism*. New York: Schocken Books, 369.

14 See Habermas, Jürgen 2011. Das Konzept der Menschenwürde und die realistische Utopie der Menschenrechte, in *Zur Verfassung Europas: Ein Essay*, Berlin: Suhrkamp, 14–15.

15 See Agamben, Giorgio 1998. *Homo Sacer: Sovereign Power and Bare Life*, translated by Daniel Heller-Roazen, Stanford, California: Stanford University Press, 69 ff.

16 For the above see Bayertz, Kurt 1996. 'Human Dignity: Philosophical Origin and Scientific Erosion of an Idea', in *Sanctity of Life and Human Dignity*, edited by Kurt Bayertz. Dordrecht: Kluwer Academic Publishers, 77.

science and technology to human dignity is not without ambivalence: if nature is degraded to mere matter, what about human nature?[17]

Two extreme positions on human dignity

As responses to the advances of biotechnology it is possible to identify two extreme and opposite positions in what regards human dignity. In one of such extremes we can locate the content of the document from 13 May 2006 of the Pontifical Council for the Family, with the title *Family and Human Procreation*. On the subject of human dignity one can read in that document the following:

> The assertion of human dignity is, undoubtedly, one of the most rich and important realities of modern civilization. Kant states the difference between thing and person; the first is a means; the second is always an end. A thing as a price and can be exchanged; persons have infinite value and admit no exchange. Christian thought not only assumes this aspect, but also shows its ground: the human person has infinite value because she is the image of God; even more, because she is loved by God.
>
> (...)
>
> The consequences from this are many and of great importance. Let us recall one of them, directly connected to our theme: the human being claims – as stated in the instruction *Donum Vitae* – to be treated as such since her conception.[18] Starting with this principle the Instruction denounces genetic manipulation in what concerns the use of embryos or *in vitro* fertilization.[19] As a person endowed with dignity the human being is to be begotten, not produced, is to come to life not as a consequence of an artificial process but in virtue of a human act in its proper sense: a union between a man and a woman deemed by its very nature to be inspired by love.[20]

The presuppositions of this conception of dignity are clear: the person as an end in itself and never as a means to an end; the person as an image of God; the person as the object of the love of God. The consequences of the same conception are also clear, according to the document *Family and Human Procreation* and, above all, the instruction *Donum Vitae*:

17 See Bayertz, Kurt 1996, 83–84.

18 See Instruction on respect for human life in its origin and on the dignity of procreation, I, 1: 'Thus the fruit of human generation, from the first moment of its existence, that is to say from the moment the zygote has formed, demands the unconditional respect that is morally due to the human being in his bodily and spiritual totality. The human being is to be respected and treated as a person from the moment of conception; and therefore from that same moment his rights as a person must be recognized, among which in the first place is the inviolable right of every innocent human being to life' (available at www.vaticano.va).

19 See Instruction on respect for human life in its origin and on the dignity of procreation, I, 6: 'Techniques of fertilization *in vitro* can open the way to other forms of biological and genetic manipulation of human embryos, such as attempts or plans for fertilization between human and animal gametes and the gestation of human embryos in the uterus of animals, or the hypothesis or project of constructing artificial uteruses for the human embryo. *These procedures are contrary to the human dignity proper to the embryo, and at the same time they are contrary to the right of every person to be conceived and to be born within marriage and from marriage. Also, attempts or hypotheses for obtaining a human being without any connection with sexuality through 'twin fission', cloning or parthenogenesis are to be considered contrary to the moral law, since they are in opposition to the dignity both of human procreation and of the conjugal union'*.

20 See Famiglia e Procreazione Umana. 2006, § 15, in Pontificio Consiglio per la Famiglia, 2007. *Famiglia e Procreazione Umana, Commenti sul documento*. Vaticano: Libreria Editrice Vaticana, 253–55.

- The human being is to be respected and treated as a person from the moment of conception, and therefore from the same moment his rights as a person must be recognized (*Donum Vitae*, I, 1);
- Prenatal diagnosis is permissible if the methods employed safeguard the life and integrity of the embryo and the human fetus and is directed towards its safeguarding or healing as an individual *(Donum Vitae*, I, 2);
- It is immoral to produce human embryos destined to be exploited as disposable 'biological material' (*Donum Vitae*, I, 5);
- Attempts or hypotheses for obtaining a human being without any connection with sexuality through 'twin fission', cloning or parthenogenesis are to be considered contrary to the moral law, since they are in opposition to the dignity both of human procreation and of the conjugal union (*Donum Vitae*, I, 6);
- The corpses of human embryos and fetuses, whether they have been deliberately aborted or not, must be respected just as the remains of other human beings (*Donum Vitae*, I, 4);
- The freezing of embryos, even when carried out in order to preserve the life of an embryo – cryopreservation – constitutes an offence against the respect due to human beings by exposing them to grave risks of death or harm to their physical integrity and depriving them, at least temporarily, of maternal shelter and gestation, thus placing them in a situation in which further offences and manipulation are possible (*Donum Vitae*, I, 6);
- Attempts to influence chromosomic or genetic inheritance aimed at producing human beings selected according to sex or other predetermined qualities are contrary to the personal dignity of the human being and his or her integrity and identity (*Donum Vitae*, I, 6);
- Heterologous artificial fertilization is contrary to the unity of marriage, to the dignity of the spouses, to the vocation proper to parents, and to the child's right to be conceived and brought into the world in marriage and from marriage (*Donum Vitae*, II, 2);
- Homologous artificial insemination within marriage cannot be admitted except for those cases in which the technical means is not a substitute for the conjugal act but serves to facilitate and to help so that the act attains its natural purpose (*Donum Vitae*, II, 6).

Let us now go to the opposite extreme. This is represented by B.F. Skinner's utopia in *Walden Two*, the utopia of a society ruled by science alone. In this society, as a consequence of experiments in selective breeding, 'the hereditary connection will be minimized to the point of being forgotten. Long before that, it will be possible to breed through artificial insemination without altering the personal relation of husband and wife. […] people will marry as they wish, but have children according to a genetic plan'.[21]

Without going that far in the goal of structuring society along the lines of science, Richard Dawkins claims, in a text with the suggestive title 'What's Wrong with Cloning?', that cloning provides a case study in the power of scientific thinking to change our minds. Dawkins says that if asked a positive argument in favour of human cloning his immediate response is to question where the burden of proof lies. According to him, 'there are general arguments based on individual liberty against prohibiting anything that people want to do, unless there is good reason why they should not'. For Dawkins, 'assuming that some people want to be cloned, the onus is on objectors to produce arguments to the effect that cloning would harm somebody, or some sentient being, or society or the planet at large'.

21 See Skinner, B.F., 2005 (1948). *Walden Two*. Indianapolis: Hackett, 133.

Dawkins rules out those arguments in an expedite way. If the harmed one is the clone herself, because perhaps she feels embarrassed or overburdened by expectations, that amounts to attributing to the clone the sentiment 'I wish I had never been born because...'. Such statements can be made, but they are hard to maintain, says Dawkins, and he further notes that those most likely to oppose to cloning are the very ones that would reject this style of argument when used in the abortion debate. As for arguments considering the harm that cloning might do to third parties, or to society at large, Dawkins says they must be strong enough to counter the general 'freedom of the individual' presumption in favour of cloning. Mere prejudice, including prejudice based upon religion, is not enough to counter such presumption. It is unjustified that religious opinions, just because they are religious, should be given any weight in public discussions on cloning.[22] Dawkins, whose position would surely apply to all techniques of artificial reproduction, appears to be defending not only individual freedom but also the freedom of scientific research.

Close to Dawkins' is the argument developed by John Harris. According to this author a fundamental principle of the morality of all democratic countries is that human liberty should not be abridged without good cause being shown. Where the liberty in question is trivial, morally dubious or morally neutral, it is plausible to accept its limitation by the popular will. But if that is not the case, then the limitation of the freedom in question is a serious matter. Admitting that decisions to reproduce in particular ways or even to use particular technologies constitute decisions of moral value then, arguably, the freedom to make them is guaranteed by the constitution of any democratic society, unless the state has a compelling reason for denying its citizens that freedom, that is, to deny them what Ronald Dworkin calls their 'procreative autonomy'. According to John Harris, no remotely plausible arguments exist as to how human cloning might pose significant dangers or threats or that it may compromise important human values. As a consequence there is a *prima facie* case for regarding human cloning as a dimension of procreative autonomy that should not be lightly restricted.[23]

John Harris claims in particular that the following cloning cases should be admitted:

- A couple in which the male partner is infertile want a child genetically related to them both and so they prefer to clone the male partner rather than opting for donated sperm;
- A couple in which neither partner has usable gametes, although the woman could gestate, want a child related to both and so they opt to use an egg cloned with the DNA of one of them;
- A single woman who wants a child prefers the idea of using all her own DNA to the idea of accepting 50 per cent from a stranger;
- A couple whose only child is dying want to de-nucleate one of her cells so that they can have another child of their own;
- A partner which has a severe genetic disease wants to use the other partner's genome so that the couple can have their own child;
- Researchers want to create multiple cloned embryos of an adult who seems to have genetic immunity to AIDS in order to isolate the gene and see if it can be created artificially to permit a gene therapy for AIDS.

22 See Dawkins, Richard 1998. 'What's Wrong with Cloning?', in *Clones and Clones: Facts and Fantasies about Human Cloning*, edited by Martha Nussbaum and Cass Sunstein, New York; W.W. Norton & Company, 60 ff.

23 See Harris, John 1998. 'Clones, Genes, and Human Rights', in *The Genetic Revolution and Human Rights, The Oxford Amnesty Lectures 1998*, edited by Justine Burley. Oxford: Oxford University Press, 85–86, 92–94.

John Harris not only considers that these cases of cloning would not be unethical or contrary to human rights or dignity; he also claims that human dignity could be compromised by the rejection of cloning in such cases.[24]

What should we think of these radically opposed conceptions?

First of all, the conception of human dignity that presents itself as the expression of the idea that the human being is to be respected and treated as a person from the moment of conception can be questioned as the basis for a constitutional concept. And this is so because this conception, being based in a metaphysical or religious conception of the person, cannot generate consensus in our plural societies. As a consequence, this person-centered conception of human dignity cannot be directly adopted as the basis for a legal principle of human dignity. Constitutional law norms and principles cannot, in fact, be the direct outcomes of a disputed moral conception since in our plural societies the state would act contrary to the human rights if it intended to enforce in a general way a particular ethics.[25]

What to say of the opposite conception, that is, the conception according to which biotechnology does not really present a challenge to human dignity? In truth it appears that authors such as Richard Dawkins and John Harris do not have a great concern with the conception of human dignity. John Harris even says that 'Appeals to human dignity are, of course, universally attractive; they are the political equivalent of motherhood and Apple pie. Like motherhood, if not Apple pie, they are also comprehensively vague'.[26] All that matters to these authors is liberty, including the autonomy of the individual. Dignity appears to be a simple function of the freedom of the individual. But it is doubtful if the freedom that is protected is not, first and foremost, the freedom of scientific research.[27]

On the other hand, although Dawkins devaluates the possibility that a clone develops feelings of the type 'I wish I had never been born because…', the fact remains that these feelings would give a new dimension to the well-known problem of wrongful life. This problem would no more be just connected to seriously defective life, in objective terms, but also to life imposed and contrary to the plans of a clone that suffers a genetic determination according to the preferences of others.[28] If the refusal to use the advances of biotechnology entitles a person to claim damages for a wrongful life perhaps the use of some of those advances can also have, in other cases, the consequence of entitling a person to claim damages for wrongful life out of genetic determinism.

The liberal vision

It seems that all liberal conceptions, notwithstanding the profound differences that separate them, share an open attitude towards some kind of what I labeled, following others, 'liberal eugenics'. Robert Nozick even speaks in this context of a 'genetic supermarket', capable of satisfying individual specifications, within certain limits, of future parents towards their children. This supermarket system would have the great advantage of not involving a centralized decision in what regards

---

24 See Harris, John 1998, 86–88, and 93.

25 See Nettesheim, Martin, 2005. 'Die Garantie der Menschenwürde zwischen metaphysischer Überhohung und blossem Abwägungtopos', in *Archiv des öffentlichen Rechts*, 130 2005, 74, 83 and 109.

26 See Harris, John, 1998, 66.

27 Harris, Jones, 1998, 64, claims that is opposition to the ban on reproductive cloning 'is based on freedom, but not on scientific freedom', but he surely doesn't bother to make any kind of differentiation between the two.

28 See Nettesheim, Martin 2005, 75.

the human types of the future.[29] Ronald Dworkin also favours liberal eugenics. The question he raises is up to what point scientific research should continue in matters of cloning and other areas of genetic engineering. According to Dworkin, the principles of ethical individualism offer the necessary guidance:[30] if playing God means struggling to improve our species the principle of each human life's equal importance 'commands that struggle', and the principle of each person's special responsibility for her own life 'forbids, in the absence of positive evidence of danger, hobbling the scientists and doctors who volunteer to lead it'.[31]

In much the same way, in his *A Theory of Justice* Rawls considers the possibility of adopting eugenic policies, although he admits that the distribution of natural assets is a fact of nature. According to Rawls, 'the pursuit of reasonable policies in this regard is something that earlier generations owe to later ones, this being a question that arises between generations. Thus over time a society is to take steps at least to preserve the general level of natural abilities and to prevent the diffusion of serious defects'. Stating that he does not want to treat questions of eugenics, Rawls nevertheless says the following: 'We might conjecture that in the long run, if there is an upper bound on ability, we would eventually reach a society with the greatest equal liberty the members of which enjoy the greatest equal talent.'[32]

These conjectures of Rawls already point out the differences among liberals in what regards a liberal eugenics. To Nozick the genetic supermarket excludes any concern with a fair distribution of genetic improvements. The same does not happen with Dworkin and Rawls.[33] In fact, Nozick considers natural resources in terms of property rights; to Rawls and Dworkin natural resources, as well as the natural talents of each one, are considered as a domain of distributive justice.

In view of the above it seems clear that liberal conceptions tend to adopt the view according to which human dignity is subordinated to liberty and individual autonomy. They also tend to exclude those views that equate human dignity with religious or metaphysical conceptions. It is possible, however, to conceive of some liberal conception of morals and politics (liberal because it adopts the principle of moral individualism as a grounding idea) that is not so steadfast in rejecting religious and metaphysical conceptions of human dignity?

In this context one should mention first of all Rawls's 'pluralist transformation'. In his book *Political Liberalism*, liberalism is no longer justified as a 'comprehensive doctrine' of a philosophical variety – as the theory of the two principles of justice developed in *A Theory of Justice* – understood as including 'conceptions of what is of value in human life, and ideals of personal character, as well as ideals of friendship and of familial and associational relationships, and much else that is to inform our conduct, and in the limit to our life as a whole.'[34] The importance of this reference to Rawls's thought is easy to understand: the intrinsic value of a comprehensive doctrine, such as the one in which the person-centered conception of human dignity makes sense, is not questioned; the

---

29 See Nozick, Robert 1974. *Anarchy, State, and Utopia*. Oxford: Blackwell, 315, note.

30 These are the principle that holds that each human life has a special kind of objective value (the principle of intrinsic value) and the principle according to which each person has a special responsibility for realizing the success of his own life (the principle of personal responsibility): see Dworkin, Ronald 2006. *Is Democracy Possible Here? Principles for a New Political Debate*. Princeton: Princeton University Press, 9 ff.; idem, 2000. *Sovereign Virtue: The Theory and Practice of Equality*. Cambridge, Massachusetts: Harvard University Press, 5–6.

31 See Dworkin, Ronald 2000, 452.

32 See Rawls, John 1971. *A Theory of Justice*, Harvard: Harvard University Press, 108.

33 The concern with the distribution of the benefits of genetics, that is, the social justice approach to genetics is developed by Buchanan, Allen Brock, Dan W. Daniels, Norman and Wikler, Daniel, 2001, 59 ff.

34 See Rawls, John Rawls 1996. *Political Liberalism*. New York: Columbia University Press, 13.

necessity for good citizens to adopt some kind or another of a reasonable comprehensive doctrine is also not questioned; what is questioned, and indeed rejected, is the possibility for a constitutional state to be guided by the precepts of such a comprehensive doctrine. As above mentioned, Rawls liberal conception as exposed in *A Theory of Justice*, is also a comprehensive doctrine. Rawls political liberalism, after its pluralist turn, certainly excludes that a metaphysical or religious conception of human dignity, considered as part of a comprehensive doctrine, could be accepted as the basis for a constitutional state. It is not certain, however, how political liberalism positions itself in face of the view that subordinates dignity to liberty.

A philosophical view that simultaneously excludes the two above mentioned radical conceptions on human dignity appears to be the one of Habermas. To this author, on the one hand, religious and metaphysical conceptions are certainly unacceptable as the basis for a constitutional state. Habermas says that:

> In pluralistic societies, these metaphysical or religious interpretations of the self and the world are, for good reasons, subordinated to the moral foundations of the constitutional state, which is neutral with respect to competing worldviews and committed to their peaceful coexistence. Under the conditions of post metaphysical thought, the ethic self-understanding of the species, which is inscribed in specific traditions and forms of life, no longer provides the argument for overruling the claims of a morality presumed to be universally accepted.[35]

Up to this point Habermas is not far from Rawls, after the latter's 'pluralistic turn'. Habermas goes beyond Rawls, however, by clearly thinking it possible to reject, on liberal grounds, the views of those that consider there is nothing in human dignity that prevents the genetic improvement of human qualities. Habermas draws a distinction between natural fate and socialization fate. Socialization fate proceeds in a 'space of reasons' that even if not widely open to the child itself in the first stages of her cognitive development can always be retroactively regained. Adolescents 'can retrospectively compensate for the asymmetry of filial dependency by liberating themselves through a critical reappraisal of the genesis of such restrictive processes'. It is precisely this opportunity that is denied in the case of a genetic determination carried out according to the parent's own preferences.[36] This kind of genetic determination violates the child's autonomy.

Habermas further thinks that pre-implantation diagnosis and stem cell research are impermissible, even if in these cases there is no question of protecting a future child's autonomy. What is at stake here is an instrumentalization of prepersonal life that interferes with the ethical self-understanding of the species, which is crucial for whether or not we may go on seeing ourselves as beings committed to moral judgment and action.[37] This stabilizing context of the ethics of the species is what seems to give sense to the intuition shared by many of us that we should not weigh human life, not even in its earliest stages, either against the freedom (and competitiveness) of research, or against the wish for a healthy child or even against the prospect of new treatments for severe genetic diseases.[38]

35 See Habermas, Jürgen 2003, 40.

36 See Habermas, Jürgen 2003, 61–62.

37 See Habermas, Jürgen 2003, 71.

38 See Habermas, Jürgen 2003, 68.

Where does this lead us?

Michael Sandel agrees with Habermas's opposition to eugenic parenting, but he considers that this opposition is not to be grounded on the framework of a liberal vision alone. In fact, Sandel admits that the defenders of liberal eugenics have a point when they argue that designed children are no less autonomous with respect to their genetic traits than children born the natural way. The question, according to liberals, is whether the parental intervention, be it eugenic or environmental, undermines the child's freedom to choose her own life plan.[39]

Sandel argues, however, that Habermas has a further argument that cuts deeper, even if it points beyond the limits of liberal considerations. This is the idea that 'we experience our freedom with reference to something which, by its very nature, is not at our disposal'.[40] To Habermas there is a 'connection between the contingency of a life's beginning that is not at our disposal and the freedom to give one's life an ethical shape'.[41] To Michael Sandel what is at stake with eugenic parenting is not only the autonomy of the child but the corruption of parenting as a social practice governed by norms of unconditional love. One could say that eugenic parenting is on the verge of a proprietary understanding of the beginning of a human life; it adopts 'a stance of mastery and dominion that fails to appreciate the gifted character of human powers and achievements, and misses the part of freedom that consists in a persisting negotiation with the given'.[42]

Habermas considers that birth, being a natural fact, meets the conceptual requirement of constituting a beginning we cannot control and stresses that philosophy, with the exception of Hannah Arendt's concept of 'natality', has rarely addressed this matter. I think Habermas has really hit an important point here by showing the connection between human life's unconditioned beginning and human freedom.[43] The questions one must address at this point are, however, the following ones: to Habermas one should ask whether his argument is not assuming an exaggerated reach of the techniques of genetic manipulation on human life while, at the same time, devaluating the pressures of socialization processes and its resistance to overcoming in the 'space of reasons';[44] to Sandel one should ask whether the option between a model of parenting based on mastery and a model open to the sense of giftedness is really an exclusive function of the advances of biotechnology.

So the question remains: is there any mode of thought from which to refuse both these radical opposite conceptions of human dignity, i.e. the person-centered and the freedom-centered conceptions? Is it possible to set up with a perspective that permits us to reject the 'totalitarian' claims, if we are allowed to call them this way, of both religious and metaphysical views, on the one hand, and of science, on the other?

The 'object-formula' and the principle of proportionality as mutually exclusive criteria

What has been said is not enough: between the 'almost everything' of the freedom of scientific investigation and the 'almost nothing' imposed by our condition as creatures of nature as a presupposition of our quality of moral beings, what has been said is simply that neither perspective towards biotechnology can occupy the whole space of the law. The definition of the limits imposed

39 See Sandel, Michael J. 2007, 80–81.
40 See Sandel, Michael J. 2007, 81 with reference to Habermas, Jürgen 2003, 58.
41 See Habermas, Jürgen 2003, 75.
42 See Sandel, Michael 2007, 83.
43 See Habermas, Jürgen 2003, 58.
44 See Ladeur, Karl-Heinz and Augsberg, Ino 2008, 22.

by the principle of human dignity to religion but also to technology and science is a legal definition. In order to clarify its scope it is necessary first to clarify that the two above mentioned extreme conceptions on human dignity also find their counterpart in the realm of constitutional law. In law the counterpart of the person-centered conception of human dignity is the 'object-formula'; the counterpart of the above mentioned freedom-centered conception of human dignity is the principle of proportionality combined with a vision of fundamental rights not only as 'optimization requirements',[45] but also as expressions of freedoms *prima facie* unlimited.

The 'object-formula' goes back to the German legal scholar Günter Dürig and his commentary from 1958 on the principle of dignity foreseen in article 1 of the 1949 German Basic Law.[46] It is necessary to distinguish four traits of the traditional understanding, developed by Dürig, of this principle: 1) human dignity involves the reception of an ethical value by positive constitutional law, which is thereby anchored on natural law; 2) furthermore the 'object-formula' implies the qualification of human dignity as an objective law norm, the 'highest constitutional principle of all objective law',[47] or even as a 'right to rights',[48] but not as an individual right; 3) this means, even if Dürig has not said it in these words, that while fundamental rights are subject to limits and can be submitted to a proportionality review human dignity is inviolable;[49] 4) it also means that the content of human dignity is evaluated from the point of view of those human actions that represent a violation of the objective law norm.[50] Human dignity is hit upon when 'a concrete person is disrespected as an object, as a simple means, as a replaceable value'.[51]

What criticisms can one address at this formula? First of all, one must question whether the 'object-formula' amounts to a generalization through law of a particular ethical conception, inspired in Kant and with Christian roots. In what regards the Kantian inspiration it is necessary to clarify that in the second formula of the categorical imperative Kant recognizes the inevitability of some functionalization of the person:[52] 'act so that you use humanity, whether in your own person or in the person of any other, always at the same time as an end, never merely as a means.'[53]

45 See Alexy, Robert 2002. *A Theory of Constitutional Rights*, translated by Julian Rivers. Oxford: Oxford University Press, 47 ff.

46 See Geddert-Steinacher, Tatjana 1990. *Menschenwürde als Verfassungsbegriff. Aspekte der Rechtsprechung des Bundesverfassungsgerichts zu Art. 1 Abs 1 Grundgesetz*. Berlin: Duncker &Humblot, 31 ff.

47 See Dürig, Günter 1958. Der Grundrechtssatz von der Menschenwürde, in Gerd Brudermüller and Kurt Seelmann, 2008, 175.

48 See Enders, Christoph 1997. *Die Menschenwürde in der Verfassungsordnung*. Tübingen: Mohr Siebeck, 501 ff.

49 See Böckenförde, Ernst-Wolfgang 2006. Die Würde des Menschen war unantastbar. Zur Neukommentierung der Menschenwürdegarantie des Grundgesetzes, in *Recht, Staat, Freiheit. Studien zur Rechtsphilosophie, Staatstheorie und Verfassungsgeschichte*. Frankfurt am Main: Suhrkamp, 380.

50 See Böckenförde, Ernst-Wolfgang 2006, 382.

51 See Dürig, Günter 1958, 182.

52 See Ladeur, Karl-Heinz and Augsberg, Ino 2008, 28–29.

53 See Kant, Immanuel 1998. *Groundwork of the Metaphysic of Morals*, translated and edited by Mary Gregor, Cambridge: Cambridge University Press, 38 (AA, IV: 429). The third formula stresses 'the idea *of the will of every rational being as a will giving universal law*' and states the principle according to which one should 'act only *so that the will could regard itself as at the same time giving universal law through its maxim*' (Kant, *Groundwork*, cit., pp. 39 and 42; AA, IV: 431, 434). The second formula is the 'self purpose formula' and the third is the 'self legislating formula'. It should also be noted that Kant himself thought the ground of the concept of dignity was in the third formula while the actual debate favors the second formula

In the second place it is very difficult to say who (or which) are the holders of human dignity.[54] Third, the object-formula gives rise to uncertainties as to which actions are contrary to dignity, as Martin Nettesheim has shown. On the one hand, human dignity admits no weighing. All that matters is the action in itself, its purposes being indifferent: no differentiations are admitted in what concerns the protection of a human life endowed with dignity. In this way torture is certainly unconditionally forbidden, whatever the ends one chooses to pursuit with it. But, in the same way, the embryo receives much the same protection as a person. However, positive law shows that a treatment contrary to dignity can have different meanings depending in which context we are placed. A prisoner is subjected to a treatment that no freeman would tolerate; public education justifies interferences in the lives of children that could not be demanded of a grown person; it is permissible, at least under certain circumstances, to interrupt medical treatment of people in a coma without the possibility of recovery. In what concerns specifically the question of extending the protection of human dignity to pre-natal life, the fetus does not receive the same protection as the embryo, as is demonstrated by the abortion issue. Fourth, those who claim that embryos are protected by the constitutional principle of human dignity, and accept that in certain circumstances the interests of scientific research can prevail over the embryo's interests, are not necessarily treating it merely as a means. In other words, accepting consideration in the context of human dignity is not necessarily the same as treating the holders of human dignity as mere objects. At last, it is possible to claim that in a sense the 'object-formula' enfeebles human dignity. This is the case if one argues that the extension of human dignity's protection to embryos is necessary in order to avoid their manipulation.[55] In such a case, the goal of avoiding the manipulation of human life leads to the manipulation of the constitutional principle that protects it.

As to the principle of proportionality, considered in the context of constitutional rights as *prima facie* unlimited freedoms, what matters is to determine whether it is possible to subject human dignity to a proportionality review in face of other constitutional values. The idea that it can be so submitted lies at the core of the freedom centered conception of human dignity. Richard Dawkins, as above mentioned, expresses this idea when he says that 'there are general arguments based on individual liberty against prohibiting anything that people want to do, unless there is good reason why they should not'.[56] On the ground of general freedom all possible courses of action would in principle be admitted, save for the existence of opposite ponderous reasons. In this context there is no place to the very idea of the inviolability of human dignity that is at the core of the 'object-formula' and the strong deontologist view that is inherent in this formula is replaced by a consequentialist view.

The replacement of the 'object-formula' understanding of human dignity by a model opened to proportionality has been much contested.[57] This is easily understandable if one bears in mind that the above mentioned four notes defining the 'object-formula' understanding of human dignity are met by its exact opposites in case we accept the consequentialist understanding of human

[see Seelmann, Kurt 2008. Menschenwürde und die zweite und dritte Formel des Kategorischen Imperativs. Kantischer Befund und aktuelle Funktion, in Gerd Brudermüller and Kurt Seelmann, 2008, 68, 73 and 77].

54 See Nettesheim, Martin 2005, 80; Ladeur, Karl-Heinz and Augsberg, Ino 2008, 29.

55 See Nettesheim, Martin 2005, 81–84.

56 See Dawkins, Richard 1998, 60.

57 This is especially true in Germany, from where comes the 'object-formula'. The great debate around the change of paradigm mentioned in the text has its origin in the replacement in 2003 of the commentary to article 1 of the Grundgesetz by Günter Dürig, the author of the so-called 'object-formula' by a new commentary by Matthias Herdegen, more open to the idea of proportionality in the realm of human dignity. See Böckenförde, Ernst-Wolfgang 2006 379 ff.

dignity. 1) First of all, according to this conception the principle of human dignity is a norm of positive law.[58] 2) Furthermore, human dignity is not simply a norm of objective law, but should be considered as a norm that establishes a fundamental subjective right,[59] or at least as norm that is used in connection with a specific basic right. 3) As a consequence, human dignity is open to weighing against other values. In the concept of human dignity one must distinguish a core which includes categorical prohibitions with a high degree of abstraction, such as the prohibitions of domestic life scouts, imprisonment life sentences and forced feeding, and a periphery in which the human dignity violation arises out of the end of a course of action, as in the cases of race discrimination. In such cases, if one diminishes the abstraction level of the criteria that determine a violation of human dignity it is possible to resort to the proportionality test.[60] 4) In the fourth place, the concept of human dignity is given not primarily on the basis of objective actions that constitute a violation of its core content but mainly by the goal of a measure that can interfere with human dignity.[61] This conception gives special emphasis to a distinction of levels of protection entailed in the legal principle of human dignity. Matthias Herdegen expresses this idea in the following way: 'Notwithstanding the claim to human dignity that inheres in every person and leads to the prohibition of certain categories of acts, the mode and measure of the protection of human dignity is open to differentiations which should acknowledge the circumstances of the case.'[62]

What criticisms can one address at this mode of understanding human dignity as a constitutional principle? In the first place, if one admits a distinction between dimensions of human dignity, which are protected according to different modes and measures, one must ask what the criteria for this distinction are.

This takes us to a second criticism: it is not the citizen, or even the Constitution, but the lawmaker, and after him the judge, who applies the proportionality test.[63] But it is the citizen, not the lawmaker nor the judge, which is to be protected by the principle of human dignity. If one adopts a consequentialist view of human dignity citizens will have difficulty to devise its content. Instead of being entrenched in the Constitution by the citizens and for the citizens, the content of human dignity will be specified by the legislator and the judge in ways perhaps the majority of citizens cannot anticipate.

We can now move to a third criticism: beneath the surface of proportionality lies the absence of reasonable criteria that enable citizens to know in advance the value of their legal positions in case of conflict with other positions or interests.[64] The logic of proportionality is in fact the logic of biopolitics.

What is the practical difference between the two modes of understanding human dignity as a constitutional concept? The difference can be shown by pointing out that according to the 'object-formula' any violation of human dignity immediately calls for the unconstitutionality of the statute or the administrative action. In contrast to the fundamental rights provisions in the Constitution, the dignity clause does not allow for a legal limitation but leads to an all-or-nothing approach and

58 See Herdegen, Matthias 2005. in *Grundgesetz. Kommentar*, edited by Theodor Maunz and Günter Dürig, 12.

59 See Herdegen, Matthias 2005, 18–20.

60 See Herdegen, Matthias 2005, 27–28.

61 See Herdegen, Matthias 2005, 28–29.

62 See Herdegen, Matthias 2005, 35.

63 See Karl-Heinz Ladeur, 2004. *Kritik der Abwägung in der Grundrechtsdogmatik. Plädoyer für eine Erneuerung der liberalen Grundrechtsdogmatik*. Tübingen: Mohr Siebeck, 15 ff.

64 See Pieroth, Bodo and Schlink, Bernhard 2006. *Grundrechte Staatsrecht II*, 22nd edition. Heidelberg: C.F. Müller Verlag, 66 ff.

gives unlimited, absolute protection.[65] Under the proportionality model human dignity entails, as is the case with fundamental rights, a limitation: Statutes may infringe human dignity, at least in the periphery of the concept, if they can be sufficiently justified under the proportionality principle. In other words, one could say that the 'object-formula' views dignity as a 'rule', applicable 'in an all-or-nothing fashion',[66] while under the proportionality model dignity is a 'principle' whose applicability to the case is a matter of consideration. This situation is further complicated by the fact that the decisions of constitutional courts frequently cite the human dignity provision in conjunction with a specific basic right, usually the right to life. As explained by Oliver Lepsius, this approach, to apply the human dignity constitutional provision partially within the area of specific basic rights, establishes a core protection of these individual rights but it also conflicts with the absolute and ultimate character of the human dignity clause.[67]

Human dignity and liberal governmentality

How to conceive of human dignity in a way that is capable of overcoming the above mentioned difficulties both of the 'object-formula' and the model of proportionality? The situation is made even more difficult as there is the temptation to resolve problems in the areas of biotechnology by means of the combination of human dignity and the right to life. An easy escape to this dilemma would be to claim that human dignity sometimes functions as an absolute rule and others as an open to consideration principle,[68] even without providing further criteria that enable us to understand when human dignity is to be viewed as a rule and as a principle. This strategy of affirming human dignity without clarifying whether it stands as an absolute rule or an open to consideration principle is manifest in some judicial decisions. I illustrate it by means of two recent decisions of the Portuguese Constitutional Court and the Brazilian Federal Supreme Court.

Portuguese law forbids the creation of embryos with the deliberate goal of using them in scientific research having therapeutic purposes, except in what concerns the remaining embryos created for purposes of artificial procreation but for which there is no 'parental project' (article 9, n. 2, of Law n. 32/2006, July 26). Furthermore in Portuguese law there is no limitation in what regards the creation of embryos for purposes of *in vitro* fertilization (article 24). On the other hand the embryos' use for purposes of scientific research is only permitted if benefits to the human kind are to be expected; the judgment concerning these benefits is to be reached by the National Council on Medical-Assisted Procreation (article 9, n. 3). The way this coheres with human dignity is certainly doubtful. Moreover, one cannot help asking oneself whether the intervention of the National Council on Medical-Assisted Procreation is opening the door to the dangers of a moral authoritarianism.[69] Constitutional Court decision n. 101/2009 has considered that it does not. According to this decision Law n. 32/2006 is not unconstitutional because scientific research only extends to those embryos which cannot be employed in parental projects and, furthermore, the

65 See Lepsius, Oliver 2006. 'Human Dignity and the Downing of Aircraft: The German Federal Constitutional Court Strikes Down a Prominent Anti-terrorism Provision in the New Air-transport Security Act', in *German Law Journal*, Vol. 7, No. 9, 2006, 769; for the contrast between absolute dignity and relative right to human life.

66 See Dworkin, Ronald 1977. *Taking Rights Seriously*. London: Duckworth, 24.

67 See Lepsius, Oliver 2006, 769.

68 See Alexy, Robert 2002, 47 ff.; Teifke, Niels 2011. *Das Prinzip Menschenwürde*. Tübingen: Mohr Siebeck, 155–157.

69 See Ladeur, Karl-Heinz and Augsberg, Ino 2008, 44.

research is only legal if it can advance the 'benefit of mankind'. Once it is known that according to Portuguese law there is no limitation in what regards the creation of embryos for purposes of *in vitro* fertilization, as above mentioned, it is questionable whether the law affords the embryos sufficient protection against instrumentalization by means of scientific research.

Brazilian law has taken a different path. Article 5 of Law n. 11.105, from the 24th of March 2005, admits, under certain conditions, the use of embryonic cells produced by *in vitro* fertilization for therapeutic and research purposes. According to the Federal Supreme Court this is not unconstitutional: the embryo is to be protected as an infra-constitutional good but not as 'a person in the biographical sense referred to by the Constitution'. There is no such thing as an embryo's 'right to a womb',[70] and so the embryo is removed from the scope of human dignity. According to the Federal Supreme Court research on embryonic cells which are no longer viable for reproductive purposes amounts to the 'celebration of life in solidarity with those who are at the margins of the concrete and inalienable exercise of the rights to happiness and living with dignity'.

Both decisions affirm human dignity as a fundamental principle and both come to adopt a rather consequentialist view of scientific research on human embryos. Is this merely a confused argument? I think these judicial decisions express a real tension between the competing claims of liberty and respect for human dignity, whose legal articulation was exposed above, and that this tension inners in the public philosophy of the liberal state.

I have already mentioned Foucault's depiction of the liberal state as introducing a 'new governmental reason', a reason built on the market envisaged as the place where truth is revealed concerning the relationship between value and price. Foucault also claims that in this new governmental reason two heterogeneous systems coexist: on the one hand there is the axiomatic of human rights; on the other hand we have the 'empirical and utilitarian way which defines, from the necessary limitation of the rulers, the sphere of independence of the ruled ones'. Beyond the permanent connections between these two systems there is one that is stronger than the other. The stronger one is the 'radical way that consists in defining the limitation of public power in terms of governmental utility'.[71]

On this view, there really is no convenient way to overcome the tensions between the deontological and the consequentialist approaches to human dignity, as this tension expresses the regression of legal discourse and its never ceasing colonization by a vision of power as management.[72]

70 See Federal Supreme Court decision of the 29th of May 2008 (ADI 3510).

71 See, Foucault, Michel 2004, 45.

72 On this, see Giacoia Junior, Oswaldo 2009. Identidades Irreconhecíveis, in *A Condição Humana: As Aventuras do Homem em Tempos de Mutações*, edited by Adauto Novaes. Rio de Janeiro: Agir, 289 ff.

Chapter 9

The Constitutional Debate on Stem Cell Research, Human Rights and Dignity: The Law and a Recent Court Ruling in Brazil

Luiz Edson Fachin

Introduction

Human life and science are not merely words with a meaning for academic debate in countries like Brazil. Strictly speaking, they deal with one of the most complex issues of our times, giving grounds to passionate discussions on scientific development and freedom of research, as well as on the concrete conditions of society itself.

What has happened in Brazil, except for historical and cultural differences, does not seem to be an exception. On the one hand, we see the rise of such arguments as the defence of the secular State, the autonomy of science as the basis for bioethics, and reproduction rights. On the other hand, we face a myriad of arguments about, *inter alia*, the existence of human life prior to birth, the therapeutic use of embryonic stem cells, and the existence of human life in the embryo.

This chapter will present the laws on embryonic stem cells, the arguments favouring and opposing the constitutional nature of the legal rule authorizing such scientific research, and the decision reached by the Brazilian Constitutional Court, which opened the doors to this new scientific horizon by a majority decision (decided by six to five opinions).

As the explanations unfold, it will be noted that the same principle – the dignity of the human person – is present in such debate, either to deny the legal possibility and the ethics of research on embryonic stem cells, and to contend that it is from scientific freedom that therapies to fight the various pathologies that afflict the very dignity of life itself may originate.

Firstly, I analyze the allegations that ascertain the human dignity as part of the fundamentals of the Republic, as expressly set forth in the Brazilian Constitution (article 1 [item III]), and even as a fundamental human right (expressly mentioned in the introduction to article 5 of the Constitution) based on the inviolable right to life.

Secondly, I examine the social and technical function of research, aiming to comply with the needs of government policies that implement the right to health, to physical integrity, and to the very dimension of living with dignity, as well as the freedom of scientific research, under provisions set forth in article 5, item IX, letter 'd' in the Brazilian Constitution. This is the course of our explanatory notes.

The aim of this chapter is to inform and examine a synthesis of the course these issues have recently taken in Brazil, both in the enactment of legal provisions and in the definition given by the Judiciary through the Supreme Federal Court in a recent ruling about the conformity of the law to the Constitution.

A key purpose is to show how any Court is not able to say what is right or what is wrong without looking at both the historical and cultural contexts of the individuals that develop their own personalities by relationships, composing a plural society, where the concept of human rights doesn't have just one meaning and where new technologies demand adequate answers.

Legal Grounds for Using Embryonic Stem Cells

Let us first examine the legal grounds which gave rise for controversy regarding research on embryonic stem cells in Brazil.

On 24 March 2005, president Luiz Inácio Lula da Silva enacted the Law No. 11105, which regulated the Federal Constitution, especially concerning 'safety norms and control mechanisms for the construction, cultivation, production, handling, transport, transfer, importation, exportation, storage, research, trading, consumption, release in the environment and discharge of genetically modified organisms and their by-products'. The law came to be known as the Biosafety Law.[1]

Prior to this 2005 law, there was a rule in Brazil banning genetic engineering of human stem cells, and the production, storage or handling of human embryos to be used as available biological

1 Law 11105 Of 24 March 2005: Below stated is a part of the legal statute that regulates items II, IV and V of article 225, paragraph 1, of the Brazilian Federal Constitution, sets forth safety norms and inspection systems for activities involving genetically modified organisms and their by-products, creates the National Biosafety Council (Conselho Nacional de Biossegurança – CNBS), restructures the National Biosafety Technical Commission (Comissão Técnica Nacional de Biossegurança – CTNBio), sets forth provisions on the National Biosafety Policy (Política Nacional de Biossegurança – PNB, revokes Law 8974 of 5 January 1995 and the Executive Order 2191–9 of 23 August 2001, revokes articles 5, 6, 7, 8, 9, 10 and 16 of Law 10814 of 15 December 2003, and includes other general provisions.

'THE PRESIDENT OF THE REPUBLIC: Let it be known that the National Congress decrees and I sanction the following Law:

CHAPTER I

PRELIMINARY AND GENERAL PROVISIONS

Article 1 – This Law establishes safety norms and oversight systems for the construction, cultivation, production, handling, transport, transfer, importation, exportation, storage, research, trading, consumption, release in the environment and discharge of genetically modified organisms and their by-products, under the guidelines of incentive to the scientific progress in the area of biosafety and biotechnology, protection of life and protection of human, animal and plant health, and compliance with the principle of precaution for the environment protection.

(...)

Article 5 – It is permitted for research and therapeutic purposes to use human embryonic stem cells produced by *in vitro* fertilization and not employed in the concerning procedure, subject to the following conditions:

I – that the embryos are unviable; or

II – that the embryos have been frozen for no less than 3 (three) years prior to the date of publication of this Law or, if already frozen at the date of publication of this Law, after a three-year lapse of the freezing date.

Paragraph One. The consent of parents will be required in all cases.

Paragraph Two. Research institutions and health service providers carrying research or therapy on or with human embryonic stem cells must submit their projects to the respective research ethics committees for approval.

(...)

Article. 41 – This law comes into force on the date of its publication.

(...)

Brasília, 24 March 2005; 184th year of the Independence and 117th year of the Republic.

LUIZ INÁCIO LULA DA SILVA, President of Brazil.'

material were also forbidden. Actually, both the genetic engineering of human germinal cells and *in vitro* interventions in human genetic material were treated as felony, subject to sentences of six to 20 years in prison.[2]

The wording of article 5 of the new law enacted in 2005 authorizes the research on embryonic stem cells, although the actual purpose of the original submitted bill was to regulate activities dealing with genetically modified organisms. Nevertheless, the theme of production, storage or handling of human embryos was added to the main bill, even though this matter, strictly speaking, bears little or no connection to the issue of GMOs (genetically modified organisms).

After a lot of discussions, public hearings and controversies, the Legislative Power approved the bill on 4 March 2005, with 60 votes against and 352 in favour of the measure. The new law authorized the research and defined embryonic stem cells as 'embryonic cells that are able to turn into any body tissue cell'.[3]

Within the universal scope encompassed by the new law (including, but not limited to, biotechnology, genetically modified organisms, biosafety and the precautionary principle), article 5 provided solely for the following permission:

> It is permitted, for research and therapeutic purposes, to use human embryonic stem cells produced by *in vitro* fertilization and not employed in the procedure, subject to the following conditions: first – that the embryos are unviable; or, second – that the embryos have been frozen for no less than three years prior to the date of publication of this Law (*i.e.* 28 March 2005), or, if already frozen at the date of publication of this Law, after a three-year lapse of the freezing date.

The consent of parents and the approval by research ethics committees were conditions previously established by law for the development of projects by research institutions and health service providers. From that date on, Brazil had a legal rule which encouraged scientific research on embryonic stem cells.

The Law is Challenged by an Allegation of Unconstitutionality

Less than two months after the law had come into force, the Federal Attorney-General of Brazil challenged the wording of article 5 in the new law as unconstitutional before the Supreme Federal Court, by means of a Direct Action of Unconstitutionality (under docket number 3510).[4]

The technical grounds for objecting to the research were, in brief, the following:

---

2 Such was the wording of articles 8 and 13 of Law 8974 of 5 January 1995, revoked by the new legislation (Law 11.105/2005). During the period between these two laws, Executive Order No. 2191-9 was issued on 23 August 2001, creating the Brazilian National Biosafety Technical Commission – CTNBio, a multidisciplinary body with collegiate powers, established for consulting purposes in the area of preparation, updating and implementation of the national policy on biosafety regarding genetically modified organisms, as well as human health protection.

3 Art. 3º, XI, Law 11.105/2005.

4 SUMMARY OF THE JUDGMENT BY THE BRAZILIAN SUPREME FEDERAL COURT

INFORMATION: The stating opinion by the Brazilian Supreme Federal Court (Supremo Tribunal Federal – STF) on the Direct Action of Inconstitutionality No. 3510, filed to ask that article 5 of the Biosafety Law be declared unconstitutional, started on 05 March 2008. The article challenged deals with the use of embryonic stem cells in researches. The stating opinion ended on 29 May 2008.

a. human life develops with, and as of, fertilization;
b. the embryo is destroyed by the use of embryonic stem cells;
c. current experiments show that adult stem cells may be used in an effective and safe manner;
d. there are no records of results from embryonic stem cells.

The petition for banning research on embryonic stem cells was based on the constitutional principle of the inviolable right to life, and on the protection granted by the Brazilian Civil Code to the rights of the unborn child from conception. During the legal debate there was also a mention of article 4 of the American Convention on Human Rights – 'Pact of San Jose, Costa Rica', of which Brazil is a signatory and which protects the right to life from the moment of conception,[5] including the allegation that such protection already existed in the Roman Law, since the rights of the foetus were guaranteed, as seen in the *Digesto* of the Justinian Code,[6] from the moment of conception.

The action was filed and assigned for proceedings by the Supreme Federal Court on 31 May 2005. After several court procedures, a public hearing was scheduled within the Constitutional Court two years later, to hear persons endowed with known expertise and authority in the field, as well as entities of the civil society. Such a hearing was set forth by the Brazilian Constitution for the Parliament, and was adopted by analogy by the Supreme Court.

Various entities and bodies of the Brazilian society participated in the debate and in the court procedures, such as the Brazilian Confederation of (Catholic) Bishops, the Institute of Bioethics, Human Rights and Gender, Brazil's Pro-Life Movement, besides obviously the Solicitor General of Brazil, defending the confirmation of the law enacted by the President of the Republic.[7]

The court session started on 5 March 2008 and ended on 29 May 2008, dismissing the direct action of unconstitutionality by a majority of voices. The opinions against the permission for researches were those of the Chief Justice (installed in office during the judgment) and of four other justices.[8]

For six justices, *i.e.*, for the majority opinion of the court, article 5 of the Biosafety Law is not liable to amendment. The majority opinion was given by justice Carlos Ayres Britto, reporting on the matter, and by justices Ellen Gracie, Cármen Lúcia Antunes Rocha, Joaquim Barbosa, Marco Aurélio and Celso de Mello.

5 Article 4. Right to Life: 1. Every person has the right to have his life respected. This right shall be protected by law and, in general, from the moment of conception. No one shall be arbitrarily deprived of his life.

6 DIGESTA (D. 1.5.7.): *'Nasciturus pro iam nato habetur, quotiens de eius commodis agitur'*.

7 PRONOUNCEMENT BY THE GENERAL FEDERAL ATTORNEY: The new General Federal Attorney, Antônio Fernando Barros e Silva de Souza, and the attorney for Brazil's National Confederation of (Catholic) Bishops (CNBB) also expressed their views, both arguing that the law was unconstitutional. For them, the Constitution guarantees the right to life, and the embryo is already a living being. Souza argued that: 'There is sound scientific conviction that human life starts with fertilization, and article 5 of the Constitution guarantees the inviolability of human life.'

8 THE JUDGMENT SESSION IS RESUMED: The stating opinion session resumed on 29 May 2008, and justice Carlos Alberto Menezes Direito stated opinion for the 'partial unconstitutionality' of article 5 of the law. The justice contended that the article required changes, so as to determine that no researches would be allowed on the embryonic stem cells unless the cells were removed from the embryo without destroying it. He stated, 'From the moment of fertilization, more precisely from the moment the sperm nucleus and the ovum nucleus are united, the embryo is already an individual, a representative of the human species, with the same genetic material of a foetus, a child, a grown-up, an old person'. For justice Menezes Direito 'the embryonic stem cells are indeed a human life, and any destination that is different from human reproduction violates the right to life'. He stated opinion against the researches.

OPINION OF JUSTICE RICARDO LEWANDOWSKI: In general lines, justice Ricardo Lewandowski stated opinion for the imposition of restrictions on stem cell researches, accepted the action partially, and

The Reporting Justice and five other justices stated opinion in favour of the permission.[9] The result

requested that the article be amended so that researches would not be allowed unless using non viable embryos, without any possibility of spontaneous division. He was opposed to researches.

OPINION OF JUSTICE EROS GRAU: Justice Eros Grau proposed amendments to the Biosafety Law in order to restrict research. The purpose of the justice was to assure that the stem cells used in the researches be solely those obtained from ova without spontaneous division, that all researches on embryonic stem cells be subject to a prior authorization by the Ministry of Health, and that the ova used be solely those from *in vitro* fertilization, exclusively for human reproduction. In the general count opinion, he opposed the researches, following the stand of justices Menezes de Direito and Ricardo Lewandowski.

OPINION OF JUSTICE CESAR PELUSO: For justice César Peluso the researches do not affront the right to life because the frozen embryos are not equivalent to persons. However, he emphasized the importance of strict inspection on the researches, pointing out the need for the proper legal tools for that purpose.

OPINION OF JUSTICE GILMAR MENDES, THE NEW CHIEF JUSTICE: The last opinion was tendered by justice Gilmar Mendes (already installed in office as the new Chief Justice of the Supreme Federal Court). He expressed reservations about the legislation, deeming that the Brazilian norm has deficiencies. Justice Mendes asserted that it is 'perplexing' to realize that this matter is ruled in Brazil by one single article of a statute. He further stated that the law fails to assign a central body to inspect the researches, under the Ministry of Health. His stand was aligned with the opinions opposing the researches.

9 OPINION OF REPORTING JUSTICE: The first opinion was given by the justice reporting on the proceedings, justice Carlos Ayres Britto, denying grounds to the action of unconstitutionality. He based his opinion on provisions of the Federal Constitution that guarantee the right to life, health, family planning and scientific research. He also stressed the spirit of brotherhood stated by the Federal Constitution for society when he defended the use of embryonic stem cells in researches seeking the cure for diseases. He used as argument in favour of stem cell use in researches the fact that human life only starts after birth. For the STF justice, 'human life is a phenomenon that takes place from birth to brain death. The embryo holds a vegetative life that precedes the brain'. The STF justice further tried to make a distinction between a frozen embryo and an embryo formed within the womb and the human person. For the reporting justice, a frozen embryo is unable to become a foetus or a human being, because it could not develop without being implanted in a feminine body. He stated opinion in favour of the researches.

OPINION OF THE CHIEF JUSTICE THEN IN OFFICE: At the same time, justice Ellen Gracie, then acting as chief justice of the STF, advanced her opinion and explained that she would follow the opinion of the reporting justice Carlos Ayres Britto as she fully agreed with him. For her, the Biosafety Law shows no vice of unconstitutionality. 'Neither the guarantee of human person dignity nor the guarantee of life inviolability can be ascribed to a pre-embryo since, as I believe, a pre-embryo not yet lodged in its natural development nest, the uterus, cannot be classified as a person.' She noted that the Brazilian legal system assigns the quality of person to a child born alive. 'On the other hand, a pre-embryo does not conform to the condition of an unborn child, since an unborn child, as the name specifies, presupposes the possibility or likelihood of birth, and that does not happen with embryos that are proved unviable or destined to be discarded.' She stated, 'I see no vice of unconstitutionality. In my belief, a pre-embryo not yet received by the uterus cannot be classified as a person.' She stated opinion in favour of the researches.

OPINION OF JUSTICE CÁRMEN LÚCIA ANTUNES ROCHA: Next, Justice Cármen Lúcia stated opinion in favour of the researches on embryonic stem cells. According to the justice, 'Their use is a form of knowledge for life. This is the nature of the scientific research on embryonic stem cells, which seeks to extend life, and not to affront it. In addition to the fact that the research does not violate the right to life, it becomes a part of human existence because it is not life'. She mentioned scientific studies indicating that the researches on embryonic stem cells capable of differentiating into any human tissue cannot be replaced by other lines of research, as those using adult stem cells, and that the discarding of cells not yet implanted in the uterus generates only 'genetic waste'. She stated opinion in favour of the researches.

OPINION OF JUSTICE JOAQUIM BARBOSA: Justice Joaquim Barbosa fully agreed with the reporting justice and stated opinion accordingly. For him, to ban the researches on embryonic cells, in terms of the law, was achieved by simple majority, *i.e.*, with six justices in favour and five justices against.[10]

Human Dignity as a Legal Value Amid the Debate

The dignity of the human person pervaded all moments of the debate and this theme is undoubtedly the cornerstone of the whole legal system. As an example, when stating opinion in favour of declaring the law unconstitutional as worded, justice Gilmar Mendes (installed as Chief Justice to replace justice Ellen Gracie) based his opinion, from the beginning, on the ethical, legal and moral issues of life and human dignity. To that extent, he further argued about the issues of abortion and euthanasia, stressing the role of the Constitutional Courts as 'houses of the people'.

He stated, in brief, that 'there is a vital element worthy of legal protection' even during the pre-birth stage, and that the Brazilian law was deficient 'in the regulation of researches and, therefore,

---

would mean 'to close the eyes to scientific progress and to the benefits likely to derive therefrom'. He stated opinion in favour of the researches.

OPINION OF JUSTICE MARCO AURÉLIO MELLO: Justice Marco Aurélio Mello stated opinion in favor of scientific researches on embryonic stem cells in Brazil. 'This not about questioning whether a pregnant woman should remain physically connected, but rather to determine the destiny of fertilized ova that would certainly be destroyed, and whether they can and should be used in an attempt to seek the progress of mankind,' he affirmed. He fully agreed with the reporting justice and stated opinion accordingly. He considered the wording of article 5 of the Biosafety Law, challenged by the Direction Action of Inconstitutionality, 'consistent with the Federal Constitution, more specifically with articles 1 and 5 thereof, and with the principle of reasonability'. Article 1, item III, of the Constitution sets forth the fundamental right to dignity of the human person, and the introduction to article 5 foresees the inviolable right to life. He also cautioned against the risk of having the STF take the role of legislator, by imposing restrictions to a law that, according to him, had been supported by 96 per cent of the senators and 85 per cent of the federal deputies, which would indicate its 'reasonability'. The justice also remarked that all positions on the supposed commencement of life were mere opinions, and he presented a list of constant discordant concepts throughout history, from ancient to modern times. For him, 'the commencement of life does not presuppose just the fertilization, but also the viability of pregnancy, of the human gestation'. He even remarked that 'to say that the Constitution protects the intrauterine life is prone to discussion, when considering [that the Constitution permits] the therapeutic abortion or the abortion of a child born out of rape'. And he concluded by saying that 'the legal cause of action depends upon a live birth' and that to throw away the embryos discarded from human reproduction would be a selfish gesture and deep blindness, since they could be used to cure diseases.

OPINION OF JUSTICE CELSO MELLO: Justice Celso de Mello also stated opinion in favour of the researches, as the law approved by the Congress gives the unviable embryos discarded 'a nobler destination'. 'All those embryos have one single destination: they are doomed to disposal as sanitary waste. Therefore, a nobler destination is assigned,' he affirmed. Regarding the statement that the law would contradict the right to life, he asserted: 'An ovum or an embryo that cannot be implanted in a uterus does not have the potential to become a human being.' The justice stated opinion in accordance with the reporting justice, *i.e.*, the action should be dismissed. According to him, the State cannot be influenced by religion. 'The enlightened opinion tendered by the eminent justice Carlos Britto will allow millions of Brazilians who are now suffering and living on the margins of life to actually exercise a basic and inalienable right, namely the right to seek happiness and also the right to live with dignity, a right of which nobody, absolutely nobody, should be deprived.'

10 FINAL OPINION RESULT: When the debates on the use of stem cells were completed, the norm of the debate was decided by 11 justices. Six of them dismissed the petition in the action of unconstitutionality of Article 5 of the Biosafety Law – that on the use of embryonic stem cells in researches.

By a slight simple majority, in May 2008, the Brazilian Supreme Court ruled as follows: the researches on embryonic stem cells do not violate the right to life, nor the human person dignity.

not compatible with the principle of proportionality in terms of prohibition of an insufficient protection'. Consequently, following such lines, the effective protection of Human Rights, of Fundamental Rights, and also of the so-called Personality Rights would demand an integral and unified protection of such rights, with a focus on the human person dignity as the central point of the axiological radiation of human values.

In view of the contemporary concept of human dignity and the relationship between the Constitution and Civil Law, it could be affirmed that the Personality Rights are actually Fundamental Rights.

Regarding this theme, both sides, attacking or defending the law that authorizes the research, *i.e.*, either seeking to declare it as unconstitutional or to uphold it as constitutional, ended up resorting to the same principle.

On the one hand, the parties defending the idea of declaring the law unconstitutional and opposing the researches tried to contend at the Supreme Court, albeit in vain, that from a legal point of view the right to life, as declared by article 5 of the Brazilian Constitution, is inviolable from the conception, and that this would further be warranted by article 4 of the new Brazilian Civil Code in force as of 2003, which protects the rights of the unborn child from the conception.

They further alleged that, from a scientific point of view, there would be a possibility of rejection, giving rise to embryonic tumours, of loss of control of embryonic cells, and that the treatment of genetic diseases could be made with adult stem cells. It was further argued that to open this door to researches would mean to transform human beings in experimental guinea pigs. They also stated that the law at least lacked a provision for the creation of a properly regulated Central Ethics Committee.

On the other hand, the parties defending the constitutional nature of the law contended that a distinction should be made between an embryo and an unborn child: whereas the Civil Code rule protects a potential being in development inside the maternal womb (*i.e.*, the unborn child), the embryo is neither a person nor an unborn child, since it is not yet implanted in the mother's uterus and its birth is uncertain.

It was further contended that the law did not authorize the researches unless the embryos represented surplus embryos from *in vitro* fertilization procedures, non-viable or frozen for over three years. In addition, the law prohibited human cloning, both therapeutic and reproductive, further banning any embryo trading. As an example, we present the opinion given by Justice Cármen Lúcia Antunes Rocha.

Under the argument of the secular State based on the Brazilian Constitution, Justice Rocha affirmed that 'the respect for the principle of dignity of the human person is ascertained by the constitutional ethics now in force'. She argued that it was a matter of living with dignity and that 'there is no violation of the right to life when researches are permitted'. In her words, 'In order to germinate, the grain has to die'. Between 'human matter waste' and the use for research, the Supreme Court justice chose not to discharge the material, since the lack of research means the certitude of no results in science.

In view of the debate on such principle, and bearing in mind that the related circumstances must not be different – considering other countries with similar legal traditions and an analogous context as regards historical, cultural and economic features – we shall now describe the legal value of said principle within the framework of the Brazilian legal system.*Personality and Fundamental Rights*

Not all of the fundamental rights are surely personality rights. Personality rights, according to Rabindranath Capelo de Souza, derive from the compound of psychosomatic and environmental facets that compose the human personality.[11] The right to due process of law, for instance, is a fundamental right, but not a personality right.

It is possible to state, along those lines, that the legal construction of Personality Rights is a subset of the wider universe of Fundamental Rights and, as such, applicable both to relationship involving the State and to those between individuals.[12]

Furthermore, in the likelihood of direct and immediate enforcement of fundamental rights in the relationship between private individuals,[13] there is no question whatsoever of the absolute restriction that results from the split between Public Law and Private Law. In other words, not only Personality Rights but also all the other Fundamental Rights are applicable to the relationship between private individuals.

It could not be otherwise. To impose an absolute restriction on the application of the principle of human dignity – endowed with constitutional status – according to Personality Right restrictions defined by ordinary laws would imply contempt for the Constitution itself and an intolerable violation of the very dignity of human persons.

It must then be reaffirmed that, regardless of the existence or lack of provision for Personality Rights other than in the Constitution itself, the dignity of the human person in the relationship between private individuals is protected by direct or indirect enforcement of the Fundamental Rights and that this is a larger universe encompassing even the Personality Rights themselves.[14]

Fundamental Rights and Justice

The focus on the perception of fundamental human rights must be made through the lens of human dignity, as a necessary goal within the core of the substantively fundamental rights.[15]

Along this line of thinking, for professor Cármen Lúcia Antunes Rocha,[16] Justice of the Supreme Federal Court of Brazil, who stated opinion in favour of the research in the judgment on the allegation of unconstitutionality, 'dignity is a basic assumption for the idea of human justice, and the entitlement to dignity should require no further effort to deserve it, as it is inherent to life and, as such, a right that precedes the State'. The dignity of the person is thus assured as a constitutional 'super-principle'.

11 Rabindranath Capelo de Souza, *O direito geral de personalidade* (Coimbra 1995).

12 J.J. Gomes Canotilho, *Curso de direito constitucional* (21st edn. Saraiva 2000), p. 372.

13 Without obviously excluding any related or consequential enforcement. In this sense, see Juan Maria Bilbao Ubillos. En que medida vinculan a los particulares los derechos fundamentales? In: Ingo Wolfgang Sarlet (coord.). *Constituição, direitos fundamentais e direito privado* (Livraria do Advogado 2006) p. 301–340.

14 Maria Celina Bodin de Moraes, Recusa à realização do exame de DNA na investigação de paternidade e direitos da personalidade. In: Vicente Barreto, *A nova família,* (Renovar 1994), p. 174. Professor Maria Celina Bodin de Moraes states: 'In contrast to the strict identification and severing of personhood rights we have the notion of a human person – and thus of his/her personhood – considered as a unitary value, consequently giving rise to the acknowledgement by the legal system of a general protection clause that will definitely encompass the full protection of personhood, in all of its manifold manifestations, having the dignity of the human person as its confluence point, placed at the apex of the Federal Constitution of 1988.'

15 On this matter, see: Ingo Wolfgang Sarlet, *A eficácia dos direitos fundamentais,* (Livraria do Advogado 1998), p. 98.

16 Cármen Lúcia Antunes Rocha, *O princípio da dignidade da pessoa humana e a exclusão social* (Speech at the XVII Conference of the Brazilian Bar Association – OAB, 29 August to 02 September 1999).

It is imperative that the State be committed to the dignity of the human person. The theme concerns the guarantees of the Democratic State under the Rule of Law and the dignity of the human person, concretely conceived,[17] as stated by article 1 of the 1988 Federal Constitution.

It should be noted that the technical and scientific development has not been able, in countries like Brazil, to promote the inclusion of everyone in the modern society. On the contrary, a kind of social Darwinism is eliminating approximately 70 per cent of the population in Brazil from such a goal.[18] They are excluded from both consumption and basic access to the Social State range of benefits. The technological wave has been much more associated with the logic of the market and the globalization processes than with the promotion of human dignity. The conversion of living beings into genetic resources generates such perplexity.

How Have we Reached this Point?

The topics presented here bear some connection to the new economics of the information age. If culture and nature are commodities in the new digital world, filled with databases, a dignified life must not simply exclude research and scientific progress.

Human dignity is imperative from an ethical and existential point of view and it is also, unequivocally, a constitutional principle and rule[19] perceived by the Brazilian legal system as the fundamentals of the Republic, pervading the whole rationality of the national legal system by its normative enforcement.

It regards, the acknowledgement by Law of a dimension inherent to every human person and this acknowledgement precedes – as a logical and ethical principle – the legal system itself. In fact, the juridical system as desired in a theoretical plan by the abstract human creation contains in itself some 'metajuridical' elements that are conditions of possibility for Law itself.

---

17 There are indeed scholars, and not a few of them, who reject the idea of dignity of the human person as an evident value, accepted by the legal system for having concrete applicability. On the contrary, some of the legal scholars ascertain that the concept of dignity of the human person would be too abstract. By refusing this view – distant from a transforming praxis – the current philosophy of Law brings an authoritative argument to provide grounds for the concrete and self-applicable nature of dignity of the human person. This is the recently disseminated paradigm of the concrete life of each subject. Under such perspective, life is no longer the first and most fundamental right to be protected by the legal system, and it rather becomes an essential condition for permitting the other rights. The concept of supremacy of the human life is thus developed, and the human life must necessarily be endowed with dignity in order to be understood as life. This paradigm imposes that life (existence) be thought of under a concrete aspect, *i.e.*, the departing point of such model is life with concrete contents, since life is, by principle, also biological. Therefore, it can be ascertained that life will never be reduced to a mere abstraction, considering its concrete physical and biological substratum. Under this perspective, the new philosophical paradigm thus demonstrates the concrete foundations for dignity of the human person, burying the critics of its supposed abstract and intangible features. See: Maturana, H.; Varela, F.A *árvore do conhecimento: as bases biológicas da compreensão humana.* [The tree of knowledge: biological bases for human understanding] São Paulo: Palas Athena, 2001.

18 The Worldwatch Institute, *State of the World 2004 – The Consumer Society* (W.W. Norton & Company 2004), p. 7.

19 On the double dimension of principles and rules inherent to the fundamental legal norms. Robert Alexy, *Teoria de los derechos fundamentales* (Centro de Estudios Políticos y Constitucionales 2002).

Nonetheless, the principle of human person dignity must address the protection of the concrete person, without reducing it to a 'virtual subject'[20] considered in an abstract manner, reputed as a mere element of the juridical relationship or center of assessment.[21]

Under such a concept, dignity is taken as an attribute referring to the human being when concretely considered. Another extremely relevant element is also inferred when reviewing the principle at issue: the dignity of the person is an imperative that derives from an ethics of alterity.

This is, perhaps, how we got this far: we have forgotten that the dignity of the person may be conceived under the double dimension of principle and value.[22] Its axiological dimension allows us to state that there is a *prima facie* prevalence of the dignity value that determines the accomplishment of rules, even though a formal *a priori* prevalence of the principle is not stated.

Paulo da Mota Pinto, a highly distinguished professor from Coimbra and a former member of the Constitutional Court of Portugal, notes the supremacy of human dignity as a value when ascertaining that:

> a true axiological imperative for any legal system derives from the assurance of human dignity, namely the acknowledgement of legal personhood for all human beings, followed by a provision of legal means (especially subjective rights) aimed at defending the refractions that are essential to the human personhood, as well as the need for protection of such rights by the State.[23]

A notion that comes from this statement is that of human dignity as a general protection of personhood, with implications for the protection of the moral, physical and psychological integrity of the human person. The inclusion of the human dignity principle in the Constitution is not – and should not – be taken as mere rhetoric on the part of the constitutional legislator: it is a constitutional rule and, as such, a binding rule.

There is no doubt that, as the dignity of the human person is a value that precedes the Law and commands it – and is further a principle taken as the fundamentals of the Republic – it ends up as a supreme value of the legal system. Consequently, it becomes a fundamental vector in the actual operation of legal precepts, both regarding Public Law and Private Law.

As the principle of the human person dignity is an unavoidable ethical and legal component to which the whole Law is subordinated, we must reexamine the precepts also under Civil Law, in view of preserving and promoting the human person dignity. The relationship between private

---

20 According to Jussara Meirelles, 'on the one hand, we have what we would call a codified person or a virtual subject; on the other hand, we have the real subject, the really human person, seen under the prism of its own nature and dignity, the 'real people' person'. (O ser e o ter na codificação civil brasileira: do sujeito virtual à clausura patrimonial. In: Luiz Edson Fachin (coord.), *Repensando fundamentos do direito civil brasileiro contemporâneo*, (Renovar 1998), p. 91).

21 Ingo Sarlet, *Dignidade da pessoa humana e direitos fundamentais na Constituição Federal de 1988* (Livraria do Advogado 2001), p. 60. Along those lines, Ingo Sarlet designates the dignity of the human person as 'an intrinsic and distinctive quality of each human being that entitles him/her to the same respect and consideration from the State and from the community, implying in this sense a set of fundamental rights and duties that secure the person from any and all acts of degrading and inhuman nature, and assure a minimum of existential conditions for a healthy life, in addition to providing for and fostering his/her active and co-responsible participation in the destinies of his/her own existence and in the life in communion with other human beings'.

22 According to Robert Alexy, the actual accomplishment of a principle is also the accomplishment of a value. In addition, both principles and values are subject to assessment, even though principles remain in the deontological domain and values in the axiological domain (*ibid*).

23 *Apud* Ingo Wolfgang Sarlet, *ibid.*, p. 88.

individuals – including and mainly regarding the exercise of any technical, scientific or economic activity – is conditioned upon the assumption of respect for the other person, taken as a concrete subject and endowed with dignity.

Thus, the respect for human dignity is undoubtedly a necessary condition for the relationship between private individuals.[24] However, dignity refers to a concrete person and, rather than being taken as an atomized and abstract individual, the person is considered in a dimension of intersubjectivity.

On our Origins

In order to position the debate within the Brazilian Supreme Court, we must now readdress one of the essential elements of this theme. It regards Kant's notion of moral autonomy, which is founded on the autonomy of will commanded by pure practical reason and leads to a formula based upon the idea that the human being must always be treated as not only a means but also as an end.[25] Even when treated as a means, it must simultaneously have an end in itself.

This widely known concept may be deemed as the core expression of the idea of human dignity in the modern thought. For Kant, it is the feasibility condition of the categorical imperative, which imposes an acting that could be risen rationally as a universal law.[26]

To treat the rational being as an end is a prior condition to support the universal possibility of commanding the individual's autonomy by practical reason. It should be immediately noted that Kant's moral theory is, in this aspect, close to what would later be deemed an ethics of alterity – even if the foundation, as well as the very manner of facing the coexistential dimension of humanity, may differ. Consequently, an act that denies the condition of an end in itself, either to the very person or to others, is not moral.

According to Kant, everything set as an end has either a price or a dignity. Whatever cannot be measured against other values and cannot have its price established has a dignity. In accordance with this thought, the person has dignity.[27]

In opposition to Greek philosophy heritage, modern reason ended up as almost exclusively reduced to an instrumental reason, leading all knowledge to a scientific bias. The belief in the possibility to forecast and control all events reduces knowledge to a notion of science that considers subject and object as separate entities with an unavoidable division between them.[28]

The instrumental reason is linear, limiting itself to draw a direct relationship between means and ends. The market is ruled by such straight-line rationality and science responds to this order of ideas and praxis likewise. Therefore, an adequate challenge deriving from the mutual symbiosis between market and scientific development is one of the easily assessable marks in the history of the market society development.

The claim to control and forecast, as supposedly assured by instrumental reason, represents the compass of modern times' regulatory pillar, spreading to all fields of knowledge – including Law. The concrete human being becomes a means for said stability, to the extent that the human being

24 Ingo Wolfgang Sarlet, *ibid.*, p. 46. The affirmation by Ingo Sarlet is quite accurate: 'The dignity of the human person means both a limit and a duty for the government powers and, as we see it, for the whole community in general, touching each and every person, and said duplicity further points to a dimension that simultaneously defends and awards dignity.'

25 Immanuel Kant, *Fundamentos da metafísica dos costumes* (Ediouro 1970).

26 Immanuel Kant, *Crítica da razão prática* (Martins Fontes 2001).

27 Immanuel Kant, *Fundamentos da metafísica dos costumes* (Ediouro 1970).

28 A split which is rejected by Kant.

is not deemed the ultimate end: the end appears within the abstraction of the formal datum named 'legal security'.

It is obviously undeniable that legal security carries a relevant value, even as a tool for the protection of personal dignity. The problem is in the inversion of values that converts security into a supreme principle, a corollary of the gap between *real* and *abstract* reached by the Law pattern built under the modern reason division.

The Re-personalization

Human dignity taken in its concrete dimensions – and not as an abstract being in a metaphysical place – finds its place in Civil Law in the so-called 're-personalization'.[29] In fact, it is possible to state that the centrality of the person in 18th century Civil Law is only identified in the discourse that fomented the Liberal Utopia, the *leitmotiv* of modern Private Law development, as explained above.

Nevertheless, it has already been demonstrated how words and reasoning centered on a purely formal element finally culminated in a rationality that made the dignity of the person be surpassed by patrimonialism and conceptualism.

Thus, to 're-personalize' the Civil Law means, according to Tepedino,[30] to place the person at the core of the preoccupations of Law. In a way, it means to readdress the idea that the human being is endowed with dignity and represents an end in itself. Nevertheless, the fundamentals differ here from the ideas defended by Kant. From the dialectics that deny the Kantian abstraction, we see the rise of a synthesis mandating the protection of the person by its condition of concreteness, of subject of necessities.

It does concern protecting the person in its coexistential dimension, with its network of relationships that composes society itself. It is impossible to conceive the individual without the others, as the protection of human dignity is always inter-individual, based on an ethics of alterity and never individualistic.[31]

The individual's personality rights are not based on abstract data of legal personality, but rather on personality as something inherent to the concrete subject. As explained above and as inferred from the words of Capello de Souza, it is a compound of psychosomatic and relationship facets, *i.e.*, it comprises the physical and psychological elements, in conjunction with the relationship between said elements and the environment – and, above all, with other subjects.

This leads to the conclusion that, if personality rights are not granted by Positive Law, it is not necessary to typify each and every right so as to insert it within the 'World of Law'. The contemporary view of the system in Law and of the normative construction methods show that there are not sufficient grounds to sustain the enforcement of Law through subsumption to rigid patterns of juridical relationships, depending on ready-made answers which fail to define the issue in each concrete case.

The personality that is to be protected by Law is thus not merely an object created by the rule. A distinction must be made between personality as a concrete datum and personality as a generic attribute allowing anyone to be part of the juridical relationship as a subject of Law.[32]

---

29 Orlando de Carvalho, *A teoria geral da relação jurídica* (Centelha 1981).

30 Gustavo Tepedino, *Temas de direito civil* (Renovar 2004).

31 We must mention the significant reflection by Maria Celina Bodin de Moraes, who bound the dignity of the human person both to freedom and solidarity (O conceito de dignidade humana: substrato axiológico e conteúdo normativo. In: Ingo Wolfgang Sarlet (coord.), *Constituição, direitos fundamentais e direito privado* (2nd. edn. Livraria do Advogado 2006), p. 107–150).

32 Jussara Meirelles, *ibid.*

The definition of personality following the abstraction that characterized the 18th century legal positivism and reached the 20th century, culminating with Kelsen, is nothing more than the normative attribution or the attribution of a function by a normative order. In other words, the 'ascension' to the condition of person would occur when the legal system 'grants' said condition. This is definitely not the personality that we are dealing with, the subject matter of the general protection detailed here.

This is due to the fact that human dignity is not something born out of positive law, integrating a dimension that, as exposed, precedes Law itself. Therefore, protection does not have its roots in the law, and it is unnecessary to list the rights that would be entitled to legal protection. Everything inherent to the personality of the concrete subject is worthy of legal protection, since it concerns the human person dignity.

To direct the central focus of personality protection to the principle of human dignity means to base those rights on the same principle that grounds fundamental rights.

We thus see how it was possible for both the defenders and the challengers of the research to resort to the same principle in order to reach completely opposite conclusions. As the principle is based on the Constitution, it is meaningful to expose, albeit briefly, this aspect of the constitutional text.

The Brazilian Constitution and Human Dignity

The 1988 Federal Constitution made Civil Law relinquish the patrimonialist stand inherited from the 19th century, especially from the Napoleonic Code, migrating to a concept under which the human development, as well as the person dignity when concretely considered, is privileged in the relationship between individuals, aiming at their emancipation.

The Constitution established human dignity as the basis of the Republic. This option placed the person in the core of the legal system preoccupation in such a way that the whole system, guided by and based on the Constitution, is directed towards the protection of the person. The constitutional norms (comprising principles and rules) are centred on such a perspective, and they thus confer a systematic unity to the whole legal system.

In opposition to the traditional and dogmatic Law, we see an inversion of the core concerns of the legal system, since the protection of the person becomes the ultimate end of Law as its full development tool. The inversion of the concern *locus* must also take place in Civil Law. This is a necessary consequence in view of the supremacy of the Constitution within the legal system. For this reason, the whole set of normative standards beneath constitutional level must adjust itself to the constitutional axiological pattern.

Within this framework and in light of the constitutional system, the patrimonial aspect, previously in the spotlight, is now moved to the background. The real estate guided codification, a mark of the 1916 Civil Code, is no longer supported by the current Constitution.[33]

Wealth has been considered as an 'attribute of personality' by many authors. Two reflections must be taken into consideration under this perspective. Firstly, the personality mentioned is the abstract personality, *i.e.*, the personality given by the legal system, making someone qualified to be a subject of rights. This is not a concrete person, a person with needs, feelings, desires, abilities, but an abstract

33 On this matter, Jussara Meirelles writes: 'Therefore, it is not difficult to conclude that the person described by the Civil Code is not the person who lives, feels and walks in our days. The personal values, the desires, and the intent to have its dignity acknowledged are not reflected in the abstraction of a figure manufactured by the system as a person, as a subject of law' (*ibid*).

category person, not to be confused with the concrete human being. Secondly, the idea that wealth is an attribute of personality leads to the idea that personality and wealth are the same thing.

In this respect, we can see confusing concepts binding wealth to the person. However, this abstract person cannot be confused with the concrete human being. Even if we were to admit wealth as an attribute of personality, we would be speaking of an abstract category, not the concrete human being. Wealth cannot thus be confused with the human person value, since the human person is not limited to one abstract category.

In this way, to privilege wealth – and contrary to what one could imagine with a superficial view of 'attribute of personality' – means to marginalize the constitutional value of the human person dignity. In the 1988 Constitution, the human person dignity acquires the status of an organizational cardinal principle within the legal system. Therefore, any positively defined or potential rule that collides with this principle, in whole or in part, is unconstitutional.

According to such ideas, any assessment of the constitutional or non constitutional nature of a statute, in view of the re-personalization mandated since 1988, must take into consideration the superiority of the human dignity protection over the patrimonial juridical relationship. By implication, this means that a statute – it must be stressed, a positively ascertained or a proposed statute – will be deemed unconstitutional if it privileges a patrimonial view rather than a concept committed with the protection of the concrete human being.

Nevertheless, according to the Brazilian Constitution, the right to life is not an absolute and fundamental right. Here are some exceptions:

a. death penalty in case of declaration of war (article 5 item XLVII of the Constitution);
b. abortion as a means to save the life of the pregnant woman (a 'necessary abortion') or when the pregnancy results from rape ('humanitarian or therapeutic abortion'), under article 128 items I and II of the Brazilian Penal Code.

Within such framework, we must see how the Brazilian Constitutional Court examined the tension between right to life, a life with dignity and scientific research.

The Role of the Brazilian Supreme Court in Permitting the Research

It is precisely along this influx that the role of Brazilian Supreme Court is established on the Brazilian contemporary horizon and, consequently, that the nexus of these considerations is found. The area filled with said concepts may reduce the defence of the Constitution to the instrumental apparatus with which, without prejudice to its relevance, the definitely ascertained constitutional text is equipped. From our point of view, the protection also implies a proactive stand, reclaiming the duty to enforce rights and not only to maintain them.

Within the scenario of a Social Rule of Law, the higher courts are assured a *locus* of significant relevance. This is due to the fact that the higher courts activities are generally committed to the discussion of controversial points, connected with constitutional matters. In general, they are also called constitutional courts, even though they may, without naming it, implement such action. This is the case of the Supreme Federal Court in the Brazilian legal system, as set forth in article 102 of the Federal Constitution.

This layout of higher courts as protectors of the Constitution, in spite of the important Roman and Germanic roots of the Brazilian law, is based on the Common Law system experience, more specifically on the example of the United States.

The role of defending the Constitution is not limited to the Supreme Court. In an indirect and general manner, each government and social body, including the citizens, is also in charge of such duty. However, the judgment rendering courts or trial courts may lack the duty of direct or immediate protection of the Constitution, even at the level of control of diffuse rights to ensure compliance with the Constitution.

Nevertheless, all those relentlessly connected with the legal submission are primarily, and above all, bound by a duty of dispensing the law while observing the Constitution. However, it is undeniable that the control has a much more direct feature when exerted by the Supreme Court, which holds a transcendent power in face of the State.

Conclusion

Here is the path followed by a controversial law to the Supreme Federal Court. The Court comes to life as an abstract defender of the Constitution, and then becomes a concrete entity, as the historical and cultural features of its decisions are unveiled.

Under the Anglo-Saxon tradition this effect is even stronger, and it is in this context that we understand the visceral connection between the constitutional jurisdiction and the democratic principle, without dismissing the formative and historical reasoning process.

In addition to a healthy reflection, the normative texts must also curb the power of the State. Accordingly, the Higher Courts – usually known as constitutional courts – also hold this control function among their competencies, and they may be at the apex of the jurisdictional scale or a political body outside the three branches of the classical power division.

The Brazilian example plays by this rule, and it was influenced by the German constitutional and jurisdictional anatomy. After the 1988 Constitution and the consequent establishment of the Superior Court of Justice [*Superior Tribunal de Justiça*], the Supreme Federal Court [*Supremo Tribunal Federal*] strengthened its constitutional jurisdiction *locus*, as the ultimate 'guardian of the Constitution'.

Such role was accomplished in the judgment analyzed, when the Supreme Federal Court fulfilled its constitutional mission. Therefore, defending the supremacy of constitutional democracy, the Court, acting as a historical agent of its own time, analyzed and authorized the stem cell research, stating a new paradigm, defending not just the text of the Constitution, nor just its abstract principles, but a transformative hermeneutics of constitutional axiology, which allowed that these principles could be fulfilled by the individuals in effective relationships and guaranteed that the biotechnology could be directed to a material access to a dignified life.

The legal examination of the constitutional nature of the law that authorizes the referred research has come to an end in Brazil. However, the debate has not ended, especially for two reasons. Firstly, only the future will show us the possible and final results obtained with scientific progress. Secondly, the discussion on life, its beginnings and its dignity will never cease.

PART VI
Balancing Privacy and Security

Chapter 10
Angels and Demons: Data Protection and Security in Electronic Communications

Pedro Ferreira

Information Society and Human Rights

We live in what is typically labelled the Information Society (third industrial revolution,[1] Third Wave,[2] Networked Society,[3] the Age of Knowledge,[4] Bit Society,[5] or Communication Society[6]). It has been an evolutionary concept: starting with the electronic age, where the personal computer began to be intensively used; followed by the information age, characterized by networked computers; and arriving in the digital era, dominated by the wide use of all kinds of networks, terminals and applications; culminating with the rise of a new digital society.

To some the digital society is defined by a particular configuration of the relationship between technology and Man, what Castells designates as a new mode of development[7] – informationalism – as 'a technological paradigm based on the augmentation of the human capacity for information processing and communication made possible by the revolutions in microelectronics, software, and genetic engineering'.[8]

It's out of the scope of the present chapter to evaluate if the new techno-economic paradigm has given way to a new 'age' or is it still a refinement of modernity, a radical modernity, according to Giddens,[9] or a liquid modernity, in the view of Bauman.[10]

However, there are important elements of the earlier modernity – such as the historical moment in which human rights were recognized – that persist into the digital society. As impressive as the digital society may be in terms of its structure around technology, the second industrial revolution

---

1 Bradford L. Smith, *The third industrial revolution, Recuil des Cours: collected courses of the Hague Academy of International Law*, 2000. The Hague: Martinus Nijhoff Publishers, 2000, p. 242.

2 Alvin Toffler, *The Third Wave*. New York: William Morrow and Company, 1980.

3 Manuel Castells, *A Sociedade em rede*. Lisboa: Fundação Calouste Gulbenkian, 2002, p. 25, footnote 30.

4 Raul Junqueiro, *A idade do conhecimento*. Lisboa: Editorial Notícias, 2002.

5 Reginaldo Rodrigues de Almeida, *Sociedade Bit*. Lisboa: Quid Juris, 2004.

6 Gérard Leclerc, *A sociedade de comunicação*. Lisboa: Instituto Piaget, 2000.

7 Manuel Castells, *A sociedade em rede*, 2002, p. 19. Fernando Redondo and Maria Redondo, talk about 'digitalism' (Fernando Redondo and Maria Redondo, Do capitalismo para o digitalismo. Porto: Campo das Letras, 2003, p. 12).

8 Manuel Castells, Informationalism, networks, and the network society: a theoretical blueprint, 2004 (http://annenberg.usc.edu/images/faculty/facpdfs/Informationalism.pdf).

9 Anthony Giddens, *As consequências da modernidade*. Oeiras: Celta Editora, 2002, p. 35.

10 Zygmunt Bauman, *Liquid modernity*. Cambridge: Polity Press, 2001, in particular, pp. 3 e 126.

has probably influenced, changed and transformed more profound and comprehensively economic activities in our way of life, than the Internet and information technologies. In many aspects, the social and economic relations based on the underlying networks are not drastically different from those of previous periods. The digital age did not create new principles for the accumulation and distribution of wealth or even change the logic of how the market works,[11] especially since the governance of the globalization remains unsolved. The economic growth of the 1990s in the last century and at the beginning of this century (the increase in the value of securities capital, the increased use of credit), based largely on the digital economy, has proved a bubble hiding explosive frailties in the economic growth (increased spending led to the deficit on balance of payments, private indebtedness and to the financial crisis) that look very similar to other economic cycles.

But, on the other hand, it is clear that much has changed, if not the significance of the information and of the networks, aspects common to most societies, at least the shape and intensity (complexity) that these two concepts (information/networks) take in modern times it's something never seen before. In other words, the novelty of the digital society is a new paradigm for the way social and economic relations make use of networks/information and how, in turn, networks/information influence and design human relations. Manuel Castells, in his trilogy,[12] conceives the new community as organized under 'the Net and the Self'. The network symbolizes the new forms of community organization linked electronically, while 'Self' refers to the ways in which individuals reaffirm their identity. The network should be a reflection of the identity-community but at the same time, identity is being confronted and defined by how it updates itself on the network.

From a legal perspective, this means that even 'traditional' personal rights are put to the test by the permanent tension existing between information/networks and community/identity. Needless to say, this tension increases the closer we get to a world where to be online is not opposed to being off-line; they are in fact continuous. What we currently have is a set of characteristics of the formal process of communication that did not exist before: screens, sensors, machines, applications that shape a virtual world that increasingly interact with the analogue reality.

One of the major consequences of this interaction is that identity is now widely avowed by technology. An increasing number of human activities are carried out through networked technological means, causing the personality to be subjected to a process of dispersion and reconstruction, where the protection offered by the analogue world is no longer present as we will discuss in this chapter.

First, in the networked world some aspects of personality decay, for the simple reason that the *locus* of existence pours through the networks at a global scale. The universalization of the Internet means, from the user's perspective, that the entire life of any person online is likely to be accessed and registered by an unspecified number of subjects anywhere in the world. Although access is local, personal information, the word, the image, the gesture, the silence is captured, processed and distributed by means of global communication.

It is true that 'being online is a fourth dimension, a logic and infinite dimension where all [..] relations are equivalent to reproduce in the physical world, as if the online universe was the projection of a shadow'.[13] But, contrary to what happens in the analogue world, in cyberspace, when we leave our home, meaning, as soon as we go online, we are marked by an invisible bar

11 See Callinicos critic to the concepts of 'informational capitalism' and 'network society' as proposed by Castells (Alex Callinicos, *Contra a Terceira Via*. Oeiras: Celta Editora, 2002, pp. 25–39), and also Boaventura de Sousa Santos, Os processos da globalização. Porto: Edições Afrontamento, 2002, pp. 56 e ss.

12 In particular *Rise of the network Society* (Oxford: Blackwell Publishers, 1996) and *The power of identity* (Oxford: Blackwell Publishers, 1997).

13 Reginaldo Rodrigues de Almeida, *Sociedade Bit*, 2004, p. 171.

code.[14] Someone, usually without our knowledge, registers what we do, where we are, with what frequency and how often.

When we connect to the world the whole world also becomes linked to us and the more time we spend online the lower our level of privacy.

Any step in the digital world easily leads to unauthorized collection and processing of personal data, the compilation of consumption profiles, the digital historical record, to trade in personal information, and to the pressure of privacy with unsolicited messages (telephone, fax or electronic mail, including SMS and MMS) which, briefly, leads to forms of direct or indirect control over people's lives.[15]

In other words, on the Internet 'anonymity is purely illusion'[16] or rather, the Internet combines the right to anonymity, the possibility of identification and the requirement of identification.[17] So that, in all propriety, it can be said that 'today it is possible – theoretically possible, fortunately – to provide the itinerary, to the minute, but without the genius of Joyce in Ulysses – of the life of a peaceful citizen, in a single day using the computer [..]'.[18] What is surprising is that new technologies are using a new language to retell our story. Now these little pieces have unfamiliar names such as caller line identification, TCP/IP (Transmission Control Protocol/Internet Protocol), cookies, RFID or e-mail address.

Hypothetically, every person and every object may one day be linked to a network and interact, consciously or not. The network will then exist as an accurate representation of reality. The passive mapping of existence today (the online activity matches the passivity of the individual seated in front of his screen) will become active (real life activity is immediately registered and read by others).

This electronic itinerary of life, even when legal, is potentially harmful to the protection of the person. Once collected and processed, this set of information allows the pursuit of a permanent control on the Internet and the users are caught between freedom and participation, on the one hand, and between communication and confidentiality on the other. Their autonomy is compressed and even the meaning of 'person' is distorted because their decisions are anticipated and instrumentalized in the benefit of others and many aspects of their privacy are controlled by others, usually without their knowledge or consent.

Thus, secondly, another threat faced by personality online is not just fragmentation but the chances of digital reconstruction of multiple personalities by any person, anywhere.

This means that analogue reality may not be directly imported to the digital because personality transmutes itself, allows for new personalities, even if they are still not recognized as such by law. In the analogue world the person is presented as 'one body, one identity'.[19] In the digital world, the person is the result of the aggregation of different data and therefore can have many different electronic personalities created in a heterogeneous way by simple technological performance or by commercial interest.

However, these different 'persons' do not enjoy the same protection that would be expected, and from which they traditionally benefit in the analogue world. The personality, disseminated as

---

14 Jerry Kang, 'Information privacy in cyberspace transactions'. In *Stanford Technology Law Review*, 50 (Spring 1988), p. 1198.

15 Luis Brito Correia, *Direito da comunicação social*. Coimbra: Almedina, 2000, p. 601, footnote 1.

16 Stefano Nespor e Ada Lucia de Cesaris, *Internet e la legge*, Milano: Editore Ulrico Hoepli, 2001, p. 81.

17 Stefano Nespor e Ada Lucia de Cesaris, Internet e la legge. 2001, p. 77.

18 José de Faria Costa, 'As telecomunicações e a privacidade: o olhar (in)discreto de um penalista'. In *As Telecomunicações e o Direito na Sociedade de Informação*. Coimbra: Instituto Jurídico da Comunicação: 1999, p. 161.

19 Subhajit Basu, 'Regulating Cyberstalking'. *Journal of Information, Law & Technology* (2) 2007, p. 10.

mentioned, distances itself from its original personal core, and witnesses a reduction, to that extent, in the degree of protection. In a virtual environment it is very difficult to know when and what kind of data are generated by the networks, or who processes them or for what purpose. On top of that, new technologies like cloud computing make personal data even more disperse, fluid and global. Since data are accessed remotely and not locally one can no longer tell which jurisdiction applies.

The inevitability of data processing on a large scale makes the decision on what others must know about us, and the accuracy of that information, even more difficult, aggravating the conditions to be imposed on free choices, because our history (the history of our choices) tends to be recorded and unified in the hands of others.

This increased availability and dissemination of personal data weakens the autonomy of its owner and extends the means of social control and surveillance,[20] public and private, over personal values and behaviours – and to the same extent, increases the risk of infringement of other fundamental rights. The danger associated with technology is not readily identifiable with a single cause or reducible to a single 'enemy'. The concentration of power and the 'instant roboting of the personality'[21] are within reach of governments and private entities. In an imperceptible way, the citizen finds himself subject to State supervision (police), on public interest grounds, or under control of private interests for commercial purposes.

Furthermore, what is most worrying is that these enormous pressures on personal autonomy do not only have an external source. The privacy risks are something that is associated with the complexity of modern life and so are inseparable from digital networks. Without communication technologies one does not exist, one cannot participate in the community, but at the same time, technology is absorbed and felt as 'Matrix' technology, which dominates without the awareness of being dominated.

Unlike the '1984' Orwellian Big Brother, the source of power lies within each one of us at the same time, it is something transcendent that is beyond control because it does not pursue individual life but simply waits until each user offers his/her life in bytes and bits.

It is true that the Internet never forgets[22] because nothing is lost, everything is registered. But one cannot imagine, at this point, how humans will be defined when any action, from birth to death, is disclosed. Any movement, any word, any image, any heartbeat will be registered and easily reproduced. Life as we know it, which is largely based on the right to forget, will be a thing of the past. The current article 6 of the e-Privacy Directive (2002/58/EC, as amended by Directive 2009/136/EC), which provides for data to be erased or to be made anonymous when it is no longer needed, will be under strong pressure and data retention exceptions will become the rule.

Psychologists have even suggested the existence of a 'Truman syndrome', alluding to the Truman show movie, where Truman Burbank, played by Jim Carrey, sees his life broadcast live 24 hours a day on television for a worldwide audience.

These two processes – dispersion/reconstruction – lead to a few interesting informational paradoxes.

---

20 Maurice Gaillard, 'Nouvelles technologies de l'information et de la communication et protection des libertés du citoyen'. In *Les libertés individuelles à l'épreuve des NTIC*. Ed. Marie-Christine Piatti. Lyon: Press Universitaires de Lyon, 2001, p. 17.

21 Fernando Condesso, *Direito à informação administrativa*. Lisboa: Pedro Ferreira, 1995, p. 113.

22 See J.D. Lasica, 'The Net never forgets', published in '21st: The culture of Technology' (http://archive.salon.com/21st/feature/1998/11/25feature.html).

Informational paradoxes

More communication, more disclosure

The risk for privacy is enhanced by particular features of the digital environment: the increase in communication/information coupled with the permanence of communication and the de-personalization of communication.

The increase of the capacity and speed of networks and access services (high-speed broadband, Wi-Fi, Bluetooth), the introduction of open platforms, increasing online activities, globalization of networks, universal connectivity, technological convergence, peer-to-peer technologies, an increased number of terminal equipments connected to the network, the increasing capacity of addressing systems (IPv6), among other things, will surely enable, on the one hand, an increase of personal devices connected to the network and, on the other, that all these devices can connect to the network permanently.

Never before have there been at our disposal so many, and such diverse, means of communication, services and sophisticated technological applications. This means that communication depends on the stage of evolution of the technological means available – terminals, networks, protocols – to their performance and especially the possibilities of access by individuals and their own skills in dealing with them. That is, the 'performance' of communication requires effective ways to transmit and access information, systems requiring large capacity, integrated and harmonized technologies, multifunctional devices and technologically neutral services. Of course, the convergence between communication, content and information technologies, together with a predominantly neutral regulation, have contributed to the democratization of technology, but at the same time, has led to an increased porosity of the personal spaces hitherto reserved.

A higher frequency of accesses derives greater exposure which, in turn, leads to further disclosure of private information. Access to online services increases the number of access points to several service providers and, as a consequence, increases the chance of intrusion. In fact, most online behaviours generate information and the exchange of information eventually has to address the question of recognition or the identity of the source of all that information.[23]

Moreover, the equivalence between the field of technical devices (technological domain) and the information field, allegedly hegemonic because it makes use of the universality of the networks,[24] leads in the end to the domain of whoever uses the technology and accesses the information. Every step in the digital world is intensively scrutinized by technology which, normally, belongs or is controlled by a third party.

Indeed, the technological dependence extends the concept of communication not only to the 'other' or 'others', properly identified, but also to communication with instruments that collect data transmitted by personal technological devices, not always in a transparent manner. Even those areas that had been in the private sphere, such as areas of residence and work, are being increasingly equipped with sensors that record all human actions, and possibly interconnects that data with the outside world.

Communication is no longer confined to personal means like the telephone but to appliances, cars, computers, and so on. Communications are not purely 'personal' but between machines,

23 Etienne Davio, 'Anonymat et autonomie identitaire sur internet'. In *Cahiers du Centre de Recherches Informatique et Droit* (16) 1999, p. 296.

24 Dan Schiller, *Digital capitalism*. Cambridge: MIT Press, 2000, p. 1.

operating in an automatic way, such as the case of a refrigerator that sends a message to the supermarket's computer when the milk runs out to add this item to the shopping list.

This entails, at the same time that we will proceed to a phase of depersonalization of communication. Unlike the analogue world in which the predominant interpersonal contacts occur face to face, electronic communication places technological devices between the interlocutors – with the reduction of any information to 'zeros' and 'ones', the personal mark of communicative relationships becomes secondary. Technology replaces nature in the mediation between Man and reality.[25]

This raises a number of issues related to the control exercised by the installation of sensors and the control of stored information.

More participation, more exclusion

The 'informational Leviathan-State'[26] is growing, and therefore, Information Society is appropriately called surveillance society.

However, data processing is not done for any obscure objective. The growing demand for identification – ID numbers, criminal records and social security numbers – is justified because a number of social benefits depend on such identification. The virtual reality of cyberspace is far more real than the analogue reality of people and objects,[27] demanding the recognition by public authorities of a 'digital public life'. Thus, the same public authorities must provide the means for such a 'digital public life' by promoting the universal access to broadband Internet. Being a citizen is seemingly becoming more and more that of being a 'cybercitizen'.

Interesting questions derive from this:

Most of our social rights are now dependable on technological means and personal electronic and computer skills. Information Society as a way of development determines, from the outset, the access conditions and possibilities of inclusion or exclusion within that society, but at the same time, technology differentiation 'promotes social differentiation inherent to the capacity of processing the information and the resulting use of knowledge, in the process of production'.[28]

Instead of magically eliminating all differences of development and inequalities of social participation, the Information Society clearly reflects these realities and may even refine them and generate new forms of exclusion, poverty (info-poverty and social sorting). These differences are expressed among those who live in space (the work place) and those who live in time (the global capital that monopolizes knowledge and supports cultural elites).[29] The latter have the power to decide the moment of connection and disconnection.[30] The former are subjected to the contingency of the digital age and require the reinstatement of new digital rights.

25 Fernando Ilharco, *A questão tecnológica*. Cascais: Principia, 2004, p. 78.

26 P. Leclercq, 'La CNIL, garante de la finalité, de la loyauté et de la securité des données personnelles'. In *Les libertés individuelles à l'épreuve des NTIC*. Ed. Marie-Christine Piatti. Lyon: Press Universitaires de Lyon, 2001, p. 111.

27 Marek Safjan, 'The right to privacy and personal data protection in the information society'. *Proceedings, European Conference on Data Protection on Council of Europe Convention 108 for the protection of individuals with regard to automatic processing of personal data: present and future. Warsaw, 19-20 November, 2001*, p. 21.

28 Victor Marques dos Santos, *Conhecimento e mudança*. Lisboa: ISCSP, 2002, p. 183.

29 Manuel Castels, *A sociedade em rede*, 2002, p. 601 and Zygmunt Bauman, *The individualized society* (Cambridge: Polity Press, 2001), p. 40 and *Liquid modernity*, 2001, p. 117.

30 Manuel Castells, *A sociedade em rede*, 2002, p. 23.

Therefore, public authorities should consider Information Society as an opportunity to reduce social inequalities expressed in info-exclusion, informative poverty and digital divide. This can only be done, in my view, by the redefinition of the Universal Service concept in two ways:

Firstly, by guaranteeing access to services and content at an affordable price (universal service, social minimum, the idea of a 'guaranteed minimum integration' following the example of minimum income).

Secondly, by ensuring freedom to provide and use services, which implies not only public policies like e-Health, e-Government, e-learning or e-safe directed to the demand side, but also broadband for all under a net neutrality principle.

More security, less freedom

The exposure of privacy increases because defence and public security interests are becoming more and more important.

The terrorist attacks of September 11 2001, and later those of Madrid and London, have jeopardized the classical system of criminal investigation. The origin, dimension and objectives of the new type of crime linked to terrorism, calls for the legitimacy of processes and other measures of public security, of which data retention would be an example, targeted at prevention and widespread surveillance. Traffic data collected by electronic communications operators could be used successfully to trace global criminals whose modus operandi reflects, only too often, the architecture of the network they use.

Moreover, there was a demand for increased integration of information gathered by police and judicial authorities in each State, in response to global and transactional terrorist networks.

To fulfil these objectives the international community and national legislators have been very active in recent years. First, with the adoption of the Convention on Cybercrime of the Council of Europe (ETS 185 of November 23, 2001) together with the Additional Protocol concerning the criminalization of acts of a racist and xenophobic nature committed through computer systems (2003) and, more recently, in the European Union with Directive 2006/24/EC of March 15 2006, which provides, among other measures, the possibility of telecommunications operators to retain the traffic data of their subscribers for a certain period of time.

These measures set off a new era in the relationship between privacy and technology. No wonder, therefore, that some say that the conservation 'of data communications in order to punish serious crimes is unprecedented and will have an historical importance'.[31]

This importance is due to the fact that the Directive 2006/24/EC avoids the test of necessity and transforms the exception (the processing of personal data for criminal investigation) into rule, subjecting all online communications to retention. This goes against the principle that such data may only be stored to the extent that it is necessary for the provision of the service, for the purpose of billing and for interconnection payments, and then, only for a limited time.[32]

31 Article 29 Data Protection Working Party Opinion 3/2006, 25.03.2006, p. 2. In the Opinion 4/2005, 21.10.2005, the same WP would say that 'The European Commission's Proposal for a Directive on the retention of data is confronting us with a historical decision' (p. 4).

32 An opinion from 'Privacy International', of 10.10.2003, comes to the conclusion that 'The indiscriminate collection of traffic data offends a core principle of the rule of law: that citizens should have notice of the circumstances in which the State may conduct surveillance, so that they can regulate their behaviour to avoid unwanted intrusions. Moreover, the data retention requirement would be so extensive as to be out of all proportion to the law enforcement objectives served. Under the case law of the European Court

The retention for months or years, of large amounts of personal data cannot be considered proportional to the objectives of criminal investigation and cannot be said to be necessary in a democratic society. A balanced community should only restrict privacy if the social welfare faces a macroscopic threat, well documented in the context of criminal prosecution, not just a mere possibility of danger.[33]

It is true that data retention is one of the most suitable means to repress violations and to ensure the gathering of evidence. It is, however, not certain that this solution is the only one or the most appropriate to fulfil the objectives of criminal prosecution. So the first question that arises is whether the community accepts the balance, not only in its legal form, but above all with its long term consequences. To what extent can democratic societies accept systems that, step by step, on behalf of that same democracy, go digging around the foundations of fundamental rights and guarantees that give support to our constitutional law system.

Taken to the limit, governments could, in the name of security, take full control of society.[34] But even outside this extreme scenario, any measure of general unrestricted surveillance can seriously jeopardize the rule of law, transforming human rights into a by-product of the criminal activity.

In other words, the potential victims are also potential suspects. By seeking enemies without a face, one begins to see the face of the enemy in each other. There is, for this reason, the risk that public security starts to prevail over privacy, leading to a situation where behavioural patterns are only changed because surveillance subconsciously leads the person to act on the basis of the surveillance.

Privacy is suspended in areas under scrutiny. This reminds us of the Panoptical effect illustrated by Michel Foucault, referring to the proposal of Bentham, where inmates of a circular prison are subject to permanent visibility. With time, the exercise of power becomes useless because it is carried by the inmates themselves.[35] The very concept of security ceases to make any sense from the moment personal relationships become the object of fear.

This scenario brought by the Data Retention Directive leads us to conclude that in the post September 11 world, 'Administration' is increasingly similar to 'Inquisition', condemning to exclusion those who do not fit the informational standards.

Unfortunately, the primacy of security over freedom may have other examples in the near future, such as the mandatory registration of subscribers, particularly pre-paid mobile cards users.

More communication, less control

With the growing intensity of communication and expanding online activities, privacy options tend to be decided by others.

Personal information provided by new technologies is being considered by businesses as an important asset. This is changing the nature of the risks perceived by the consumers. Actually, until now, the largest databases were public, territorially located and limited to a particular population. However, with the globalization of economic activities, there are now enormous databases in the

---

of Human Rights, such a disproportionate interference in the private lives of individuals cannot be said to be necessary in a democratic society.' (http://www.statewatch.org/news/2003/oct/Data_Retention_Memo.pdf).

33 A. Etzioni, 'A contemporary conception of privacy', *Telecommunications and Space Journal*, Vol. 6, 1999, p. 82.

34 On the subject please see 'Dayse de Vasconcelos Mayer, Os acontecimentos de 11 de Setembro de 2001 e a sua projecção sobre os direitos fundamentais', *Revista da Faculdade de Direito da Universidade de Lisboa*, Vol. XLIII, (2) 2002.

35 Michel Foulcault, *Vigiar e punir*, 27ª ed., Petrópolis: Editora Vozes, 2003, p. 166.

hands of large multinationals, including telecommunications companies, airlines, search engines and distant selling business, which are potentially universal and outside democratic control.

I would like to point out that the global commerce of personal data is fully in line with Information Society objectives, which are based on the re-orientation of the traditional public tasks towards the privatization of risk, until now assumed by the Welfare State, and the privatization of public economic activities and services.

Moreover, privatization and deregulation open the way to less scrutiny of the economic activities (self-regulation and Internet as a non-legal space) and allowing them greater opportunities to forum shopping, making use of the 'variable geometry of the Internet'[36] by the choice of location for the provision of services (a global shopping mall).

For such businesses, privacy is considered a cost because they have to guarantee a certain level of data protection for their customers. The traditional view is that these requests for protection and security, with the associated costs, are generating economic inefficiencies,[37] which can be reduced by forum shopping.

At the same time, business entities have an extra incentive for data processing. In a world increasingly competitive and flooded with information, with a range of products and services which are not always easy to differentiate, the consumers' attention ends up being the scarcest resource.[38] To capture every potential customer becomes increasingly important and any kind of commercial advantage, however insignificant, is highly valued.

The customization of services is, of course, one of the most suitable means for achieving this objective, requiring it to have at their disposal consumer profiles based on more and more detailed personal data, so the goods and services can be tailored to the needs of the individual consumer. Again the idea of a 'social sorting', but in this case for commercial purposes.

More security, more data processing

The privacy paradox increases when, in order to achieve greater opacity, one has to offer greater transparency.

Almost all communication technologies have a double face: they offer anonymity but, at the same time, they require an increasing amount of data to ensure that anonymity. The guarantee of privacy and other personality values (encryption) require the disclosure of these values (identification and authentication).

The sophistication of the means of attack and disclosure of personal information increases simultaneously with the development of security systems and protection technologies. That is, the very technology used for protection ends up generating a new set of personal data. The higher the level of protection and recognition required the more data is needed. For instance, biometric

36 Manuel Castels, 'Internet', liberdad y sociedad, Lección inaugural del curso académico 2001-2002 de la UOC, 2001, p. 4 (http://www.uoc.edu/web/esp/launiversidad/inaugural01/intro_conc.html). The variable geometry it is one of the means that businesses make use of, benefiting from the inherent competition between legal systems and, by de-locating their businesses, they look for legal paradises where they can cut on costs at the expenses of human rights.

37 About the analysis of the privacy as an economic variable please see article from Eli M. Noam, 'Privacy in telecommunications'. *New Telecom Quartely*, 1995.

38 Fernando Ilharco, *A questão tecnológica*, 2004, p. 151.

authentication,[39] namely fingerprints, the iris pattern, voice features, have the effect of multiplying the data related to the technology used.

Proportionality is the predominant idea that should govern the relationship between security and data processing. Data processing should only take place when the imperatives of security so require, in full implementation of the principle of proportionality, excluding for instance the uses of biometric technology if only because it is attractive, fashionable and simple.[40] This type of data processing also requires the implementation of particular security measures and a strict control of the principle of purpose, criteria that would be highlighted should the law provide for the mandatory requirement of authorization by data protection authorities.

Privacy as a fatality

The paradoxes I have just listed are present in any situation where choices have to be made, particularly in the amount and type of personal information we have to provide in order to have a digital existence.

However, these choices always involve a privacy cost that is inherent to our life in society and Marek Safjan illustrates this with the vision of a man hiding behind a wall of privacy, eager to know everything about his neighbour who, in turn, also lurks behind the wall of privacy and is also eager to learn everything from the other neighbour.[41]

Drawing a life plan involves, as Alasdair MacIntyre reminds us, making the world we live in the most predictable possible, eventually, knowing as much as possible about others. But on the other hand, this plan requires a certain degree of opacity and unpredictability; otherwise we will be reduced to the creations of other people's projects,[42] losing all singularity and dignity.

Therefore, the real problem lies in determining the balance between predictability and transparency or opacity and unpredictability.

We cannot live with the 'obsession of the vitrification of reality'[43] as Faria Costa called, the domain of absolute transparency, and we cannot relinquish a public space and run the risk of becoming prisoners of our own subjectivity.[44] It is like trying to level a scale without really knowing what to put on either of the plates.

Personal communication requires transparency, carrying with it a potential for building itself as a public space where it can be shared by others.[45] But, now, with the ubiquity and permanent

---

39 See study from the OECD *Working Party on Information Security and Privacy* da OCDE DSTI/ICCP/REG(2003)2/FINAL – 'Biometric-based technologies', of 30.07.2004.

40 In a decision taken in 8.04.04, the CNIL, the French data protection agency, confirmed that only an undeniable imperative of security could justify the existence of databases with fingerprints.

41 Marek Safjan, *The right to privacy and personal data protection in the information society*, 2001, p. 20.

42 Alasdair MacIntyre, *After Virtue*. Notre Dame: University of Notre Dame, 2002, p. 104.

43 José de Faria Costa, 'Os meios de comunicação – correios, telégrafo, telefones ou telecomunicações –, o segredo e a responsabilidade penal dos funcionários'. In *Boletim da Faculdade de Direito da Universidade de Coimbra*, Vol. LXXII, 1996, p. 144.

44 Hannah Arendt, *A condição humana*. Lisboa: Relógio D'Água, 2001, p. 73.

45 José Engrácia Antunes, 'A hipótese autopoiética'. In *Juris et de Jure: nos vinte anos da Faculdade de Direito da Universidade Católica Portuguesa*. Porto: UCP, 1998, p. 1277, by reference to Luhmann, says that 'social systems are noetic systems, whose reproductive base is the sense: this means that their components are not individual human beings, but communications'.

connectivity it is possible to communicate beyond the community, making communication an area where the distinction between private and public is blurred and where the chances of personal affirmation are intermittent and permanently changed, if not, inconsequential.

With the absence of time and allocation of space between local and global, what is public becomes privatized and what was imperative becomes interactive,[46] so there is a risk that privacy is not a choice but an obligation to be alone, because the desire for common values also becomes impossible.

Privacy as a product of social exclusion cannot therefore be evaluated positively, because social life becomes nothing more than the arithmetic sum of partial encounters and of individual worlds permanently exposed but never coupled. The very concept of space fades away with the possibility of relationships at a distance (no space), instantaneous (no time), so that the 'inhabitant of the tele-optic metacity is no longer able to distinguish the here and now, the private and public'.[47] Probably for the first time in human history, one can be alone in a crowd and select to whom it connects,[48] but the shattering of community relations in small private spaces leads to the denial of the public and, with it, the denial of the private.[49] We may not be far from a world, not beyond good and evil as Nietzsche sought, but beyond public and private.

But what world is this? The answer is not easy but if we look carefully, this problem is identical to the balancing of rights well known from constitutional law. What is new is the intensity within which this balance has to be made, every day in the lives of millions. The normal consumer protection measures may not be enough. The ordinary means of redress through the courts does not work here. It is therefore important to determine, in general, the limit to the balancing between technology and human rights: the very terms in which that balance should be made.

In this respect, an idea is paramount: Human rights must be at the service of the person, as a universal citizen, that finds in the network the conditions for full development.

The image of man opened to global communication, but isolated in front of the computer (connected to a network), which has been previously referred to in the example of the two neighbours, does not necessarily lead to the justification of the post-modernist isolationism.

We don't believe man should be an appendix to the machine, a 'human posthuman' to use the words of Fukuyam[50] and Dominique Lecourt,[51] plundered of sensations and human contact, reduced to a freedom within its own prison. This would, as we saw, lead to privacy as a fatality and disconnection from the network as the only available option.

The networking requires, therefore, a whole new concept of interpersonal dynamics (interconnectivity) where the otherness is available in terms of global networks, a world totally communicating, interactive and participant, only possible through the free flow of information insensitive to space, time and social, cultural, economic and political conditions. But insensitive does not mean integrated. To communicate is above all to build public spaces, thereby allowing enduring ties between men. As Arjun Appadurai pointed out, 'it is wrong to assume that electronic communication is the opium of the people'.[52] The openness and sharing means that the digital person is no longer definable by secret or anonymity alone, but by communicating, by informing

---

46 Alain Finkielkraut e Paul Soriano, *Internet: o êxtase inquietante*, [s.l.]: Fim de Século, 2002, p. 15.

47 Paul Virilio, *A velocidade de libertação*. Lisboa: Relógio D'Água Editores, 2000, p. 85.

48 Stéphane Callens, 'La société de l'information: une société de surveillance?' In *La Société de l'information entre mythes et réalité*. Bruxelles: Bruylant, 2005, p. 306.

49 Hannah Arendt, *A condição humana*, 2001, p. 76.

50 Francis Fukuyama, *O nosso futuro pós-humano: consequências da revolução biotecnológica*. Lisboa: Quetzal Editores, 2002.

51 Dominique Lecourt, *Humano pós-humano*. Lisboa: Edições 70, 2003.

52 Arjun Appadurai, *Dimensões culturais da globalização*. Lisboa: Teorema, [1996], p. 18.

and being informed, by establishing new personalities in virtual worlds. Personal data should, therefore, only be revealed and shared by others to the extent necessary to fulfil those interests.

Human dignity is therefore not a formal concept. Human dignity does not satisfy itself with the passive information in the possession of a passive person; it is only fully understood when that person possibly uses it as knowledge and communication and as a way for social accessibility.

So, secondly, human rights are the foundations not only of the digital society but especially of the Information and Knowledge Society.

The increasing ability to communicate creates a greater amount of information. However, more and more means of access and technological artefacts do not mean in themselves more knowledge. Sometimes, we may face an excess of technology and an excess of information. Indeed, heeding Paul Virilio's warning, too many technical interfaces may turn a super-equipped valid person into an equipped handicapped person[53] a 'terminal-citizen' 'submitted to machines, with which, it says, dialogues'.[54] Or, too much information may lead to a 'freedom of disinformation',[55] to an 'illusion of knowledge'[56] and the erosion of the powers of democratic participation. Fortunately, reality shows that the Digital Society also values democratic principles and struggles for freedom, pluralism and equality. In this sense it's a society of knowledge and exchange of information (the 'land of choice for freedom'[57]). Recent examples in the Middle East and North African countries show how effective the use of information technologies can be to promote civil engagement in the political process.

The Information Society should be aimed at socially and informationally valid citizens, requiring the full implementation of the right of access to communication (and information). The network has to be filled by personal 'experience' otherwise it will end up as 'pure technology'[58] devoid of identity, meaning and value. The relationship between man and communication necessarily has to be an ethical relationship.

Conclusion

As pointed out by Martin Buber (1878–1965) when referring to the new technological artefacts: 'Man faced the terrible fact that he was the father of demon whose master he could not become',[59] that is why the use of new technologies renders us all to the opposing forces of 'liberation and servitude'.[60] On the one hand, Man is dependent on the machine and to a certain extent it is its slave because technology has an imperceptible control of his life. But, at the same time, technology is

53 Paul Virilio, *A velocidade de libertação*, 2000, p. 32.

54 Paul Virilio, *A velocidade de libertação*, 2000, p. 44.

55 Victor Leitão, 'As tecnologias da informação e as novas leis da comunicação social'. In *Sub Iudice* (15, 16), 1999, p. 162.

56 Gil Baptista Ferreira, *Linguagem e modernidade*. Lisboa: Livros Horizonte, 2003, p. 103.

57 Giovanna Corrias Lucente, 'Internet e libertà di manifestazione del pensiero'. *Il Diritto dell'informazione e de XVI* (4–5, Luger/Ottobre) 2000, p. 599.

58 Anna Maria Szczepanska, 'Searching for the virtual community'. In *Proceedings of IRIS 24, August 11–14, Bergen, Norway 2001*, p. 10.

59 Martin Buber, *Between man and man* [2007], p. 188. First published by Routledge & Kegan Paul, 1947.

60 José Augusto Sacadura Garcia Marques, 'Telecomunicações e protecção de dados'. In *As Telecomunicações e o Direito da Sociedade de Informação*. Coimbra: Instituto Jurídico da Comunicação, 1999, p. 90 e Garcia Marques e Lourenço Martins, *Direito da informática*. Coimbra: Almedina, 2000, p. 76.

freedom, seduction and communication, thus, satisfying human needs and providing knowledge. Angels and demons eat at the same table of electronic communications.

There is no definitive solution for this dilemma and the most suitable legal solutions should be found for each jurisdiction. At the same time, a few principles, on top of the existing ones in most of the legal regimes, could be implemented as a way to ensure a minimum level of personal data protection.

Firstly, the role of the 'guarantee' and an effective regulation must always prevail over the privatization of personal rights and self-regulation;

Secondly, the limitation of general surveillance, especially in the field of data retention and greater control of the data collected for security purposes;

Thirdly, an increased international protection;

Fourthly, a broader definition of e-inclusion in order to include consumer awareness and the necessary tools for consumers to protect and enforce their privacy;

Fifthly, the strengthening of the principle of consent and control over personal information in two ways: by setting a clear right to be forgotten when the conditions of the legitimacy for processing data are no longer present obliging the controller to remove that data wherever it is located; and by requiring that data controllers make available effective means to access (check, change, correct, delete) personal data online and by recognizing the right to retrieve the data when the service is ended, allowing it to be passed to another service provider.

Chapter 11

Privacy, Security and New Technologies: A Brazilian Approach to Privacy Issues in the Public Security Field

Mario Viola de Azevedo Cunha and Danilo Doneda

Introduction

In this chapter we will analyse the conflict between the right to privacy and security in the use of new technologies for the fight against crime, with a special emphasis on the Brazilian scenario. Despite the fact that public security is, on the one hand, an important value, privacy, on the other, is a fundamental right recognized by most modern constitutions that needs to be equally protected. The main challenge is, therefore, to establish a balance between the need to ensure public security and the protection of individual privacy.

After the end of the Second World War, and primarily as a response to the use of personal information to identify ethnic groups, the right to privacy was promoted to the status of a human right. The right to privacy, once secluded to matters involving personal communications and expectations of secrecy, ended up being included in several international documents regarding the protection and promotion of human rights, such as the Universal Declaration of Human Rights, the European Convention on Human Rights and the American Convention on Human Rights, which ensured that 'No one shall be subjected to arbitrary interference with his privacy, family, home or correspondence, nor to attacks upon his honour and reputation. Everyone has the right to the protection of the law against such interference or attacks.'[1]

Nowadays, with the advent of the internet, a new facet of the right to privacy is being threatened, when personal information is – through the use of new technological tools – shared and collected for a wide range of purposes, including the fight against crime.

A good example of this 'security threat' to privacy took place after the terrorist attacks of September 11, 2001, in the US, which changed the perception that nations had regarding privacy and data protection, especially when national security issues were at stake. They interrupted the development of the right to privacy (and, consequently, of the data protection regulatory framework), having impact not only in the US, but also in the European Union and even in the Southern Hemisphere – including Brazil, which is the focus of this chapter. Taking this scenario into account, this article will analyse the threats to privacy posed by new technological tools for the fight against crime, with a special emphasis on the experience in the Southern Hemisphere.

1 Article 12 of the Universal Declaration of Human Rights. In the same sense, see Article 8 of the European Convention of Human Rights and Article 11 of the American Convention of Human Rights.

After September 11 era: US measures against terrorism, PNR Agreements and other initiatives[2]

Immediately after the tragic events of September 11, the US Congress approved two pieces of legislation which, to a large extent, imposed restrictions to individual privacy and data protection.

The first one was the US Patriotic Act, of October 2001 (*Uniting and Strengthening America by Providing Appropriate Tools Required to Intercept and Obstruct Terrorism Act of 2001*),[3] which granted unrestricted access to any databases, both private or public, and also the interconnection of such databases to a series of governmental agencies and bodies.[4] Moreover, this Act authorized, for example, the access by governmental agencies to the history of phone calls, emails, medical and financial files, amongst many other powers.

Another piece of legislation enacted after the terrorist attacks was the Aviation and Transportation Security Act,[5] which imposed upon all air companies operating flights to and from the US the duty to disclose passenger data (PNR Record) to the Customs and Border Protection Administration (CBP) before the departure of airplanes. The Act had an extraterritorial effect, since airlines would transfer personal data of their customers collected outside the US, while they were in the territory of the departing countries, out of the US.[6] Such extraterritorial effect led to an international agreement between the US and the European Union, the so-called US-EU PNR Agreement which, apart from the criticism it deserves, tried to ensure an adequate level of data protection for EU citizens flying to the US, as we will discuss in the next topic.

This situation had also produced effects in Brazil. Although Brazil has not yet adopted a general data protection law, as will be examined in a further section of this chapter, the Brazilian government announced in 2005 that it had authorized air companies to send PNR data of passengers flying from Brazil to the US, and that it would start negotiations with the US Government for a US-Brazil PNR Agreement in the basis of reciprocity.[7] Nevertheless, such agreement never took place and PNR data from Brazilian passengers has been transferred to the US government without any data protection guarantees.

---

2 Some parts of this section were published in a previous work. See Mario Viola de Azevedo Cunha. 'Privacy, Security and the Council Framework Decision 2008/977/JHA'. *Law Technology*. World Jurist Association (2010), volume 43, issue 4, pp. 1–19.

3 Available at http://epic.org/privacy/terrorism/hr3162.html (01.03.2010).

4 Stefano Rodotà, *La vita e le regole – Tra diritto e non diritto* (Feltrinelli, 2006) 82.

5 Available at http://frwebgate.access.gpo.gov/cgi-bin/getdoc.cgi?dbname=107_cong_public_laws&docid=f:publ071.107.pdf (01.03.2010).

6 The rules of the Aviation and Transportation Security Act regarding the transfer of PNR Records to the CBP were implemented by a regulation adopted in July 2002 and amended in April 2005. See Section 122.49.b, title 19 (Customs Regulation) Code of Federal Regulations, concerning Passenger Name Record Information. Available at http://cfr.vlex.com/vid/122-passenger-name-record-pnr-information-19649183 (12.06.2009).

7 According to the Brazilian newspaper *O Globo*, the Brazilian government authorized air companies with an office in Brazil to transfer to the US Department of Security information about Brazilian passengers with the US as a destination. The final agreement, analysed by the Itamaraty (Brazilian Ministry of Foreign Affairs), has not yet been signed. However, a provisional solution, based in reciprocity, in respect of international Law and of the prohibition of discrimination of specific groups, requires air companies to share information supplied by their passengers when they book the tickets, such as: name, dates of arrival and departure, itinerary, payment methods and e-mail address. See 'O Globo'. O mundo. 'Governo brasileiro aceita compartilhar informações de passageiros com destino aos Estados Unidos'. Published in 26.02.2005.

The US-EU PNR Agreement[8]

As we have mentioned, the US Aviation and Transportation Security Act, as a consequence of its extraterritorial effects and its impact on individual privacy, sparked lively reactions in many EU member states and led to negotiations between the European Union and the US. The aim of these negotiations was to ensure an adequate level of data protection in the transfer (and further processing) of PNR data, according to EU standards. Following the latter, airlines which share this information with US authorities would be subject to penalties applied by the national data protection authorities, as in most EU member states such practice would violate data protection laws.

The debate of privacy *versus* security was evident. The negotiations were concluded in 2007 after two previous attempts (one void by the European Court of Justice and the other an interim agreement). This 2007 Agreement, however, was severely criticized, since from a data protection viewpoint it reduced the guarantees already well consolidated at European level. Recently, the Council of the European Union, after the entering into force of the Lisbon Treaty which changed the decision making and law making process in the European Union, decided to send the Agreement for discussion and approval by the European Parliament.[9] The latter has thus approved a new agreement which replaced the 2007 agreement,[10] giving 'green light' to 'U.S. authorities to collect and use PNR data for the prevention or fight against serious transnational crime and terrorism'.[11]

The terrorist attacks in Madrid and in London

The debate privacy *versus* security gained even more importance after the terrorist attacks in Europe (Madrid – March 2004; London – July 2005), and which rendered the exchange of personal data of citizens between law enforcement authorities an essential tool for the international co-operation against terrorism and organized crime. In the European Union the exchange of information by police forces of the member states of Europol[12] and of the Schengen agreement[13] are just some examples of this new justification for the transnational flow of personal data.

This situation of 'insecurity' led again the US Government to require the Society for Worldwide Interbank Financial Telecommunication (SWIFT) to send to US authorities information about international financial operations concluded around the world, fact that motivated new negotiations between the EU and the US. The agreement was initially rejected by the European Parliament, but latter approved, 'allowing sharing EU citizens' bank data with the US authorities'.[14]

---

8 For a deep analysis of the US-EU PNR Agreements, see Marco Botta and Mario Viola de Azevedo Cunha, 'La protezione dei dati personali nelle relazioni tra UE e USA: le negoziazioni sui trasferimento dei PNR' (2010), *Diritto dell'informazione e dell'informatica*, Vol. 26, nº. 2, 315–41.

9 Available at http://www.europolitics.info/europolitics/ep-asked-to-approve-eu-us-passenger-name-record-agreement-artb263317-46.html (19.02.2010).

10 Council of the European Union. Council adopts new EU-US agreement on Passenger Name Records (PNR). PRESSE. 9186/12. Luxembourg, 26 April 2012. http://www.consilium.europa.eu/uedocs/cms_data/docs/pressdata/en/jha/129806.pdf (05.05.2013).

11 European Union Delegation to the US. European Parliament Gives Green Light for PNR Agreement with the U.S. Available at http://eurunion.org/eu/2012/European-Parliament-Gives-Green-Light-for-PNR-Agreement-with-the-U.S.html (29.05.2012).

12 See http://www.europol.europa.eu/index.asp?page=home&language= (12.06.2009).

13 See http://www.hri.org/docs/Schengen90/ (12.06.2009).

14 Digital Rights in Europe. SWIFT agreement adopted by the European Parliament. EDRi-gram - Number 8.14, 14 July 2010. Available at http://www.edri.org/edrigram/number8.14/swift-20-adopted-

Again there is no agreement in place between Brazil and the US, although the collection of data regarding SWIFT transactions of Brazilian citizens has been taking place and such data are sent to US Authorities without any control.

New technological tools for the fight against crimes

In the context of these exchanges of personal information, many EU states, at the national level, have implemented new technological tools which, according to them, play an important role in the fight against crime and in the promise of security. CCTV, Body Scanners and DNA databases containing DNA samples of criminals are the most well-known tools adopted by law enforcement authorities around the world, including Europe. Such use, however, is not free of criticism.

Regarding DNA databases, the European Court of Human Rights decided in the Marper case that the storage of DNA samples of two British citizens who were criminally indicted but later considered not guilty (for different reasons), violated article 8 (the right to privacy) of the European Convention on Human Rights and, as a consequence, required the British government to destroy such samples.[15]

Another technology that has been largely implemented, especially in the UK is the so-called CCTV (Closed-circuit television), used for the purposes of *prevention and persecution of crimes and for the maintenance of public order*.[16] A research published in June 2002 estimated that there were by that time more than 4 million cameras integrated to the main CCTV system in the UK, with 500,000 of them located in London.[17] A more recent research, published in 2011, questions this estimate by affirming that there are now 'only' 1.85 million cameras in the UK.[18] It is not by chance that the UK has the highest number of CCTV cameras per inhabitant in the world.[19]

Finally, another technology that has recently been tested in airports, with the aim of increasing the security in flights is the so-called Body Scanner.[20] This technology is already being tested in Manchester Airport in the UK[21] and in Amsterdam Airport in the Netherlands. Nevertheless,

european-parliament (29.05.2012).

15 European Court of Human Rights. Case of *S. and Marper v. The United Kingdom* (Applications nos. 30562/04 and 30566/04) – Judgment of 4 December 2008. Available at http://cmiskp.echr.coe.int/tkp197/view.asp?action=html&documentId=843941&portal=hbkm&source=externalbydocnumber&table=F69A27FD8FB86142BF01C1166DEA398649 (13.04.09).

16 National CCTV Strategy, October 2007. UK home Office. Available at http://www.crimereduction.homeoffice.gov.uk/cctv/National%20CCTV%20Strategy%20Oct%202007.pdf (29.05.2012).

17 Michael McCahill and Clive Norris. *Urbaneye: CCTV in London*. Working Paper nº 6. June 2002. Centre for Criminology and Criminal Justice. University of Hull. Available http://www.urbaneye.net/results/ue_wp6.pdf (29.03.2012). P. 20.

18 Graeme Gerrard and Richard Thompson. 'Two million cameras in the UK'. *CCTVImage*, N. 42, Winter 2011. Available at http://www.securitynewsdesk.com/wp-content/uploads/2011/03/CCTV-Image-42-Winter-2011.pdf (09.06.2012). P. 12.

19 See also http://www.ico.gov.uk/for_organisations/topic_specific_guides/cctv.aspx (29.05.2012). 'The UK has more CCTV cameras per person than anywhere else in the world and the use of CCTV raises data protection and wider privacy concerns.'

20 Security Scan at Amsterdam Aiport Schiphol no privacy issues. Available at http://www.schiphol.nl/Travellers/AtSchiphol/CheckinControl/SecurityChecksUponDeparture/SecurityScan.htm (29.05.2012). 'Schiphol is the only airport in the world with Security Scans provided with a screening technology that safeguards personal privacy. A computer analyses images instead of a human operator by means of harmless millimeter wave technology.'

21 See http://www.manchesterairport.co.uk/manweb.nsf/Content/xraytrail

the discussions regarding the adoption of these new technologies at the European level are just beginning.[22]

In Europe, differently from Brazil as we will see in the following sections, law enforcement authorities have to comply with data protection rules when processing personal data for the fight against crime.[23]

The Brazilian Data Protection Framework

Brazil has no general data protection regulation[24] and its data protection legal framework is based mainly on privacy constitutional provisions and sectorial data protection rules. The Brazilian Constitution recognizes in its article 5, X, the rights to private life, intimacy, honour and image as fundamental rights. The same article 5 guarantees the protection of other aspects of privacy (article 5, XI, XII, XIV),[25] creating in clause LXXII a new judicial remedy to grant citizens free access to their personal data, the writ of Habeas Data.[26] The Brazilian Civil Code adopted a similar position, including in its article 21 the right to privacy as a 'right of personality'. However, the only rule dealing with data protection, besides the Habeas data, is the Brazilian Consumer Code,[27] which articles 43 and 44 regulate the maintenance of databases and consumer files and establish a number

22 See, for instance, European Union Agency for Fundamental Rights. *The use of body scanners: 10 questions and answers*. July 2010. Available at http://fra.europa.eu/fraWebsite/attachments/FRA_Opinions_Bodyscanners.pdf (09.06.2012).

23 See Resolution on the use of body scanners for airport security purposes adopted by the European Privacy and Data Protection Commissioners' Conference 29, 30 April 2010, Prague. Available at http://www.tietosuoja.fi/uploads/z1k164nuv.pdf (09.06.2012).

24 In this sense are the words of Maria Celina Bodin de Moraes in the introduction she made for the Portuguese translation of RODOTÀ, Stefano. A vida na sociedade da vigilância – Privacidade Hoje. Op. cit. P. 12. 'The Brazilian choice, however, was not yet decided. It is expected that the same level of respect for human dignity, enshrined in art. 1, III of our Constitution, as well as the Private Law tradition that supports our system, in addition to a call for globalization through rights, would allow the option for an approach close to the European model, through a legislation based on principles.' Unofficial translation by the authors.

25 See Privacy and Human Rights 2006. An international survey of Privacy Laws and Developments. Electronic Privacy Information Center (Washington, DC, USA) and Privacy International (United States of America, 2006). Available at http://www.privacyinternational.org/article.shtml?cmd[347]=x-347-559539. Accessed 24 November 2008. 'Article 5 of the 1988 Constitution of Brazil – 1. provides that 'the privacy, private life, honour and image of people are inviolable, and the right to compensation for property or moral damages resulting from their violation is ensured'. 2. The Constitution also holds the home as 'inviolable,' and 'no one may enter therein without the consent of the dweller, except in the event of flagrante delicto or disaster, or to give help, or, during the day, by court order'. 3. Correspondence and electronic communication are also protected, except by court order 'for purposes of criminal investigation or criminal procedural finding of facts'. 4. 'Access to information is ensured to everyone and the confidentiality of the source shall be safeguarded, whenever necessary to the professional activity.'_5. Finally, the Constitution provides for habeas data, which guarantees the rights: a) to ensure the knowledge of information related to the person of the petitioner, contained in records or databanks of government agencies or of agencies of a public character; and, b) for the correction of data, when the petitioner does not prefer to do so through a confidential process, either judicial or administrative.

26 BESSA, Leonardo Roscoe. 'O Consumidor e os Limites dos Bancos de Dados de Crédito'. *Biblioteca de Direito do Consumidor V*. 25. Revista dos Tribunais, São Paulo, 2003. P. 107.

27 The Complementary Law 105/01 (Lei Complementar nº 105/2001) regulates the exchange of negative information between financial institutions and the Brazilian Central Bank.

of rights for consumers.[28] The Consumer Code, firstly, recognizes the consumers' right to be informed by the data controller[29] that their personal data is being processed (Article 43, paragraph 2). This communication has to be made before such data is made available in the public domain,[30] in order to allow the consumer to exercise his/her rights of access and rectification and the other rights guaranteed by Article 43.[31] Accordingly, if the data controller does not communicate this to the consumer in a reasonable time, he/she will be able to claim damages.

The Consumer Code also recognizes the rights of access[32] and rectification,[33] giving consumers the possibility to access any personal information stored and rectify it if they find any inaccuracy (Article 43, caption and paragraph 3).[34] In cases where the data controller does not allow consumers to exercise such rights, they will be able to claim damages and to exercise them through ordinary proceedings (Article 43, paragraph 4) or to use the above-mentioned Habeas Data writ.[35] Moreover, article 43 paragraphs 1 and 5 states that any negative information about a consumer which can restrict access to credit shall not be stored for more than five years.[36] Again, if the data controller fails to comply with such an obligation, consumers will be able to claim damages and to request the exclusion of the respective information through ordinary courts.

It is important to note that a Law was recently adopted by the Brazilian Parliament (Law n° 12.414 of 9 June 2011), converting into law the interim measure 518 of 30 December 2010, which regulates the creation and access to databases of information about payments, regarding natural and legal

28 The Consumer Code does not bring a definition of personal data, however, it applies to both natural and legal persons. See Article 2: 'Consumer is any individual or body corporate who acquires or uses any product or service as an end user' (Unofficial translation available at http://www.caxias.rs.gov.br/procon/site/_uploads/codigo_defesa_consumidor_ingles.pdf. Accessed 26 October 2010.

29 Although the Code establishes a common liability for both the data controller and the supplier of goods or services that included the consumer's data in a database, the Brazilian Superior Court of Justice states that the only responsible for such communication is the data controller (Digest n° 359 of the Brazilian Superior Court of Justice).

30 There is no mention in the Consumer Code about the moment in which the communication has to be done. However, both doctrine and jurisprudence agree that the communication has to give the consumer enough time to exercise his rights before his personal data is available in the public domain. Nevertheless, there is a local law in Rio de Janeiro that establishes the period of 10 days as a reasonable one (Law n° 3.244, 6 September 1999). Available at http://www.alerj.rj.gov.br/processo2.htm. Accessed 28 September 2008.

31 Benjamin, Antonio Herman Vasconcelos et al. *Código Brasileiro de Defesa do Consumidor comentado pelos autores do anteprojeto*. 9. ed. Forense, São Paulo, 2007. p. 405.

32 Ibid. p. 413.

33 Ibid. p. 416.

34 The right of deletion is implicit, since in the case there is any information in the database which is wrong or where the storage limit is over, the consumer will be able to request the deletion of such information.

35 The proceedings of Habeas data remedy were regulated by Federal Law n° 9.507, 12 November 1997. Available at http://www.planalto.gov.br/ccivil_03/Leis/L9507.htm. Accessed 20 September 2008.

36 In a recent ruling, the State Court of Appeal of Rio de Janeiro decided that the deadline for the storage of personal data regarding a debit in a consumer credit database is three years, instead of five years. According to the Court the Civil Code reduced the limitation of action for debt to three years and, for that reason, personal data related to debts cannot be stored longer than that period (Appeal n. 0011679-53.2009.8.19.0203, 6th Civil Section, judgment of 14 July 2010). Such reasoning goes in the same direction of Article 43(5) of the Consumer Protection Code: 'Paragraph 5. – Extinguished the time for collecting consumers' debts, the respective Credit Protection Services shall no longer provide any information that might prevent or make it difficult to consumers a new access to credit operations before suppliers.'

persons, with the aim of creating positive credit history.[37] Since the Consumer Code dealt mainly with data regarding unpaid debts, this Act provided for the registration of consumer financial data in general and included a reasonable set of typical data protection principles and procedures.[38]

This Law establishes that the treatment of consumers' financial data would be possible only with the consent of the data subject (Art. 4) and, among other issues, regulates which kind information can be stored (Art. 3, §2 and §3), data subjects' rights (Art. 5), duties of the data processor (Art. 6), supervision of the databases (Art. 17) and liability in case of damages (Art. 16).

Despite the lack of a comprehensive data protection framework, many Brazilian courts have recognized not only the protection of the traditional dimension of the right to privacy ('the right to be let alone') but also the protection of the informational aspect of privacy ('the ability of people to control information about themselves') and of the right to self-determination ('the individuals should have the capacity to decide about circumstances that affect them').[39]

It is worth noting that the purpose principle, which is one of the core principles of all data protection laws, is not expressly recognized in general terms by the Brazilian legislation.[40] However, in a famous Superior Court of Justice case, reported by Justice Ruy Rosado de Aguiar, the purpose principle was used as a limit for the processing carried out by consumer credit databases:

> The Credit Protection Service (SPC), which has been set up in several cities by trade organizations of merchants and shopkeepers, has the aim of informing its members about the existence of outstanding debt of a purchaser seeking for new financing.
> The benefits deriving from it, in terms of agility and security of commercial transactions, are obvious while it is also difficult to deny the seller the right to find out about the credit status of his client, and to share with others the data he has about him.
> This activity, however, because of its social importance and serious effects deriving from it – since even for applying for work in the public sector a SPC negative certificate has been required – must be exercised within proper limits, so that once it reaches its purpose it does not become cause and reason for greater social harm than the benefits it sets out to pursue.[41]

However, according to the Consumer Protection Code, the compilation (creation) of a database containing personal data is not subject to any authorization from a public authority or from the data

---

37 Available at http://www.planalto.gov.br/ccivil_03/_Ato2011-2014/2011/Lei/L12414.htm. Accessed 10 June 2011.

38 Another Law, regarding the access to information contained in government archives was recently adopted and has also some provisions regarding the processing of personal data (Law nº 12.527 of 18 November 2011).

39 See Federal judge decision in the Case 2009.61.00.007033-0, Federal Jurisdiction of São Paulo. Apud Doneda, Danilo; Viola de Azevedo Cunha, Mario. *Notes about Vehicle Monitoring in Brazil and Europe from a Data Protection Perspective*. op. cit. p. 319.

40 Law nº 12.414 of 9 June 2011, to a certain extent, recognizes the purpose principle.

41 *Apud* Doneda, Danilo; Viola De Azevedo Cunha. *Risk and Personal Information: the Finality Principle and Data Protection in the Brazilian Legal System.* op. cit. p. 146. 'The authors of the Draft Consumer Protection Code, when addressing the issue of access of suppliers to consumer data stored in consumer files or databases, established the existence of "consumption needs" as a legitimacy criterion, which is nothing more than the accomplishment of the principle of finality. In other words, according to them, the request for personal data must be linked to a specific deal to be carried out by both parties involved (the service provider and the consumer) (the service provider and the consumer) (Benjamin et al., 2001. p. 389/390).'

subject.[42] In this scenario, the Brazilian Ministry of Justice opened in 2011 a public consultation regarding a draft bill of a general data protection law.[43] This draft bill follows, in general terms, Directive 95/46/EC.

However, as we will see in the next topic, although not having general data protection rules, or specific rules applying to the use of personal data for surveillance purposes, both private and public bodies in Brazil have been using technology to monitor people and to process their personal data.

Monitoring Technologies in Brazil[44]

Email monitoring in the workplace

In 2004 an internal regulation of the House of Representatives provided specific rules for the use of e-mail by their deputies and staff.[45] The fact that the Information Technology Centre of the House is competent enough to regulate and supervise e-mail systems, and is entitled to gather evidence on potential unauthorized uses, has raised some concerns on potential privacy violations of congressmen's e-mails.

Still regarding the monitoring of e-mails, the 9th Regional Labour Court has ruled that auditing or monitoring an employee's computer is an illegal violation of the secrecy of electronic communications.[46] According to this decision, any employer's labour agreement allowing such monitoring practices is considered void. Any monitoring shall only be authorized upon a prior court order. Another decision, issued by the 10th Regional Labour Court,[47] held that the right of privacy and the right to the secrecy of correspondence and electronic communications are inviolable. As a consequence, evidence obtained by infringing these rights will not be admissible.

However, the highest Brazilian Labour Court (*TST – Tribunal Superior do Trabalho*) has ruled a series of cases regarding privacy and corporate e-mail in a different direction. The Court stated that an employee does not have a reasonable expectation of privacy when using his corporate email account. Only the personal or private e-mail account based on its own server can take advantage of the constitutional and legal protection of privacy; corporate e-mails, based on resources supplied by the employer follow a different rule and, according to this Court, it is possible for the employer to monitor employee use of a corporate e-mail account in the workplace.[48] These rulings were

42 Article 43, paragraph 2 of the Consumer Protection Code – 'If not requested, the consumer shall be communicated in writing about the inclusion of his name in any reference file, index card, register, personal and consumer data.' Unofficial translation available at http://www.caxias.rs.gov.br/procon/site/_uploads/codigo_defesa_consumidor_ingles.pdf. Accessed 26 October 2010.

43 See http://culturadigital.br/dadospessoais/apresentacao-2/. Accessed 18 January 2011.

44 Parts of this section were included in a previous work. Notes about Vehicle monitoring in Brazil and Europe from a data protection perspective (co-authors: Mario Viola de Azevedo Cunha e Danilo Doneda). In Rodrigo Firmino, Fabio Duarte e Clovis Ultramari (editors). *ICTs for Mobile and Ubiquitous Urban Infrastructures – Surveillance, Locative Media and Global Networks*. IGI Global: Hershy, 2011. pp. 312–23.

45 Câmara dos Deputados, Portaria No. 96, August 20, 2004.

46 TRT9 – 5ª T., RO 5568/2002, Rel. Juíza Janete do Amarante, j. 20.02.2003, DJ 04.04.2003.

47 TRT 10 – 13.000613/2000, issued on October 9, 2001.

48 Tribunal Superior do Trabalho, 1ªTurma, Relator: João Oreste Dalazen, RR - 613/2000-013-10-00, DJ - 10/06/2005. Available at http://brs02.tst.gov.br/cgi-bin/nph-brs?s1=3896444.nia.&u=/Brs/it01.html&p=1&l=1&d=blnk&f=g&r=1. In another important decision in 2006, the same TST stated that video monitoring in the bathrooms of one company is illegal, as a violation of employees' privacy. Tribunal Superior

confirmed by the TST itself, based on the idea that a corporate e-mail account, provided by the employer, does not provide an expectancy of privacy to the employee and the privacy constitutional provisions do not cover it.[49]

Government Databases, Wiretapping and Geolocation Tecnologies

In 18th November 2011 Law n. 12.572 on access to public information was approved. The law aims at enforcing the right stated by the Federal Constitution of free access to public information. This law deals not only with federal public bodies but also with all spheres of the Federal State and, to a certain extent, with private bodies when they process public information.

In 1996, a law regulating wiretapping was enacted.[50] Official wiretaps are allowed for 15 days, renewable on a judge's order for another 15 days, and can only be resorted to in cases dealing with the investigation of serious crimes punishable by imprisonment, such as drug or contraband smuggling, corruption, murder and kidnapping. The granting of judicial eavesdropping, authorized by judges, was previously an ad hoc process without any legal basis.[51] But now, procedures involving legal wiretapping are treated in confidentiality, which means that access to recordings and transcripts is restricted to the judge and the parties involved in the procedure.

In principle, investigative powers to instruct criminal procedures are restricted to the judiciary police, which is an auxiliary body of the Judiciary Branch. The Public Prosecutor Office (*Ministério Público*) is the entity officially competent to bring criminal actions of a public nature. There is still a controversy, based on different interpretations of the Brazilian Constitution, over whether the Public Prosecutor Office should be entitled to initiate criminal investigations. Such controversy is under review before the Supreme Court,[52] although in some individual cases the Court has already recognized this power to the Public Prosecutor Office.[53] A decision that would allow prosecution attorneys to promote criminal investigations could weaken privacy rights, as it would make possible privacy violations within the investigations conducted by them, as long as the judicial control over such investigations is bypassed. On the other hand, a decision denying such investigative powers to prosecution attorneys would certainly nullify several criminal procedures currently initiated, and in which such powers have been employed, such as corruption cases involving judges, police chiefs and politicians.

The Brazilian Penal Code was amended in 2000 to criminalize certain informational crimes.[54] The insertion of false data into an information system is punishable by a prison sentence of two to 12 years.[55] Unauthorized alteration of an information system is punishable by detention from three months to two years.[56] The Brazilian Penal Code and Brazilian Penal Procedural Code were also

---

do Trabalho, AIRR 1660/2003-044-03-40.1, DJ – 05/05/2006. Available at http://brs02.tst.gov.br/cgi-bin/nph-brs?s1=4028070.nia.&u=/Brs/it01.html&p=1&l=1&d=blnk&f=g&r=1 (09.06.2012).

49 Tribunal Superior do Trabalho, 7ªTurma, Relator: Ives Gandra Martins Filho, AIRR – 1542.2005-055-02-40, DJ June 06, 2008. Available at http://brs02.tst.gov.br/cgi-bin/nph-brs?s1=(4431080.nia.)&u=/Brs/it01.html&p=1&l=1&d=blnk&f=G&r=1 (09.06.2012).

50 Federal Law No. 9,296, July 24, 1996.

51 'Brazil Makes Police Phone-Taps Legal', Reuters World Service, July 24, 1996.

52 Extraordinary Appeal (*Recurso Extraordinário*) nº 593727, Brazilian Supreme Federal Court.

53 See, for instance, Habeas Corpus 97969 / RS, decided on March 1st, 2011. Brazilian Supreme Federal Court, 2nd Chamber.

54 Federal Law No. 9,983, July 14, 2000.

55 *Id.* at Article 313-a.

56 *Id.* at Article 313-b.

amended in July 2003[57] in order to strengthen sanctions corresponding to the violation of copyrights, and to criminalize the unauthorized distribution of copyrighted works through cable, optical fibre, satellite, radio waves or any other means. Changes in the Penal Procedural Code facilitated search and seizure procedures, thereby minimizing the defendant's rights. As a consequence, criminal lawsuits have been initiated by the Brazilian Association of Record Producers (ABPD) against suspects of illegal online music distribution. According to the ABPD's website,[58] which has been monitoring the Brazilian Internet since 1999 – even before the amendments of the Penal Code were enacted. Such practices could represent potential privacy violations, since the interception of Internet communications is allowed only with a judge's order.[59]

In 2007, the numbers of wiretappings in Brazil were estimated at between 300,000[60] and 409,000,[61] mostly without judicial order. In addition, the Federal Police and a private software company had developed a wiretapping system called *Guardião* (guardian). This system, which has being used by the Federal Police, was criticized after the disclosure of some of its functionalities such as the remote and automated monitoring of up to 3,000 telephone lines, both land and mobile ones.[62]

In 2006, the Brazilian National Traffic Council adopted a regulation (CONTRAN Resolution 212/2006)[63] requiring that every licensed Brazilian vehicle shall have an RFID[64] chip and that all the major highways and urban areas will be covered by an extensive array of RFID sensors. In order to make use of these chips, this regulation also creates a nationwide automated system for identifying vehicles (SINIAV), which includes a centralized database of every monitored vehicle's wanderings.

Such a regulation is not unique in the sense that it is part of a group of regulatory initiatives which, in the recent past, made Brazil one of the most active countries in making use of technological measures available to control its population and in providing as much as possible data for administrative purposes. The measure, however, does not seem to consider a series of probable pitfalls related to privacy and data protection issues.

Organizing a rather large population in one of the largest countries in the world has always been one of the main challenges of the Brazilian public administration. To make goods and services, either public or private, arrive in Brazil's most inner locations is a rather usual problem and a fact of life for many people residing in remote areas. That has also probably been a cause for the concentration of both population and capital in south eastern Brazil.

So, with the 'arrival' of technologies capable to keep track of the actions and whereabouts of people, the application and development of these technologies started to be seen by many policy-makers as the next logical step. Thus, several projects are already being implemented, such as the biometrical authentication of voters by the electronic voting machine in all Brazilian's elections;

57 Federal Law No. 10,695, July 1, 2003.

58 Associação Brasileira dos Produtores de Discos. Available at http://www.abpd.org.br (09.06.2012).

59 Brazilian Constitution, Title 2, Chapter 1, Article 5, XII.

60 Consultor Juridico, 'Invasão de privacidade, Trezentos mil brasileiros estão com telefone grampeado', October 27, 2007. Available at http://www.conjur.com.br/static/text/60835,1 (09.06.2012).

61 Aranha, Raquel, 'Excesso de escutas telefônicas ameaça direito à privacidade', April 25, 2008, available at <http://www.fecomercio.com.br/pagina.php?tipo=21&pg=675>.

62 Ordem dos Advogados do Brasil, 'Denuncia a escuta telefonica veem endo usada como medida preiminar de investigacao', available at <http://www2.oabsp.org.br/asp/jornal/materias.asp?edicao=113&pagina=3117&tds=7&sub=0&sub2=0&pgNovo=67>.

63 Resolution 212/2006 – Contran. Available at http://www.denatran.gov.br/download/Resolucoes/RESOLUCAO_212.rtf (09.06.2012).

64 Radio-frequency identification.

the unique ID for civil identification that comes with an all-new plastic-made and chip-powered ID card and a central database, according to the RIC project;[65] as well as the SINIAV project.

One could argue that since the SINIAV uses only RFID technologies, it is less effective (and less dangerous) in terms of 'mobile surveillance' than the systems which use other geolocation technologies, as recognized by David Lyon.[66] Nonetheless, through the interconnection of the information processed by SINIAV with other governmental databases already under control of the Brazilian National Traffic Department, it will be possible to use the system not only for geolocation but also for law enforcement purposes, for imposing sanctions to drivers or even to collect taxes. David Lyon presents two interesting examples which show how location information of vehicles can be used for law enforcement:

> On-board navigation systems for cars, transponders for electronic tolls at bridges or tunnels or on private highways, and the increasing use of 'black box' sensors in cars offer multiple possibilities for generation mobile data. California resident Scott Knight, for example, was convicted in 2001 after a hit-and-run death when his OnStar system reported an airbag inflation. And Acme Rent-a-Car in New Haven fined drivers $150 when their GPS system showed they had been consistently speeding (Schawartz 2003).[67]

There is also the possibility that information processed under the SINIAV framework is transferred to private parties, as has been the case with other databases managed by the Brazilian National Traffic Department, since this kind of information is very useful for some industries. For example, 'How fast the driver was travelling could affect insurance premiums or invoices from car rental companies'.[68]

Despite all the concerns about privacy and data protection that arose when analyzing the SINIAV, no judicial action against it or the regulation which established the system has been brought in Brazilian courts (this is probably due to the fact that SINIAV has not been implemented yet).[69]

Due to security concerns, the number of surveillance cameras in public and private places has increased significantly in Brazil. A number of regulations have been implemented in this regard. The City of São Paulo, for instance, passed a Municipal Law mandating the installation of signs notifying the public of the existence of surveillance cameras, both in public and private areas. Recorded images are meant to be confidential and protected under law.[70] Failure to comply with the installation of warning signs may subject infringers to statutory fines.

DNA Databases

Recently, a new law[71] allowing the collection of the genetic profile as a kind of criminal identification was adopted.

---

65 Registro único de identidade civil.

66 David Lyon. *Identifying Citizens: ID Cards as Surveillance*. Cambridge, UK: Polity Press, 2009. p. 13.

67 David Lyon. op. cit. p. 17.

68 Ibid. p. 24.

69 In the Brazilian National Traffic Department adopted an Act (Portaria n. 570 of 27 June 2011) establishing rules and the minimum requirements for certification and approval of products within the SINIAV framework.

70 São Paulo City Municipal Law No. 13,541, March 24, 2003.

71 Law nº 12.654 of 28 May 2012.

This law establishes that data related to the collection of the genetic profile shall be managed by a special criminal audit unit,[72] and that genetic data stored in such databases cannot reveal information regarding somatic or behavioural traits of people, except for gender information, observing constitutional rules and international agreements regarding human rights, human genome and genetic information. Moreover, such data will be protected by secrecy and those who allow the processing of these data for a purpose different than the ones provided for by this law will be civil, criminally and administratively liable. Finally, those convicted for a crime committed intentionally, with violence against a person, or of a serious nature, or even for heinous crimes, will be compulsorily submitted to genetic profile identification.[73]

Conclusions

One of the great challenges of the 21st century in the field of data protection is, therefore, to protect the right to privacy of individuals not only when their personal data are transferred for commercial purposes, but also when they are transferred for uses related to the public interest (fight against crime). Another important challenge is to find a balance between the need to ensure security and the fundamental rights of privacy and data protection.

This discussion, which is in the political arena in Europe since the terrorist attacks, has not gained yet the necessary support in Brazil. However, as announced by the Brazilian Ministry of Justice in August 2010, a bill of general data protection law is intended to be submitted to the Brazilian Congress this year – after a public consultation process which took place in 2011.

In the meantime, it is up to jurists and academics to draw the attention of the Brazilian society for the risks to individual privacy posed by the deregulated use of personal data for security purposes.

72 Article 2.

73 See Articles 2 and 3.

PART VII
Emerging Issues

Chapter 12
Proposing a Right to Identity within the International Framework of Human Rights: Issues and Prospects

Norberto Nuno Gomes de Andrade and Paul De Hert

In all cases, it remains to be debated whether the interests of agents are best expressed in the language of a claimed right to identity.[1]

Introduction

Forgotten and neglected for several decades by both the jurisprudence and the legal doctrine, the right to personal identity has been the target of a recent revival movement.[2] The legal 'revitalization' of the right to identity is, to a very large extent, connected with the revolutionary changes brought by recent technological developments,[3] namely with the so-called information revolution[4] and the digitization of the human person.[5] These technological progresses have equipped people with a new set of tools through which to express and represent their identities, rendering the latter increasingly fluid and dynamic. Further to the novel and fascinating ways through which identities can be constructed and communicated, these technologies also aggravate the dangers threatening identity, intensifying the ways through which a person's identity can be detected, distorted, deleted,

1 Roger Brownsword, 'Friends, Romans, and Countrymen: Is There a Universal Right to Identity?' *Law, Innovation and Technology* 1, no. 2 (2009): 226.

2 The previous and inaugural movement of conceptualization of the right to identity was conducted by the Italian legal doctrine and jurisprudence during the 1980s and 1990s. Before that, one should also quote the work of De Cupis. See Adriano De Cupis, *Il Diritto All' Identità Personale* (Milano: A. Giuffrè, 1949). For a detailed explanation of the Italian jurisprudential creation of the right to identity, see Giorgio Pino, *Il Diritto All'identità Personale : Interpretazione Costituzionale E Creatività Giurisprudenziale*, Ricerca (Bologna: Il mulino, 2003). For a thorough examination of the historical precedents of the right to identity, encompassing the Roman period, the Middle Ages and the nineteenth centuries, see Norberto Nuno Gomes de Andrade, *The Right to Personal Identity in the Information Age. A Reappraisal of a Lost Right* (European University Institute, 2012).

3 As Oreg correctly observes, this is not the first time that transformations of this kind generate new legal conceptions. This was also the case with the introduction of photographic cameras in the late 19th century, and which impact in the American society led Samuel Warren and Louis Brandeis to develop the concept of 'Right to Privacy' (famously defined as 'the right to be let alone'). See Elad Oreg, *Right to Information Identity* (2011); and Samuel D. Warren and Louis D. Brandeis, 'The Right to Privacy', *Harvard Law Review* 4, no. 5 (1890).

4 Luciano Floridi, 'A Look into the Future Impact of ICT on Our Lives', *The Information Society* 23, no. 1 (2007).

5 Norberto Nuno Gomes de Andrade, 'The Right to Privacy and the Right to Identity in the Age of Ubiquitous Computing: Friends or Foes? A Proposal Towards a Legal Articulation' in *Personal Data Privacy and Protection in a Surveillance Era: Technologies and Practices*, ed. Christina Akrivopoulou and Athanasios Psygkas (Hershey, PA: Information Science Publishing, 2011).

concealed, stolen, misappropriated, impersonated, falsified and misrepresented, rendering it increasingly vulnerable.

In order to understand the impact and the significance of the information revolution on human identity, Floridi, an Italian philosopher, distinguishes four major historical revolutions in science, based not on the technologies involved but on the intellectual findings that each of them presented. These revolutions changed not only our understanding of the external world but also our conception of who we are. They were the Copernican revolution, which displayed humanity from the centre of the universe; the Darwinian revolution, which showed that all species of life have evolved over time from common ancestors through natural selection, thus displaying humanity from the centre of the biological kingdom; and the Freudian revolution, which underlined that the mind is also unconscious and that we are very far from being Cartesian minds entirely transparent to ourselves. The fourth revolution, and the one that matters the most to our study, is what Floridi calls 'the informational turn' – that is, the next step in the process of dislocation and reassessment of humanity's fundamental nature and role in the universe. It is the acknowledgement that we may be informational organisms (*inforgs*) among many others, significantly but not dramatically different from natural entities, agents and smart, engineered artefacts.[6]

Following Floridi's informational ontology, we – as informational elements – live in the so-called 'infosphere', i.e., the informational ecosystem constituted by all informational entities. The idea that we have, utterly and irreversibly, become information (or 'inforgs') is also behind Roger Clarke's notion of 'digital person'[7] and Rodotà's concept of 'networked persons'.[8] Further than the simple digitization of information we are thus moving towards the outright digitization or 'informational-ization' of the human person.[9] Information and Communication Technologies (ICT), especially the ones related with the creation and development of the Internet, have revolutionized the way our identities are perceived, presented and projected.[10] Specific aspects of one's identity are, today, channelled as bits and bytes into computer networks, often in completed automated ways through algorithms and other computing processes, reaching wider audiences and geographies.

In the same way that identities can be presented and expressed through informational processes, they can also be misrepresented and distorted. As Brownsword explains, developments of this kind provoke various kinds of 'identity crisis', as for example the concern that our identities should not be assumed or 'reconstructed' by others.[11] In fact, due to the technological progresses associated with the establishment and consolidation of the information revolution, not only the ways to define

6 See Luciano Floridi, 'The Information Society and Its Philosophy: Introduction to the Special Issue on the Philosophy of Information, Its Nature, and Future Developments', *The Information Society* 25, no. 3 (2009).

7 Roger Clarke, 'The Digital Persona and Its Application to Data Surveillance', *The Information Society* 10, no. 2 (1994).

8 S. Rodotá, 'Data Protection as a Fundamental Right', in *Reinventing Data Protection?*, ed. Serge Gutwirth, et al. (Dordrecht; London: Springer, 2009).

9 Andrade, 'The Right to Privacy and the Right to Identity in the Age of Ubiquitous Computing: Friends or Foes? A Proposal Towards a Legal Articulation'.

10 Sherry Turkle, *Life on the Screen. Identity in the Age of the Internet* (New York: Simon & Schuster, 1995). The author argues that the interaction between people and computers is causing a new sense of identity to emerge, one that is decentred and multiple.

11 Brownsword, 'Friends, Romans, and Countrymen: Is There a Universal Right to Identity?, 224. As the scholar adds, research suggests that 'three in four young internet users are concerned that their identity is reconstructed using personal data from various sources', see EC Health and Consumers Directorate-General, 'Data Collection, Targeting and Profiling of Consumers for Commercial Purposes in Online Environments' (Brussels 2009), 8.

and represent but also the means to violate personal identity (theft, distortion, misrepresentation, impersonation, etc) have become – to a very large extent – a matter of data processing and information management. The laws regulating the processing of personal information seem, in effect, to be one of the most adequate legal instruments through which to protect personal identity.

In order to understand the challenges posed to the legal regulation of personal identity and the importance of re-activating and re-conceptualizing a right to identity, namely within the scope of data protection and privacy laws, one needs to first understand how new (and prospective) technological developments are changing the old premises and paradigms of identity. Here, we should expand our analytical lens beyond the immediate present and peek into the future, looking into the changes that the so-called Ambient Intelligence (AmI) or Ubiquitous Computing environments[12] (i.e., post-Internet scenarios) will bring to personal identity.[13] This will be the object of our next section (section 2). In the third section we will discuss a series of authors that argue in favour of a re-conceptualization of the right to identity: Pino, Sullivan, Andrade, Oreg and others. This doctrinarian movement is intimately connected to the ever expanding and more flexible manner through which law has been addressing and regulating identity. In fact, the law has endowed individuals with more and more legal tools with which they can influence and change aspects of their identity. Individuals are now entitled to break the chains of their affiliations, modify their names, and change their nationality and sex.[14]

In section 4 we discuss the legal framework on human rights law, assessing the argument advanced by certain authors that a proper protection of identity aspects through existing legal instruments is lacking. The section is followed by a discussion of policy initiatives that call for new Information Society rights (section 5). Section 6 discusses several examples of recent human rights initiatives (regarding Internet access, regarding the elderly, regarding water and regarding data protection) in order to address the feasibility of a new right to personal identity. The seventh section concludes the contribution.

12 For further details on the vision of AmI, see Emile Aarts, Rick Harwig, and Martin Schuurmans, 'Ambient Intelligence,' in *The Invisible Future : The Seamless Integration of Technology into Everyday Life*, ed. Peter J. Denning (New York: McGraw-Hill, 2001).; E.H.L. Aarts and Stefano Marzano, *The New Everyday: Views on Ambient Intelligence* (Rotterdam: 010 Publishers, 2003).; Werner Weber, Jan M. Rabaey, and E.H.L. Aarts, *Ambient Intelligence*, 1st ed. (Berlin; New York: Springer, 2005).; G. Riva et al., *Ambient Intelligence: The Evolution of Technology, Communication and Cognition Towards the Future of Human-Computer Interaction*, Emerging Communication, 1566–7677 (Amsterdam; Oxford: IOS Press, 2005).; H. Nakashima, H. Aghajan and J.C. Augusto, *Handbook of Ambient Intelligence and Smart Environments*, 1st ed. (New York: Springer, 2009); Norberto Nuno Gomes de Andrade, 'Technology and Metaphors: From Cyberspace to Ambient Intelligence', *Observatorio (OBS*) Journal* 4, no. 1 (2010).

13 For a detailed account of how AmI impacts on the way human beings express and construct their identities, see Bibi van den Berg, *The Situated Self. Identity in a World of Ambient Intelligence* (Nijmegen: Wolf Legal Publishers, 2010).

14 Alain Pousson, 'Domicile Et Identité. "Je T'aime, Moi Non Plus",' in *L'Identité De La Personne Humaine. Étude De Droit Français et le Droit Comparé*, ed. J. Pousson-Petit (Bruxelles: Bruylant, 2002), 529; P. De Hert, 'A Right to Identity to Face the Internet of Things' (at http://portal.unesco.org/ci/fr/files/25857/12021328273de_Hert-Paul.pdf/de%2BHert-Paul.pdf. Also on the CD of Commission Nationale française pour l'Unesco, Ethique et droits de l'homme dans la societé d'information. Actes, synthèse et recommandations, 13–14 septembre 2007, Strasbourg., 2008), 12.

Changes to Personal Identity due to AmI and Ubiquitous Computing

AmI and Ubiquitous Computing represent a vision of the form and means that computing will take in the near future. They convey the idea of an aspiring reality – automated, intelligent, imperceptible and omnipresent – a foreseeable future stage in which the current Internet – as a network of computers – will gradually become a network of objects,[15] enveloping the physical environment.[16] Requiring little deliberate human intervention and encompassing a wide array of different emerging technologies (mobile sensors, radio frequency identification [RFID] tags, software agents, nanotechnology, etc), AmI consists of a technological ecosystem in which 'people will be surrounded by intelligent and intuitive interfaces embedded in everyday objects around us'.[17] One of the most remarkable shifts entailed in these prospective scenarios is the fading of (traditional) computers from our visible physical environment and consciousness. In their place we will have the deployment of a prolific number of devices and machines (such as tags and sensors) capable of recognizing a given person and his situational contexts, adapting to the user's needs and anticipating his desires without conscious mediation. AmI will thus be characterized by, on the one hand, its invisibility, discretion and unobtrusiveness and, on the other, its sensitivity, interactivity and responsiveness to the human person.

The AmI scenarios and the Ubiquitous Computing settings will exert a profound impact not only on our sense and definition of personal identity, but also on how we express and shape it. These novel and technological environments will transform how personal identity will be captured, represented and conveyed to others by a) massively increasing the digitization (and thus collection, storage and processing) of personal information; b) blurring the distinction between the physical and the digital realms, rendering our identities more and more traceable, profiled and networked; c) fragmenting and multiplying one's identity into various distinct and partial ones; and d) deploying a set of advanced instruments to track and monitor users and, therefore, displaying a more encompassing and sophisticated capacity to identify, distinguish and classify each human being.[18] Regarding the latter, there is the concern 'that various kinds of identifying technologies (particularly of a biometric nature) should not erode our privacy or compromise our human dignity'.[19]

Personal identity will thus become, increasingly more, dispersed, multiple, ubiquitous, de-centred and (tendentiously) everlasting (i.e., permanently registered).[20] Traces, traits, aspects and attributes of our identities – all digitized and processed by an infinitude of intelligent devices – will thus be dispersed through the physical-digital environment and scattered through smart

15 Unesco has termed this vision of 'Internet of Things'.

16 Ubiquitous Computing represents thus 'a vision of processing power so distributed throughout the environment that computers per se effectively disappear', Adam Greenfield, *Everyware: The Dawning Age of Ubiquitous Computing* (Berkeley, CA: New Riders, 2006), 1.

17 Information Society Technologies Advisory Group – ISTAG, 'Orientations for Workprogramme 2000 and Beyond' (1999). ISTAG report 1999, in which the term 'ambient intelligence' was coined.

18 'In a world of "Internet of Things", it will be easier to establish new relationships, but also to identify people, since all possible everyday objects will be part of a network' De Hert, 'A Right to Identity to Face the Internet of Things', 10.

19 '… and perhaps, most disturbingly, we are concerned that genetic and neuroscientific technologies should not undermine our understanding of who and what we are as humans', Brownsword, 'Friends, Romans, and Countrymen: Is There a Universal Right to Identity', 224.

20 Norberto Nuno Gomes de Andrade, 'Right to Personal Identity: The Challenges of Ambient Intelligence and the Need for a New Legal Conceptualization', in *Privacy and Data Protection. An Element of Choice.*, ed. S. Gutwirth, et al. (Dordrecht; London: Springer, 2011).

objects. Identity will also become de-centred, gradually escaping our own control and sphere of command. The collection of personal data by external entities (governments, public institutions, law-enforcement authorities, private entities, commercial companies, etc), as well as by other people, leave data subjects with less and less control over the construction, representation and projection of their personal identities. In addition, more and more profiles and other identity representations will be constructed by AmI machines and agents. The intermediate character of the modern information environment (mediated by a wide range of different actors: Internet's access providers, search and filter services, content hosts and database operators, each one with their own interests and motivations) will only render identity more dependent on 3rd parties' intermediaries (and many times under a singular channel controlled by a monopolistic body).[21] This trend will only tend to increase with AmI, thus intensifying the dangers posed to identity, such as the ones of simulation, impersonation, misrepresentation and identity theft. In addition, identity elements will tend to become indefinitely preserved in databases, registered and stored (potentially) *ad finitum*. Finally, personal identity will also become multiple. Rather than rigid and uniform, there is an ongoing social change according to which identity is increasingly understood as being multifaceted and context-dependent.[22] The different contexts in which we act, the various roles we assume, and the technological environment that provides for a newer and greater number of different roles and contexts are the fundamental factors behind this multiplicity of identities.[23] Internet (and its forthcoming conversion into an AmI space) will thus disrupt the traditional connection between one person and one identity (i.e., its alleged unicity and stability), rendering it increasingly fluid, undetermined, variable and fragmented. People, in effect, tend to – more and more – present different and dissociated identities.

Without being able to proof a causal link, we assume that the technological changes discussed above have contributed to a recent doctrinarian movement interested in understanding the role of identity in our society and in law. The following section sketches the main contributions to this re-launch and re-conceptualization of the notion of identity and its legal casting. Most authors underline the importance of identity and show, each in their own way, how identity formation works. Some authors add to this a specific argumentation about identity in the law, its uniqueness and relationship with other legal notions such as privacy and freedom of expression.

The Right to Identity as Conceptualized in Recent Scholarship

From 2000 on Italian author Giorgio Pino has been writing extensively on identity. His work, especially his article 'The Right to Personal Identity in Italian Private Law: Constitutional Interpretation and Judge-Made Rights', describes how a right to identity was recognized in Italy by

21 For a more detailed development of this argument (intermediation), see Oreg, 'Right to Information Identity'.

22 Ibid.

23 Behind this fundamental change, three factors assume particular relevance: roles, context and technology. The diversity of contexts and roles are the two main factors behind our tendency to multiplicity. This tendency is being exacerbated by the technological progress and conditions that characterize modern life. See Andrade, 'The Right to Personal Identity in the Information Age. A Reappraisal of a Lost Right'.

judges,[24] legal theorists and then by the legislator.[25] This right to personal identity, first developed in case law, is commonly described as the right everybody has to appear and to be represented in social life (especially by the mass media) in a way that fits with, or at least does not falsify or distort, his or her personal identity. Due to a tendency towards an expansive legal protection of the various aspects of human personality and to the striking diffusion of the mass media in past decades, the right was understood to protect the interest that everybody has to be represented with his/her real identity, i.e., with the identity that appears in concrete and unequivocal circumstances of social life. The recognition of the right expresses the claim that one's (ascertainable) cultural, professional, religious, political, social experiences should not be distorted, misrepresented, falsified, confused, contested, or the like, by means of the ascription of false (even if not necessarily defamatory) statements or acts.[26] In brief, the right to personal identity means the protection of individual personality against false representations elaborated by the mass media, or displayed in databases.

In his work, Pino discusses these developments and characterizes this right to personal identity as a multiform and adaptable right, flexible enough to grant legal protection to different situations.[27] In addition, Pino analyses different laws and issues that are strongly linked to the idea of personal identity: intellectual patrimony, sexual identity, the right to oblivion, and the right over

24 Italian case law during the last quarter of the twentieth century literally created the right to personal identity. The landmark case that introduced the right to identity in Italy is the Pretura Roma 6-5-1974 *Pangrazi* and *Silvetti v. Comitato Referendum*). Pino summarizes the case as follows: 'The facts of the case are quite interesting. In the days of the referendum propaganda about the abrogation of divorce in Italy, the anti-divorce committee, for the purpose of its campaign, used the picture of a man and a woman working in the country. The picture was meant to evoke a "traditionalist" atmosphere (and old-style family) and was of course associated with an anti-divorce message. The problem was that, first of all, the picture was taken without the consent of the people portrayed; in the second place, they were not married; finally, and what is more, they were in favour of the existing divorce legislation', Giorgio Pino, 'The Right to Personal Identity in Italian Private Law: Constitutional Interpretation and Judge-Made Rights', in *The Harmonization of Private Law in Europe*, ed. M. Van Hoecke and F. Ost (Oxford: Hart Publishing, 2000), 234.

25 For a detailed overview of the construction of the right to identity by the Italian jurisprudence, see Pino, *Il Diritto All'identità Personale : Interpretazione Costituzionale E Creatività Giurisprudenziale*.

26 In effect, this is the commonest definition of the right to personal identity, which can be read in the decision of the Corte di Cassazione, I, 22.6.1985, n. 3769, in Nuova giurisprudenza civile commentata, I, 1985, pp. 647–54. This Court decision explicitly recognized the autonomy of the right to personal identity, and rooted its normative foundations, in art. 2 of the Italian Constitution in conjunction with article 3(2). Moreover, in 1994, the Corte Costituzionale (n.13) followed the same line of argument.

27 In emphasizing the autonomy of the right to personal identity, the scholar stresses three distinctive features of the right to identity. First, the protection afforded by the right to personal identity can only be invoked if a false representation of the personality has been offered to the public eye. Taking into account that personal identity can be violated also by the attribution of false statements that are not necessarily defamatory, the right to identity is thus considered different from reputation related rights. Bearing in mind that the legal protection of personal identity concerns the correct exposure of the personality to the public eye and not the interest of the subject not to be exposed, the right to identity is also considered different from the right to privacy. Second, the right to personal identity refers to a concept of personal history that must be interpreted only in a factually-objective way. The object of the right is the social projection of the personality, as can be ascertained using an ordinary duty of (professional) care (this point has been clearly expressed by Tribunale di Roma, 27.3.1984 (in Giurispudenza italiana, 1985, I, 2, p.13 ff) and Corte di Cassazione, n.3769, quoted), and not personal ideas and thoughts that have never been publicly exposed or actually revealed in concrete acts. Third, the right to personal identity is 'relational' in character: it protects the interest to preserve the social image one has concretely revealed.

personal data.[28] Regarding the latter, and taking into account the broad definition of 'processing' and 'personal data', data protection law seems to cover, Pino holds, all the most important cases of violation of personal identity that have been brought to court.[29]

In 2008 and 2009, Claire Sullivan, following a legal perspective and within a transactional context, embarks on a full-length study of digital identity. Sullivan identifies the emergence of a distinct and new legal concept of identity, linking it closely to the notion and regime of property. Her study demonstrates that an individual's digital identity presents characteristics of property that ought to be subject to legal protection. By defining 'identity theft' through the lens of this emergent concept, Sullivan analysis shows that digital identity amounts to property capable of actually being stolen and criminally charged. Sullivan then turns to human rights law. She observes that although the right to identity – in the context of the National Identity Scheme (NIS) in the United Kingdom[30] – arises in specific form – as a right to digital identity (defined as the right of an individual to an accurate, functional, unique transaction identity), it is part of a broader right to identity under international law. This right should not be understood as a privacy related right. On the contrary, Sullivan believes that the overwhelming focus on privacy in international legal scholarship and jurisprudence has undermined the actual importance and relevance of the right to identity. Following Neethling,[31] Sullivan argues that the right to identity is infringed by untrue or false use of indicia of identity, whereas the right to privacy is infringed by the association of an individual with personal facts, contrary to the wishes of that individual. Contrarily to the right to privacy, and given its fundamental right nature, derogations to the right to identity cannot be justified on public interest grounds and can only take place in exceptional circumstances. Based on this reasoning, the author asserts that the right to identity applied within its scope provides better, and more appropriate, protection than the one afforded by the right to privacy.

In passing we note Sullivan's interesting association between digital identity and legal personality. Sullivan argues that 'token identity' (a defined and limited set of information which determines an individual's identity for transactional purposes) should be considered a legal person.[32] In effect, the scholar asserts that the concept of token identity established under the UK NIS fits the concept of legal personhood. As the author states:

> Token identity "exists only as an abstract capacity to function in law, a capacity which is endowed by law because it is convenient for law to have such a creation". Although the lawmaker may not have made a conscious decision to create token identity, let alone endow it with legal personality,

---

28 As a matter of fact, the Italian law on personal data makes an explicit reference to personal identity. L. 675/1996, art.1. 'La presente legge garantisce che il trattamento dei dati personali si svolga nel rispetto dei diritti, delle libertà fondamentali, nonché della dignità delle persone fisiche, com particolare riferimento alla riservatezza e all´identità personale'.

29 Giorgio Pino, 'L'identità Personale', in *Trattato di Biodiritto*, ed. S. Rodotá and P. Zatti (Milano: Giuffrè, 2010), 9. Pino, in effect, has also studied the impact of data protection laws on identity and its protection, see Giorgio Pino, 'Il Diritto All'identità Personale Ieri e Oggi. 'Informzione, Mercato, Dati Personali', in *Libera Circolazione e Protezione Dei Dati Personali*, ed. R. Panetta (Milano: 2006).

30 Established under the Identity Cards Act 2006 (repealed in the meantime by the Identity Documents Act 2010).

31 J. Neethling, J.M. Potgieter, and P.J. Visser, *Neethling's Law of Personality* (Durban: Butterworths, 1996).

32 Clare Sullivan, 'Digital Identity – the Legal Person?', *Computer Law & Security Review* 25, no. 3 (2009).

> the legislation has crystallized the concept and through the operation of the scheme, it has been endowed with legal personality.[33]

Sullivan thus establishes a crucial distinction between the physical person and the (digital) information that is associated with that person: [a]lthough there is a national connection with a human being, it is the information which plays the crucial role in the transaction, not the individual to whom it is presumed to relate'.[34] As we shall see in the following, the concept of information lies at the basis of two other proposed re-conceptualizations of the right to identity, namely the ones by Andrade and Oreg.

In a context of new and upcoming technological developments and challenges, Andrade – in his study *The Right to Personal Identity in the Information Age. A Reappraisal of a Lost Right*[35] – conceptualizes the right to personal identity as a right that encompasses, controls and protects a series of different types of information related to or constitutive of our personal identity (digital, genetic, neural). Following a postmodern conception of identity (as anti-essentialistic, dynamic and multiple), and grounded upon the fundamental values of dignity, autonomy and self-determination, the right to personal identity is presented and defined as the right to be different, inimitable and unique; the right to be different, not only from others but also from oneself. Further to a right over information, this right to identity is presented and developed as a right that regulates a series of identity movements and transformations between different ontological levels of 'being' (possible ↔ real; actual ↔ virtual). Thus, the right to identity is the right to have one's identity attributes registered (real → possible), as well as the right to be recognized and identified (possible → real) according to those defining features. The right to identity also encompasses the right to be represented as one wishes (virtual → actual) – that is, the right not to be misrepresented; the right to delete and recreate oneself (actual → virtual), an identity movement that encompasses the right to be forgotten (and, consequently, the right to start again); and the right to multiple identities (virtual → actual) – that is, the right to create, control and uphold different identities in digital environments. Based on the fundamental idea of multiplicity, Andrade proposes a new approach to existing laws and in particular laws on privacy and data protection. The author proposes to elaborate a regulatory framework through which the user can articulate and use different identities, beginning with the 'holonym' (master identity), which comprises all of a person's possible nyms, i.e., all aspects, elements and attributes of their personal identity.[36] The regulatory proposal would focus not on the information itself (surpassing the personal/non-personal dichotomy), but on the sources of information, i.e., on the various and separate identity categories to which different streams of information would correspond to.

In his discussion of the legal framework, Andrade shows how existing laws and courts' decisions have lagged behind, addressing and regulating identity through a series of outdated

33 Ibid., 233.

34 Ibid., 233.

35 Andrade, 'The Right to Personal Identity in the Information Age. A Reappraisal of a Lost Right'.

36 This macro-identity is then composed of the following forms: 'lexonyms' (civil, legal identities); 'meronyms' (attributes, partial and contextual identities); 'endonyms' (identities created by oneself), which include autonyms, pseudonyms (concealed identities) and heteronyms (different identities); and, finally, 'exonyms' (external and imposed identities). This new regulatory model allows the data subject to control the links and connections between her various 'nyms', encompassing, in particular, the right to keep one's pseudonym separate from another one; the right to create and uphold heteronyms; the right to avoid one's exonym from being traced to one's lexonym; or one's meronym separate from one's autonym, among other possible set of connections and relations.

'dogmas' and 'paradigms' (namely the ones of immateriality, notoriety [or publicity], visibility, ex-post intervention [remediation] and authenticity).[37]

Again we find an argument to conceive 'a' right to identity as an autonomous legal instrument. By drawing attention to the importance of keeping the right to identity, privacy and data protection explicitly defined and separated, Andrade proposes two important criteria (procedural/substantive and alethic/non-alethic) through which these different rights can be distinguished and articulated. Hence, the scholar distinguishes data protection, on one side, from privacy and identity, on the other, qualifying one as procedural and the other as substantive. Regarding the difference between the rights to identity and privacy, the scholar distinguishes between personal information that qualifies alethically (from αλήθεια [aletheia], the Greek word for truth) from the one that does not. Andrade argues that personal data encompassing a set of true facts related to the data subject should be protected under the right to privacy, whereas personal information that is not necessarily truthful (that is, which is false or de-contextualized) should be covered by the right to identity.[38] As a way to test the usefulness of the alethic criteria, Andrade devotes particular attention to the implications of automated profiling technologies, arguing that the conceptual clarification of both the rights to identity and privacy will be crucial in order to protect and promote the autonomy and self-determination of the human person.[39]

In his 2011 article *Right to Information Identity*,[40] Elad Oreg equally starts his analysis with looking more closely at the idea of information as a pivotal concept. This legal scholar anchors (and, in a way, substantiates) the notion of identity to information, arguing that the current legal protection of information-identity is partial, incidental and insufficient. Identity-related information is spread out through various branches of law (privacy, intellectual property, freedom of expression, slander, etc) that fail to cover the wide array of dangers threatening identity. In effect, the extent to which information-identity can be distorted, impersonated, filtered, deleted and concealed demands thus the conceptualization of a right to identity, grounded in solid conceptual and normative foundations.

In this light, Oreg argues in favour of the conceptualization and recognition of a new, independent and explicit legal principle of a 'right to information identity', that is, the 'right of an individual to the functionality of the information platforms that enable others to identify and know him and to remember who and what he is'.[41] The right to information identity is depicted as

37 Andrade's analysis is based on a comprehensive historical account of the legal regulation of personal identity, comprising the Classical Roman period, the middle Ages and the nineteenth/twentieth centuries.

38 Andrade, in this way, demonstrates how the right to privacy is currently being overstretched, covering the legal protection of personal data that should, in reality, be assigned to the right to identity. According to the more delimited conceptualization of the right to privacy proposed in the scholar's analysis, Andrade argues that the right to identity should also be contemplated and enshrined within the EU data protection regulatory framework.

39 Further to this theoretical framework, Andrade's thesis also presents the foundations for an identity-regulatory system that grants the individual with the necessary and operational means to manage, control, aggregate, disaggregate, change and delete his or her multiple identities. According to the author, this proposed model ensures respect for one's privacy and for the free development of one's identity, mitigating most of the threats that current data collection practices pose to individual autonomy (such as the misuse of personal information, self-censorship, behavioural chilling effects and misrepresentation of personal identity), while allowing the user to reap the benefits of the massive collection and processing of personal information, such as improved search engine results and relevant targeted advertising.

40 Oreg, 'Right to Information Identity'.

41 This right is conceived as a 'person's right to the functionality of the platforms that accommodate comprehensive, continuous and dynamic knowledge about him, and which enables others to ascribe this

a person's right to the existence of his information identity, i.e., as a right to exist (as information) in the 'mind' of others (persons, institutions, State). This right is not conceptualized as a right 'stricto sensu', but as a principle which – in Hofheldian terms – gives expressions to all legal norms – 'freedoms', 'rights', 'immunities' and 'powers', etc – that are intended to promote the identity interests and values protected by such principle. As Oreg explains, this right imposes limitations upon various players whose conduct affects these platforms; it prohibits them from behaving in ways that damage it, such as impersonating, distorting, falsifying, deleting, hiding, filtering and destroying identity-related information.[42]

Oreg explains the inherent and the instrumental justifications (psychological significance for others, efficiency, incentive and accountability, trust, community, democracy) for the establishment of a right to identity. In his work we find a general outline of the right to information identity, its protected values and interests, its influence on diverse contemporary legal doctrines, and a 'future research' agenda capable of providing a more concrete and detailed explanation of this fundamental principle (the right to identity is depicted not as a specific rule, but as a broad standard which requires further discretion in implementing it in concrete situations). Oreg, in addition, not only presents and defines the right to identity, it also differentiates it from other rights (right to good reputation, right to privacy, freedom of expression), contributing also to the autonomization of the right to identity.

In Paul Bernal's *The Right to Online Identity* (2012)[43] we find a strong defence of a (specific) right to an online identity. In the same way that people have a right to internet access, Bernal argues that they should also have a right to an online identity. According to the author, online identities should be understood as something more complex than a matter of authentication of a link from an online actor to a real person. Online identities are, instead, complex, multifaceted and constantly developing, bearing both similarities and significant differences from 'real-world' identities. The recognition and assertion of an online identity is perceived as a pre-requisite for any individual to take part and to function fully in modern life.

Bernal constructs his 'right to online identity' as encompassing three clusters of specific rights: the right to create, to assert and to protect that identity; as well as the right to control the links between the online identity and the real identity behind it.[44]

---

information to him, when meeting him' (ibid., 53.). Although the author refers to the conceptualization and recognition of a new right, it is important to bear in mind that the right to identity is not a new right. In fact, its normative foundations have been built centuries ago and its explicit enshrinement in written law occurred in the twentieth century.

42 The scholar lists and develops the many dangers posed to identity by both traditional and modern information environments (intermediation, simulation, impersonation and identity theft, among others), calling also the attention to the increasing importance assumed by the phenomena of pseudonyms and multiple identities.

43 Paul Bernal, 'The Right to an Online Identity', *Available at SSRN: http://ssrn.com/abstract=2143138* (September 7, 2012).

44 In a tri-partite structure, Bernal's right to an online identity is thus composed by a creation, an assertion (relationship between online identity and the real-world identity) and a protection of online identities processes. The first part of the right to an online identity is the right to create such an identity. The right to create an online identity, which should be in the hands of the individual rather than determined by a specific authority, whether governmental or corporate, is deemed as fundamental to proper functioning in the online world, as well as to the full functioning in the real world, which now requires the full use of the online world. This right includes the right to Internet access as the latter cannot exist if the former is taken away. As the author explains, the right to an online identity reinforces the arguments against blocking or banning people

An important idea underlined by Bernal is the need to specifically protect the online identity rather than protecting the owner/user of that online identity, i.e. the real person behind it.[45] This requires protecting online identities without (necessarily) revealing the links to the corresponding offline identities.

It is important to note that the author does not define the rights to create, assert and protect online identities as purely legal ones, but as 'natural' rights, emerging from the needs of individuals and communities. Similarly to Oreg, Bernal thus states that the rights forming the right to identity should function as principles, from which legal rights and regulations could then be derived. Taking into account that the protection of and the control over an online identity includes rights over the data associated with that online identity, Bernal argues – similarly to Andrade – that the right to be forgotten can be directly derived from a right to an online identity.[46]

---

from the use of the Internet upon, for example, suspicion of copyright breeches. These copyright-related bans or convictions should thus be weighted much more carefully than they tend to be today.

The second part of the right to an online identity is the assertion of the latter. Here Bernal advocates a perspective shift according to which authentication processes should be a question of the users asserting their identities rather than the service providers demanding these identities. From the right to assert one's identity and the idea that identity should be under the control of the individual, the scholar derives the concept of 'disclosure minimization', similar to the data protection's concept of data minimization (a user's right to only provide the information necessary to use a given service); and the concept of 'identity compartmentalization', i.e., a user's right to separately maintain a number of compartmentalized online identities for use in different circumstances. The assertion of identity online, enshrined as an online operational right, could thus reduce the current levels of privacy intrusion. It could also provide users with the means to assert their own intellectual property rights online and to enter into contracts online.

The third key part of Bernal's right to online identity is the right to protect that online identity. Here the author distinguishes and develops two broad categories of protection required by an online identity: protection from harm or damage to that identity, such as damage to reputation, exclusion, deletion, protection from impersonation and protection of the links between the online and offline identities. The latter means that the building of tracking and tracing systems into the technical infrastructure of the Internet should be strongly resisted. The protection of the links between the online and offline identities also means that the balancing of rights involved in any decision to reveal these links should be weighted heavily in favour of not disclosing them. As Bernal remarks, '[i]t is important to understand, however, that this is and should be a balancing act, and that the revelation of the links between the online and the offline should and would be appropriate where the harm is sufficiently significant'.

45 As a possible solution, the scholar suggests the development of specific resolution systems to address disputes relating to 'online-only' problems, as well as the possibility of redress in an online or 'anonymized' form being provided before enforcement is made upon the real person. For this purpose, the law online should reflect equivalent laws offline. As Bernal clarifies, '[u]ltimately, of course, should the dispute require it, the forum could move offline, with links revealed and more conventional law brought into play'.

46 Along the lines of Andrade and Oreg, Bernal also examines the possibilities of multiple online identities, shared online identities and pseudonymity, setting out possible approaches to each of these concepts under the taxonomical umbrella of the right to an online identity. In effect, the right to protect the links between the online and offline identities implies, according to the author, a right to pseudonymity (i.e., a right to use a name other than your real name in your functioning on the internet). This right bears important implications to the way that Internet is currently being structured. Bearing in mind the need to have control over when and how one's identity is used – whether by assertion or in answer to a demand – as well as the need to protect that identity and its links to the offline identity, Bernal argues against the idea of an enforced 'real name' policy for the internet, considering it deeply problematic. This 'real name' policy, for example, has been implemented by Social Networking sites such as Facebook or by national governments as the South Korean one.

In adopting an approach that draws on the moral philosophy of Alan Getwirth, Roger Brownsword in his 2009 article *Friends, Romans, Countrymen: Is there a Universal Right to Identity* debates the conceptualization of a right to identity as a universal right (i.e., a right that should be recognized as universally binding). By thinking through the logic and concept of agency, and namely by following Gewirth's seminal claim that 'agents are rationally bound to respect the freedom and basic well-being of one another'[47] (which constitutes, according to the author, 'the best shot that we have at arguing for universal rights'[48]), Brownsword asserts that 'each agent is able to claim a right to respect for their own distinguishable and distinctive personal identity'.[49] In other words, 'it is because we are agents, and only because we are agents, that we each have rights and responsibilities to recognize and respect the different and distinctive personal identities that we assume'.[50]

Looking at Brownsword's construction in more detail, the scholar argues that although we need a shared identity to ground and to universalize our rights claims, one of these claimed rights is the right to develop our own distinctive identity (distinguishing oneself from other agents). Within the freedom presupposed in the conditions of agency, 'each agent claims a right to be respected as (…) the author of his or her own distinctive personal identity'.[51] In developing this identity claim, which 'is largely designed to protect an agent's autonomy, particularly in relation to the authorship and ownership of one's own personal identity (the claim to be recognized and respected as 'the agent that I am')',[52] Brownsword articulates an agent's right to identity.[53]

The author thus argues that the right to be recognized as an agent constitutes an eminently suitable articulation of a distinctive universal right to identity.[54] Based on such right, Brownsword discusses the issue of surveillance, detective (identifying) technologies and profiling. Regarding the latter, the scholar refers to an agent's right to correct his profile, the right to challenge a profile that he believes misrepresents his identity or that is used in a way that treats him unfairly, or even the right to complain against a profile that, although accurately reflecting his prior record and pattern of consumption, subtly constrains his choice, exposing him to a particular stream of behavioural advertising and, consequently, impeding the agent to experiment or to 're-invent' himself. In other words, the profile is in line with his identity but the agent claims a reserve right to be free to modify

47 Brownsword, 'Friends, Romans, and Countrymen: Is There a Universal Right to Identity', 226. Alan Gewirth, *Reason and Morality* (Chicago: Chicago University Press, 1978). Brownsword explains that the Gewirthian argument is typically 'presented in three principal stages, starting with a rational and self-conscious agent identifying the generic needs of agents (or the generic conditions of agency), progressing to the formulation of a necessary rights' claim to such conditions, and concluding with the agent accepting an unavoidable duty to respect such conditions', Brownsword, 'Friends, Romans, and Countrymen: Is There a Universal Right to Identity?, 227–28. In his reasoning, Brownsword also assumes the setting of a community of rights. That is, a community oriented towards Gewirthian principles, one which demands respect for each agent's freedom and basic well-being, thus committed to the fundamental principles of respect for the essential conditions and context of agency (or what the scholar terms the 'agency commons': well-being, security, freedom).

48 Brownsword, 'Friends, Romans, and Countrymen: Is There a Universal Right to Identity', 225.

49 Ibid., 226.

50 Ibid., 226.

51 Ibid., 241.

52 Ibid., 241.

53 'As an agent, I have an identity, an essential purposive similarity, with all other agents, but (a) I have a right to be recognized and respected as the particular agent that I am; (b) I have a right to construct the distinctive particularities of my agency in my own way; and (c) I have a right that others do not unfairly or inaccurately represent the particularities of my agency' (ibid., 241).

54 Ibid., 246.

his identity.[55] As the scholar observes, '[i]nsofar as these rights claims are ones that should be made by any agent (…), in any community of rights, they are universal'.[56] The author nevertheless does not provide a strong and definite conclusion regarding the right to identity. Brownsword argues that the appropriateness of addressing the novel threats posed by new surveillance and information technologies by asserting a right to identity is not altogether clear. These hesitations are legitimate but do not necessarily have to lead to a deadlock. Most authors discussed so far pay attention to problems and risks associated with a strong recognition and protection of modern identity practices. Bernal, for instance, calls the attention to the complications associated with the use of identity online, namely the sharing of one online identity by several 'real' people, the transfer of online identity from one person to another, the regime applied to an online identity when the corresponding physical person dies, the use of fake, effectively fraudulent identities, and the need to address them.[57] Nevertheless, and as alerted by Bernal, these problems do not undermine the need to understand, accept and establish the right to an online identity.[58]

This discussion brings us to an important point. Next to the question whether there is need for the recognition of a new right (to identity) and whether such a right will bring more good than bad, there is a discussion about the possible ways to frame such a new right, in such a way that the right is either absolute or not, and encompasses some identity aspects or all identity aspects. A reflection of these and other questions is contained in De Hert's 2007 *A Right to Identity to Face the Internet of Things?*

Paul De Hert analyses the need to create or recognize a specific 'right to identity' in light of the threats posed to the individual by the so-called 'Internet of Things' (that, broadly speaking, equates to the Ambient Intelligence and Ubiquitous Computing scenarios previously analysed).[59] Following Hildebrandt's work, De Hert identifies profiling as the most important threat to identity posed by the Internet of things. Profiling creates new possibilities to manipulate people into certain behaviours without providing them adequate feedback of how their data have been used (or abused), fitting people into new idem identities that they cannot control and that they are often not aware of.

55 Ibid., 247.

56 Ibid., 247.

57 This is the case of identities that are just automated programmes ('bots') and the so-called 'astroturfing' practice, i.e., the establishment of a 'fake' grassroots movement by using fake identities to suggest a groundswell of opinion As the author exemplifies, the US tobacco industry has been reported to have used the technique, see http://www.guardian.co.uk/environment/georgemonbiot/2011/feb/23/need-to-protect-internet-from-astroturfing

58 As the scholar states: 'My conclusion is that there are a number of identity concerns that are likely to be prompted by modern science-based, high technology societies. Some of these concerns cannot be translated as rights, certainly not as rights to identity. However, many of the kinds of acts (such as identity theft, identity suppression, biometric marking and monitoring, and so on) that prompt the articulation of a claimed right to identity are an appropriate cause for concern in a community of rights … in all cases, it remains to be debated whether the interests of agents are best expressed in the language of a claimed right to identity' (Brownsword, 'Friends, Romans, and Countrymen: Is There a Universal Right to Identity)', 226.

59 'The term 'Internet of Things' has come to describe a number of technologies that enable the Internet to reach out into the real world of physical objects. The Internet of things predicts a world where billions of everyday objects are linked in a network and are intercommunicating', De Hert, 'A Right to Identity to Face the Internet of Things', 2. In a world of 'Internet of Things', computing is enabled to melt invisibly into the fabric of our business, personal and social environments, supporting our economic, health, community and private life' European Commission EC, 'From Rfid to the Internet of Things. Pervasive Networked Systems (DG Information Society and Media)' (Brussels 2006). ftp://ftp.cordis.europa.eu/pub/ist/docs/Ka4/au_conf670306_buckly_en.pdf

De Hert constructs his right to identity based on Ricoeur's distinction between ipse and idem identity. As explained by the author, and supported by the works of Ricoeur and Hildebrandt, ipse (or self) is the irreducible sense of self of a human person, the reflexive consciousness of oneself; whereas idem (or sameness) identity is the objectivation of the self that stems from comparative categorization.[60] The legal recognition of identity as a right should thus be understood in dynamic terms, encompassing both ipse and idem identity, i.e. the double tension of personal identity. The right to identity should thus allow for this double movement, one towards resembling the other and comparing oneself to others (one needs the outside world and other people to construct his or her identity), and one differentiating and distinguishing oneself in a perspective of individualization. In stressing the positive (and constructive) aspects of identity, De Hert alludes to the need to clearly distinguish the right to identity from the classical or first generation (shielding) human rights, such as privacy:

> [u]pholding identity is not only an issue of shielding persons against intrusions by governments and other actors, but also an issue of making identity formation possible. A formulation of an identity right as a first generation human right would not pay enough respect to the positive nature of the relationship between ipse and idem identity.[61]

Moreover, De Hert identifies specific identity-related issues that are not covered or protected (nor should they be) by the right to privacy, namely the following: choice of family names, sexual identity and choice, recognition of a right to oblivion, biomedical implants; enhanced testing of new-borns and ethno-screening with the purpose of avoiding health-risks, conception outside the body and the issue of giving birth anonymously, human enhancement (for instance, extreme life prolongation); dual nationality; right to cultural identity. The author, along with Prins,[62] argues that these novel issues and new developments can have an important impact on our understanding of identity and call for a new balancing of interests. Moreover, and in order to properly conduct this balancing, there is the need to go beyond the established rights and concepts such as privacy, liberty, autonomy and discrimination, recognizing thus an explicit right to identity as an aspect of the human dignity in the EU Charter on Fundamental Rights.[63]

In the sense that people cannot function without identity ('[t]o have an identity is like living, breathing, having a healthy life, to be able to feel and think'), De Hert defends the straightforward recognition of identity as a right protected by international human rights.[64] Regarding its implementation, De Hert lists and discusses several options. The first option is to conceive such a right as an asset of the right to human dignity recognized in Article 1 of the 2000 EU Charter on Fundamental Rights.[65] A second option is to use as a model Article 8(1) of the 1990 United Nations Convention on the Rights of the Child: 'State Parties undertake to respect the right of the child

60 Paul Ricoeur, *The Course of Recognition* (Cambridge: Harvard University Press, 2005).; M. Hildebrandt and Serge Gutwirth, *Profiling the European Citizen: Cross-Disciplinary Perspectives* (New York: Springer, 2008), Chapter 15.

61 De Hert, 'A Right to Identity to Face the Internet of Things', 13.

62 J.E.J. Prins, 'Een Recht Op Identiteit', *Nederlandsch juristenblad* 82, no. 14 (2007): 849.

63 Also in this sense, see ibid.

64 De Hert argues that such recognition would be consistent with the human rights perspective defended by Amartya Sen and Martha Nussbaum in their mutual and respective work. See Amartya Sen, *On Ethics & Economics* (New York: Blackwell, 1987).; Martha Craven Nussbaum, *Upheavals of Thought. The Intelligence of Emotions* (Cambridge: Cambridge University Press, 2001).

65 Also in this sense, Prins, 'Een Recht Op Identiteit'.

to preserve his or her identity, including nationality, name and family relations as recognized by law without unlawful interference. Another option is to recognize a specific right to identity at the level of ethics, for instance by recognizing it in the Unesco's Code of Ethics for the Information Society, which is still in its preparatory phase.[66] A final option, and the most original one presented by the scholar, is to draft a specific legal right to identity in a broader manner. For this purpose, and faithful to the need to include both ipse and idem identity in its formulation, De Hert suggests the following definition: 'States Parties undertake to respect the right of each person to preserve and develop his or her ipse and idem identity without unlawful interference.'

Amidst the various options presented, De Hert – nevertheless – does not provide a definite solution, leaving the question unanswered about the need and desirability to recognize and develop a general right to identity within the current international human rights framework. The scholar, in effect, argues that the recognition of a legal right to identity might have undesirable consequences, such as heightening the tensions between personal and collective identities, together with those shaped by race, ethnicity, nationality, religion, gender and sexuality.[67]

Identity in international human rights law

In the foregoing discussion of arguments about the need for more recognition of identity, we saw that some authors advanced the view that current human rights law did not frame identity issues, values and conflicts in a satisfactory way. In this section, we take a brief look at this legal framework, in order to better understand this argument.

As a starting point is that identity, as such, does not figure in all existing human rights documents, with the exception of the 1989 UN Convention of Rights of the Child.[68] Article 8(1)[69] of this Convention establishes that: 'State Parties undertake to respect the right of the child to preserve his or her identity, including nationality, family relations as recognized by law without lawful interference.'

Article 8(2) goes further, and asserts that: 'Where a child is illegally deprived of some or all of the elements of his/her identity, States Parties shall provide appropriate assistance and protection, with a view to speedily re-establishing his or her identity.'

Despite the fact that the term 'identity' is not defined, important identity elements are expressly mentioned – nationality, name and family relations – and, following article 7(1) of the same Convention, are to be registered at birth: 'The child shall be registered immediately after birth and shall have a right from birth to a name, the right to acquire a nationality and, as far as possible, the right to know and be cared for his or her parents.'

The history behind the adoption of a specific right to identity within the international framework of Human Rights is linked to Argentina and to the initiative carried out by the 'Abuelas de Plaza de

66 Concrete proposals for the adoption of legal rights when the existing ones, such as privacy, are insufficient, can also be found in Yves Poullet and Jean-Marc Dinant, 'The Internet and Private Life in Europe: Risks and Aspirations', in *New Dimensions in Privacy Law: International and Comparative Perspectives*, ed. Andrew T. Kenyon and Megan Richardson (Cambridge: Cambridge University Press, 2006).

67 For a critical and sceptical view of the concept of (individual) identity and its understanding as a dynamic process, see S. Gutwirth, 'Beyond Identity?', *IDIS – Identity in the Information Society* 1, no. 1 (2009).

68 UN Convention on the Rights of the Child, Nov. 20, 1989, 1577 UNTS 3.

69 For a more detailed analysis of the inclusion of Article 8 of the Rights of the Child Convention, as a result of a proposal by Argentina, see Sharon Detrick, ed. *The United Nations Convention on the Rights of the Child. A Guide to the 'Travaux Préparatoires'* (Dordrecht/Boston/London: Martinus Nijhoff Publishers, 1992).

Mayo', the grandmothers and mothers of the children 'disappeared' during the 1976–1983 military dictatorship. The Abuelas claim that during that period hundreds of children (allegedly around 500) were removed from their birth families and given new legal identities as children of other parents. This practice was, furthermore, supported by a set of Argentinean adoption laws which allowed for children's true identities to be concealed and false ones to be created. The campaign for the restoration of these lost identities conducted by the Abuelas resulted in the Argentinean proposal of a right to identity[70] in the UN Convention on the Rights of the Child, namely to the inclusion of articles 7, 8 and 11 (designated as the Argentine clauses). This campaign also resulted in Argentina's recognition of a constitutional right to identity and in the implementation of an open adoption system,[71] as well as in the location and restoration of the true identity of 106 'disappeared children'.[72]

The 1950 European Convention of Human Rights (ECHR) of the Council of Europe is one of the main key texts regarding human rights. The document does not mention the term 'identity' in any context. The jurisprudence of the European Court of Human Rights (ECtHR) has however derived the right to identity from its interpretation of Article 8 ECHR on the right to privacy.[73] The ECtHR has ruled that the right to respect for private life covers an individual's physical and social identity, such as gender identification, name, sexual orientation and sexual life, and the right to personal development and personal autonomy. In *Peck v. UK*,[74] the Court 'held that elements such as gender identification, name, sexual orientation, and sexual life are important elements of the personal sphere protected by Article 8' and that '[t]he Article also protects a right to identity'.[75] In effect, in *Tysiac v. Poland* (Application no. 5410/03 Judgement 20 March 2007), the ECtHR reiterated 'that "private life" is a broad term, encompassing, inter alia, aspects of an individual's physical and social identity including the right to personal autonomy, personal development and to establish and develop relationships with other human being and the outside world'.[76] The ECtHR emphasized not only the negative and protective dimension of the right to respect for one's private life (protection against unwanted intrusions into people's private classical sense of keeping a person's private space intact), but also a more positive and 'constructive' aspect of this right. The inclusion of a right to develop one's personality within the right to respect for one's private life operated by the developing

70 The original draft proposal was as following: 'The child has the inalienable right to retain his true and genuine personal, legal and family identity. In the event that a child has been fraudulently deprived of some or all the elements of his identity, the State must give him special protection and assistance with a view to establishing his true and genuine identity as soon as possible. In particular, this obligation of the state includes restoring the child to his blood relations to be brought up'. See ibid., 292.

71 See Lisa Avery, 'A Return to Life: The Right to Identity and the Right to Identify Argentina's "Living Disappeared"', *Harvard Women's Law Journal* 27(2004).

72 For further details on the work of the Abuelas and the search process of their grandchildren, see www.abuelas.org.ar/english/history.htm

73 The full text of the article is as follows:

1. Everyone has the right to respect for his private life and family life, his name and his correspondence.

2. There shall be no interference by a public authority with the exercise of this right except such as is in accordance with the law and is necessary in a democratic society in the interests of national security, public safety or the economic well-being of the country, for the prevention of disorder or crime, for the protection of health and morals, or for the protection of the rights and freedoms of others.

74 *Peck v United Kingdom* [2003] All ER 255, C003 36 EHRR 719, [2003] EMLR 287.

75 Ibid., para 57, citing *PG and JH v United Kingdom* ECHR 2001-IX.

76 For a detailed analysis of this and similarly related case-law, see Jill Marshall, *Personal Freedom through Human Rights Law?: Autonomy, Identity and Integrity under the European Convention on Human Rights*, International Studies in Human Rights, V. 98. (Leiden ; Boston: Martinus Nijhoff Publishers, 2009).

jurisprudence of the ECtHR stresses this positive and constructive dimension of this right in the sense of 'such personality being developed not only "alone" but also in our relationship with others and the outside world'.[77] The Court, in effect, has held that the right to respect for private life 'comprises also, to a certain degree, the right to establish and develop relationships with other human beings especially in the emotional field, for the development and fulfilment of one's own personality'.[78] As Pino summarizes, this norm has been interpreted by commentators as one that protects the individual against attacks on physical or mental integrity or moral or intellectual freedom, attacks on honour and reputation and similar torts, the use of a person's name, identity, and the disclosure of information protected by the duty of professional secrecy.[79]

Despite the absence of an explicit reference to the right to identity in the ECHR, one can safely state that this right is deemed as fundamental in the context of the Convention. As Sullivan asserts:

> [i]t is clear that like the Universal Declaration, the ECHR is based on recognized, intrinsic human rights like dignity and autonomy in the sense of self-determination, which form the basis for the right to identity. Although the right to identity is not specifically covered by any particular article in the ECHR, it nevertheless is a fundamental human right which underpins the ECHR.[80]

Underlying the ECtHR's stance on personal identity is the understanding of the latter as a narrative, a continuous process of creating and recreating our own life story. In fact, it is the idea of identity as a narrative endeavour that explains the ECtHR open and progressive approach towards sexual identity rights (namely in the cases of sex change) and the right to access information relating to one's birth and childhood existence.

The international legal framework of human rights has also contributed to the re-conceptualization and modernization of the right to personal identity by adapting it to new technological developments, namely in the field of genetics. Human Rights legal instruments and texts have thus endorsed the concept of genetic identity (and genetic integrity),[81] protecting the person not only as an individual per se, but also as a depositary of the genetic heritage of the human species. In effect, 'the individual is protected as a depositary of the genetic heritage of the species and the right to genetic identity protects the interests of future individuals and of the human species over time'.[82] Nonetheless, it is important to note that the relevance and weight attributed to the

---

77 Jill Marshall, *Personal Freedom through Human Rights Law?: Autonomy, Identity and Integrity under the European Convention on Human Rights*, International Studies in Human Rights, V. 98. (Leiden ; Boston: Martinus Nijhoff Publishers, 2009).

78 App. 6825/74, X v. Ireland, 18 May 1976, Decisions and Report of the Commission, 5, 1976, p. 86 ff.

79 Pino, 'The Right to Personal Identity in Italian Private Law: Constitutional Interpretation and Judge-Made Rights', 7. See also F. Jacobs and R. White, *The European Convention on Human Rights*, 2nd ed. (Oxford: Clarendon Press, 1996).; Louise Doswald-Beck, 'The Meaning of the "Right to Respect for Private Life" under the European Convention on Human Rights', *Human Rights Law Journal* 4 (1983).; Louke G. Loucaides, 'Personality and Privacy under the European Convention on Human Rights', *British Yearbook of International Law* 61 (1990).

80 Clare Sullivan, 'Privacy or Identity?', *Int. J. Intellectual Property Management* Vol. 2, no. No. 3 (2008): 297.

81 These are the cases of the Universal Declaration on the Human Genome and Human Rights (UDHGHR), which served as the building block for the UNESCO 2003 International Declaration on Human Genetic Data (IDHGD) and the 2005 Universal Declaration on Bioethics and Human Rights (UDBHR); and the Oviedo Convention on Human Rights and Biomedicine.

82 Hélène Boussard, 'Individual Human Rights in Genetic Research: Blurring the Line between Collective and Individual Interests', in *New Technologies and Human Rights*, ed. Thérèse Murphy (Oxford;

concept of genetic identity (as the right to identity encompassing genetic characteristics) are not extrapolated. Genetic attributes are seen as only a part (albeit important) of someone's identity, not equating to the whole of the identity itself. The International Declaration on Human Genetic Data stresses this point, referring to personal identity in its article 3 as encompassing not only the genetic components of each individual, but also the 'complex educational, environmental and personal factors and emotional, social, spiritual and cultural bonds with others'.

Human Rights Language in Recent Policy Documents regarding the Internet[83]

The previous sections show that the step towards the recognition of a new right is not unthinkable. We have recognized rights in many documents. In one important document there is a right to identity for children. Such a right is lacking, but a brief discussion of European human rights case law shows that identity falls within the recognized rights sensibilities. So why not make the implicit explicit and the half proposition (identity rights for children) into a full proposition (identity rights for all)? Overseeing policy initiatives with regard to the Information Society, one senses a development towards such a full step. We will discuss some of these policy documents and observe that, although not all focus on identity, all address issues that can be related to identity.

In recent years one can indeed observe that the debate about Internet rights has conquered the policy fora. The debate is not always on a right to identity (or the need to recognize it) but on rights, that can be considered as partly overlapping (see our section 2), such as the right to have access to the Internet and the right to freedom of expression on the Internet.

In May 2011, Frank La Rue, the UN Special Rapporteur on the freedom of expression, explored key trends and challenges to the freedom of expression through the Internet.[84] This proved to be a turning point in the discussion. Having analysed the impact of the Internet in the contemporary world, in particular on the Arab protests, he concluded that 'the Internet has become an indispensable tool for realizing a range of human rights'.[85] He emphasises that there should be as little restriction as possible to the flow of information via the Internet, short of a few exceptions provided for in the international human rights law. Further he argues that ensuring universal access to the Internet should be a priority for all states. Article 19, a London-based NGO defending freedom of expression, immediately hailed the report as a milestone development and urged all governments to fully implement its recommendations.[86]

In his report La Rue shows that freedom of expression (and perhaps a number of other rights) protects both the Internet content and connectivity against unlawful interference. But in order to fully enjoy the use of the Internet, a maximum level of connectivity must be ensured. La Rue therefore 'reminds all States of their positive obligation to promote or to facilitate the enjoyment of the right to freedom of expression and the means necessary to exercise this right, including

New York: Oxford University Press, 2009), 259.

83 The following sections borrow in part from Paul De Hert and Dariusz Kloza, 'Internet (Access) as a New Fundamental Right. Inflating the Current Rights Framework?', *European Journal of Law and Technology* (EJLT) vol. 3, no. 3 (2012)., Available at http://ejlt.org//article/view/123

84 UN Human Rights Council, *Report of the Special Rapporteur on the promotion and protection of the right to freedom of opinion and expression, Frank La Rue*, 6 May 2011, A/HRC/17/27, http://www2.ohchr.org/english/bodies/hrcouncil/docs/17session/A.HRC.17.27_en.pdf.

85 Idem, p. 22.

86 Article 19, *UN: ARTICLE 19 calls for global access to the internet*, press release, 21 October 2011, http://www.article19.org/resources.php/resource/2790/en/un:-article-19-calls-for-global-access-to-the-internet.

the Internet'. He further clarifies that the States should adopt effective and concrete policies and strategies to make the Internet widely available, accessible and affordable to all.[87]

An interesting thing about La Rue is that his report suggests a rights talk but he does not really insist on creating an explicit right to the Internet (access). He only asks 'to make the Internet widely available', 'facilitate technology transfer to developing states', not to exclude persons with disabilities or linguistic minorities, and to include 'Internet literacy skills in school curricula'.[88]

A more explicit turn towards the language of rights and human rights is taken at other policy fora. A coalition called *Internet Rights and Principles* has launched its 10 Internet Rights and Principles[89] and currently drafts a *Charter of Human Rights and Principles for the Internet*.[90] Brazil considers its own comprehensive legal statute on the Internet governance, including individual rights.[91]

In this spirit, the EU Digital Agenda foresees to 'issue a Code of EU Online Rights by 2012 that summarizes existing digital user rights in the EU in a clear and accessible way'.[92] This would be a listing exercise rather than creation of any new rights. (We judge this from a statement 'summarizes'.) In March 2012, the Council of Europe has adopted its own Internet governance strategy,[93] built on its 2011 *Declaration on Internet Governance Principles*[94] and its *Recommendation on the protection and promotion of the universality, integrity and openness of the Internet*.[95] The ambitious document pays special attention to right to Internet access for all (action I); privacy and data protection (action III), rights of children and young people (action VI) and combating cybercrime (action VI). It aims at 'developing a charter of rights for Internet users', among others. In the section on privacy and data protection, the text states amongst others that the Council should aim at promoting 'the development of measures and tools for children and their families to better manage their privacy and personal data and, in this connection, *their identity*, such as by using pseudonyms on the Internet' (italics added) and that the Council should strive for 'developing human rights-based data protection guidelines for States, the private sector and civil society in the light of trends and challenges posed by the Internet'.

The language of rights is also very present in a recent Resolution, *The Promotion, Protection and Enjoyment of Human Rights on the Internet*, adopted by the UN Human Rights Council in July 2012.[96] The short resolution affirms that 'the same rights that people have offline must also be protected online, in particular freedom of expression, which is applicable regardless of frontiers and through any media of one's choice', but does not call for 'new' human rights.

---

87 UN Human Rights Council, *Report*..., op. cit. p. 19.

88 Idem, p. 22. Cf. paras 85–88.

89 Cf. http://irpcharter.org/campaign.

90 Cf. http://irpcharter.org/charter.

91 Cf. http://direitorio.fgv.br/civilrightsframeworkforinternet.

92 European Commission, *A Digital Agenda for Europe*, op. cit., p. 13.

93 Council of Europe, *Internet Governance – Council of Europe Strategy 2012–2015*, Strasbourg, 15 March 2012, CM(2011)175 final.

94 Council of Europe, Declaration of the Committee of Ministers on Internet governance principles, https://wcd.coe.int/ViewDoc.jsp?id=1835773.

95 Council of Europe, *Recommendation of the Committee of Ministers to Member States on the protection and promotion of the universality, integrity and openness of the Internet*, Strasbourg, 21 September 2011, CM/Rec(2011)8.

96 Resolution L13 – The Promotion, Protection and Enjoyment of Human Rights on the Internet – adopted by consensus by the Human Rights Council on Thursday, July 6, 2012. See http://geneva.usmission.gov/2012/07/05/internet-resolution/

The policy documents that we have reviewed equally denote a series of interesting common arguments and positions. There is a concern both for the social aspects of technology ('access for all') and the more traditional civil liberties side of it ('protection against intrusion and censorship'). The language of human rights is predominant in most documents, although not all favour the recognition of new ones, but insist on the application of the 'old ones'. In this context identity is mentioned as an important value, but not as a specific issue that needs to be protected by a new *sui generis* right.

Human Rights Arguments Against and in Favour of a Right to Identity

There are different modes of regulating and protecting technologies, including powerful non-legal ones.[97] Hence, the case for a fundamental rights approach has to be made strong. But one needs to be not too fundamentalist about fundamental or human rights either. These rights are far from static. They evolve, simply because they reflect developments in the society, rather than eternal truths or state of beings of human kind. Protecting non-human entities, such as legal persons, animals and, why not, even the climate is not unthinkable. 'It depends'.

The current system is characterised by the expanding and evolving nature of human rights. The international human rights system has advanced greatly since the Universal Declaration of Human Rights (1948) was first adopted. Since the adoption of the Declaration, the codification process regarding the definition of new rights and new international principles has continued. This expanding nature is still producing ramifications in the 21st century. With the ever-changing nature of society, human rights face a need for continuous evolution in order to address new challenges.[98] Human rights are situated rights: they take shape in certain societies at certain moments of time. Brownsword and Goodwin argue that in the future, where human rights remain the dominant language for moral reasoning – and there is every reason to expect that they will – technological developments are likely to force the creation of new human rights. To believe these authors, new rights that look to be on the horizon include the right to genetic privacy, the right to a unique identity and also the right to Internet access.[99]

Vinton Cerf, co-designer of the TCP/IP protocol is sceptic about protecting the Internet access by means of human rights.[100] There is a high bar for something to be considered a human right. The modern western 'human rights ideal' can be summed up as follows: *prima facie* everyone has an equal legitimate claim to those tangible and intangible goods and benefits most essential for human well-being.[101] In other words, in the classical perspective, these rights are understood as basic moral guarantees that people in all countries and cultures allegedly have simply because they

97 Browen Morgan and Karen Yeung, *An Introduction to Law and Regulation* (Cambridge: Cambridge University Press, 2007).

98 Marco Odello and Sofia Cavandoli, eds., *Emerging Areas of Human Rights in the 21st Century: The Role of the Universal Declaration of Human Rights* (Routledge,2001), 3.

99 Roger Brownsword and Morag Goodwin, *Law and the Technologies of the Twenty-First Century* (Cambridge: Cambridge University Press, 2012). Cf. e.g. Murray who explicitly call for the right to access the Internet. A. Murray, *A Bill of Rights for the Internet*, available at http://theitlawyer.blogspot.be/2010/10/bill-of-rights-for-internet.html

100 Vinton G. Cerf, 'Internet Access Is Not a Human Right', *New York Times*, January 4 2012. http://www.nytimes.com/2012/01/05/opinion/internet-access-is-not-a-human-right.html?_r=3&ref=technology.

101 Steven Greer, *The European Convention on Human Rights. Achievements, Problems and Prospects* (Cambridge: Cambridge University Press, 2006), 2.

are people.[102] Cerf illustrates that the things that we call human rights must be among the things humans need in order to lead healthy, meaningful lives, like freedom from torture or freedom of conscience. The Internet is valuable as a means to an end, but not as an end in itself. He concludes with a nice example: 'at one time if you didn't have a horse it was hard to make a living. But the important right in that case was the right to make a living, not the right to a horse.'[103] Cerf is more favourable of protection of Internet access by means of civil rights even though the same argumentation applies. Civil rights are different from human rights because they are conferred upon us by law, not intrinsic to us as human beings.

In order to better understand Cerf's position and his rejection of human rights claims, it is useful to remember that calls for a fundamental right status for the Internet are not unique but axiomatic for the wider domain of all human rights. There is indeed a general trend of NGOs and other stakeholders to continuously demand for the creation of more human rights. Baxi gives the example of interest groups of international airlines, hotels and travel agents who assiduously lobby the UN to proclaim a universal human right of tourism.[104] Claims for the recognition of new fundamental rights should always be carefully examined. If they are rashly accepted, it could lead to a practice of fragmentation and constant increase of human rights.[105] Inflation of rights could then diminish the value of other existing rights. Inclusion of new rights in the international human rights framework is only justified if there is a substantial added value to the protection offered by existing rights and when there is a consensus that a high level of protection is strictly necessary. Next, as recognition of any right requires codifying, any codification would bring difficulties to define its scope, to choose the proper generation of a right as well as the correct legal instrument for regulation and – finally – would risk becoming out-dated.[106]

102 James Nickel, *Making Sense of Human Rights: Philosophical Reflections on the Universal Declaration of Human Rights* (Berkeley: University of California Press, 1987).; cited in Andrew Fagen, 'Human Rights, Internet Encyclopaedia of Philosophy', http://www.iep.utm.edu/hum-rts.

103 Cerf, 'Internet Access Is Not a Human Right'.

104 Upendra Baxi, 'Too Many, or Too Few, Human Rights?', *Human Rights Law Review* 1, no. 1 (2001).

105 Paraphrasing Easterbrook, in going too much into detail, one might end up with 'a right to a horse'. Easterbrook argued that there was no more a 'law of cyberspace' than there was a 'law of the horse'. The dean of Chicago Law School was proud that they did not offer a course in 'the law of the horse' but rather only those 'law and …' courses that 'could illuminate the entire law'. The best way to learn the law applicable to specialized endeavours is to study general rules. Frank H. Easterbrook, 'Cyberspace and the Law of the Horse', *University of Chicago Legal Forum* 207(1996).; Lawrence Lessig, 'The Law of the Horse: What Cyberlaw Might Teach', *Harvard Law Review* 113, no. 2 (1999).

106 Kuner discusses pros and cons of various possibilities for a proposed international data protection framework. They are equally important for a possible right to the use of the Internet. Each approach to harmonization has its strengths and weaknesses. A convention can produce a greater degree of harmonization, since it results in a single text that is legally binding on States that enact it, but such binding nature can make States reluctant to do so. A convention can also be subject to reservations made by States that are party to it, which can result in a diminution of the very harmonization that the convention was supposed to accomplish, and a convention can be difficult to amend in the face of changing practices or technological evolution. A model law allows States more flexibility in implementation, which may incline them to adopt it, but this very flexibility can result in a lack of harmonization in implementation. Guidance documents and contractual terms and conditions can be adopted more swiftly and be taken up by a large number of parties, but their legally binding nature is of a lesser value than that of a multilateral convention.' Christopher Kuner, 'An International Legal Framework for Data Protection: Issues and Prospects', *Computer Law & Security Review* 25, no. 4 (2009). Let us imagine that the Charter of Fundamental Rights of the European Union – the most recent instrument in the field – were drafted today. It would most likely not include an explicit right to the use

As an example, *sui generis* human rights for elderly people are being debated as the existing international instruments have failed to address adequately the needs of these people.[107] As another example, a distinct right to water and sanitation was recognized by the United Nations and a handful of international human rights instruments. Although it has been argued that this right could be easily interpreted from the rights to housing and health, there are a few reasons why it merits a separate recognition. First, water and sanitation are primary needs and nowadays many people still suffer from a lack of both. Second, not all aspects of the access to water and sanitation are covered by existing rights, in particular the rights to housing and health. The scope of sanitation goes well beyond prevention of contamination of drinking water supplies and wastewater drainage. It is also about ensuring hygiene and safe water storage.[108]

As a third example, one could also think of the new right to data protection in the EU, both in Art 8 of the EU Charter of Fundamental Rights and in Art 16 of the Treaty on the Functioning of the European Union. This recognition can be approved for at least two reasons. First, there were considerations with regard to the legitimacy of the EU data protection framework. The 1995 Data Protection Directive[109] has only an internal market dimension and lacked a fundamental rights justification. With a separate fundamental right for data protection this dimension is added. Second, the existing right to privacy did not suffice. Data protection explicitly protects values that are not at the core of privacy, such as the requirement of fair processing, consent, legitimacy and non-discrimination. Data protection laws serve a multiplicity of interests, which in some cases extend well beyond traditional conceptualisations of privacy.[110] What these examples have in common is that additional prominence and visibility has been given to the subject matter of protection. In result, it is easier and more practical to claim these things. On top of that, from the viewpoint of efficiency, an explicit recognition creates responsibilities and tools to ensure observance and to oversight enforcement, including soft mechanisms like monitoring.

The argument of visibility explains why we do not follow Cerf, who is more favourable of protection of Internet access by means of civil rights (*above*), and this for two reasons. First, we believe that identity passes the threshold defined by Cerf, that of 'things humans need in order to lead healthy, meaningful lives'. The incorporation of a right to identity in Article 8 of 1989 UN Convention of Rights of the Child, the case law with regard to Article 8 ECHR and the writings discussed above leave no doubt about the essential status of identity for meaningful human living. The view of many authors that proper identity protection, both against intrusions (negative aspect)

---

of the Internet, but its Art 11 – for the sake of clarity – would include wording like 'through any media of her choice'. That would explicitly include the Internet and/or its successors.

107 Paul De Hert and Eugenio Mantovani, 'Specific Human Rights for Older Persons? The Inevitable Colouring of Human Rights Law', *European Human Rights Law Review*, no. 4 (2010).; Emilio Mordini and Paul De Hert, eds., *Ageing and Invisibility*, Ambient Intelligence and Smart Environments, Vol. 7 (IOS PRESS, 2010).; John Williams, 'An International Convention on the Rights of Older People?', in *Emerging Areas of Human Rights in the 21st Century: The Role of the Universal Declaration of Human Rights*, ed. Marco Odello and Sofia Cavandoli (London: Routledge, 2001). Williams explicitly asks 'if children have special protection, why not older people?'.

108 Centre on Housing Rights and Evictions, *The human right to water and sanitation: Legal Bases, Practical Rationale and Definition*, 2008, p. 6, http://www.wsscc.org/sites/default/files/publications/cohre_legal_basis_for_right_to_water_and_sanitation_2008.pdf.

109 Directive 95/46/EC of the European Parliament and of the Council of 24 October 1995 on the protection of individuals with regard to the processing of personal data and on the free movement of such data.

110 Cf. P. De Hert and S. Gutwirth, 'Data Protection in the Case Law of Strasbourg and Luxembourg: Constitutionalisation in Action', in *Reinventing Data Protection?*, ed. Serge Gutwirth, et al. (Dordrecht; London: Springer, 2009).

and with a view of allowing identity formation and control (positive aspect), cannot be guaranteed by existing legal instruments, including privacy, cannot be ignored.

Second, we are sceptical about the legal instrument of civil rights. Contrary to civil rights, human rights are not derived from the citizenship of any country, or the membership of any nation, but are presumed to be claims or entitlements of every human being. They create what Amartya Sen calls 'imperfect obligations' that fall broadly on anyone who is in a position to help, contrary to civil rights that are dependent of the country of which a person is a citizen.[111] Human rights are strong ethical pronouncements as to what should be done, rather than recognitions of existing things and they indicate that something needs to be done for realization of these recognized freedoms that are identified through these rights. 'One thing they are not are claims that these human rights are already established *legal* rights, enshrined through legislation or common law'.[112] When their content is of some importance and when the claim can survive open scrutiny, such human rights can serve as agenda's for new laws and policies. More pragmatically, there is the growing capacity of human rights law to create responsibilities and tools to ensure observance and to install oversight enforcement, including soft mechanisms like monitoring. Turning something into a fundamental right does not only guarantee it a place in policy agendas, but, more often, triggers enforcement mechanisms such as reporting, mainstreaming and legal redress, that more and more States are willing to accept whenever they recognize new human rights instruments. Under a human rights rational, the right to identity should not only shield against intrusions, but also be protected in a more positive way. It should be understood as including the right to be provided with the necessary conditions for identity to be shaped and developed, allowing not only for identity recognition but also (and especially) for identity formation. In addition to its negative dimension, as a right to be protected from intrusions or infringements on one's identity, a properly drafted right to identity (as a fundamental human right) would also encompass a positive obligation for third parties (namely the States and others), that is, the right to be endowed with the indispensable means to forge, develop and sustain one's identity.[113]

For many reasons we believe that Article 8 of 1989 UN Convention of Rights of the Child could form an acceptable starting point for the future discussion. Both the first and the second paragraph are phrased in such a way that positive and negative rights obligations are implicit. The first paragraph enumerates certain identity aspects ('including nationality, family relations') without excluding others. There is a strong case to amend this by adding 'online identity' to this non-exclusive list. The first paragraph would then state: 'State Parties undertake to respect the right of every one to preserve his or her identity, including nationality, online identity and family relations as recognized by law without lawful interference.'

Of course this is just a proposal, one which raises many questions: 'where (in which Treaty or Convention such a right should be accommodated?'; could all on-line problems identified higher (access to the Internet, right to be forgotten) be sufficiently addressed by these wordings? The precedent is there. What is good for our children is also good for the rest of us. There is, so we

---

111 Amartya Sen, *The Idea of Justice* (London: Allen Lane, 2009), Chapter 5, 143–4. See on the importance of these vague duties also Chapter 17, 373–6.

112 Ibid., Chapter 17, 357–8.

113 This important facet of the right to identity is connected to the Court's development of 'positive' obligations, which – in our particular case – affirm the State's duty of assisting and contributing to the creation and formation of one's identity. At the level of the human rights framework, the obligation imposed to states of creating conditions (either social, technical or legal) to enable the flourishing of one's identity renders the right to identity an extremely efficient and compelling juridical instrument.

believe not a principled objection against generalizing an intuition, as can be illustrated by the Argentinean Constitution having recognized a general right to protection of identity (see *above*).

Conclusions

After a discussion of the impact of new technologies (Ambient Intelligence and Ubiquitous Computing) on identity and its legal framework, this contribution discussed several new writings on the importance of identity and online identity in our society. A close reading of a plurality of authors revealed certain common positions, insights and arguments regarding the right to identity. Several scholars share a number of important findings and assertions regarding the right to identity, as well as open questions. These are the case of the following:

- The intrinsic informational nature of identity;
- The importance and the need to take into consideration the phenomena of multiple identities, i.e., to maintain separate identities;
- The identification of specific identity-related concerns, threats and dangers that: a) are not covered by the existing legal framework, namely by the right to privacy or other rights; b) that demand specific legal protection; and c) that require a new balancing of interests;
- The identification of the issue of profiling as one of the most serious concerns and perils to the expression and representation of one's identity, carrying also the dangers of unconscious behaviour manipulation;
- The distinction between this right to identity and similar ones, such as freedom of expression, privacy and data protection (the autonomy argument);
- The argument that the overstretched focus on the right to privacy has, to a certain extent, overshadowed or even neglected the right to identity;
- The legal protection of identity (interests, values) conceptualized as a legal principle more than a right, from which other legal rights and regulations could be derived;
- The importance of taking into account the tension between ipse and idem identities in the conceptualization of the right to identity;
- The derivation of the right to oblivion (also termed right to be forgotten) from the right to identity;
- The argument in favour of an explicit and specific right to identity and the debate about the need and desirability of considering it (or upgrading it to) a human right.

The remainder of this chapter then focused on this last question, debating a human rights-based approach to the emergent right to identity. For this purpose, we first reviewed the latest developments concerning the right to identity in the field of international human-rights framework and found a growing, but not comprehensive, recognition of this right. Secondly, we analysed the need and advantages (as well as possible disadvantages) of a human rights-based approach to the right to identity. In this light, we propose a comprehensive right to identity as full-fledged human right, along the lines of Article 8 of 1989 UN Convention of Rights of the Child, but this time for all citizens, and for both offline and online ones.

Chapter 13
Legal Implications of the Privatization of Cyber Warfare

Lucas Lixinski

Introduction

One of the most important emerging topics related to militarization and the conduct of war is that of cyber warfare.[1] As technological capacity grows, populations and governments alike become more and more dependent on reliable internet connections and information placed only in the cyberspace. The whole financial market can no longer function without the internet and computers. The same can be said of air traffic and other sectors that would at first sight seem less network-dependant, such as energy distribution systems and hospitals. The fact that computers are so depended upon makes these sectors of human activity particularly vulnerable if their computers or networks were to be shut down.

Additionally, the internet is essentially a civilian place. Over 90 percent of all internet infrastructure is civilian-owned, and these communication capabilities are used for civilian and military purposes alike, blurring the civilian/military distinction that is so essential to the conduct of warfare.[2] In that sense, the privatization of war, or the reliance upon contractors, Private Military and Security Companies (PMSCs) and other similar actors for the performance of duties that once fell under the exclusive domain of the State and its armed forces overlaps substantially with cyber warfare efforts.

In May 2009, the U.S. Presidency published a report called 'Cyberspace Policy Review – Assuring a Trusted and Resilient Information and Communication Infrastructure'. In this report, the White House recognized that the U.S. had lagged behind in its response to the growing threat of cyber attacks, and it went on to highlight the importance of cooperation with the private sector.[3] This has spurred a surge among military contractors and IT companies who started recruiting personnel and preparing themselves for the opening of tender processes before the U.S. military.[4]

It has been reported that all major U.S. military contractors have contracts in the field of cyber warfare with the military and intelligence agencies. These companies have also been cooperating towards building a 'Cyber Range', or a duplicate of the internet where they can test offensive and defensive techniques for cyber warfare.[5]

1 Also known as internet warfare, cyber war, and information warfare, among other synonyms. For the purposes of this chapter, these terms will be used interchangeably, unless otherwise indicated.

2 Susan W. Brenner and Leo L. Clarke, *Civilians in Cyberwarfare: Conscripts*, 43 *Vanderbilt Journal Of Transnational Law* 1011 (2010).

3 See Stuart S. Malawer, 'Cyberwarfare: Law and Policy Proposals for U.S. and Global Governance', available at <http://papers.ssrn.com/sol3/papers.cfm?abstract_id=1437002> (last accessed March 3, 2012).

4 See Christopher Drew and John Markoff, 'Contractors Vie for Plum Work, Hacking for U.S.', *New York Times*, May 30, 2009.

5 Id.

Along these lines, the United States Special Operations Command (USSOCOM) has, in its strategic plan for 2009, outlined the need for investment in cyber warfare capacity. However, unlike the White House report, this one focuses on the development of in-house capacity for cyber warfare and, more specifically, network-centric capabilities.[6]

What happens, then, when cyber warfare is privatized, when a contractor working simultaneously for the U.S., French and Saudi Arabian governments can, from his office in a commercial neighbourhood in London, set off an attack that disrupts the entire telecommunications grid of say, China? Who is responsible for the attack? And, more importantly, what happens when, by disrupting the telecommunications system, one satellite happens to fall back into the atmosphere, crashing into a school in South Korea, killing dozens of innocent children? Who bears responsibility for these issues? Is it the British government, for letting this person use its cyberspace to launch the attack? Is it one or all of the government of the States under whose service this contractor acts? Is it the Chinese government, to whom the satellite belonged?

These are some of the questions this chapter explores. This contribution deals with the topic of the privatization of cyber warfare and the legal consequences of violations of international humanitarian law (IHL) and human rights perpetrated in cyber conflict scenarios.

The discussion of this contribution will play out against a broader background of the impact of new technologies upon human rights, in particular with respect to relations between developed and developing countries. It has been suggested that cyber warfare is a valuable tool in the hands of militarily weaker states (which is the majority of developing countries) to try to level an otherwise deeply asymmetrical military battlefield. More specifically, because cyber war is much cheaper to undertake than conventional warfare, developing countries are in a better position to counter imbalances in military might against other adversaries.[7]

What does this mean in terms of regulation? Is this statement a means to suggest that, in the name of the emancipation of developing countries, cyber warfare should go unregulated? I would suggest no. While it is true that cyber warfare is relatively cheap to undertake, it is also true that a lot of the technological innovation that drives it still comes from developed countries. To imply that countries like the United states should enhance their cyber war capabilities in order to counter the possibility of developing countries catching up and mounting attacks against US structures (a form of cyber deterrence) is to make an unacceptable concession to American Exceptionalism (and the thinly veiled imperialism behind it).

This contribution's central thesis is that the seeming regulatory vacuum of cyber warfare in international law does little in the way of creating an opportunity for developing countries' countering of empire. Asymmetries existing in warfare in general, while diminished in some instances (and increased in others), are still essentially replicated in the context of cyber warfare, because of the concentration of technology in countries of the Global North. Countries in the Global South are actually in a position to benefit from stricter regulations of this type of war. To suggest that countries in the Global South would be at an advantage is nothing but a means to coopt international law once again as a means to cover-up (and ultimately justify) a hegemonic project stemming from the Global North.

6 See United States Special Operations Command, USSOCOM CIO Strategic Plan 2009, available at <http://www.socom.mil/SOCOMHome/newspub/pubs/Documents/CIO_Strategic_Plan-2009.pdf> (last accessed March 3, 2012).

7 Todd C. Huntley, 'Controlling the Use of Force in Cyber Space: The Application of the Law of Armed Conflict during a Time of Fundamental Change in the Nature of Warfare', 60 *Naval Law Review* 1 (2010); and Jack Goldsmith, 'The pervasive cyberthreat that goes unchallenged', *The Washington Post*, 26 November 2011.

The chapter will be structured as follows: the first part will look generally at cyber warfare, exploring the modalities in which it occurs, and the possibilities for its regulation, both in international humanitarian law and general international human rights law. Cyber-attacks differ substantially from each other, in that not all cyber-attacks meet the necessary threshold for calling international humanitarian law into application. There are, however, several rules that should be observed even when the gravity of such an attack does not amount to an 'act of war'.

The second part is a reflection on the privatization of cyber warfare. It starts by examining policy developments that discuss the structuring of cyber warfare, as well as the argument of the supposed inextricability of the private sector from this area of the military. It then analyzes the issue of accountability of 'private cyber warriors' for acts that violate human rights and humanitarian law.

Cyber Warfare

The aim of this part is to refute the idea of the 'legal vacuum' of cyber warfare under currently existing international law, an idea that many have been quick to affirm.[8] While it is true that more specific rules are necessary to address the specificities of cyber warfare, it is an exaggeration to say that there are no applicable rules that can help deal with certain situations, should they arise before a specific instrument is completed.

However, before debating this issue, it is important to understand what falls under the category 'cyber attack', and the effects of different types of technology-based warfare.

Fighting a Cyber War

Cyber war falls under the broader definition of 'information warfare'. Information warfare, according to military sources, falls into three categories: (1) acts aimed at 'maintaining information superiority while protecting against counter-information warfare'; (2) 'using information as a weapon against the enemy', or (3) the use of information systems to enhance the effectiveness of the use of force.[9]

The first two categories refer more broadly to intelligence and information gathering, whereas the third one refers to 'technology-based warfare' in a narrow sense. There are two main types of action that can be described as 'technology-based warfare', and that rely heavily on the cyberspace. The first one is what is known as 'network-centric combat'. In this type of combat, soldiers are normally deployed to the field. The big difference is that they rely heavily on intelligence information and technology that enhances their capabilities, such as Global Positioning System packages, constant communication links with information units away from the theatre of war who keep feeding the soldiers with useful intelligence, equipment that can pick up on radio transmissions and from that determine the position and movement of enemy combatants, among others.[10]

8 See for instance 'U.S. Joint Chiefs of Staff, Questions Abound in Cyber Theater of Operations, Vice Chairman Says', available at <http://www.jcs.mil/newsarticle.aspx?ID=106> (last accessed March 3, 2012).

9 As cited by Davis Brown, 'A Proposal for an International Convention to Regulate the Use of Information Systems in Armed Conflict', 47 *Harv. ILJ* 179, 184 (2006).

10 For an explanation of network-centric warfare, see Stuart H. Starr, 'Toward a Preliminary Theory of Cyberpower', in *Cyberpower and National Security* 43, 59–60 (Franklin D. Kramer, Stuart H. Starr and Larry K. Wentz eds.) (2009). On the dependence of network-centric warfare on intelligence gathering, see Tim Shorrock, *Spies for Hire: The Secret World of Intelligence Outsourcing* 162–3 (2009). Martin C. Libicki questions whether network capabilities actually enhance combat performance, and concludes that there is no

While this is an important use of technology and the internet to enhance combat capabilities, it is not cyber warfare in the strict sense. However, there are specific implications to be taken into account here. For instance, the definition of combatant defines a combatant as a person engaging directly in hostilities.[11] Until recently, this meant only the soldiers in the theatre of conflict, as any information was given to them prior to actual combat, and therefore intelligence agents did not participate in hostilities. However, direct and constant communication links imply that people far from the actual theatre of conflict, sometimes sitting in offices thousands of kilometres away in a civilian zone in a different country, are also participating moment by moment in hostilities. Are these people also to be considered combatants? While they cannot physically engage with enemies, they are an indispensable part of the capabilities of the soldiers on the field to engage enemies, and can make a significant difference in the outcome of a war, as they serve practically as the 'super eyes' of soldiers. Another example of this kind of activity is the use of remote control-operated drones that can bomb a target without the need for someone to be physically present to launch or detonate it.[12]

I submit that they should be considered combatants, to the extent that they in fact willingly contribute to the conduct of hostilities. The consequence of them being considered combatants is that the communication links they use, as well as their equipment, are legitimate military targets, either through cyber attacks or physical strikes (for instance, bombing the building where the computers used for information gathering and transmission are). But this finding means that the equipment cannot be placed amidst civilian property or otherwise protected property, as defined by international humanitarian law rules.

These techniques of information warfare are highly sophisticated, requiring equipment that is developed by wealthy countries in the Global North, and therefore out of reach for most of the world. This type of technologically-enhanced military capability therefore counters the suggestion that combat asymmetries could be evened out by developing countries; if anything, in fact, these asymmetries are further enhanced. Therefore, regulation that ensures this technology is used within certain boundaries, and in respect of basic principles of IHL (much in the same way as international law regulating biological warfare) is imperative.

But the most important type of technology-enabled warfare for our purposes is what is known as cyber attacks. Any attempt at defining a cyber attack would necessarily be broad and rather vague, but a working definition would be attacks conducted with the primary use of the internet with the goal of inflicting temporary or permanent harm to information systems, with or without consequences to the physical support of these systems or any other physical objects connected to them.

Some of the tactics used in cyber warfare include: espionage and intelligence gathering; 'web vandalism', or attacks aimed at defacing web pages, or causing servers to collapse by flooding it with innumerable requests through what is known as 'Denial of Service' (DoS) attacks (which

---

measurable impact on combat effectiveness. See Martin C. Libicki, 'Military Cyberpower', in *Cyberpower and National Security* 275, 284 (Franklin D. Kramer, Stuart H. Starr and Larry K. Wentz, eds) (2009).

11 For a list of definitions of 'combatant' extracted from military handbooks, see Thomas C. Wingfield, 'International Law and Information Operations', in *Cyberpower and National Security* 525, 534 (Franklin D. Kramer, Stuart H. Starr and Larry K. Wentz, eds) (2009).

12 Questioning the morality of using drones to promote targeted killings, see Roger Cohen, 'An Eye for an Eye', *The New York Times*, February 25, 2010.

is what happened in Estonia in 2007,[13] and in the Russia-Georgia conflict in 2008);[14] the posting of propaganda on the internet;[15] distributed DoS attacks, which is a much stronger version of a normal DoS attack, in which a single person controls – through spyware software, worms and other malicious software – a large number of computers, which are all used to launch a DoS attack against a larger system; and disruption of equipment by, for instance, disrupting the communications system of precision bombs,[16] or paralyzing software that controls the cooling system of a group of satellite antennas.[17]

The disruption of equipment can happen through the launching of viruses into the operational systems of the equipment to be affected, or by launching an Electronic Magnetic Pulse weapon against the targeted structures (that is, the building where the computers that command the equipment is). While this is an effective and seemingly 'least destructive' alternative to the bombing of a building, it can also cause a lot of collateral damage, as the pulse will affect all computers within a certain radius of its deployment, which can affect vital civilian systems.[18] Another technique is the use of computer attacks to add imaginary targets to enemy computers (causing the enemy to waste efforts and weapons).[19]

Cyber attacks can be of two types, according to their consequences: there are cyber attacks the consequences of which are limited to the virtual world (such as attacks on websites and DoS attacks),[20] while others may cause very tangible damage in the physical world (e.g., stopping a

---

13 See Edward Skoudis, 'Information Security Issues in Cyberspace', in *Cyberpower and National Security* 171, 177–8 (Franklin D. Kramer, Stuart H. Starr and Larry K. Wentz, eds) (2009); and Thomas C. Wingfield, 'International Law and Information Operations', in *Cyberpower and National Security* 525, 531–3 (Franklin D. Kramer, Stuart H. Starr and Larry K. Wentz, eds) (2009).

14 On the Russia-Georgia conflict, see Lesley Swanson, 'The Era of Cyber Warfare: Applying International Humanitarian Law to the 2008 Russian-Georgian Cyber Conflict', 32 *Loy. L.A. Int'l & Comp. L. Rev.* 303 (2010).

15 See Martin C. Libicki, *Conquest in Cyberspace: National Security and Information Warfare* 30 (2007).

16 In this specific example, the precision bomb becomes an indiscriminate weapon, and serious collateral damage can be done by it, so the lawfulness of such use of a cyber attack is questionable. See William Church, 'Information Warfare', 837 *International Review of the Red Cross* 205 (2000).

17 This is only a sample list. Many authors have created their own lists, more or less comprehensive than this one. See Martin C. Libicki, *Conquest in Cyberspace: National Security and Information Warfare* 31 (2007) (with a very useful diagram), and again at 79–87; Christopher C. Joyner and Catherine Lotrionte, 'Information Warfare as International Coercion: Elements of a Legal Framework', 12 *EJIL* 825, 836–9 (2001).

18 See William Church, 'Information Warfare', 837 *International Review of the Red Cross* 205 (2000).

19 See Martin C. Libicki, *Conquest in Cyberspace: National Security and Information Warfare* 52 (2007); and William Church, 'Information Warfare', 837 *International Review of the Red Cross* 205 (2000). Martin Libicki, a representative from the private military industry who wrote the book used in this article, tells an interesting anecdote in this sense: '[…] When Winston Churchill during World War I proposed dragging battleship silhouettes in the water, sceptics replied that the Germans would eventually realize that they were being tricked; he responded that henceforth they would doubt their eyes whenever they saw any such silhouette, whether real or fake.' *Id.*

20 See David E. Sanger, 'U.S. Steps Up Effort on Digital Defenses', *New York Times*, April 27, 2009. This is what he reported on the use of these techniques in the context of the Georgia-Russia conflict of 2008: 'In August 2008, when Russia invaded Georgia, the cyberattacks grew more widespread. Georgians were denied online access to news, cash and air tickets. The Georgian government had to move its Internet activity to servers in Ukraine when its own servers locked up, but the attacks did no permanent damage.'

country's electrical power distribution system, or causing a nuclear plant to collapse by disrupting its computer-operated cooling system).[21]

Some of the effects that can be obtained through cyber warfare are: (1) the destruction or disruption of infrastructure systems; (2) distracting the military, or diverting its energies, from detecting physical impending attacks[22] (referred to in military circles as 'hybrid warfare');[23] (3) intelligence theft;[24] (4) general effects on military and civilian morale, which can be a side effect of an attack on another target, or the primary objective (such as propaganda built into governmental websites, or simply the psychological effect of having some concept of 'social integrity' breached from abroad).

These means of cyber warfare are certainly not exclusive to developed countries, and have in fact been deployed by developing countries. However, it is noteworthy that the advantage in the instances in which cyber warfare techniques were in fact used still rested with the wealthier party to the conflict, simply because they had more means available to them also for the conduct of cyber warfare. Again, the suggestion that combat asymmetries could be corrected by cyber warfare fails, and developing states are put at a disadvantage.

All these forms of cyber warfare, as well as their different effects and the different form of classification, indicates that there are very different degrees of intensity of a cyber attack. Consequently, there will also be different legal responses to these different degrees. I will now analyze these different possible legal responses.

The Matter of the Applicable Law

International Humanitarian Law

Cyber warfare can happen both in times of peace and times of war.[25] Whether it happens during wartime or peace time will determine the legal regime applicable. Also, one has to take into account the different legal perceptions of each individual act of cyber warfare which, even out of context, can be seen as triggering different regimes.

Depending on the way an act of cyber warfare is legally perceived, there will be a different applicable regime. If an act of cyber war is seen as an act of use of force, then general principles of international humanitarian law should apply. If, on the other hand, one does not look at these acts as meeting the legal threshold for characterizing these acts as an 'armed attack' initiating an armed conflict, then the applicable regime should be the incipient international law on cybercrime and the general regime of international human rights law.

---

21 See Gregory J. Rattray, *Strategic Warfare in Cyberspace* 19 (2001).

22 See William Church, 'Information Warfare', 837 *International Review of the Red Cross* 205 (2000) (pointing out the possibility of engaging in such actions against civilian infrastructure prior to the start of hostilities, as a means to delay physical conflict).

23 See David E. Sanger, 'U.S. Steps Up Effort on Digital Defenses', *New York Times*, April 27, 2009.

24 For instance, it has been reported that in March 2009 a spy network using computers located mainly in China has retrieved classified information from computers of governments and private organizations in 103 countries, including computers of Tibetan exiles. China has denied any participation in these events. See Ministry of Foreign Affairs of the People's Republic of China, 'Foreign Ministry Spokesperson Qin Gang's Remarks on the So-Called Chinese Cyber-Spy Ring Invading Computers in Countries', available at <http://www.fmprc.gov.cn/eng/xwfw/s2510/2535/t555337.htm> (last accessed March 3, 2012); and Wikipedia, Cyberwarfare, available at <http://en.wikipedia.org/wiki/Cyberwarfare> (last accessed March 3, 2012).

25 See William Church, 'Information Warfare', 837 *International Review of the Red Cross* 205 (2000).

The definition of international conflict as a threshold for the application of IHL has been determined to be any situation in which a state's armed forces breach the sovereignty of another state.[26] In this sense, a cyber attack, if conducted by persons not enlisted in a state's military forces, could not conceptually be an armed attack. However, one commentator has noted that 'the reference to armed forces is more logically understood as a form of prescriptive shorthand for activity of a particular nature and intensity'.[27] Taking this factor into account, and in light of the principles and purposes of IHL, one is led to conclude that an armed attack is an assault upon another state with military means to impinge upon territorial integrity and political independence.[28] This definition can naturally extend to cyber warfare that is aimed at provoking direct destruction of property or loss of life in the physical world, to the extent one of the effects of these actions is precisely to cause internal unrest and weaken the governmental structure. It encompasses therefore actions aimed at, for instance, altering an airport's air traffic control system (which could lead to airplane collisions), but not necessarily acts aimed at defacing a governmental website.

Moreover, if one chooses to apply IHL, one has to consider the questions of territory as a requirement for the determination of IHL regime. How is the international character of a cyber conflict to be determined? Is it to be presumed, or should there be some criteria for this determination? The 'place' where the conflict takes place, for instance, cannot be deemed a determining factor, for the computers engaged in the conflict need not be in the territories of the conflicting states.

Also, cyberspace can in itself be referred to as a new environment for military action, and it has been assimilated to the global commons (outer space and the oceans are the most common references) in the literature about it.[29] There are certain differences, of course, at least to the extent that rules governing the oceans do create some sort of jurisdictional allocation, but the rules governing outer space are more easily applicable. And these become very relevant for analogical application: the core international treaty regulating the use of outer space explicitly determines that all activities (for our purposes, particularly military activities) of non-governmental entities in outer space must be authorized and continuously supervised by states parties to the relevant treaties. States are responsible for activities undertaken in outer space by governmental and non-governmental entities alike.[30] It further determines that states are responsible for damage caused

26 See Thomas C. Wingfield, 'International Law and Information Operations', in *Cyberpower and National Security* 525, 526–31 (Franklin D. Kramer, Stuart H. Starr and Larry K. Wentz, eds) (2009); and Michael N. Schmitt, 'Wired Warfare: Computer Network Attack and Jus in Bello', 846 *International Review of the Red Cross* 365, 372 (2002).

27 See Michael N. Schmitt, 'Wired Warfare: Computer Network Attack and Jus in Bello', 846 *International Review of the Red Cross* 365, 372 (2002).

28 Another definition characterizes an armed attack as an act or attempt to destroy, kill or injure, but this definition can be easily mistaken by the use of force by a state's police internally, which surely does not fall within International Humanitarian Law. See Michael N. Schmitt, 'Wired Warfare: Computer Network Attack and Jus in Bello', 846 *International Review of the Red Cross* 365, 373 (2002).

29 See Franklin D. Kramer, 'Cyberpower and National Security: Policy Recommendations for a Strategic Framework', in *Cyberpower and National Security* 3, 12 (Franklin D. Kramer, Stuart H. Starr and Larry K. Wentz, eds) (2009); Martin C. Libicki, *Conquest in Cyberspace: National Security and Information Warfare* 31 (2007); and Stuart H. Starr, 'Toward a Preliminary Theory of Cyberpower', in *Cyberpower and National Security* 43, 48 (Franklin D. Kramer, Stuart H. Starr and Larry K. Wentz, eds) (2009).

30 See *Treaty on Principles Governing the Activities of States in the Exploration and Use of Outer Space, including the Moon and Other Celestial Bodies, Article VI*. The full text of the provision is the following: 'Article VI. States Parties to the Treaty shall bear international responsibility for national activities in outer space, including the Moon and other celestial bodies, *whether such activities are carried on by governmental agencies or by non-governmental entities*, and for assuring that national activities are carried out in conformity

to another state simply if the object that caused the harm has been launched from their territory.[31] Rules governing outer space thus offer interesting insights and can be applied analogically to the regulation of cyber space.

One must be aware of differences, however. Possibly one of the reasons why responsibility for the acts of private entities is so easily attributable to the state in the outer space context is that outer space endeavours are large and costly enterprises, and the state from which one such enterprise is launched would hardly be able to deny knowledge of it; when it comes to cyber attacks, however, any person with a home computer can launch one such attack, as long as they have the necessary skills and training. This difference of scale and accessibility must be taken into account when trying to draw this parallel, but I suggest that the parallel can be drawn nonetheless, precisely because of the aspiration to protect a common space that is not subject to territorial borders.

Another important question is that of attribution. Assuming a cyber attacker does not identify herself/himself, how can this identification be done? Tracing the attack back is a long and often futile exercise, as most cyber traffic goes through a wide range of computers in disparate parts of the world, being hardly linear.[32] Also, even if an attack can be traced back to a certain country, it is nearly impossible to determine whether the source is a state- or a privately-owned computer.[33]

Therefore, it would be nearly impossible to attribute an attack through these means. Even if attribution were possible, tracking the attack down to its source computer would not necessarily resolve the problem. For one, this computer may be just a smokescreen created by spyware software for the real attacker. Also, as private military contracting expands into cyberwar, to find that the computer responsible for the attack is one of a private military company does not say much, particularly if this company renders services to more than one state. The attacks of March 2009 in which intelligence computers in 103 countries were hacked and had information stolen by computers that could be traced back to China is an example. Even though the attacks were traced back to China, the Chinese government denied any involvement in the acts, and that more or less ended the affair, as there are no means to effectively prove that the attacks were commanded by Chinese authorities.

Further, the fact that there was no response to these attacks may serve as evidence of state practice in not considering them as armed attacks, at least not to the extent that it may trigger the

---

with the provisions set forth in the present Treaty. *The activities of non-governmental entities in outer space, including the Moon and other celestial bodies, shall require authorization and continuing supervision by the appropriate State Party to the Treaty*. When activities are carried on in outer space, including the Moon and other celestial bodies, by an international organization, responsibility for compliance with this Treaty shall be borne both by the international organization and by the States Parties to the Treaty participating in such organization' (emphasis added).

31 *Id*., Article VII. The full text of the provision is the following: 'Article VII. Each State Party to the Treaty that launches or procures the launching of an object into outer space, including the Moon and other celestial bodies, and *each State Party from whose territory or facility an object is launched, is internationally liable for damage to another State Party to the Treaty or to its natural or juridical persons* by such object or its component parts on the Earth, in air space or in outer space, including the Moon and other celestial bodies' (emphasis added).

32 See Thom Shanker and David E. Sanger, 'Privacy May Be a Victim in Cyberdefense Plan', *New York Times*, June 12, 2009 (making the case that this may even imply that to counter a cyber attack may require entering the 'cyber territory' of third nations).

33 Recent U.S. efforts to try to determine the source of foreign-originated scans into American industrial databases illustrate this point. It has been reported that, even though it was possible to ascertain that the probing came from China, it was not possible to determine whether it came from the Chinese government or a non-State actor. See David E. Sanger, 'U.S. Steps Up Effort on Digital Defenses', *New York Times*, April 27, 2009.

application of Article 51 of the UN Charter (as a use of force) or international humanitarian law. Thus, one may be led to the conclusion that different forms of cyber attack will constitute armed attacks or not depending on the pervasiveness of their effects. Documented cyber attacks have so far done little more than blocking access to or defacing certain websites, and there have also been some alleged thefts of intelligence information. None of this, however, seems to be enough to trigger a military countermeasure, cybernetic or otherwise, which lends further credence to the notion that these forms of cyber warfare at least cannot be deemed to be armed attacks. If a cyber attack, however, ever has effects causing the loss of civilian life and/or property, the response might be stronger. Another possible interpretation is simply that a sufficient causal link between the attacks and the Chinese authorities could not be established. The analogical application of rules on outer space, however, would help shed light onto this situation, as all that would be required would be to determine that the computers were located in China.

If IHL applies, then naturally the concepts of 'protected person' and 'protected property' apply as well, meaning that all attacks directed at non-military cyber structures are to be considered in violation of IHL principles. In this sense, one has to consider that cyber warfare cannot thus be conducted from a civilian building, as the building naturally becomes a legitimate military target due to the presence of the cyber warriors.

Likewise, the computer systems of hospitals and essential public utilities such as power plants cannot be targets of cyber attacks, since they are considered as protected property by rules of international humanitarian law.[34] Most of the common examples of scenarios of cyber attack are therefore examples of acts that violate general principles of international humanitarian law.

If a cyber-attack, however, happens outside of the context of a conflict, and does not amount by itself to an act of use of force, then the rules and principles of international humanitarian law do not apply. Instead, the applicable regime will be that of general human rights law and specific rules on cybercrime.

International Human Rights Law

Human rights rules will be applicable as general principles of law, requiring, for instance, that privacy and freedom of expression and information be protected when cyber attacks imply breaking into databases and public and private websites. The situation during the Georgia-Russia conflict,[35] in which access to newspaper websites was denied, is an example of a violation of a human rights rule, as it violated the freedom of expression (seen as the freedom to impart and to receive information) of Georgians.

The early 2010 Google-China controversy is an example of violation of privacy by cyber warfare means, even though ultimately the attacks were directed at a private company, and not at a state. China was allegedly trying to gain information on political activists within its own territory. To this extent, should political opposition in China ever take upon arms, and start an internal

---

34 There are several rules in Additional Protocol I to the Geneva Conventions protecting: installations containing dangerous forces, including most power plants (Article 56); cultural property (Article 53); medical facilities (Article 12); religious buildings (Article 53); farms and crops (Article 54). See also Michael N. Schmitt, 'Wired Warfare: Computer Network Attack and Jus in Bello', 846 *International Review of the Red Cross* 365, 385 (2002).

35 For more on cyber warfare in the context of this conflict, see Daniel T. Kuehl, 'From Cyberspace to Cyberpower: Defining the Problem', in *Cyberpower and National Security* 24, 36 (Franklin D. Kramer, Stuart H. Starr and Larry K. Wentz, eds) (2009).

conflict in the country, any act such as those against Google and Gmail could be considered an act of cyber warfare in the context of an internal conflict, and in violation of human rights.[36]

Other possibilities for human rights violations arising out of cyber attacks refer to the effects of these attacks upon the physical world. For instance, a cyber attack that leads to the disruption of the power grid of a hospital, causing the loss of patients' lives, can be considered a violation of the right to life. Similarly, a cyber attack that leads to the explosion of a factory and the spilling of toxic content into a river, polluting the water source of a certain city or village, can be seen as a violation of the right to private life, according to a similar precedent of the European Court of Human Rights.[37]

The examples so far are restricted to civil and political rights. Naturally, there are many instances in which economic, social and cultural rights are affected, in part as the counterpart to a civil and political right. In the hospital case, for instance, the right to health is affected; in that of the pollution, the right to a safe environment is being impinged upon. Other examples may include the right to food and water in the case of cyber attacks affecting food distribution schemes, or the right to culture, with the denial of access to information. Be it as it may, acts of cyber warfare have a very tangible impact upon human rights, particularly when the targets of attacks are not military objectives.

When it comes to the enforcement of these rules, however, a serious problem arises in meeting the jurisdictional threshold of most human rights adjudicatory and quasi-adjudicatory bodies, and to connect the case to a state party to a human rights instrument. That is, it is difficult to argue that in the hypothesis of Afghani victims of a cyber attack launched by France in which access to Afghani and foreign media was denied (violating therefore freedom of expression) that the affected Afghani citizens were at any moment under the jurisdiction of France. It has already been established that it is very difficult to establish jurisdiction in the case of aerial bombings,[38] and the same negative of jurisdiction can be transplanted to the context of cyber attacks.

Cybercrime rules, on the other hand, have very limited reach in offering redress to victims of cyber attacks. They offer states tools to prosecute and punish the perpetrators of cyber attacks that fall under the states' jurisdiction, but do not offer remedies to the victims other than the indirect effects of prosecution and punishment of perpetrators. And this set of rules is only applicable to non-state actors, being unclear whether an attacker acting with state support would be subject to the same rules.

Among the different sets of potentially applicable rules to the general context of cyber warfare, international humanitarian law seems to offer the best structure for dealing with cyber attacks. However, this set of rules is not applicable at all times, as a certain threshold must be met to trigger the application of IHL principles. Further, the application of IHL rules to private actors engaging in cyber war is difficult. I will now look at the possibilities for holding private actors engaging in cyber war accountable for their actions.

---

36 See Wikipedia, Google China, available at <http://en.wikipedia.org/wiki/Google_China> (last accessed February 25, 2012).

37 See European Court of Human Rights, *Case of López Ostra v. Spain* (Application no. 16798/90), judgment of 9 December 1994.

38 See in this sense the seminal case of the European Court of Human Rights. ECtHR, *Bankovic* et al. *v. Belgium* et al. (Application no. 52207/99), Admissibility Decision (Grand Chamber); and Georg Ress, 'Problems of Extraterritorial Human Rights Violations – The Jurisdiction of the European Court of Human Rights: the Bankovic Case', 12 *Italian Yearbook of International Law* (2002).

Privatizing Cyber Warfare: E-Mercenaries?

This part will discuss emerging strategies regarding cyber warfare (offensive and defensive) in a few countries and NATO. It will also discuss whether the involvement of non-state actors in cyber warfare is similar to their involvement in the broader military, or if there is something peculiar to cyber warfare that requires a greater or smaller involvement of the private sector. I will then move on to analyzing issues of accountability and responsibility for actions undertaken by these private individuals in the context of cyber warfare that violated international humanitarian law or human rights rules.

Emerging Strategies on Cyber Warfare

The United States has in many aspects taken the lead in the development of cyber warfare. Even though a report issued in April 2009 said that the issue was not addressed properly within the U.S. military, and that there was no real structure for cyber warfare,[39] there have been reports that prior to that the U.S. has engaged in offensive cyber attacks at least twice: once in penetrating Iran's nuclear program for intelligence gathering and another for deploying false intelligence to attract members of Al Qaeda into an ambush.[40]

The United States has also developed a plan that was to be put into effect shortly before the U.S. invasion of Iraq, and that would consist of freezing billions of U.S. dollars of Saddam Hussein's bank accounts, amounting to a financial paralysis of the country that would prevent Hussein from purchasing new weapons, and even paying the troops. This plan was halted, however, because of the financial turmoil it could create in the Middle East. This collateral damage was deemed excessive in relation to the benefits of a successful cyber attack.[41] The United States Department of Defense has since worked on defining principles for offensive cyber war, but its efforts seem to be riddled with doubt.[42]

At the same time, some measures have been adopted by the U.S. Military, in creating special divisions to address cyber warfare. For instance, the Air Force has created the 57th Information

---

39 See David E. Sanger, 'U.S. Steps Up Effort on Digital Defenses', *New York Times*, April 27, 2009.

40 See FOX News, Report: U.S. Already Conducting Cyberwarfare, available at <http://www.foxnews.com/story/0,2933,518259,00.html?loomia_ow=t0:s0:a16:g12:r1:c0.333394:b25402662:z0> (last accessed February 28, 2012). This act, however, can be classified as perfidy, which is a clear violation of the principles governing the conduct of warfare. See also Davis Brown, 'A Proposal for an International Convention to Regulate the Use of Information Systems in Armed Conflict', 47 *Harv. ILJ* 179, 202–207 (2006). Regarding Brown's contribution, his draft proposal for an international instrument is particularly relevant, especially Article 23, which reads as follows: 'Art. 23. The use of information systems to invite the confidence of an adversary to lead it to believe that an individual, location, or facility is entitled to protection under the law of armed conflict, with intent to betray that confidence, constitutes perfidy, and States shall be forbidden from engaging in such acts.'

41 See John Markoff and Thom Shanker, 'Halted '03 Iraq Plan Illustrates U.S. Fear of Cyberwar Risk', *New York Times*, August 1, 2009. A very similar strategy was devised during the invasion of Kosovo, and also halted because deemed illegal. U.S. Department of Defense legal counsel also found that the general rules of international armed conflicts would apply to any cyber operation, and it was based on these rules that they decided for the illegality of the freezing of Slobodan Milosevic's bank accounts. For this report, see Martin C. Libicki, *Conquest in Cyberspace: National Security and Information Warfare* 258 (2007).

42 See U.S. Joint Chiefs of Staff, Questions Abound in Cyber Theater of Operations, Vice Chairman Says, available at <http://www.jcs.mil/newsarticle.aspx?ID=106> (last accessed February 27, 2012).

Aggressor Squadron, based in the Nellis Air Force Base (Nevada) and the Army has created the Network Warfare Battalion.[43]

Cyber-attacks were also reportedly considered with regard to the intervention in Libya in 2011. The goal of such attacks would be to break through firewalls of the Libyan government's networks in order to 'sever military communication links and prevent the early-warning radars from gathering information and relaying it to missile batteries aiming at NATO airplanes'.[44] Ultimately, though, a decision was made against the use of cyber warfare means, because of the precedent it would create for other nations. Deterrence thus played an important role in avoiding the open use of cyber warfare techniques by a government.[45]

In June 2009, the UK government released a report on cyber security, reaching essentially the same conclusions as the U.S. report, in the sense that the UK also believes itself to be underprepared for the event of a cyber conflict, and it highlights the need for international cooperation on the matter.[46]

The North Atlantic Treaty Organization (NATO) has also stepped up to discuss the issue of cyber warfare. Triggered by the attacks against Estonia in 2007, the Cooperative Cyber Defense Center of Excellence (CCDCOE) was created in Estonia in 2008, receiving shortly thereafter the status of International Military Organization before NATO.[47] This young institution has engaged in discussing the legal implications of cyber warfare (most notably with conferences on the topic), but it has so far failed to offer concrete policy and legal guidelines.

That these countries and NATO are leading the way in attempts to regulate cyber warfare is not surprising, and points precisely in the direction of this chapter's central thesis: they are the ones leading the way because they are the ones with the resources to actually wage cyber warfare. I suggest the concern with the regulation of cyber warfare stems not so much from a fear of being exposed to attacks coming from 'rogue developing countries', but from a need to deter one another. It is somewhat worrisome that developing countries do not seem to be participating in any main fora for law-making in this arena, as the rules could easily be drafted in a way that prevents developing countries from even considering developing cyber warfare capabilities, while giving free rein to a few developed countries to do so (in the name of international peace and security, for instance).

The larger part of these policy-level developments, when they even mention the possibility of using private contractors in cyber warfare, seem to mention that the involvement of the business sector is important.[48] They fail, however, to offer and explanation as to why. The indispensability of the connection between the private sector and government in information warfare efforts has not been argued persuasively in the literature on the field.

43 See Corey Kilgannon and Noam Cohen, 'Cadets Trade the Trenches for Firewalls', *New York Times*, March 10, 2009.

44 Eric Schmitt and Thom Shaanker, 'U.S. Debated Cyberwarfare in Attach Plan on Libya', *The New York Times*, October 17, 2011.

45 *Id.*

46 See Stuart S. Malawer, 'Cyberwarfare: Law and Policy Proposals for U.S. and Global Governance', available at <http://papers.ssrn.com/sol3/papers.cfm?abstract_id=1437002> (last accessed March 3, 2012).

47 See 'Cooperative Cyber Defense Center of Excellence, Homepage', available at <http://www.ccdcoe.org/> (last accessed March 3, 2012).

48 See in particular Gregory J. Rattray, *Strategic Warfare in Cyberspace* 363–4 (2001) (part of a long chapter explaining the full evolution of cyber warfare policies in the U.S., and repeatedly mentioning the matter of private sector involvement, but not justifying the need for it).

One of the most commonly advanced arguments is that the private sector is better positioned than the government when it comes to incorporating and responding to fast-evolving technologies.[49] This is part of the general argument in favour of privatization of warfare in general, and is one that can hardly stand on its own. While it is true that the governmental military apparatus of many countries is being gradually replaced by the private sector, this does not necessarily have to do with the ability of the private sector to adapt to change in a quicker pace. Research in the field of political science regarding the operation of private military contractors has shown that they have not necessarily represented a major increase in the evolution of military technique, at least not one that outdoes what the governmental military could have accomplished on its own.[50] There is also the risk that computer systems of private companies will be more vulnerable than governmental computer networks simply because smaller companies do not have the same resources to invest in high computer security as the government, a factor that further challenges the idea of greater technical expertise of the privatized cyber military.[51]

Also, the costs of private contractors are not necessarily lower than the ones of a governmental employee. What does happen, especially in the intelligence sector, is that individuals will have large amounts of financial resources invested by the government in their high-level training and, as soon as the training is complete and a high security clearance is obtained, these individuals will leave their jobs with the government only to return to governmental buildings as contractors.[52] Therefore, in this specific case, by creating such favourable conditions to the privatization of warfare, the government is in fact losing the resources it invests in training of high level military and intelligence agents.[53]

Another argument for the privatization of warfare is that the private sector is more often than not the primary target of cyber attacks, and therefore its involvement is inevitable and indispensable.[54] However, an analysis of the principles of IHL applicable to situations of cyber conflict easily ruled out the possibility that the private sector be legitimately targeted by cyber attacks. In fact, if anything the private sector should be clearly differentiated, as computers launching cyber attacks become legitimate targets for cyber and physical attacks. If these computers are located in a commercial building shared with other companies, there is actually a risk of collateral damage on civilian property caused precisely because cyber warfare has been privatized.

---

49 See Tim Shorrock, *Spies for Hire: The Secret World of Intelligence Outsourcing* 174 (2009) (describing the account of one IT specialist hired by the U.S. military who described the technology around him as a 'colossal letdown').

50 See P.W. Singer, *Corporate Warriors – The Rise of the Privatized Military Industry* 154–7 (2008).

51 *Id.*, at 163.

52 See generally Tim Shorrock, *Spies for Hire: The Secret World of Intelligence Outsourcing* 28–29 (2009). On the privatization of intelligence services, see also Simon Chesterman, 'We Can't Spy… If We Can't Buy!': The Privatization of Intelligence and the Limits of Outsourcing 'Inherently Governmental Functions', 19 *EJIL* 1055 (2008); and Simon Chesterman, 'Intelligence Services', in *Private Security, Public Order: The Outsourcing of Public Services and Its Limits* 184 (Simon Chesterman and Angelina Fisher, eds) (2009).

53 See P.W. Singer, *Corporate Warriors – The Rise of the Privatized Military Industry* 76–78 (2008).

54 See Stuart H. Starr, 'Toward a Preliminary Theory of Cyberpower', in *Cyberpower and National Security* 43, 65 (Franklin D. Kramer, Stuart H. Starr and Larry K. Wentz, eds) (2009); Gregory J. Rattray, *Strategic Warfare in Cyberspace* 328 (2001); and Daniel T. Kuehl, 'From Cyberspace to Cyberpower: Defining the Problem', in *Cyberpower and National Security* 24, 41 (Franklin D. Kramer, Stuart H. Starr and Larry K. Wentz, eds) (2009).

One final argument is that the same networks and 'cyber highways' are used for civilian and military purposes alike.[55] One 1996 estimate indicated that over 95 percent of military communications happened over commercial communications systems.[56] While this is an argument that deserves some attention, it does not necessarily justify the privatization of these services. The fact that cyber *security* is public-private by definition does not imply that the cyber *military* should also be public-private.[57] It does call for increased efforts in protecting networks in general, and may perhaps justify closer cooperation in defensive cyber warfare, but it by no means justifies the delegation of offensive cyber warfare capabilities to the private sector.

Therefore, despite policy-level rhetoric aimed at justifying the privatization of cyber warfare as an essential step if sufficient cyber capabilities are to be acquired, there seems to not be a convincing argument justifying privatization as a necessity, rather leaving it as an option. Despite the way in which the rhetoric goes, it seems that the privatization of cyber warfare in countries such as the United States is inevitable, especially if one considers that currently over 70 percent of the U.S. intelligence budget,[58] along with considerable parts of its general defense budget, are already spent with contractors, which makes the formation of cyber capabilities exclusively within the regular state military a near-impossible task.

Accountability Issues Regarding the Privatization of Cyber Warfare

Quite a lot has been already discussed on the issue of the privatization of war and the responsibility of states and private military companies for legal breaches undertaken by these contractors.[59] I do not intend to re-open this discussion here in detail, as it would be far beyond the purposes of this chapter. However, I will draw on elements developed so far with respect to the general

55 See Michael Likosky, 'The Privatization of Violence', in *Private Security, Public Order: The Outsourcing of Public Services and Its Limits* 11, 17 (Simon Chesterman and Angelina Fisher, eds) (2009) (noting that the internet was created out of a public-private partnership); P.W. Singer, *Corporate Warriors – The Rise of the Privatized Military Industry* 100 (2008); Tim Shorrock, *Spies for Hire: The Secret World of Intelligence Outsourcing* 164 (2009); and Thomas C. Wingfield, 'International Law and Information Operations', in *Cyberpower and National Security* 525, 535 (Franklin D. Kramer, Stuart H. Starr and Larry K. Wentz, eds) (2009).

56 See Richard W. Aldrich, 'The International Legal Implications of Information Warfare', *Airpower Journal* (Fall 1996).

57 See Franklin D. Kramer, 'Cyberpower and National Security: Policy Recommendations for a Strategic Framework', in *Cyberpower and National Security* 3, 4 (Franklin D. Kramer, Stuart H. Starr and Larry K. Wentz, eds) (2009).

58 See Tim Shorrock, *Spies for Hire: The Secret World of Intelligence Outsourcing* 18–19 (2009).

59 A small sample of the literature can be found on Issue No. 863 of the *International Review of the Red Cross* (2006), which is dedicated entirely to the topic of Private Military Companies, as well as one issue of the *European Journal of International Law*, Vol. 19(5) (2008). It has also been the object of a project within New York University's Institute for International Law and Justice. See Institute for International Law and Justice, 'Project on Private Military and Security Companies', available at <http://www.iilj.org/research/PrivateMilitaryandSecurityCompanies.asp> (last accessed March 3, 2012). There is also another project, being conducted by a consortium of universities under the leadership of the European University Institute, on the topic of the legal implications of the use of private military contractors (PRIV-WAR Project). This chapter is written in the context of this project. Many working papers related to this topic are available on the Project's webpage. See PRIV-WAR, 'Home', available at <http://priv-war.eu/> (last accessed March 3, 2012). See also Alexandre Faite, 'Involvement of Private Contractors in Armed Conflict: Implications under International Humanitarian Law', 4(2) *Defence Studies* (2004).

legal scenario as a means to inform the discussion when it comes specifically to cyber warfare contractors, drawing the analogies and making the necessary differentiations, should it be the case.

The instruments being proposed for the regulation of cyber warfare fail to take into account the participation of non-state parties in these conflicts and operations, which has been identified as a major defect in the deterrent effect of these instruments.[60] One exception is a proposal, by Davis Brown, that proposes a total ban on the uses of private companies for cyber warfare activities.[61]

The available tools for accountability naturally depend on who is called upon to respond for the acts of private contractors. If one wants to call upon the state, then it is imperious to prove that the actions of the contractor were undertaken under command of a state entity. This option can give rise to remedies in the hiring state, or in the state where the attacks happened or of the nationality of the victims (subject to rules on immunity of jurisdiction and enforcement of judgments), or even in a state with which the company or individual undertaking the attack is connected (in which case procedural tools that allow for the state to be named a single or co-defendant must be available).

If one thinks of seeking the company for redress, then it is necessary that states regulate the activities of companies operating within their territories and dealing with cyber warfare. This is one of the requirements of the Cybercrime Convention (Council of Europe),[62] that determines that national legislation be enacted to combat illegal action over the internet that originates from a computer based on the state party's territory.

The applicable legal regimes also have an important role to play in the possibilities for redress. While the application of IHL rules imposes an obligation on states to provide for internal remedies for grave breaches of international humanitarian law (which is the case of an attack against protected property, even if by cybernetic means),[63] it only provides for domestic remedies, there being few (if any) avenues for the enforcement of IHL in international fora, at least in principle.

---

60 See Tim Stevens, 'Cyberwar and Global Law', in *Ubiwar – Conflict in N Dimensions*, available at <http://ubiwar.com/2009/09/05/cyberwar-and-global-law/> (last accessed March 3, 2012).

61 Davis Brown, 'A Proposal for an International Convention to Regulate the Use of Information Systems in Armed Conflict', 47 *Harv. ILJ* 179, 217 (2006). The relevant provision is the following: 'Art. 10. States shall launch information attacks from only information systems operated by lawful combatants. States shall not use the information systems of noncombatants or nonparties to the conflict as proxies for such attacks. States shall take reasonable measures to prohibit and prevent such attacks by private persons.'

62 For a comment on the effectiveness of this instrument regarding cyber security, see Clay Wilson, 'Cyber Crime', in *Cyberpower and National Security* 415, 430 (Franklin D. Kramer, Stuart H. Starr and Larry K. Wentz, eds) (2009); and Harold Kwalwasser, 'Internet Governance', in *Cyberpower and National Security* 491, 515–16 (Franklin D. Kramer, Stuart H. Starr and Larry K. Wentz, eds) (2009).

63 The provision on grave breaches common to all Four Geneva Conventions (Articles 50, 51, 130 and 147 respectively), as well as the provision of Additional Protocol I (Articles 11 and 85) state this obligation. The common text is the following: 'Grave breaches to which the preceding Article relates shall be those involving any of the following acts, if committed against persons or property protected by the Convention: wilful killing, torture or inhuman treatment, including biological experiments, wilfully causing great suffering or serious injury to body or health, and extensive destruction and appropriation of property, not justified by military necessity and carried out unlawfully and wantonly.' The text is different in the Additional Protocol, and has slight variations in the Fourth Geneva Convention, which adds extra elements. Because the Fourth Convention refers to the treatment of civilians, it is also important to add its full text here: 'Art. 147. Grave breaches to which the preceding Article relates shall be those involving any of the following acts, if committed against persons or property protected by the present Convention: wilful killing, torture or inhuman treatment, including biological experiments, wilfully causing great suffering or serious injury to body or health, unlawful deportation or transfer or unlawful confinement of a protected person, compelling a protected person to serve in the forces of a hostile Power, or wilfully depriving a protected person of the rights of fair and regular

On the other hand, international human rights adjudicatory and quasi-adjudicatory bodies can address these situations, even if only from the perspective of seeking redress from the state, and not directly from the private actors under state command. If one considers that human rights courts have successfully used international humanitarian law as tools to enhance the application of human rights instruments, IHL can also be an important tool.[64]

There is one hypothesis in which international action can be pursued directly against the contractor, and that is the hypothesis in which the state can sue the contractor internationally for, e.g., overstepping the boundaries of the contract and causing indiscriminate harm, in violation of IHL and human rights norms and the main contract. There has been one case in which a private military contractor has been internationally sued by the state (Sandline by the government of Papua New Guinea).[65] Even though this specific case referred to an issue of payment, matters of violation of IHL and human rights rules can also be the object of arbitration, as long as the respect for these rules is an integral part of the contracts (as they should be).

Concluding Remarks

A lot of the currently existing principles of international humanitarian law and human rights law, as well as specific regimes regarding cyber crime, can be applicable by analogy, even though they fail to provide answers to all possible scenarios. Rules regulating the global commons, especially those on the outer space, also offer some possible source of inspiration, but important differences must be taken into account, potentially diminishing the reach of such analogies. Nevertheless, in the absence of a clear framework, they offer a much-needed point of reference.

Specific rules, therefore, are a necessity in the field of cyber warfare. But these should be drafted with the participation of developing countries, so as to try to avoid that asymmetries existing in the current laws of war are repeated in the regulation of cyber warfare, and that rules that come into existence apply equally to both developed and developing countries.

Emerging proposals have so far largely overlooked the issue of the privatization of this type of conflict, which has been progressively advanced as a policy issue, despite there being no compelling reasons why the privatization of war is a necessity. It is necessary that future regulatory proposals look at the issue of privatization of war, avoiding that indiscriminate cyber attacks occur and affect

---

trial prescribed in the present Convention, taking of hostages and extensive destruction and appropriation of property, not justified by military necessity and carried out unlawfully and wantonly.'

64 See Hans-Joachim Heintze, 'On the Relationship between Human Rights Law and International Humanitarian Law', 86 *International Review of the Red Cross* 789 (2004); William Abresch, 'A Human Rights Law of Internal Armed Conflict: The European Court of Human Rights in Chechnya', 16 *European Journal of International Law* 741 (2005); Amna Guellali, Lex Specialis, 'Droit International Humanitaire et Droits de l'Homme: Leur Interaction dans les Nouveaux Conflits Armes', 2007 *Revue Génerale de Droit International Public* 539; Noam Lubell, 'Challenges in applying human rights law to armed conflict', 87 *International Review of the Red Cross* 737 (2005); Louise Doswald-Beck and Sylvain Vité, 'International Humanitarian Law and Human Rights Law', 293 *International Review of the Red Cross* 94 (1993); Fanny Martin, 'Application du Droit International Humanitaire par la Cour Interaméricaine des Droits de l'Homme', 83 *International Review of the Red Cross* 1037 (2001); David S. Weissbrodt and Beth Andrus, 'The Right to Life During Armed Conflict: *Disabled Peoples' International v. United States*', 29 Harvard *International Law Journal* 59 (1988); and Liesbeth Zegveld, 'The Inter-American Commission on Human Rights and International Humanitarian Law: A Comment on the Tablada Case', 324 *International Review of the Red Cross* 505 (1998).

65 For an account of this litigation, see P.W. Singer, *Corporate Warriors – The Rise of the Privatized Military Industry* 192–96 (2008). The full text of the contract is an appendix to the book. *Id.*, at 263–70.

negatively the lives of innocent civilians and other parties not involved in the conflict. Ideally, the engagement of non-state actors in cyber warfare should be simply prohibited, or state responsibility should be strict, meaning that the state should be engaged by any act of cyber warfare that can be traced back to its territory.

The potentials of technological warfare are increasingly high, and the new domain of cyberspace promises a true revolution in terms of military capabilities. Legislators must, however, impose clear limits on this revolution, so as to avoid unnecessary and disproportionate injury in the name of a type of warfare that may in many instances resemble a video game, but that has a very real and potentially catastrophic reach.

Chapter 14
Internet Content Filtering in Latin America: Reasons and Impacts on Freedom of Expression[1]

Joana Varon Ferraz, Carlos Affonso Pereira de Souza, Bruno Magrani and Walter Britto

Introduction

In December 2010, the Venezuelan Congress approved a bill to regulate access to content and the use of Internet in the country. The bill was proposed to amend the Law on Social Responsibility in Radio and Television (*Ley de Responsabilidad Social en Radio y Televisión*, also known as Ley *Resorte*), which already restricts content broadcast by radio and television stations. Under this amendment, access to websites that distribute messages or information that 'may be contrary to national security' or that seek to 'discredit legitimately constituted authorities' may be restricted. Moreover, it establishes that Internet Service Providers ('ISPs') would be required to establish mechanisms capable of restricting the dissemination of messages, access to portals and disclosure of information related to the actions foreseen under this regulation. According to Reporters Without Borders, such provisions would enable indiscriminate Internet filtering mechanisms in clear detriment of freedom of access to information.[2] As reported by NGO Espacio *Público*:

> the project contains serious deficiencies regarding good legislative practice, which allows officials who have the responsibility of enforcing this legal instrument to act arbitrarily and discretionarily, which constitutes per se a violation of the human right of freedom of expression and leads to a selective and interested enforcement.[3]

In Mexico, the Party of the Democratic Revolution (*Partido de la Revolución Democrática*) has submitted a bill on the monitoring and regulation of the use of social networks in the country. According to the bill, the mere exchange of information that helps others to violate the law would be considered a crime. Norberto Nazario, the proponent of the bill, claimed it was intended to help monitor and hamper the way drug cartels are using the net. Mexican Internet users had a critical reaction to the proposal: many have asserted that the law would serve as a mere excuse for the government to increase surveillance; they have even used the term 'Big Brother' to refer to the position the police has sought to take.

Also very critical, in April 2011, the Ministry of Justice from Colombia has presented a bill that intends to regulate Internet content. The text allows ISPs to remove or block access to content

1 This article is an abridged version of the original one, published in Spanish under the name 'Filtrado de contenido en America Latina: razones e impactos en la libertad de expresión', in Bertoni, Eduardo (org.), 'Hacia una Internet libre de Censura', <http://www.palermo.edu/cele/pdf/internet_libre_de_censura_libro.pdf>, accessed 29/06/2012.

2 <http://www.rsf-es.org/news/venezuela-la-ley-resorte-se-extiende-a-internet/> accessed 28/06/2012.

3 <http://www.espaciopublico.org/index.php/noticias/1-libertad-de-expresi/939-ley-resorte-restringe-la-libertad-de-expresion-en-internet-y-medios-electronicos> accessed 28 June 2012.

preventively, in case someone claims that such content violates copyrights. Civil society has expressed its concerns about the law, calling it the Colombian version of the French *Hadopi* Law,[4] which provided a three-strikes procedure to suspend the Internet connection for violation of copyrights.

In Brazil, in 2007, access to YouTube was blocked for a few hours under a court decision issued on a privacy/image violation claim involving Daniela Cicarelli, a Brazilian celebrity. She had been exposed in an amateur video that captured intimate moments of her and her boyfriend at a beach. Though not so recent, the Cicarelli case turned out to be paradigmatic among Brazilian jurists, and triggered the debate about how internet regulation could foster the protection of rights in the digital environment.[5]

The right of every citizen to seek, receive and share information is protected under the Universal Declaration of Human Rights and the International Covenant on Civil and Political Rights (ICCPR). Specifically regarding Latin American countries, the Pact of San José, officially known as the American Convention on Human Rights, which was ratified by most countries of the region, establishes rules on censorship at article 13. Similarly, the Tunis Agenda also recognizes these rights within the Information Society, item 42 reaffirms their commitment to 'the freedom to seek, receive, impart and use information, in particular, for the creation, accumulation and dissemination of knowledge'. Most importantly, the same item affirms that:

> measures undertaken to ensure Internet stability and security, to fight cybercrime and to counter spam, must protect and respect the provisions for privacy and freedom of expression as contained in the relevant parts of the Universal Declaration of Human Rights and the Geneva Declaration of Principles.[6]

However, despite the fact that freedom of expression depends on the free flow of information, there is a tendency for national and regional laws and judicial orders to intervene in the end-to-end architecture of the Internet, preventing the free flow of information and thus undermining the rights of every citizen to freedom of expression and privacy.

There is a tendency towards increasing online censorship, as several Latin American governments and governments around the world[7] have proposed legal texts that impose: criminalization of

---

4 The HADOPI (*Haute Autorité pour la diffusion des œuvres et la protection des droits sur internet*) is the French governmental agency dedicated to copyright enforcement. The law that created it in 2009 was heavily criticized for the provision of measures that could lead to the blocking of the internet connection if a certain user repeatedly violated copyright law.

5 It is worth noting that judge Enio Santarelli Zuliani, from the Appeals Court of the State of São Paulo, after ordering the blocking of the website and being aware of the national attention the case had gathered, issued a second decision ordering the urgent reestablishment of access to the website. In his decision he mentioned that the first decision had the positive effect of proving that national and international internet companies could comply with judicial orders and as no legislation had been issued in the Brazil on the matter, his decision fostered the debate over the internet regulation (see <http://g1.globo.com/Noticias/Brasil/0,,AA1413590-5598,00.html> accessed 28 June 2012).

6 <http://www.itu.int/wsis/docs2/tunis/off/6rev1.html> accessed 28/06/2012.

7 Recently, a huge polemic has risen around the Stop Online Piracy Act (SOPA). Introduced in the US House of Representatives in the end of 2011, the bill would expand enforcement of copyright in the online environment, through measures such as making unauthorised streaming of copyrighted content a crime, barring search engines, requiring ISPs to block access to websites and so on. Opponents say that it infringes First Amendment rights as it constitutes a clear act of Internet censorship, besides crippling the Internet and threatening whistle-blowing initiatives. Even a coalition of Internet giants (Google, Yahoo, Amazon, Wikipedia, etc.) has considered blacking out as a protest against SOPA.

legitimate expressions; liability of intermediaries; disconnection of users based on copyright violation or transmission of illegal information (such as pornography, drug trafficking, cyber-attacks, etc.), or even legislation that establish arbitrary mechanisms to filter, block and remove content from the net.

All those provisions are rather reprehensible, as they not only jeopardize the fundamental rights to privacy and freedom of expression of citizens, but also pose a threat to some of the key elements of the network architecture, such as neutrality and openness. Meanwhile, though developed countries have already established a legal framework for the Internet, the movement in Latin America is still recent. Such context provides more room for reflection, as the criticism of previous foreign legislation can be educational on what went wrong in those experiences and lead to a more balanced perspective on how to avoid the same pitfalls and at the same time guarantee that freedom-related issues will be taken into account with a regional perspective.

At this point in time, in which Latin American countries are beginning to regulate the internet, this chapter aims to explore recent legislation, court decisions and Internet policies in Brazil, Argentina, Chile, Colombia, Mexico and Venezuela,[8] focusing on filtering and content removal cases. It will attempt to evaluate whether the most recent approaches have been consistent with the guaranteed protection of the right to freedom of expression. The chapter is organized into five sections: (I) a brief analysis of the meaning of filtering and the fine line that separates it from violation of freedom of expression; (II) a brief overview of studies on the current situation of online freedom of expression in these countries and future trends; (III) analysis of the legal provisions of these countries concerning (1) universal and (2) neutral access to the Internet's infrastructure, as well as (3) access to content and their impact on filtering practices; (IV) filtering and Internet Service Providers liability; and (V) conclusion.

The Meaning of Filtering

Just as the advances in technology have led to an unprecedented and immeasurable access to information, technical innovations also provide ways of controlling the flow of information in the networks. It is necessary to take into account that part of this control has been driven by the need to maintain and improve the quality and security of services in the network, such as screening out spam and viruses. Thus, the key question is: to what extent is it possible to allow such control in the flow of information in order to guarantee both the well-functioning of the network and the protection of fundamental rights? Nonetheless, if it is true that efforts are being made to use technology to block content that is considered unwanted, a second question, as important as the first one, would be: what is 'unwanted' content?

A UNESCO report called *Freedom of Connection, Freedom of Expression: The Changing Legal and Regulatory Ecology Shaping the Internet* addresses this problem. As information and communication flows online, it may use several Internet related protocols and pass through various points in the Internet network until it reaches the user's access devices. Taking this into

8 We have selected these six countries because they are the top six in the list of countries by nominal GDP in Latin America (1st Brazil, 2nd Mexico, 3rd Argentina, 4th Venezuela, 5th Colombia and 6th Chile). At first, the selection included only five countries. Chile was added to the list because it was the first country to approve a network neutrality law. Cuba was also an interesting option for the subject, but it had to be excluded due to the lack of data available. Even though all the countries will be analyzed, the current version of this essay contains more information on Brazil, given the nationality of the authors.

consideration, the mentioned Report indicates that the most common points at which filtering practices can be applied include:[9]

> Gateways to the Internet backbone: State-directed implementation of filtering and blocking technologies may be carried out at the backbone level, which constitutes the foundation of the network, such as international gateways in order to eliminate access to certain content throughout an entire country.
> Internet Service Providers: There is a dangerous tendency to have ISPs filter illegal or immoral content, or prevent search results from specified websites. These providers also filter spam and attempt to prevent infection by malware for reasons of stability and user protection.
> Institutions: Companies, libraries, schools etc. can filter content on the basis of their own criteria and for their own purposes, and/or on the basis of guidelines from state authorities.
> Individual Computers: Each person may install filtering software on their own computer to restrict the ability to access certain content and/or protect their safety.
> Law Enforcement: Actions are also taken against users who engage in practices that are considered illegal on the network, such as fraud, unlawful sharing of music etc.

Therefore, Internet content can be regulated through those technical approaches implemented at different levels of access to the network. The UNESCO report seeks to find out precisely whether the content regulations have clear and reasonable limits for a potential filtering method and whether the filtering methods have taken into consideration at least the legal provisions, or have instead been developed to influence culture and politics by determining which content should be controlled, consumed or produced, promoting excuses such as censorship of political speech, abusive protection of copyright, etc.

Finally, it is important to highlight that filtering techniques are not precise, i.e., it is almost impossible to block specific content without affecting others. However, many of the mechanisms used to regulate and censor information are increasingly more sophisticated and sometimes use many layers of control, which are often hidden from the common user, who will probably not even notice that the information is being filtered. So there are questions that still remain unanswered: Is filtering really necessary? If so, under which circumstances? What content should be controlled and in which way? What is the adequate level of transparency? The balance between the technical need of filtering practices, the political and social need and the respect for freedom of expression are the topics we intend to approach in our analysis of the policies, laws, court decisions and practices of the six selected countries.

Brief Overview of Freedom of Expression in Latin America: Recent studies and future trends

Among many reports on freedom of expression on the internet, some conclusions can be reached when focused specifically on the Latin American region.

Freedom House, in collaboration with the United Nations Democracy Fund (UNDEF), has released a report entitled 'Freedom on the Net, a Global Assessment of Internet and Digital

9 Adapted from Dutton, William H., Dopatka, Anna, Hills, Michael, Law, Ginette and Nash, *Victoria, Freedom of Connection – Freedom of Expression: The Changing Legal and Regulatory Ecology Shaping the Internet* (November 29, 2010): 28–29, http://ssrn.com/abstract=1654464.

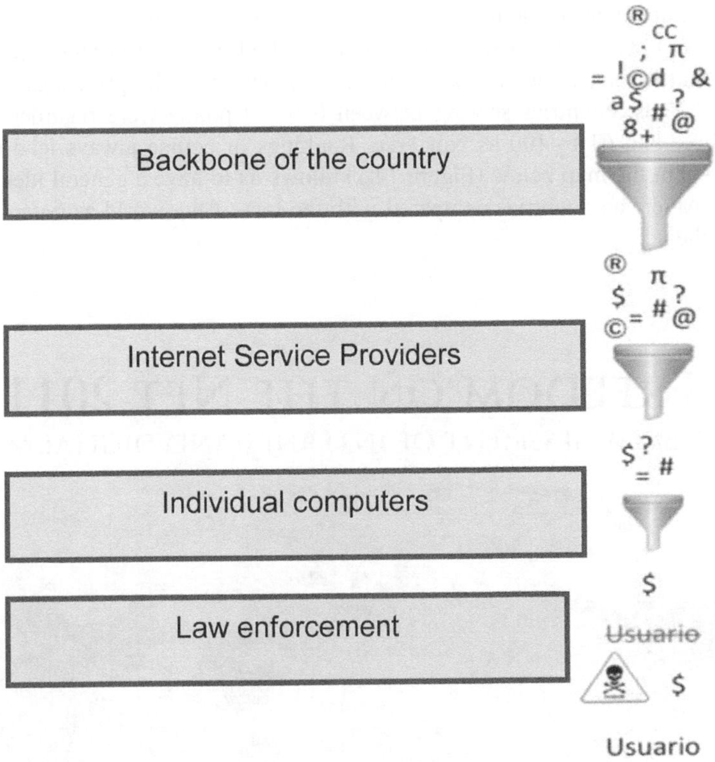

Figure 14.1 Where Filtering Methods can be Applied

Source: Prepared by the authors based on the UNESCO report[10]

Media'.[11] Covering the period from January 1, 2009 to December 31, 2010, it comprised a series of interviews and surveys divided into the following thematic groupings:

- Obstacles to Access: including infrastructural and economic barriers.
- Limits on Content.
- Violations of User Rights: including legal protections and restrictions on online activity; surveillance and limits on privacy and prosecution of online activity.

The answer to each question received a score from 0 (best) to 100 (worst) allowing for comparative analysis among the countries surveyed. The report is based on the definition of freedom of expression provided by article 19 of the Universal Declaration of Human Rights. Accordingly, the project evaluates the freedom of transmission and exchange of news and other politically relevant communications, as well as the protection of user's rights to privacy and freedom to express their ideas on the net from both legal and extra-legal repercussions arising from their online activities.

10 Ibid.

11 Sanja Kelly and Sarah Cook (eds), 'Freedom on the Net: a Global Assessment of Internet and Digital Media' (Freedom House, 18 April 2011) <http://www.freedomhouse.org/sites/default/files/FOTN2011.pdf> accessed 29 June 2012.

The project considers that freedom of expression may only be restricted in some strictly defined circumstances, and provided that such restrictions are both transparent and implemented in line with international human rights standards, the rule of law, and the principles of necessity and proportionality. Thus, countries scoring between 0 to 30 points were regarded as Free, 31 to 60 as Partly Free and 61 to 100 as Not Free. Rankings of course always lead to questionable generalizations, but the map below (Figure 14.2) allows us to have a general idea of the position of some Latin American countries compared with the rest of the world as regarding freedom of expression on the net.

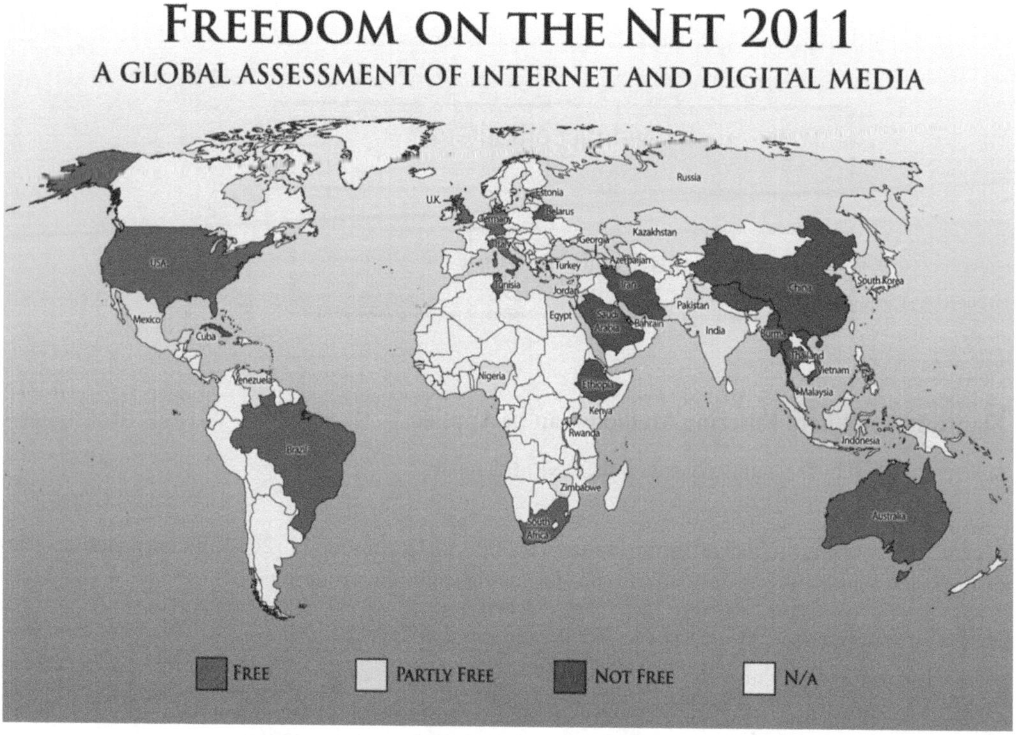

Figure 14.2 Global Assessment of Internet and Digital Media

Source: Freedom on the Net 2011, Global Assessment of Internet and Digital Media, Freedom House, http ://www.freedomhouse.org/sites/default/files/FOTN2011.pdf.

As the map indicates, from the Latin American countries, Freedom House's investigation only includes Brazil, Mexico, Venezuela and Cuba. Only Cuba is identified as a Not Free country, while Mexico and Venezuela show some restrictions to freedom and Brazil respects the possible limits to freedom of expression. The law in force in these countries is compared with the laws and practices of other countries, such as China, Iran, Saudi Arabia and Cuba (which are known to be extremely repressive with respect to this issue, approaching 100 points and equating this score with totally unacceptable limits; this has led to some criticism as to what can actually be considered a free country in the ranking).

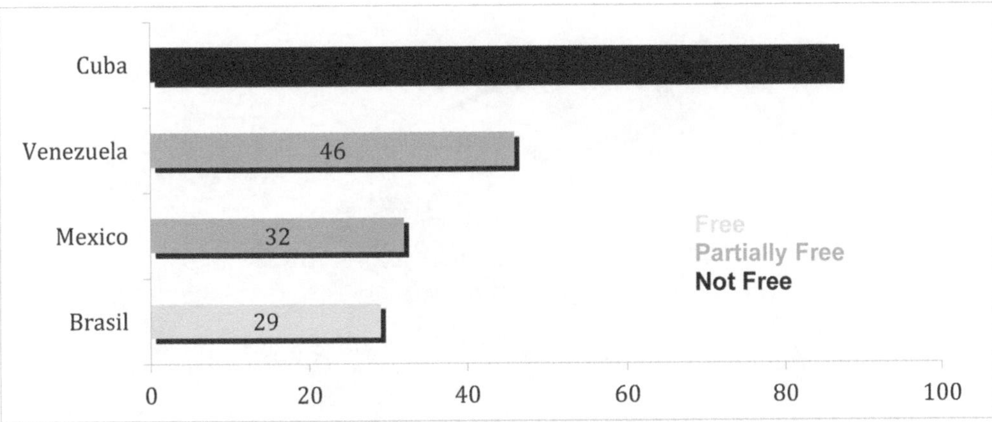

Figure 14.3 Online Freedom of Expression in Latin America

Source: Freedom on the Net 2011, Global Assessment of Internet and Digital Media, Freedom House

Figure 14.3 shows the scores of each of the Latin American countries that were included in the report, revealing significant differences between the scores of Brazil, Mexico and Venezuela. With a less complex methodology, but based on a survey of empirical cases of censorship on the net, Reporters Without Borders also published a report in March 2011 where, among the Latin American countries, Cuba was identified as an enemy of the Internet and Venezuela as a country under surveillance, as shown in the map below (Figure 14.4).

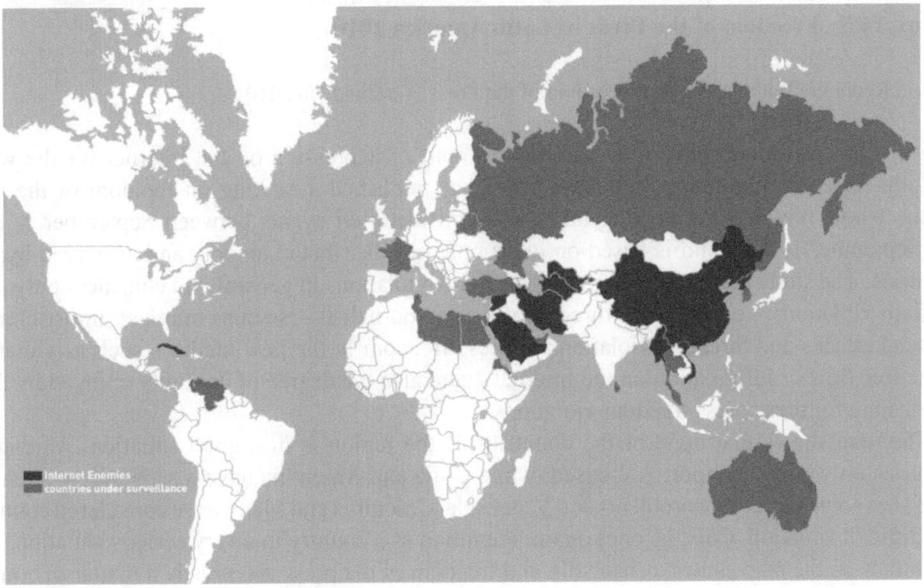

Figure 14.4 Internet Enemies 2011

Source: Reporters Without Borders for Press Freedom, Internet Enemies, March 2011, http://12mars.rsf.org/i/Internet_Enemies.pdf.

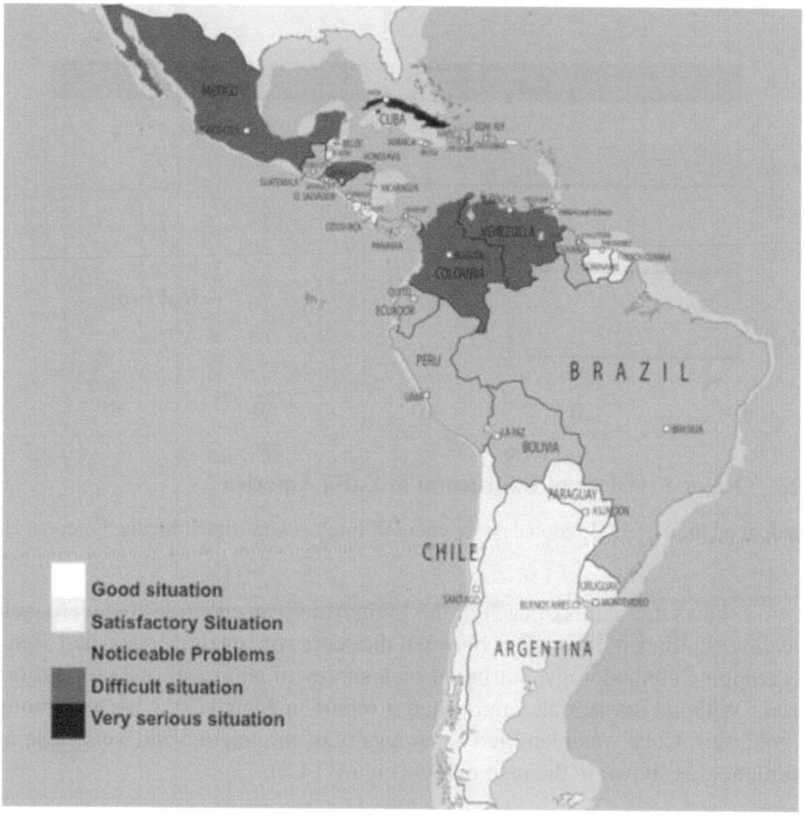

Figure 14.5 Freedom of the Press in Latin America 2010

Source: Reporters Without Borders, Freedom of the Press Worldwide in 2010

Even though we do not have final data on freedom of expression on the Internet for the whole of Latin America, Reporters Without Borders has published a ranking on freedom of the press for the whole region. This ranking takes into consideration events between September 1, 2009 and September 1, 2010 and is based on questionnaires distributed among, and answered by, 178 countries. The study does not address human rights violations in general and considers only press freedom violations, i.e. violations directly affecting journalists – such as murders, imprisonment, physical attacks and threats – violations to press freedom in the new media – such as violations of the free flow of information on the Internet – and also the degree of impunity enjoyed by those responsible for these press freedom violations.

The map shows that none of the countries of the region is in a good situation. Among the countries on which the report is focused, while Chile and Argentina have a satisfactory situation, Brazil has some noticeable problems and Venezuela, Colombia and Mexico are considered countries in a difficult situation. Cuba is, once again, identified as a country in a very serious situation.

In fact, as the map shows, censorship and freedom of the press are already a matter of concern in the region. As the region increases its Internet penetration rates in the population, we should be watchful to avoid that such a critical profile be extended to all the other spaces of freedom of expression, which go beyond freedom of the press.

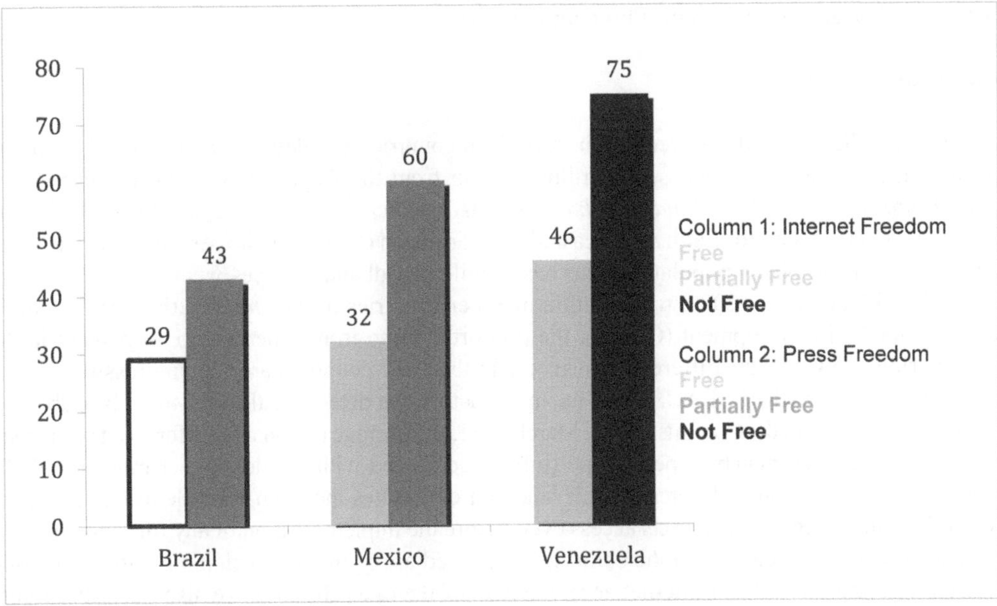

Figure 14.6 Freedom of Expression on the Internet vs. Freedom of the Press in some Latin American Countries

Source: Freedom on the Net 2011, Global Assessment of Internet and Digital Media, Freedom House

In this sense, interestingly enough, Freedom House's investigation compares its freedom of expression on the net rates with another study which applied a similar methodology but dealt only with freedom of the press. Figure 14.5 highlights that there is a considerable difference in the performance of those countries on the rates of the two studies, with censorship to freedom of the press attaining even more concerning numbers. As the digital divide is bridged and the press activities and flow of information increasingly depend on the net, the question remains whether those high rates of press repression may potentially pose a threat to the future of online freedom of expression in the region. We should keep in mind and closely watch this possible trend to prevent it from becoming a reality.

It is also important to add that the mere absence of investigations about freedom of expression on the Internet including complete data for all the Latin American countries is already worrisome per se. Even though other regions of the world have inspired greater concern in this regard given the existence of serious violations to human rights, we should not ignore what has happened and what may happen in the future of the Internet in Latin America, particularly in the current context of redefinition of the regulatory frameworks for the Internet in the region.

Analysis of Legal Provisions on Filtering Practices

Universal Access Policies

Bridging the digital divide between Latin American countries and developed countries is still one of the region's major challenges. According to data from the Regional Broadband Observatory (*Observatorio Regional de Banda Ancha* or ORBA), which was launched in May 2011 by the Economic Commission for Latin America and the Caribbean (ECLAC), the percentage of the Latin American and Caribbean population who has mobile broadband services went from 0.2 percent in 2005 to 4.7 percent in 2009, while within member countries of the Organization for Economic Cooperation and Development (OECD), the proportion rose from 5 percent to 49 percent in the same period. However, the differences in access in the same countries are also impressive.

Still according to the ECLAC, one of the main factors that determine the take-up of broadband is its price. According to the Commission, in March 2011, the average regional price for fixed broadband was 72.8 dollars per megabyte per second (mbps), compared with 5.9 dollars per mbps in OECD countries, which is a huge difference. This situation constitutes the main obstacle to free access to network content, because it restricts access even before the implementation of any filtering method.

Faced with this situation, all the countries examined are trying to develop regulations focused on guaranteeing the right to Internet access. Some of them, as Brazil, have also been discussing regulations to improve quality of access, concerning quality patterns for broadband to the telecommunications services. Establishing the right to access is indeed a priority issue, whether analysing laws that have recently entered into effect or bills that are still being debated. It is worth highlighting that there is still little competition among Latin American Internet Access Providers, which is a common consequence of a not always very well conducted privatization processes or of the existence of state monopoly providers. Therefore, government strategies to expand access can sometimes be contradictory, with some allowing too much leeway to the Internet Service Providers while not properly facing the monopoly situation.

In addition to these technical and economic issues that prevent universal access to the net, there are also economic interests from telecom companies, as access providers, to bypass the principle of net neutrality, topic addressed in a separate section.

Network Neutrality

Even though net neutrality is actually a technical concept concerning network administration, the principle of net neutrality clearly interferes with the access to content and may also, although it isn't its primary objective, protect freedom of speech when dully guaranteed. To analyse how the network neutrality principle has been implemented and debated in different countries, we will first briefly describe its general meaning and the basic problem to which this principle refers; then, we will present a comparative chart of how the principle was applied or is being discussed in the different countries included in this study; and finally, we will provide a comparative analysis of the alternatives.

Network neutrality is a principle of network architecture that establishes that all Internet data must be treated equally, i.e. without favouring any application, content or service provider.[12] Thus, it is possible to ensure the free flow of information, without discrimination on the grounds of origin, destination, protocol or content. To implement this principle, Internet Access and Service

12 Barbara van Schewick, 'Towards an Economic Framework for Network Neutrality Regulation' (2007) 5 *Journal on Telecommunications and High Technology Law* 329.

Providers must transport data packets in a neutral manner, without favouring certain contents and disfavouring others.[13] While Internet service providers have no general incentive to discriminate against data packets that are carried through their networks,[14] several studies have shown that access providers have discriminated against traffic at least for three reasons: to increase their own profit, to manage bandwidth on their network or to exclude content that is contrary to the company's policies.[15]

Network neutrality is frequently threatened by a provider who signs commercial agreements to favour or degrade certain content, based on its commercial interests or relationships. This may happen, for example, with Voice over IP (VOIP) services that may directly compete with an Internet Access Provider that also offers telephone services. Or when an Access Provider is also a cable TV company and feels threatened by certain online video content, so it slows down the speed at which those packets are delivered. Moreover, on the pretext of managing traffic, providers may also discriminate against packets and establish other tiers of quality for a certain service, to the detriment of others, including the charge of a higher fee, as if imposing a toll on certain types of content, such as more expensive plans to have higher-speed connections specifically for video packets. Some argue that competition policies would ensure that even though providers do not respect network neutrality, users could still choose those that offer the services they need for the fairest price. Truth is, however, that in our countries, in light of what has been explained in the previous section regarding infrastructure and access, and given the lack of transparency in traffic management, there is no level of competition that can guarantee the consumer rights of users. Therefore, the purpose of the network neutrality principle is to guarantee the right of Internet users to access the content, services and applications and to avoid the inappropriate blocking or filtering of content for political or economic reasons, among others.

With respect to these issues, Chile was the first country in the world to approve a specific law about the subject. Despite this fact, the USA had already established general rules on network neutrality in 2004, which were laid down by their telecommunications regulatory entity, the Federal Communications Commission (FCC). The FCC's statement established the guiding principles of the telecommunications industry, based on the four freedoms that constitute the central core of any future laws on neutrality. These are:

> (a) consumers should have access to their choice of legal content. (b) [should be entitled to] run the applications of their choice. (c) attach any devices they choose [to their broad band Internet access service] and (d) should receive meaningful information regarding their service plans.[16]

To visualize how a significant part of the FCC rules and of the Chilean law has influenced the legislative proposals of the countries examined, we have prepared the following chart (3.1). The first three columns of the chart deal with the laws and legislative proposals of Argentina, Chile and

---

13 Tim Woo and Cristopher S Yoo, 'Keeping the Internet Neutral?: Tim Wu and Christopher Yoo Debate' < http://papers.ssrn.com/sol3/papers.cfm?abstract_id=953989> accessed 29 June 2012.

14 If users foreseen freedom to access content and services as a value added factor, the bigger the freedom, the higher will be the value of the product and, as a result, users would migrate to the ISP that would provide more services.

15 Barbara van Schewick and David Farber, 'Point/Counterpoint: Network Neutrality Nuances' in (2009) 52 Viewpoints 31 < http://www.thei3p.org/docs/events/WESIINetNeutrality2.pdf> accessed 29 June 2012.

16 Federal Communications Commission, 'Notice of Proposed Rulemaking 09-93' < http://hraunfoss.fcc.gov/edocs_public/attachmatch/FCC-09-93A1.pdf> accessed 16 August 2011.

Table 14.1 Comparative Table of Legislations and Legislative Proposals about Network Neutrality in Argentina, Brazil, Chile, Colombia, Mexico and Venezuela

Chile	Argentina	Colombia	Brazil	Mexico	Venezuela
Law No. 18168 of 2010 Section 24 H. – Concessionaires of the telecommunications public utility providing services to Internet Access Providers together with these providers (in the understanding that Internet Access Providers shall make reference to any natural or artificial person providing commercial connectivity services between users or their Internet networks): a) May not arbitrarily block, interfere with, discriminate against, hinder or restrict the right of any Internet user to use, send, receive or offer any legal content, application or service on the Internet, or any kind of legal Internet activity or use. In this sense, they shall offer to each user the service of Internet access or connectivity to the Internet Access Provider, as applicable, which may not make an arbitrary distinction between content, applications or services on the basis of the origin or ownership thereof, according to the relevant Internet connection configuration as per the contract in force with the users.	Argentine House of Representatives Bill 1159-D-2011 SECTION 1. – Internet Service Providers, which comprise any natural or artificial person providing commercial connectivity services between users or their Internet networks, and any companies providing connectivity to Internet Access Providers: a) May not arbitrarily block, interfere with, discriminate against, slow down or restrict the use, sending, receipt or offer or any legal content, application or service on the Internet by any user of this service, or any other kind of legal Internet activity or use.	Law No. 1450 of 2011 Section 56. Neutrality on the Internet. Internet Service Providers. 1. Internet Service Providers may not, notwithstanding the provisions of Law No. 1336 of 2009, block, interfere with, discriminate against or restrict the right of any Internet user to use, send, receive or offer any lawful content, application or service on the Internet. In this sense, they shall offer to each user Internet access or connectivity, which may not make an arbitrary distinction between content, applications or services on the basis of the origin or ownership thereof. Internet Service Providers may make offers according to the needs of the market segments or their users based on their use and consumption profiles, and this shall not be understood as discrimination.	Bill – Internet Civil Framework (Marco Civil da Internet) Section 10. The person responsible for the transmission, switching or routing of Internet traffic as the duty to treat data packets in an isonomic way, regardless of their content, origin and the use of the service, terminal or application, and it is forbidden to establish any kind of traffic discrimination or degradation other than that which would constitute a technical resource necessary to provide appropriate services, in accordance with the regulations issued by the National Telecommunications Agency (ANATEL) about the guarantee of network neutrality and its preservation.	Bill to amend the Federal Telecommunications Law (Ley Federal de Telecomunicaciones) Section 44 XVI. Where public telecommunication network concessionaires provide Internet access, whether land or mobile-based, they shall ensure unrestricted network traffic and shall abstain from blocking, discriminating against, hindering or restricting the right of users to access, read, send, receive, hire or offer any lawful content, service or application.	None

In any case, concessionaires of the telecommunications public utility and Internet Access Providers may take any measure or action that may be necessary for purposes of traffic management and network administration, within the exclusive area of activity that has been authorized to them, provided the above is not intended to conduct actions that affect or may affect fair competition. Concessionaires and IAPs shall endeavour to preserve the privacy of the users, safeguard their users against viruses and ensure security on the network. Additionally, they may block access to certain content, applications or services, only upon express request of the users and at their expense. Under no circumstance may this block arbitrarily affect providers of Internet services and applications. b) Such concessionaires and Internet Access Providers may not limit the right of users to add or use any kind of instruments, devices or equipment on the network, provided they are legal and do not harm or adversely affect the network or the quality of the service.	b) Internet Service Providers and companies providing connectivity to Internet Access Providers may not limit the right of users to add or use any kind of instruments, devices or equipment on the network, provided they are legal and do not harm or adversely affect the network or the quality of the service. c) Internet Service Providers and companies providing connectivity to Internet Access Providers may take any measure or action that may be necessary for purposes of traffic management and network administration, within the exclusive area of activity that has been authorized to them, provided the above is not intended to conduct actions that affect or may affect fair competition. Additionally, they may block access to certain content, applications or services, only upon express request of the users and at their expense. Under no circumstance may this block arbitrarily affect providers of Internet services and applications.	2. Internet Service Providers may not limit the right of users to add or use any kind of instruments, devices or equipment on the network, provided they are legal and do not harm or adversely affect the network or the quality of the service. 3. Internet Service Providers shall offer to the users parental control services for content that is against the law, and shall provide users with clear information, in advance, regarding the scope of such services. 4. Internet Service Providers shall publish on their website information about the Internet access offered, the speed and quality of the service, making a distinction between national and international connections, and shall include information about the nature and guarantees of the service. 5. Internet Service Providers shall implement mechanisms to preserve the privacy of the users, protect them against viruses and ensure security on the network.	Single paragraph. In the provision of an Internet connection, whether as a free service or for a price, it is forbidden to monitor, filter, analyse or supervise the content of data packets, except in the cases expressly admitted by law. ANATEL's Rules and Regulations Section 59. Internet Access Providers are precluded from blocking or according a discriminatory treatment to traffic of any kind, such as voice, data or video, regardless of the technology used. § 1° The prohibition put forth on this article's caput does not impede adoption of traffic blocking or managing when these prove indispensable for maintaining network and service safety, and stability.	Internet Access Providers that are not concessionaires but make use of a public telecommunication network shall also abide by the provisions in this paragraph.	

Chile	Argentina	Colombia	Brazil	Mexico	Venezuela
c) Concessionaires and Internet Access Providers shall offer, at the expense of the users requesting it, parental control services for content that is against the law, ethics or moral conventions, provided the user receives clear information, in advance, regarding the scope of such services. d) Concessionaires and Internet Access Providers shall publish on their website information about the Internet access offered, its speed and the quality of the connection, making a distinction between national and international connections, and shall include information about the nature and guarantees of the service. The user may request that the concessionaire or Internet Access Provider, as applicable, deliver such information at its own expense, in writing and within a 30-day term as from the relevant request.	SECTION 2.- All ISPs shall publish on their website information about the Internet access offered, its speed (both uploading and downloading speed), and quality of the connection, making a distinction between national and international connections, and shall include information about the nature and guarantees of the service. Bill S-1491/11 Section 1. – Telecommunications service providers and Internet Access Providers may not block, interfere with, discriminate against, hinder or restrict the right of any Internet user to use, send, receive or offer any legal content, application or service on the Internet, or any kind of legal Internet activity or use. No hierarchy or priority in the Internet information or services may be established. The quality of the service offered may not be impaired by any traffic management measures adopted. Users may have access to all the content without the intermediation of Internet Access Providers.	6. Internet Service Providers shall block access to certain content, applications or services, only upon express request of the users. Paragraph. The Communications Regulatory Commission (Comisión de Regulación de Comunicaciones) shall regulate the terms and conditions for the implementation of the provisions of this section. The initial regulation shall be issued within six months following the entry into force of this law.	§ 2° The criteria for the blocking or managing of traffic presented on §1° of this article must be previously informed to all subscribers and broadcasted to all who might be interested, including publications at the Providers' website. § 3° The blocking or managing of traffic must respect the Subscribers' privacy, communications sigil and free and wide competition.		

	Section 2. – Telecommunication service providers shall offer to each user the service of Internet access or connectivity to the provider, which may make no arbitrary distinction between content, applications or services. Section 3. – Telecommunications service and Internet Access Providers may take any measure that may be necessary for purposes of traffic management and network administration, exclusively within the area that has been authorized to them, provided the above does not affect fair competition.				

Colombia, and are filled with the same colour because of the strong influence of the Chilean law. Brazil and Mexico have adopted different approaches and are therefore identified with other colors.

As a supplement to the previous analysis, Table 3.2 shows how the general principles laid down in the regulations issued by the Federal Communication Commission influenced the different regulation models for network neutrality in the region. Following, Table 3.3 provides a comparative view of the regulatory panorama on the six countries.

Table 14.2 Comparative Table of FCC's Basic Freedom Models for Network Neutrality and the Legislation and Legislative Proposals of Chile, Argentina, Colombia, Brazil, Mexico and Venezuela

FCC's Basic Freedoms for Network Neutrality	Chile	Argentina	Colombia	Brazil	Mexico	Venezuela
Freedom of access to any legal content	Section 24, H, a).	Bill 1159-D-2011, section 1, a).	Law No. 1450 of 2011, section 56, 1.	Bill – Internet Civil Framework, section 10, heading.	Bill to amend the Federal Telecommunications Law, section 44.	None*
		Bill S-1491/11, section 1.		ANATEL's Rules and Regulations, section 59, heading.		
Freedom to run any legal application	Section 24, H, a).	Bill 1159-D-2011, section 1, a).	Law No. 1450 of 2011, section 56, 1.	Bill – Internet Civil Framework, section 10, heading.	Bill to amend the Federal Telecommunications Law, section 44.	None
		Bill S-1491/11, section 1.		ANATEL's Rules and Regulations, section 59, heading.		
Freedom to connect any device which does not interfere with the operation of the network (Carterfone)	Section 24, H, b).	Bill 1159-D-2011, section 1, b).	Law No. 1450 of 2011, section 56, 2.	Not included in a specific neutrality provision.[2]	Not included in a specific neutrality provision.	None
				Not included in a specific neutrality provision**.		
Access to thorough information about service plans (transparency)	Section 24, H, d).	Bill S-1491/11, section 2.	Law No. 1450 of 2011, section 56, 4.	Bill – Internet Civil Framework, section 8, IV.	Not included in a specific neutrality provision.	None
				ANATEL's Rules and Regulations, section 59, paragraph 2.		

* See n 16. ** The fact that this freedom is not contemplated in a specific neutrality provision does not mean that it may not be provided for in another rule.

Table 14.3 Comparative Table of other Key Issues in the Legislations and Legislative Proposals of Chile, Argentina, Colombia, Brazil, Mexico and Venezuela

	Chile	Argentina	Colombia	Brazil	Mexico	Venezuela
Is there an exception to the neutrality principle for purposes of technical or security management?	Yes. Section 24, H, a).	Bill 1159-D-2011 Yes. Section 1, c.	No.	Yes. Section 10, heading.	No.	Not applicable
		Bill S-1491/11 Yes. Section 3.		Yes. Section 59, paragraph 2.		
Are providers obliged to provide parental control services at the request of users?	Yes. Section 24, H, a).	Bill 1159-D-2011 Yes. Section 1, c.*	Yes. Section 56, 3.	No.	No.	Not applicable
		Bill S-1491/11 No.		No.		

* The section in question does not contemplate the possibility of having the user request a security block from the provider.

Content Regulation

Although access to the Internet has only recently been the object of debate in the laws of the Latin American countries in question, these legal provisions do not ensure unrestricted access to the content on the Web. Provisions regarding network neutrality do not guarantee such access, either, as they leave a space for legal restrictions to be applied. Therefore, it is important to explore what types internet content regulation are being tackled by legislators in the region. First, we need to examine the general freedom of expression guarantees; then, we need to find out what the legal restrictions are and whether these are compatible with the minimum restrictions acceptable for the specific legal system.

Frank La Rue – the UN Special Rapporteur on freedom of expression – in his report about the promotion and protection of the right to freedom of expression on the Internet, prepared after a series of consultations and meetings held throughout the world, explains that a restriction to online content could be imposed as an exceptional measure 'if it passes a three-part, cumulative test',[17] namely:

- it must be provided by law, which is clear and accessible to everyone;
- it must be proven as necessary and the least restrictive means required to achieve the purported aim (principles of necessity and proportionality);
- it must pursue one of the purposes set out in article 19, paragraph 3, of the International Covenant on Civil and Political Rights.[18]

Strictly speaking, article 19 of the International Covenant on Civil and Political Rights is one of the most important provisions that should be borne in mind when addressing the issue of filtering and how it should be articulated with freedom of expression. Paragraphs 2 and 3 thereof state:

> 2. Everyone shall have the right to freedom of expression; this right shall include freedom to seek, receive and impart information and ideas of all kinds, regardless of frontiers, either orally, in writing or in print, in the form of art, or through any other media of his choice.
> 3. The exercise of the rights provided for in paragraph 2 of this article carries with it special duties and responsibilities. It may therefore be subject to certain restrictions, but these shall only be such as are provided by law and are necessary:
> (a) For respect of the rights or reputations of others;
> (b) For the protection of national security or of public order, or of public health or morals.
>
> That is to say, freedom of expression is not an absolute right and may be subject to legal restrictions provided they are very specific and only to the extent necessary to meet the requirements mentioned before. Additionally, the UN Special Rapporteur holds that any legislation involving these restrictions must be applied by a body that is independent of any political, commercial or other unwarranted influences in a manner that is neither arbitrary nor discriminatory; and even so, there should be adequate safeguards against the abusive application of restrictions.

---

17 La Rue, Frank, Report of the Special Rapporteur on the promotion and protection of the right to freedom of opinion and expression, <http://www2.ohchr.org/english/bodies/hrcouncil/docs/17session/A.HRC.17.27_en.pdf>, accessed 29 June 2012.

18 Idem. Also a valid reference is article 13 of the American Convention on Human Rights, which concerns freedom of thought and expression and prohibits, in its second paragraph, any kind of previous censorship under the same triple test as the one provided in art 19 para 3 of article 19 of the International Covenant on Civil and Political Rights.

Taking these requirements into account, we have developed a critical examination of content regulations in the countries in question,[19] properly divided in three kinds of content that are usually subject to regulation or filtering practices:

a. Regulation of content that is against equality and the reputation of others: racist and xenophobic content, incitement to terrorism or genocide, hate speech, libel, slander and defamation;
b. Regulation of content that violates copyright;
c. Regulation of sexual content.

The purpose was to enquire whether they truly seek to ensure respect for the reputation and the fundamental rights of others, as well as protect national security, public order, health and morals, in a way that is compatible with freedom of expression. Our analysis[20] has demonstrated that the arbitrary use of the law, for example by penalizing legitimate expressions, has caused serious restriction of rights. An analysis of these regulations and considerations about the way in which they have been implemented is of utmost importance. The reason is the following: notwithstanding the efforts undertaken by the countries in question to guarantee the right of access and neutrality on the web, it has fallen upon the courts in Latin America to play an important role in deciding what must be filtered or blocked on the web, together with the ISPs that receive content removal requests. As previously examined, this approach may prove inappropriate and dangerous for freedom of expression.

The chart below (Figure 14.7) displays the information taken from 'Google Transparency Report'[21] and displays the number of requests to remove content in Brazil, Argentina, Mexico, Colombia and Chile. Brazil, for example, is at the top of the list among all Latin American countries where requests for content removal from Google have been made.

According to the information provided by Google, the number of requests for content removal is higher in Brazil mainly because of the popularity of Orkut.[22] Most of them involved allegations of defamation and impersonation. The chart below (3.5) shows the percentage of items removed in Brazil, broken down by reason. According to Google's report, 76 percent of requests were complied with in the second half of 2010; this amounts to 12,363 items removed from the Internet. Among these, most of them were due to infringement of copyright, mainly related to a court order for the removal of 18,000 photos from the photo-sharing website Picasa. In addition 546 removals were related to defamation through content posted mostly at Orkut and YouTube. Other cases are presented in the chart below (Figure 14.7).

19 A full set of comparative tables of country regulations is available in the annexes.

20 For a full analysis of this regulation, please, refer to the original version of this article: 'Filtrado de contenido en America Latina: razones e impactos en la libertad de expresión', in Bertoni, Eduardo (org.), 'Hacia una Internet libre de Censura', <http://www.palermo.edu/cele/pdf/internet_libre_de_censura_libro.pdf>, accessed 29 June 2012.

21 <http://www.google.com/transparencyreport/> accessed 29 June 2012.

22 Orkut is a social network created by Google in 2004. It has been the major social network in Brazil up to 2011 (see http://www.orkut.com.br/Main#MembersAll for demographics).

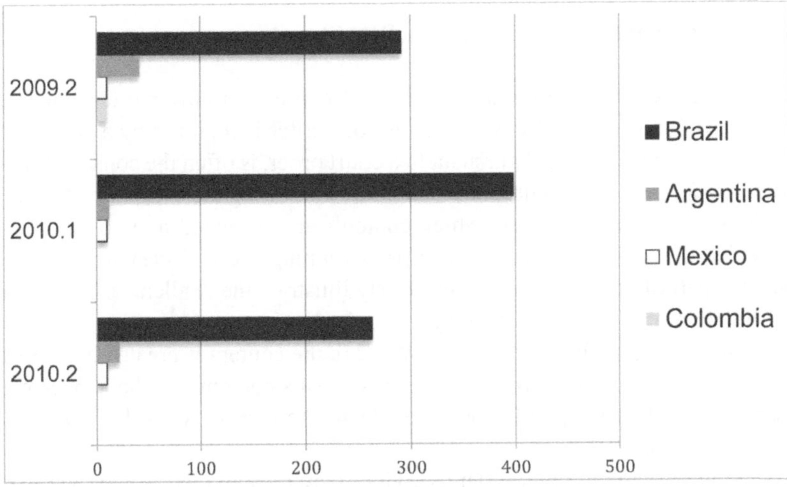

Figure 14.7 Number of Content Removal Requests from Google (Six-month evaluation, from July 2009 to December 2010)

Source: Google Transparency Report, available at http://www.google.com/transparencyreport/

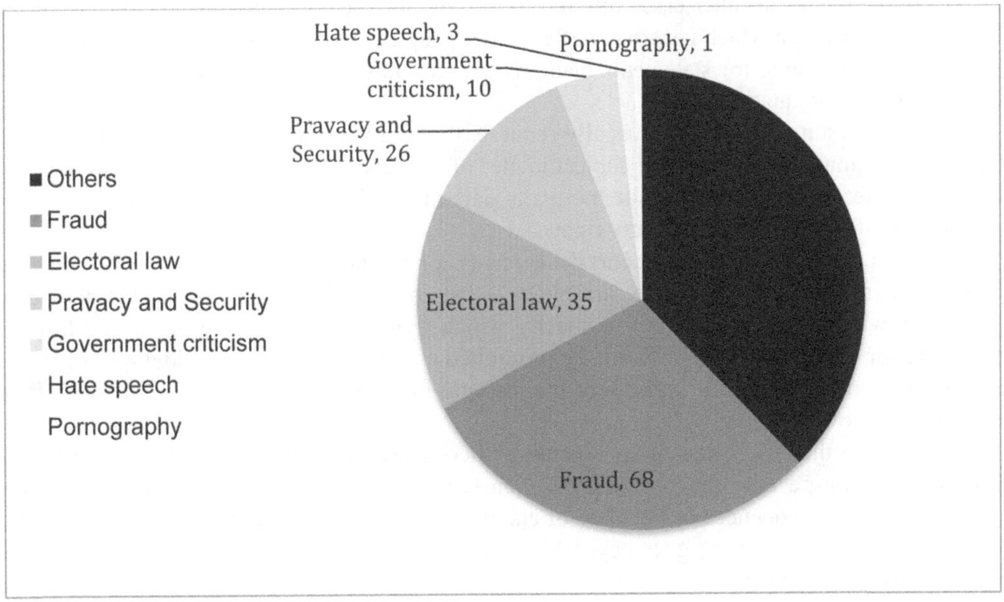

Figure 14.8 Removed items in Brazil, February 2010 (except for copyright)

Source: Data from 'Google Transparency Report'.

Note: These are partial data, as copyright cases are not accounted, because the total amount of such is particularly higher of the other removals and would cause graphic distortions that would render it impossible to make a visible comparison between the categories. The cases represented in the chart did not amount to more than 100 items individually; 11,588 items were removed due to allegations of copyright infringement in Brazil.

Filtering and the Role of the Internet Service Providers[23]

The debate on the effects of filtering and freedom of expression may not leave aside the role of Internet service providers, especially when the use of a filter is required by a court order. Content filtering by ISPs, when implemented pursuant to a court order, is often the consequence of damages suits for compensation and the prohibition to continue exhibiting the content on the web. This part of our analysis will focus on providers which contents are produced in a collaborative way, that is to say, in which the users (and not the company running the website) are responsible for the greater (if not all) part of content. Those sites clearly illustrate the challenges brought about by the protection of freedom of speech and other rights on the Internet.

In such websites, commonly referred to as Web 2.0, the content is created by users themselves, by uploading photographs, videos, music files or texts. This content may have been created by the users and/or be owned by them, and should be adapted to comply with the terms of the content license for that particular website.

Nevertheless, when images, texts and music videos are created by others or when the copyright belongs to a third party – and the use thereof is not contemplated by copyright exceptions and limitations – the authorization must be requested. Lacking an authorization to disclose or in the event of other unauthorized uses of the work, irrespective of the identity of the user that disclosed the unauthorized contents, the individuals or companies exploiting those collaborative websites, i.e. the Internet service providers, might be prosecuted for improper use of such content.

The same applies to other cases referred to in previous sections – involving content outside the scope of copyright which negatively affect other people – regarding the possibility of holding service providers liable for statements made by their users showing prejudice based on gender, ethnicity, sexual orientation etc.

In those lawsuits, the Plaintiff usually requests the judge to award damages and to prohibit the use of the materials that are the subject matter of the proceedings. That prohibition, imposed on the provider operating the website, normally determines that the penalty shall apply to every subsequent infringement of third party rights.

The main difficulty with these court decisions is compounded by the lack of specificity as to how the filtering process should be carried out. Most court decisions only oblige the defendant to comply with the ruling, but fail to specify which terms should be used to put the filter in place, the sort of expression that should be prohibited etc. In the absence of guidelines regarding the methods to be applied to implement the filtering mechanisms, providers are authorized to establish their own criteria.

Even though the lack of specificity regarding filtering criteria is the basic problem, there are at least three other aspects worth considering in connection with filter management, which may help understand the consequences of this type of claim for damages. We may hold that court-ordered filtering (i) is ineffective; (ii) goes beyond the specific limits for which it was sought; and (iii) impairs network neutrality.[24]

---

23 It is important to note that both connection providers and service providers are included under the term ISP. The distinction between them is pretty clear in the Brazilian Draft Bill Proposition on Civil Rights Framework for Internet ('Marco Civil da Internet'), which gives different responsibilities according to the kind of ISP. In this session, we will tackle only the service providers, for we believe connection providers shouldn't have any kind of filtering whatsoever, except for that utterly necessary for technical reasons and for the network maintenance.

24 These three negative effects of filtering mechanisms have already been examined, though from a different perspective, in: Carlos Affonso Pereira de Souza, Pedro de Paranaguá Moniz and Sérgio Branco

Filtering devices are regarded as ineffective because, at the present state of technological development, it is impossible to guarantee with some degree of accuracy that certain content will not be available in collaborative websites. This is because the means used to circumvent filters are simple and constantly updated. Hence, blocking specific materials becomes, in fact, a constant chase after new ways to evade rules and control techniques.

In the case of collaborative websites that, following a judicial resolution, are required to put in place filtering mechanisms, without any indication as to methodology, the individual or company operating the website is charged with the obligation to create the adequate conditions for the content at stake not to be uploaded again by the users of the site. Even though the prohibition may be established in the rules governing the use of the site, under the terms and conditions for use, they are actually rendered effective by means of a source code, i.e. the technological devices which have a strong impact on the effects of the regulation.[25] Even if there is an order requiring the removal of the complete website – as was the case in Brazil, when YouTube was banned for a few hours due to a complaint regarding image rights – there are nevertheless technological means which allow users to access those sites using, for instance, a proxy server[26] and thus, circumventing filtering regulations.

Besides, it is important to underscore that the prohibition that stops certain websites from showing specific content does not prevent other sites from exhibiting the same content, even outside the scope of the country's jurisdiction. As a result, the damage inflicted by the online presence of unwanted material is not eliminated. This is precisely the third test suggested by Lawrence Lessig in the decision issued in Napster's case:[27] how effective would it be to file a claim for damages in order to suspend the activity of a file exchange network when the perfect filtering mechanism is not yet available? Users would respond to such court decision by simply migrating to other websites, where the potential damage will continue.

In Brazil, the Court of Justice of the State of São Paulo has had the chance to hear a case in which the company Anima Producciones Audiovisuales Ltda., owner of the copyright to the movie 'Pelé Eterno', which portrays the life and career of the homonymous footballer, filed a claim requesting the removal of the movie clips that were posted on YouTube. According to the case record, more than 100 video clips had already been created by users, some including comments, new images, remixing or mash ups etc. The judgment considered that such practices constituted unlawful uses of the intellectual work.[28] The following is a transcript of the most relevant section of the judgment:

> 5. Based on the foregoing, protection is given in advance and the defendants are required to remove the content from their websites, under the penalty of paying a daily fine of $1,000.00. The pecuniary award shall not be applicable in the case of videos which are already available online, as blocking them would be technically impossible. Therefore, the defendants shall not be liable for the potential dissemination of such content through alternative 'links' in other sites or portals,

---

Vieira Júnior 'Neutralidade da rede, filtragem de conteúdo e interesse público: reflexões sobre o bloqueio do site Youtube no Brasil' (2007) 246 *Revista de Direito Administrativo* 67.

25 See Lawrence Lessig, *Code and other Laws of Cyberspace* (Basic Books 1999).

26 'Brasil Telecom Censura a internet no Brasil bloqueando acesso ao YouTube' available at <http://www.softwarelivre.org/news/8219> accessed 15 August 2011.

27 Lawrence Lessig. Expert Report on *A&M Records Inc vs Naspter Inc*, United States District Court, Northern District of California, June 2000 http://cyber.law.harvard.edu/works/lessig/nap/napd3.doc.html> accessed 28 June 2012).

28 TJSP, Agravo de Instrumento no. 497 958 4/7-00; rel. Des. Testa Marchi; ruled in 13 March 2007.

> including the replacement of the video by third parties in the sites of the defendants, all of the above without prejudice to any award of damages that may be granted.

The lack of a network control center – which in itself is very positive – prevents the adoption of filtering mechanisms that would cover all forms of online content viewing, making it hard to impose liability for videos that may be accessed online[29] through alternative links[30] and which are impossible to block. It is worth pointing out that such decentralization has allowed an unprecedented level of cultural pluralism and freedom of expression in the mass media.

Tim Berners-Lee, considered the 'father' of the World Wide Web, when mentioning the perspectives that could be adopted to build its architecture, noted that:

> Among the market-oriented inspirations and the humanist ideals, we realized that adopting a control perspective would be a wrong decision. The network has been designed in such a way that there is not a single center where users must register their new servers or request authorization to upload new content. Anyone can create a new server or upload new content (...) In technological terms, should there be a point of control, it would rapidly become a bottleneck for the growth of the Internet, which as a result would never reach the intended scale. Its most important trait was to be free from control.[31]

Therefore, we might conclude that orders requiring the implementation of content filtering mechanisms are, as a general rule, not very effective. But even worst, such solutions also have a negative impact on technological development through the Internet.

These effects are especially true when we realize that the filtering tends to go beyond the specific limits for which it was required, as the mechanisms implemented to comply with court orders often end up restricting access to additional content that was not meant to prohibit.[32] For instance, if the filtering mechanisms are based on key-words, other materials which were lawfully inserted in a cooperative website will probably be affected by those restrictions for using the same terminology. The same problem would affect works which have identical or very similar titles. This shows that filtering mechanisms still need to be improved to guarantee a minimum level of safety.

29 Since the prosecution was against Google Brazil Internet Ltda, the request included not only the removal of parts of the film from YouTube, but also the elimination of the website Google Videos, both operated by the defendant.

30 It seems to be consensus within national and international doctrine that the person who creates a link to a certain webpage cannot be responsible for the content you'll find there. This understanding is based mainly on the fact that the targeted page can be changed even though the author is unaware of it. The dynamics of accountability for such a simple behaviour would generate not only a disincentive to make connections between webpages, a common practice, but also monitoring practices not compatible with many activities developed online under the flag of freedom of expression. See also Flip Petillion e Sophie Huart, 'La responsabilité des intermédiaries dans la violation des droits d´auteurs' in Droits Intellectuels: à la rencontre d´une stratégie pour l´entreprise (Bruylant 2002) 553, 577–9.

31 Tim Bernes-Lee, Weaving the Web: The original design and ultimate destiny of the World Wide Web by its inventor (HarperCollins 1999) 99.

32 The blocking of websites that reported Mars space exploration by a NASA car robot is a famous example of inefficient filtering. Most of the filters placed on home computers to control navigation of children prevented access to websites that contain the word 'sex'. In English, joining the words 'Mars' (Mars) and 'Exploration' (Exploration), the result is the word sex, so all the corresponding search results were blocked. See <http://query.nytimes.com/gst/fullpage.html?res=9D00E2D8163BF937A25756C0A9669C8B63> accessed 15 August 2011).

It is interesting to note, as a further proof of the uncomfortable position in which Internet content providers find themselves, that anyone who feels impaired by the undue removal or filtering of content may bring an action to have their work featured on the web once again. In sum, our hypothetical scenario began with only one aggrieved party (the author of a piece of work that is available without the relevant authorization). Then there appeared a second aggrieved party whose problem resulted from the solution adopted to remedy the damage inflicted on the first party, i.e. by the filtering mechanism.

This scenario considerably reduces the chances for innovation on the Internet, as new providers may simply not adopt new business models for fear that they might be held liable for the actions of their users. Regarding copyright infringements, if peer-to-peer network operators were held liable, this could discourage the development of such technology, which clearly has many uses other than the commission of crimes, as was established in the Betamax case.[33]

Finally, and reinforcing the negative effects of filtering mechanisms implemented as a result of legal actions, it may also be observed that in the claims for damages filed in Latin American courts, especially in Brazil, the aggrieved party often brings action against the service provider that hosts the content. As a result of this practice, the provider that operates a collaborative website is under constant threat of further legal actions. It is to be expected that, as a measure to prevent further legal action, service providers will enhance surveillance of content posted on the website by users. Nonetheless, the criteria for assessing harmful material and the rights of third parties are not clear. In the absence of consistent criteria, the provider will probably choose to block the controversial content instead of maintaining it. Such a decision will not only impoverish the content on the website, but will also impose a sort of censorship that determines what may and may not be accessible through the World Wide Web.

With regard to this uncanny situation in which the provider acts as an intermediary between users and the general public, which includes potential victims, Brazilian copyright specialist Ronaldo Lemos mentions that:

> Regarding the intermediary's liability in Brazil, it is surprising that, unlike other countries, no legal criteria have been established for releasing intermediaries from liability or for holding them liable upon notification. Therefore, Internet access providers work under conditions of uncertainty and fear regarding possible court decisions; as a result, they are more likely to remove the content without assessing the legitimacy of the request, since they do not have incentives to act otherwise. It should be noted that there is no 'safe harbor' system in the country that can release the provider from liability by complying with certain requirements'.[34]

As Ronaldo Lemos has further pointed out, 'a large part of the content in the web, though legitimate, has no legal protection at all … by threatening intermediaries, it is likely that content that is legitimate will be removed from the web without further consideration'.[35] In fact, due to these tendencies, a perilous vicious cycle has developed:

---

33 The US Supreme Court decision on Sony Corp. of America v. Universal City Studios, Inc. is often regarded as one the of the most important copyright US case law. According to such decision, the making of individual copies of complete television shows for the single purpose of time shifting is protected under the fair use clause and therefore is not to be regarded as a copyright infringement. (For more information, see: http://en.wikipedia.org/wiki/Sony_Corp._of_America_v Universal_City_Studios,_Inc., accessed 28 June 2012)

34 Ronaldo Lemos. 'Direito', Tecnologia e Cultura (Editora FGV 2005) 125.

35 Ibid.

Based on these trends, it would not be exaggerated to affirm that the future of innovation on the Internet is threatened by the adoption of filtering techniques and claims for damages. This scenario does not encourage new business models or innovation. The balance between the protection of legitimate rights (such as honour, copyright etc.) and the freedom to engage in innovative activities that depend on technology – and which may help guarantee other rights, such as citizenship and freedom of expression – is at risk. It is of utmost importance to bring these themes to discussion, particularly at this stage of Internet regulation in Latin America, in order to guarantee an Internet based on liberty, openness and net neutrality.

Conclusions

Internet content filtering is an issue that is difficult to grasp. While it is true that these mechanisms imply a restriction on freedom of expression, at the same time there are some legal reasons that may support filtering, such as the fight against child pornography. However, these reasons have been used to justify excessive and abusive filtering practices. Thus, arguments of copyright protection and prohibition of defamation have been the basis, in a misguided way, for censorship mechanisms that, despite being categorically banned by international treaties signed by Latin American countries, have been adopted by national governments and companies intending to restrict the free flow of communication in the world wide web.

Even though most of the analyzed countries aren't classified by the main international reports as 'Free Speech Enemies', the region has a history of censoring traditional press, which may indicate a tendency to also censor content on the web. This possibility must be our main concern as the region overcomes the digital gap and begins to regulate network practices and to debate access policies, net neutrality and intermediaries' responsibilities laws.

Indeed, the analysis of implementation of content regulations has shown that even though countries only have specific provisions about filtering in statutes dealing with child pornography, the existing regulation that is not specifically targeted at the Internet has nevertheless been applied to the Web. An example of a threat to freedom of expression is the use of criminal provisions that protect honor as an instrument to filter political content (in Mexico, Venezuela and Colombia, mainly, but also in Brazil). Other reasons for undue filtering are generally related to copyright protection. That's the case, for example, of the lawsuits against service providers that have been addressed in our analysis, especially those against social networks and search mechanisms. Brazil and Argentina[36] are prominent examples of the tendency by users to prosecute the providers (usually in cases of crimes against honour) asking for the removal and filtering of content and, possibly, monetary compensation.

It is important to note that this chapter has mainly used information derived from court orders, because data about intentional filtering undertaken by governments or private entities prior to any request is not available. The absence of this kind of information is even more alarming given the goal to guarantee the observance of the principles of freedom of speech, openness and net neutrality on the net.

For all these reasons, regardless of the argument that justifies the use of a filtering mechanism, ensuring transparency is always fundamental, meaning that the Internet user should always be informed about the usages of filtering mechanisms and its reasons. Note that, as of connection

36 <http://www.google.com/transparencyreport/governmentrequests/AR/?p=2010-12> accessed 12 August 2011.

providers, there should be no possibility of filtering specific content, since they must be guided by the principle of net neutrality when managing the network, abstaining from granting special treatment to any kind of content.

On the other hand, if there's a judicial order for the removal of content, it is important that the user, when trying to access the removed content, be informed that it has been blocked and why it has been blocked. This kind of provision could at least be a part of the judicial orders which, in fact, for eventual lack of judges' technological knowledge, have been determining excessive and abusive removals. To avoid this, the judge must know that if filtering a given content is inevitable, it must be based on objective criteria, with solid standards that minimize the discretion of the person that implements the filtering and require transparency in every step. All in the intent to avoid blockades or filters that go beyond the specific content that should be removed.

Ultimately, the discussion regarding whether a specific content on the Web should be filtered is key to the future of the Web and is also essential for the adoption of regulations that can ensure that its nature and architecture remain free and open. The debate about the decisions made and how they are applied helps us realize how complex this issue is. Furthermore, the same debate provides guidance to understand and evaluate those options that have achieved significant progress towards the control of behaviour and the prevention/compensation of damages resulting from content posted on the Internet.

Internet crimes, privacy, e-commerce and freedom of expression are only a few of the aspects involved in the debate over content filtering on the Web. This broad range of issues reveals how the discussion on filtering mechanisms cuts across different fields of knowledge and affects the way in which we deal with different aspects of law enforcement in the light of technological progress.

Table 14.4 Internet Service Access

		Brazil	Venezuela				Colombia	Argentina	Chile	Mexico
Internet Access Right	Laws	Internet Civil Framework	Decree No. 825 of 2000.	Law on Social Responsibility in Radio, Television and Electronic Media	Constitution of the Bolivarian Republic of Venezuela	Organic Law on Telecommunications (Ley Orgánica de Telecomunicaciones)	Law No. 1341/09.	Decree No. 554/97	Constitutional Reform Project establishes Internet access right.	Bill on Internet users' rights
		PEC 6/11 – Internet access as a constitutional right (Acceso a Internet como Direito Constitucional)								
		Broadband National Plan (Plano Nacional de Banda Larga)					Bill No. 149/Senate		More about the bill here: http://bit.ly/TuhYZB	
	Cases and case law									

		Brazil	Venezuela	Colombia	Argentina		Chile		Mexico
Network Neutrality	Laws	General Telecommunications Law (Lei Geral de Telecomunicações)	Network neutrality in Venezuela	National Development Plan (Plan Nacional de Desarrollo), section 56	Bill No. S-1491/11	Bill No. 1159-D-2011	Law No. 20453.	Network neutrality regulations	About network neutrality in Mexico: http://bit.ly/VfsPZt
		Internet Civil Framework, sections 2, IV; 9 and 12.							Telecommunications Law, (Ley de Telecomunicaciones) section 44.
	Cases and case law								

14.2A Content Regulation

<table>
<tr><th></th><th></th><th>Brazil</th><th colspan="2">Venezuela</th><th colspan="3">Colombia</th><th colspan="2">Argentina</th><th colspan="2">Chile</th><th>Mexico</th></tr>
<tr><td>Hate crimes</td><td></td><td>Racial Crimes Act, sections 1 and 20.
Criminal Code, sections 140 to 141.
Law No. 8.072/90, section 2.
Brazil Constitution, Articles 5, XLII; 3, IV.
Law No. 2889/56, sections 1 and 3.</td><td colspan="2">Law on Social Responsibility in Radio, Television and Electronic Media (Ley de responsabilidad social en radio, televisión y medios electrónicos), section 28.</td><td>National Constitution, Articles 11 et seq.</td><td>Criminal Code, sections 102, 144, 147, 201 et seq.</td><td>Intl. Convention on the Eradication of All Kinds of Racial Discrimination (Convención Internac. sobre la Eliminación de Todas las Formas de Discrimin. Racial.)</td><td>Law No. 23592</td><td>Decree No. 1086/05</td><td>Anti-Terrorism Act (Ley Antiterrorismo)</td><td>Anti-Genocide Act (Ley de Ge-nocidio</td><td>Federal Law to Prevent and Eliminate Discrimination (Ley federal para prevenir y eliminar la discriminación)

Criminal Code</td></tr>
<tr><td></td><td>Cases and case law</td><td>Marcelo Valle Silveira Mello case.
Mayara Petruso case.</td><td>Government investigates blog

Venezuela</td><td>Public prosec investigates website

Colombia</td><td colspan="2">Nicolás Castro case.

Argentina</td><td>Piedad Córdoba case.

Chile</td><td></td><td>Mexico</td><td></td><td></td><td></td></tr>
</table>

Table 14.2A continued

		Brazil			Venezuela		Colombia				Argentina	Chile		Mexico
Child pornography; obscene and sexually explicit material	Laws	Children's Charter (Estatuto de la Niñez), sections 240 to 241-D.	Criminal Code, sections227, 228, 230, 234 and 215	Bill No. 494/08.	Organic Law on the Protection of Children and Adolescents (Ley Orgánica de Protección al Niño, Niña y del Adolescente, LOPNA)	Law on the Protection of Children and Adolescents in Establishments for the Use of Internet, Videogame and other Multimedia Systems (Ley para la Protección del Niño y del Adolescente en Salas de Uso de Internet, Videojuegos y otros Multimed)	Criminal Code, section 218.	Law No. 679 dated August 3, 2001 on Child Abuse and Pornography in Internet, sections 7, 8 and 10.	Law No. 1336 of 2009	Optional Protocol to the Convention on Child Rights (Protocolo Facultativo de la Convención sobre los Derechos del Niño) on children trafficking, child prostitution and use of children in pornography.	Bill No. S-0256/11	Law No. 19927 Bill for the amendment of the Criminal Code and the criminalization of child pornography in virtual media	Bill Against Child Seduction in Virtual Media	Criminal Code, section 202.

	Cases and case law	Operação carrossel	A few years ago, an investigation was carried out in connection with pornographic videos involving adolescents that had been posted in YouTube. The information on the case was silenced after finding out that the videos had been posted by the teenagers involved.	Paul Anthony Brailsford case.	In January 2011, Criminal Court No. 23 of Medellin Circuit Court sentenced Wilson Hernando Daza Duque to 10 years' imprisonment for a pornography crime involving minors. Investigators found out that Daza Duque, a music teacher aged 34, had created an account in social networks with the purpose of contacting minors. He then photographed those minors and threatened them with disclosing their pictures. When this crime was reported, the Investigation Technical Team of the Office of the Attorney General of Colombia searched the teacher's house and detained him. Even though Daza Duque pleaded guilty, his sentence was not reduced because the victims were minors. We are not aware of the existence of any specific laws that prohibit obscene and sexually explicit materials on the Internet.				

Table 14.2A continued

		Brazil				Venezuela	Colombia				Argentina	Chile	Mexico
							Neither are we aware of any general rules on this matter that may be applicable to the Internet environment. Decision T-391-07 of the Constitutional Court analysed the sexually explicit and coarse language used by a radio station and held that: 'The authorities have the power, established by the Constitution, to put in place reasonable and adequate limitations on the social spreading of this kind of language, thereby protecting the rights of third parties. However, this does not mean that they are entitled to hamper their broadcasting through the mass media by censorship.' We understand that, if the Constitutional Court maintains its current regarding case law, this criterion may be applied to obscene and sexually explicit contents on the Internet.						
Intellectual property	Laws	Copyright Law, sections 7, XIII; 33; 41; 101-109.	Law on Software	Decree No. 1355/94	Brazil Constitution, Article 5, XXVII.	Special Law on Information Technology Crimes (Ley Especial contra los delitos informáticos)	Berne Convention.	Law No. 23 of 1982.	World Intellectual Property Organization (WIPO) Copyright Treaty.	WIPO Performances and Phonograms Treaty		Reform of Intellectual Property Law	Mexican Copyright Law (Ley de Derechos Autorales Mexicana)

		Brazil	Venezuela	Colombia				Argentina		Chile	Mexico
	Laws			National Constitution, Article 61 et seq.	Criminal Code, Title VIII.	Common Regime on Copyright and Related Rights (Régimen Común sobre Derechos de Autor y Derechos Conexos.)	Law No. 44 of 1993.				
	Cases			Guillermo Veléz case							
Slander and libel (defamation)	Laws	Criminal Code, sections 138-145. Election Code, sections 324, 325 and 326.	The provisions on crimes against reputation contemplated in the Criminal Code could be applicable.	Criminal Code, section 220 et seq.				Law No. 26551	About Law No. 26551	Criminal Code	Civil Code
	Cases and case law		Noticiero Digital case. Jesús Majano case. Cristian Fuentes case.	Cláudia Lopez case.	Alfredo Molano case.						

Table 14.2A continued

		Brazil	Venezuela			Colombia		Argentina		Chile	Mexico
Slander and libel (defamation)	Laws	Criminal Code, sections 138-145 Election Code, sections 324, 325 and 326	The provisions on crimes against reputation contemplated in the Criminal Code could be applicable.			Criminal Code, section 220 et seq.		Law No. 26551	About Law No. 26551	Criminal Code	Civil Code.
	Cases and case law		Noticiero Digital case.	Jesús Majano case.	Cristian Fuentes case.	Cláudia Lopez case.	Alfredo Molano case.				
General prohibitions	Laws	Bill No. 84/99 – Cybercrimes	General Banking Law (Ley General de Bancos.)			Newsletter N.o 1 Legal Information and Communic-ation Technologies (Tecnologías de la Información y la Comunic., TIC.)	Habeas Data Law.	BILL No. S-0209/09			
	Cases and case law		Parallel dollar case. El Liberal Venezo-lano case								General laws on telecommunica-tions in Mexico.

Table 14.3A Content Blocking, Content Removal, Filtering

		Brazil	Venezuela			Colombia	Argentina	Chile	Mexico
Service blocking based on 2.0 web	Laws								
	Cases and case law	Cicarelli Case	Engineer arrested for his twitter comments	Citizens arrested for express-ing their opinion on twitter	Media commission requests prosecutor's office to investigate internet social networks	The closing, blocking or limitation of the access to certain Internet sites may be ordered in two scenarios: for prevention purposes, in order to stop minors from accessing web pages that might affect their development and education, or at the request of subscribers or users. In cases of child pornography and related crimes, as these are illegal conducts, access blocking is the Internet service provider's obligation and is also a penalty that may be applied by the relevant authorities.	Law No. 25690/02		
Web page blocking	Laws	Bill No. 7439/2010	Law on Social Responsibil-ity in Radio, Television and Elec-tronic Me-dia (Ley de responsabi-lidad social en radio, televisión y medios elec-trónicos.)	Law on the Protection of Children and Adolescents in Establishments for the Use of Internet, Videogame and other Multimedia Systems (Ley para la Pro-tección del Niño y del Adolescente en Salas de Uso de Internet, Videojuegos y otros Multimedias.)		Resolution 1732 of 2007 issued by the Com-munications Regulatory Commission (Comisión de Regulación de Comunicaciones), sections 113 and 114. Decree No. 1524 of 2002, section 6-5. Law 679 of 2001, section 4.			–
			Law on the Protection of Children and Adolescents in Establishments for the Use of Internet, Videogame and other Multimedia Systems.						

Table 14.3A continued

		Brazil	**Venezuela**	**Colombia**	**Argentina**	**Chile**	**Mexico**
Web page blocking	Cases and case law	In general, the cases of content blocking are related to the protection of privacy, or to pain and suffering or property damages caused by contents posted on the Internet. We have no information on specific cases.	The users of the ABA – CANTV (telecommunications company owned by the State of Venezuela) service often (at least one Friday per month) submit complaints because they cannot access certain websites. The most commonly affected sites are blogs hosted in Blogger or WordPress, and the websites Noticiero Digital (www.noticierodigital.com) and Chigüire Bipolar (www.elchiguirebipolar.net.) The government does not acknowledge the existence of any blocking mechanism.	In November 2010, a webpage was closed by the judicial police. At that time, it was reported that a Colombian operation that investigated child pornography had authorized the closing of 5,000 webpages, after finding that photographs and videos were digitally downloaded using Internet connections. Another reported event was Teléfonica-Telecom's blocking of an Internet page known as rapidshare, with a traffic of 60,000 visits, based on 'ethics policies and requirements by the Ministry of Information and Communications Technologies.' Last, in 2010, the Constitutional Court ordered Dejusticia to remove the personal information and references of a girl from its website. In this case, the homosexual partner of the girl's mother wanted to adopt the girl, and the situation was being analysed further to a guardianship suit in which our organization had initiated a citizen intervention action.			
'Notice and Take Down'	Laws	Copyright Law, sections 102-110. Bill No. 84/99. – Cybercrimes	Law on Social Responsibility in Radio, Television and Electronic Media (Ley de responsabilidad social en radio, televisión y medios electrónicos.)				
	Cases and case law			In Colombia, there are no specific legal provisions based on the principle of 'notice and take down.' There is, however, a general application of the 'notice and take down' principle among technicians, based on the widespread practice in the US, and in case that a free trade agreement was signed with that country.			

		Brazil		Venezuela	Colombia	Argentina	Chile	Mexico
Reporting mechanisms	Laws	Private: Safernet;	Public: Federal Public Ministry- Anti-Cybercrime Group.	Public: The Law on Social Responsibility in Radio, Television and Electronic Media (Ley de responsabilidad social en radio, televisión y medios electrónicos) and the National Telecommunications Commission (Comisión Nacional de Comunicaciones, CONATEL.)	There is a series of steps to be followed to report, control and follow up Internet sites with child pornography content. The first step is to report complaints to the units specialized in sexual offences at the prosecutor's office. If the report is sustained, the usual proceedings are initiated at the Investigation Technical Team (Cuerpo Técnico de Investigación, CTI), the division of the prosecutor's office charged with the allocation of cases. The public prosecutor and the relevant commission are appointed to conduct the criminal investigation.			
		National Campaign Against Paedophilia in the Internet.	The Federal Public Ministry is governed by Law No. 75/93.					
	Cases and case law	Safernet admits reports on the following issues: child pornography, racism, advocacy or incitement of crimes against life, xenophobia, neo-Nazism, animal mistreatment, religious intolerance, homophobia and human trafficking. Reports for offensive content may be submitted with the Federal Public Ministry.			Internet Sano, a governmental project with cooperation from the private sector.			

Table 14.3A continued

		Brazil	Venezuela		Colombia		Argentina	Chile	Mexico
Libraries and Internet cafes	Laws		Law on the Protection of Children and Adolescents in Establishments for the Use of Internet, Videogame and other Multimedia Systems (Ley para la Protección de Niños, Niñas y Adolescentes en Salas de Uso de Internet, Videojuegos y otros Multi-medias), sections8 and 10.	Law on the Prohibition of War Videogames and Toys (Ley para la Prohibición de Videojuegos y Juguetes Bélicos.)	Law No. 1336 of 2009, s 4.				
	Cases and case laws								Data on Internet cafes in Mexico. http://bit.ly/V4Glc8

Table 14.4A Licenses and Liability

		Brazil		Venezuela	Colombia	Argentina	Chile	Mexico
ISPs' Liability	Laws	The ISP company may be created as any other legal entity. It must be clearly stated that one of the activities contemplated in the corporate purpose is the provision of access or information services on the web. Should the Internet access service be provided via radio or by means of ADSL technology, a license issued by the National Telecommunications Agency shall be required.	Internet Civil Framework.	Law on Social Responsibility in Radio, Television and Electronic Media (Ley de responsabilidad social en radio, televisión y medios electrónicos.)	Law No. 1341 of 2009, sections 10 and 15			Federal Telecommunications Law (Ley Federal de Telecomunicaciones.)
Browser and content providers' liability	Laws	Internet Legal Framework (Marco Civil da Internet.)	Copyright Law (Lei de Direitos Autorais.)	Law on Social Responsibility in Radio, Television and Electronic Media (Ley de responsabilidad social en radio, televisión y medios electrónicos.)				

Chapter 15

Nanotechnology, Human Rights, Patent Law and the Global South: A Brief Overview

Ana Nordberg

Introduction

Starting from a Global South perspective, this chapter presents a brief overview of the potential of nanotechnology to serve either as vehicle for broader attainability of human rights or to undermine current efforts. Particular attention is drawn to the complex interconnected issues of ensuring even access to the benefits of technological development and the need to maintain adequate levels of economic incentive to innovation. The present chapter begins with a short characterization of nanotechnology followed by the description of the current key fields of scientific research, state of the art and expectations for the future. The second part explores the social and economic relevance of nanotechnology and its implication for the Global South. In the third part, social, ethical and legal aspects of nanotechnology are framed in terms of human rights issues. The fourth part devotes closer attention to an analysis of the current patent rules intended to safe keep accessibility while confronted with the new challenges brought by nanotechnology inventions. Throughout this chapter, it will be sustained that nanotechnology poses normative challenges implying the need to re-evaluate the functioning of exclusions, exceptions and limitations to patent rights as mechanisms for safekeeping accessibility.

Nanotechnology

Nanotechnology is an umbrella denomination that designates technologies involving the manipulation of matter at the nanoscale (below 100 nanometers). A nanometer (nm) is equivalent to 10^{-9}m or 0.000000001m, in order to offer a sense of proportion it is usual to point out that one nanometer is about 1/80000 of the diameter of the average human hair or the equivalent to 10 hydrogen atoms.

The study and manipulation of matter at the nanoscale enables building structures and new materials at atomic, molecular and macromolecular scale. Such activities are not a question of mere scaling down since at nanoscale the properties of materials reveal differences due to two main reasons: firstly, quantum effects can dominate the behaviour of matter at the nanoscale, particularly in the lower ranges and thus affecting the magnetic, optical, and electrical behaviour of materials; and secondly, nanomaterials have a relatively larger surface area when compared to the same mass of matter in larger forms. These characteristics open the possibility to new uses of known materials, and the creation of novel functional materials. Nanotechnology is an interdisciplinary technological field where the distinction between disciplines such as physics, chemistry and biology becomes less clear. Such characteristics have consequences to the overall legal regulation of these technological advances.

At the present moment the exact meaning of the terms Nanoscience and Nanotechnology is still contentious among the scientific community. Such ambiguity, translates into the inexistence of a widely accepted legal definition of nanotechnology. In the absence of uniformity, the present work uses as main reference the definition formulated by the European Patent Office (EPO):

> The term nanotechnology covers entities with a controlled geometrical size of at least one functional component below 100 nanometers in one or more dimensions susceptible of making physical, chemical or biological effects available which are intrinsic to that size. It covers equipment and methods for controlled analysis, manipulation, processing, fabrication or measurement with a precision below 100 nanometres.[1]

This choice is justified not only by the topic of this chapter – the interface between human rights and patent law – but also by the fact that the above definition was the basis for the current formulation of subclass B82Y of the International Patent Classification (IPC),[2] thus embedding it with an aura of international consensus.

Key Fields of Scientific Research, State of the Art and Expectations for the Future

Nanoscience is considered a horizontal or enabling scientific field, since its advances typically can be applied to and developed in a wide range of scientific disciplines. Correspondently, nanotechnology is considered a converging technology that combines expertise from different scientific disciplines and applies in conjunction technologies originally developed in different industrial and technological sectors. Technological advances afforded by nanotechnology will typically have horizontal, cross-industry applications, and lead to overall progress in a wide range of technological areas and in certain cases possibly even determine the emergence of new industries.

Currently, the most promising fields of research concern medical and pharmaceutical applications, information technologies, energy production and storage, novel materials, food, water and environment, and security and law enforcement. To name a few examples: information technologies and telecommunications already use nanotechnology to obtain faster, smaller and more energy efficient devices; the use of nanotechnology in the medical sector is producing remarkable results particularly in improved drug delivery systems, medical diagnostic and therapeutic tools; finally, solar cells technology is expected to significantly benefit from nanotechnology leading to the wide scale use of solar energy as a major power source.

Several nanotechnology based consumer products are currently available on the market such as cosmetic products, textiles, metals, electronic devises and construction materials.[3] These are

---

1 Definition of patent class Y01N (out of use since May 2011). EPO archive <http://forums.epo.org/espacenet-archive/topic405.html > accessed 15 December 2011.

2 The IPC is a hierarchical classification system used to classify and search patent documents according to technical fields. The IPC legal base is The Strasbourg Agreement, which entered into force in 1975. On June 2011, the Strasbourg Union had 61 Member States. However, according to the WIPO, it is currently used in more than 100 countries, making it the 'the lingua franca' of patent classification (<www.wipo.org> accessed 1 December 2011).

3 Currently there is lack of reliable data regarding the number of products on the market incorporating nanotechnology. An on-line nanotechnology consumer products inventory counts 1317 nanotechnology consumer product or product lines on the market by March 2011. The inventory is based on internet available information release by the manufactures. Product lines using the same nanotechnology are only counted once and the inventory does not account for industrial products or research tools. The authors acknowledge the

mainly improvements of existing products (evolutionary nanotechnology). However, in the future developments of major importance are expected, meaning new or radically improved products, steaming from technological advances that from current time perspective will consist of a leap forward in our technological development (revolutionary nanotechnology).

Social and Economic Relevance: Everyone Aboard the Nanotech-Train

With the USA, EU and Japan currently occupying the leading carriages, followed by Korea, China and Russia, not only is every nation claiming a place aboard the 'nanotech-train', every country is making considerable effort to secure the best possible seat. These technologies are expected to grant competitive advantage to the economies that first master them. Worldwide official documents and political rhetoric indicate a widespread perception that the nanotechnology industrial wave can bring changes to the world development and economic power status quo. Nanotechnologies have been described in a European Commission staff working paper[4] as a promising candidate to become the next and sixth Kondratieff wave.[5] The European Commission officially expressed concerns over the possibility of industry across the EU losing competitiveness should it fail to either lead, or follow closely, other economies in the development of nanotechnology.[6] Nanotechnology has been ranked a priority in economical and industrial development policies both at national and supranational level. In recent years governments have elaborated Nanotechnology action plans and policies. According to the literature, by 2005 62 countries had or were in the process of initiating and implementing national nanotechnology initiatives (18 of them transitional and 19 developing);[7] 16 countries had at least groups or individual researchers working in nanotechnology (three transitional and 12 developing, including one least developed country) and 14 additional others had shown official interest in promoting research in this area (one transitional and 13 developing, including three least developed countries).[8]

---

possibility for a considerable margin of error; see the Project on Emerging Nanotechnologies <http://www.nanotechproject.org/inventories/consumer/analysis_draft/> accessed 1 December 2011. Another inventory 'provides an overview of how nanomaterials and nanostructuring applications are used today in industrial and commercial applications across industries' listing 196 industrial products or applications. The authors 'note, that this database is a work in progress' <http://www.nanowerk.com/products/products.php> accessed 1 December 2011.

4 Angela Hullmann, *The economic development of nanotechnology – An indicators based analysis* (European Commission, DG Research, Unit Nano S&T – Convergent Science and Technologies 2006)

5 Kondratieff proposed a theory of long waves, or cycles, of economic boom and bust published in the 1920s, reputably these cycles were first named Kondratieff waves by Joseph Schumpeter in *Business Cycles* (1939). Joseph Schumpeter *Business Cycles: A theoretical, historical and statistical analysis of the Capitalist process* (first published 1939, Porcupine Press 1989).

6 Communication from the Commission to the Council, The European Parliament and The Economic and Social Committee, 'Nanosciences and nanotechnologies: An action plan for Europe 2005–2009', Brussels, 7.6.2005 (COM (2005) 243 final).

7 Donald Maclurcan, 'Nanotechnology and Developing Countries. Part 1: What Possibilities?' (2005) 1, *AZoNano: Online Journal of Nanotechnology*, <http://www.azonano.com/azompdf.asp?ArticleID=1428&heading= Nanotechnology>; and 'Part 2: What Realities?' (2005) 2, *AZoNano: Online Journal of Nanotechnology*, <http://www.azonano.com/azompdf.asp?Article ID=1429&heading=Nanotechnology>, accessed 15 December 2011.

8 Noela Invernizzi, Guillermo Foladori and Donald Maclurcan, 'Nanotechnology's Controversial Role for the South' (2008) 13: 1 *South, Science, Technology and Society* 123, 124.

Since nanotechnology entered the political agenda in the first years of the 21st century, specific and direct public and private funding of research and development projects has grown from marginal or non-existent to priority area of investment in research. A private consulting survey reports that by 2010 the annual public investment on nanotechnology research and development worldwide had reached 10 billion US dollars, and predicts a 20 percent increase of investment until 2013. Between 2000 and 2011 governments worldwide have invested more than 67.5 billion US dollars in nanotechnology funding. If corporate research and various other forms of private funding are taken into account, it is estimated that by 2015 nearly a quarter of a trillion US dollars will have been invested in nanotechnology.[9]

However, despite the enthusiasm and optimism created around the promises of a revolutionary technological wave these are still yet to become reality. Simultaneously, the scientific community has been recommending caution pointing out that the unrestrained development of nanotechnology may pose high risks for human health, environment and earth eco-systems, further adding that those risks are currently to a large extent unknown and unpredictable. Currently, safety issues are a main concern and as far as the EU is concerned regulatory authorities have stressed the importance of maintaining and applying a precautionary principle regarding nanotechnology safety issues[10] while promoting complementary research concerning ethical, legal, social and governance aspects.

Developing World and Nanotechnology: The Global South Not Only is Joining the Train but Claiming a Seat at the Leading Carriages

The characterization of nanotechnology as being the next industrial wave was not ignored by the Global South. It is likely that developing countries[11] have interpreted such characterization in official documents and public investment policies of the most developed nations as a signal to follow suit, allocating resources to take advantage of what appears to be a unique opportunity to recover in merely a few years from centuries of delay on the development race.

Commentators have mentioned that such hope may be misguided by the assumption that technological innovation by itself can lead to social and economic development, and may not take into account predicaments such as the dependency theory,[12] according to which 'one country's industrial revolution is another country's underdevelopment and these are two sides of the same coin of world capitalist development'.[13] Schummer points out that under the predicament of such theory

---

9 Tim Harper, 'Global Funding of Nanotechnologies and its impact' (2011) Cientifica <http://cientifica.com/wp-content/uploads/downloads/2011/07/Global-Nanotechnology-Funding-Report-2011.pdf> accessed 15 December 2011. According to the author the report was based on official national documents and confirmed by the World Economic Forum's annual Global Competitiveness Report 2011. See Klaus Schwab (ed.), *The Global Competitiveness Report 2011–2012* (World Economic Forum 2011).

10 See: European Commission Staff Working Document, Summary of legislation in relation to health, safety and environment aspects of nanomaterials, regulatory research needs and related measures, Brussels, 17.6.2008 (SEC (2008) 2036).

11 Terms such as 'developing world' and 'developing countries' are contentious, for this reason in this chapter such terms will be used for countries or regions with low or medium state of development according to the human development index (HDI) put forward by the United Nations Development Programme. The HDI is a composite index that combines per capita GDP with life expectancy and educational standards, and is currently the most consensual.

12 Joachim Schummer, 'The Impact of Nanotechnologies on Developing Countries' in Fritz Allhoff and others (eds), *Nanoethics: The Ethical and Social Implications of Nanotechnology* (Hoboken 2007) 294 ff.

13 P. Hudson, *The Industrial Revolution* (Arnold 1992) 20, quoted by Schummer n 12, 295.

even assuming that nanotechnology will be in fact the next industrial revolution wave it would, as any the previous ones, necessarily reinforce the existing development gap rather than diminish it.[14] Along this pessimistic view, it also has been observed that cutting edge technologies are expensive and inappropriate for the existing realities of the developing world and for this reason they are often viewed with scepticism by developing circles.[15] Others consider that promoting investment in nanotechnology in countries such as Brazil and India brings forth the danger to divert financial resources and political focus from the basic needs of the large poor population in these countries.[16] Another voiced concern is the possibility that the high level of investment needed to acquire new procedures and skill are likely to exacerbate the existing divisions between rich and poor.[17]

Sceptic views of development through emerging technologies present valid points: it may be ill advised to place too high hopes on new technologies. To anchor policies on the expectation that technological development by itself will be a quick fix to all human development issues is at best a leap of faith. Also, mimicking industrial policies from the North may deter governments from taking more appropriate, attainable and immediate options to manage each country specific developing needs. However, such pessimism is susceptible to simple counter argumentation. Assuming that such predictions are correct and dependency is inevitable, it can be equally validly argued that if developing countries refrain from investing in science and technology the development gap will deepen to an even greater extent. The industrial capability developing countries have succeed in acquiring so far will become obsolete if such industries fail to modernise and keep pace with technological development. Furthermore, changes in technology and production will dictate changes in the needs for natural resources. There is a high probability that nanotechnology technological advances will provide alternatives to the use of certain basic commodities, and thus either make redundant or severely reduce the demand for natural resources that are currently an important source of income for some countries in the Global South.

Like other emerging technologies, nanotechnology can be both relevant to address specific challenges faced by developing countries and be part of sustainable development policies and practice in developing countries, in particular for those who already have a relevant scientific and industrial capability. Data collected by the World Economic Forum, seems to reinforce an optimistic view of development through investment in emerging technologies, showing that while competitiveness in advanced economies has stagnated over the past seven years, it has improved in many emerging markets that invested in such technologies.[18]

To a certain extent national authorities in the Global South appear to subscribe to this view. A summary analysis of official documents and political discourse shows that the Global South is investing in building nanotechnology research capability, not merely to keep pace with the North but with tailor-made objectives adapted to specific needs and challenges, such as: First,

14 Schummer n 12, 295.

15 Mark Malloch Brown, 'Foreword' in United Nations Development Programme (ed.), *Human Development Report: Making new technologies work for human development* (Oxford University Press 2001) iii.

16 Katie Mantel 'Developing nations "must wise up to nanotechnology"', Science and Development Network (Interview with Andrew Scott and others, London, 4 September 2003) <http://www.scidev.net/en/news/developing-nations-must-wise-up-to-nanotechnology.html> accessed 15 December 2011; and Andrew Scott, 'Nanotechnology and Nanoscience' (response from stakeholders n. 77, The Royal Society and Royal Academy of Engineering 2003) <http://www.nanotec.org.uk/evidence/77a AndrewScott.htm> accessed 15 December 2011.

17 The Royal Society and Royal Academy of Engineering, *Nanoscience and Nanotechnologies: Opportunities and Uncertainties* (London 2004) ch 6.

18 Schwab n 9.

seeking more efficient and less expensive solutions to specific major socio-economic problems, including economic dependence on the international market value of natural resources, sanitation, clean water supply and combat of epidemic diseases; Second, modernize the existing industries, increasing short term competiveness and preventing long term redundancy; and finally, find new markets and market niches, not heavily patented and still relatively unexplored, that can serve as future exporting goods and thus improve the commercial balance.

In the impossibility of a more detailed analysis, three countries in different continents with diverse historical backgrounds and distinct internal political approaches are worth a brief mention as interesting examples. China, Brazil and Russia are part of the six largest non-OECD economies known collectively as BRIICS's[19] and, despite profound historical differences, share some common characteristics such as: abundance of natural resources, wide territorial base, large and relatively young population and a respectable scientific community.[20] Generally, these countries have seen the potential of nanotechnology and thus have channelled public funds to research in this area, while making efforts in improving the ability to translate scientific successes into commercial products.

In 2011 China became the country with the highest investment in nanotechnology research in terms of Purchasing Power Parity (18 billion US dollars or approx. 14.4 billion euro), surpassing even the USA. Although, in terms of actual investment adjusted for currency exchange rates, in 2011 China has spent only 1.3 billion US dollars (approx. 800 million euro), while the US has spent 2.18 billion US dollars (approx. 1.6 billion euro) during the same period.[21]

Russia has also become one of the major public investors in nanoscience and nanotechnology research with the establishment in 2007 of the Russian Corporation of Nanotechnologies (RUSNANO) along with a scheduled governmental investment of 130 billion roubles. The organization has an explicit focus on the commercialization of nanotechnology, and essentially functions as a venture capital fund, investing in selected projects in exchange for equity stakes (lower than 50 percent). The finance support is long term (over 10 years), and at the end of such period equity stakes will be sold following the logic of retrieving investment costs and not with the commercial approach of maximizing profit. From 2007 to 2009, RUSNANO had approved 61 projects, committing to invest 92.4 billion roubles (approx. 2.4 billion euro), and in the coming years RUSNANO predicts as outcome of the program that the volume of nanotechnology production will reach 900 billion roubles (approx. 19.8 billion euro) per year by 2015, which signifies a significant increase from the 4-5 billion roubles (approx. 88 million euro) registered in 2009.[22]

---

19 Brazil, Russia, India, Indonesia, China and South Africa.

20 According to OECD data these countries show high old age support ratio (number of people of working age per person of pension age) that ranges between double and six times the average of OCDE countries (currently 2.1). Despite some of their infra-structural weaknesses and considerable internal inequities, these countries also have respectable high education institutions in scientific fields and produce (home or abroad) a considerable number of relevant scientific publications. Regarding the level of tertiary attainment – the proportion of the population with a qualification at bachelor's degree level or above – only Russia with a 54.2 percent rate of tertiary attainment in population aged 25–64 is at the same level as most OCDE countries. However, in absolute terms due to their large population all these countries possess a large amount of scientists and qualified workers. See Organization for Economic Co-operation and Development *Countries statistic profiles* (2011 OECD).

21 Harper n 9, 4. The author uses the Short system of large-number names, in which the term *billion* refers to *a thousand millions* (10^9).

22 ObservatoryNano *Economic Report Public Funding of Nanotechnology* (2010, Spinverse), ch 3.4 <http://www.observatorynano.eu/project/document/1838> Accessed 15 December 2011.

Brazilian authorities have elected nanotechnology as a priority area in industrial development. A federal program for development of nanoscience and nanotechnology was created in 2003 with the general goal of creating and developing new products and processes in nanotechnology, implementing them in order to increase the competiveness of the industry and also building human capacity to benefit from the economic, technological and scientific opportunities offered by nanotechnology.[23] According to official data, the Brazilian government has directly invested 160 million reais (approx. 65 million euro) during 2000–2007 in nanotechnology research. Adding to the investments from the private sector, it is estimated that the total investment amounts to 320 million reais (approx. 130 million euro).[24]

In 2005, Brazilian President Lula da Silva delivered a speech at the official opening of the Brazilian National Program for the Development of Nanoscience and Nanotechnology, which in a certain way summarizes the strategic vision of the Brazilian authorities concerning nanotechnology. The Brazilian President expressed the view that investment in science, technology and educations is the safest and best investment as it produces an almost immediate return. Lula da Silva, also linked scientific and technological development to human progress, irradiation of poverty and reduction of social inequities and declared that 'science and technology are instruments essential to economic development and constitute the basic priority of our government'.[25]

Investment in nanotechnology by the Global South started early to produce remarkable results. In the period ranging between 1999 and 2004, China ranked 3rd, Russia 11th, India 13th and Brazil 20th in the ranking of nanotechnology scientific publications indexed by the Science Citation Index (SCI).[26] When the relative scientific quality of the publications is taken into account as measured by a pre-defined number of citations threshold, these countries perform equally well, accounting for 12 percent of core papers and 22 percent of citing papers in nanoscience and materials.[27] However, in terms of number of patents, indicators suggest that patent activity has not accompanied scientific success given the strong concentration of patents in the most developed countries.[28] In 2005 the European Union, Japan and the United States had contributed to 84 percent of all nanotechnology patents, while the BRIICS accounted only for 2.6 percent.[29]

Overall it can be observed that the investment in nanoscience and nanotechnology research and development is not a prerogative of the most industrialized nations. Instead, these nations face solid competition from emerging economies that see in cutting edge technologies an opportunity to acquire a competitive advantage by claiming their stake in the field at an early stage.

---

23 Ministério da Ciência e Tecnologia 2009 <http://www.mct.gov.br/index.php/ content/view/27137.html> accessed 3 December 2009.

24 Agência Brasileira de Desenvolvimento Industrial, *Panorama nanotecnologia* (2010 ABDI).

25 Luiz Inácio Lula da Silva, *Discurso do presidente da República Luiz Inácio Lula da Silva, na cerimônia de lançamento do Programa Nacional de Desenvolvimento da Nanociência e Nanotecnologia, Campinas, São Paulo, 19 de agosto de 2005* (translated from original) <http://www.mct.gov.br/index.php/content/view/14842.html> accessed 1 December 2011.

26 Angella Hullmann, 'Who is winning the global nanorace?' (2006) 1 *Nature Nanotechnology*, 81.

27 Masatsura Igami and Ayaka Saka, 'Capturing the evolving nature of science, the development of new scientific indicators and the mapping of science' (2007) OECD Science, Technology and Industry Working Paper 2007/1 <http://www.oecd.org/dataoecd/11/40/38134903.pdf> accessed 3 November 2011.

28 Susan Schneegans (ed.) *The UNESCO Science Report, 2010: The Current Status of Science around the World* (UNESCO 2010).

29 Hélène Dernis, Dominique Guellec and Maria-Pluvia Zuniga-Lara, *The OECD Compendium of Patent Statistics 2008* (OECD 2008) 16–17.

Every Rose has its Thorns: Nanotechnology and Human Rights

Nanotechnology promises to change the world and solve many of the most important global challenges of our time. Emerging technologies of such magnitude, recipient of large amount of public and private funding, are bound to generate heated regulatory debate. A debate that in itself is crucial, not only for the future development of the technology but also for the fulfilment of the predicted return of such investments: much is dependent on public and political understanding and acceptance of technology. General mistrust can dictate consumer's choices and future political options, delaying for decades the availability of a technology in consumer products.

Most of the topics raised are neither novel, nor exclusive to nanotechnology, but rather reflect timeless human interrogations and concerns in face of the uncertainty brought by technological change. In general terms the issues under debate relate to concerns typical of human rights, such as: unfair distribution of the economic benefits associated with technology; uneven access to the benefits of technology; consumers, workers and environmental safety; negative social and anthropological impact of the technology; privacy and informed consent. Each of these topics, although intrinsically interconnected, can be analyzed using either a social, ethical or a legal perspective. The latter is a commonly used classification that is believed to offer the benefit of a clear analytic framework.[30] This chapter will attempt to conjugate this classification with a human rights perspective by framing the issues that form part of the nanotechnology debate in terms of potential either to strengthen or threaten human rights attainability.

For the purposes of this chapter, human rights are to be understood in its broader sense, including not only a normative perspective based on a formalistic classification of rights, but also an ontological perspective. In this broad sense, the concept of human rights encompasses those rights codified as such in international and national legal sources, plus any right that can conceptually be constructed as an inalienable right based on core universal values intrinsically connected with the human condition and inherent to all human beings. However, for sake of clarity, such human rights *lato sensu* will be framed in terms of possible correspondence to the UN human right system, since it is the result of the possible, even if imperfect, international consensus on the matter.[31]

Social Aspects of Nanotechnology: Preparing the Stage For the Nano (R)Evolution

Nanotechnology is generally profiled as either the next evolutionary step in industrialization or even as a disruptive technology originating the next cycle in the industrial revolution: the nano revolution. Either way, new technologies with wide cross-sector applications necessarily imply a certain degree of social changes. Among the main social issues currently under debate particular attention has been devoted to: (1) public acceptance; (2) workers, consumers and environmental safety; and (3) access to nanotechnology. Translating these issues into human rights concerns,

30 The classification is used widely in EU documents, studies and reports. See for all: Angela Hullman, *European activities in the Field of ethical, legal and social aspects (ELSA) and governance of nanotechnology* (European Commission, DG Research Unit Nano and Converging Sciences and Technologies 2008).

31 The UN human right system main legal instruments comprises the United Nations Universal Declaration on Human Rights, adopted by the General Assembly on December 10, 1948, General Assembly Resolution 217A (III), U.N. Doc. A/180 (UDHR); the International Covenant on Political Rights Adopted and opened for signature, ratification and accession by General Assembly resolution 2200A (XXI) of 16 December 1966, entry into force 23 March 1976 (CPR); and the International Covenant on Economic, Social and Cultural Rights, Adopted and opened for signature, ratification and accession by General Assembly resolution 2200A (XXI) of 16 December 1966, entry into force 3 January 1976 (CESCR).

these would mainly correspond to social and economic human rights, such as those codified under the International Covenant on Economic, Social and Cultural Rights.[32]

Public acceptance has been generally debated as an economic issue in terms of marketing goods and services; however it also has a human rights dimension. Acceptance is connected with information and knowledge over the safety of nanotechnology products and consequences of long-term exposure to them; it is in this sense a right to information issue. Rights cannot be fully enjoyed and exercised without access to knowledge and information. Thus, although in the commercial context it may be contentious to speak of an absolute right to information, such right necessarily underlines any construction of inalienable right based on the value of human dignity. Public acceptance is crucial for the future development of any new technology, dictating not only consumer behaviour and preferences, but also public and private investment decisions. Negative public perception can have devastating consequences, delaying technological development for decades. Several studies on risk communication and risk perception have found the existence of a high level of scepticism and resistance to nanotechnologies in the EU.[33] In the EU the issue has been linked with a low level of understanding of the technology by the general public,[34] thus justifying the allocation of considerable financial resources to national and EU sponsored programs in this area.[35] The issue of public acceptance is not merely a European concern. Often countries that prioritize nanotechnology in their industrial policies have also included in their national nanotechnology policies measures to disseminate knowledge through the general public, such as popular science publications, public conferences and exhibitions, thematic web pages and plans to introduce the topic in basic education programs.

Workers, consumers and environmental safety are currently central issues in the nanotechnology debate and a major worldwide concern for regulatory authorities. In normative terms, these concerns can generally be linked to the right to an adequate and progressively improved standard of living, as well as to a right to health that cannot be attained without taking into account environmental protection. The right to safe and healthy working conditions is protected under article 7 (b) CESCR, while consumer and environmental safety can be included under the 'right to a standard of living adequate for the health and well-being' of individuals and families.[36] The latter is developed in the CESCR as the right to adequate standard of living and the continuous improvement of living conditions,[37] and the right to 'the enjoyment of the highest attainable standard of physical and mental health'[38] that includes both 'the improvement of all aspects of environmental and industrial hygiene'[39] and 'the prevention, treatment and control of epidemic, endemic, occupational and other diseases'.[40]

The debate concerning nanotechnology safety gain public notoriety with the publication of the Royal Society and Royal Academy of Engineering 2004 report, which raised the question whether

---

32 CESCR n 31.

33 Kate Seear, Alan Petersen and Diana Bowman, *The Social and Economic Impacts of Nanotechnologies: A Literature Review, Final Report Prepared for the Department of Innovation, Industry, Science and Research* (Monash University 2009).

34 Communication from the Commission to the Council, The European Parliament and The Economic and Social Committee, *Nanosciences and nanotechnologies: An action plan for Europe 2005–2009*, Brussels, 7.6.2005 (COM (2005) 243 final).

35 Hullman 2008 n 30, 7.

36 Art. 25 UDHR n 31.

37 Art 11 (1) CESCR n 31.

38 Art 12 (1) CESCR n 31.

39 Art 12 (2) (b) CESCR n 31.

40 Art 12 (2) (c) CESCR n 31.

nanotechnology components or applications (such as, for example, nanoparticles and carbon nanotubes) have a direct impact on the natural environment and on human health and wellbeing.[41] The EU has stressed the importance of maintaining and applying a precautionary principle while supporting further scientific studies and regulatory initiatives.[42] International organizations have also been active in the field, and for the most part agree with the need for caution and further research regarding safety issues. To mention a few examples, the OECD established a Working Party on Manufactured Nanomaterials in September 2006; and the Food and Agriculture Organization of the United Nations has convened, together with the World Health Organization, a joint expert meeting to 'develop global guidance on adequate and accurate methodologies to assess potential food safety risks that may arise from nanoparticles'.[43]

Technological development naturally leads to interrogations over the possibility of uneven access to its benefits, and the need to ensure effective universal realization of the right 'to enjoy the benefits of scientific progress and its applications'.[44] Individual and collective access to the benefits in terms of human development and the distribution of the economic advantages brought by nanotechnology remain a concern often raised. A report prepared for the United Nations Industrial Development Organisation (UNIDO) and published in 1997 is perhaps one of the earliest publications to consider the potential implications of nanotechnologies in aggravating the gap between developed and developing countries.[45] Since then, different macro-economic reports concerning the effects of nanotechnology on international trade and world commerce have been published emphasizing potential negative effects in less industrialized economies, such as possibly facing high barriers to enter the nanotechnology market while simultaneously losing their main source of income due to the redundancy of their currently valuable natural resources.[46]

The possibility of nano-divides and nano-districts and their potential dangers has been observed. Nano-districts refer to the possibility that these technologies will emerge in small geographic areas, also referred to as 'clusters'.[47] Nano-divides refer to the possibility that nanotechnologies may come to have a negative social-economic impact, exacerbating existing internal social inequalities in both developed and developing nations and aggravating the gap between developed and developing nations.[48] One of the main concerns is affordability, since concentration of intellectual property rights, know-how and industrial capacity, may lead to de facto market monopolies and the temptation to practice high prices that generally cannot be afforded by the Global South.

New horizontal technologies imply new production methods and techniques and require the use of highly specialized work force. They may thus entail the danger of suddenly excluding entire segments of the population from the labour market. It follows that those segments risk being

41 The Royal Society and Royal Academy of Engineering n 17.

42 COM(2005) 243 final n 33 and SEC(2008) 2036 n 11.

43 Food and Agriculture Organization of the United Nations and World Health Organization, *FAO/WHO Expert meeting on the application of nanotechnologies in the food and agriculture sectors: potential food safety implications, Meeting report* (FAO/WHO 2010).

44 Arts 27 (1) UNDHR and 15 CESCR n 31.

45 P. McKeown and others, *Nanotechnology* (Emerging Technology Series: New and Advance Materials, UNIDO 1997).

46 *Action Group on Erosion, Technology and Concentration, Nanotech's 'Second Nature' Patents: Implications for the Global South* (Special Report – Communiqués No. 87 and 88, ETC group 2005).

47 Philip Shapira and Jan Youtie, 'Emergence of Nanodistricts in the United States: Path Dependency or New Opportunities?' (2008) 22(3) *Economic Development Quarterly* 187.

48 Robert Sparrow 'Negotiating the Nanodivides' in Graeme Hodge, Diana Bowman and Karinne Ludlow (eds) *New Global Frontiers in Regulation: The Age of Nanotechnology* (Edward Elgar, 2007) 87–107.

denied the right to 'the opportunity to gain his living by work',[49] with the aggravated risk that the realization of such right through 'technical and vocational guidance and training programmes'[50] may encounter barriers connected with the high complexity of the technology.

Ethical Aspects of Nanotechnology: The Age of the Homo Chimaera

The ethical debate concentrates on possible future revolutionary advances of nanotechnology that advance the possibility to change the very anthropological definition of human being, bringing forth the danger of new forms of social exclusion and eugenic trends in society. It comprises, among others, important subjects that can be framed in terms of basic human rights, such as: the protection of human dignity, freedom and equality;[51] non-discrimination;[52] right to privacy;[53] informed consent regarding medical acts;[54] freedom of thought, conscience and religion;[55] and freedom of opinion and expression.[56]

In the coming years, nanotechnology is expected to provide considerable advances in prosthetics, organ replacement, reconstruction surgery and genetic therapy. These advances may go beyond the concept of therapy understood as restoration of abilities and functions to the species typical level, introducing widespread artificial human enhancement. It is an old dream of mankind to acquire abilities typical of other species, such as flying, under water breathing, self-regeneration, or enhanced hearing, sight and olfaction. The possibility to artificially improve or enhance oneself will likely be appealing to many, and be regarded as harmless and conceptually similar to the current cosmetic surgeries and treatments. However, it raises major ethical questions, such as those concerning nano-exclusion and eugenic trends in society. In a world where it is possible to correct any disability and enhance natural abilities, social and labour market discrimination of those who do not wish or are not able to access enhancement is likely to occur.[57] Simultaneously, the ability of society to accept and integrate persons who fall short of the average typical abilities of the species may experience a setback.[58] The mere possibility of 'enhanced' humans co-existing with 'natural' humans would likely create societal disruption and perhaps even call for the need to reformulate the concept of human being. Every human being has the right to be considered a person before the law[59] and every person is entitled to enjoy human rights protection.[60] Nanotechnology evolutionary manipulation of human DNA hypothetically may enable a wide range of modifications to the human body. The availability of such technology would raise complex philosophical and legal questions. Establishing

49 Art 6 (1) CESCR n 31.

50 Art 6 (2) CESCR n 31.

51 Art 1 UDHR n 31.

52 Art 7 UDHR n 31.

53 Arts 12 UDHR and 17 CPR n 31.

54 Art 7 CPR n 31.

55 Arts 18 UDHR and 18 CPR n 31.

56 Art 19 UDHR and 19 CPR n 31.

57 Laura Cabrera, 'Nanotechnology: Changing the Disability Paradigm' (2009) 8(2) *International Journal of Disability, Community & Rehabilitation*; and Fritz Allhoff, Patrick Lin, James Moor, and John Weckert 'Ethics of Human Enhancement: 25 questions & Answers' (2010) 4.1 *Studies in Ethics, Law, and Technology*, 1 <http://works.bepress.com /palin/9> accessed 10 December 2011.

58 Geert Van Calster, 'Regulating Nanotechnology in the European Union' 3.3 (2006) *Nanotechnology Law & Business*, 356.

59 Art 6 UDHR n 31.

60 Art 2 UDHR n 31.

a legal concept of person and determining the beginning and end of a person life is a complex legal matter subject to constant vivid debate in most jurisdictions. This subject has always remained very sensitive due to its deep political and religious roots. Radical enhancement technology will add further difficulties, which begin with determining if an enhanced human is still a *homo sapiens sapiens* and by definition a legal person. To what extent is the concept of human being defined by biological identity and/or by societal and environmental interaction? And, if a human being is to be defined by societal and environmental interaction, would a being with, for example, infrared vision and telepathic abilities necessarily experience and interact differently? Philosophical interrogations concerning human enhancement have important legal ramifications concerning the legal concept of person and its boundaries. Not only is it problematic to determine if an enhanced human is still a human, other questions emerge, such as: Is it possible to measure and accurately determine the boundaries of 'humanity' without infringing the principle of non-discrimination? Will human rights apply unchanged to radically enhanced humans? Do equity and the principle of justice and equality imply (or not) that different entities should be treated differently?

Another technological development that may soon be available and be the source of concern is the possibility of implanting the human body, cloths or any other object with virtually undetectable nano-tag mechanisms able to measure, store and relay large quantities of data. While nano-tags can be used in unlimited beneficial contexts, they nevertheless raise important ethical and legal issues such as respect for personal privacy, human dignity, informed consent, and accountability for public or private abuses.[61]

Many advocate strong and restrictive regulation as the answer to avoid the pitfalls of scientific and technological development. However, the same technologies can be used in different contexts. What is qualified has enhancement while applied to a healthy person, may be merely therapeutic if used in a different individual; and what is intrusive for some, may enhance the quality of life of others. Restrictions to scientific development and use of technology imply interference with freedom of opinion and thought in its component of freedom of scientific research,[62] as well as with the overall human right to enjoy the benefits of scientific progress.[63] Such restrictions need careful consideration, they can only be legitimized based on the protection of human dignity, however the over expansion of this principle may be disruptive to the human rights system.[64]

Legal Aspects: Regulating the Infinitely Small and Largely Unknown

New technological waves imply changes in the social reality regulated by the law. This does not mean that nanotechnology stands in a legal void. The existing legal and regulatory framework remains applicable, however it is vital to consider the appropriateness of extending its application to nanotechnology research, nanotechnology products and nanotechnology induced social phenomena. An out-dated and inadequate legal framework may lead to unbalanced and conflicting

---

61 The Royal Society and Royal Academy of Engineering n 17, 53–54.

62 Arts 18 and 19 CPR n 31.

63 Art 15 CESCR n 31.

64 In the EU there are on-going efforts to harmonize national initiatives in this area, such as the Commission Recommendation on a code of conduct for responsible nanosciences and nanotechnologies research, Brussels, 07/02/2008 (C (2008) 424 final). This is not a legally binding document but a mere recommendation providing guidelines to Member States 'as they formulate, adopt and implement their strategies for developing sustainable nanosciences and nanotechnologies research' (art 1). The final text benefited from extensive public debate but has nevertheless been criticized for being too vague.

decisions which pose a danger to the realization of the right to equality of treatment by the law and justice system.[65]

An additional concern to the general realization of human rights is that without the corresponding obligations human rights would be reduced to mere political declarations. In order for human rights to become incrementally attainable, enforceable and enforced, the regulatory framework needs to be updated so as to effectively reflect the protection of such rights. The insufficiency of safety regulations and the lack of international harmonization raise concerns. On the one hand, the possibility for national divergences can restrict de jure or de facto international trade. On the other hand, the absence of, or the existence of, permissive regulations in some countries could, in a world of global commerce and Internet trade, endanger consumer safety worldwide. The lack of scientific consensus regarding potential dangers and long term exposure effects undermines the efforts to evaluate and adapt safety regulations. As mentioned previously, considerable attention is being devoted to the study of safety issues, although critical voices have noted that not enough funding is being channelled to such projects.

The right to own private or collective property,[66] as well as the right to the protection of and the right to benefit from 'moral and material interests resulting from any scientific, literary or artistic production of which he is the author'[67] are usually seen as the consecration of intellectual property rights as human rights. In the case of nanotechnology, the protection of the research results is of considerable strategic importance. The nature of the technology and the considerable resources invested in research are leading all actors involved to actively seek intellectual property rights protection and presumably to actively enforce their rights, all in all giving rise to new challenges to the patent system. In order for inventors and investors to be able to collect the fruits of their labour and investment, the patent system needs to be constantly adapted to new technological developments. International harmonization and international cooperation mechanisms between patent offices, international instruments of protection against infringement of intellectual property rights, and technology transfer mechanisms are matters that need continuous improvement efforts. On the other side, the trend for companies and research institutions to engage in strong intellectual property rights strategies are often seen as potential barriers to the fulfilment of other human rights, such as right to access and benefit from technology in general and the right to health in particular.

Nanotechnology, Patent Rights and the Accessibility Debate

As succinctly described in the previous sections, nanotechnology may facilitate solutions to make human rights de facto attainable for a large part of underprivileged populations – either directly through technical innovation, or indirectly through macro-economic effects – but interrogations over possible overall negative human rights repercussions persist. This section will further examine the issue of the right to health and its intersection with patent rights, taking nanotechnology inventions as the reference point.

Several different conceptual frameworks have been used to analyse the interface between intellectual property right(s), and the right to health and access to healthcare and medicines. These can be divided into (1) conflict, (2) coexistence and (3) 'beyond conflict and coexistence'.[68]

65 Arts 7 UNDHR and 14 CCPR n 31.

66 Art 17 UDHR n 31.

67 Arts 27 (2) UNDHR and 15 (b) CESCR n 31.

68 Laurence Helfer and Graeme Austin, *Human rights and intellectual property mapping the global interface* (CUP 2011) 64–81.

The conflict of rights framework considers both rights individually, confronting the patent right with the right to health, including under the latter a right of access to patented inventions (e.g. medicines). These rights are confronted in terms of relative hierarchical value, seeking to develop rules to solve situations where a conflict of norms may exist. In a certain sense this is a legal dogmatic approach, destined to find interpretative solutions to the application of existing normative provisions to factual situations. The coexistence framework, on the other hand, underlines that both fields of law have separate but coexistent objectives – to provide for incentive to innovation while improving accessibility. This framework allows for a broader analysis that can serve as guidance for future legislative changes or treaty negotiations. Alternative constructions, beyond conflict and coexistence, understand patent rights not as a property right but instead constructed as a human right. To a certain extent, this is also a conflict framework entailing a constitutionalization perspective, in the sense that it involves a confrontation between different human rights by reference to their basis for legitimacy and relative precedence.

Without ignoring the existence of potential or actual normative conflicts, patent rights will be analyzed in this chapter as part of the access paradigm, complementing other rights in promoting accessibility.

The traditional understanding of the repercussion of patent rights in terms of accessibility has justified the implementation in the patent system of mechanisms destined to introduce a balance between incentive to innovation and access. Within the patent system exclusions and exceptions to patentability and limitations to the exercise of patent rights assume the function of gatekeepers of accessibility.[69] These restrictions have a long historic presence in patent legislation and are currently internationally recognised under article 27 of the TRIPS agreement.[70]

The traditional views of confrontation and coexistence described above, understand the right to health as a static right and not as an incremental progressive right, largely ignoring the importance of innovation and the devastating consequences to the attainability of the right to health should the incentive for innovation be reduced or undermined. Health is often described as a public good, by definition non-excludable, meaning that individual use cannot limit the benefit to others.[71] However, the same can be said about technological knowledge. Inventions are public goods privatized by means of a legal institute, the patent. In strict dogmatic terms, the right to health is a public right, unlimited by nature and addressing primary public authorities, while intellectual property rights have a private law nature and primarily concern the protection of private economic interests.[72] Following this line of reasoning, there are few arguments to support the inclusion of intellectual property rights in the UN catalogue of human rights,[73] unless a distinction is made between fundamental and non-fundamental human rights.[74] Under this view, the inclusion of the human rights discourse in the patent system debate is even counterproductive by promoting an

69 For a general reflexion on patent law and accessibility see Jens Schovsbo, 'Increasing Access to Patented Inventions by post-grant measures' (2009) 36 *Science and Public Policy* 609.

70 Agreement on Trade-Related Aspects of Intellectual Property Rights, contained in an Annex to the Marrakesh Agreement Establishing the World Trade Organization, signed in Marrakesh, Morocco on 15 April 1994.

71 Johanna Gibson, *Intellectual Property, Medicine and Health: Current Debates* (Ashgate 2008) 80.

72 Willem Grosheide, 'Intellectual property rights and human rights: related origin and development' in Willem Grosheide (ed.), *Intellectual Property and Human Rights: A Paradox* (Edward Elgar 2010) 3, 21.

73 Rochelle Dreyfuss 'Patents and human rights where is the paradox?' in Willem Grosheide (ed.), *Intellectual Property and Human Rights: A Paradox* (Edward Elgar 2010) 72, 73.

74 Grosheide n 72, 20.

adversarial perspective or 'zero-sum game' between rights holders that hides the existence of common interests[75] and prevents a global analysis of the accessibility problem.

However, an alternative view is possible. The right to health is a complex access right. It includes a right to access all the direct and indirect determinants of health.[76] It includes access to health facilities, goods and services; environmental factors, such as access to clean water, food and basic sanitation; and access to information.[77] If the right to the highest possible attainable standard of health is understood as an incremental right,[78] then the availability of adequate levels of incentive to innovation necessarily becomes a central element of the right to health paradigm. Without technical innovation and incentives to invest in such innovation, this right to health cannot be fulfilled. Under this view the legislator's choice does not lie between (1) to protect investment of pharmaceutical companies by the grant of patents or (2) to guarantee effective access to medicines to poor populations by reducing or eliminating such protection. Instead, the real attainable public policy options are to determine what is more beneficial: (1) less expensive medicines and medical instruments or (2) new medicines that are more efficient and less toxic, as well as novel methods and instruments for treatment and diagnosis that are more precise, faster and safer. The challenge is whether it is possible to pursue and attain both objectives simultaneously and if so, how. Detractors of the patent system remark that patented inventions marketed under monopolistic conditions are necessarily more expensive than equivalent goods sold in a competitive market, thus concluding that the elimination or restriction of patent rights is necessary to ensure access to health. Assuming the correctness of such statement, it should be added that without the incentive provided by a marketing monopoly companies might refrain from investing in research and development since there would be no guarantee of retrieving such investment. Naturally, this argument requires innovation to be a function of the availability of patents, something that typically these sectors contest. However, if we accept that in the absence of patents the incentive to industrial innovation could be achieve by alternative means and that companies would continue to invest in research – for example in order to compete in the market by introducing new products and improving product quality – in such a case commercial logic would dictate that there would be a strong incentive to keep research and industrial know-how secret. Patent law provides incentive for knowledge dissemination since the grant of patents is made conditional to the disclosure of technical information. Such has been a long-standing justification of patent rights. Currently, sufficient disclosure is a mandatory obligation under article 29 (1) of the TRIPS agreement, according to which, in order to be granted a patent, the applicant has to describe the invention in a manner at least sufficiently clear as to allow others to be able to understand its functioning and reproduce it. Allowing others to build upon the shared knowledge is an important function of the patent system as a mechanism for promoting innovation, and often an overlooked one in the accessibility debate. Without patents forcing the disclosure of such vital knowledge, commercially valuable information would be kept secret and scientists bound by contractual obligations would be prevented from publishing their results. It has been argued that recent research demonstrates that patent law indirectly causes delay to publication

---

75 Dreyfuss n 73, 90.

76 The right to the highest attainable standard of health contains the following interrelated and essential elements: availability, accessibility, acceptability and quality. The ICESCR also implies among others the obligation for the states to adopt appropriate measures towards the full realization of this right. See UN Committee on Economic, Social and Cultural Rights (CESCR), *General Comment No. 14: The Right to the Highest Attainable Standard of Health (Art. 12 of the Covenant)*, 11 August 2000,E/C.12/2000/4.

77 Gibson n 71, ch 3.

78 The principle of progressive realization, applicable to all rights protected under the ICESCR, implies that States must take steps to achieve progressively full realization to the maximum of its available resources.

of scientific results.[79] Without contesting such conclusion, it should be noted that such does not invalidate the beneficial role of patents in the dissemination of knowledge, since the alternative – generalized use of trade secrets – would have in the current economic and technological framework even more restricting results.[80] The more complex the technology is, the more relevant this function becomes. Reverse engineering always implies duplication of efforts and resources. However, while in simple mechanical inventions it may be a relatively easy and non-expensive task, the more complex and recent a technology is the more expensive and time consuming such exercise becomes. Nanotechnology is often developed by long-term projects employing interdisciplinary research teams and using expensive research instruments and tools, making reverse engineering extremely costly and lengthy.

An incremental right to the highest possible attainable standard of health necessarily implies innovation. It is thus an oversimplification to consider mechanisms destined to promote innovation – such as patents – to be major obstacles to public health policies, or to address the subject of balancing innovation and access as fundamentally separate realities.

Nanotechnology Patent Landscape Accessibility Implications

Nanotechnology inventions concern more than the mere scaling down of existing technologies, thus while nanotechnology patents tend to experience some of the difficulties present in the scientific field(s) of origin they face specific challenges.

Overall, nanotechnology patents display a number of distinct characteristics concerning ownership, subject-matter of protection and scope of protection, namely: (1) a tendency to seek patent protection at early stages; (2) broad and often overlapping patents are being issued over technology building blocks and research tools;[81] (3) patent ownership is highly concentrated, and remarkably nanotechnology major patent owners are not commercially orientated entities, but rather universities and public funded research institutions;[82] (4) patent thickets have been identified at least in carbon nanotubes, metal nanoparticles, ceramic nanoparticles dendrimers, quantum dots, fullerenes and nanowires.[83]

The literature generally argues that nanotechnology patent landscape is different from other important technological developments.[84] The nature and potential of the technology in itself, together with the considerable investment that this technology requires, is leading all actors involved to actively seek intellectual property rights protection at very early stages of the research process when a possible commercial application may be vague and distant. How actively and aggressively are those rights being enforced is currently unknown and a matter for debate. There

79 Gertrui Van Overwalle 'Reconciling patent policies and university mission', (2006) 13 *Ethical Perspectives*, 231.

80 Regarding the conditions that dictate the use of trade secrets see David Friedman, William Landes and Richard Posner 'Some economics of trade secret law' (1991) 5 *Journal of Economic Perspectives*, 61; and Wesley Cohen, Richard Nelson and John Walsh, 'Protecting Their Intellectual Assets: Appropriability Conditions and Why U.S. Manufacturing Firms Patent (or Not)' (Working Paper No 7552, National Bureau of Economic Research, 2000).

81 Douglas Sylvester and Diana Bowman, 'Navigating the Patent Landscapes for Nanotechnology: English gardens or Tangled Grounds?' (2001) 726:2 *Biomedical Nanotechnology: Methods in Molecular Biology* 359.

82 Mark Lemley, 'Patenting nanotechnology' (2006) 58 *Stanford Law Review* 601.

83 Lux Research, *The Nanotech Intellectual Property Landscape* (Lux Research 2005).

84 Lemley n 82.

is an observed general tendency to broad interpretation of the concept of invention that results in blurring the distinction between invention and discovery. This is a consequence of the nature of technological development that has rendered the traditional legal conceptual framework less useful and the work of patent offices more difficult. The nature of the patent exam procedure entails the general tendency for broad patents to be granted at the dawn of emerging technologies. 'It is widely stated that changes in the nature of basic science have rendered more "basic science" patentable than previously was the case.'[85] The issue is not new, nor specific to nanotechnology patents, but it is likely that if such tendency persists it will have relatively more severe consequences due to the specific nature and cross sector application of nanotechnology inventions. Broad and overlapping patents, conjugated with a tendency for research institutions to seek patent protection for basic research at an early stage may hamper future research and the public availability of the benefits nanotechnology.[86]

Traditionally, universities were not particularly active in seeking patent protection for their inventions, but surprisingly rank as the top patent owners in nanotechnology-related inventions.[87] Universities often work on first generation research, i.e. research that opens the field for later commercially driven research. Thus, such patenting activity is bound to fall upon basic blocks of the technology that in other technological waves were left in the public domain. This may create obstacles to further research and technology innovation in developing countries since, as the available data shows, such patents are owned in their majority by research institutions and large corporations located in developed countries. However, it should be noticed that these adverse consequences may be mitigated by new and more dynamic models of technology transfer, collaborative research projects, and the Global South's on-going investment efforts in nanoscience and nanotechnology research.

Patent thickets can be described as an unintended formation of dense interconnected and often overlapping intellectual property rights with different owners. Thickets are often a consequence of the above-mentioned broad and overlapping patents and can cause prohibitive costs for cross-license schemes (royalty stacking), and thus endanger the economic viability of new products and serve as anti-competitive barriers.

The mentioned nanomaterials entail the potential to cross sector unlimited industrial and commercial applications, including in the medical sector, thus patent thickets in this area lead to accessibility concerns. Although such claims need to be observed with caution, the nature of this technology points in such direction. On the other hand, observed excessive concentration of patent ownership may give rise to different anti-commons issues, possibly originating not only barriers to entry in the market, but also deterring third parties from conducting research in the field.

---

85 Lionel Bently and others, *Exclusions from Patentability and Exceptions and Limitations to Patentees' Rights* (WIPO Standing Committee on the Law of Patents 2006), 31.

86 Gavin Clarkson and David DeKorte, 'The Problem of Patent Thickets in Convergent Technologies' (2006) 1093 *Annals of the New York Academy of Sciences* 180; and Joel D'Silva, 'Pools, Thickets and open Source nanotechnology' (2009) 31 *European Intellectual Property Review* 300.

87 In the US the Bayle-Dole Act allowed public funded research organizations to retain intellectual property rights over their research, encouraging them to assume and establish a technology transfer function and thus changing the university research paradigm from an *open science model* to a *licensing model.* In Europe a similar trend has been observed. See Bayle-Dole Act (US 1980) University and Small Business Patent Procedures Act (December 12, 1980) codified in U.S.C Title 35 part II, chapter 18 § 200-212. For an analysis of evolution of different models of research and technology transfer see Laura MacDonald and others, *Management of intellectual property in publicly-funded research organisations: Towards European Guidelines* (Expert Group Report, European Commission, 2004).

Broad and overlapping patents result in legal uncertainty. Concerns have been voiced that the availability to the public of major developments in vital sectors such as medicine and pharmaceuticals, energy and information and communications technology may be delayed due to complex and lengthy multi-jurisdiction patent related litigation. Litigation activity has been growing in the US and is expected to explode and spread to other major jurisdictions in the coming years.[88]

Despite the dark scenario drawn by comments and data collections, the fact that developing countries are investing in building nanotechnology capabilities, leading to a respectable number of publications in this subject, might point out to a brighter picture. Also, it is possible that the existence of early, broad and overlapping patents might not become a major factor in delaying the development of the technology since the lack of knowledge regarding toxicity and long-term effects may become the major factor delaying the use of the technology. Currently, more research is needed on this matter before definitive conclusions can be stated.

Exclusions, Exceptions and Limitations to Patent Rights as Mechanisms to Protect Accessibility

Patent rights are not absolute in nature. A patent is merely a right to exclude others from the commercial exploitation of a certain subject-matter,[89] and is subject to several statutory limitations. Firstly, time limitation – a minimum duration of 20 years has been imposed by the TRIPS agreement[90] and such limit is currently generally adopted as the patent term.[91] Secondly, limitations regarding the object of the right can be found in practically all jurisdictions – only inventions must be patentable.[92] Thirdly, moral and *ordre public* considerations may impose that certain inventions cannot receive patent protection,[93] including 'diagnostic, therapeutic and surgical methods for the treatment of humans or animals'[94] and 'plants and animals other than micro-organisms, and essentially biological processes for the production of plants or animals other than non-biological and microbiological processes'.[95] Fourthly, limitations to the exercise of the patent right for public interest reasons may lead, for example, to the granting of compulsory licenses.[96] These public policy limitations, which were adopted in a considerable number of jurisdictions, reflect the need to safe keep general societal needs or public goods in face of the attribution (adjudication) and exercise of private rights. A study commissioned by the WIPO found that, in 2010, 84 jurisdictions had limitations to patent rights based on morality and *ordre public*, while the patentability of 'therapeutic, surgical and diagnostic methods for treating humans or animals' was restricted in 79 countries.

In patent law, exclusions and exceptions are adaptation rules, providing room for including ethical and social equity considerations in the system governing the grant of patents. In this sense, such limitations assume a function of gatekeepers of accessibility allowing the introduction of

88 Sean O'Neill and others, 'Broad claiming in nanotechnology patents: Is litigation inevitable?' (2007) 4 *Nanotechnology L. & Bus.* 29; Sylvester and Bowman n 80.

89 Art 28 TRIPS n 70.

90 Art 33 TRIPS n 70.

91 For active substances of medicines the reduction of commercial exploitation time induced by lengthy regulatory approval processes in many jurisdictions is compensated by the availability of a patent extension/ supplementary patent certificate. However this does not extend the patent term.

92 Art 27 (1) TRIPS n 70.

93 Art 27 (2) TRIPS n 70.

94 Art 27 (3) (a) TRIPS n 70.

95 Art 27 (3) (b) TRIPS n 70.

96 Arts 30 and 31 TRIPS n 70.

public policy considerations on the patent system, in order to mitigate possible adverse results in terms of general access to and availability of industrial knowledge and innovation.

The limitation of patentability to inventions prevents the grant of the commercial exploitation monopoly over scientific knowledge. Under such rule only technological innovation is patentable, scientific discoveries or theories are excluded from or considered unsusceptible of private ownership and thus left in the public domain. The second set of limitations provide for an exception from the general patentability rule, determining that certain inventions that would otherwise be patentable are unsusceptible of being the object of such right.

Nanotechnology, if proven to be a major leap forward in technological development, will necessarily entail social changes and the emergence of the need to apply previously existing normative structures and concepts to new realities and phenomena. Technological change throughout history has brought forth moral and ethical dilemmas that require normative translation at some stage. Nanotechnology inventions, due to their particular nature, pose new challenges to the patent system since many of the technologies being currently developed blur the line between patentable and non-patentable subject-matter. The distinction between what can be considered an invention and thus patentable and, for example, a non-patentable discovery is becoming less clear.

Nanotechnology also challenges patentability exceptions by rendering the operative concepts of legal norms less useful. In order to apply either exceptions to patentability of inventions (Europe) or limitations to the exercise of the patent right (USA), different patent jurisdictions rely on a distinction between methods for treatment and diagnostic methods practiced on the human body, on one side, and products used in such activities, on the other side. Regarding nanotechnology inventions, such distinction is increasingly difficult resulting in the ability of the technology to circumvent such limitations.

Nanotechnology and the Exception from Patentability for Methods for Treatment and Diagnosis

The patentability exception of methods for treatment and diagnosis is allowed by the TRIPS Agreement but not subject to harmonization. It has been adopted in several jurisdictions, and can be described as holding a function of guardian of accessibility to medicine. In Europe it is stated in article 53 (c) of the European Patent Convention (EPC).[97] Although the formulation and *ratio legis* of this norm has been a matter for doctrinal debate, it can be said that in its current formulation and interpretation by the European Patent Office (EPO) boards of appeal, it has as objective and function to guarantee the attainability of the right to health by safekeeping access to methods for treatment and diagnosis. The norm is thus intended to simultaneously protect the freedom of the medical practitioner to apply any known methods for treatment and diagnosis, and to ensure the right of the patient to receive any methods for treatment and diagnosis available, appropriate and efficient for his/her condition. It does so by keeping such methods under a regime of exception from the general rule that determines that all inventions, new, inventive and susceptible of industrial application can be object of a patent right. The EPC model inspired the legislation of many jurisdictions[98] however it is a matter for discussion if the solution adopted in article 53 (c) EPC is in fact the most

97 'European patents shall not be granted in respect of: […] (c) methods for treatment of the human or animal body by surgery or therapy and diagnostic methods practised on the human or animal body; this provision shall not apply to products, in particular substances or compositions, for use in any of these methods.' Art. 53 (c), Convention on the Grant of European Patents (European Patent Convention) of 5 October 1973 as revised by the Act revising the EPC of 29 November 2000.

98 The Patent Co-operation Treaty (1970) and the WIPO Model Law for Developing Countries on Inventions (Geneva, 1979) are also credited as important sources of influence.

appropriate. It can be questioned whether such function is actually being fulfilled by the norm, as it can be discussed whether excluding economic incentive to innovation in the field of methods for treatment and diagnosis does not in fact compromise the realization of the right to the highest attainable standard of health, understood as an incremental and progressive right.

Nanotechnology adds to this debate the fact that the nature of this technology further blurs the line between what may or not fall under the exception, creating increased patentability options and the possibility to avoid the prohibition almost completely.[99] Nanotechnology due to its nature may be difficult to subsume to the operative concepts of article 53 (c) of the EPC, as interpreted currently by the EPO. The distinction between methods, products or apparatus may turn out to be artificial regarding most nanotechnology inventions, since often a nanotechnology invention can be described both as an apparatus 'nano-machine' and as a chemical compound. Thus, allowing the overall circumventing of the legal provision.[100]

Conclusion

The right to the highest attainable standard of health, understood from a global and dynamic perspective, necessarily includes the need to promote investment in scientific research and industrial innovation in the medical and pharmaceutical sector. Without such innovation the incremental development of generalized attainment of the right to health cannot be achieved. The patent system has an important role to play in providing incentives to such investment.

Nanotechnology is recognized as a promising field of technological development, one that can bring hope to solve many of the major health problems that humanity is currently facing, both in developed and developing countries. However the nature of the technology poses normative challenges that require careful consideration. Among the latter is the need to re-evaluate the functioning of exclusions, exceptions and limitations to patent rights as mechanisms for safekeeping accessibility.

---

99 Herbert Zech, 'Nanotechnology – New Challenges for Patent Law?' (2009) 6 *SCRIPTed* 144 <http://www.law.ed.ac.uk/ahrc/SCRIPT-ed/vol6-1/zech.asp> accessed 14 December 2011.

100 Angela Follett and Teresa Lavoie, 'Delivering macro-quality IP protection for nanosized therapeutics' (2008) 5 *Nanotechnology L. & Bus.* 163.

Index

For Product Safety Concerns and Information please contact our EU representative GPSR@taylorandfrancis.com Taylor & Francis Verlag GmbH, Kaufingerstraße 24, 80331 München, Germany